STUDIES IN ECONOMIC PLANNING
OVER SPACE AND TIME

CONTRIBUTIONS
TO
ECONOMIC ANALYSIS

82

Honorary Editor

J. TINBERGEN

Editors

D. W. JORGENSON

J. WAELBROECK

NORTH-HOLLAND PUBLISHING COMPANY – AMSTERDAM · LONDON

AMERICAN ELSEVIER PUBLISHING COMPANY, INC. – NEW YORK

STUDIES IN ECONOMIC PLANNING
OVER SPACE AND TIME

Edited by

GEORGE G. JUDGE
TAKASHI TAKAYAMA

University of Illinois

1973

NORTH-HOLLAND PUBLISHING COMPANY – AMSTERDAM · LONDON

AMERICAN ELSEVIER PUBLISHING COMPANY, INC. – NEW YORK

© NORTH-HOLLAND PUBLISHING COMPANY – 1973

Library of Congress Catalog Card Number: 73 75536
    ISBN North-Holland:
           Series: 0 7204 3100 X
          Volume: 0 7204 3184 0
ISBN American Elsevier: 0 444 10515 8

Publishers:

NORTH-HOLLAND PUBLISHING COMPANY – AMSTERDAM

NORTH-HOLLAND PUBLISHING COMPANY, LTD. – LONDON

Sole distributors for the U.S.A. and Canada:

AMERICAN ELSEVIER PUBLISHING COMPANY, INC.
52 VANDERBILT AVENUE
NEW YORK, N.Y. 10017

PRINTED IN THE NETHERLANDS

Introduction to the series

This series consists of a number of hitherto unpublished studies, which are introduced by the editors in the belief that they represent fresh contributions to economic science.

The term *economic analysis* as used in the title of the series has been adopted because it covers both the activities of the theoretical economist and the research worker.

Although the analytical methods used by the various contributors are not the same, they are nevertheless conditioned by the common origin of their studies, namely theoretical problems encountered in practical research. Since for this reason, business cycle research and national accounting, research work on behalf of economic policy, and problems of planning are the main sources of the subjects dealt with, they necessarily determine the manner of approach adopted by the authors. Their methods tend to be "practical" in the sense of not being too far remote from application to actual economic conditions. In addition they are quantitative rather than qualitative.

It is the hope of the editors that the publication of these studies will help to stimulate the exchange of scientific information and to reinforce international cooperation in the field of economics.

The Editors

Preface

The economics profession has over the last two decades been to some extent preoccupied with the specification and analysis of models for understanding the processes and institutions underlying economic development and growth and providing a planning framework within which people and their governments may achieve their social and economic aspirations. Although these models have been valuable in helping us to understand the process of development and growth and the possible economic and social consequences of using alternative strategies or instruments, the need for comprehensive and systematic quantitative analysis at the regional, inter-regional, national, and international levels has become increasingly evident. Against this backdrop of a rich and varied set of models and methods of analysis and a need for quantitative knowledge at the various structural decision levels over the range of centralized-decentralized allocation schemes, the modest purpose of this book is to report the results of research concerned with economic decision problems over space and time and to show how the models and methods may be applied, interpreted, and the information used.

Our first thought was to publish a volume of applications that would correspond to the models developed in our book *Spatial and Temporal Price and Allocation Models*. However, we decided to go outside of this conceptual framework and have included applications involving models such as macro econometric, recursive programming, and regional and dynamic input–output analysis. In order to show the practicability and usefulness of these models and results over a spectrum of centralized-decentralized allocation schemes, geographical locations, and scale and mix of endowments of resources, technology and utility function(al)s, we have sought and included applied work from a wide range of countries and political and economic systems. However, the research applications included are intended to be neither all inclusive nor exhaustive. Rather they are only a subjective sample of a very rich possibility set.

We wish to acknowledge the wonderful cooperation of our partners in this venture. Thanks to their efforts most of the papers were either new research results or rewritten for this volume. Their rapid responses to our requests for sometimes significant revisions in length and substance permitted us to complete the book pretty much on schedule. We wish to also thank Carol Daggett who through her competent and efficient help kept the letters and manuscripts flowing and retyped many of the first or second round papers. For the editors, this has been a joint effort, and the order of the appearance of our names has nothing more than alphabetical significance.

George Judge

Takashi Takayama

Contents

Part II Linear Planning Models over Space and Time

A. Spatial Programming Models

B. Spatial and/or Temporal Programming Models

CHAPTER 1

Introduction

The concept and activity of "economic planning" is no longer monopolized by economies characterized by a centralized allocation scheme. Rather, this activity pervades the range of centralized–decentralized allocation systems or economies and cuts across decisionmaking activities at the individual, regional, national, and international choice levels. Correspondingly, perhaps in recent times starting with Keynes, there have been significant increases in the range of economic models which seek to upgrade our understanding of economic processes, institutions, the strategies and the decisionmaking processes. These models, such as Leontief's input–output analysis and Dantzig, Koopmans *et al.*, activity analysis framework, have permitted allocation problems to be cast in a new form and opened new approaches to their analysis. Extensions and refinements of traditional models along with new approaches to old problems have in addition permitted the space and time dimensions to be explicitly introduced.

Meanwhile, back in the real world, these models and methods formed the basis for much of the work done in local, regional, national and international economic planning agencies. This action-oriented work has made it clear that although the models that have been developed and analyzed have been valuable in helping us understand the process of development and growth or the economic and social consequences of alternative strategies or instruments, for many problems it is not enough to be able to identify the system of interrelationships, but one must also know the magnitude or range of magnitudes involved. Thus, it has become increasingly apparent that in order to understand, to identify the set of alternative actions and to solve some of the production and allocation problems for economies characterized by the range of centralized–decentralized decision schemes, comprehensive and systematic quantitative analyses are necessary. In addition, for many problems it is not sufficient to analyze a system at one point in time but for decision purposes one must be able to say something about the time path of the alternative choices and outcomes. Given this situation, the purpose of this book is to present quantitative research results that have been completed in the last decade, which (i) provide a basis for gauging the adequacy or applicability of our conceptual models and analyzing techniques, (ii) indicate how these models and techniques may be applied and interpreted, and (iii) generate information that may be used as a basis for choice.

Although the contributors to this volume are widely distributed over the world and the topics are varied, the majority of the papers deal with a variation of the market-oriented allocation system. Thus, we have no illusions that this book covers all aspects of applied research in economic planning that is available at this time. Rather, as indicated in the preface, this is only a partial collection of papers available which make use of recent economic models and methods in trying to learn from experience and data.

Organization and critique of contents

The book is organized in four parts with the partitions being a function of the tools used, and the problem focus of the papers. In Part I some aspects of the philosophy of the planning venture are presented; the actual use of both optimizing and descriptive models in planning is discussed and evaluated; static and dynamic input–output models are reviewed and applied. In Part II papers relating to applications of the classical transportation, the linear activity analysis and recursive programming models are presented and the results interpreted and evaluated. In Part III application of non-linear (quadratic) programming models involving space and time are presented and evaluated for a variety of problems and economic environments, and a conceptual framework for analyzing problems of international trade is presented. In Part IV applications of both programming and econometric models are given, and the usefulness of these models and results for public and private planning purposes are emphasized. Although an attempt has been made to group papers with common focuses or emphases, the great diversity of the manuscripts chosen means that the variability within each Part is perhaps as great as that between.

In the first paper in the first set of papers in Part I, Tinbergen discusses the philosophical and methodological issues in economic planning in India and gives his interpretation of socialism and economic planning under mature socialism. In the second paper, Sebestyén reviews agricultural planning models used in Hungary after the second world war and brings out in sharp relief the difference in emphasis and focus of hierarchical planning models of centralized allocation schemes and more decentralized planning models. Maki and Angus discuss the objectives and content of models used for sectoral and regional planning and presents some attempts at model implementation and application. In the fourth paper Miller reviews economic adjustment activities undertaken by the U.S. Department of Agriculture for policy purposes and gropes for more efficient ways of organizing the research and decision activities. In the next paper, Herman considers the problem of minimum unemployment production planning on a world basis and uses a combination of semi input–output and programming reasoning. In the last paper in the first section of Part I, Frisch considers economic planning for the Arab Republic.

In the second section of Part I, four papers employing regional, inter-regional input–output models and dynamic input–output models are presented. In the first paper Ricflcr reviews interregional input–output analyses and points to the future directions of research in this area. Polenske in the second paper notes how important the multiregional trade is for each State by using U.S. regional and interregional input–output data, and develops a multiregional input–output analysis based on this information. Czamanski in the third paper explores ways of clarifying linkages between industries in reference to urban—regional complex development planning. In the final paper in Part I Tsukui analyzes the Japanese economy in the first half of the 1960's by using a dynamic input–output model and attempts to answer the question of whether or not the Japanese economy followed the turnpike and if the growth path around the turnpike is stable.

Throughout Parts II and III, the basic tools used are mathematical programming methods such as linear programming and quadratic programming. The tools are used in a semi-centralized sense in that the total transport costs or total revenue throughout the economy or a part thereof are to be minimized or maximized in linear programming cases, or the net social payoff or net revenue throughout the economy is to be maximized in quadratic programming cases. In a centrally planned or controlled economy, these optimization concepts are perhaps not as unfamiliar as they are in a decentralized economy. In a market oriented economy, in employing these semi-centralized optimization concepts, we are forced either to accept a certain philosophical stand that the economy or a part thereof has an implicit purpose to minimize or maximize a certain objective (teleological view), or to simply accept that the economy efficiency will be attained if a minimum or a maximum of the objective is attained (efficiency view). How well these semi-centralized optimization concepts serve for the efficient operation of the economy is to be judged referring to the papers in Parts II and III.

Part II is divided into two parts. The first part contains four papers using linear programming tools for analyzing problems involving space. The first paper by King, Cassetti and Kissling reflects the recent use of geographers of linear optimizing models and deals with a coal transportation allocation problem in the Great Lakes region in the United States and an agricultural product transportation optimization problem in New Zealand. The second paper by Guedry deals with a multi-commodity spatial analysis of the feed grains sector in the United States and uses the results to evaluate regional support price differentials in use. In the next paper Judge, Havlicek and Rizek use the linear activity analysis model to determine the optimum level of slaughter and geographical flows for livestock products in the United States. The fourth paper by Leunis and Vandenborre analyzes the interregional allocation of the U.S. soybean industry by using the linear programming method. In the fifth paper Buchholz summarizes research works done by West German scholars and researchers in the fields of farm management and agricultural marketing and points out possibilities for future works in these fields. In the last paper in this section Weinschenck, Henrichsmeyer and Hanf review their research in regional and interregional models for the agricultural sector of the West German economy.

The second part of Part II deals mainly with applied research done by utilizing recursive linear programming (RLP) models developed by Day and his associates. Day in the first paper summarizes the theory and historical development of the applied works using RLP methods. In the second paper, Abe reports the results of RLP to the Japanese and the U.S. iron and steel industries and derives conclusions such as the rationality of their efforts to grow. Nelson analyzes the U.S. iron and steel industries over time and space by using RLP. Singh in the last paper in Part II applies RLP to Punjab agriculture to see if the tool is effective to less developed countries in understanding and planning agricultural development.

In spite of the productive efforts of many researchers, an impasse was reached in developing regional aggregative LP models. The impasse is reflected by the result that either aggregated results of linear programming applied to micro-units or those applied to regions using the representative farm concepts tend to deviate from the historical data by a large margin. Perhaps this was the basic reason R. Day developed RLP. Instead of following RLP and restricting the activity levels by the upper and lower bounds, Takayama and Judge, à la Samuelson, introduced regional market demand functions so that the activity levels can be adjusted endogenously to price changes. This market oriented approach has been used widely recently and some of the research results using this framework are reported in Part III.

In Part III the first part deals mainly with spatial — interregional and international — programming models, and the second part is concerned with spatial and temporal — finite time horizon — programming models.

In the first part of Part III, four papers analyze spatial pricing and allocation problems of agricultural commodities for various countries. The first paper by Sasaki investigates the rationality and efficiency aspects of the present pricing allocations of poultry, pork, and milk in Eastern Japan under the assumption that the information generated by this type of analysis is highly demanded by the policy and decision makers in the Federations of Agricultural Cooperatives of Japan, the central government, and prefectural governments. Lee and Seaver analyze the spatial pricing and allocation situation of poultry in the Northeastern United States and investigate its stability. Zusman, Melamed, and Katzir in the third paper, deal with a spatial pricing and allocation analysis of EEC trade policies for the Mediterranean winter oranges and develop a comparative static analysis of the effects of various policy alternatives on the prices and export–import quantities of various countries in the EEC and those countries contiguous to the EEC, also producing winter oranges. In the final paper in the section, Schmitz and Bawden develop a comparative static spatial analysis to the international wheat economy.

In the second part of Part III we have four papers dealing with temporal and/or spatial programming models. Guise of Australia and Aggrey-Mensah of Ghana analyze the Australian banana market with reference to some policy alternatives the Board of Australian Banana Producers considered implementing in the later 1960's. Weekly demand functions are used in generating a time path of prices, demand quantities, and carry-over quantities over the fifty-two week period. In the second paper a spatial and temporal quadratic programming model is employed by Guise and Flinn to determine an optimum pricing and allocation of water in a river basin for three different uses of water and over four seasons of a year. In the third paper Kottke analyzes the problem of determining an optimal spatial and temporal price and allocation of dairy products in the Northeastern United States dairy industry which is characterized as a combination of competitive and mixed components. The Indian rice and wheat pricing and allocation policies are analyzed by Pandey and Takayama for the Fourth Plan Period of India by using modified versions of the temporal quadratic programming model. The final paper by Pant and Takayama deals with the rice and wheat economy of India by using the Leontief Input–Output Analysis, linear programming, and spatial and temporal price equilibrium models. The objectives and results of the Pant, Pandey and Takayama papers serve to point up the wide gap between scholastic research work and recommendations and policy implementation by responsible governmental decision making bodies in India. In the last paper of this section, Samuelson reviews the fundamental core of international trade theory, locates Hume as the originator of the theory itself, and consistently pursues the theory through Ricardo and Marshall and completes his logical clarification of the general equilibrium aspect of the international trade theory. The partial equilibrium nature of spatial and/or temporal *price* equilibrium models is all too patently clear and is a challenge to all of us to develop ways to mitigate this restriction in both theory and practice.

Part IV contains four papers. Except for one paper, linear programming techniques are used as tools in analyzing some relevant private and public problems. In the first paper, one of the early initiators of mathematical programming approaches in the field of agricultural economics, Earl O. Heady attempts a long range projection of interregional optimal water allocation for the continental United States by using an interregional linear programming model. In the next paper Swanson and Narayanan evaluate the effect of alternative agricultural systems on water quality by taking one small watershed as their project site. This is a prototype of modeling in this field, but the simplicity of the model and the implications appear impressive and promising. In the third paper Baker proposes a linear programming model to solve a capital budgeting and financial management problem faced by individual producing firms. In the fourth paper Correa uses the macroeconomic model approach in his attempt to estimate manpower requirements or manpower demand functions in seventeen U.S. industries. This is one step forward to forecasting or planning the national manpower requirements once the other side of the Marshallian scissors, the supply functions, are successfully estimated.

PART I

NATIONAL AND INTERNATIONAL PLANNING MODELS

A. ECONOMIC PLANNING

CHAPTER 2

Some thoughts on mature socialism*

JAN TINBERGEN

Netherlands School of Economics

1. Introduction

It is a great honour for me to have been invited to give this year's Nehru
Memorial Lecture; for me, it is also a great occasion. India is by far the
largest country of the non-committed world and many of my friends like
myself are aware of how much depends on where India goes. Jawaharlal
Nehru decisively influenced India's future path. Under his guidance India
was the first of the non-committed countries to embark upon a planned
development. In the Second Five Year Plan this country chose in favour of
a "socialistic pattern of society". Having been, since my student days, a
member of the democratic socialist party of my own country, I took a keen
interest in the road chosen by this great country. For to-day's occasion I
could not think of a better subject than the one announced, that is, Some
Thoughts on Mature Socialism.

It is a good habit to start an address with a definition of the subject
and a layout of the address. In my case this seems to be the more necessary
since the word socialism in our days covers a variety of versions and also as
I have added an unusual adjective. Although I propose to elaborate somewhat on the origin and the history of socialism a bit later, I see some convenience in formulating my own definition of socialism now. I see it as the
institutionalization of solidarity among human beings and as the recognition
that in last resort the community is responsible for the welfare of its members.
Its opposite is individualism in the sense of each individual being responsible
for his or her own welfare. The word socialism, having been derived from

* This paper was presented as the Jawaharlal Nehru Memorial Lecture 1970 and is
published here with the permission of the author and the Jawaharlal Nehru Memorial Fund.

the same root as the word society, in my opinion stands for this task of society to maximize the welfare of its members.

The word mature, in my mind, stands for using as much human experience as possible in order to avoid inconsistencies in behaviour; especially to avoid doing things which one later deplores.

The subjects I propose to take up in an attempt to elaborate on my theme are (1) Some lessons from socio-economic history; (2) Some features of the history of socialism; (3) Scientific socialism as I see it now; (4) Actual and possible contributions of socialist ideas to Indian development and, finally, (5) Actual and possible contributions of socialist ideas and of India to world development. I apologize for the ambitious suggestions implied. I will take up these subjects one by one.

2. Some lessons from socio-economic history

Socialism was launched, as a set of ideas, about a century and a half ago. Some of the facts used as a basis for Marxian scientific socialism were registered about a century ago. Since then society has further developed, with development of science and technology as one of the driving forces. Technological development has indeed been unprecedented and today's production methods are infinitely more complicated than those of a century ago; also the size of productive units has grown enormously. Very impressive contributions have been made to the wellbeing of the population of the developed countries and some modest contributions to the wellbeing of the poorer sections of the world. Increasingly also negative effects have emerged, especially by the change in technology of armament. Other dangers are the deterioration of human environment, the dangers of drugs and the problems created by the population explosion.

The last century has also added to our social experience. New social structures have come into existence, under the impact of two main forces and a number of secondary ones. The two main forces are the labour movement and the movement for national self-determination. The new structures appear in different forms. In the highly developed countries stepwise social reforms have prevailed; in the less developed part of Europe sudden changes have occurred of which the creation of the Soviet Union was the most important. All over the world — with few exceptions — nations have liberated themselves from foreign domination and empires have been dissolved as in the case of the Austrian-Hungarian empire after World War I or been transformed as in the case of the British and French empires after World War II.

The new structures were inspired by theories and hence constituted experiments from which we have been able to learn. The lessons we learned have often been starting points for other changes, forward or backward, depending on the nature of the experiences.

It is of particular interest to list experiences relevant to socialist ideals. In the early phases of the socialist movement the social structure aimed at was fundamentally different from the free-enterprise free-market system more or less prevailing around 1850 in the then most developed countries. According to these theories, private ownership of the means of production should be changed into community ownership; free competition into central planning. Incomes should be distributed much more equally and as a consequence all citizens would have access to the boons of culture. In the new, classless society the forces making for war would have disappeared. This picture I will indicate as 'primitive' socialism, as distinct from mature. As announced, we will discuss later in some more detail the history of socialist ideas. For a better understanding of that history and of what I mean by maturity we will discuss first some of the experiences gained from the changes introduced.

A positive experience Western Europe has made is the possibility of stepwise change, implying that each step is a partial change and not necessarily a fundamental one. The introduction of social legislation, progressive tax systems, a long series of new public tasks and, in particular, anti-cyclical policies are examples of successful partial changes contributing to the welfare of the socially weak groups.

An experience of a mixed character is the one with changes in ownership. State-owned enterprises and co-operative enterprises have not been universally successful. No doubt Soviet experience has shown that production is possible without private ownership of the means of production. Whether that production is more efficient than private production cannot be derived from the Soviet experiment, however, since fair competition between the two types had not been arranged. Even in Western countries comparisons in efficiency between privately and publicly owned enterprises have rarely been made, since as a rule an industry is either completely private or completely public. The few cases I know of where public and private units existed side by side in fair competition do not show much of a difference in efficiency. In my own country the state coal mines, in existence since 1902, probably were a bit better than the private mines, whereas the state farms were doing a bit less well than comparable private farms. Ownership seems to matter much less than the quality of management.

In the West, another experience has shown that ownership can be and has been stepwise socialized. Professor Undén from Sweden analysed the concept of private ownership and showed that it can be seen as a bunch of decision rights, each of them showing a range of alternatives. In the course of the last century the extent of the ranges has been clearly reduced by a large number of public laws, such as social legislation, tax legislation, quality requirements, price regulations and so on. It is misleading, therefore, to say that in the West private property still prevails as if the situation had not changed since 1870, say. The freedom to decide on a number of issues — working hours, wages, taxes, prices — has been reduced quite substantially for the private sector and, in addition, the public sector has been expanded [1].

A third experience worth mentioning is the one of centralized decision making. With the increased complexity of technology and of products, more decision power must be laid at lower levels, both in enterprises and in administration. Delegation of power is efficient and, at the same time, enhances democracy. The experiences made in big enterprises everywhere and in central planning in Eastern Europe run parallel. The picture that emerges is one of decision making at a number of different levels [8].

A fourth experience refers to some limits to equalization. Human beings are different from each other; as we knew, of course. Acquired qualities are partly innate, partly the result of a learning process. About a century or half a century ago we had become rather optimistic about the learning process. We believed that if only the bad material environment in which workers' children lived were changed, they would be able fully to develop their personality, both with regard to their capabilities and with regard to their taste. While this holds true indeed for a portion of the total population, it is not that simple for others. It either takes a longer time or it does not happen at all. On top of this a tendency has developed for a change in tastes which poses some real cultural problems to the developed world. We are living in a cultural crisis with many aspects and we hope to learn from other civilizations in order to solve these problems. There are many aspects to this change in tastes; the one that concerns us most is a downgrading of some human values which for my generation meant very much. Of course we have to deal here with problems which have been with mankind for a few thousand years and there was some naïveté about them in socialist as well as in liberal circles — both in the European and in the American sense.

A final major experience I want to remind you of is the strength of nationalism. To be sure, nationalism is a positive force during certain stages of development. It is a positive force in supporting the struggle against foreign domination and it is positive to the extent that it means overcoming tribalism and provincialism, that is a broadening of loyalties. What we desperately need in the present era is, however, internationalism, and in principle socialism always went in for it: "proletarians of all countries, unite!" Reality has been a terrible and most dangerous disappointment, however. A heavy burden of guilt rests on social-democrats for their failing to avoid the First World War. Unfortunately there is no clear evidence that communists are doing better.

3. *Some features of the history of socialism*

As I already said, the ideas of socialism go back to the first half of the nineteenth century, when Robert Owen and several French thinkers tried to find an alternative to free enterprise societies. Their values were, of course, partly inherited from previous philosophers. They were essentially humanitarian and enlightened. They tried to give new content to the "fundamental equality of all human beings", a concept with a particularly fascinating history. Perhaps the oldest version is of a religious character and has been expressed as "equality before God". Later politico-juridical versions have been developed resulting in "equality in court" and universal franchise. For socialists the socio-economic aspect became central; one version of the latter is the rejection of exploitation of one human being by another. Later on I will try my best to give a more general interpretation.

The attitude of enlightenment meant that socialists wanted to use the fruits of scientific development as distinct from all sorts of superstitions. It was of course Karl Marx who claimed to bring scientific socialism as distinct from utopian; meaning that he claims to have proved that socialism by necessity will emerge out of capitalism. This transition he sees as one phase in a longer term development activated by scientific and technological development, or, as he says, the productive forces, which bring to explosion antiquated social structures, that is, structures preventing new technologies from being applied.

The word socialism has had a tremendous appeal to Western workers and later, more generally, to the oppressed elsewhere. This appeal has also been abused by such groups as the "national-socialists" − a contradictio in terminis − and some French politicians. Unfortunately the accusation of abuse has also been used against people of a truly socialist conviction. This is a consequence of the dynamics of thought and society. Around 1900 one form of revisionism was started by the German socialist Bernstein [2] and then a long series of revisionists have followed; I only mention Tito and Khrushchev.

While dramatic discussions had already taken place before World War I, a decisive split between the revolutionary and the reformist wings occurred as a consequence of the events in 1917 in Russia. In the so-called October revolution (November, according to our calendar) power was taken over by the Bolsheviki or, as we now say, communists, followed by a series of internal power struggles within the communist ranks, with Stalin as the victor. It was a matter of considerable controversy whether this development — I mean Russia emerging as the first socialist country — was in line with Marxist thought, where socialism was assumed to be the fruit of a highly developed capitalism. There was doubt even whether Marxist theories were at all fitting for a predominantly agricultural society as Russia was in 1917. No doubt the greatest difficulties of the Soviet regime have been in the field of agriculture, a matter of importance to India. As an alternative, Maoist thought starts from the village as the avant-garde in the socialist struggle.

In the meantime the Soviet Union has become a major industrial power, though at the cost of immense sacrifices in consumption, especially during the thirties, and notwithstanding the murderous war imposed on them by the German 'national socialists'. In the fifties Soviet development has been quite remarkable, although still surpassed by recent Japanese development, but in the sixties the need for some decentralization of decision making became clear.

Decentralization of a more pronounced character had already been introduced in Yugoslavia, where not only the market, but also labour management has been introduced, implying forms of industrial democracy not existing in either Western or Eastern Europe.

Within the official Eastern European bloc some of the decentralization reforms accepted by the Soviet Union spread, and in some respects tried to go further. The Czech version was blocked by military intervention, whereas the Hungarian and Romanian versions did not cause difficulties. In Hungary probably the most sophisticated new internal decentralization was tried out, whereas the Romanian case is one of more national independence from the bloc.

Thus, the river of socialist ideas has split into a large number of branches. The social-democrats adhere to parliamentary democracy and to stepwise transformation of society. The communists of all brands stick to the idea of the monopoly of one party. The Chinese look at the peasants as the innovators; the European communists at the industrial workers. The Yugoslavs have given considerable power to works councils. The official Eastern

European bloc sticks to state-owned production units, but is shifting decision power from the state to these units.

The discussions between the representatives of these branches have been troubled by emotional outbursts. As you know, emotions restrict our capability to think objectively, that is scientifically. The names given to each other reflect the emotions of the discussants. One of the names called is "bourgeois", evidently a bad word. Another is "revisionist". You are no doubt aware that many socialists consider the word revisionism also a bad word and few revisionists announce themselves as such; usually they are called that by others. To me it seems that no scientist should ever reject revision of any theory if observation shows that the theory does not fit the facts. It is the essence of science that it consists of a series of revisions. In the history of socialism we observe, however, a succession of splits between revisionists and orthodox, with a danger of orthodoxy degenerating into doctrinairism and a danger of revisionists becoming opportunists. A scientific approach implies, though, the possibility of a free discussion and of fair experiments. I am not sure, to say the least, that experiments with public enterprises in Western countries and with private enterprises in Eastern European countries have always been fair. My own conclusion from the history of socialism is that in order to remain scientific socialists we must accept revisions, in the light of experience, of the means to attain the goal. The goal remains the same, however, and its core is solidarity among human beings to be reflected in our social structures.

4. Scientific socialism 1970: a view

Let me now try to give my own interpretation of socialism in todays's world. I apologize for the technicalities involved and will soon return to plain language. You will not be amazed that as an economist I take as my starting point the theory of welfare economics. This chapter of economic science attempts to formulate the conditions that have to be fulfilled in order to maximize social welfare, under the restrictions given by nature and technology (or the "productive forces"). Of course, the outcome depends on how we define social welfare. In this definition some of our humanitarian values must be expressed. I believe that large sections of a modern community are accepting these values, which I will sketch out later.

Let me add first that the real problem of welfare economics is not only to state the conditions to be fulfilled by the maximum, but to interpret these conditions in terms of the institutions which together will let these conditions materialize. This group of institutions may also be called the optimum social order or regime and this I take to be identical to the mature socialist order. Indeed it is derived from our value system while using all scientific information available.

Our value system finds its expression in the social welfare function. I submit we have to think of it as the sum total of all individual welfare or utility functions. I use the word utility as the broadest concept of human satisfaction and hence use the expression welfare as synonymous with it. Both must take into account what psychology and sociology have taught us and not stick to material wellbeing only. In what I said the sum total of all individual welfare reflects the element of solidarity: everybody's welfare counts. The shape I give to individual welfare functions reflects my view on that old concept of the fundamental equality of all human beings. Each individual welfare or utility function contains variables and coefficients. Variables may be the individual's consumption, an index (or several indices) representing his job, and one or more indices representing his abilities and his needs. Among the latter are the size of his family or his professional needs. The coefficients indicate the intensity of the influence of the variables on his satisfaction or welfare. I interpret the fundamental equality of human beings as the equality of these coefficients for all individuals. This is an assumption, a working hypothesis. Since the variables may differ from person to person, all observable differences among human beings which science has shown us are accounted for. So in a way my approach to the subject of equality is that I assume equality unless observation shows inequality for instance in abilities and needs. Among the variables some of these abilities and needs may be given; the problem of the best social order is to so choose the job and the consumption of each individual as to maximize total social welfare. Of course the brevity of the formulation leaves unanswered a number of questions, but I hope it has the advantage of emphasizing the essence. I should add that, on the one hand, there are a number of lacunae in our knowledge which have to be filled by further research, but that, on the other hand, some conclusions about the optimum order can be drawn without some of my assumptions or our knowledge.

The advantage of using welfare economics as a starting point to define a mature socialist order consists of using the same method as the one applied by the most sophisticated defence of liberalism offered in the past. In this way the definition of socialism can be seen as a critique of liberalism based on criticizing the assumptions made for its justification. In fact it is mostly because of antiquated assumptions regarding the production process that the liberalist view must be rejected.

In our critique a distinction must be made between what I shall call ultraliberalist practice and the liberalist theory as defended by Pareto and his followers. Ultraliberalist practice not only defended free enterprise and free markets, but even the principle of 'each for each', which is the rejection of income redistribution. This cannot be justified, however, by welfare economics, and even a man like Milton Friedman recognizes this. Income redistribution is necessary anyway and is already implicit in Pareto's optimum situations. But with today's production processes the general decentralization in decision making typical for free enterprise and free markets is no longer optimal. This is due to the increased indivisibility of capital goods and to external effects. Both require decision making on higher levels for the activities showing these features. Often external effects can also be seen as a consequence of indivisibilities. So the pollution of air and water, often described as an external effect of motor traffic and chemical production, can be seen as a consequence of the indivisibility of the earth's atmosphere and the earth's rivers and seas system. What has emerged from new technologies as well as from a better understanding of the operation of economies is a long list of activities which are government tasks and cannot be left to private decisions. Private armies and police, or competing issuing banks once existed, but we understood early on that they are not the best way of taking care of external and internal security or of our need for a sound monetary system. To-day we recognize that large parts of transportation, energy and water production and education cannot be left to private decision making; that the government has to regulate unstable markets, the total volume of demand, the rate of investment, and to provide macroplanning and a good deal of information and communication. Thus we arrive, on the basis of the new productive forces, at the conclusion that a mixed economy is better than the extreme of decentralization. In the light of experiences I discussed before, complete centralization is an inferior method too. Both state ownership and central micro-planning have their drawbacks. The remaining problems of an optimum order are problems of degree, rather than problems of principle. Here we find quite a few unsolved problems, for instance those of the right system and level of taxes, depending on the outcome of further research. The problem is related to the problem of the optimal job and income distribution. Elsewhere [16] I have tried to show that this optimal distribution can be said to imply the well-known slogan: "from each according to his abilities, to each according to his needs", but that this requires a tax system which we are not yet able to administer. In the meantime we have to use 'second best' tax systems. May I add that in my opinion the concept of an optimum income distribution will have to replace the concept of the elimination of exploitation. One dramatization of these unsolved problems is the question of whether we can avoid mass misery during take-off. So far the masses suffered in each type of take-off we know: the British around 1800, the Russians around 1930 and the Indians right now. I am coming back to this vital issue later.

From my view on the optimal or mature socialist order I derive two conclusions which I want to emphasize. The first conclusion is that we should not stick to doctrinaire views based on antiquated theories, sometimes on scientific views of a hundred years ago. It is essential to science and hence to scientific socialism that our minds are open instead of closed and that we are tolerant instead of narrow-minded. There is a message involved for socialist political parties. Intolerance and the tendency to form small sectarian parties is not in conformity with solidarity, apart from being against the spirit of science. One condition has to be fulfilled in order to re-unite socialist parties; the condition that a clear and vigorous policy be followed. I hope to specify the contents of such a policy later.

The second conclusion refers to the developments to be expected in both Western and Eastern societies. If we accept the broad Marxian view that the economic forces determine to a large extent the superstructure of a social and political nature, we must expect that all societies have a built-in tendency to move towards the optimum. Since the optimum is somewhere between the completely decentralized and the completely centralized structure, we must expect a movement which will reduce the differences between the originally liberalist and the primitive socialist structures. This is what we actually observe in Europe. Already we have started a dialogue between economists of Eastern and Western Europe about a number of common problems, such as which decisions to centralize and which not. If this is the picture in Europe, isn't it tragic then that in Asia the tendency prevails to fight a struggle of life and death? Persuasion, not violence, should be the way to decide upon social structure.

As a last remark on my view of scientific socialism as of 1970, let me add that it also has an important international aspect, to be discussed later.

5. *Actual and possible contributions of socialist ideas to Indian development*

I may now try to sketch out what actual and potential contributions socialist ideas are making or may make to the development of India. As your President Mr. Giri said on July 6, 1970, "we are pledged to establish a socialistic pattern of society by democratic means", and he warned that "our people must realize that it is hard work alone which can bring about equality through increasing prosperity" [5]. To avoid any misunderstanding let me start the subject by saying that not only socialist ideas but also non-political ideas of technicians, employers and educators will have to play their part, a very important part even.

Socialist ideas, however, have an important part to contribute in shaping the general structure of society in developing countries and hence also in India. Thus, it is a simple truth that tax evasion is contrary to solidarity and hence rejectable. It is a truth officially recognized in this country that the caste system is also rejectable, for the same reason. Among the most important aspects of a society's general structure is inequality among individuals with regard to their starting point in life. "Equal chances" is a slogan already accepted by liberalism, but which did not materialize during the rule of this political principle; socialists should try to dig more deeply here. Partly they have done so in their pleas against inherited property or against property of capital goods generally. As I tried to make clear, the Western alternative to complete nationalization as advocated by Eastern European programmes is gradual socialization of property rights. In a way this Western viewpoint is reflected in Myrdal's [10] recommendations with regard to land property. He is in favour of tax measures and a minimum property rather than either nationalization or a ceiling. A quantitative assessment of the possibilities here, and the influence of a steeply progressive land tax on tax revenue as well as productivity in agriculture, seem to be useful. In addition a study of which other types of property can be tackled the same way should be considered.

Another way of reducing the inequality of chances has been long recognized to be education. Here all countries, rich and poor, are facing the same problem. For developing countries the problem is even more important than for developed countries. As we know by now, the trouble for the least educated groups of population is that education starts long before schooling. Just as is the case with nutrition the harm to underprivileged children is already done at very young ages and the organizational problem is how to reach these young children by schemes of improvement. Quite apart from this difficulty there is the urgent need for more effective methods of education than the traditional ones: less learning by heart and more teaching to understand, less passive listening and more active participation.

A third way of attaining equality in opportunities is to create more employment. I am coming back to this later, in the framework of some suggestions on development policies as I see them. These I am now going to make.

Foremost in our minds must still be agriculture not only because such a large portion of Indian population is rural, but also because, as Minister Jagjivan Ram told the Second World Food Congress in my home town [13], "agriculture is becoming as much a source of capital and investment as industry". In this context Mr. Ram of course also mentioned the Green Revolution, which has given rise to new hopes, but also to new problems. The small farmer needs special attention, partly by appropriate credit facilities. Together with other inhabitants of rural areas he may profit from a number of so-called intermediate technologies and from further research on the use of sunlight and wind. Such research has obtained higher priority now that the dangers of ecological disequilibria are spreading and some allegedly modern techniques may have to be restricted in order to save human environment.

While it remains true that development requires industrialization, the first source of industrialization in many developing countries is better use of existing capacity. This in turn requires expansion of demand and here trade policies of the developed countries are the bottle-neck. The choice of new industries should be more employment-oriented and hence labour-intensive industries; again the bottle-neck of trade policies has to be eliminated. The plea I just made in favour of labour-intensive industries has been criticized by many colleagues of mine. I am glad to find the President of India, in his statement of June 10, before ILO on my side [5]. I also think my collaborator B. Herman has collected new evidence showing that from one million rupees both more income and more employment can be obtained if invested in labour-intensive or intermediate than if invested in capital-intensive activities [6].

In the field of industrialization the multinational firm and the joint venture remain important. Since this also is an old subject of discussion let me only say this: just as much as the possibility of trade to mutual advantage exists, as our Soviet friends put it, investment to the advantage of both parties is possible.

But the contribution to employment to be expected from industry is not large in the near future. A much larger contribution could be obtained from an expansion of building. From a humanitarian point of view an enormous volume of building is desirable. In the restricted economic sense it is not too attractive a proposition, although opinions are somewhat changing, now that some of the indirect (external) effects of better housing have been estimated. Again international cooperation will be a way out, especially, for instance, if the execution of the Basic Development Plan of the Calcutta Metropolitan District is to be assured. Among international housing experts there is a beginning of support for such a special project.

A last word about Indian development. Western socialists openly and Eastern Europe implicitly, by their own behaviour, thoroughly sympathize with the efforts made by the Government of India to stimulate family planning. It is part of doing away with superstitions.

6. *Contributions of socialist ideas and of India to world development*

I quoted Marx about antiquated social structures which stand in the way of modern productive forces and hence have to disappear. None of our social structures is more antiquated than the international structure, which is almost the jungle. It is heartening to quote Mr. Apa B. Pant, India's High Commissioner in Britain, speaking in his personal capacity: "Basically, India thinks of only 'one world' " [11]. May I add another quotation, from Mahatma Ghandi who said: "The conception of my patriotism is nothing if it is not always ... consistent with the broadest good of humanity at large" [4].

In my own way I would say the same things by elaborating on what I announced as the international component of mature socialism. The proposition that in the optimal social order some decisions have to be taken on higher levels than the enterprise or the individual level can be further specified. The level should be high enough so as not to leave sizeable external effects. For some types of decision the level of a city may suffice — think of traffic regulations — ; for others the level of the nation is required — think of education. Finally there are decisions which can only be properly made at supra-national levels, some at world level only.

This is true for commodity agreements for world-market products; it is also true for other trade decisions and for decisions on financial flows between developed and developing nations. The urgent need for such collective decisions exists, first of all, in the field of development policies. Minister Swaran Singh was quite right when in this summer's Ecosoc session he said: "... I sincerely hope that our partners from developed countries would not hesitate to exercise the necessary political will and assume additional responsibilities, which alone will make it worth while for the developing countries to plan their future course of development within the framework of a global strategy" [14]. When discussing Indian development I have already indicated several subjects where India can go ahead only if the developed countries play their part.

Recently more socio-economic subjects have come up where some international authority will be needed. The multinational enterprises will have to be under some public control and supervision will be needed of air or water polluting activities and other activities threatening our future environment. These are questions of importance to all of us, whether from developed or from developing countries.

Of course the oldest and most urgent need for collective decisions is in matters of peace or war. I have already mentioned our disastrous experiences with nationalist attitudes. Here socialist attitude all over the world is still pitifully immature, not to speak of other political parties. Perhaps business is ahead of politicians. Why do we have multinational firms but hardly any multinational authorities where they are needed?

Another way of presenting this fundamental problem is to state that a tremendous discrepancy has developed between man's intellectual capabilities and his moral capabilities. Politically we have not been able so far to unite, whereas the world we have created with our brains requires that unity for our survival. It requires statesmen (or women, of course) of the greatest stature to take the first steps here. I think of steps as they have been taken in my continent by Jean Monnet. Here, also, stepwise changes seem to be the most promising, but the dilemma is that we do not have much time. Could U Thant or Professor von Weizsäcker be right, who give us only ten years [15, 17]?

I am now coming to my last subject, the role India can play in world development. Here also the first steps may be the application of international solidarity with regard to neighbours. It may encourage the world enormously if cooperation with Pakistan could be extended. I am thinking of further cooperation in the basins of the Indus and the Bramaputhra rivers. Economic cooperation often is a good start for wider cooperation. This was also Jean Monnet's thesis. I take some encouragement from our experiences at home, although I apologize for the comparison: in my part of the world countries are so small as to be comparable to the states of this great country, sometimes to parts of states. The experience at home is that immediately after World War I the relationship between Belgium, our neighbour, and the Netherlands was one of great distrust. I remember that in 1920 our newspapers interpreted the construction of a four-track railroad near Antwerp as the intention of Belgium to invade Holland. This distrust did not have any basis, as it appeared later on. During World War II we concluded the Benelux Union between Belgium, Luxembourg and the Netherlands and this was one of the starting points of the European Economic Community. Often the problems between neighbours are the most difficult problems: a common frontier by definition constitutes a source of friction.

India's influence extends much further, because of its cultural contribution and the size of its population. As the leading country among the developing countries of the non-communist world India has been, and I am sure will be, instrumental in pushing other nations. The Prime Minister Mrs. Indira Gandhi [3] admirably put one of the issues at stake when in the Second World Trade Conference in New Delhi she said: "The question before the advanced nations is not whether they can afford to help the developing nations, but whether they can afford *not* to do so". By so speaking she showed that she sees the world situation better than most Westerners. Even though it is correct to state, as the Pearson Report [12] does, that by far the largest effort needed for world development has come and still has to come from the developing countries, the bottle-necks at the moment are to be found in the lukewarm attitudes of the developed countries in matters of trade and of financial transfers. When speaking about what India should do for her own development I pointed out already that the fuller use of her industrial capacity, the extension of labour-intensive industries and the execution of the Calcutta Plan are all blocked by these bottle-necks.

Numerous are the contributions made by Indian scientists and Indian industrialists to international development. It would be impossible for me to give an equilibrated account of these performances. At most it could be the list of the representatives of these two areas of activity I had the good luck to meet, a small sample taken from the fields in which I have been active myself. Even this, time would not permit. But speaking of samples, I cannot help mentioning Professor P. C. Mahalanobis, the father of the famous sample surveys and of planning models [9], thanks to whom I was once received by Prime Minister Nehru. Then, speaking of Indian contributions to world development, I want to remind you of all Dr. P. S. Lokanathan did. Neither could I overlook mentioning Mr. Tarlok Singh without whom Indian planning cannot be conceived of. I am sure the younger colleagues in my sample will forgive me that I do not mention them individually. Many of them made and are making substantial contributions to our understanding of development and planning. And it is my loss, of course, that as a rule a sample does not include all members of the population from which it is drawn.

Even though, as the Polish joke goes, production is only the brief interval between the construction of a plan and the evaluation of its execution, planners have become aware that the execution of a plan is of some importance and that managers are quite useful people, especially if they are able to export, although not only in that capacity. In a developing country one of the most precious capabilities a manager may have — or else may have to acquire — is to employ people, which gradually has become more difficult than to use machines.

Jawaharlal Nehru was the architect of India's foreign policy, the policy of non-alignment. In a world threatened with polarization because of the East–West conflict this was a wise policy because it was an attempt to create a more stable pattern of thinking. This was understood in the West only much later. For its influence to grow this policy needs an economically strong non-committed world and this is one more reason in favour of a thorough policy of development for the Second Development Decade.

India can enhance her position as a mediator between extremists of East and West also by elaborating her brand of socialism, using to the full all that modern science has to teach us about the optimal social order and applying that knowledge with the courage characteristic of great men such as Gandhi and Nehru. As Myrdal's research has shown, the gap between principles and practice is bound to be strong in a developing country and this is one of the challenges: to bring practice closer to the principles.

It is my opinion that the various social systems of the world move in convergent directions. But if this is not the view of others, may I finish by commenting on a famous poem by Rudyard Kipling [7]. In his time we spoke of East and West in a different sense. Today we call South what he meant by East. Today East stands for the communist world; and even that world now seems to have an East and a West. Instead of thinking of two cultures we may have to think of three or even four. The line of Kipling's poem always quoted is not too encouraging: "Oh, East is East, and West is West, and never the twain shall meet". My wife, who knows literature better than I, reminded me of the complete text, not so generally known:

"Oh, East is East, and West is West, and never the twain shall meet,
Till Earth and Sky stand presently at God's great Judgment Seat;
But there is neither East nor West, Border, nor Breed, nor Birth
when two strong men stand face to face, tho' they come from the ends of the earth!"

In my own words: if, in mutual respect, East, South and West understand they are all responsible for the world's survival, they must forget borders, birth and . . . creed! Or, rather, they must be aware of one common creed: that we have a common interest in survival, still to be organized.

References

[1] Adler Karlsson, G., Funktionssocialism, Oskarshamn 1967 (Swedish; an English translation is now available).

[2] Bernstein, E., Die Voraussetzungen des Sozialismus und die Aufgaben der Sozial-demokratie, Stuttgart 1904 (German).

[3] Gandhi, Mrs. I., Report on UNCTAD II, Geneva 1904.

[4] Gandhi, M. K., Address in Rangoon, 1929, cf. T. K. N. Unnithan, Some Problems of Social Change in India in Relation to Gandhian Ideas, Groningen/Djakarta 1956, p. 109 ff.

[5] Giri, V. V., India News, July 11, 1970, and International Labour Conference 1970, address on June 10.

[6] Herman, B., On the Problem of the Optimal Use of Factors, Netherlands Economic Institute, Division for Balanced International Growth, Rotterdam, May 1970.

[7] Kipling, R., Ballad of East and West, cf. Louis Untermeyer, The Pocket Book of Story Poems, New York 1945.

[8] Kornai, J., Mathematical Planning of Structural Decisions, Amsterdam 1967 (Original: Hungarian, 1965).

[9] Mahalanobis, P. C., The Approach of Operational Research to Planning in India, Indian Statistical Series, No. 18, Calcutta 1963.

[10] Myrdal, G., Asian Drama, New York 1968.

[11] Pant, A. B., India News, June 27, 1970.

[12] Pearson, L. B. and co-members of the Commission on International Development, Partners in Development, New York 1969.

[13] Ram, J., Address at Second World Food Congress, FAO, Rome, 1970.

[14] Swaran Singh, India News, July 18, 1970.

[15] U Thant, Ten Crucial Years, Statement at Conference sponsored by the Institute for Man and Science, 4 May 1969.

[16] Tinbergen, J., A Positive and a Normative Theory of Income Distribution, to be published by the International Association for Research in Income and Wealth.

[17] von Weizsäcker, C. F., Zugänge zur Friedensforschung. Soziale und politische Perspektiven. Bergedorfer Gesprächskreis zu Fragen der freien industriellen Gesellschaft, Protokoll Nr. 35, Hamburg, 1970 (German).

CHAPTER 3

On models of planning regional development in Hungary

JOSEPH SEBESTYÉN

Institute of Agricultural Economics, Budapest, Hungary

1. An overview

Regional planning as a sphere of planning the national economy appeared in an early phase of development of a planned economy in Hungary. In 1949–50, the National Planning Office organized its county filials and a central Section for Territorial Planning for the direction of their activity. This central group, which included among others the present author, tried to develop methods for regional planning, starting with a system of regional balances, the majority of which was meant for agriculture.

The tendency toward over-centralization and a growing rigidity in the direction of the national economy that prevailed until 1957 turned spatial planning into a framework for distributing tasks and resources not decided upon in detail by ministries. The 1960's brought a step-by-step extension of the sphere of independent decision making of the Councils as agents of planning for a hierarchy of areas.

The past system of economic direction and planning led to great spatial uniformity in agriculture. Today a process of specialization is unfolding among the large-scale cooperative farms, similar to the development which took place on State farms. Major factors of this process are new facilities of a biological and technical character, the growing scarcity of labor, due to ageing of the farming population, to the rural exodus of past years and the preference of youth for non-agricultural jobs, which is related to the costs of substituting for labor, and the imbalance in our price system. Guiding this process in a right direction is not only a matter of agricultural policies; at least so much depends on the development of rural areas as places to work and live in.

Dispersion of industrial production over the country has progressed during the past years, and has changed the face of the countryside in various regions. Regional development has, however, often been regarded as equal to industrialization. Due to this simplification, important aspects have been neglected in many cases.

2. Methods used for regional analysis

The work that has been carried out in our country in the field of regional analysis and planning is considerable but, as to the methods used, is mainly of traditional character. At this point let me mention only recent examples.

A project by Bartke [2], concerned with the spatial structure of Hungarian industry, has already been computerized. This study measured efficiency as a relation between the actual net product of different industries and the norms established, an aggregate of such figures being the characteristic of the area. Another study by Bognár [4], which is still within the frames of traditional statistics, extends the field of investigations and gives a method of assessing the production and consumption aspects of national income by counties.

Discussions concerning the requirements of more efficient planning led some people to shift to mathematical methods. Major areas of application to spatial analysis in Hungary have been production functions, input–output analysis and mathematical programming. The following are examples of different types of applications in each field.

2.1. Production functions

Krekó *et al.* [8] presented the relationship between wheat yield and meteorological factors in a county;

Sebestyén [11] calculated the relationship between farm output and major factors of production, per unit of acreage, for an overall sample of cooperative farms and for the subsamples referring to Eastern and Western Hungary;

Sebestyén [19] studied the relationship between total volume of output and factors of production in the cooperative sector of agriculture in 1965 and 1970 at the national and county level.

2.2. Input–output analysis

Sebestyén [11] analyzed representative farms in a county assuming both autarchic conditions and free inter-farm flows of intermediate products;

Sebestyén [16] studied the distributions of technical and inverse coefficients for a sample of cooperative farms, and compared the subsamples for Eastern and Western Hungary;

Csepinszky *et al.* [5] developed an input–output table for the economy of a county.

2.3. Mathematical programming

Sebestyén [11] computed the optimum composition of crops in areas characterized by different values of Thornthwaite indices and analyzed the formation of two types of differential rent;

Sebestyén [17, 18] derived the optimum structure of production, with changing prices and regional normative supply functions, for several counties;

Jándy [6] analyzed the optimal geographical flows of fertilizer;

Bikics *et al.* [3] investigated the optimum location of a network for distributing oil products.

3. Types of mathematical models for spatial planning

Mathematical models of spatial planning have often been built upon the use of a single mathematical tool. At an early date a model of planning over space had been conceived as a system described by formulae of different mathematical disciplines, due to involvement in the complicated problems of Hungarian agriculture. Consequently, the multi-period model of spatial location described by Sebestyén [12] dealt with agriculture and a detailed version [14], although aimed at generality, also appeared as a model of planning agricultural production. These models involved non-linear production functions, structural interdependence and optimization according to a linear or a linear fractional objective function.

3.1. The model of centralistic planning

At the end of the 1950's, a number of economists and politicians were aware that the centralistic direction, which still prevailed, should be transformed into a more decentralized type but the characteristics of the new system and, consequently, the possible paths to be followed were not quite clear. Thus, the approach toward a model of decentralized planning by developing first a model for centralistic planning specified for a sector seemed to be worth trying. The result was the model described by Sebestyén [14].

The assumptions were the following: (a) optimality is required at all levels of hierarchy, including spatial hierarchy; (b) the optima for the units of a level of hierarchy must be derived from the optimum of a higher level; (c) the conflicts of interest between levels of hierarchy may find a reconciliation by certain choices; (d) criterion of efficiency for all levels of hierarchy is the productivity of social labor.

According to these assumptions, a model covering ten years could be built at the highest level of hierarchy as follows:

(1) The national final demand is to be specified for each year of the planning period;

(2) The subvectors of national final demand, relative to a certain year and denoted by y_t, are to be premultiplied by certain Leontief inverses R_k of the national economy, k covering 3 or 4 years of the planning period while the coefficients of R_k are characteristic to a system of technologies assumed by planners to prevail during the kth subperiod;

(3)
$$R_k y_t = x_t \qquad (1)$$

where the vector of social product x_t embraces x_t^a as a subvector relative to agriculture. We get the vector of demand in agricultural products d_t^a for the sector model by deducing from x_t^a the quantities of agricultural products serving for intermediate goods within agriculture;

(4) A decision outside of the sector model states the share of agriculture from certain resources, elements of y_t, e.g. investment goods. These quantities appear here as upper bounds;

(5) The technical coefficients of the system of constraints and that of the objective function are weighted averages of those specified for the next lower level of hierarchy;

(6) The resources existing within agriculture at $t = 1$ are simple aggregates for which obsolescence and a policy of sorting out or scrapping is considered.

At the lowest level of the hierarchy, at the farm level, the basic assumptions may be met in the following way:

(i) There exists for each commodity produced within the framework of a certain system of farming, a non-linear function of productivity of social labor involving natural conditions as variables for crops with other variables being considered in their equivalents of social labor;

(ii) There exists an optimum technology for each commodity at a certain location giving a maximum of productivity of social labor at the respective location. In the case of animal products the optimization techniques require a combination of calculus and linear programming;

(iii) The farms cannot be forced to consider technologies other than those giving the maximum of productivity of social labor at the location in question;

(iv) The farms may be autarchic or use inter-farm flows as far as intermediate goods of agricultural origin are concerned;

(v) The farms of a certain area constitute one unit of the hierarchy level above them and the output of that unit given by the optimum computed for the hierarchy level in question serves for a subset of the constraints. The supply of resources is derived in the same way for a particular group of farms, while other constraints are farm-specific.

The solutions computed for all levels of hierarchy use a transportation model to determine the flows of goods connected with systems of farming based on inter-farm cooperation when such systems were selected by the computer as components of optima for locations.

On the basis of general considerations, many objections can be raised against a centralistic type of model by going through the details of the formulae which represent principles often spoken of by traditional planners but not enforced as a consistent system.

Instead of enumerating the reasons why a model representing centralism cannot support national planning well enough, let us state that another type of model for spatial planning of the national economy which *builds up* the national optimum plan from optima for lower levels of hierarchy is needed if we take decentralized decision-making seriously. A variant of such models had been described by Sebestyén [15].

3.2. The model based on decentralized decision-making

The main characteristics of such a model are the following:

(1) The managers of any unit have, and are also able, to make decisions about future action by working out their plan;

(2) Different systems of assumptions and/or goals may serve for starting points. Thus different plans may be optimized for a certain unit but one of them must be selected for realization;

(3) The managers of the areas belonging to the next level of hierarchy also have to develop their own plans and these must include the plans of the units below as entities;

(4) The selection of one of the optima computed for one unit may occur by the rules of optimization developed for the next higher level of hierarchy.

By using a procedure that complies with the above requirements, one could build up optimum plans for any level of hierarchy superior to another, under the conditions set by the economic reform started in 1968.

4. Some problems of model building for regional planning

There exist two main types of regional plan in Hungary. One of them is elaborated by the National Planning Office and is called a regional plan of the national economy. The 19 counties and the capital have been grouped into 6 large units. Thus the goals, requirements and actions of the national plan also are disaggregated into 6 sets. These plans are worked out for long and medium range.

If we consider that the economic reform transformed the managers of the farms, industrial or other firms or various institutions to independent decision-makers responsible for their actions, their present situation may be more attractive for a model builder interested in planning over space. These units no longer receive orders from above but they are influenced by prices, taxes, subventions, credit conditions and demand–supply relations. (Of course, partly different rules are valid for a number of firms and institutions supplying social, cultural or communal services.) This leads to the problems of planning faced by firms and by the Councils administering different areas.

4.1. Relations between councils and firms

Different types of firms can be found within an area administered by a Council. They may be owned by the State (state farms and non-agricultural firms), by a group (e.g., cooperative farms), or by a community. A state-owned firm may be subordinated to a ministry or to a council.[1]

The councils elaborate medium and long-term plans. The plan of a county council covers items such as the following:

(1) The goals set by the council in connection with the development of the firms and other institutions subordinated to it;

(2) The services to be rendered to firms or institutions subordinated to other authorities by units subject to the council;

(3) The goals set by the councils of the districts, towns and villages situated within the boundaries of the county;

[1] In 1970, the firms subordinated to different ministries employed 90% of the labor force of the State-owned industry, the rest falling upon firms subordinated to Councils, [20].

(4) The actions to be made in connection with goals of firms or institutions not subject to the council;

(5) The resources and means which may or must be mobilized to fulfil the plan.

These items mean that the goals, requirements, supplies appearing in the plans of operations or development of the decision units, e.g., firms are integrated into the plan set up by the council for purposes of development of a whole area. This implies a system of flows of information, in order to have the necessary co-ordination between plans developed by the National Planning Office, the ministries, firms and institutions and by the councils.

4.2. A model for planning development of a county

The formulation as a mathematical programming problem covering several periods, where one period may consist of one or more years, seems to be a reasonable approach and the model described by Sebestyén [15] may serve as a starting point.

4.2.1. The variables

In agriculture, the variables identified by type of ownership, geographical location etc. may stand for different feasible or optimum plans of units, or rather aggregates of units.

The variables for industry may be represented by variants of development plans of existing firms and new establishments already decided upon or still under discussion.

Development plans of communal and other services and infrastructure elaborated by councils for districts, towns and villages, as well as other projects developed by ministries or other organizations may constitute a third group of variables.

The variables that represent producing units are denoted by x_j while y_j stands for variables grouping plans for services, building of residential quarters, social-cultural establishments and infrastructure. The variables z_j^t include inflows like imports of goods for investment or consumption, labor force coming from other regions either to become residents (z_{jh}^t) or as commuters (z_{jc}^t). Subventions to sectors of the sphere of production and credits may be denoted by r_j^t.[2]

---

[2] The variables without a superscript t are considered for the whole planning period while those with the superscript t, like z_j, relate to a subperiod, and eventually to a single year. The superscript t above matrices and column vectors denotes the time dimensions of the constraints.

4.2.2. The constraints

Resources like land, farm or factory buildings, etc. are denoted by b^t_{11}, and the requirements of the variables appear as elements of the matrices A^t_{x1}, A^t_{y1} and A^t_{z1}. Under these definitions the relationship becomes:

$$A^t_{x1} x + A^t_{y1} y + A^t_{z1} z^t \leqq b^t_{11}. \tag{2}$$

Land is a scarce resource since reclamation can hardly cope with the needs of urbanization and infrastructure development. A distinction by quality is of great importance.

The labor constraint is as follows:

$$A^t_{x2} x + A^t_{y2} y - z^t_h - z^t_c \leqq b^t_{12}. \tag{3}$$

Labor constitutes a great problem for the regional planners. The demographic picture is rather unfavorable since very low rates of natural increase[3] combined with coefficients of net reproduction less than unity and ageing, particularly in agriculture, means a shortage of labor in the next decade all over the country. It seems not to be possible to speed up technical change to cope with such a situation, without drastic changes in the structure of production. This is a burning problem, especially in agriculture, where the changes proposed by technologists are very expensive while the anticipated shifts in the structure of production might affect the interests of the consumers and the balance of payments.

The balances for services, housing, social-cultural and infrastructural establishments are:

$$A^t_{x3} x - y + A^t_{h3} z^t_h + A^t_{c3} z^t_c \leqq 0. \tag{4}$$

The balances of commodities which include goods for consumption, for investment and intermediate products are represented as

$$B^t_1 x + B^t_2 y - z^t \leqq 0, \tag{5}$$

[3] Rates of natural increase, 3.0 per thousand on the national level in 1970, had a spatial variation as follows [20]:

Classes of rate of natural increase (per thousand)	Number of regions in a class	Share of regions in a class from total population (%)
< 0	1	18.81
$0 \; - 2.0$	5	20.39
$2.1 \; - 4.0$	5	17.09
$4.1 \; - 6.0$	7	30.50
$6.1 \; \leqq$	2	13.21

where the coefficients of B_1^t and B_2^t appear with either positive or negative signs.

Lower bounds in supplies could be considered for some agricultural products from sources within the county. Due to slowly changing customs of consumption, goods such as pork, poultry and eggs are also produced by families not engaged in agricultural occupations.[4] About 50 % of industrial workers are now residents of villages and have only partially liquidated their agricultural past.

The group of financial balances includes constraints for incomes and for sources of development. The constraints for incomes must be differentiated according to groups of population and, in some cases, according to areas within the county. These relations may be represented as

$$C_1^t x + C_2^t y \geqq b_2^t, \tag{6}$$

where b_2^t represents the minimum volume of earnings required for a planned level of living standards.

Capital formation appears in the model according to the regulations that became valid in 1971 and relate to both firms and councils.[5] These constraints are expressed by

$$D_{x1}^t x + D_{y1}^t y \leqq b_{31}^t. \tag{7}$$

The positive coefficients of D_{x1}^t and D_{y1}^t stand for requirements of capital to be invested while the negative ones refer to capital formation. The right-hand side represents the contribution by the state and can be regarded as a policy variable. Thus, variants of the optimum plan for the county may be produced by parametrizing b_{31}^t. The coefficients of D_{x1}^t and D_{y1}^t also represent policies because the variants of the plan for a certain unit may heavily differ, due to the application of different possible rules for capital use. Some of these variants of plan may be elaborated by the unit in question while others may be produced by the planners of the County Council and the solution of the regional model is expected to select the variant to be realized from the point of view of a regional optimum.

Subventions to certain sectors or enterprises are also a source of development and may be specified as

$$D_{x2}^t x + D_{y2}^t y \leqq b_{32}^t, \tag{8}$$

---

[4] In 1970, 54% of the slaughter weight of hogs were produced by families. The figures for poultry and eggs were 51 and 73%, respectively. However, most of the output of the families was used for their own consumption. The share of sales from their 1970 production was 12% for hogs, 7% for poultry and 19% for eggs [10].

[5] See [1].

with

$$r_1^t = b_{32}^t. \tag{9}$$

The term b_{32}^t may also appear as a policy variable and changed parametrically.

The balance of credits also has a right-hand side to be regarded as a policy variable:

$$D_{x3}^t x + D_{y3}^t y \leqq b_{33}^t \tag{10}$$

with

$$r_2^t = b_{33}^t. \tag{11}$$

To complete the balance of capital formation, we may add (7), (8) and (10) with (9) and (11) taken into consideration:

$$D_{x1}^t x + D_{y1}^t y - r_1^t - r_2^t \leqq b_{31}^t, \tag{12}$$

where the right-hand side continues to be a policy variable that changes according to a parameter.

4.2.3. The objective function
The optimization may occur with different objective functions. The minimum of the volume of social labor to be consumed by the plan is one of the choices. Different optima could be reached by maximizing the incomes of the population or capital formation in the county as the criterion of optimization. Even such an objective function should not be excluded which would maximize the amount to be channeled to funds for development of the councils.

4.3. The central model

The role of the central model is the selection from the series of regional solutions of one and only one for each region such that the sum of these regional optima adds up to an optimum solution at the national level.

The variables u_{kn} of the central model are the optimum solutions for the kth county computed according to the different objective functions and parameter values belonging to the various characteristic points. Another group of variables denoted by w_n^q refers to foreign trade.

The system of constraints consists of balances for commodities, for labor, the financial balances, foreign trade and finally the choice constraints.

The balances of commodities

$$S_p^t u + Q_d^t w^q = d^t, \tag{13}$$

equate national final demand with production, exports and imports. Upper and lower bounds for foreign trade by markets of goods may be set on the basis of long-term agreements and forecasts:

$$Q_f^t w^q \lesseqgtr f^t. \tag{14}$$

The financial balances embrace contributions by state, specific subventions and credits for development

$$\begin{bmatrix} C_1^t \\ C_2^t \\ C_3^t \end{bmatrix} u \leq \begin{bmatrix} c_1^t \\ c_2^t \\ c_3^t \end{bmatrix} \tag{15}$$

where the magnitude of the figures at the right-hand side may depend on government decision. This allows for parametric solutions on the national level with the choice assigned to the politicians.

Another financial constraint is the balance of payments

$$Q_p^t w^q \geq m^t. \tag{16}$$

The migration of labor force in terms of resettlement and commuting between counties is represented by

$$L_d^t u - Z_{hk}^t w^h - Z_{ck}^t w^c = 0 \tag{17}$$

$$Z_{hk}^t w^h + Z_{ck}^t w^c \leq v_k^t \tag{18}$$

$$Z_{ck}^t w^c \leq v_{ck}^t \tag{19}$$

$$v_{ck}^t \subset v_k^t, \tag{20}$$

where L_d^t represents a matrix of labor deficiencies in certain regional plans, Z_{hk}^t and Z_{ck}^t stand for 'labor imports' of the kth county by resettlement and commuting, v_k^t denotes the labor surplus in the kth county and v_{ck}^t represents those people in the kth county who are inclined to commute into other counties.

The selection of one and only one optimum plan for each region occurs according to the following conditions:

$$\sum_{n=1}^{N} u_{kn} = 1, \tag{21}$$

with

$$u_{kn} = \text{either } 0 \text{ or } 1. \tag{22}$$

$$\sum_{n_q=1}^{N_q} w_n^q = 1; \quad \sum_{n_h=1}^{N_h} w_n^h = 1; \quad \sum_{n_c=1}^{N_c} w_n^c = 1; \tag{23}$$

$$w_n^q, \ w_n^h \text{ and } w_n^c \text{ are equal to either } 0 \text{ or } 1. \tag{24}$$

This all-zero-or-one integer problem may be considered for Case A in solving the central model. Here, the matrices Q^t, Z^t_{hk} and Z^t_{ck} represent segments of feasible policies on the national level for foreign trade and for moving of labor force. Like the regional optima, they refer to total volumes and one of the variables considered for each segment must enter into the solution optimal on the national level.

Another possibility of treatment leads to a mixed integer zero-or-one optimization (Case B). If we interpret Q^t, Z^t_{hk} and Z^t_{ck} having coefficients relative to units, further being timed not only in the dimension of constraints but in the dimension of variables too, with vectors of continuous variables for foreign trade w^t_q and for relocation of labor w^t_h and w^t_c, our central planning model gains much in flexibility.

In Case B, the selection of variables entering into the optimum solution occurs according to the following conditions:

$$\sum_{n=1}^{N} u_{kn} = 1, \tag{25}$$

$$u_{kn} = \text{either } 0 \text{ or } 1, \tag{26}$$

$$w^t_{qn}, \ w^t_{hn} \text{ and } w^t_{cn} \geqq 0. \tag{27}$$

As far as interregional flows of goods and labor are concerned, the origins and destinations may be determined by submodels. These submodels can be used separately or built in as part of the central model.

The objective function of the national model may assume several economic categories: social labor, national income, subventions and contributions to regional development funds by State etc. The first and the third one should be minimized while the second is maximized. In the author's opinion, minimization of the volume of social labor should generally be preferred to the others.

4.4. The requirement of indivisibility

As discussed by Sebestyén [15] and Kazareczki–Sebestyén [7], the computer is required to select one and only one plan from the number of possible optima available for each region. Indivisibility has often been treated by authors discussing spatial planning models, and in this context we should mention Mennes *et al.* [9] and Vietorisz [21]. The reason for considering indivisibility has been in most cases of a technical or technico-economic character, although Vietorisz [21] noted the 0–1 character of the choice among projects.

In the author's opinion, a policy, or a strategy, is a consistent system with organic interdependences. Thus, a plan reflecting such a policy or strategy also is a consistent, interdependent system, in both the qualitative and quantitative sense. Consequently, a plan, as the policy or strategy behind it, is indivisible. Segments from different plans cannot generally be welded successfully into a new and consistent plan. This also holds for plans developed by optimization techniques.

On the other hand, these indivisible plans are specified for certain units to which the relative policy or strategy is valid. If we have enough indivisible, possibly optimized, variants of plans for each component of a macro-unit ranking higher in a hierarchy, we can select one for each unit so that they can be put together and appear as a feasible or even optimum plan.

We should consider that, under the economic reform, the firms and the councils administering different units of the country have become independent in making often rather complex decisions, bearing at the same time the responsibility for such a consistent system of decisions reflected by a properly elaborated plan. Consequently, the integration of their plans should occur by meeting the requirement of indivisibility.

5. A case study in multi-regional planning and price policies

The measures of the economic reform in Hungary could not eliminate the imperfections of the price system. A standing topic of discussion has been the structure of production and its change with respect to prices. Although the reasoning of the managers of large-scale farms still differs from that of computers fed by mathematical models, the computations started in 1966 have provided results worthy of consideration.

The last phase of the project described by Kazareczki–Sebestyén [7] was aimed at getting answers to these questions:

What kind of structure would be optimal in the 19 counties under prices set by the reform?

How would increases of prices for milk, beef and hogs affect these optimum structures?

How much subvention would be needed in the particular counties and for the products considered?

Could the optima based on different price structures or policies be integrated into a national plan?

How would increasing requirements in earning foreign currency affect the spatial structure of production, prices and subventions?

5.1. The model

Except for the state farms, the project covered crop production and animal husbandry of the country. The models of the particular counties had 12 to 21 constraints for land quality, 6 for labor, 6 for machinery, with 45 to 55 in total. A financial constraint prescribed the coverage of fixed costs and the amount of revenue claimed by rural people engaged in any form of agricultural production including, for example, factory workers living in villages and keeping hogs and poultry. Consumption of milk, pork, poultry and eggs by the households of the producers also were included as lower bounds.

Starting with 1968 levels, prices were changed parametrically: one by one first and later 3 prices at the same time but at different speeds.

The results of the optimum solutions were put together in a central model with food balance constraints for commodities, upper bounds for foreign markets and lower bounds for export earnings less import expenses in foreign currencies. In addition, there were constraints for choosing one from the optima computed for each county. The balance equations for food contained 1975 consumption on the right-hand side. The lower bounds for earnings in foreign currencies were increased parametrically. The objective function to be minimized referred to the amount of subvention to cover increases in milk, beef and hog prices.

The problem required a 0–1 mixed integer solution. Since no such computer program was until recently available in Hungary, a simple linear programming routine was used. To our pleasant surprise, many solutions were 0–1 integers for the regional variables and from the point on where the pressure upon the foreign currency constraints became binding, the standard linear programming routine allowed a linear combination of two plans for only one region while for the other 18 regions the 0–1 character had been preserved. We interpreted this fact as the expression of goodness inherent in this type of model and the usefulness of this framework was proven by several hundreds of runs. Thus we may hope that such models as the one sketched in sect. 4 of this paper would soon become tools of regional and national planning practice.

The following tables try to give some information concerning the results. Table 1 stands for a map of regional price policies, each 'price policy' being represented by the levels of the 3 prices subject to change. A column refers to a solution of the national model while the rows refer to the regional solutions that became components of the national optimum. Milk prices are given in Ft/liter, for beef and hogs in Ft/kg live weight.

Table 1

Equilibrium county prices for milk, beef and hogs under two alternative solutions of the national model

No. of county	National model, solution no. 1			National model, solution no. 12		
	Milk (Ft/l)	Beef (Ft/kg)	Hog (Ft/kg)	Milk (Ft/l)	Beef (Ft/kg)	Hog (Ft/kg)
1	4.22	24.15	23.53	4.99	27.35	24.32
2	3.72	22.07	23.02	6.19	32.36	25.56
3	3.70	22.00	23.00	4.04	23.43	23.35
4	3.70	22.00	23.00	3.70	22.00	23.00
5	3.70	22.00	23.00	3.70	22.00	23.00
6	3.70	22.00	23.00	3.70	22.00	23.00
7	3.70	22.00	23.00	4.38	24.82	23.70
8	3.70	22.00	23.00	3.70	22.00	23.00
9	3.98	23.18	23.29	3.98	23.18	23.29
10	3.70	22.00	23.00	3.70	22.00	23.00
11	3.70	22.00	23.00	3.70	22.00	23.00
12	3.70	22.00	23.00	3.70	22.00	23.00
13	3.70	22.00	23.00	3.70	22.00	23.00
14	3.92	22.91	23.22	4.13	23.80	23.45
15	3.70	22.00	23.00	3.70	22.00	23.00
16	3.70	22.00	23.00	3.70	22.00	23.00
17	3.70	22.00	23.00	3.70	22.00	23.00
18	4.14	23.85	23.46	4.74	26.34	24.07
19	3.70	22.00	23.00	3.70	22.00	23.00

According to agricultural statistics, [10], the national averages of prices paid by state purchasing agencies in 1970 were 4.08 for milk, 24.82 for beef and 23.81 for hogs. Thus, optimization of policies does not seem to be a wild dream.

Table 2 shows elasticities of the minimum amount of subventions to farm prices with respect to changes in the value of export excess over imports on dollar markets. The figures for the first 12 solutions with the national model are enumerated.

The results from this case study are being prepared for submission to discussion. Two statements should be mentioned here.

Firstly, this case study tested the multi-level planning model described in sect. 4 of this paper from the point of view of crucial characteristics. Thus, with the recently established computing facilities, such planning is a practical possibility.

Table 2

Elasticity of subventions to milk, beef and hog prices with respect to changes in the value of export excess over imports

No. of solution	Per cent
1	8.13
2	7.94
3	7.31
4	9.00
5	8.27
6	8.43
7	9.38
8	6.63
9	5.54
10	5.52
11	5.82
12	6.97

Secondly, under the conditions prevailing, and anticipated to prevail in Hungary, agricultural policies and development strategies might more efficiently be planned within a framework like that described in sect. 4, for a general, multi-sectoral–multi-level planning over space and time.

References

[1] A népgazdaság irányitási rendszere, 1970, Közgazdasági és Jogi Kiadó, Budapest. (The system of management of national economy.)

[2] Bartke, I., and Mrs. P. Tóth, 1971, A magyar ipar térszerkezetének hatékonysági modellje. (The efficiency model of the spatial structure of Hungarian industry), O.T.-Tg. I., Budapest.

[3] Bikics, Mrs. I., Gy. Meszéna and J. Szép, 1967, A köolajtermékelosztóhálózat telepitési programjainak meghatározása matematikai módszerekkel. (Determination of the program of location of a network for distribution of oil products, by using mathematical methods.) Döntési modellek. Közgazdasági és Jogi Kiadó, Budapest.

[4] Bognár, Mrs. J., 1971, A megyénként realizált és felhasznált nemzeti jövedelem számitási módja. (The method of calculation of national income realized and consumed by regions), O.T.-Tg.I., Budapest.

[5] Csepinszky, A., T. Kovács and Z. Novák, 1971, Vas megye kisérleti ágazati kapcsolati mérlege, 1968. (The experimental interindustry model of county Vas for 1968.) Paper read at the II Hungarian Conference on Interindustry Analysis.

[6] Jándy, G., 1961, Mütrágyaszállitás optimális terve. (An optimum plan of fertilizer transportation), UVATERV, Budapest.

[7] Kazareczki, K. and J. Sebestyén, 1970, Goals and problems in national planning of

agriculture, 1968. In: Economic Models and Quantitative Methods for Decisions and Planning in Agriculture, Iowa State University Press, Ames.

[8] Krekó, B., G. Párniczky, L. Pintér and E. Theiss, 1958, Korreláció- és trendszámitás. (Correlation and trend analysis.) Közgazdasági és Jogi Kiadó, Budapest.

[9] Mennes, L. B. M., J. Tinbergen and G. Waardenburg, 1969, The Element of Space in Development Planning, North-Holland, Amsterdam.

[10] Mezögazdasági statisztikai zsebkönyv, 1971, KSH, Budapest. (Pocket-Book of Agricultural Statistics.)

[11] Sebestyén, J., 1960, Optimumszámitások alkalmazása a legkedvezöbb termelési szerkezet meghatározására. (Optimization to find the most favorable structure of production), 19. sz. MTA. Mezögazdasági Üzemtani Intézete, Budapest.

[12] Sebestyén, J., 1960, A mezögazdasági termelés optimális területi elhelyezése. (The optimum spatial location of agricultural production), Statisztikai Szemle, 12. sz.

[13] Sebestyén, J., 1962, Matematikai módszerek alkalmazása a mez˝gazdasági termelés vizsgálatában. (Application of mathematical methods to the analysis of agricultural production), Akadémiai Kiadó, Budapest.

[14] Sebestyén, J., 1962, A short sketch of a mathematical method of planning of agricultural production. Bulletin 2, Institute for Farm Economics, Budapest.

[15] Sebestyén, J., 1963, Some thoughts on a spatial model for development purposes, Regional Science Association, Papers XII, Lund Congress.

[16] Sebestyén, J., 1967, On structural analysis in agriculture. Bulletin 15, Research Institute for Agricultural Economics, Budapest.

[17] Sebestyén, J., 1967, Egy területi árhatásvizsgálat néhány eredménye. (Results of a spatial price analysis.)

[18] Sebestyén, J., 1970, Facts for planning. Bulletin 29, Research Institute for Agricultural Economics, Budapest.

[19] Sebestyén, J., 1972, Agricultural production functions by regions. (In preparation for publication.)

[20] Területi statisztikai zsebkönyv, 1971, KSH, Budapest. (Pocket-Book of Regional Statistics).

[21] Vietorisz, Th., 1963, Industrial development planning models with economies of scale and indivisibilities, Regional Science Association, Papers, XII, Lund Congress.

CHAPTER 4

Development planning

WILBUR R. MAKI and JAMES E. ANGUS

University of Minnesota

1. Introduction

1.1.

Development planning usually is associated with the efforts of the less developed countries in planning for programs of sectoral and regional development. However, lagging regions and distressed areas in mature economies are increasingly the subject of special legislation and programs for reducing disparities in unemployment, income and economic growth [55]. Analytical and information-producing capabilities are being formulated for projecting future levels of employment and population and relating these projections to alternative regional development strategies.

Much of the emphasis in the construction and application of development planning models is upon four of five basic factors accounting for national and regional growth, namely, transportation access to resources and markets, capital formation and its financing, skill formation and educational planning, land ownership and control, and external resources for obtaining capital and imports. In addition, the so-called external effects of economic growth are becoming increasingly important in the choice of particular development strategies and programs [20].

1.2. Macroeconomic growth

The basic factors in economic development are approached from several different planning viewpoints. The first approach is one of macroeconomic growth and the selection of an economic growth rate consistent with the supply of foreign and domestic savings and foreign exchange [9]. Both econometric and planning models are used in the preparation of data and information for development planning. The planning models range from simple input–output tables to large-scale linear and dynamic programming models.

Macroeconomic growth models for development planning include both optimizing and non-optimizing types. For some models, objective functions, such as total external financing, are maximized or minimized. The optimizing models generally are used in 15-to-20 year perspective planning, while the non-optimizing models are used in the 5-year intermediate-term planning.

1.3. Sectoral planning

The second approach to model construction and implementation is from the viewpoint of sectoral planning. The sectoral models are available for countries with a substantial degree of central planning and control to assure balance of demand and supply in each sector and to set minimal levels of investment [1]. Macroeconomic models are a source of certain parameters and constraints, such as the total final demand for domestic production, for these models.

Sectoral planning emphasizes the investment requirements for achieving optimal levels of production and consumption. Because of intersectoral linkages, certain investment levels must be attained, not only in the critical export-producing industries, but, also, in the residentiary industries upon which both the export-producing industries and the domestic labor force depend for essential services. Most sectoral models are confined, however, to the agricultural and manufacturing sectors [28]. Recently, the education sector has received growing attention in development planning [9, 46].

1.4. Project analysis

Development planning also involves consideration of alternative public investments under project analysis [46]. Typically, project cost-benefit analysis is approached on a single project basis without explicit consideration of project impacts upon other projects, and it is concerned with the direct effects of an individual project on a given area. If the context of development planning is national rather than local, then project feasibility depends, not simply on addition to local income, but net addition to national income and well being. In either case, the basic criterion for feasibility is that capitalized net benefits are positive. Project analysis in the context of development planning, however, involves new approaches in measurement and model-building that account for both intangible and external effects of individual project implementation [52].

1.5. Regional planning

Regional planning is another facet of development planning, and one emphasized in this chapter [7, 21]. Regional models are prepared to assess the types of activities most appropriate for decentralization of industry and population, the investment requirements for regional development under alternative national growth objectives, the social costs of urban and regional growth, the area impacts of alternative regional development proposals, and the infrastructure and service requirements of growing metropolitan areas [4, 6, 12, 15, 19, 20, 22, 25, 29 – 31, 48].

Development planning at the regional level is viewed in terms of multi-state or multi-province regions where the planning emphasis is upon export-base expansion. However, area planning on a multi-county scale is an important dimension of regional development insofar as area planning emphasizes the quality of local environment for industry and population. Social investment in a favorable physical and economic environment is a necessary, if not a sufficient, condition for achieving a viable regional economic base [26].

Economic models for regional development planning are grouped under four major headings, namely, regional product and income, industry location, area impact analysis, and investment allocation. Under each of the four headings, elements of macroeconomic growth, sectoral planning, and project analysis models are introduced into existing regional models as a means of implementing and extending a regional systems approach to subnational development planning and analysis.

2. Regional product and income

2.1.

Changes in regional product and income are one measurable outcome of regional development. To illustrate the design and implementation of a system for measuring and assessing changes in regional product and income accounts, an interindustry transactions table is presented which provides the data base for constructing a multi-sector model of a regional economy [17].

An input–output table of the Iowa economy provides the actual data for the illustrative model.

2.2. Interindustry transfers

To simplify the presentation, the gross social product of the given region is adjusted to a $ 10 billion base-year level. The gross outputs of the two primary sectors, household and capital consumption, are equivalent to the regional gross product in the given region (table 1).

Table 1

Illustrative interindustry transactions in a regional economy of $ 10 billion gross regional product

Originating sector	Intermediate purchases						Final demands				
	Manufacturing		Services								
	Agriculture	Agriculture-related	Other	Regulated industries	Trade construction and other services	Total ($ million)	Household expenditures	Government purchases	Private capital formation	Exports	Gross output
Agriculture	2123	2186	106	1	14	4430	135	5	2	1629	6205
Manufacturing:											
Agriculture-related	260	347	35	4	39	685	942	16	186	2058	3886
Other manufacturing	104	177	526	53	313	1173	54	155	377	7	2234
Services:											
Regulated industries	175	95	77	88	275	710	457	56	29	147	1398
Trade, construction and other services	604	98	90	135	881	1808	3450	538	319	359	6472
Subtotals	3266	2903	834	281	1522	8806	5038	770	913	4200	7875
Distribution of business income:											
Households	2040	541	763	496	3460	7300		769			8068
Government	176	65	97	179	748	1265	716	281			2261
Capital consumption	183	119	170	331	447	1250	684				1932
Imports	541	68	369	110	298	1576	1162	160	414		3812
Gross outlay	6205	3886	2234	1398	6474	20197	8068	1980	1327	4201	35768

Source: See, Ref. [26].

While the input–output data for the illustrative region were prepared originally for a single region (i.e., Iowa), a two-region input–output model may be used as a means of acquiring an initial set of regional input–output coefficients.[1] These coefficients, when adjusted for internal domestic, i.e., interregional trade, are reduced below the corresponding coefficients in the national input–output table.

In the one-region input–output table, commodity exports, together with export-related services, are equivalent to nearly half of the gross output of the agriculture and agriculture-related sectors. Total imports are slightly smaller than total exports, which results in a net money inflow to balance the current trade account with the rest of the nation [37, 40].

A system of regional product and income accounts to deal with inter-account balances is derived from the data summarized in the interindustry transactions table. Thus, the gross regional product of $ 10 billion, which results from the remunerative outputs of regional resources, is represented by $ 7.5 billion of primary input originating from the household sector and $ 2.5 billion originating from the capital consumption. Total household income, which includes state and local income payments, is $ 8.1 billion, while total capital accumulation exceeds $ 1.9 billion. Because of a lack of profitable investment opportunities in the region, $ 607 million, or 31 %, of the total capital accumulation flows out of the region. The regional product and income accounts thus include intersectoral transfers among both current and capital accounts.

2.3. Social accounting system

By rearranging the flow categories of regional product and income under the five column headings, a regional social accounting matrix is obtained. The intersectoral transfers in a social accounting table are illustrated by the flow chart of income transfers between principal social accounting categories (fig. 1). The flow chart shows (1) the total value of all inter-account transactions, by originating accounts, and (2) the total value of transfers between each pair of accounts. The $ 7.5 billion of income payments from the production to the consumption sectors, for example, is shown as a money transfer from the production to the consumption accounts.

---

[1] A computer programming routine for a two-region input–output model was prepared at Iowa State University and used, subsequently, in developing state-level input–output tables for Minnesota, North Dakota and Iowa. Details of model construction are covered in forthcoming report [27].

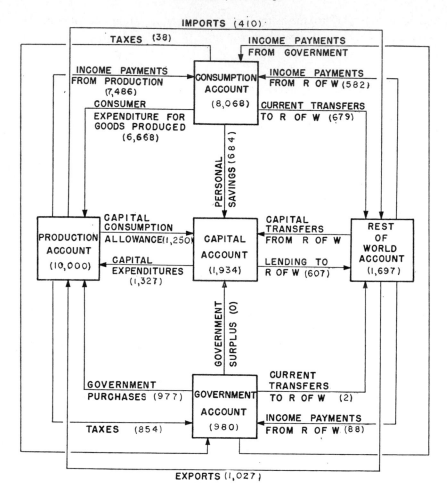

Fig. 1. Illustrative inter-account money transfers in a regional economy of \$ 10 billion gross regional product.

2.4. Simulation model

The system of regional product and income accounts is implemented for development planning purposes by means of a regional model for simulating year-to-year changes in each of the regional-social accounts. This model is built around the basic Leontief input–output equation

$$X = AX + Z, \tag{1.1}$$

where X = vector of sector outputs, Z = vector of sector final demands, and A = matrix of interindustry flow coefficients. Output is expressed as a function of final demand by the form

$$X = BZ, \tag{1.2}$$

where $B = (I-A)^{-1}$, the inverse of the Leontief matrix.

The first equation in the model relates capacity of plant and equipment to the previous year capacity by the form

$$X_t^K = X_{t-1}^K + (A_1)^{-1}(I_{t-1} - A_2 K_t), \tag{2.1}$$

on which the capacity constraint is represented simply by two components — the first-of-year existing capacity and the within-year additions to capacity.[2] The latter includes a certain amount of needed replacement expenditures, represented by the term, $A_2 K_t$, and annual business investment, which is a function of available capacity, capital stock and demand, i.e.,

$$I_t = A_2 K_t + A_1(A_3)^2 X_{t-1}^D - A_4 X_t^K. \tag{2.2}$$

While replacement investment is a function of capital stock, investment in new plant and equipment is viewed as a function of the imbalance between present capacity requirement, $A_4 X_t^K$, and the capacity requirement anticipated for next year, $A_1(A_3)^2 X_{t-1}^D$. In the first four years of model simulation, the matrix A_3 is given. Beginning with the fifth year, however, the coefficients are recomputed for each year. Each diagonal element is computed as an average of 1 plus the rate of growth in output demanded in the previous four years.

Annual investment, finally, is bounded by the form

$$A_2 K_t \le I_t \le A_5 K_t. \tag{2.3}$$

The upper bound represents certain financial and technical constraints that limit the rate of growth of capital stock. The lower bound sets a floor on capacity. Thus, gross investment must be enough, at least, to replace depreciated plant and equipment.

The third major equation relates household expenditures to lagged disposable income by the form

$$h_t = a_1 a_2 (y_{t-1})^D. \tag{2.4}$$

In this abbreviated form of a household consumption function, the scaler variable, a_2 (which is computed, beginning with the fifth year, as 1 plus

---

[2] The reader is referred to [25] for a detailed description of each element in the model.

the growth rate of disposable income in the previous four years), relates expected current income to lagged income. A portion of the expected income, a_1, is spent, while the remainder, $1-a$, is saved.

If the derived household expenditure is less than the household expenditure in the previous year, the value of h_t is increased by a portion of the difference. The new value of h_t then becomes

$$h_t + a_3(h_{t-1} - h_t), 0 < a_3 < 1. \tag{2.5}$$

This restriction has the effect of dampening excessive fluctuations in h_t.

Total final demand is computed next by using the form

$$Z_t = A_6 h_t + A_7 I_t + (A_8)^t E_0 + A_9 t_{t-1} + A_{10}(a_4)^t f_0. \tag{2.6}$$

In this equation, the column vector of parameters A_6 is updated each year by assigning certain growth rates to the coefficients. The coefficients are normalized so that the sum of the elements equals one.

Given the final demand vector, the input–output equation is used to calculate the demand for sector outputs. Thus,

$$X_t^D = A_{11} Z_t. \tag{2.7}$$

The vector Z_t in this case excludes the import sector.

Available labor resources by sector are calculated by using the form,

$$L_t = A_{12} A_{13}(L_{t-1})^E. \tag{2.8}$$

Beginning with the fifth year of the simulation, the growth rates are computed each year as the average of the four previous years' rates. Thus, the labor force in a sector is determined by the projected employment, $A_{13}(L_{t-1})^E$; it is adjusted to allow for normal levels of employment by the matrix A_{12}.

Again, as a gross simplification of regional structures, upper and lower bounds,

$$A_{14} L_{t-1} \leqq L_t \leqq A_{15} L_{t-1}, \tag{2.9}$$

are placed on the labor force. These bounds reflect institutional restrictions on the percentage change in the labor force from year to year. Thus, with a limited labor force, a corresponding upper bound to output is given by the expression

$$X_t^L = A_{16}(A_{17})^t L_t. \tag{2.10}$$

Realized output is the minimum of output demanded, maximum output of the labor force, and minimum output allowed by plant and equipment capacity. Hence,

$$X_t^R = \min(X_t^K, X_t^L, X_t^D). \tag{2.11}$$

Thus, the actual, or realized, output of a sector is the output demanded, unless the labor force and the capacity of plant and equipment are too small to produce the specified output. That is, for each sector, the minimum of the sector's elements in the three vectors, X_t^K, X_t^L, and X_t^D is selected.

Employment is a function of realized output in the equation

$$L_t^F = [A_{16}(A_{17})^t]1^{-1} X_t^R, \qquad (2.12)$$

which follows directly from eq. (2.10). Thus, a demand-oriented sequence of product and resource flows is assumed.

The next five equations are self-explanatory, given the appropriate definitions; i.e.,

$$K_{t+1} = K_t + I_t - A_2 K_t. \qquad (2.13)$$

$$V_t = A_{18} X_t^R; \qquad (2.14)$$

$$G_t^S = A_{19} X_t^R + A_{20} K_t; \qquad (2.15)$$

$$G_t^F = A_{21} X_t^R + A_{22} K_t; \quad \text{and} \qquad (2.16)$$

$$C_t = V_t - (A_2 K_t - A_{23}(A_{24})^t L_t^E) - (G_t^S + G_t^F + A_{25} X_t^R). \qquad (2.17)$$

The last variable, unallocated value added, is obtained by subtracting from total value added, V_t; the following: (a) depreciation allowances, $A_2 K_t$; (b) wage and salary payments, $A_{23}(A_{24})L_t^E$; (c) state and local taxes, G_t^S; (d) federal taxes, G_t^F; and (e) autonomous retained earnings, $A_{25} X_t^R$. Autonomous retained earnings are a minimum amount of earnings retained. Finally, the unallocated portion is divided between uses, namely, dividends and proprietoral income and additional business savings (i.e., savings in addition to depreciation allowances and autonomous retained earnings).

A matrix, A_{26}, is derived for the purpose of dividing the unallocated value added between the two alternative uses. The diagonal matrix is computed by the equation,

$$A_{26} = [(I_t - A_2 K_t)I][(I_t)I]^{-1}. \qquad (2.18)$$

In this equation, I is the identity matrix and $(I_t - A_2 K_t)$ is the vector of net investment. Thus, the ith diagonal element of A_{26} is the ratio of net investment to gross investment in the ith sector. If gross investment is made up entirely of the replacement of old plant and equipment, then net investment is zero, and the corresponding element of A_{26} is zero. If new additions to sector capacity are large, then the corresponding element A_{26} will be close to one.

The remaining five equations in the basic series are used in computing business savings and personal income payments (S_t and Y_t^B,) personal income (Y_t^P), taxes (t_t), and disposal income (Y_t^D). These equations are

$$S_t^B = A_2 K_t + A_{25} X_t^R + A_{26} C_t; \tag{2.19}$$

$$Y_t^B = A_{23}(A_{24})^t L_t^E + (I - A_{26})C_t; \tag{2.20}$$

$$Y_t^P = i Y_t^B + a_5 t_{t-1} + (a_6)(a_4)^t f_o \tag{2.21}$$

$$t_t = i G_t^s + a_7 y_t^P \tag{2.22}$$

$$Y_t^D = (1 - a_7 - a_8)y_t^P. \tag{2.23}$$

The 23 basic equations (plus the auxiliary equations) form a complete recursive system. Given the initial values of the exogenous variables, the values of the endogenous variables are derived as functions of time, lagged endogenous variables and current endogenous variables calculated earlier in the sequence of equations.

A flow diagram of the structure of the regional development model is presented in fig. 2. The exogenous and lagged endogenous variables are of order zero and appear in the first column. The current endogenous and lagged endogenous variables are enclosed in circles. Variables of order one are dependent upon variables of order zero. Variables of order two depend upon variables of order zero or one, or both. In general, variables of any order greater than one are dependent upon only those variables of a lower order. Thus, the values of nine series of variables are needed, initially, to obtain the values of all subsequent series of variables for the given year. In the simulation process, the outputs of year (t) become the inputs of year ($t+1$).

The model can be divided into two parts linked together by the fifth-order eq. (2.11). The equations of orders one through four are mainly concerned with determining the level of production, while equations of orders six through 10 are mainly concerned with the distribution of income created in the production process.

In terms of the computer experiments based on the regional simulation model, the well-being of the region is the result of two important factors — its resource productivity and its terms of trade with the rest of the world. Given this conceptual bias, the production account and the rest-of-world account thus become important means of describing the internal mechanisms of regional growth [10, 16]. Moreover, estimates of relationships between the rest-of-world account and the product account, and changes

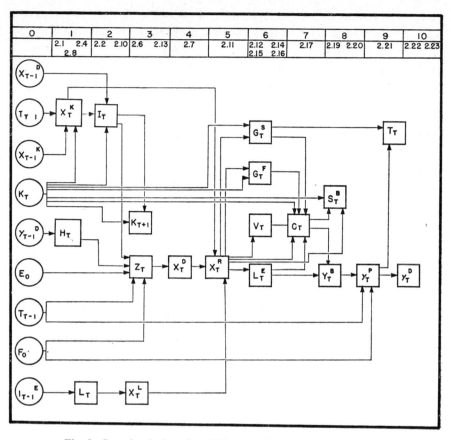

Fig. 2. Causal ordering of variables in regional development model.

in these relationships, are the empirical measures for achieving year-by-year consistency among the nine series of variables needed to initiate the computer runs of regional growth patterns based on alternative productivity and trade assumptions. Thus, the input–output table and the social accounting system are used as means of reconciling a wide range of economic projections used in regional development planning.

2.5. Industry location

Results of the computer simulations apply to the total region which, in effect, is considered to be a 'point' economy. Important differences within the region with respect to industry location are ignored. Also ignored are intra-regional trends in the spatial distribution of population and employment. Concentration of employment and population in the metropolitan core area, however, is a major issue in the debate over balanced national growth policy [14, 39, 45, 53].

The intra-regional distribution of employment is handled by means of a shift-share model in which the components of employment change are estimated for each sub-region relative to the region as a whole [3, 26]. Hence, the development region is disaggregated, first, into an exhaustive set of sub-regions. National growth and industry mix components of employment change then are estimated from employment projections for the overall region, which are generated by the regional product and income simulation model [24].

Derivation of the regional-share effect is carried out with the aid of regression analysis. Cross-section data for the base year are utilized to explain the variance in the regional share effect among sub-regions. Independent variables in the regression equations are lagged one period, which makes the model recursive. Thus, given base year employment and projections of the components of employment change in each sub-region, the future distribution of employment within the development region can be derived [15].

Employment projections based on the shift-share sub-model are a continuation of present trends in employment distribution, which represents the metropolitan concentration alternative as opposed to an urban growth option based on a policy of focused decentralization [14, 31]. To examine alternative distributions of employment, corresponding to alternative urban growth options, the shift-share employment projections are altered by utilizing a simple economic base sub-model. This approach involves the reduction of employment levels in the metropolitan core area in line with a lower employment growth rate than that projected by the shift-share model. The reduction in core area employment is then allocated to other subregions in accordance with the urban growth option under consideration. In terms of the focused decentralization option, a large percentage of the reduction in core area employment would be allocated to sub-regions with intermediate-size cities which have a long-run potential for self-sustaining growth.

The shift-share projection model provides a means of examining the distribution of industry employment within a large development region. Examination of particular sub-regions or areas for regional development planning, however, involves the use of models which consider a variety of economic variables, in addition to employment. For example, the evaluation of industry location incentives which are sufficiently attractive to affect existing patterns of industry and population distribution requires models with a capability for assessing the location impacts of changes in material costs and supplies, or market locations.

Computer programs are available for determining the location impact of assumed changes in material costs or availability, or market locations, as a result of a resource development project [18]. While these programs yield changes in the overall efficiency of an industry's location pattern, they are primarily applicable to transport-oriented manufacturing industries, and to development planning rather than industrial firm location.

In the programmed models of industry location, a given number of raw material sources, production points and market areas are prescribed. Each material source and production point has a specified unit cost and for each market a linear demand curve for the product is given, also. Transportation costs between any of these points consists of a flat terminal charge plus a specified line-haul charge. Given, too, is the number of units of material required for one unit of product.

Within the regional simulation model, the introduction of a programmed sub-model makes possible the assessment of intermediate-size cities (of 50 000 to 500 000 population) as alternative production centers in a large metropolitan-centered development region [2, 31]. The large, multi-state development region thus is viewed as a minimal-size unit for effective development planning. The development sub-region, which focuses on an intermediate size city, becomes, however, an appropriate scale for public intervention in terms of specific incentive programs to redistribute industry and population within the region [34−36].

3. Area impact analysis

3.1.

Area impact analysis is an important application of industry location and product-income simulation models in regional development planning [6]. In this section, however, the focus is upon potential extensions of the preceding models in terms of measuring the social and spatial incidence of national and regional economic growth.

A series of activity components in an extended regional systems model for area impact analysis are identified as follows: (1) population; (2) demand; (3) output and employment; (4) earnings and income; (5) capital improvements and financing; (6) facility location; (7) land use; (8) environmental management; (9) public financing; and (10) public policy.[3] In the regional model, population change is viewed as an intervening variable that triggers a series of subsequent changes in demand, output and employment, and other activity components. Submodels are formulated and implemented to deal with each of the activity components and inter-relationships between components are represented quantitatively.

Of particular concern in area impact analysis are the internal linkages of three broad service systems − the producer/provider system, and the distribution system. These three systems can be, and are being, stimulated by public intervention. They are strongly dependent, however, upon the export-producing activities in the region. Both the spatially-dispersed activities, such as agriculture, and concentrated manufacturing activities are identified in considerable spatial and sectoral detail in the regional submodels.

3.2. *Input–output sub-model*

The producer/provider system includes both the export-producing activities and the residentiary activities dependent upon the export-producing activities. Estimation of the individual elements in the producer/provider model of the development subregion is implemented in two stages. In the first stage, a conventional input–output sub-model provides a framework for estimating other relationships and variables within the producer/provider model.

Preparation of an extended input–output table for area analysis is accomplished with the aid of the two-region model cited earlier. The regional transactions table is disaggregated into two sub-regions, using the same procedures as were applied in the case of the two-region model. Thus, derivation of a sub-regional input–output table also is a process of successive decomposition of inter-industry flows from nation to region and from region to sub-region or impact area.

The extended input–output framework provides the context for deriving the second-stage analytical procedures. First, research areas are identified which represent logical extensions of a primarily resource-oriented approach to regional development planning. However, because of the conceptual and operational limitations of the input–output framework, research areas and activity components are described in terms of three broad groups of

---

[3] An activity component is essentially a group of related equations which are programmed sequentially and which relate to a particular group of activities in the development region. The 10 equation groups are specified for the pilot study subregion focusing on the Fargo-Moorhead SMSA in West Minnesota and Eastern North Dakota.

producer/provider sub-models, rather than only the input–output sub-model.

In the expanded study design, the input–output table represents only one segment of the total regional system (activity component 3), and even then, the representation is quite partial for development planning purposes. Moreover, to the extent that the preparation of a sub-regional input–output table depends upon low cost access to an existing regional or national input–output study, the industry classification must conform with prevailing standards. Thus, the 1963 U.S. input–output table and the employment projection series to the year 2020, which were prepared by the U.S. Office of Business Economics, provide the criteria for delineating the industry groups in the two-region (and two-sub-region) input–output models [50, 51].

3.3. Resource access sub-models

The next five sub-models are grouped together because of their close association with the input side of the input–output sub-model. Each of the five sub-models focuses upon the flow of production inputs from resource owners to the producer/provider system and the flow of income payments from the producer/provider system to resource owners.

The land allocation sub-model (activity component 7) provides for two patterns of land allocation — a rural and an urban. Important data sources for the land allocation sub-model in Minnesota are (1) a recently completed state land use inventory, which shows current land use, by a 40-acre unit, and (2) an area land type survey, which delineates key surfacial and subsoil characteristics of land for urban and rural development. Thus, the sub-model provides a framework for relating existing land-use inventories to projected future land-use patterns associated with projected future product-output levels for the sub-region [8].

In the private investment and financing submodel (activity component 5), individual establishments are geocoded and grouped into four-digit industry classifications for analytical purposes. Of primary importance is the specification and estimation of capital, labor and entrepreneurial inputs into primarily export-producing activities. This sub-model, therefore, is closely linked to other resource access sub-models and to the facility location and public financing sub-models.

The facilities location (activity component 6) sub-model relates primarily to the location of public facilities in the sub-region. Hence, linkages between the transportation–communication networks and the size and spacing of area facilities are important considerations in accounting for emerging patterns of land use, including conversion of rural-agricultural land into urban-industrial uses in the periphery of urban centers.

Public facility location is a key policy instrument in the sub-regionalization of state and federal service delivery systems [32, 42]. Federal-state cooperation is envisioned in the channeling of public facility expenditures to a limited number of local, area and sub-regional service centers. However, such cooperation will require a certain degree of inter-agency collusion in the preparation and implementation of area infrastructure budgets [44].

In addition, public facility location influences the spatial distribution of private sector services, particularly medical and other professional services. Thus, the level and range of service inputs flowing into the input–output sub-model will depend upon the data and procedures of the infrastructure and services sub-model.

The earnings and income (activity component 4) sub-model translates output levels into corresponding levels of labor earnings and other income payments. This sub-model, in the economist's view, is demand, rather than supply, oriented. Employment depends upon output and, indeed, it is derived from output by using output–employment relationships. And, the level of total income payments depends upon the level of employment in each sector. Thus, market-based input–output projections of future output levels determine the corresponding future levels of earnings and income.

A population sub-model (activity component 1) for generating area population distributions, by age and sex, is used in projecting future employment levels that are influenced also by population supply (as well as labor demand) considerations. Inter-area migration within the region is influenced by relative employment, income and consumption prospects. Hence, demand-based output projections are constrained by consumer considerations outside the conceptual and factual domain of the sub-regional input–output sub-model [23].

The environmental management submodel (activity component 8) deals largely with environmental services inputs for other resource access sub-models. Data on residuals recycling and disposal are processed by this sub-model, which, also, will include geocoded public facility input–output coefficients and constraints.

3.4. Service delivery submodels

The remaining submodels listed earlier are primarily demand-oriented. They are concerned with service delivery linkages within the producer–provider system.

In contrast with the resource access sub-models, the service delivery sub-models are influenced greatly by national considerations as well as local considerations. Hence, many of the explanatory variables accounting for subregional shifts in levels of investment, population, trade and public policy are dominantly exogenous to the pilot study sub-region.

The private investment and financing sub-model cited earlier includes the capital and institutional accounts of the sub-regional economy. Flow of funds data provide an indication of the net savings position of the sub-region [13, 37, 40]. Private capital formation is the demand-oriented component of the sub-model. In addition, public financing institutions (activity component 9) establish constraints on the supply side of service delivery insofar as the current year's public infrastructure outlays will induce private capital formation in the agricultural, processing, manu-facturing and other private sectors of the sub-regional economy.

Other demand-oriented components of the producer/provider system are represented by the demand sub-model (activity component 2). Projected sub-regional household consumption depends upon projected population, earnings per worker, and persons supported per worker. Hence, the popula-tion–consumption sub-model is linked to the employment–income sub-model through earnings and labor force participation ratios.

A sub-regional household expenditure function is derived as a means of allocating a portion of total sub-regional income to given producing sec-tors in the form of household expenditures for a specified mix of consumer goods and services. Thus, an additional series of consumption accounts are introduced through the population–income sub-model.

In addition, trade and transportation activities link the input–output sub-model to export markets. Transportation services are provided for moving sub-regional products to demand centers outside the sub-region. Thus, the demand-oriented trade–transportation activities are linked directly to the supply-oriented public facility location sub-model.

Finally, a public program sub-model (activity component 10) introduces current and projected public policy considerations into the overall producer/provider model. Public program impacts may originate largely from out-side the region; they, too, relate to demand-oriented dimensions of the sub-regional model.

3.5. Linkage and feedback

Each of the 10 submodels thus becomes a building block in the construction of the sub-regional producer/provider model. Feedback from one stage to the preceding stage is obtained by use of iterative procedures that ultimately will provide for man–machine interaction in dealing with changing external conditions [54].

Consumer/user system sub-models are included, also, in the extended equation system. These systems involve the use of behavioral relations for predicting changing consumer and user responses to the outputs of the producer/provider system. Involved in the transformation of producer outputs for consumer use is some concept of an end-in-view of the consumption process — measurable outcomes that add up to improvements in the quality of life in the development subregion. Hence, a third-stage consumer 'input–output' submodel is envisioned in the research design that relates a 'service access' sub-model to an 'outcome delivery' sub-model.

A final major component of sub-regional impact analysis model is the distribution system which determines the incidence of benefits and costs of sub-regional growth and development. Presently, sub-regional institutions, primarily local governments, are engaged in limited income redistribution. Sub-regional development efforts, however, are likely to favor some redistribution of the income and assets of a region between metropolitan core area and peripheral areas. Projections of alternative futures, when related to proposed programs and projects of rural–urban development, are one means of focusing on the distributional implications of development planning activities.[4] Eventually, the overall sub-regional model will include a series of distribution system sub-models for identifying the spatial and functional location of probable gainers and losers of alternative sub-regional development proposals.

4. Investment allocation

Investment programming activities are represented in both the private and the public financing sub-models of the regional simulation model. Also, the sectoral planning models cited earlier are concerned about investment allocation. In this section, the development planning process is depicted in terms of implications for establishing an investment allocation capability in the regional systems model.

---

[4] More active citizen participation in the development planning process is one factor in the emergence of a new sub-field of "distributional planning". For a planning-oriented discussion of the increased emphasis on distributional issues, see: William K. Tabb, Alternative futures and distributional planning, Journal of the American Institute of Planners 38, 25–42, January 1972.

An activity analysis approach to the programming of capital expenditures in a sub-regional economy was applied in the modeling of a low-income rural area in South Kentucky [41]. In this case, the programming model is similar to the 'process-analysis' type model for sectoral planning in less developed countries [1, 9]. However, labor requirements in the sub-regional model are detailed to a far greater extent than in earlier sectoral planning models and labor is viewed as a limiting factor.

Four categories of labor (i.e., managerial, clinical, skilled and unskilled) are identified. The unskilled category is further differentiated into six (two-month) sub-categories because of its seasonality.

The objective of the model is to minimize the total external funds required for area development to achieve given target levels of income and employment under the program. Thus, the study findings show that to implement a development program designed to raise per capita incomes in the area by, say, 5.6 % per annum (or $ 48 million for the area), fixed investment by outside agencies of $ 37 million is required for the total 10-year program.

The programming model applied to the South Central Kentucky development area expands greatly the total number of variables and equations representing a sub-regional economy.[5] Also, the inclusion of alternative income and population targets for the development area implies certain consumption goals, which are related to both income and population targets. Associated with these targets are certain external exchange and industry mix requirements and/or outcomes.

References

[1] Adelman, I. (ed.), 1969, Practical Approaches to Development Planning, Baltimore: The Johns Hopkins Press.

[2] Advisory Commission on Intergovernmental Relations, 1972, Multistate Regionalism, A-39, Washington, D.C.: U.S. Government Printing Office, April, 1972.

[3] Ashby, L. D., 1965, Growth Patterns in Employment by County, 1940–1950 and 1950–1960, Vols. 1–8, Washington, D.C., U.S. Govt. Printing Office.

[4] Barkin, D. and T. King, 1970, Regional economic development: The river basin approach in Mexico, Cambridge Latin American Studies No. 7, New York and London: Cambridge University Press.

[5] Barnard, J. R., 1967, Design and Use of Social Accounting Systems in State Development Planning, Iowa City, Iowa: Bureau of Business and Economic Research, University of Iowa.

[5] The model format has 586 activities (columns) and 239 balance equations (rows), of which 247 activities are 'slack' variables and 124 rows are 'dummy' equations for exports.

[6] Barnard, J. R., J. A. MacMillan and W. R. Maki, 1969, Evaluation models for regional development planning, Papers Regional Science Association 23, 117–138.

[7] Boudeville, J. R., 1966, Problems of Regional Economic Planning, Edinburgh University Press.

[8] Center for Real Estate and Urban Economics, 1968, Jobs, People and Land: Bay Area Simulation Study (BAAS), Berkeley: University of California, Institute of Urban and Regional Development.

[9] Chenery, H. B. (ed.), 1971, Studies in Development Planning, Cambridge: Harvard University Press.

[10] Edwards, C. A., 1970, Simple two region simulation of population, employment and income, Agr. Econ. Research, April 1970.

[11] Fox, K. A. and T. K. Kumer, 1966, Delineating functional economic areas, in: Research and Education for Area and Regional Development, Iowa State Center for Agricultural and Economic Development, Ames: Iowa State University Press.

[12] Hamilton, H. R. *et al.*, 1969, Systems Simulation for Regional Analysis On Application River-Basin Planning, Cambridge, Mass.: The MIT Press.

[13] Hansen, W. L. and C. M. Tiebout, 1963, An intersectoral flow analysis of the California economy, The Review of Economics and Statistics XLV, no. 4, 509–518.

[14] Hansen, N., 1971, Intermediate Size Cities as Growth Centers: Applications for Kentucky, the Piedmont Crescent, the Ozarks and Texas, New York: Praeger Publishers.

[15] Harris, C. C., Jr. and M. C. McGuire, 1969, Planning Techniques for Regional Development Policy, Journal of Human Resources 4, Fall.

[16] Hartman, L. M. and D. Seckler, 1967, Toward the application of dynamic growth theory to regions, Journal of Regional Science 7, 2, 167–173.

[17] Hirsch, W. A. (ed.), 1966, Regional Accounts in Policy Decisions, Baltimore: The Johns Hopkins Press.

[18] Hoover, E. M., 1967, Some programmed models of industry location, Land Economics 43, 3, 303–311.

[19] Hurter, A. P. Jr. and L. N. Moses, 1964, Regional investment and interregional programming, Papers Regional Science Association 13, 105–120.

[20] Isard, W. *et al.*, 1972, Ecologic-Economic Analysis for Regional Development, New York: The Free Press.

[21] Isard, W. and J. H. Cumberland, 1961, Regional Economic Planning, Paris: Organization for Economic Cooperation and Development.

[22] Levin, C. L., J. B. Legler and P. Shapiro, 1970, An Analytical Framework for Regional Development Policy, Regional Science Study No. 9 London and Cambridge, Mass., MIT Press.

[23] Lowry, I. S., 1966, Migration and Metropolitan Growth: Two Analytical Models, Los Angeles: University of California, Institute of Goverment and Public Affairs.

[24] Maki, W. R. and R. E. Suttor, 1966, Analysis for area development planning, in: Research and Education for Regional and Area Development, Iowa State Center for Agricultural and Economic Development, Ames, Iowa: Iowa State University Press, 193–214.

[25] Maki, W. R., R. E. Suttor and J. R. Barnard, 1966, Simulation of Regional Product and Income with Emphasis on Iowa, 1954–1957, Iowa Agr. and Home Econ. Exp. Sta. Res. Bull. 548, September.

[26] Maki, W. R., 1968, Infrastructure in rural areas, in: Rural Poverty in the United

States, President's National Advisory Commission on Rural Poverty, Washington, D.C.: U.S. Government Printing Office, pp. 86–109.

[27] Maki, W. R. *et al.*, Minnesota Interindustry Transactions, 1963: Comparisons with Iowa, North Dakota and the Rest of U.S., Department of Agr. and Applied Economics, University of Minnesota (in process).

[28] Michigan State University Simulation Team, 1971, A Generalized Simulation Approach to Agricultural Sector Analysis — With Special Reference to Nigeria. Prepared under U.S. Agency for International Development Contract No. AID/csd-1557-Agriculture Sector Models, Michigan State University, East Lansing, Michigan, November 20.

[29] Miernyk, W. H. *et al.*, 1967, Impact of the Space Program on a Local Economy: An Input-Output Analysis, Morgantown, West Virginia: University Library.

[30] Miernyk, W. H. *et al.*, 1970, Simulating Regional Economic Development: An Interindustry Analysis of the West Virginia Economy, Lexington, Mass.; D.C. Heath.

[31] Neutze, G. M., 1965, Economic Policy and the Size of Cities, Canberra: The Australian National University.

[32] Ostrom, V., 1969, Operational federalism: organization for the provision of public services in the American federal system, Public Choice 6, Spring.

[33] Pavelis, G., 1972, Planning Natural Resource Development: An Introductory Guide, Agriculture Handbook No. 431, U.S. Department of Agriculture, Washington, D.C.

[34] Perloff, H. S. and L. Wingo, Jr. (eds.), 1968, Issues in Urban Economics, Baltimore: The Johns Hopkins Press.

[35] Pickard, J. R., 1967, Dimensions of Metropolitanism, Urban Land Institute, Washington, D.C.

[36] Resources for the Future Staff, 1966, Design for a Worldwide Study of Regional Development: A Report to the United Nations on a Proposed Research-Training Program, Baltimore: The Johns Hopkins Press.

[37] Romans, T. J., 1965, Capital Exports and Growth Among U.S. Regions, Middletown, Conn.: Wesleyan University Press.

[38] Sazama, G. W., 1970, A benefit-cost analysis of a regional development incentive: state loans, Journal of Regional Science, December, 385–396.

[39] Shacker, A. S., 1971, Israel's development towns: evaluation of national urbanization policy, Journal of the American Institute of Planners 37, 6, 362–372.

[40] Shane, M., 1972, The Flow of Funds Through the Commercial Banking System, Minnesota–North Dakota, University of Minnesota Agr. Exp. Sta. Bull. 506, St. Paul, Minn.

[41] Spiegelman, R. G., E. L. Baum and L. E. Talbert, 1965, Application of Activity Analysis to Regional Development Planning, Technical Bulletin No. 1339, U.S. Department of Agriculture.

[42] Sundquist, J. L., 1969, Making Federalism Work, Washington, D. C.: The Brookings Institution.

[43] Swanson, C. V. and R. J. Weldman, 1970, A simulation model of economic growth dynamics, Journal of the American Institute of Planners 36, 5, 314–322.

[44] Tietz, M. B., 1968, Towards a theory of urban public facility location, Papers Regional Science Association 21, 35–51.

[45] Thompson, W. R., 1972, The national system of cities as an object of public policy, Urban Studies 9, 99–116.

[46] Tinbergen, J., 1967, Development Planning, New York: McGraw-Hill Book Co.

[47] Ullman, E. L., M. F. Dacey, H. Brodsky, 1969, The Economic Base of American Cities, Seattle, Washington: Center for Urban and Regional Research, University of Washington.

[48] U.S. Dept. Agriculture, 1969, Evaluating the Economic Structure of a Rural Area Demonstration of an Input–Output Analysis, ERS-386.

[49] U.S. Department of Commerce, Area Redevelopment Policies in Britain and the Countries of the Common Market, Economic Development Research Area Redevelopment Administration.

[50] U.S. Department of Commerce, 1969, Input–Output Structure of the U.S. Economy: 1963 Volume 1 — Transaction Data for Detailed Industries, Office of Business Economics.

[51] U.S. Department of Commerce, 1972, Employment, Population and Income Projections to year 2020, Prepared by U.S. Office of Business Economics for Water Resources Council, Washington, D.C.

[52] Westphal, L. E., 1971, Planning Investments with Economies of Scale, Amsterdam: North-Holland Publ. Co.

[53] Weitz, R., 1965, Rural development through regional planning in Israel, Journal of Farm Economics 47, 634–651.

[54] Wood, M. K. and D. E. Labovitz, 1969, Chapter 5 Appendix: Implementation of the Korean sectoral model, in: Irma Adelman (ed.), Practical Approaches to Development Planning, Baltimore: Johns Hopkins Press, pp. 135–143.

[55] Wood, W. D. and R. S. Thoman (eds.), 1965, Areas of Economic Stress in Canada, Kingston, Ontario: Industrial Relations Center, Queen's University.

Economic adjustment research for policy guidance: an example from agriculture

THOMAS A. MILLER

Economic Research Service, USDA

1. Introduction

Almost daily a number of "what if" questions are raised by public policy-makers in the U.S. Department of Agriculture. Many policy questions are of this type: What would be the probable acreage and production of wheat next year if proposed changes are made in the Government wheat program? How would these wheat production changes affect the production of feed grains? How much will the proposed feed grain program cost the Government? What will be the most likely effects of proposed programs on aggregate farm income and resource use? Answers to such questions are a necessary ingredient in the formulation of effective farm policies and programs.

Such questions have always been responded to by regional and commodity policy specialists who, knowing agriculture and economics, brought informed judgment to bear on the question. Often, the responses of such specialists were not based on formal analysis of the specific policy question at hand but were more in the nature of a by-product of their jobs, which required them to be informed on certain resources, commodities, types of farms, etc. Thus, such specialists drew logical inferences from available data and research results, and seasoned these with informed judgments as required by the particular situation and problem.

Effective policy guidance is not possible without the data and results of ongoing research and the informed judgment of specialists. However, policy specialists often face an extremely complex set of relationships and questions due to the sensitive balance between the production and marketing requirements of many agricultural commodities. Many of today's researchers and administrators are placing increased emphasis on formal economic models for the development of timely economic intelligence. These models help the policy specialist by providing a systematic way of bringing more quantitative facts and relationships to bear on the policy question than the human mind alone can analyze. In this context, formal analytical models complement the traditional process of policy formulation.

In response to the need for formal economic models to help guide policy formulation, the Farm Production Economics Division of the USDA's Economic Research Service has developed a specially designed research activity. This research activity is not confined to any one programming or statistical model. Rather, it utilizes a system of models, techniques, and analytical procedures to aid in the analysis and evaluation of policy proposals.

Three characteristics distinguish the FPED research effort: (1) the use of a complementary system of tools, (2) the team approach involving a group of researchers working on a common problem, and (3) the continuity of the effort over time. The integrated research system provides the capability to make maximum use of all available research resources — models, data, and the informed judgment of a group of specialists.

The objective of the FPED research effort is to estimate short-run production and resource use under alternative Government programs and changing economic and technical conditions. The estimates are primarily of United States totals, but are also made for major producing areas and farming situations. The analysis is designed to yield timely, short-term estimates (one or two years) of the aggregate production response that would likely result from changes in a variety of factors including prices, costs, technologies, and Government programs. The estimates include assessment of the impacts on farm income and U.S. Treasury costs. The current emphasis of the research effort is on major crops such as cotton, wheat, feed grains, and soybeans. Livestock are considered only to the extent that their inclusion contributes to more accurate crop acreage and production estimates — no regional or national estimates of livestock production are made.

The production response estimates are not forecasts as such. Rather, these estimates are the probable or 'most likely' year to year production response expected under specified alternative conditions. Thus, the models are used to quantify the likely impact on production, resource use and farm income of given or assumed alternative conditions rather than to predict those conditions and then estimate the most probable outcome.

2. APAS — An analytical system

2.1.

The system of models and procedures utilized by FPED is called the Aggregate Production Analysis System (APAS). This system brings together data from many sources, several econometric techniques, and individual informed judgment and technical skills. Its design is based on three primary considerations: (1) flexibility — the system must be able to answer a wide variety of questions; (2) sufficiently refined — reasonably accurate estimates are required; and (3) timely — the system needs to provide answers in a short period of time [5, p. 2]. The organization of the system and the tools that make it up are constantly being revised and improved as policy issues change, as the data base changes, and as experience is gained concerning the nature of the system and the contribution of each component to the overall research mission.

2.2. An overview of APAS

APAS began in 1964 with the development of a specific, formal model called the National Model of Agricultural Production Response [15]. While the dimensions of APAS were not fully envisioned at that time, it was generally agreed that a truly effective response to policy questions would require a system of models and a marriage of formal and informal approaches. Indeed, early experience with the National Model suggested that no model could provide all of the quantitative intelligence on aggregate production response that policy makers require. Some policy questions relate to a long-term 5 to 10 year adjustment process. Other questions are concerned with the immediate or short-term response to commodity programs. Some are best responded to by using regression techniques, others by linear programming and still others by budgeting, simulation, and the study of individual or representative farms. As a result, the capability to do relevant policy analysis is enhanced by an integrated research system that can make use of many research resources [17, p. 1534].

A schematic diagram of APAS is shown in fig. 1. The process of policy analysis begins at the bottom of the figure with the introduction of a policy question. An analytical process is set in motion as the question is interpreted and translated into a research question. The translation involves identifying the appropriate variables and relationships to be manipulated and those to be estimated; deciding what method or methods of analysis

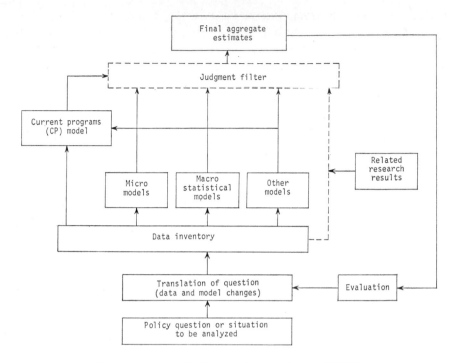

Fig. 1. Aggregate Production Analysis System (APAS).

seem most promising; and changing data as required. The accumulation and adjustment of data takes place in the box labeled 'Data inventory'.

The dashed line leading upward from the inventory box represents the more informal methods of policy research. As already explained, policy researchers have traditionally responded to policy questions by drawing together inferences from available data and research, and seasoning these with informed judgment. APAS builds on this traditional base by adding a set of formal models — shown on the left side of fig. 1. The estimates obtained from using both formal models and informal methods are funneled into the box marked 'Judgment filter' where they are weighed, condensed and interpreted before arriving at a final estimate to be passed on to policy makers. In this way, final estimates benefit from the informed judgment of the specialists doing the research work as well as from the formal analysis of particular policy questions. The human element in evaluating policy questions is retained and utilized in much the same way that it has always been, with the formal analysis system (APAS) being used to strengthen this process.

Any of several different formal models may be used to respond to a given policy question. Most important among these models is the Current Programs (CP) model. APAS also includes three additional types of models: (1) micro or farm level budgeting and linear programming models, (2) macro statistical or econometric models, and (3) other models such as interregional competition models. Each of these will be discussed in more detail later. Note from fig. 1 that these last three types of models may be used both for making final estimates and for developing input data for the CP model.

The accuracy and usefulness of the results are continuously evaluated to improve the system through the feedback loop of fig. 1. This feedback process may suggest changes in the models or tools included in the system, the data included, and the particular technique used for a specific question.

The use of sound judgment, both in interpreting the results and in applying the models, is possibly the most important component of the system. Unfortunately, it is easy to become overconcerned about small-order errors in the data at the expense of ignoring the limitations of models and how they are applied. For example, regression models may relate variables indicative of incentives but completely ignore the role of profit. In representative firm models, profits may be maximized with little allowance for risk or other factors in the utility function, or for variation in costs, yields, etc. A continuing process of evaluation and judgment plays a major role in APAS in maintaining a balanced approach towards realistic estimates.

The data inventory underlying the system deserves special attention. A significant portion of the research effort is devoted to developing and maintaining the data inventory for each of the major producing regions of the United States. This data inventory (1) serves the data needs of APAS for both formal models and informal responses and (2) is frequently made available to other research workers to service the data needs of a wide variety of research topics.

2.3. The current programs model

The Current Programs (CP) Model forms the core activity around which the rest of the work is developed. The current version is designed primarily to make estimates of the impact of Government commodity programs on the acreage and production of major crops for one or two years in the future. Its make up and logic have been previously described by Schaller and others [2, 5, 14, 17, 23] and will be summarized here only to describe the current configuration.

The CP model is based on the cobweb principle that current production depends on past prices, while current prices depend on current production. This cobweb principle is applied through the use of recursive linear programming which simulates farmers' decision making under a variety of conditions, treating each year as a separate profit-maximizing decision problem [3, 4, 16]. The programming model is designed to be aggregative in perspective while retaining as much micro detail as possible within practical limits of cost, time, and research manageability. The units of analysis are multi-county areas shown in fig. 2. Many of these areas are further broken down into aggregate resource situations. Currently, the national CP model includes 111 resource situations covering the major crop producing areas of the United States. Each is represented by a separate programming submodel.

There is a considerable variation in the programming matrices used to represent these different resource situations even though they all involve identical assumptions. Each matrix includes the major crops produced in the area and various interrelated enterprises. Separate activities are included for any Government programs open to farmers. The enterprise budgets underlying the cropping activities reflect current production technologies, average weather and an average level of management and efficiency. The total U.S. response to a given change in a parameter is estimated by summing the results from each of the sub-models.

Four types of constraints are employed in the programming matrices: (1) physical restraints which include cropland and irrigation water, (2) institutional restraints based on Government program provisions which include restrictions due to allotments, bases, and land to be maintained in conserving use, (3) technological restraints which generally limit the solution level of a specific practice such as the acreage of continuous corn consistent with current technology, and (4) flexibility restraints which play a primary role in determining the accuracy of the estimates. The flexibility restraints, as described by Day [4] and Schaller [16], appear in the matrices in the form of upper and lower bounds on individual crop enterprises or on groups of enterprises. Flexibility restraints are used to reflect the probable limits on farmers' aggregate response from one year to the next due to the host of unquantified restraints within which farmers actually operate; they are important because of the small number of physical and institutional restraints contained in the model. Various techniques are used to estimate flexibility restraints — from informed judgment to multiple regression. The method used depends upon the reliability and availability of data [9]. The flexibility restraints are usually re-estimated for each major change in any of the model's parameters.

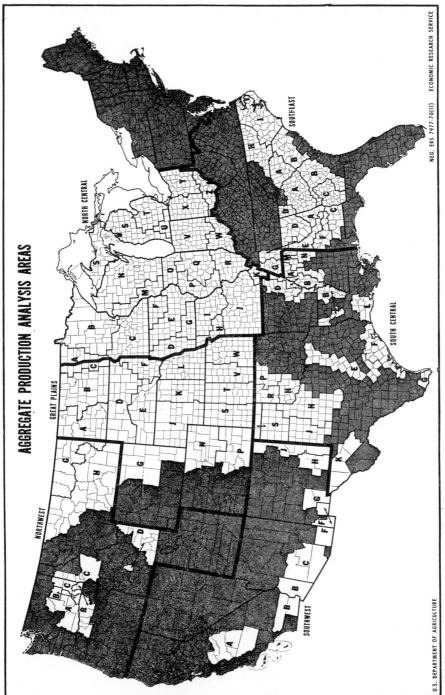

Fig. 2.

Analyses using the CP model normally include all resource situations, involve identical problems and assumptions, and end with U.S. total estimates. Much of the remainder of APAS is built around developing and servicing the requirements of this core activity. The CP model furnishes one common denominator upon which an effective teamwork approach can be based. None of the other tools of APAS is currently coordinated to this extent.

2.4. Micro models

Micro models or techniques may be used for policy questions when timeliness is critical. Two micro techniques are commonly used. Partial budgeting is the simplest, utilizing the same budget information used in the CP model. Examples of the use of partial budgeting include comparing corn and soybean budgets for several resource situations to determine the impact of alternative price relationships and similar comparisons to determine the profitability of farmer participation in various voluntary acreage diversion programs.

A second type of micro analysis utilizes linear programming models of representative farms. These models may contain activities and restrictions that cannot be used in more aggregate models. Usually, flexibility restraints are omitted. A few such matrices may be easily solved to determine the set of interrelationships faced by actual farmers as they make decisions concerning how to respond to Government programs. Results identify the type of reaction farmers may make, what resources are particularly limiting, and what alternatives appear most profitable. As suggested in fig. 1, this information is useful in answering policy questions and is also useful in structuring the CP model to analyze certain issues. Modifications are often made in the CP model after programming representative farms uncovers key factors underlying farmer response to a specific policy variable.

2.5. Macro statistical models

Formal statistical methods are used in APAS in two basic ways. The CP model utilizes a number of statistical point estimates in determining the flexibility restraints. Often these take the form of least-squares regression estimates of crop acreages for the next year. These point estimates become the final estimates for situations in which their estimated variance is low, or for situations where the CP model is expected to add little to their accuracy.

In addition to the flexibility restraint use, statistical methods are often used to analyze participation in voluntary Government commodity programs, the impact of program changes on acres planted, and changes in crop acres where the impact of program variables is minor. Such estimates have the advantage of providing the related variance and confidence interval statistics.

2.6. Other models and techniques

A number of other models and techniques are used in APAS as required by various policy questions. These techniques are represented by 'Other models' and by the dashed line in fig. 1. For example, the CP model budgets have been used to analyze general cropland retirement programs and related interregional competition questions. For this work, all of the budgets were combined in one programming model with no flexibility restraints. This model estimated the concentration of retirement in various geographic areas and the accompanying shifts in the production of crops when land was retired under alternative payment criteria [25, 26].

Capability has also been developed to make aggregate estimates of the impact of proposed policies whenever time is not available to use one of the other models in APAS. Many policy questions must be answered in one or two days. The procedure used in this situation is perhaps best described as an ability to make prompt responses by the systematic utilization of the best available results from other APAS models. The overriding restraint is the time frame set by the policy official asking the question. The particular technique is then chosen with the goal of making the best estimate possible within this time frame.

The continuum of procedures that have been used in such instances ranges from the purely informal component of APAS to the analysis of the most important resource situations with the CP model. Other model results are often interpolated and extrapolated. Even though formal models cannot be used on every policy question, having the framework set up and the data inventory up-to-date permits more useful responses within a short time constraint than would otherwise be possible. In such cases, APAS constitutes a stock of knowledge upon which expert judgment and opinion can be based. Currently, the number of policy questions handled via short time frame techniques is about equal to the number answered with the CP model. The climate within which public policymakers operate suggests that a significant number of issues will always need to be decided in very short time frames.

3. APAT — A research team

3.1.

Early experience with the national model by the Farm Production Economics Division indicated that a research team approach was required to provide the estimates needed by policymakers in time for them to be used in the policy formulation process. As a result, a research team was formed within FPED called the Aggregate Production Analysis Team (APAT). This team of agricultural economists has had the primary responsibility for the research effort since early 1967.

3.2. An overview of APAT

Currently, six of the team members (regional analysts) are located at land-grant universities in each of the different producing regions of the United States shown in fig. 2, and four analysts are located in Washington, D.C.[1] Location of the team members in different producing regions of the U.S. allows them to gain firsthand experience and knowledge of agricultural conditions in the different regions. Such knowledge can contribute to the analytical process in terms of more realistic models. Regional analysts often collect economic intelligence that may be useful to policymakers and, without any formal analysis, forward it to Washington for evaluation. In this manner APAT brings sources of economic intelligence, developed both through the formal analysis system (APAS) and informally outside of the system, to bear on policy questions. Geographical separation has not been a problem in any of the major functions carried on by APAT; rather the benefits from such separation have been substantial. The 'grass roots' contact with agriculture and the integration of expert opinions and quantitative analyses are strong points of the research program.

The members of APAT have research responsibilities that are broader than those suggested by APAS alone. Working with other FPED personnel, they strive to achieve complementarity between the APAS activity and other research carried out by the Division. They also are a source of technical

---

[1] The current regional analysts are: Southeast, W. C. McArthur, Athens, Ga.; North Central, Jerry A. Sharples, W. Lafayette, Ind.; South Central, P. L. Strickland, Stillwater, Okla.; Great Plains, Thomas A. Miller, Fort Collins, Colo.; Northwest, LeRoy C. Rude, Pullman, Wash.; and Southwest, Walter W. Pawson, Tucson, Ariz. The four Washington, D.C. analysts are W. Herbert Brown, Milton Ericksen, Rod Walker, and Herbert R. Hinman.

advice for other professional workers in closely related research, with special emphasis on aggregate supply analysis and regional adjustment studies. Thus, the team members have the opportunity to become economic intelligence specialists with unique geographic and commodity proficiencies. The store of knowledge accumulated from activities and responsibilities outside of APAT, as well as that resulting from APAT research, provides the basis for contributing to the policy making process in a direct and significant manner.

3.3. Operating characteristics of APAT

A division of labor has evolved among the various team members. The various components of the CP model are developed and maintained by the regional analysts in their respective regions. The CP model work is coordinated in Washington, D.C. All team members collaborate at regional and national levels in planning research objectives, analytical procedures and the calendar of work for APAS analyses. The regional analysts have responsibility for setting up the CP model to best encompass the relationships of their region, as long as comparable assumptions are used, specified problems are analyzed, and timeliness goals are met. Around this core activity all APAT analysts have the responsibility of adding the most appropriate models to APAS that are necessary to treat current issues. Thus, a national general cropland retirement model may be developed in Washington, a national Feed Grain Program statistical analysis completed in the Corn Belt, and a representative farm analysis initiated in the Great Plains. At the same time, all members of APAT may be working closely on a particular question involving the CP model. In this manner, the flexibility requirement noted in sect. 2 is achieved and maintained, both in respect to models and in respect to researchers.

Another division of labor exists between the Washington analysts and the regional analysts. The Washington analysts identify most of the questions to be researched from their firsthand contact with national policy making officials. They also handle the job of communicating and explaining the results of the analyses to policy making officials. The regional analysts, on the other hand, devote a higher proportion of their research effort toward assembling a stockpile of basic knowledge. They have the opportunity to remove themselves from the day-to-day routine of agricultural policy formulation in Washington. This opportunity allows them to perform more of the detailed analytical work in APAS.

The APAS data base is maintained by all members of the team. The

Washington analysts accumulate and tabulate data that is most efficiently collected at the national level. Included are official Government farm program participation and expenditure information, Agricultural Census information, and the results of various national farm surveys. The regional analysts collect and maintain information that is available on a state or regional basis, including FPED farm cost survey information, state Statistical Reporting Service information, and other data available in Agricultural Economics Departments at state universities and other research organizations. Data series that are unique to, or required by, specific tools in APAS are maintained by the particular analyst doing the research.

4. The nature of the results

4.1.

Actual applications of the models included in APAS, the nature of the results, and the way in which the information has been used in the policymaking process help provide an understanding of the capabilities of the system. The FPED research effort has led to many and varied reports, both published and unpublished. These results have been made available to the Secretary of Agriculture and other policymaking officials for consideration in making annual farm program decisions; the results have also contributed to the body of knowledge in agricultural economics literature.

4.2. An example of the CP model work

APAT provides a significant amount of intelligence that is not reflected in publications. Many of the estimates, particularly those derived from the current programs (CP) model described in sect. 2 and symbolized on the left side of fig. 1, are transmitted in the form of memos and verbal communi-

---

Footnotes to table 1

[1] Net weight, including micronaire premium of 45¢.

[2] Estimated July 1, 1972, wheat parity price of $ 2.98.

[3] The maximum set-aside percentage. The producer is assured of being able to set-aside 10%. An additional 5 or 10 % is at the Secretary's option.

[4] The original payment rate. A producer is also eligible for a rate of $ 0.80 for corn and $ 0.76 for sorghum if he reduces 1972 plantings of corn and sorghum two acres below 1971 levels for each one acre of additional set-aside. A non-controlled crop can be planted on the second acre taken out of corn and sorghum.

Table 1

Program assumptions underlying APAT analysis of 1972 set-aside program

Item	Alternative					
	1	4	5	9	11	14
Substitution						
Grains	Yes	Yes	Yes	Yes	Yes	Yes
Soybeans	No	No	Yes	Yes	Yes	Yes
Barley in the program	No	No	No	Yes	Yes	Yes
Loan rates						
Corn ($/bu)	1.05	1.05	1.05	1.31	1.05	1.05
Sorghum ($/cwt)	1.73	1.73	1.73	2.24	1.79	1.79
Barley ($/bu)	0.81	0.81	0.81	1.08	0.86	0.86
Wheat ($/bu)	1.25	1.25	1.25	1.56	1.25	1.25
Soybeans ($/bu)	2.25	2.25	2.25	2.25	2.25	2.25
Cotton (¢/1b) [1]	19.5	19.5	19.5	19.5	19.5	19.5
Set-aside, required (%)						
Feed grain program	25	25	25	25	25	25
Wheat program	85	85	85	83	83	83
Cotton program	25	25	25	20	20	20
Payment rate, required set-aside						
Corn ($/bu)	0.32	0.32	0.32	0.50	0.40	0.40
Sorghum ($/bu)	0.29	0.29	0.29	0.48	0.38	0.38
Barley ($/bu)	0	0	0	0.40	0.32	0.32
Wheat ($/bu) [2]	1.73	1.73	1.73	1.73	1.73	1.73
Cotton, upland (¢/1b)	0.15	0.15	0.15	0.15	0.15	0.15
Set-aside, additional (%)						
Feed grain program	0	15	0	20	10	20 [3]
Wheat program	0	0	0	0	75	75
Cotton program	0	0	0	0	0	0
Payment rate, additional set-aside						
Corn ($/bu)	0	0.54	0	0.80	0.52	0.52 [4]
Sorghum ($/bu)	0	0.51	0	0.75	0.49	0.49 [4]
Barley ($/bu)	0	0	0	0.65	0.42	0.42
Wheat ($/bu)	0	0	0	0	0.94	0.94
Cotton, upland (¢/1b)	0	0	0	0	0	0
Farmers' expected prices						
Corn ($/bu)	1.10	1.15	1.10	1.31	0.95	1.15
Sorghum ($/cwt)	1.85	1.93	1.85	2.24	1.62	1.93
Barley ($/bu)	0.85	0.89	0.85	1.08	0.78	0.89
Wheat ($/bu)	1.25	1.25	1.25	1.56	1.25	1.25
Soybeans ($/bu)	2.75	2.75	2.75	3.00	2.50	2.75
Cotton lint ($/cwt)	22.00	22.00	22.00	25.00	25.00	25.00
Cotton seed ($/ton)	54.00	54.00	54.00	54.00	54.00	54.00

cations to decision makers in Government. Seldom do such CP model estimates reach the formal publication stage.

An example is provided by a summary of the CP model work relating to Government commodity program decisions for the 1972 crop year. Planning for this work began in December, 1970, with preparation of a study guide to coordinate the work of APAT members participating in the effort. Changes in the commodity programs brought about by the 1970 Farm Act reduced the reliability of some existing APAS methods for estimating land use, acreage and production response to commodity program variables. Accordingly, new procedures were added to APAS and extensive modifications were made in the CP model to recognize the different ways for achieving production control.

A total of 14 alternative specifications of the 1972 Government commodity (set-aside) programs were analyzed by APAT. The assumptions underlying six of the more significant alternatives analyzed are shown in table 1. Under the 1970 Farm Act, policy officials annually must make numerous commodity program decisions. For 1972 decisions were made on (1) whether to allow feed grains, wheat, and soybeans to be substituted for each other for the purpose of maintaining farm base and allotment history, (2) whether to include barley in the feed grain program, (3) the level of loan rates, (4) the amount of the required set-aside and its payment rate, and (5) the amount of additional set-aside to be authorized, if any, and its payment rate.[2] Table 1 shows APAT assumptions concerning these variables for six alternative 1972 analyses.

CP model estimates of acreage and production of major crops in the U.S. under alternative 1 assumptions for 1972 had been prepared by April 1971. As shown in table 1, this alternative assumed a minimum 25 % set-aside requirement for corn and sorghum, 85 % set-aside for wheat, and 25 % set-aside for cotton. No additional set-aside was assumed for any crop. A medium level of farmer price expectations was assumed with corn priced at $ 1.10 per bushel. Acreage and production estimates under alternative 1

---

[2] The Agricultural Act of 1970 provides for production control through the use of a 'set-aside' concept. Participation in the program is voluntary with participating producers required to set-aside or keep out of production an acreage on their farm determined as a proportion of their historical base or allotment. After this set-aside requirement is met, producers receive program benefits and are free to plant the remaining acreage on the farm to whatever crop or crops they wish.

In addition to the minimum set-aside requirement, producers may be allowed to set-aside an additional acreage for payment. Under the Act, the Secretary of Agriculture has the responsibility each year to set loan and payment rates and to determine acreages to be set-aside.

Table 2

Estimates of 1972 major crop acreage and production for six set-aside alternatives, United States [1]

	Unit	1971	Alternative					
			1	4	5	9	11	14
All feed grains								
Planted	Mil. A.	128.4	122.9	120.5	121.5	118.2	118.1	115.2
Harvested	Mil. A.	106.3	106.6	104.5	105.4	100.5	102.4	99.9
Yield	T./A.	1.93	1.92	1.90	1.91	1.97	1.93	1.88
Production	Mil. T.	205.3	203.5	198.9	201.4	198.2	197.2	187.7
Corn								
Planted	Mil. A.	74.1	72.5	70.5	71.4	69.4	69.6	64.9
Harvested	Mil. A.	63.8	62.2	60.4	61.2	59.5	59.4	55.5
Yield	Bu./A.	86.8	86.2	86.2	86.5	88.7	86.7	86.1
Production	Mil. bu.	5540	5365	5206	5294	5282	5153	4777
Wheat								
Planted	Mil. A.	54.6	57.4	56.1	57.4	55.6	53.4	52.4
Harvested	Mil. A.	48.5	51.8	50.7	51.8	50.3	48.4	47.6
Yield	Bu./A.	33.8	29.6	29.7	29.6	30.0	32.0	32.1
Production	Mil. bu.	1640	1534	1506	1533	1506	1548	1529
Soybeans								
Planted	Mil. A.	43.2	47.8	46.4	48.9	45.1	42.5	47.4
Harvested	Mil. A.	42.4	46.6	45.3	47.8	43.9	41.5	46.3
Yield	Bu./A.	27.6	28.2	28.1	28.2	28.1	28.3	28.2
Production	Mil. bu.	1169	1317	1275	1346	1237	1176	1307
Cotton								
Planted	Mil. A.	12.4	12.7	12.4	12.4	12.9	14.7	12.5
Harvested	Mil. A.	11.5	11.9	11.7	11.9	11.9	13.9	11.9
Yield	Lbs./A.	442	490	490	490	490	475	480
Production	Mil. bales	10.5	12.2	12.0	12.2	12.2	13.8	11.9
Set-aside								
Feed grain	Mil. A.	18.2	20.2	26.8	20.2	38.0	32.5	37.4
Wheat	Mil. A.	13.5	15.1	15.1	15.1	14.7	19.9	19.9
Cotton	Mil. A.	2.1	2.6	2.6	2.6	1.6	2.1	2.1
Total	Mil. A.	33.8	37.9	44.5	37.9	54.3	54.5	59.4

[1] The CP model described in sect. 2 was used directly in preparing estimates for alternatives 1, 4, 5, 11 and 14. Alternative 9 estimates are extrapolations of other CP model results.

assumptions are shown in table 2, along with comparable 1971 data. Estimated production was about 1.5 billion bushels of wheat, 5.4 billion bushels of corn and 203 million tons of corn, grain sorghum, oats, and barley. Set-aside under the assumed program was estimated at 37.9 million acres.

Since the estimated production of wheat and feed grains was larger than anticipated 1972 demands, APAT began analyses of program provisions that would hold production to lower levels. By the end of June, 1971, five additional situations had been evaluated with the CP model including alternative 4 which allowed farmers an additional 15 % set-aside for feed grains (see table 1). As shown on table 2, the 6.6 million acres additional set-aside obtained under alternative 4 did not reduce major crops correspondingly as there was a less than one-to-one relationship between increased set-aside acreages and the decrease of major crop acreages. Results showed that additional set-aside acres reduced minor crops while leaving major crops virtually unchanged. This finding was consistent with the basic structure of the set-aside program which allows farmers freedom to expand the acreage of their most profitable crop(s) at the expense of other less profitable crops.

Alternative 5 evaluated a program provision intended to encourage shifting corn acreage to soybeans. It was hypothesized that farmers were planting additional corn acreage in order to protect their corn base history for future years. Alternative 5 assumed soybeans could be substituted for such corn with no loss of history. CP model results showed a small 1.1 million acre decrease in corn and an increase in soybeans under this provision as shown in comparing alternatives 1 and 5 on table 2. This feature was later included in the feed grain program announced by USDA officials.

During the summer and fall of 1971, APAT used existing CP model results to make prompt responses to a number of questions faced by USDA policy makers considering the final details of the 1972 commodity programs. These questions included: What would be produced on a regional basis if the conserving base requirement[3] were eliminated for participating farms in 1972? How would soybean acreage respond to prices above the $ 2.75 per bushel level assumed for the initial CP model solutions? What would be the acreages of major crops if barley was included in the feed grain program and the set-aside requirement raised to 35 or 40 % of the feed grain base? Each of these questions was evaluated using the existing CP model estimates, results of other work completed or under way in APAS and most importantly, the informed judgment of APAT members.

---

[3] Each farmer's conserving base relates to his historical acreage of cropland in conserving use, i.e., hay, cropland pasture, other soil conserving cover crops, and summer fallow. This acreage must be maintained on each farm participating in the set-aside program, in addition to the set-aside requirement.

USDA announced tentative details of the 1972 commodity programs in November, 1971. The programs contained many of the provisions APAT had evaluated as means for balancing production and anticipated demands. Barley was included in the feed grain program, soybean substitution to protect base history was permitted, and up to 20 % additional feed grain set-aside was allowed at a corn payment rate of $ 0.52 per bushel.

In December, APAT was asked to estimate the likely production response that would result from 25 % higher wheat and feed grain loan rates and corresponding increases in set-aside payment rates. This issue arose in response to a bill introduced in the Senate to increase feed grain and wheat loan rates 25 %. These assumptions are shown in table 1 as alternative 9. Based on CP model analyses already completed at that time, APAT was able to respond to this question within three working days. Results suggested that by increasing set-aside payments to achieve about 54.3 million acres set-aside, feed grain acreage could be held to about 118 million acres. However, the Treasury cost of this program increased substantially due to the higher loan rates and increases for both set-aside acreages and payment rates.

Five more situations including alternatives 11 and 14 were evaluated early in 1972 using the CP model. Alternative 11 analyzed the situation where farmers expected relatively low prices under the announced 1972 program and the Secretary did not accept the 10 % additional set-aside that was offered by farmers.[4] Alternative 14 assumed a program nearly identical to the final one announced by USDA in January, 1972. It includes a provision that farmers can qualify for a higher set-aside payment rate by reducing corn and sorghum two acres below their 1971 level for each acre of set-aside. A non-controlled crop such as soybeans could be planted on the second acre taken out of corn and sorghum. As shown on table 1, alternatives 11 and 14 also included the provision announced by USDA in January to allow additional set-aside of up to 75 % of the allotment on wheat farms.

APAT estimates under alternatives 11 and 14 are shown in table 2. These estimates suggest the additional set-aside offered by farmers would need to be accepted by the Secretary in order to reach the 1972 announced feed grain set-aside goal of 38 million acres. The estimates also suggest that the 'two for one' provision would result in over 4 million acres being shifted

---

[4] The program announced in November, 1971, by USDA contained the provision that a farmer could agree to set-aside up to 35 percent of his corn-sorghum base during the February sign-up period. At this time, he can also offer to set aside an additional 10% of his corn-sorghum base acreage. The Secretary of Agriculture would announce by mid-March whether to accept this additional offer.

from corn to soybeans. Since they are based on the actual 1972 program provisions announced by USDA, the results from alternative 14 will be compared with actual 1972 data by APAT to evaluate the realism of models and procedures.

Such work is typical of CP model use during the past three years. Results are generally made available through staff reports and papers within USDA. Particular options of Government commodity programs and different price expectations are analyzed and results are made available in time to be considered by policymakers in structuring the respective commodity programs for the year ahead.

4.3. Publication of CP model results

Three reports based on CP model results have been published. These are a report on the impact of alternative cotton programs by Strickland et al. [20], a report by Brown [1] on the response of soybeans to farm program changes, and a report by Miller [8] on 1972 Great Plains production response.

The report by Strickland et al. examines the impact of alternative Government cotton programs on the acreage and production of cotton and other crops in the Cotton Belt, as well as the effects on farm income and associated Government costs. Several alternative cotton programs, including continuation of the 1969 program, were evaluated for the 1970 crop year. Specific factors evaluated included the level of cotton support payments, the effect of marketing quotas, and the impact of changes in the cotton loan rate and market price. The estimates included in this report were originally prepared in response to questions from USDA officials concerning alternative specifications of the 1970 cotton program. The information compiled in the report was also used extensively as background material during the formation of the Agricultural Act of 1970. The report provides an excellent picture of the nature and scope of the APAT research activity relating to cotton [20].

Brown estimated the U.S. planted acreage of soybeans with expected prices from $ 1.80 to $ 2.50 per bushel using CP model results and a regression model based on 1946–69 data [1]. Changes in soybean acreage caused by reductions in the feed grain loan rate and changes in the domestic cotton allotment were also estimated to determine the interrelationships between the production of soybeans, feed grains and cotton.

CP model results were the basis for the estimates of the 1972 Great Plains production response to the Agricultural Act of 1970 reported by

Miller [8]. This paper utilized a statistical model to identify the relationship between changes in the set-aside requirement and aggregate cropland use. CP model estimates for the Great Plains based on this statistical relationship were presented.

4.4. Publication of the 1970 budgets

The data base underlying APAS consists of some items that have usefulness outside APAS as well as within the system. The best example is provided by the crop enterprise budgets that provide input data for the CP model. Nationally, there are 665 budgets for all major crops in the producing areas shown in fig. 2. These budgets have been published in a series of ERS publications titled 'Selected U.S. Crop Budgets — Yields, Inputs, and Variable Costs' primarily for the use of other analysts and researchers [6, 10,13, 19 24]. The comparability of the estimated crop yields and variable production costs, both within and among the major crop-producing areas of the United States, make the budgets well suited for interregional competition studies. Current plans are for constantly updating this APAS budget data.[5]

4.5. Other publications

Two studies have been reported which utilized the statistical models of APAS. The first study identified the relationship between the acreage of wheat planted and the level of Government wheat allotments under the Agricultural Act of 1965 [11]. Regression point estimates were made of wheat acreage planted as a function of the wheat allotments. These estimates not only explained how wheat programs have worked historically but also provided input to the flexibility restraints of the CP model. The second regression study reported an extensive examination of the Government feed grain program for the 1961–69 period [7]. Three factors found to be important in affecting the acreages farmers actually diverted under the voluntary program were: (1) the maximum portion of the feed-grain base farmers were allowed to divert, (2) payment rates for voluntary diversion, and (3) the relationship between the total support rate and the market price. The study contained guides for predicting farmer response to similar voluntary programs and identified variables for consideration in improving some of the other APAS models.

---

[5] A computerized budget generation technique is now being employed for preparation of budgets. This technique provides an efficient and accurate method of generating, maintaining, and updating enterprise budgets.

In response to the continuing interest in general long-term cropland retirement as a means of controlling agricultural production and increasing farm income, a series of studies have been completed analyzing this proposal [22, 25, 26]. This work made use of the same budget data used for the CP model. Different cropland retirement criteria were evaluated for their impact on farm income, resource adjustment, Government cost, and social and economic conditions in rural communities. A major policy implication is that crop production and the location of acres retired can be affected substantially depending on which criterion is used. Another policy implication is that to be efficient in retiring production, payments per acre retired should not be limited, but should be related directly to the productivity of land.

Members of APAT have published several other articles and papers that draw on various parts of the analytical system. Slaughter evaluated the impact of payment limitations to farmers on the effectiveness of supply adjustment and income distribution [18]. This study made use of data concerning commodity program payments to individual farmers and suggested that payment limitations above the $ 10,000 level would probably not impair the effectiveness of the programs in adjusting supply and would have only very nominal effects on income distribution. Pawson evaluated transferable non-domestic cotton acreage allotments as a means of allowing shifts to occur in the geographic pattern of production in response to technological changes [12]. Miller evaluated several different flexibility restraint procedures on the accuracy of recursive programming models [9]. This article contained suggestions for the proper use of flexibility restraints and their determination under a range of conditions and assumptions.

These publications suggest the applications of APAS have been many and varied; they reflect the flexibility of the system to provide a wide range of formal economic intelligence in a timely manner.

5. *Problems and proposed changes*

5.1. *Limitations of the analytical system*

Often, an analytical model or research system is criticized because the model builder failed to identify the boundaries of the model's capabilities. With APAS there may be a tendency to conclude that, given the flexibility and versatility of the system, it can provide answers to all questions concerning policy issues. A summary of the current limitations and scope of the activity points out the fallacy of such a conclusion.

Except for Government commodity programs, APAS does not explicitly include many of the institutional or structural variables that affect production response. It does not consider the impact of the changing political power of agriculture, changes in the importance of farm organizations, centralized decision making from vertical and horizontal integration, or other basic changes in the structure of agriculture. APAS also fails to incorporate subjective factors such as likes and dislikes of farmers or the impact of anti-government feeling into the analysis. Although some of these variables may be implicitly represented by the flexibility restraints, their specific impacts as independent variables are difficult to estimate.

The present configuration of APAS limits the research effort primarily to short-run (one or two year) analyses of production. Consequently, APAT is able to say little about the longer-run impact of alternative policies. The supply response and production orientation of the system fails to consider demand factors; such failure may lead to a lack of relevance in the information generated by the system. Limitations also stem from the failure to consider many of the linkages between crop and livestock decisions in production response, as well as the failure to recognize detailed restraints in equipment capacity, labor, and capital. Such limitations may be explained by a lack of data. However, they render the CP model an extremely naive portrayal of the actual decision making climate faced by farmers. Although such naive portrayals are not necessarily lacking in usefulness, resulting analyses may be lacking in depth.

Data problems are severe. Information on the prices expected by farmers, expected yields, costs and cropping practices, and physical and institutional restraints is difficult to obtain. The high costs of nation-wide surveys as well as the abstract nature of some concepts limits the precision of their estimation. Although recursive programming is based on the profit motive, little is known about profit relations required to induce aggregate shifts from one crop to another. Flexibility restraints present their own special and complex problems to the analyst; they are especially difficult to estimate when new program features are to be evaluated. And the problems of aggregation error in the CP model can be recognized but never solved. Such problems lead to error in many aggregate production response models and APAS is no exception.

Finally, there is the limitation of time. Many questions could be answered within the APAS framework if adequate lead time were available to do substantial research. Unfortunately, such time is seldom available. Trade-offs between time and accuracy must continually be made in organizing the research activity. Decisions must often be made that reflect the best judgment available at that time with only limited consideration of precision or reliability in the normal econometric sense.

5.2. More general models

Some of these limitations can be dealt with. Several models or techniques are being considered for possible addition to the analytical system. These include use of the Delphi process to elicit or bring together the opinions of experts, the addition of stochastic or probabilistic dimensions to the models, and the use of simulation techniques to more accurately estimate response to some program variables.

There is also the consideration of doing additional analyses outside the area of production response. Often, questions concern the final, overall impact of a particular policy as well as the initial farm impact. Such questions imply more intensive or general economic analysis on key policy issues. Domestic demand and exports, prices and food costs, farm income, Government costs and welfare factors need to be evaluated along with the current production response estimates. The systems approach to model building has been found useful in production response analysis — a logical extension would be to expand this system to consider all of the implications of particular policy measures.

5.3. Improved problem identification

APAT has been constantly faced with a timing problem. Often when policymakers define a problem and ask a question, it is too late to do substantive research. Providing more lead time for analytical research is a constant challenge. Attempts to meet this challenge are in two categories.

First, there is the possibility of searching out or anticipating longer-run and more general policy issues facing the rural public and devoting research resources to their possible solution. There are two possible payoffs from this activity. The anticipated policy issues may actually be the basis of questions asked by policy makers at a future date — thus, significant research can be completed by the time the policy issues develop. The more probable outcome is that the particular questions researched will not be asked directly, but furnish results that can be extrapolated to answer specific questions. Looking ahead and anticipation of future policy issues appears appropriate for a portion of the effort in policy research groups such as APAT.

Second, APAT has enjoyed a measure of success in establishing under-standing and communication with the users of the information so that they appreciate the need for lead time and the need to anticipate policy problems. Establishing this rapport takes time, skill, and patience, but possibly other model builders could learn from APAT's experience. The possible payoffs in the opportunities to do relevant policy research are potentially large and worth the effort. Success in this direction may be APAT's most important contribution toward increasing the role of economic intelligence in the policy making process.

References

[1] Brown, W. Herbert, 1971, Soybeans: Acreage Response to Price and Farm Program Changes, USDA ERS-473, July.

[2] Day, R. H., 1962, An approach to production response, Agr. Econ. Res. 14, 134–148, October.

[3] Day, R. H., 1961, Recursive programming and supply prediction, in: Agricultural Supply Functions, Estimating Techniques and Interpretation, eds. E. O. Heady, C. B. Kehrberg and S. Staniforth, Ames: Iowa State University Press, pp. 108–125.

[4] Day, R. H., 1963, Recursive Programming and Production Response, Amsterdam: North-Holland Publishing Company.

[5] McArthur, W. C. and P. Leo Strickland, 1968, Production adjustment research for policy guidance — the national model approach, paper presented at the Southern Farm Management Research Committee Meeting, Atlanta, Georgia, June 18, 1968.

[6] McArthur, W. C., 1971, Selected U. S. Crop Budgets: Yields, Inputs and Variable Costs — Volume 1, Southeast Region, USDA ERS-457, April.

[7] Miller, T. A. and S. H. Hargrove, 1970, Factors Affecting Acreage Diverted Under the U. S. Feed Grain Program, USDA ERS-453, November.

[8] Miller, T. A., 1971, Estimates of 1972 Great Plains production response to the Agricultural Act of 1970, in: Proceedings 1971, Western Agricultural Economics Association, Squaw Valley, California, July.

[9] Miller, T. A., 1972, Evaluation of alternative flexibility restraint procedures for recursive programming models used for prediction, Am. J. Agr. Econ. 54, 68–76, February.

[10] Miller, T. A., 1971, Selected U. S. Crop Budgets: Yields, Inputs and Variable Costs — Volume 3, Great Plains Region, USDA ERS-459, April.

[11] Miller, T. A., 1968, The relationship of wheat planted to wheat allotments in the Great Plains, Agr. Econ. Res. 20, 57–63, April.

[12] Pawson, W. W., 1969, Transferable non-domestic cotton acreage allotments, in: Proceedings 1969, Western Agricultural Economics Association, Corvallis, Oregon, July, pp. 86–89.

[13] Rude, L. C., 1971, Selected U. S. Crop Budgets: Yields, Inputs and Variable Costs — Volume 4, Northwest Region, USDA ERS-460, April.

[14] Schaller, W. N., 1968, A national model of agricultural production response, Agr. Econ. Res. 20, 33–46, April.

[15] Schaller, W. N., 1967, New horizons in economic model use: an example from agriculture, Statistical Reporter, no. 67-12, June, pp. 205–208.

[16] Schaller, W. N., 1965, Predicting Regional Crop Production, An Application of Recursive Programming, USDA Tech. Bull. 1329, April.

[17] Sharples, J. A. and W. N. Schaller, 1968, Predicting short-run aggregate adjustment to policy alternatives, Am. J. Agr. Econ. 50, 1523–1536, December.

[18] Slaughter, R. W., Jr., 1969, Payment limitation: Effect on supply adjustment and income distribution, Am. J. Agr. Econ. 51, 1233–1236, December.

[19] Strickland, P. L. and R. L. Harwell, 1971, Selected U. S. Crop Budgets: Yields, Inputs and Variable Costs — Volume 5, South Central Region, USDA ERS-461, April.

[20] Strickland, P. L., W. H. Brown, W. C. McArthur and W. W. Pawson, 1971, Cotton Production and Farm Income Estimates Under Selected Alternative Farm Programs, USDA ERS Agr. Econ. Rep. 212, September.

[21] U. S. Department of Agriculture, 1967, The National Farm Model, The Farm Index, 6, 4–5, November.

[22] Vermeer, J. and R. W. Slaughter, Jr., 1968, Analysis of a General Cropland Retirement Program, USDA ERS-377, May.

[23] Worden, G. and F. Able, 1968, A national model of agricultural production response, paper presented at the North Central Farm Management Research Committee Meeting, Chicago, Illinois, March 11–13, 1968.

[24] Worden, G., R. D. Tompkin, R. A. Benson, W. G. Bursch and B. M. Buxton, 1971, Selected U. S. Crop Budgets: Yields, Inputs, and Variable Costs — Volume 2, North Central Region, USDA ERS-458, April.

[25] Zepp, G. A. and J. A. Sharples, 1971, General Cropland Retirement Analysis of Four Alternatives, USDA ERS-462, April.

[26] Zepp, G. A. and J. A. Sharples, 1970, General cropland retirement: retiring low-net-return acreage vs. retiring high-cost production, Agr. Econ. Res. 22, 89–95, October.

CHAPTER 6

Unemployment and the international division of labour*

B. HERMAN

Netherlands Institute of Economics

1. The problem

Mounting unemployment on a global scale remains one of the most important problems in the world today. The phenomenon has two aspects: Conjunctural Unemployment, which prevails in western countries, where its recurrence is due to a malfunctioning of the system which can be remedied with the correct application of policy measures known to us for almost 40 years; and Structural Unemployment, prevailing in the LDC's, which cannot be solved by traditional policy measures applicable to developed countries. In what follows we will deal with the second aspect.

The problem of unemployment generally is to be considered in the context of unsatisfied needs. Since satisfaction of human needs, in the world at large, is constrained by availabilities of resources, unemployment of factors is not to be allowed. Viewed in this context the level of activity attained by full use of factors, refers to all goods and services necessary to satisfy the complex of human needs. Therefore, priorities, in the sense of choice between commodities, become a hollow concept since it is not a question of producing as many commodities on the list as is possible given the resources, but of allocating the resources to production of all commodities at as high a level as it is technically feasible. Once that consistency between resources and uses is satisfied, minimization of unemployment of different factors should be attained by means of a proper spatial allocation of the different production lines. The main implication of this is that the problem must be approached at world level, that is, no space can be left out.

* Mr. Mahfuzur Rahman, M. A., improved the English of this paper. My thanks to him. Errors, of course, are entirely mine.

The model described in sect. 2 aims at allocating the set of activities (without limiting their number in advance) to the set of spaces (also, as detailed as is found convenient) in such a way that total demand is satisfied up to the extent bounded by the capital availabilities (capital being understood as a combination of physical plus human capital) and that idleness of factors and costs are minimized.

The model, in effect, describes an optimal world industrialization programme. It will be proven that this will be conducive to the maximum potential absorption of un- and under-employed manpower and moreover, that the algorithm is also conducive to fastest consistent income growth rates.

The two assumptions are (1) that capital (and the property of it) is mobile while labour should be given employment on the spot, and (2) that there are no impediments to trade.

2. The model

We will make use of a conceptual frame which might be generally called "correspondence models" [8, 9]. These are intrinsically static models where two sets are mapped upon each other. The result of the mapping will be a function called transformation equation characterized by a one-to-one correspondence between elements of both sets over the whole range, a matching that satisfies certain constraints optimizing certain targets. This set-up is general enough to cover a large variety of problems and will be used here for sector planning at world level. The pattern to be found out corresponds to an ideal development path, meaning full capacity utilization.

Intuitively, the method is as outlined in fig. 1.

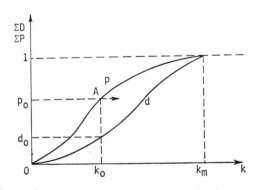

Fig. 1.

Let us assume that the two universes are (i) the universe of spaces and (ii) the universe of activities. Elements of each universe are characterized by a unique value of k. The distribution functions of both universes are known, being the frequencies of appearance (obviously cumulative) expressed in homogeneous units. The problem is then, either, (i) to allocate activities characterized by $k \leq k_o$, for which there is a demand $\sum D = d_o$, to the most suitable countries, or, (ii) to select for those countries characterized by $k \leq k_o$, which offer a productive capacity $\sum P = p_o$, the most suited activities, in such a way that the path can be followed till k_m where all activities are indicated to all spaces. This ideal path must optimize certain targets at space levels and at world level.

It must be pointed out here that it is intrinsic in the model that every infinitesimal space will become specialized in its optimal activity. Therefore, it will be necessary to import all other goods produced by the other activities allocated to the other countries. Hence, the word 'activity' should always be understood as an activity producing perfectly mobile goods, meaning, both the outputs as well as the inputs of that activity are mobile. (For the treatment of immobilities, see sect. 2.4 below.)

Let us pass now to the specification of the model. For the sake of simplicity, we will assume that capital can be written down as a scalar, thus avoiding the more complicated vectorial description needed if we introduce several classes of capital. Generality is not sacrificed since the same set-up can be used, either for each type of capital we might wish to distinguish or for an aggregation of all classes of capital if their 'prices' (or the weights) are known. This second alternative is the one that we will actually implicitly refer to and the one that will be used in the empirical illustration, where the weights are exogenously imposed.

2.1.

Let the universe of spaces be described by

$$P(^ak) = P(S \leq {}^ak_o) = \sum_{{}^ak_j=0}^{{}^ak_j={}^ak_o} {}^aU_j = {}^aU_o \ldots (jcJ), \tag{1}$$

that is, productive capacity, P, of countries, S, with capital endowments per unskilled worker smaller or equal to ${}^ak_o$, is represented by the stock of unskilled workers, ${}^aU_o$, available at those spaces with ${}^ak_j \leq {}^ak_o$.

$$\sum_{{}^ak_j=0}^{{}^ak_j={}^ak_J} {}^aU_j = {}^aU_T, \tag{2}$$

where the total manpower to be given employment, ${}^aU_T$, is equal to all available unskilled workers from all countries, $0 \leq {}^ak_j \leq {}^ak_J$.

$$\sum_{{}^ak_j=0}^{{}^ak_j={}^ak_o} {}^aU_j{}^ak_j = {}^aK_o, \tag{3}$$

or, total capital endowment of countries poorer than ${}^ak_o$ is computed by 'definite integration' of the 'function' of distribution of capital over those countries; and similarly,

$$\sum_{j=0}^{j=J} {}^aU_j{}^ak_j = \sum {}^aK_j = {}^aK_T \tag{3'}$$

if we 'integrate' over the whole range of countries, we get the total world wealth, as the whole area under the distribution.

Individual countries within the set of spaces relate to one another by

$$h_j = {}^af({}^ak_j, \alpha, \beta) \tag{4}$$

with

$$h'_k > 0 \tag{5}$$

and

$$h''_{kk} < 0 \tag{5'}$$

and

$$\alpha = \phi({}^ak_j), \tag{6}$$

with

$$\alpha'_k \geq 0, \tag{7}$$

where h_j = labour productivity in country j, $(Y_j/{}^aU_j)$, depends on ${}^ak_j$ = capital available per worker in country j, and α = efficiency indicator which might be independent of ${}^ak_j$ if equal efficiency is assumed throughout the world, or positively dependent on ${}^ak_j$ if the dictum "the sloppier, the poorer" is considered to be relevant.

From eq. (4), we are able to derive

$$\frac{w_j}{r_j} = \frac{h_j - {}^ak_j h'_j}{h'_j} = F({}^ak_j) = \frac{{}^af'_U({}^ak_j)}{{}^af'_K({}^ak_j)} \tag{8}$$

where

$${}^af''_{UU} > 0 \tag{9}$$

$${}^af''_{KK} < 0, \tag{9'}$$

which tell us that (1) factor prices, w_j and r_j, prevailing in country j are uniquely determined by the factor productivities in country j; and that (2) factor productivity is uniquely determined by the capital equipment available to every worker.

There are J countries, where J is a large number. Each country differs from the rest only in ${}^ak_j$. Hence, any two spaces with similar ${}^ak_j$ can be aggregated.

This characterization, therefore, allows for considering that only one demand pattern and one production function per commodity prevails for all countries.

2.2. The universe of commodities

In section 2.1. above we did not need to define the size of nations affecting distribution function (1), since the size of spaces is known. Size of sectors is not given but it depends on demand for goods produced by those sectors. Hence, in this section we will describe the set of goods, parallel to the description in sect. 2.1. of the universe of spaces, assuming that we know already the size of the sectors. Sect. 2.3. will be devoted to how we have determined those sizes.

Let the universe of activities be described by

$$D(^{r}k) = D(G \leqq {}^{r}k_{o}) = \sum_{^{r}k_i=0}^{^{r}k_i={}^{r}k_o} {}^{r}U_i = {}^{r}U_0 \ldots (i \subset I), \tag{10}$$

that is, the demand, D, for goods, G, with capital requirements per unit of unskilled worker smaller or equal than $^{r}k_0$, is represented by the requirements of unskilled workers, $^{r}U_0$, needed for production of those activities with $^{r}k_i \leqq {}^{r}k_0$.

$$\sum_{^{r}k_i=0}^{^{r}k_i={}^{r}k_I} {}^{r}U_i = {}^{r}U_T \tag{11}$$

where the total number of jobs, $^{r}U_T$, is equal to all requirements of unskilled manpower needed to produce the whole range of commodities $0 \leqq {}^{r}k_i \leqq {}^{r}k_I$.

This means that:

(1) There are I activities (see sect. 2.4.), where I is a large number.
(2) Each activity i produces one good, i.
(3) The amount of good i (or size of sector i when put in terms of workers required) is equal to the demand for good i.
(4) Demand for good i is determined by factor availabilities; for its endogenous estimation, see sect. 2.3. The pattern of demand for the I goods is described below.
(5) Each activity can be uniquely characterized by its specific capital intensity, $^{r}k_i$. Hence, one single technology is accepted for production of each good, there being no factor reversals, no innovations, no substitution, and no scale effects.
(6) Any two goods can be aggregated provided they are similar in $^{r}k_i$.
(7) Goods are understood to cover actually a bunch of physical goods, to be specified below (sect. 2.4.).

Total capital requirements are found by 'integration' of the 'function' of distribution of demand through the whole range of demanded goods:

$$^rK_T = \sum_{i=0}^{i=I} {}^rK_i = \sum {}^rU_i \frac{{}^rK_i}{{}^rU_t} = \sum {}^rU_i {}^rk_i.$$ (12)

Similarly, by means of 'definite integration' we may compute in general the requirements of scarce factors needed for production of any subset of commodities contained between $^rk_0 \leqq {}^rk_i \leqq {}^rk_v$:

$$^rK_v = \sum_{{}^rk_i = {}^rk_0}^{{}^rk_i = {}^rk_v} {}^rU_i {}^rk_i,$$ (12')

when the subindex, v, refers to the upper end of the segment.

Moreover, commodities are governed by the following technological laws:

$$^rU_i = u_i {}^sX_i$$ (13)

where ^rU_i = already defined, u_i = unskilled-labour input-coefficient of good i, and ^sX_i = supply of good i to be explained below, sect. 2.3.

$$^rK_i = {}^rk_i {}^rU_i = {}^rk_i u_i {}^sX_i = c_i {}^sX_i$$ (13')

where c_i is the capital/output ratio of commodity i.

Finally, individual sectors are connected to one another by

$$h_i = {}^rf({}^rk_i, \alpha, b)$$ (14)

with

$$h'_k > 0 \quad \text{and} \quad h''_{kk} < 0$$ (15)

where α and b are parameters and h_i, the productivity of labour engaged in sector i is defined as $Y_i/{}^rU_i$, this ratio being the composite of the capital intensity of a sector times its capital productivity,

$$\frac{{}^rK_i}{{}^rU_i} \frac{Y_i}{{}^rK_i}.$$

2.3. The demand pattern

Let demand be specified by

$$^dX_i = d_i X$$ (16)

where ^dX_i = demand of commodity i, d_i = share of commodity i in total demand ($\sum d_i = 1$ and $d_i > 0$), and

$$X = \sum_i {}^dX_i = \text{total demand for all } I \text{ goods.}$$ (16')

Vector (d) is the pivot of the whole thing we are trying to build up. From each billion dollar product, it tells us how much will be food, how much clothing, and so on, for the I commodities. Thus, our problem is not just to find out Max X subject to given factor endowments ^aK_T and ^aU_T (eqs. (2) and (3)) and subject to given technological constraints (eqs. (13) and (13′)), but also to take into consideration the demand constraints (eq. (16)). Vector (d) enables us to decide how this total feasible product will be distributed into all goods required to satisfy needs. Needs might be taken from the pattern of actual preferences (revealed by the market, but subject to present suboptimal levels); alternatively, they can be inferred from wishes of the population, however expressed, in a normative pattern, if changes in actual demand patterns are assumed to be possible. When opting for the normative pattern, we are implicitly assuming that unit-income elasticities of demand prevail at every space for each commodity. In other words, all human beings, whatever their income levels, require the same proportion of a good to satisfy a given need. The unit-income-elasticity hypothesis does not imply that a need is necessarily to be satisfied by a fixed amount of a good, but that, given a need, common to all human beings, the productive system supplies goods to satisfy it up to a certain level, and this level of satisfaction is equal for all persons. When and if factors get accumulated, this level will be higher, and more of a good will be used to satisfy the need for it. But, again, every one will get more, irrespective of his income.

We will now describe how X is fixed. Applying X to our exogenously fixed vector (d), we will get the maximum potential level at which every commodity can be supplied (eq. (16)), that is, making

$$^dX_i \equiv {}^sX_i. \tag{17}$$

Once ^sX_i is known, applying eqs. (13), where u_i and ^rk_i are technical data, we get factor requirements. These are stated in an ordered manner in distribution function (10), which implicitly contains (d).

Assuming that capital is not redundant, we try to get such a level of activity as to occupy all available capital

$$\sum_j {}^aK_j = {}^aK_T = {}^rK_T = \sum_i {}^rU_i^r k_i. \tag{18}$$

For (18) to hold,

$$^sX_i = Qd_i, \tag{19}$$

where Q is a constant defined as

$$Q = \frac{^aK_T}{\sum d_i u_i k_i} = \frac{^aK_T}{[(^rK_T)_{10^9}]}, \tag{20}$$

the denominator being the amount of capital required to produce, say, a billion dollar product of a mix described by the vector d_i. This way of fixing the level of activity taking into account only resource availabilities and not income maximization, comes from the consideration that world resources are finite. That would apply also to natural resources if we make ^aK refer to this type of resource and not simply to physical and/or human capital (see sect. 2.5.4. below). What matters is the satisfaction of disaggregatedly specified needs (subject to resource availabilities) and not maximization of a grossly aggregated income figure (see sect. 2.5.2, below).

Evidently,

$$\sum {}^sX_i u_i k_i = {}^rK_T \qquad (21)$$

when

$$^rK_T = {}^aK_T, \qquad (18)$$

and for that last equality, demand will be satisfied up to the extent of feasible supply,

$$^sX_i = {}^dX_i. \qquad (17)$$

From that level of activity, we derive the level of employment creation

$$\sum_i X_i u_i = {}^rU_T \qquad (11 \text{ and } 13)$$

which might be expected to be smaller than the stock of labour:

$$\sum D(^rk) \equiv {}^rU_T < {}^aU_T \equiv \sum P(^ak). \qquad (22)$$

2.4.

We have described, thus, the distribution of spaces (sect. 2.1.) and the distribution of commodities (sect. 2.2.) having devoted sect. 2.3. to explaining how we fixed the size of each activity. Before passing to the correspondence between both distributions, we will describe in this section the meaning and coverage of the concept of activity, sector, industry, commodity, etc., which were thus far used interchangeably.

Each of the I activities, for which the optimal location will be chosen, is actually a complex of activities. Attached to each industry producing a perfectly mobile good (hence, choice of its location is possible), we have a bunch of activities producing goods that show certain (or full) immobility, so that no such choice is possible, since their location is fixed.[1]

Immobilities can be of two sorts: output of an activity may be immobile when its transport costs (in the widest sense) are prohibitively high. By input-immobile activities we refer to those heavily dependent on natural resources. Of the two other classical factors (or neo-classical if we incorporate human capital into total capital), labour will also be immobile as well as the above referred natural resources, but labour is spread — though not evenly — over the whole world while the same cannot be said about natural resources, which must be exploited on the privileged spot. Hence, whenever a good cannot travel internationally or it is dependent on natural resources specifically bound to a spot, we will consider it as being produced by an immobile activity. Mobile goods will then be those among the ones that participate in international trade that depend mainly on capital (mobile) and labour (to be given employment on the spot, hence immobile, but available everywhere).

Goods, in general, will require other goods, besides primary factors, for their production. Of the goods used by a certain activity as material inputs, those which were considered above as mobile are not necessarily to be produced in the space chosen to carry out that activity, since that space can always get mobile goods by means of international trade. But the space would have to produce domestically all other goods required as material inputs, when these other goods are produced by immobile activities defined above.

The complications of inter-industry deliveries and transport costs introduced here do not come about merely because they add realism to the model. The main reason is teleological: the aim of this model is to minimize unemployment by means of activity selection. Now, mobile activities (mainly industrial ones) account for about only 10 % of employment opportunities given in the world at large to the active population. (10 % is an average; the range is from 5 % to 25 %, from the least- to the highly-industrialized countries.) Thus, a large part of the employment opportunities will lie in the immobile sector, either in the output immobile activities as construction, trade, services, or in the input immobile ones, as primary exploitation of natural resources, mainly agriculture.

Whenever we refer to $^r k_i$ as the capital requirements per unit of unskilled worker given employment in activity i, it should be understood as the capital

---

[1] We distinguish only 2 classes of goods, but one may think of a more refined classification in 3, 4 or more mobility classes. Our choice is based on previous research [4]. For an example of allocation when goods are classified into more than 2 mobility classes, see [1].

intensity of the bunch composed by sector i plus all the immobile sectors attached to it. This capital intensity is a weighted average where the weights given to each immobile sector are taken from the IP-OP relationships. More specifically, we define the capital requirements of activity i as:

$$^r k_i = \frac{k^i + \sum_n B_n^i k_n}{1 + \sum_n B_n^i} \tag{23}$$

where k^i = capital intensity of mobile sector i, k_n = capital intensity of immobile sector n (originally, immobile activities were called national, hence the subindex n, which runs from 1 till N)[2], and B_n^i = semi-input-output[3] demand coefficient of immobile good n required for production of one unit of commodity i (see [1] for a method of their computation). All other coefficients affecting the set of activities, as u_i or c_i are to be understood also as weighted averages similar to (23), where, for example u^i will be the labour coefficient of mobile sector i and u_i, the labour coefficient of the whole bunch.

Activity levels and factor requirements of every bunch are thus made up of two parts: a direct factor requirement corresponding to the level of a mobile sector itself plus an indirect requirement of factors corresponding to the levels at which the attached immobile activities will be working.

As an example, and because it is of our immediate concern, employment creation will be of two sorts: Jobs at an international activity the country specializes in for exports and jobs at national activities expanded domestically to support the export industry. The activity level of the bunch is:

$$^s X_i = (1 + \sum_n B_n^i) X^i \tag{24}$$

where X^i is the level of activity of industry i alone.

The direct employment creation would have been, were we not using the 'bunch' approach:

$$^r U^i = u^i X^i \qquad \text{(As in eq. (13))}$$

The indirect employment creation comes immediately as the difference:

$$^r U_i - {}^r U^i.$$

---

[2] By national sectors we understood those which showed only output immobilities, therefore, our immobile class is an extended sub-set.

[3] See Tinbergen and Bos [7] where the concept was launched (footnote on p. 108).

Alternatively, the indirect level of output is

$$^sX_i - X^i = X^i \sum_n B_n^i,$$

from (24)

and the indirect employment creation, then, becomes:

$$(X^i \sum_n B_n^i) \frac{\sum_n B_n^i u_n}{\sum_n B_n^i},$$
(25)

where u_n = labour coefficient of immobile sector n, and $(\sum_n B_n^i u_n)/(\sum_n B_n^i)$ = average labour coefficient of all immobile activities attached to sector i. Of course,

$$^rU_i - ^rU^i \equiv X^i \sum_n B_n^i \frac{\sum_n B_n^i u_n}{\sum_n B_n^i}.$$

2.5. *The correspondence of both sets*

The correspondence of both distributions is the operation by which optimal activities are indicated to countries (or optimal locations are found for industries). In sect. 2.3. we have found the overall extent of the feasible employment creation, which already, when compared with present employment opportunities (eq. (22)), can give us an impression of the improvement to be expected at world level, when factors are used more efficiently. But the minimization of un- and under-employment, for those spaces that actually suffer from it, can only be done, within the extent of the overall feasible bound, by a proper allocation.

Hitherto, correspondence models have assumed that both universes had continuous distribution functions with known and manageable mathematical shape. (By manageable, we mean few, say two, parameters.) But we found that reality is too complex to be fitted into the straitjacket of mean and variance. Therefore, we will work with the 'frequency' distributions as stated in eqs. (1) and (10). The way in which the distributions are described in these two equations does not enable us to make use of the elegant mathematical language used in former models, since we cannot concisely specify the shape of the distributions. However, this does not preclude the possibility of finding the equivalent to the correspondence function and showing it to be optimal in as much as it satisfies demand and technical constraints when hitting the income and employment targets. The advantage of this approach lies in the fact that we will be working with all the infor-

mation without neglecting that part of it which deviates from theory if we had been fitting a function to our data. The disadvantage is that, in order to show the shape of the distribution, we must show the distribution itself in tabulated form. We will do that in sect. 3, concentrating now on the principles governing the correspondence.

Looking at fig. 1, intuitively it would seem appropriate to allocate activities up to k_o to countries up to k_o. Or, stated more generally, given the actual distribution of endowments and the chosen distribution of requirements, to allocate activities to countries in such a way that ^rk_i approach ^ak_j as close as possible. A principle, thus, can be enunciated, paraphrasing Heckscher and Ohlin, as follows: Up to the extent conditioned by the fulfilment of an overall demand constraint, countries should specialize in the production of those activities whose factor requirements match most closely with the country's factor endowments. Let us now take four points in succession.

2.5.1. The employment effect

The application of the principle would obviously be conducive to the largest employment of labour with the most careful use of domestically available capital. This may sound unnecessary since at the end of the introductory sect. 1, we stated as the first general assumption governing the whole exercise, that capital is mobile. Still, without relaxing this assumption, for practical implementation purposes we may recognize that capital transfers, at short term, may involve certain difficulties, and that LDC's may do well relying on transfers from rich countries only to cover shortages, not for core investments.

Moreover, through the industrialization process, LDC's will change their factor proportions since (again look at fig. 1, this chapter) activities up to k_o have a demand, expressed in number of jobs, equal to d_o, which is not enough to give employment to all workers, p_o. Hence, if they want full employment, they must move right from point A, taking up activities with increasing k, up to the extent shown by the demand curve. Then, changes in factor prices must be forthcoming. The application of the principle will minimize labour idleness putting on each group of countries the smallest burden in implementing those factor price changes.

One may argue that if the first group of countries with $k \leq k_o$ takes up activities with k somewhat larger than k_o, the second, immediate group of countries, itself with k somewhat larger than k_o, is not anymore able to take up production of its most suited activities. Against this, however, we can argue that the game can go on as long as all participants keep playing. Only by a systematic right shift can we select the k_i that fits better with a specific k_j (obeying the imposed demand pattern), that makes the distribution of the burden most equitable for all groups of countries, if by burden we mean either dependence on transfers from abroad or policy means to change factor prices according to the new task distribution. As it is in the interest of all, it pays to keep all participants playing. This is a kind of implicit solidarity hypothesis.

2.5.2. *The income effect*

One may wonder whether at all it is in the general interest to play this game. Full employment of labour might be a very appealing target, but, indeed, we feel that there must also be some beneficial income effects to be derived from the strategy suggested, to make the game worthwhile.

Let us make the hypothesis that income depends on capital investments.[4] Those investments will be made out of current flow of income. Therefore, if we want to maximize, dynamically, to-morrow's income, we must begin by trying to maximize to-day's income. Let us say that investable income is that part of income which remains after paying wages and salaries.

From section 2.2, we use eq. (14), and define the investible resources per man, z, as

$$z = h - w = \frac{Z}{U} = \frac{Y}{U} - \frac{W}{U} \, , \tag{26}$$

and try to maximize the flow of investible resources per unit of capital:

$$\text{Max } \theta = \frac{z}{k} = \frac{Z}{U} \frac{U}{K} \, . \tag{27}$$

To do so, we calculate:

$$\frac{\mathrm{d}\theta}{\mathrm{d}k} = \frac{\mathrm{d}\left(\frac{z}{k}\right)}{\mathrm{d}k} = \frac{1}{k^2}\left[k\frac{\mathrm{d}z}{\mathrm{d}k} - z\right].$$

As

$$\frac{\mathrm{d}z}{\mathrm{d}k} = \frac{\mathrm{d}(h-w)}{\mathrm{d}k} = \frac{\mathrm{d}h}{\mathrm{d}k} - 0 = \frac{\mathrm{d}h}{\mathrm{d}k}$$

we get

$$\frac{\mathrm{d}\theta}{\mathrm{d}k} = \frac{1}{k^2}\left[k\frac{\mathrm{d}h}{\mathrm{d}k} - (h-w)\right]$$

---

[4] We venture to make it because capital includes human capital, so, in capital accumulation, training programmes for skill formation are implicit.

and from $d\theta/dk = 0$, we find that the condition

$$h - k\frac{dh}{dk} = w \qquad (28)$$

must hold, enabling us to find out the activity characterized by $k = k^*$ that maximizes dynamically income growth subject to a given level of salaries, w. Now, higher w will mean a larger value of the intercept in eq. (28). Because of the shape of eq. (14) (described in eq. (15)), that would mean that the sector selected will have higher capital intensity, because $dw/dk = -kh'' > 0$, since $h'' < 0$, as defined in eq. (15) above.

Therefore, we may safely conclude that, in absence of demand constraints, sectors of increasingly higher k should be allocated to richer countries — where w will be higher (eq. (9)) — in order to maximize national income growth.

For a more comprehensive treatment of the income effects and of the trade-offs between income and employment, see Herman [3]. There, however, no treatment is made of the international harmonization of income targets when a demand constraint is active. It might very well be that, for the activity that maximizes income of a specific country, there is not enough demand. It might also be that the demand constraint forces a shift to the right away from the proper activities in order to satisfy employment targets in poorer countries. Then, the country under reference would not be able to select its optimal activity from the point of view of its own optimal income growth. We believe that here our solidarity hypothesis would be again necessary and we may qualify our contention about maximum income as follows: Maximum income is not only the maximum consistent with full employment within the country but also consistent with growth rates between countries, in such a way that this other type of collective burden is equitably distributed among countries forming a harmonious complex of (national) income targets. This statement is to be interpreted only as indicative of that our proposed strategy does not have harmful effects on aggregated income.

2.5.3. The cost effects

Hitherto, we dealt with three of the elements that are a 'must' in every model, namely, full utilization of factors, income effects and demand satisfaction. On these three scores, our suggested strategy performs well. But the game can only be kept going if a fourth element is taken into account: Every good must be supplied by the cheapest producer (see qualifications below).

Commodity i when produced by country j, will cost:

$$P_{ij} = {}^r k_i r_j + w_j,\qquad(29)$$

expressed in US \$ per units of merchandise produced by one man, where r_j and w_j are defined in eq. (8), sect. 2.1.

Then P_{ij} should be minimal (though not necessarily the lowest) for a fixed i, if we want to get:

$$\min E = \sum_i \sum_j P_{ij} U_{ij},\qquad(30)$$

where E is a kind of world expenditure in all commodities.

With the strong condition stated above, we hit (30) if

$$P_{ij}(i = j) < P_{ij}(i \neq j),\qquad(31)$$

and then, it follows immediately that

$$U_{ij} \begin{cases} > 0 & \text{for } i = j \\ = 0 & \text{for } i \neq j \end{cases}\qquad(32)$$

will hold.[5]

However, demand may force the mechanism to deviate from (31)–(32) and still achieve (30). The reasons for deviating are that a specific cheapest producer of a given good may not have enough productive capacity to satisfy demand for that good, therefore, a second cheapest should come to share part of the task; it might also be that a given producer is the cheapest for more than one commodity, thus, obviously, more producers must come forward to carry out the required supply; this last argument implies that there might be countries which are not the cheapest producers of any commodity at all, and still they should get some task to perform if we want to achieve our employment and income targets at country and world levels.

In order to minimize eq. (30) without imposing the strong condition (31), let us design a two-entry tableau similar to the one used in [2] as an accounting device to carry out the computation in an ordered manner. As above, eq. (12′), sub-index v, refers to the summation through the interval $[v-1, v]$. The grouping is made following the common sense dictum for clustering: the contiguous element, of value immediately higher than v, is not included in the group if its inclusion means an enlargement of the variance around the mean of the group. In this way, a cluster of industries is allocated to a group of countries, allowing for a healthy diversification of

---

[5] Of course, by means of eq. (13), U's can always be converted into X's and then eqs. (30) and (32) may look more familiar.

production, instead of the somewhat unrealistic specialization of individual countries in single commodities. Let's assume that, by grouping, we made the number of groups of countries equal to the number of clusters of activities. It goes without saying that it is definitely not necessary to have these numbers equalized.

Table 1

Groups	1	2	...	j	...	J	Requirements
Clusters							
1	U_{11}	U_{12}	:	U_{1j}	:	U_{1J}	$\Sigma_j U_{1j} = {}^rU_1$
2	U_{21}	U_{22}	:	U_{2j}	:	U_{2J}	$\Sigma_j U_{2j} = {}^rU_2$
:	...	...	:	...	:	...	....
:	...	...	:	...	:	...	....
i	U_{i1}	U_{i2}	:	U_{ij}	:	U_{iJ}	$\Sigma_j U_{ij} = {}^rU_i$
:	...	...	:	...	:	...	....
:	...	...	:	...	:	...	....
I	U_{I1}	U_{I2}	:	U_{Ij}	:	U_{IJ}	$\Sigma_j U_{Ij} = {}^rU_I$

Avail-abilities $\Sigma_i U_{i1} = {}^aU_1$ $\Sigma_i U_{i2} = {}^aU_2$ ... $\Sigma_i U_{ij} = {}^aU_j$ ... $\Sigma_i U_{iJ} = {}^aU_J$ $\Sigma_j {}^aU_j = {}^aU_T = {}^rU_T = \Sigma_i {}^rU_i$

Of course, the order of rows and columns is fixed, as can be derived from fig. 1, that is country columns are ordered according to the ranking

$$ {}^ak_1 < {}^ak_2 < \ldots < {}^ak_j < \ldots < {}^ak_J \tag{33} $$

and industry rows, ordered according to the ranking

$$ {}^rk_1 < {}^rk_2 < \ldots < {}^rk_i < \ldots < {}^rk_I, \tag{33'} $$

hence, applying the principle stated at the introduction to this section, we begin allocating activity-cluster 1 to country-group 1 up to the extent allowed by the productive capacity of group 1 and we go on, either allocating the rest of cluster 1 to group 2 or filling up the rest of group 1 with cluster 2 until the whole pie is eaten up when cluster I is allocated to group J. What we fill up, thus, are all the cells in or around the main diagonal.

This operation may look like the application of the Hitchcock problem suggested in [6, sect. 3.4] for spatial allocation of activities, since, using the parlance of linear programmers, our accounting device would be equivalent to finding a first basic feasible solution by way of the north-west corner rule. What gives our problem a special nature is the fact that our matrix of costs shows very well defined regularities. Making good use of the knowledge on regularities in our matrix of costs, may be enough to hit right away at the optimal solution with the first basic feasible solution around the main diagonal. This feature of regularities in costs would discourage feeding a computer with all the data and getting the solution by a mere application of well-known algorithms, since, because of the size of the problem, avoiding iterations is of utmost importance. Moreover, for policy purposes, our suggested strategy offers a rationale in terms of attractive goals, not a cold solution of a computer exercise.

The built-in regularities in the matrix of costs are easy to analyse from the definition of its general element given in eq. (29).

(a) Because of being the rows ordered according to increasing ${}^r k_i$, (33′), for a fixed j, P_{ij} will tend to be increasingly larger in the north/south direction of the tableau. This is so obvious that does not add much information.

(b) What is more interesting, is to fix i and see the behaviour of P_{ij} for the different j's. Because of being the columns ordered according to increasing ${}^a k_j$, (33), w_j and r_j will show an opposite behaviour in regard to each other (see eqs. (9) and (9′)). Fixing ${}^r k_i$ and taking into account the described trends of w_j and r_j, we can easily visualize the structure of P_{ij} and thus reject a priori as non-optimal any first basic feasible solution found in or around the north-east/south-west direction, since it would not follow the row minimum, nor the column minimum, nor the matrix minimum rules.

We might check the optimality of our main diagonal solution by means of the socalled "u-v" method, where the u's and v's are arbitrary numbers depending on P_{ij}. The difference

$$P_{ij} - (u_i + v_j) \tag{34}$$

indicates the increase in costs the world must be willing to pay to allow countries to engage in activities away from their corresponding place in the main diagonal. Because of the above explained regularities in the cost matrix, difference (34) will tend to be very large towards the north-east and southwest extremes, and it will tend to zero in cells around the main diagonal. That means that solutions around the main diagonal will be of the type of the so-called multiple solutions, which is encouraging enough as not to impose the strong condition (31) when optimizing (30).

In general, we may say that difference (34) is an index of comparative advantages when we generalize the 2-commodity, 2-country model into an I-commodity, J-country model. P_{ij}'s (eq. (29)) are not indexes of comparative advantages since they compare only country- or commodity-wise. But difference (34) makes the comparison country- and commodity-wise.

2.5.4. *The environment effects*
A world industrialization programme as suggested here might have an impact on environment. Since factual information is not yet available, we will mainly indicate how to fit this information, whenever available, into the framework of our methodology. There are two types of environmental effects: (a) exhaustion of natural resources, and (b) pollution.

We have dealt with the first type of effects in 2.3, above. As more information on wealth becomes available, our definition of capital endowment must accordingly change. This variable will be instrumental in fixing the feasible level of activity. Some refinements would be necessary to accommodate the non-reproducible resources together with the conventional reproducible ones (i.e., labour and capital).

On the second type of effects, we might distinguish three origins:

(1) From production: As in the case of employment, income and cost effects, the pollution effect of a given solution might be also estimated. Depending on the regularity of the distribution of pollution propensities across sectors, a system for equitably allocating this new type of burden might be devised; this may force the solution to deviate from the main diagonal solution.

(2) From transportation: The industrial specialization implied in the proposed allocation algorithm will be conducive to a substantial enlargement of the transport flows. In order to optimize these trade flows, the pollution propensity of the transport activity might be introduced as a constraint in the minimization programme. This might end up in less specialization at lower levels of employment and income and higher costs.

(3) From consumption: Information on individuals' propensities to pollution by consumption of certain commodities might find its correct place when constructing the demand vector, if fear of pollution is large enough to allow for changes in tastes.

3. *An empirical illustration*

The model described in sect. 2 is indicative of the type and volume of data necessary to attack the problem. In the absence of complete data, sect. 3 will be devoted only to putting some flesh on the skeleton described above for illustrative purposes, and not to empirical testing of the model. We are well aware of the fact that, for raw data, more statistical work should be done by proper institutions, and for processed data, better estimation procedures than ours can be applied. We relied extensively on the data collected for the exercise reported in [2].

3.1. The universe of spaces

We collected information for 122 spaces, the level of disaggregation being higher for LDC's than for rich countries.

Total capital was estimated, first, applying countries' capital-output ratios to countries' total product. Then, skilled manpower was converted in dollar terms and added up. A portion of this stock was supposed to be required to carry out what we called the "autonomous" immobile activities. This autonomous capital requirements were estimated assuming a linear relationship between (a) remunerations to capital paid by immobile sectors and (b) per capita capital endowments; the linear regression being based on two observations: India and Western Germany.

Total labour (that is, pure labour, or manpower minus skill) and labour for mobile activities were not estimated but taken from sources. What is added here to the figures reported in [2], is the estimation of un- and under-employment, taken from the country percentages offered by Turnham and Jaeger in 'The Employment Problem in LDC's,' OECD, Development Centre, Paris, December 1969.

In this way, the stock of workers for mobile activities plus the stock of unemployed workers is supposed to be free to be engaged in either industrial sectors or in immobile activities expanded to support industrialization. The 122 spaces were aggregated in nine groups according to their similarities in capital availability per worker. We took this measure of capital endowments to make results of this exercise comparable with those reported in [2]. The 9 groups are made out of the following countries:

1a — A considerable number of African countries; Bhutan, Greenland, West Irian, Laos, Nepal, Virgin Islands, Yemen, Falkland Islands, etc.
1b — China, South Korea, Nigeria, Pakistan and others.
1c — India, Indonesia, Madagascar, Bolivia, Thailand and others.
2 — Twenty countries including Spain, Turkey, UAR.
3 — Seventeen countries including Brazil, Mexico, Yugoslavia.
4 — Seven countries including Japan, Colombia, South Africa, Greece.
5 — Eastern Europe, Uruguay and Liberia.
6 — USSR.

7 — Western Europe and Israel.
8 — Argentina, Australia, Canada and New Zealand.
9 — USA with Puerto Rico and Canal Zone.[6]

We show in table 2, a summary of this information where individual countries are grouped.

Glancing at this table we may notice that our problem is not anymore to get better employment for the 150 million workers already engaged in industry ("better" in terms of income, or costs, etc.) but to get efficient employment for 230 million workers, amount which implies absorption of 75 million people, presumably redundant in off-industrial sectors.

Table 2

Distribution of endowments

Group	1	2	3	4	5	6 = 4+5	7	8	9 = 1/100 ×(7×8)	10 = 7−9
1	380	2002	801	66	63	129	2448	83	2040	408
2	64	164	49	5	6	11	319	81	257	61
3	104	225	60	6	5	11	505	79	400	105
4	140	173	69	12	1	13	759	77	585	175
5	166	114	50	6	..	6	618	76	467	151
6	417	235	109	11	0	11	1746	72	1252	494
7	631	296	118	24	0	24	2851	66	1885	966
8	126	62	20	4	1	5	706	55	390	316
9	842	210	81	18	0	18	4557	34	1552	3004
Total	2869	3480	1357	152	76	229	14508		8828	5680

Column 1: RGDP 10^9 US $.
Column 2: Population 10^6 men.
Column 3: Active population 10^6 men.
Column 4: Active population mobile activities 10^6 men.
Column 5: Un- and under-employed 10^6 men.
Column 6 = 4+5: Labour for mobile activities and bunches 10^6 men.
Column 7: Total capital 10^9 US $.
Column 8: Percentage required autonomous immobile activities.
Column 9 = 1/100(7×8): Capital for autonomous immobile activities 10^9 US $.
Column 10 = 7−9: Capital for mobile activities and bunches 10^9 US $.

[6] For a description of sources and an explanation of intriguing features of this classification and complete list of countries, the reader is referred to [2].

In table 2 we have quantified eqs. (1) through (3). For eq. (4) needed to derive (8), we may fit our data into the following type of function $h = e^{\alpha - \beta/k}$ which gives us

$$h = e^{\alpha - 9.3/k}. \tag{4'}$$

Since α is the parameter which shifts the function up- or downwards, it might be taken as a measure of efficiency, since with a larger α, a fixed k_o will result in a higher h. If efficiency in one way or another is supposed to be related with the degree of development, we may try to find a functional relationship for eq. (6), in which case, in (7) only the inequality sign would hold. The advantage of this operation lies in the fact that a given level of income with a fixed h can be achieved with smaller capital expenditures, at the same employment level. For this purpose, we may make use either of new statistical evidence (to be collected) on nations' efficiency, or of estimates already available, as the famous Leontief's 3 to 1 relationship between American and non-American workers. Exercises with this class of production function where technological innovations of the capital-saving type are a function of capital endowments, will not be reported here, however.

It may be worthwhile mentioning that the elasticity of factor substitution of function (4') varies from zero to one-half as k varies from 9.3 to infinity. Parameter β might be interpreted as the bare minimum capital equipment a worker requires to be efficient. Below this point, labour's marginal productivity is negative, pointing towards capital transfer policies. The behaviour of the elasticity of substitution would indicate that countries where capital is more abundant tend to replace labour by capital. At the other end, labour abundant countries will face certain rigidities, probably due to the fact that certain minimum capital equipment is conditio sine qua non for a labourer to be productive, hence, those countries cannot replace capital by labour further than a certain minimum. From eq. (4') we may derive what for the illustrative purposes of this exercise will be considered as the equilibrium wages and rentals at each country. These are shown in table 3.

Table 3

Factor prices (w in 10^3 US$/man; r in %)

Groups	1	2	3	4	5	6	7	8	9
Wages (w_j)	−1.0	−0.5	−0.0	0.5	1.0	1.5	3.5	4.5	8.5
Rentals (r_j)	47.0	28.5	22.5	15.5	20.0	14.0	8.5	4.5	3.0

3.2. The universe of commodities

For this set of data, we have also relied on what was our main source in [2], namely, Sweden's input-output table as computed by Höglund and Werin. Capital requirements (stocks) were computed from the remunerations to capital (flows) assuming an uniform yield. Skill requirements were standardized into dollar terms. Total capital requirements are the addition of both (for details, see [2]). What matters for this exercise, is the suggested bunches approach. Applying the definitions given in sect. 2.4. above, and making use of our preliminary results on mobility as reported in [4], sectors were classified into mobile and immobile. From the 127 sectors of the Swedish input-output table, 88 were considered mobile and 39 immobile. For a list of immobile sectors and their main characteristics, (k_n and u_n), see [5].

Applying a computational procedure as described in [1], the bunches of immobile activities, complementary to each mobile sector, were computed. Then, weighted averages of the kind formulated in (23) were computed to find the capital intensity and labour coefficients of each bunch.

For the demand vector, d_i, we took total demand for mobile goods in Sweden. By total demand we mean final plus intermediate demand. Exports have been subtracted and imports added. Thus, we avoid particular features of the Swedish productive structure which might be due to its historical specialization. If for the production statistics we had reason to rely on one single source (hollowness of the factor reversal concept, etc.) and to prefer the Swedish material (reliability, enough sectoral disaggregation, disaggregation of primary inputs mentioning labour classified by skills, etc.), the same cannot be said of the demand pattern. Several patterns were tried out, either from different sources (rich, intermediate and poor countries) and/or averaging them, etc.; there was no a priori reason to prefer these patterns to the Swedish. We favoured the Swedish pattern because its level of disaggregation was consistent with the production statistics. Anyway, what matters is to have a vector $\{d\}$, and the whole quantitative illustration could have also been made with a demand pattern which would follow the author's preferences as, for instance, $d_i = 0$ for $i =$ weapons and ammunition, etc., assuming that changes in tastes can be pushed so far.

Thus far, we got enough material as to perform the operations indicated between (18) and (22), in order to fix the level of activity X_i of every activity and its factor requirements. The level of activity, Q, (eq. (20)) that makes (18) an equality was found to be 1.8×10^{12} US \$. Introducing it in eq. (16), we got the sectoral activity levels, X_i. Using X_i in eq. (21) we got the sectoral capital requirements and using it in eq. (13), we found out the employment creation. By means of eq. (11) we could calculate inequality (22), as:

$$'U_T = 214 \times 10^6 \text{ men} < 229 \times 10^6 \text{ men} = {}^a U_T.$$

By means of eq. (25) we may compute the employment directly created by the industrialization programme and the employment created in the immobile sectors expanded to support such an industrialization programme.

Table 4

Supply and demand of labour (10^6 men)

Active population for mobile activities	153	Labour for mobile activities	102
Un- and underemployed	76	Labour for supporting immobile ones	112
Total labour available	229	Total labour required	214

We proceed then to cluster the 88 activities into 9 clusters, where the size of each one is made to coincide as much as possible with the size of the corresponding group of countries (size, in terms of number of workers). See table 5 below for a summary of clusters' main characteristics.[7]

Table 5

The distribution of requirements

Characteristics	$'K_i\,(1)$ 10^9 US \$	$'U_i\,(2)$ 10^6 men	$'U^i\,(3)$ 10^6 men	$'U_i-'U^i\,(2\text{--}3)$ 10^6 men
Clusters				
1	1.813	111	60	51
2	324	15	7	8
3	225	9	5	4
4	434	15	6	10
5	176	6	2	3
6	311	9	4	5
7	1.015	27	12	15
8	178	4	2	2
9	1.202	19	6	13
Total	5.680	214	102	112

Comparing table 5 with table 2, notice that the dispersion of $'k_i$ is smaller than the dispersion of ${}^a k_j$, that is, the smallest $'k_i$ is much larger than the smallest ${}^a k_j$ while at the other end, $'k_i$ more or less coincide with ${}^a k_j$.

[7] The reader interested in the composition of the clusters is referred to [5].

With this, all relationships affecting the universe of commodities are quantified. An attempt to quantify eqs. (14) and (15) can be found in [3]. An exercise of the type described in sect. 2.5.2., to find the optimal activity for income growth when no overall demand constraint is active, could have been performed. It would have shown the discrepancies between a nationalistic approach as compared with a strategy that takes into account what the others might be willing to do. But, for the time being, nothing on this will be reported.

3.3. The correspondence on both universes

We must first compute the matrix of costs where each element is to be found applying eq. (29).

Table 6

Matrix of costs (all figures in 10^3 US $, except r_j in %) (rounded to nearest 0.5)

Groups			1	2	3	4	5	6	7	8	9
		w_j	−1.0	−0.5	−0.0	0.5	1.0	1.5	3.5	4.5	8.5
	k_i	r_j	47.0	28.5	22.5	15.5	20.0	14.0	8.5	4.5	3.0
Clusters											
1	16.5		7.0	4.0	3.5	3.0	4.0	4.0	4.5	5.5	9.0
2	22.5		9.5	6.0	5.0	4.0	5.5	4.5	5.0	5.5	9.5
3	25.5		10.5	6.5	5.5	4.0	5.5	5.0	5.5	6.0	9.5
4	28.5		12.5	7.5	6.5	5.0	6.5	5.5	5.5	6.0	9.5
5	31.5		14.0	8.5	7.0	5.0	7.0	6.0	6.0	6.0	9.5
6	34.0		15.0	9.0	7.5	5.5	7.5	6.5	6.0	6.0	9.5
7	37.5		17.0	10.0	8.5	6.0	8.5	7.0	6.5	6.5	10.0
8	47.0		21.0	13.0	10.5	7.5	10.5	8.0	7.5	7.0	10.0
9	62.5		28.5	17.5	14.0	10.0	13.5	10.5	8.5	7.5	10.5

Now, we build a two-entry tableau as designed in table 1, sect. 2.5.3, above. To do so, inequality (22) between supply and demand of labour must be made equal, as it is indicated in the south-east corner total of that tableau. This can be done in several ways, and none would be more reasonable than to assume that Country-Group 1, which is the largest and where unemployment is more rampant would still remain with some unemployment. We have seen that Group 1 has 63 million unemployed (table 2) and we have estimated the redundant labour to be about 15 million (table 4). We assume, thus, that Group 1 will try to create employment for this portion of their labour force by means of appropriate choice of labour intensive techniques in construction and agriculture. We do not go deeper on this, here. Anyway, the bunches approach here followed might create employment for 4 out of every 5 presently redundant labourers.

Table 7

The correspondence tableau (10^6 workers)

Groups	1	2	3	4	5	6	7	8	9	^rU_i
Clusters										
1	110.8	–	–	–	–	–	–	–	–	110.8
2	3.7	10.8	–	–	–	–	–	–	–	14.5
3	–	0.3	8.6	–	–	–	–	–	–	8.9
4	–	–	2.6	12.6	–	–	–	–	–	15.2
5	–	–	–	0.8	4.8	–	–	–	–	5.6
6	–	–	–	–	1.3	7.8	–	–	–	9.1
7	–	–	–	–	–	3.2	23.7	–	–	26.9
8	–	–	–	–	–	–	0.1	3.7	–	3.8
9	–	–	–	–	–	–	–	1.2	18.0	19.2
^aU_j	114.5	11.1	11.2	13.4	6.1	11.0	23.8	4.9	18.0	214.0

Computing the $(u-v)$ numbers, we check optimality in terms of supply at minimum costs. Other procedures would be needed in order to show optimality in terms of the equitable distribution of the burdens we mentioned in sect. 2.5.1 above, namely, dependence on transfers from abroad or necessary changes in factor prices. We will not report about these, here. Below, in table 8, one may find the increases in unit-costs, that the world must be willing to pay in order to allow countries to take up sectors that deviate from the main diagonal rule (see eq. (34)).

Table 8

$[P_{ij} - (u_i+v_j)]$ (in 10^3 US \$)

Groups	1	2	3	4	5	6	7	8	9
Clusters									
1		1.0	1.5	2.5	2.0	3.0	4.0	3.5	6.0
2			0	0.5	0	1.0	1.5	2.5	3.5
3	0.5			0.5	0	0.5	1.5	2.0	3.0
4	1.0	0.5			0	0	0.5	1.5	2.0
5	2.5	0.5	0			0	0.5	1.0	1.5
6	3.0	1.0	0.5	0			0	0.5	1.0
7	4.0	1.5	0.5	0	0			0.5	0.5
8	7.5	3.0	2.0	0.5	1.5	0.5			0.5
9	14.5	7.0	4.5	2.5	3.5	2.0	0.5		

A quick glance through table 8 would suggest that country-groups may do well choosing industries from those included in their own corresponding clusters but, also, they might consider industries of the adjacent clusters since the problem has a considerable number of multiple solutions all around the main diagonal, which is one of the optimal solutions.

3.4. Final remark

The illustration given here is, admittedly, simplistic. We are far from suggesting that a world industrialization programme is a matter to be treated as a computer exercise. More details are necessary. Data on wealth should be collected. Equilibrium factor prices are to be estimated by sophisticated methods. Huge data collection systems must be organized to improve our knowledge about production functions. Hence, we would certainly not dare to suggest that a given country, drafted here, say, into Group 4, should look at Cluster 4 to find out which are its most suited activities.

What we do venture to suggest is that the exercise is worth-while doing in earnest (that is, with enough detailed information) since it will provide us with a picture of an industrial structure which would definitely be better than the present one. That picture would, of course, like all pictures, be static. But dynamic models, with all their sophistication, may be useless for planning purposes since the coefficients used in their equations imply future developments (as technological innovations, income yields of planned ventures, capital accumulation processes, factor price changes, modification in tastes, etc.), and estimation of these coefficients may fall more in the realm of prophecy or wishful thinking than in actual planning. A normative static model, on the contrary, might indicate a first objective which we should try to achieve, without implying that, once we reach it, the whole exercise cannot be carried out again with new information in order to define the next objective. Following the advice of Goudriaan, when a bridge breaks down, it is more useful to study the humble statics of a well-built new bridge than the elegant dynamics of the crumbling process of the old one.

References

[1] Herman, B., L. B. M. Mennes and J. G. Waardenburg, 1969, Some exercises with a simple model for world development planning, in: H. C. Bos, ed., Towards Balanced International Growth, Amsterdam, North-Holland Publishing Co, 69–92.
[2] Herman, B. and J. Tinbergen, 1971, Planning of international development, in Proceedings of the International Conference on Industrial Development, Budapest, 1970:

Progress and Planning in Industry, Institute of Industrial Economics, Hungarian Academy of Sciences, Budapest, 1971.

[3] Herman, B., 1973, On the choice of the optimal industry: a check of a controversy, Weltwirtschaftliches Archiv, forthcoming.

[4] Herman, B., 1971, Commodities classification by mobility as means for international structural forecast, paper read at the European Meeting of the Econometric Society, Barcelona, September 1971.

[5] Herman, B., 1972, Employment creation through international division of labour, background paper for the annual meeting of the UN Committee for Development Planning; ILO-Geneva; April 1972.

[6] Mennes, L. B. M., J. Tinbergen and J. G. Waardenburg, 1969, The Element of Space in Development Planning, Amsterdam, North-Holland Publishing Co.

[7] Tinbergen, J. and H. C. Bos, 1966, Modelos Matemáticos del Crecimiento Económico, Madrid, Edit. Aguilar., (English version available).

[8] Tinbergen, J., 1968, The optimal international division of labour, Acta Oeconomica Academiae Scientiarum Hungaricae 3.

[9] Tinbergen, J., 1970, A positive and a normative theory of income distribution, The Review of Income and Wealth, Series 16, 3, 221–234.

CHAPTER 7

Planning for the United Arab Republic*

RAGNAR FRISCH †

University of Oslo

1. Introduction

I don't know very much about the conditions in the other countries of the Arab Nation, but I believe that, through my several stays in Egypt, I have come to know something about the conditions for economic and social development in the United Arab Republic. This knowledge has made me confident that the Republic has a great economic and social future provided its economy is planned in a wise way.

This love of and faith in the Republic gives me the privilege, or rather makes it my duty, to express my frank opinion on certain aspects of its planning system that can, in my opinion, be considerably improved. What I have particularly in mind is to base final decisions on a scientifically worked out global plan frame with optimality computations. I might even say that such an improvement is a conditio sine qua non for a speedy and safe economic development of the country. This improvement should by all means be put into effect and implemented as soon as possible.

If this is not done in the present situation characterized by a strong determination to do something to foster rapid economic progress, it is inevitable that one will run into improvisations that may create unforeseen difficulties of such dimensions as to seriously disturb economic stability. Unforeseen balance of payments problems is only one example of these difficulties.

* Public lecture delivered on 8 February 1964 in the Egyptian Society for Political Economy, Legislation and Statistics, at the invitation of Cairo University. This paper first appeared in The Economics of Planning, 1965, pp. 29–42 and is published here with permission of the author and the editor of the journal.

Since this paper was partly addressed to politicians it is formed in rather elementary terms. But behind it there is considerable computation on empirical data, which were needed in order to determine the shapes of the curves in the basic policy chart.

2. Work that has been done and work that needs to be done

The technique for the elaboration of a global and optimal plan frame has been the main concern of the Operations Research Center in the Cairo Institute of National Planning, and it is this work I would like to tell you something about.

The work stems from what the President explained to me in private conversations four years ago. His main theme was "I want to know how to plan". Our work since then has aimed at answering this question. And we believe that now we are in a fairly good position to produce an answer.

The general line of approach has been mapped out by me, but the implementation of the ideas is the work of several Egyptians. A list of them with my grateful acknowledgement is given in an earlier publication. Of the names in the earlier list I must in particular mention Dr. Ibrahim Abdel Rahman.

The work in its most recent stage is due to Dr. Salah Hamid, the powerful Director of the Operations Research Center, to Dr. Nazih Deif, Under-Secretary of State in the Ministry of National Planning[1], who has provided us with the data, to Dr. Salib Roufael, Professor in Ain Shams University and to Mrs. Mary Naguib, who has been in charge of the electronic computer in the Operations Research Center. In a general way we have also profited by remarks made by Dr. Mahmoud Shafie.

Before embarking on a description of the technique for elaborating a global and optimal plan frame, I must state quite explicitly that this technique only aims at being an *aid* for decisions on the economic policy, just like the compass is an aid for the master of a ship when he decides what course to follow. The final decisions on economic policy must, of course, reside with the top level authorities. But the technique of a global and optimal plan frame is a necessary condition for making wise decisions. It is an indispensable compass for steering the economy.

A development plan contains a great number of different aspects. Even if we aggregate the details into broad categories, we are left with a considerable number. When the work is coded for an electronic computer (even a relatively small one such as the IBM 1620 now available in the Cairo Operations Research Center), we are able to include a great number of different aspects, even several hundred. It would only lead to confusion if I should try to speak here about all the aspects that have been included in our Cairo work, so I will concentrate on the most basic aspects of the economy.

[1] Subsequently Minister of Economy and Treasury.

Foremost among these aspects are: the increase in national income seen in long perspective, the protection of the balance of payments and the level of private consumption[2] over the years in the immediate future. These three aspects gear into each other, and our first task has been to express in figures how they gear into each other.

3. First aspect: The national income

When we speak of the increase in national income, the first thought that comes to your mind is probably the target of doubling the national income in ten years. I think that this target is excellent as a stimulus to effort. It is a whip that will force everybody concerned with the development of the economy to use his imagination and to do his utmost.

But the simple figure which will measure the national income in any specific year, such as 1970, can not be taken as the basis for the machinery of scientific planning. To focus all attention on the year 1970 and disregard what is happening after that date, will lead one astray. The perspective must be much longer when one has to decide what actions to take this year or in any specific year in the immediate future. I think it was a very wise decision to start the building of the High Dam. But this is not because of the contribution which the High Dam may make to the national income in the particular year 1970, but because the Dam will yield a great contribution to national income over a very long period, virtually an indefinite time into the future. Similarly for the decision to build a thermal power station. With normal maintenance the power station will yield good service for 50 or more years. So we must concentrate our attention on the accumulated income which an investment will create. We must take the sum of all the annual incomes which the investment will create in all the years of the whole life expectancy of the real capital goods that emerge from the investment.

If increase in national income is what is wanted, the scientific planner who is to give advice on how to shape a five year plan, must look for that particular pattern of action in the plan period which will produce the highest possible accumulated income creation over all the future years until the

---

[2] Government consumption is in most countries smaller in size, perhaps around 10% of private consumption, and may, therefore, be disregarded when we concentrate on the three most basic aspects.

effects of the plan period action, particularly the effects of the plan period investment startings[3], have tapered off and finally have been exhausted.

Only in this way can the national income aspect be rationally worked into a global and optimal plan frame.

4. Second aspect: The balance of payments

4.1.

The optimal action in a plan period is, of course, subject to a number of conditions. Foremost among them is the condition which stems from the concern about the balance of payments.

In all essentials the annual balance of payments is the total value of the goods and services that have left the country in a given year, minus the total value of the goods and services that have entered into the country in that same year. This difference is a clear cut concept that can be observed statistically with a fairly high degree of accuracy. When we speak of the annual balance of payments, it is the export-import difference we should concentrate on. If we begin to think in terms of financial concepts, such as the contraction of a loan abroad or the paying back of a loan, there is a great risk that we will be led astray and end up with confusion and mistakes. For instance, the mere contraction of a loan abroad has no effect on the balance of payments. Nothing at all will really happen to the balance of payments until we start to draw on this loan. What will happen when we start to do so? We may perhaps use part of the new loan to pay back an old indebtedness. If we do, this in itself has no effect on the balance of payments. It only means that we have, pound by pound, changed one kind of indebtedness into an other kind. It is only at the moment when we use part of the new loan to pay for imports of goods and services, that something really happens. And the thing that now happens can, pound by pound, be measured by the value of the goods imported. A similar argument can be made regarding the financial transactions involved in the

---

[3] One must distinguish between investment starting and investment sinking. Investment starting in any given year is the total outlay which it is estimated that the projects started that year will have entailed when they are finally completed at some future date. Investment sinking in any given year is the value of goods and services that were actually used (that were 'sunk') that particular year in order to carry towards completion projects which were started that year or some previous year. The distinction between investment starting and investment sinking is absolutely essential in an analysis that is to be truly dynamic.

export of goods from the country. Therefore, in the end, the net effect on the annual balance of payments in any given year is essentially the total value of goods and services exported this year minus the total value of goods and services imported this year.

This difference may be positive, negative or zero. It is positive if the country has exported more than it has imported. It is negative in the opposite case. And it is zero if total exports equal total imports. If gifts to or from the country occur, a correctional term must be entered to account for these unilateral transfers.[4]

The annual balance of payments in a given year is the same as the change that has taken place this year in the country's net creditor position with the rest of the world. If the annual balance of payments in a given year is positive, the country's net creditor position with the rest of the world has improved this year. If the annual balance of payments is negative, the net creditor position has become worse.

If we consider the accumulated balance of payments, that is to say, if to the annual balance of payments in the first year of the plan we add the annual balance of payments in the second year of the plan and to this we add the annual balance of payments in the third year of the plan, and so on up to any given year where we want to stop, this accumulated sum is equal to the total change, i.e., the total improvement or worsening that has taken place in the country's net creditor position with the rest of the world since the beginning of the plan period up to the year where we stopped the accumulation. Since we may stop the accumulation in any year, we see that if the annual balance of payments in each year is given, it is an easy matter to compute what the accumulated balance of payments, and hence the country's net creditor position with the rest of the world, will be in any future year reckoned from the beginning of the plan period.

This accumulated balance of payments is an extremely important aspect of the national economy. In a country which is going through an economic development process, the accumulated balance of payments will begin negative and will get worse and worse from year to year. It will become more and more negative because the country is heavily importing in order to build up its real capital equipment through investment. This will continue until a certain year when the peak load on the accumulated balance of payments, that is the peak load on foreign indebtedness, is reached. From this year on the accumulated balance of payments may go on im-

---

[4] Interests and dividends to or from foreign countries are classified with the unilateral transfers.

proving because now the fruits of the investments start to emerge. The expected peak load on the accumulated balance of payments which is caused by action in the plan period, is an extremely important figure, that the planners and the responsible politicians must study carefully and correctly.

4.2. The peak load on foreign indebtedness can be foreseen

To any given distribution of investments over the various sectors of the economy and over the various years in the plan period, and to any given pattern of private consumption and government use of goods and services in the various years of the plan, will correspond a certain size of the peak load on the accumulated balance of payments. That is to say, a certain size of the highest foreign indebtedness reached is a consequence of the investment and consumption policy that was carried out in the plan period. It is possible to compute in figures with a fair degree of accuracy how high a peak load on foreign indebtedness will follow from a given investment and consumption policy in the plan period. It is possible to do it, and we have done it. In performing these computations we have taken account of all effects, direct as well as indirect. We have equations that will tell us with a fair degree of accuracy what the peak load will be for any given size of investments and private consumption in the plan period. Once a given constellation of the five year plan is fixed, we can foresee with a fair degree of accuracy what the peak load on net foreign indebtedness will be, and we can foresee when this peak load will occur.

A lack of understanding of this has been a weak point in economic planning in many underdeveloped countries. I am seriously concerned about this, because this lack of understanding may lead to an investment and consumption policy that will cause balance of payment surprises of a critical order of magnitude.

It is as if in a military operation one should fail to evaluate correctly the enemy's strength. The reason for the too optimistic estimates often made, is, I believe, that there is a temptation to reckon only with direct effects that are immediately visible and attract attention, while the indirect effects can only be estimated after a patient study of a global economic decision model for the country.

There is for example a popular belief that if goods and services needed for consumption or investment purposes can be provided by domestic sectors of production, these goods and services will not fall as a burden on the balance of payments. This is a fundamental mistake. If all indirect effects are taken account of, one will find that the burden on the balance of payments is much higher than what appears prima facie. This failure to consider indirect effects is the great danger.

The fact that we are able to compute the total effect on the size of the peak load on foreign indebtedness and the year when it will occur, when we have given the investment and consumption policy in the plan period, is important. But there is another fact that is still more important from the viewpoint of rational planning. We are also able to perform the computation in the reverse direction. By this I mean the following.

4.3. A ceiling on the peak load of foreign indebtedness

Suppose that we put a ceiling on the peak load of foreign indebtedness. That is to say, we will allow the foreign indebtedness to go up to a certain point, but not beyond this point. We can express it by saying that we put a lower bound on the accumulated balance of payments. This lower bound will be a condition put on the kind of consumption and investment policy we are allowed to follow in the plan period. There are, of course, still a great variety of such policies that are open to us, but they must be chosen in such a way that they do not break the ceiling that has been imposed on the peak load of the foreign indebtedness.

When this ceiling on the peak load of foreign indebtedness is given, we are able to determine in figures an optimum constellation of the investment and consumption policy in the plan period. That is to say an investment and consumption policy which is such that it will − according to our estimate − produce the largest size of accumulated national income creation which it is possible to attain when the ceiling on the peak load of foreign indebtedness is given. The more liberal we have been when we put the ceiling on the foreign indebtedness, that is to say the deeper we have allowed the country to go in foreign indebtedness, the higher it will be possible to reach in accumulated national income creation, provided, of course, that the funds borrowed are wisely used. And the more stringent we have been when we put the ceiling on the peak load of foreign indebtedness, that is to say the smaller peak load we have allowed for the country's foreign indebtedness, the smaller will be the maximum size which we can reach in accumulated national income creation.

5. Third aspect: The private consumption

5.1.

The way in which our concern about the private consumption comes into the picture can be illustrated as follows. Take for example the curve marked 140 in the Basic Policy Chart (fig. 1). I shall later have more to say about these down-sloping curves, but for the moment take the particular curve marked 140 as an illustration.

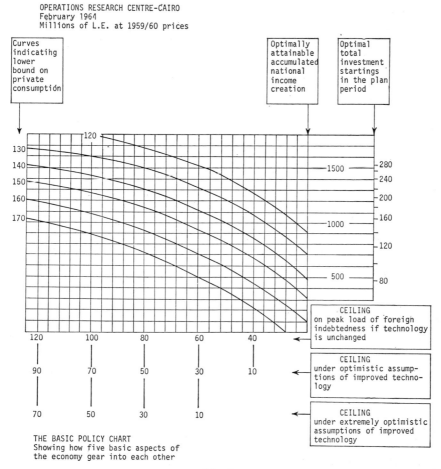

Fig. 1.

Figures and curves for the Basic Policy Chart resulting from actual computations made for the Egyptian economy are available but have not been published. The figures given in the appended chart are different from the actual ones and are here given only for the purpose of illustration. Anyone familiar with the United Arab Republic economy will see that the figures given here are much smaller than those applicable in the realistic situation. The figures given in the chart will, however, give a good illustration of what can be achieved through a rational form of optimality in national planning.

The figures and curves in the Basic Policy Chart have been worked out by Dr. Salib Roufael who has done a most excellent job in this connection.

Let us start by reading off the point 60 on the horizontal axis (the upper row of figures immediately below the horizontal axis). This indicates a ceiling of 60 millions on that part of the Egyptian foreign indebtedness which will follow when we have decided on the optimal action to be taken in the plan period 1965–70, optimal in the sense of maximizing accumulated national income creation.

From the point 60 we move vertically up until we hit the downsloping curve marked 140. And from this point we move horizontally to the right until we hit the first vertical axis. Here we read off the value[5] 1125. This reading means that if we impose the condition that the peak load on the part of foreign indebtedness due to action in the plan period, is not to be more than 60 millions and if the consumption policy in the plan period is to be such as to assure an annual private consumption of not less than 140 millions, then we can, if the investment policy in the plan period is determined in an optimal way, reach an accumulated national income creation of 1125. Note that 1125 is not the annual income in any single year, but the sum of national incomes over all the years covered by the life expectancy of the capital goods created through investment startings in the plan period.

Similarly we read off from the chart that, if the ceiling on the peak load of foreign indebtedness is as stringent as 40, and the consumption policy is still characterized by 140, we will only be able to reach an optimal accumulated income creation of about 850. And if the ceiling is as liberal as 80, we will be able to reach an optimal accumulated national income creation of about 1300.

5.2. Different alternatives for the consumption policy

All the explanations given so far refer to a situation where we have decided to follow a policy pattern with respect to private consumption characterized

---

[5] The figure 1125 is not printed in the chart, but 1000 is, and there is one horizontal line at the level 1100 and one at 1200. The vertical marked 60 is seen to intersect the downsloping curve 140 between the horizontal at 1100 and that at 1200. We judge by the eye that the intersection takes place when we have moved about one quarter of the way between 1100 and 1200. Hence the result is 1125.

by the downsloping curve marked 140 in the Basic Policy Chart. This policy was defined by the condition that total annual private consumption in any year in the plan should never fall below 140 millions. If we had decided to follow a more drastic austerity policy by imposing a lower bound of only 130 millions on private consumption, we would have been able to reduce the burden on the foreign indebtedness. But still the situation would have been precisely the same as before. To any given ceiling on the peak load of the foreign indebtedness, will also now correspond a certain optimal value of the accumulated income creation. The only difference is that now we have to use the curve marked 130 in the Basic Policy Chart.

For instance, let us again start on the horizontal axis at the point indicating a ceiling of 60. Moving vertically up to the consumption curve 130, and then to the right, we read off an optimally attainable accumulated national income creation of 1325. This accumulated national income creation of 1325 is considerably higher than the one we were able to attain when we imposed the same ceiling 60 on the peak load of foreign indebtedness, but adopted the more liberal consumption policy of 140.

6. *A fourth aspect*: *Total investment startings in the plan period*

An optimal economic policy has, of course, many aspects to it other than national income creation, protection of the balance of payments and concern about private consumption. One of these other aspects is the total size of investment startings in the plan period.[6] This is a fourth of the basic aspects of the economy which we will now draw into the picture. This total size can be read off from the second vertical axis, in the Basic Policy Chart. We note for instance that to the peak load ceiling on the foreign indebtedness of 60 corresponds on the curve 140 an accumulated national income creation of 1125 and a total plan period investment starting of about 180.

This means that if the ceiling on the peak load of foreign indebtedness is given as 60 and the lower bound on private consumption is 140, and we determine the investment and consumption policy in the plan period in such a way as to maximize the accumulated national income creation under the conditions stated, we will find that we need to make a total investment starting in the plan period of some 180 millions. The composition

---

[6] For the distinction between investment starting and investment sinking, see the footnote above.

of these 180 millions is not arbitrary but must conform to an optimal pattern.

This figure, 180 millions, will, of course, depend on the nature of the investment projects that are available in the list of projects among which we are to make the optimal pick. All layers of the population should be encouraged to help extending in a useful way the list of projects from which the optimal pick is to be made. The mere inclusion of a project in this list is, of course, not tantamount to assuming that the project is to be accepted. Whether or not it is to be recommended for acceptance is precisely what the optimality analysis is intended to bring out.

Similarly, if we put on a peak load ceiling of 80 and a consumption bound of 140, we read off from the chart that the optimal total investment starting will be about 220. Similarly if we had used the consumption curve 130 or some of the other consumption curves.

7. How should high level planning discussions begin?

By a little exercise one will quickly learn to make readings in the chart and thereby see at a glance how four extremely important aspects of the planned economy gear into each other, namely: (1) Optimally attainable accumulated national income creation, (2) ceiling on the peak load of that part of the foreign indebtedness which is due to action in the plan period, (3) lower bound on annual private consumption in any year in the plan period, and (4) total investment startings in the plan period. When using the chart we have two 'degrees of manoeuvrability' in the sense that when any two of the four aspects are assumed given, we can read off what the other two aspects are estimated to be in an economy whose structure is as that depicted by the numbers printed in the Basic Policy Chart.

The planning procedure at the high political level ought to begin by asking: What point in the Basic Policy Chart should we aim at?

This is a much more rational approach than to let the authorities — low level or high level authorities — proceed directly to deciding on specific measures, one by one, say deciding on whether or not some specific investment projects are to be accepted. Such detailed decisions must, of course, finally be made, but they should only come at a much later stage, after the Basic Policy Chart has been thoroughly discussed at the high political level.

The chart is like a budget-frame for the total economic policy. If one does not begin by studying this budget-frame, but start by ad hoc decisions on a number of details, it is practically certain that one will sooner or later run into very serious unexpected difficulties.

Since any point in the Basic Policy Chart will simultaneously define four of the most basic aspects of the five year plan, any responsible politician will be able to say which one of the points (i.e. small square cells) in the chart he prefers the most. He will even be able to rank the points in a preference order.

The recording of the preferences can be done as follows: One will give each voter a total sum of, say, 100 points and ask him to distribute these points in any way he prefers over the small square cells of the chart. These votes will be collected and processed by adding the votes distributed in the cells. And this summarized view of the voters will be presented for top level decision on which specific point is to aimed at. This procedure is both rational and democratic.

8. A fifth aspect: Improved technology

8.1.

In the ceiling figures indicated along the heavy horizontal axis is not included the effect of an improved technology. This represents a fifth aspect. Under an optimistic assumption about the possibility of realizing a gain through improved technology, the ceiling figures may perhaps be reduced by 30, that is to say, instead of the figure 60 one may use the figure 30, and so on. These optimistically amended figures are printed in the horizontal row below the figures that belong to the heavy horizontal axis. If we can make this optimistic amendment, we find that a ceiling of 30 on the peak load of foreign indebtedness and an austerity policy corresponding to the consumption curve 130 will make room for a total plan period investment starting of about 225.

If one wants to be extremely optimistic about the possibility of an improved technology, one may perhaps reduce the ceiling figures by a further 20 as indicated in the bottom row under the horizontal axis. Using these figures one finds that a ceiling of 30 on the peak load of foreign indebtedness and the strong, but not excessive austerity policy of 135 will make room for a total plan period investment starting of about 240. It must be emphasized that this is a highly optimistic view.

The technology factor has in the present analysis only been treated by a very rough estimate. It is possible to study this factor in a much more precise way by including into the optimality analysis what I call infra investments, i.e. investments which aim at changing the coefficients that express the needs for inputs into production sectors or aim at changing other coefficients in the decision model used. I have discussed this in greater detail in other papers. It will make the programming analysis at least quadratic and can only be handled by the use of a bigger electronic computer.

8.2. *Further aspects*

It is possible to add still more aspects in the Basic Policy Chart, for instance the accumulated employment creation due to action in the plan period. This can be done by adding another vertical axis parallel to the axis of the accumulated national income creation. One might even add more aspects to be represented in the chart by more vertical axes. The number of 'degrees of maneuvrability' in the chart would remain the same, namely two.

9. *The second and third phases of the decision process*

When the first phase of the decision process is completed by using the Basic Policy Chart, we can proceed to the second phase. We can now make several new specific runs on the computer and present more details, all of which pertain to the situation where the ceiling on the peak load of the foreign indebtedness and the lower bound on private consumption are fixed at the levels that were decided upon through the decision technique of the Basic Policy Chart. We can make what we call a stochastic sensitivity analysis by changing at random some of the data to test the precision of the analysis. In this way we can determine a number of different solutions that are equally optimal from the practical point of view. We can work out, say, 10 different alternatives regarding the phasing of the investments in the various sectors over the plan period. In the Operations Research Center we have worked out a tentative voting chart intended for voting on 10 such alternatives.

Again we may let each voter be alloted a sum of 100 points to be distributed over the 10 alternatives in the way which best suits his preferences. And again a final top level decision will fix the alternative to be chosen.

In a third phase of the decision process one will study tables that show how a much larger number of aspects of the economy — perhaps 100 or 200 aspects — gear into each other. The study of such tables will lead up to the final stage where decisions are made about individual investment projects and about other detailed planning questions.

10. Conclusion

To conclude I would like to say that a rational plan frame work of the kind suggested here will mean millions and millions to the Republic and will do away with a large part of the balance of payment hazards now experienced. It will also activate a close cooperation between top level authorities and the analytical experts. In the end this will be a decisive factor in the economic and social development of the country.

B. STATIC AND DYNAMIC
INPUT–OUTPUT MODELS

CHAPTER 8

Interregional input–output: a state of the arts survey

ROGER F. RIEFLER*

University of Pittsburgh

1. Introduction

Empirical studies of spatial interdependence fall into two broad and over-lapping classifications (see Meyer [56]). First, historical and behavioral analysis, which tends to be the less comprehensive of the two approaches, emphasizes the dynamic and unstable elements of spatial interaction. This approach does not usually invoke a formally comprehensive or consistent conceptual framework. It tends to be piecemeal and short-run oriented in its approach. Forecasts based on this approach typically emphasize the plausibility (with respect to past behavior) of projections. Second, a quantitatively oriented analysis has developed which stresses a logically comprehensive and rigorous conceptual framework. The emphasis in this approach centers on the stability and consistency of the posited framework. Forecasts are evaluated chiefly in terms of their consistency.

These two approaches are not mutually exclusive; they can and should be combined to obtain an overall picture of the interregional or regional economy. (See, for instance, Henderson and Krueger [33].) When combined, the historical and behavioral approach must be adjusted to take account of the observed complexities and comprehensive scope of spatial interaction, while the quantitative approach must be modified to take into consideration shifts and changes in the pattern of spatial interaction.

This chapter will survey the development and application of a quanti-

* The author wishes to acknowledge the assistance of his colleagues at the university as well as William Miernyk and Karen Polenske, both of whom constructively criticized earlier drafts of this endeavor. Due to the very nature of a study such as this, however, all errors of commission and omission remain the author's.

tative model of spatial interdependence, interregional input–output analysis.
Sects. 2 and 3 will briefly outline the conceptual and empirical heritage
of this model. Sect. 4 will be devoted to an analysis of the basic criticisms
of the model as a theoretical construct, as an empirical tool and as an input
or vehicle for policy evaluation. This section will also discuss the extension
of the basic model and the combination of this particular quantitative construct with historical and behavioral analysis. The final section, sect. 5,
outlines a specific extension of the basic model currently being pursued.
It serves not only to emphasize the continuity of contemporary interregional input–output research with the past and the flexibility of the basic
model in analyzing the wide gamut of problems encountered in regional
planning, but it serves as a prediction of the general direction further investigations will take.

2. The interregional input–output model

The objectives of any interregional input–output model are to identify
empirically and to analyze the interindustry and interregional linkages
between two or more spatially defined economies. As such, the intellectual
heritage or lineage, as well as currently available alternative conceptual
formulations, can be found in two broad fields of economics. The mutual
interdependence of two or more trading regions (interregional linkages) is
of course at the foundation of international economics. Works such as
Ohlin's classic International and Interregional Trade [70] represent the intellectual forebears of today's interregional input–output model while
trade multipliers, terms-of-trade analysis and balance of trade accounts all
vie with the input–output model for identifying and analyzing interregional
linkages. Analysis of interindustry linkages in the interregional framework,
of course, can be traced directly to the pioneering work of Leontief on
regional input–output [47]. Various alternative models from regional
economics encompassing location theory, comparative cost analysis, industrial complex analysis and various linear programming formulations
compete with interregional input–output as a tool for identifying and analyzing interindustry linkages.

International trade models applicable to the general interrelations
between two economies are typically of a highly aggregative nature. This
characteristic, while facilitating empirical and analytical application sub-
sumes much detailed information into such broad concepts as total exports,
total imports and overall marginal propensities to import. These models

also tend to neglect the spatial elements of trade (for exceptions see Isard and Peck [40], Isard [41] and Metzler [55]) and its interindustry dimensions. Much the same comments can be made with respect to the available regional models. Economic base, multiplier and comparative cost models, for instance, make use of partial equilibrium methods and aggregation; as such these methods lend themselves quite readily to empirical application, but they are vulnerable to the usual disadvantages of partial equilibrium analysis (Meyer [56], pp. 30–32). Linear programming techniques (or to use the broader term, activity analysis), location and industrial complex analysis, while at the conceptual level formulated to analyze general interregional and interindustry linkages, have been severely constrained at the empirical level by data availability.

The basic advantages of interregional input–output analysis are its comprehensive use of the available data on production and trade, its disaggregative nature and (therefore) its potential as a starting point for supplementary analysis. In contrast to other regional models it is empirically applicable, and general in nature. In contrast to international trade models it is disaggregative in nature and explicitly recognizes the spatial dimension of trade. Not only is the basic model, in the form of the inverse or multiplier matrix, a useful tool for analyzing regional and interregional growth paths, but the gross flows table itself provides a systematic depository or account for factual information and the direct technical matrix provides the raw data necessary for the implementation of specialized studies such as linear programming, location, industrial complex, economic base, regional income and interregional trade analysis.

Interregional input–output models represent a disaggregation of the standard Leontief national model [47]. A new dimension, the region, is introduced and commodity and service flow data are delineated by both industry and region of origin and destination. The basic flow and structural equations are given below (Isard [36]):

$$_rX_i - \sum_{s=1}^{n} \sum_{j=1}^{m} {}_{rs}x_{ij} = \sum_{s=1}^{n} {}_{rs}Y_i \qquad \begin{matrix} (r, s = 1, 2 \ldots n) \\ (i, j = 1, 2 \ldots m) \end{matrix} \qquad (1)$$

where $_rX_i$ represents the total output of industry i in region r, $_{rs}x_{ij}$ represents the flow from industry i in region r to industry j in region s, and $_{rs}Y_i$ represents that part of the final demand for i in region s satisfied by output from region r,

$$_{rs}x_j = {}_{rs}b_j \, {}_sX_j \qquad (2)$$

where $_{rs}b_{ij}$ represents the spatial input coefficient indicating the amount of i from region r needed per unit of output by industry j in region s.

Substituting eq. (2) into (1) yields:

$$_rX_i - \sum_{s=1}^{n} \sum_{j=1}^{m} {}_{rs}b_{ij} {}_xX_j = \sum_{s=1}^{n} {}_{rs}Y_i \qquad \begin{array}{l} (r, s = 1, 2 \ldots n) \\ (i, j = 1, 2 \ldots m) \end{array} . \qquad (3)$$

This system of equations, given regional final demands, can be solved for regional outputs, the solution being given by:

$$_rX_i = \sum_{s=1}^{n} \sum_{j=1}^{m} {}_{rs}B_{ij} {}_{rs}Y_j \qquad \begin{array}{l} (r, s = 1, 2 \ldots n) \\ (i, j = 1, 2 \ldots m) \end{array} \qquad (4)$$

where $_{rs}B_{ij} = [I-b]^{-1}$ and I is the identity matrix.

The unique assumption of this interregional model, as opposed to the standard Leontief national model is the assumed stability of the spatial input coefficients, the $_{rs}b_{ij}$'s defined by eq. (3). These coefficients are assumed to be stable over time when projecting future output and output multipliers.[1] The significance of this assumption can be illustrated if we let $_sa_{ij}$ represent the regional technical coefficient expressing the amount of input from industry i, wherever located, required per unit of output of industry j in region s and $_{rs}t_{ij}$ equal the proportion of the total amount of i needed for industry j in region s supplied by industry in region r, ($\sum_{r=1}^{n}$ $_{rs}t_{ij} = 1$). Then

$$_{rs}b_{ij} = {}_{rs}t_{ij} {}_sa_{ij} \qquad \begin{array}{l} (r, s = 1, 2 \ldots n) \\ (i, j = 1, 2 \ldots m) \end{array} . \qquad (5)$$

Eq. (5) demonstrates that the assumption of stability for the spatial input coefficients actually entails two separate assumptions. First, consistent with national and regional input–output models, the regional technical coefficients ($_sa_{ij}$'s) are assumed to be fixed. Second, the trade coefficients expressing industrial spatial trading relationships are assumed stable.

The model originally formulated by Isard [36] and summarized by eqs. (1) to (4) may be considered the 'ideal' interregional input–output model; that is, from a descriptive and analytical viewpoint the model is the ideal interregional input–output archetype (Riefler [77], p. 25). Although this ideal model was originally formulated in 1951, its empirical application has been somewhat restricted by the lack of adequate data. For the United States consistent data from which the spatial input coefficients ($_{rs}b_{ij}$'s) could be directly computed are not available. Even where regional studies have

---

[1] This assumption of stability, as in the case of all input–output models can be relaxed if the necessary data are available. (e.g. If time series data are available on flows, the assumption of a linear homogenous relationship could be replaced by using 'marginal' coefficients (see Tiebout [84]).)

provided statistics necessary for the computation of the $_s a_{ij}$'s of eq. (5), the existing body of transportation data have not been and are not adequate enough to allow general identification of the $_{rs}t_{ij}$'s.

There have been four distinct approaches to an empirically applicable simplification of the ideal interregional model.[2] Each has partially sacrificed the descriptive and analytical content of the ideal formulation in order to achieve a workable model in light of currently available data. Each is summarized below in terms of its reformulation of eq. (5).

The first approximation to the ideal interregional input–output model was a reformulation of the Leontief regionally balanced model (Leontief [48]) by Moses [66]. Although the original Leontief model was intranational in character, Moses' transformation of the basic model converted it to an interregional format.[3] The model rests upon the distinction between 'regional' or 'local' industries and national industries. For the former it is assumed that production and consumption balance at the local level; there are no interregional flows. A national industry is one for which this balance is achieved only on a nation-wide level. Interregional flows for these latter commodities are estimated by:

$$_{rs}\hat{b}_{ij} = (_s a_{ij} \, _s X_j)_r L_i /_s X_j \quad ^4 \tag{5a}$$

where $_s a_{ij}$ represents the regional technical coefficient, $_s X_j$ represents the output of j in region s, and $_r L_i$ is a location coefficient calculated by $_r L_i = (_r X_i / X_i)$ and $_r X_i$ and X_i represent output of i in region r and the nation respectively.

---

[2] Throughout this chapter, due to space limitations we will focus rather narrowly on the specific genre, interregional input–output models. For a more comprehensive review see Miernyk [60]. For alternative approaches to the ideal interregional model falling outside our narrow purview see for instance Moses [68], Isard [40], Fox [22] and Henderson [32].

[3] The original Leontief formulation was intranational or intraregional in the sense that it did not link regions together. It treated all regional exports of a national industry as going to a national pool and all imports as being drawn from this pool. There is no rationale presented to establish preferential paths for interregional trade; quite the opposite, Leontief's definition of national goods precludes any a priori attempt at arriving at such paths. Leontief assumes national goods to be transported free of charge and to encounter no spatial friction (Moses [66], pp. 45–51). The Moses reformulation presents a rationale for preferential interregional paths (see eq. (5a)).

[4] All estimates of the ideal model's coefficients are "hatted". To simplify exposition only those equations designed to approximate interregional, interindustry flows are presented. Interregional flows to final demand would be estimated in an analogous fashion.

The Leontief–Moses model will not only characterize a region as either a net importer or exporter of a given national commodity, but will also indicate the geographic origin of the net imports or the destination of the net exports. The advantage of this model, of course, is that it requires no data on actual trade flows ($_{rs}x_{ij}$'s or $_{rs}t_{ij}$'s). Against this advantage must be set several disadvantages. Foremost is the question of whether a meaningful hierarchy of regions and industry detail can be identified so as to minimize cross-hauling of goods and facilitate the identification of local and national industries (Isard [37]). If such a hierarchy cannot be found, the model will grossly underestimate the importance of interregional trade to regional development. A second disadvantage is the limitation inherent in the assumption of a constant locational pattern for national industries. There is no a priori reason to anticipate that, as final demand changes, all regions will expand or contract output in fixed proportions. Third, the model fails to explicitly consider a most crucial aspect of spatial economics, the friction of distance.

A second approximation to the ideal interregional input–output model has been formulated by Leontief with the collaboration of Strout [49]. For this model interregional coefficients are estimated by eq. (5b):

$$_{rs}\hat{b}_{ij} = (_{r}X_i \cdot {}_{s}U_i / X_i)_{rs}Q_i / {}_{s}X_j \, {}_{s}a_{ij} \qquad (5b)$$

where $_{r}X_i$ and X_i represent the output of i in region r and nationally respectively; $_{s}X_j$ represents the output of j in region s; $_{s}U_i$ represents the total internal input (production plus imports minus exports) of good i in region s; $_{s}a_{ij}$ is the regional technical coefficient, and $_{rs}Q_i$ is a (constant) location coefficient.[5]

Like the Leontief–Moses model this formulation estimates interregional coefficients without actual data on interregional flows. The Leontief–Strout model, however, does not require the a priori identification of local and national industries and it does allow the cross-hauling of commodities between regions. Like the Leontief–Moses model the location coefficients are assumed constant, but unlike that model the authors explicitly recognize

---

[5] This location coefficient, which is really a locational preference coefficient can either be estimated from available flow data or by the following equation:

$$_{rs}Q_i = (_{r}E_i + {}_{s}K_i) \, _{rs}d_i \, V_i \qquad (5b')$$

where $_{rs}d_i$ represents the inverse of the per unit transport costs from region r to region s, $_{r}E_i$ represents a parameter characterizing the relative position of r versus all other regions as a supplier of i, $_{s}K_i$ represents a parameter characterizing the position of region s versus all other regions as a user of i, V_i represents a dummy variable (equal to zero if no shipments are expected, otherwise equal to one).

the influence of distance on commodity flows through the computation of these coefficients (see footnote 5).

The third method to approximate the ideal interregional model is exemplified in the work of Moses [67] and Chenery [11, 12]. The Moses–Chenery model estimates the interregional flows of eq. (5) by:

$$_{rs}\hat{b}_{ij} = {}_s a_{ij} \, {}_{rs}t_i, \tag{5c}$$

where the trade coefficients are computed by $_{rs}t_i = {}_{rs}Z_i/{}_sZ_i$, and $_s a_{ij}$ represents the regional technical coefficients, $_{rs}Z_i$ represents the amount of good i purchased by all region s industries and final demand from region r $(= \sum_{j=1}^{m} {}_{rs}x_{ij} + {}_{rs}Y_i)$, and $_sZ_i$ represents total purchases of good i by all industries and final demand sectors in region s from all regions. $(= \sum_{r=1}^{n} \sum_{j=1}^{m} {}_{rs}x_{ij} + \sum_{r=1}^{n} {}_{rs}Y_i)$.

The advantages of this model are basically its consistency with published statistics on interregional commodity flows and its ability to capture crosshauling of commodities. On the negative side, however, the model assumes both the stability of regional trading patterns and the uniformity of trading relationships for all sectors or industries within a region. This model applies to all industries in a region a spatial pattern for a particular commodity which is the average pattern for the region as a whole.

A final reformulation of the ideal interregional model has been advanced by Riefler and Tiebout [76, 77]. This model estimates interregional flow coefficients by eq. (5d):

$$_{rs}\hat{b}_{ij} = {}_{rs}t_i({}_s a_{ij} - {}_{ss}a_{ij}), \tag{5d}$$

where $_{ss}a_{ij}$ represents the amount of region s output of good i purchased per unit of output of industry j in region s, and $_{rs}t_i = {}_{rs}Z_i/\sum_{\substack{r=1 \\ r \neq s}}^{n} {}_{rs}Z_i$. The advantage of this model over the Moses–Chenery formulation is that while the model, in common with all interregional input–output models, assumes that interregional trading patterns by types of input are constant, it assumes that interregional, but not intraregional trading patterns are identical for each industry in a region. The disadvantage of this model is that it requires a regional input–output table and internal flow matrix to determine the $_s a_{ij}$'s and $_{ss}a_{ij}$'s of eq. (5d).

In summary, then, the regional analyst concerned with identifying and analyzing interregional and interindustry linkages has five variants of input–output models to choose between. Ranking these models in terms of data requirements would find the ideal Isard model at the top, followed by the Riefler–Tiebout, Moses–Chenery, Leontief–Moses and Leontief–Strout models.[6] A ranking by informational content would be similar, the only alteration being the reversal of the Leontief–Moses, which does not allow cross-hauling, with the Leontief–Strout model, which does. Unfortunately the analyst usually does not have the luxury of a free choice amongst the models. If data on interregional output flows are not available by region and industry of origin and destination, the ideal Isard model is precluded from use. Statistics on interregional flows by region and industry of origin and region of destination allow the use of either the Riefler–Tiebout or Moses–Chenery model although the former requires knowledge of intra-regional flows by industry of origin and destination. Finally, in an area where flow statistics on interregional trade are not available recourse to the Leontief–Moses or Leontief–Strout model will result. Sect. 3, by surveying the available empirical studies, gives an indication of the propensities to apply these various conceptual formulations.

3. Applications of the interregional model

Given the enormous data requirements of an interregional input–output model, it is not surprising to discover that relatively few applications of the model have been undertaken. Moreover, of those studies which have been completed, one is immediately impressed with not only the variety of conceptual models applied, but the diversity of regional foci, the varia-tions in industrial sectoring of the basic model and the differences in research goals or objectives of the authors. This part of our survey is devoted to cataloging the basic models with respect to their conceptual framework, regional identification and sectoring plan. This cataloging is limited to model applications in the United States. (For examples of ap-plication to other areas see Ministry of International Trade and Industry [63], Hartwick [29], Brodersohn [8], Chenery et al. [11], Polenske [73].) Sect. 4 evaluates the methods used as well as the research goals of the in-vestigators.

There have been eleven interregional input–output studies applied using United States data. These studies illustrate four of the basic models

---

[6] Since at least four versions of the Leontief–Strout model exist, the ranking of this model in terms of data requirements is rather imprecise. This ranking refers to the simplest version of the Leontief–Strout model; use of the equation contained in footnote 5 would significantly advance the model's rank.

delineated in sect. 2:[7] four studies use the 'ideal' Isard model, five the Moses–Chenery formulation, one the Riefler–Tiebout framework and two a Leontief–Strout approach. It is significant to note that, despite the paucity of data on industrially defined interregional trade flows, only two applications of a Leontief–Strout gravity-type formulation and none of the Leontief–Moses model, the two models which require no commodity flow data, have been attempted.

Three of the four studies applying the Isard-type ideal model have emphasized interregional flows of agricultural products. The first of these, by Carter and Heady [9, 31], traced 1954 interregional flows of nine agricultural sectors between ten census regions. Although the complete model contains twenty-two sectors, only the nine agricultural sectors are regionally defined; the thirteen non-farm industries (emphasizing agricultural processing and supplying industries) are defined only on a national basis. A second Isard formulation emphasizing agriculture was published by Martin and Carter [54]. This two region, northern and southern California, 1954 model contains 10 agricultural sectors, 5 agricultural processing industries and 12 "other" sectors for each region.

The third study emphasizing agriculture is more recent in origin. Carter and Ireri have linked state input–output matrices for California and Arizona into a two region interregional model for 1958 containing, for each state, ten agricultural sectors, five agricultural processing industries and eleven other sectors [10, 35]. The objective of this study is to determine "the technical water requirements of different sectors in California and Arizona and how ... these requirements [are] related to economic activity within California and between California and Arizona". ([10], p. 140.)

The final application of the ideal interregional model has been advanced by Lee *et al.* [45, 46]. Their model is a three region disaggregation of the Tennessee economy for 1964 containing, for eastern, central and western areas of the state, twenty-five industrial sectors defined basically at the two digit Standard Industrial Classification (SIC) level. Unlike the above three Isard-type models, which relied on published and unpublished data on interregional flows, the Tennessee group surveyed firms to identify interregional

---

[7] While no study has utilized the Leontief–Moses framework completely, several of the studies cited below do assume certain sectors to be regionally balanced or local in nature. In addition, Isard has experimented with the intranational version of the model [37] and Leontief [50], [51], Polenske [72] and Boulanger [5] have applied the original intraregional (Leontief [48]) formulation of the model to an analysis of the impact of changes in federal expenditures. The intraregional nature of these studies (viz., flows are not designated by both originating and terminating region) preclude their inclusion as an interregional model application.

flows by region and industry of origin and destination. Since the survey process relied on the "rows only" approach utilized by Hansen et al. in their California regional study [27], no cross check of flow entries from the purchase side was utilized. This method also precluded the computation of spatially defined technical coefficients.

The earliest United States application of the Moses–Chenery model, of course, was that advanced by Moses in the same article which contained the conceptual framework of the basic model [67]. The empirical application, using 1947 data, divided the United States into three regions and defined, for each region, eleven industries at the one digit SIC level. Moses' empirical work basically had the twofold objective of illustrating the basic theoretical model using available transportation (Interstate Commerce Commission railroad waybill) statistics and testing the stability of the interregional commodity flows.

A second application of the Moses–Chenery framework was published by Wonnacott in 1961 [93]. Although this analysis of Canadian–American dependence in 1949 represents an international application of the interregional model, the spatial proximity of the two trading partners, the magnitude of their trade as well as relatively unfettered nature of trade dictates its inclusion in our interregional survey. Although the basic conceptual framework applied is the Moses–Chenery model ([93], p. 27–32), the availability of a Canadian import matrix allowed such imports to be identified both by industry of origin and industry of destination ([93], p. 67–68). Thus, at least partially, Wonnacott was able to modify the model in the direction of the Riefler–Tiebout and Isard models. Thirty-five industries were defined for each country at, with some exceptions, the two digit SIC level.

Greytak has designed an interregional, interindustry input–output model, based on the Moses–Chenery formulation, "within which regional delineation is a variable controllable by the analyst" ([25], p. 156). He has implemented this approach in two published studies [25, 26]. Both empirical models contain, for each region, twenty-three industries defined basically at the two digit SIC level and are applied using 1958 and 1963 national input–output statistics. The first study [25] encompasses nineteen regions, eighteen substate areas of Appalachia and the Ozark region and a rest-of-the-United States region.[8] The second study contains eight regions,

---

[8] A gravity-type formulation was used to allocate interareal flows of each extractive and manufacturing commodity to substate areas of origin and destination. Thus, although the basic model uses actual data on commodity flows, recourse to a Leontief–Strout formulation must be made for substate allocation. This first study also used 1958 national input-output coefficients, the second, 1963 national coefficients as published by the Department of Commerce [87, 88, 90].

encompassing whole states or groups of states, exhausting the spatial area of the United States [26].

The most recent application of the Moses–Chenery model, and undoubtedly the most ambitious, has recently been published by the Harvard Research Project and the Economic Development Administration of the Department of Commerce (Polenske, [74] and ch. 9 below). This 1963 model contains 44 regions (defined as states or group of states) and 86 sectors (78 producing industries, 61 of which produce commodities for which interregional flows are delineated). Although, like the other applications of the Moses–Chenery model, national input–output coefficients were used to estimate most regional technical coefficients, these regional coefficients were built up, where possible, from a weighted aggregation of a 370 sector national table and as such reflect differences between regions in intra-sector industrial output mix ([74], Part IV).[9]

The only application of the Riefler–Tiebout interregional model was published in 1970 ([76], see also [77]). This study basically linked existing regional input–output and intraregional flow studies of California and Washington, both based on survey data, thereby developing a two state interregional model for 1963. The endogenous matrix contained 31 Washington industries and 22 California industries. The availability of both an export and import matrix, for Washington industries, delineating industry of origin and destination for all interstate flows emanating or terminating in Washington State, respectively, facilitated the application of the Riefler–Tiebout framework.

Davis, in his 1963 study of water resource dependencies among the western states, utilized the Leontief–Strout gravity flow model to predict origins and destinations for net commodity trade between eight regions (Arizona, California, Colorado, New Mexico, Nevada–Idaho, Montana–Wyoming, Oregon and Utah–Washington) [17, 18]. For each region fifteen sectors were defined utilizing basically two digit SIC categories or combinations of two digit industries. Emphasis, of course, was placed on industries with significant water requirements. Where possible existing regional (state) tables were utilized for intrastate flows.

The final application of the interregional input–output model, also utilizing the Leontief–Strout framework, was reported by the CONSAD

---

[9] National coefficients were relied on for manufacturing and some service industries. For agriculture, mining and construction various sources of secondary information were utilized to determine regional coefficients. In addition to delineating 1963 interregional flows the Harvard Project projected final demands to 1970 and 1980 and derived interregional trade flows and sector outputs for these years.

Research Corporation in 1968/69. [14] The model was implemented as part of the U.S. Department of Transportation's Northeast Corridor Transportation Project. Actually this study utilized three different versions or 'runs' of the basic Leontief–Strout model. All three versions used 1963 data contained in various Bureau of Census publications; projections were made for 1965, 1970 and 1975. All three versions also emphasized regions encompassed by the Northeast Corridor. The first run contained four regions (based on Bureau of the Census production areas) and nine industrial sectors (agriculture and minerals, trade, energy, "other services", basic metals, final metals (2), basic non-metal, final non-metal). The second version had five regions (states or groups of states) and the same nine sectors. The final run contained fifteen regions, eleven corridor regions or "superdistricts" and four "rest of the U.S." regions, and fifteen sectors (including eight sectors in manufacturing). Two interesting aspects of the CONSAD study are its use of an intraregional location model to extend the basic interregional model and the application of an econometric model, formulated at a higher level of aggregation, to test the interregional input–output model [14]. Emphasis throughout the report, of course, is focused on transportation requirements.

4. Evaluation: Theory and applications

Interregional input–output models represent a logical culmination to an evolutionary process begun with the original Leontief national input–output model. By combining the industrial disaggregation of this original Leontief model with the spatial disaggregation common to its immediate forebears, regional input–output models, the interregional model has inherited the restrictive theoretical assumptions of its progenitors. In addition, however, this youngest progeny of the general input–output family displays its own unique assumptions both at the theoretical level, as outlined in sect. 2, and at the empirical level, as indicated in sect. 3. It is the purpose of this section to evaluate these unique aspects of the interregional model. For a critical discussion of the assumptions of the original Leontief national and regional framework the reader is referred to Isard [44], Dorfman [19], Chenery and Clark [13], Ghosh [23], NBER [69], and Miernyk [58]. An excellent critique of the regional model, both at the theoretical and applicative level, is contained in Miernyk [60].

The unique aspect of the interregional model, of course, is its ability to capture interregional intersectoral trade flows and hence allow the estimation of not only interregional impact (i.e. the impact of an increase in final demand for the output of Region A on the economy of Region B), but also the interregional 'feedback' (i.e. the repercussions this induced expansion in Region B has back on Region A and so on). As mentioned in sect. 2, the crucial assumption necessary for isolation of these interregional effects is the stability of the $_{rs}b_{ij}$'s, the spatial input coefficients of eq. (3). As eq. (5) further demonstrates, this assumption can be decomposed into the assumption of fixed regional technical coefficients and stable trade coefficients.

The assumption of fixed technical coefficients need not detain us. This assumption is common to not only interregional, but also national and regional models, although as Tiebout has pointed out [83], the assumption may be more dubious when applied at the regional or interregional level. It can, however, be relaxed for forecasting purposes (see below). More serious is the assumption of stable trade coefficients. To quote Miernyk:

"Even with constant technology, changes in scale [may] alter regional input patterns. At a given stage of regional development, for example, a region might import packaging materials and containers. When regional output reaches a level which will support local production of such inputs, and if it is possible to produce them locally at a profit, capital will be attracted to the region. The result is a shift from imported to locally-produced inputs. Similarly, at an early stage of its development a region might be an exporter of raw materials. Later, these outputs can be sold to regional processors and manufacturers." [60]

There is no theoretical necessity for the existence of stable trade coefficients. Several authors have investigated the various variables effecting the spatial pattern of interregional trade over time (Moses [66], Part II, and Isard [42, 44], ch. 5, [36], pp. 322–326, [38]). The question of stability for the trade coefficient is more an empirical than theoretical issue however. Input–output models represent an empirically applicable approximation to the general structure of the economy. The crucial issue, therefore, is not whether it is theoretically possible or likely for spatial input coefficients to be constant over time, but rather whether the posited economy, be it intra-regional or interregional, acts or responds as if the relevant coefficients are stable. It must be emphasized that input–output, as an empirical model, must be judged on the basis of its ability to predict the reaction paths and structure of the economy over time.[10] The only relevant judgment, there-

---

[10] Regional reaction paths may be defined as the effects on income, employment and/or output resulting from a given change in the level of economic activity. See Moore [64].

fore, must rest on a comparison of the model's structure and predictive power with the structure of the actual economy and predictive ability of alternative conceptual approaches to that structure.

Moses [66] and Riefler [77] have investigated the stability of trade coefficients over time using United States rail data. Both studies found some variation in the coefficients, but concluded that this variation, which increased as the time span lengthened, did not invalidate the model for short to medium term (1–5 year) forecasts. Suzuki has examined the stability of the structure of interregional flow of goods using more comprehensive Japanese data [82]. He found a high degree of stability in actual inter-regional flows during the 1962–64 period. For longer-term projections or forecasts the assumption of fixed spatial input or technical coefficients can be relaxed by using methods suggested by Tiebout ([84], p. 337) and Miernyk et al. [59, 60]. Relaxation of the assumption of fixed trade patterns could be accomplished using methods suggested by Suzuki ([82], pp. 208–209).

Before turning to a critique of the available empirical interregional studies it is necessary to address ourselves to an issue raised by Miller [61, 62]. Miller questioned whether the ability of interregional input–output to capture interregional feedbacks, as defined above, justified the time, effort and expense of collecting the data necessary to implement the basic framework. Miller's results, which were obtained by means of a simulation approach rather than an actual interregional table and therefore were labelled "experimental", suggested "that the overall percentage error involved in using a simple single-region input–output model in a true two-region interregional context is remarkably small over a very wide range of representative situations . . ." (Miller [62], p. 49). His conclusions indicate that where two regions are not closely linked (i.e. where significant leakages exist) a regional input–output model may suffice while, at the other extreme, if two regions are closely linked a simple correlation rule can be employed to correct for underestimation due to neglect of interregional feedbacks.

Miller's results have not gone unchallenged. Miernyk points out that Miller's basic data came from "a variety of sources which could not be expected to show actual interregional linkages" [60]. Both Greytak [25] and Lee et al. [45] have used their actual interregional models to refute Miller's conclusions. In addition, of course, Miller's criticism refers only to the magnitude of interregional feedbacks; an interregional model is still necessary if one wants to isolate the 'pure' interregional impact of, for instance, California's rapid growth on the Washington State economy.

Despite its brevity, the enumeration of existing interregional input–output studies contained in sect. 3 illustrates the hallmark of empirical work in this area, its diversity. Not only do the various studies illustrate each of the conceptual models outlined in sect. 2, but they differ as to the number and size of regions included, dating, sectoring plan, purpose or objective and method of data generation. While such diversity illustrates the flexibility of the basic interregional model (and in several cases the ingenuity of the investigator), it does make an overall evaluation of available studies a hazardous undertaking. Given the growing length of the interregional input–output bibliography, however, such an evaluation or 'taking stock' is certainly desirable.[11]

Which of the various models presented in sect. 2 of this paper best describes the interregional reaction paths of a given economy? As demonstrated by Hartwick [30] and Riefler [77] the Isard model summarizes interregional interactions in a more precise way than any of the alternative conceptual frameworks. Given the availability of interregional trade data denominated by both industry and region of origin and destination and given the adoption on an input–output framework, the Isard model is clearly the superior vehicle for simulating interregional reaction paths. The Isard model then, as indicated in sect. 2, is clearly the ideal model or the standard against which alternative formulations must be measured. Sect. 2 did this at the conceptual level, but in actual implementation how close do these alternatives come to the ideal?

Unfortunately the diversity of the available studies makes any concrete answer to this question impossible. The lack of regionally and industrially denominated trade statistics have forced most of the investigators to use an approximation to the Isard model and, of course, also preclude any comparison of their estimates to actual intersectoral and interregional flows. Differences in regional definitions, sector definitions and dating also preclude comparisons between alternative conceptual frameworks. California, for instance, has been used as one region in the Moses–Chenery model of Polenske [74] and ch. 9, in the Riefler–Tiebout model [76], in a Leontief–Strout gravity formulation by Davis [17] and in an Isard-type formulation by Carter and Ireri [10, 35]. In each case, however, not only have the "other" regions of the interregional structure been different, but the number, treatment and definition of sectors have differed and the date of application has varied. Such diversity makes impossible an analysis of

---

[11] To facilitate the evaluation attention is focussed only on the interregional variant of the basic input–output framework. For a slightly broader approach see Tiebout [83], Edelstein [20] and Miernyk [60].

the 'power' of the various models to approximate the Isard ideal. The problem is further compounded by the lack of 'follow-up' studies to test the congruence between predicted and actual regional reaction paths.

Polenske has conducted two tests of available models. In her 1966 study, three models, a Leontief–Strout gravity model, the Moses–Chenery or "column coefficient" model and a "row coefficient" model[12], were used to estimate interregional flows of fresh fruits and vegetables in the United States [71]. Although the gravity model produced the most accurate results when compared to actual shipments, the other two alternatives were not far behind. Polenske's 1969 study again tested the same three models; this time a complete interregional input–output framework (the 1963 Isard-type Japanese study) was utilized as a test vehicle [75]. All tests revealed the row coefficient model to be inferior, but "no discernible difference in the overall predictive ability of the column coefficient and the . . . gravity trade models [was found].   Both models give reasonable estimates of Japanese regional production" ([75], p. 14). Further tests of the available approximations to the Isard model will have to await better data on trade flows and not only more, but comparable applications of the various models.

While most investigators have had recourse to national input–output coefficients for certain cell entries in the interregional matrix, if only to act as a check or constraint on survey-generated data, some studies have utilized national technical coefficients to describe regional production functions (for example see Greytak [25] and CONSAD [14]). The use of national coefficients, often aggregated to reflect the unique interregional sectoring plan, and 'adjusted' national coefficients greatly simplifies model implementation and reduces the cost of data collection. Against this benefit, however, must be weighed the cost of lost information due to uniquely regional product mixes and differences in industrial structure. Studies by Czamanski and Malizia [15] and Shaffer and Chu [78] suggest that such losses are quite significant. As the former study concludes:

"It appears . . . that while national input–output tables cannot be used for purposes of regional studies without considerable adjustments, acceptable results can be achieved . . . [if one] (1) exclude(s) the tertiary sectors through

---

[12] The fixed row coefficient model basically assumes fixed interregional sales patterns. It is the Moses–Chenery model applied to output rather than input patterns; in terms of eq. (5c), the trade coefficient becomes $_{rs}t^*{}_i = {}_{rs}x_i/{}_rX_i$ and instead of using regional technical coefficients $(_sa_{ij})$, regional sales coefficients are applied. For an application see Riefler [77], pp. 50–51, 68–69.

aggregation; . . . (2) use(s) field surveys in order to obtain input–output coefficients for (a) primary industries, and (b) industries in which the regional economy is specialized." ([15], p. 73.)

Clearly then, ". . . the nonsurvey methods may prove useful supplements to survey studies . . . [but] it seems that, at the moment, there is still no substitute for a good survey-based study" ([78], p. 96). It must be added, however, that neither of these two studies tested the informational loss inherent in the use of highly disaggregated national matrices, such as the 370 sector 1963 national model, to estimate regional technical coefficients (U.S. Department of Commerce [89]). This large table was used, for instance, by the Harvard Economic Research Project to estimate most regional cell entries in its interregional model. The growing use of survey-based interregional studies as well as better and more comprehensive data on regional economic activity and interregional trade patterns bodes well for the continuing improvement in the statistical implementation of the available interregional models.

As far as the present author knows, no dynamic interregional input–output model has been implemented. Such a model would, through the use of a capital coefficient matrix allow for investment in new productive capacity as part of the endogenous model instead of relegating it to exogenous final demand as done with static models. Both Moses and Harris have attempted to extend temporally the forecasting capabilities of the basic interregional input–output framework through the use of linear programming techniques (Harris [28] and Moses [68]).[13] Since such methods preclude the cross-hauling of commodities, a phenomena found in all data on trade flows, such studies while relating capital expenditures to output and allowing for the shifting location of industries as well as the migration of people must be considered as first approximations to a dynamic interregional input–output model. Harris's model especially, by treating 100 industrial sectors and over 3000 counties thus minimizing the probability of cross-hauling and utilizing Almon's dynamic national input–output model [1, 2], does promise to contribute to our knowledge of the dynamic aspects of the interregional economy.

In the light of the above noted diversity in conceptual model availability as well as data and method of implementation, it is not surprising

---

[13] Numerous interregional (linear) programming models have been advanced, some with significant industrial disaggregation, both at the conceptual and applied level. Since these fall outside the specific purview of this study they are neglected although they may, in the future, provide a useful supplement to the static interregional input–output model.

to finally note that in the past twenty years the purpose of model application has varied significantly. Although it is difficult to place a model as comprehensive and flexible as interregional input–output into a single teleological category, it does appear that empirical applications of the basic framework do fall into three broad classifications. Ordering the available studies in roughly a chronological way we find: (1) academic studies, (2) impact studies and (3) "other" studies.

The best exemplar of the academic approach to model application is Moses' classic study [67]. The objective of these earlier studies was basically to demonstrate the applicability of the evolving conceptual models. Emphasis was placed on the ability of the gross flows table and direct coefficient matrix to provide an economic accounting system or description of the basic dimensions of the interregional economy. The use of the inverse or multiplier matrix to trace regional and interregional interactions or reaction paths was outlined and the relationship between the multiplier matrix and the scalar Keynesian multiplier was investigated as well (Ghosh [23], pp. 89–90). In a sense this first phase of implementation emphasized the applicability of the basic model and its explicative content.

With the second, or impact, stage of development application broadened beyond the halls of academia. Complete studies during this period were typically published in monograph form by various government agencies and applied research centers (for example see Carter and Heady [9] and Martin and Carter [54]). No longer did the professional journals publish the basic tools, the analytical matrices, but rather they were used to summarize the results of the application of those tools to specific problems. Emphasis shifted from the simulating of hypothetical changes in exogenous or final demand to the forecasting or prediction, either ex ante or ex post, of actual changes in the interregional economy. Attention centered on such problems as the interregional impact of a cessation of Vietnamese hostilities (Leontief *et al.* [50]), the impact of California's rapid postwar growth on the Washington State economy (Riefler and Tiebout [76] and Riefler [77]), the impact of shifts in the final demand for agricultural output (Carter and Heady [9] and Martin and Carter [54]), and the impact of the Tennessee Valley Authority on the structure of the Tennessee economy (Lee *et al.* [46]). In a sense it is with the advent of this phase of development early in the 1960's that interregional input–output models successfully achieve their 'niche' in the regional economist's toolkit of basic models. The structure and analytical power of the model in its various conceptual formats is generally acknowledged as are its basic weaknesses or restrictions; emphasis is now placed on application.

The current or "other" phase of model implementation can be roughly divided into two parts. The first group encompasses those who have adapted or suggested the adaptation of the basic interregional model to analyze such specific problems as water usage (Carter and Ireri [10, 35] and Davis [17, 18]), pollution (Leontief [52], Stillson [81]), and intensive versus extensive interregional growth paths (Tiebout [84]). Here emphasis is not placed on the basic model (as with the academic approach), or the highly mechanistic use of the various descriptive and analytical matrices; rather these basic summary tables of interregional interaction are themselves extended to address a specific issue, often an issue of current policy interest. In a sense, the analytical results of the impact approach are considered as an intermediate input for futher analysis by these investigators.

The second group includes economists such as Leven *et al.* [53] Harris [28] and CONSAD [14] who have used the interregional input–output model as an input to a more general analysis of interregional reaction paths. These studies have basically recognized the complementarity between the interregional input–output model and other spatial constructs to analyze such problems as the growth and the location (and relocation) of economic activity.[14] Such approaches emphasize the flexibility of the basic input–output model as well as its ability to digest and insure comparability in the results of a wider, multi-model approach to regional development. These studies, in terms of our earlier dichotomy, combine the behavioral approach with the quantitative.

This evaluation of the available applications of interregional input–output has of necessity been somewhat brief. Our aim has been more to critique overall accomplishments rather than specific studies. While such an overview is dictated by space limitations, it also reflects the author's limited knowledge of studies currently being conducted as well as the almost 'oral traditition' of much of the past work in the field. Looking at the past twenty years of research, however, it appears that the greatest weakness of empirical application of the interregional input–output model lies in the diversity of approach, data utilization and time frame. Such differences preclude detailed comparisons of the available investigations as well as any linking together of results or precise evaluation of the analytical power of the various conceptual formulations or methods of application. The greatest strength, however, is also an outcome of this diversity; the overall trend has been towards the refinement of methods, the improvement and increased availability of regional and interregional data, the extension and

[14] See sect. 5 for a further suggestion in this direction.

increasing flexibility in model application, and the increased orientation of model application towards policy questions. It appears that we can safely predict a growing use of interregional input–output analysis at the macro-regional level to analyze the overall growth path of the interregional economy and at the micro-regional level to analyze the distribution of this growth between various economic entities and locations.

5. A prediction: Future uses of interregional input–output

Our review of the interregional input–output literature of the past twenty years has identified three slightly overlapping periods or phases of development. The first ten year period, beginning with Isard's seminal study on the ideal interregional model [36], focused on the conceptual 'refinement' of the model to take into account currently available data on interregional commodity flows. Although some mechanistic simulation, involving the use of national technical coefficients and fragmentary trade data, was undertaken the major research objective appears to have been the elucidation of a particular conceptual model. In the second decade more attention has been devoted to the empirical application of the available models. With a few major exceptions, these empirical applications have been spatially selective or partial in their formulation. The studies have been largely limited to interregional economies which remain significantly 'open'. The California–Washington Study referred to above, for instance, while bringing into the endogenous matrix 28 % of Washington's interstate exports and 13 % of those of California, leaves the remainder of interstate, to say nothing of foreign exports, outside or exogenous to the model (Riefler and Tiebout [76], p. 146). While for regional analysis it is probably acceptable to leave the foreign trade sector exogenous to the model, the same cannot be said for interstate exports and imports.[15] They represent significant 'leakages' from the interregional system.

The spatial partiality of most existing interregional studies has severely restricted their application. Authors have used their basic models in (1) analyzing regional production patterns, (2) isolating important interregional linkages, (3) computing (partial) interregional output or employment multipliers and (4) undertaking (partial) impact studies. While such applications do yield interesting and challenging results, it must be admitted that the limited scope of analysis (especially in light of the huge data, time

[15] See sect. 4 above.

and budget requirements of such a study) and uniformity of results seem to indicate rapidly diminishing returns to further extension of these 'partial' studies unless dictated by and constructed to meet specific policy requirements. Further complicating the picture, as indicated above, is the lack of comparability between these 'partial' studies: difference in sectoring, in regional definitions and treatment of certain flows. Even for policy purposes an economy of effort, such as that suggested by Czamanski and Malizia [15], seems indicated.

These facts, combined with the recent availability of more comprehensive interregional studies and better regional and interregional statistics have ushered in the third phase or the "other" phase referred to in sect. 4. As indicated there, significant progress has already been made in this new direction in the past five years; hopefully this progress presages further developments. This part of our survey outlines one direction in which such progress is likely to be directed.

Ohlin, writing in the 1930's, demonstrated the intimate relation between trade theory and location theory [70]. The baton was picked up by Isard in his pioneering article on interregional input–output; the very first paragraph of that article emphasizes the relationship of his subject matter to general location theory. He stated that interregional input–output would "permit an attack upon a specific set of significant problems which logically fall within the jurisdiction of a general theory of location and space economy" ([36], p. 318). Again, echoing Ohlin's statements, Isard in 1954 stated that "clearly a general and comprehensive location theory and a general comprehensive trade theory are one and the same" ([41], p. 319). Isard was not alone during the 1950's in recognizing this relationship, most research designed at extending the basic interregional model or adapting it for application recognized this intimate association (see, for instance, Moses [68]). At the empirical level, the locational implications of interregional input–output was emphasized, but only partially applied, in Isard and Kuenne's study of the impact of steel agglomerations [39].

By the late 1950's, however, the baton was being fumbled if not dropped; the use of interregional input–output in formulating and testing a general location theory was being neglected. Rather than the interregional model providing a framework for a general location theory, causation ran the other way – the tools of location theory were used to reduce the stringent data requirements of the interregional model.[16] Thus Tiebout, in 1957, pointed out that the main use of regional and interregional input–output

[16] For instance, the use of a location coefficient to estimate regional or interregional cell entries or the use of a gravity-type model to simulate interregional flows.

techniques in regional analysis was for local impact, regional balance of payments, and interregional flows studies [83]. The failure of interregional input–output to live up to its promised potential as a tool of locational analysis can be traced to three causes.

First, and probably foremost, has been the failure of interregional input–output studies to encompass an area wide enough so as to approximate a closed system. Too much of the interregional economy was relegated to the exogenous imports and exports column to allow for the development and testing of a truly general model of spatial determinants. The more open the interregional model, the greater weight placed on the local (non-transportable) environment as a locational factor versus transportable inputs and outputs (the 'access' factors). Thus, for instance, in the three-region Tennessee interregional model, material resources play a significant factor in determining what locates where (Lee *et al.* [46]). A model including other areas, however, would permit investigation of such problems as why wool processing industries locate in eastern Tennessee versus similar areas in Kentucky (or vice versa); here the key would be access and a more comprehensive location model could be developed.

Second, several of the larger interregional models have generated flow data on the basis of location quotients, income potential and linear programming techniques rather than direct observation (see, for instance, Davis [17] and Greytak [25]). All these approaches rely on an implicit (usually untested) general location theory and as such, the resulting interregional table cannot be 'reversed' to examine its locational implications. Third, and probably most significant for future developments, the static nature of the presently available interregional input–output studies severely restricts any locational analysis. Any investigation which is based on a given interregional table tries to 'explain' the given locational pattern of industry (the dependent variable) as a function of input and output access, availability of non-transportable materials and the agglomeration–repulsion dichotomy (the independent variables). At a point in time, however, the spatial pattern of output represents a mosaic based on both past and present locational decisions. As has been stressed in the literature on location theory, the decision to locate new capacity at a given point and the decision to relocate capacity are based on a different calculus due to the durability of plant (Hoover [34], ch. 2). Hence, any investigation of locational determinants based on a single static interregional study centers on the 'average' impact of the independent variables (e.g. distance) rather than the 'marginal' influence. For the steel industry, for instance, the availability of coking coal and, to a lesser extent, iron ore inputs would have a far greater role in explaining the present overall industry pattern than changes in that pattern.[17] While this shortcoming of the interregional model for locational analysis might be overcome through the use of a dynamic interregional input–output model, the availability of an interregional table for more than one time period, and/or the availability of information from subsidiary models it is probable that, at least for the next few years in the United States as indicated in sect. 4, it will remain a constraint. The studies, cited in sect. 4, by Moses, Riefler and Suzuki, which have demonstrated the stability of interregional trade coefficients over time indicate that while this constraint should be recognized, even a static comprehensive interregional model could add to our knowledge of locational determinants and serve as a basis for the analysis of change in the locational mosaic.

Developments in the United States in the past decade have done much to obviate the first two shortcomings of interregional models for locational work and hopefully represent a step in removing the third obstacle to the evolution of a more general, empirically applicable, location theory. Although originally formulated as an approximation to the ideal Isard interregional model, the Leontief–Strout model, through the use of the location coefficient in eq. (5b), contains an implicit location theory. Given the availability of interregional flow data use of eq. (5b') (contained in footnote 5), which the authors originally intended for estimation of location coefficients in absence of such data, provides an entree for an explicit comprehensive locational analysis. The availability of the Harvard Economic Research Project's interregional input–output model, utilizing actual trade flow data and uniquely determined, regionally defined, technical coefficients for 44 areas encompassing the entire United States, provides the empirical foundation necessary to implement the locational content of the Leontief–Strout model. Utilization of these data and the model should facilitate the identification, at a moment in time, of the locational 'sensitivity' of each industrial sector to the availability of local markets and local inputs, agglomeration economies, as well as the industry's access to dispersed markets and transferable inputs.[18] The continuing compilation, by the Departments of Commerce and Transportation, of interregional commodity

---

[17] The development and refinement of the basic oxygen and electric furnace has decreased reliance on coke inputs. The pelletizing of ore plus the more flexible scrap-iron ore mix required by the new furnaces have significantly diminished input access as a locational factor. The overall result has been a trend in location towards market access.

[18] For location analysis eq. (5b) of the Leontief–Strout model could be adjusted, for instance, to take into account recent work on agglomeration economies in the form of industrial complexes. (See, for example, Isard and Kuenne [39], Czamanski [16], and

trade statistics, hopefully indicates that, in the not too distant future, analysis of change in the influence of these locational factors can be accomplished.

Such analysis is crucial if regional planners hope to analyze economic behavior in a spatial setting. As succinctly stated by Horst Siebert:

"Regional expansion is . . . connected with changes in the economic landscape. In the process of economic growth shifts in demand occur, new resources are discovered, the tranportation system is improved, production costs are reduced, and factor intensities change due to new production possibilities and different growth rates of the factors of production. All these events force the individual entrepreneur to reconsider his location and may very well lead to a relocation of resources in space. Thus the economic landscape is the result of economic growth. On the other hand, it is also one of the important determinants of economic development. The growth rate of a region depends on the allocation of resources in space at a certain moment of time, and it is therefore strongly influenced by the individual location decisions. Consequently regional growth theory [and regional policy] has to take into account the analysis of the economic landscape." [79, p. 5]

The potential application of interregional input–output analysis to location theory, as briefly outlined in this section, is meant not only to indicate

---

Bergsman *et al.* [3].) One form of adjustment might be:

$$_{rs}X_i = \left[\frac{(_rX_i -_r U_i{}^c) \, (_sU_i -_s X_i{}^c)}{X_i} \right] _{rs}Q_i$$

where $_{rs}X_i$ represent shipments of good i from region r to region s, $_rX_i$, X_i represent the output of i in region r and nationally, respectively, $_{rs}Q_i$ is defined as a location coefficient, $_sU_i$ represents the total input of i in region s, and $_rU_i{}^c$, $_sX_i{}^c$ represent the total input (output) of i into (from) industries, in region r and s respectively, which are part of the ith complex.

Similarly the residually estimated $_{rs}Q_i$'s of the above equation could be divided into their component parts by first 'deflating' these coefficients for transportation costs (or distance),

$$_{rs}L_i = \frac{V_i \,_{rs}Q_i}{_{rs}d_i}$$

where $_{rs}L_i$ is defined as the 'distance deflated' location coefficient and the remaining variables, $_{rs}Q_i$, V_i and $_{rs}d_i$, are as defined in eq. (5b′) (footnote 5). The $_{rs}L_i$'s could then be related to the availability of local inputs. Such an approach would enable an interindustry comparison of sensitivity with respect to (1) agglomeration economies (as measured by the 'complex' analysis), (2) the importance of market and supply access and, finally, (3) the availability of local inputs.

a specific avenue of ongoing research, but is also included to demonstrate both the flexibility of the basic model and the potential for synthesis of the model's results with constructs from other areas of regional economic theory. It is this flexibility, this potential, which makes interregional input–output a valuable tool to the regional planner both at the macro-planning level (i.e. as a set of regional economic accounts and as an 'impact' tool for analyzing the overall effect, including interregional 'spillovers', of broad national and/or regional policies), at the individual program level (i.e. the effect of a highway program, a pollution abatement program, etc. on aggregate regional growth), and at the micro-planning level (i.e. changes in the economic landscape).[19] It is this flexibility, this potential, then, which is the hallmark of current interregional input–output analysis and enables us to conclude on a much more optimistic note as to the future than Tiebout did approximately fifteen years ago [83].

References

[1] Almon, Jr., C., 1963, Consistent forecasting in a dynamic multi-sector model, The Review of Economics and Statistics, XLV, 148–162.

[2] Almon, Jr., C., 1966, The American economy to 1975, New York, Harper & Row.

[3] Bergsman, J., P. Greenston and R. Healy, 1971, The agglomeration process in Urban growth, Working Paper 200-2, Washington, The Urban Institute.

[4] Bos, H. C., 1965, The Spatial Dispersion of Economic Activity, Amsterdam, North-Holland Publishing Company.

[5] Boulanger, D. R., 1969, The Implications of Vietnam De-escalation for the commonwealth of Massachusetts, EDA Report No. 15, Harvard Economic Research Project.

[6] Bourque, P. J., 1971, An input–output analysis of economic change in Washington State, University of Washington Business Review, 5–22.

[7] Bramhall, D., 1961, Projecting regional accounts and industrial location: Reflections on policy applications, Papers of the Regional Science Association, 7, 89–117.

[8] Brodersohn, M. S., 1965, A multiregional input–output analysis of the Argentine economy, Buenos Aires, Institute Torcuato di Tella, Centro de Investigaciones Economicas.

[9] Carter, H. O. and E. O. Heady, 1959, An input–output analysis emphasizing regional and commodity sectors of agriculture, Ames, Iowa State University, Agricultural and Home Economics Experimental Station.

[10] Carter, H. O. and D. Ireri, 1970, Linkages of California-Arizona Input–Output Models to Analyze Water Transfer Patterns, in: A. P. Carter and A. Brody, eds., Applications of Input–Output Analysis, Amsterdam, North-Holland Publishing Company, 139–167.

[19] See U.S. Department of Commerce [91] for an interesting statement on the possible uses of interregional input–output for regional planning.

[11] Chenery, H., P. G. Clark and V. Cao Pinna, 1953, The structure and growth of the Italian economy, Rome, U.S. Mutual Security Agency.

[12] Chenery, H., 1956, Inter-Regional and International Input–Output Analysis, in: Tibor Barna, ed., The Structural Interdependence of the Economy, New York, John Wiley and Sons, Inc., 341–356.

[13] Chenery, H. and P. G. Clark, 1959, Interindustry Economics, New York, John Wiley and Sons, Inc.

[14] CONSAD Research Corporation, Impact Studies: Northeast Corridor Transportation Project, v. II and III, Pittsburgh, Prepared for the U.S. Department of Transportation, January 1968 and January 1969 respectively.

[15] Czamanski, S. and E. Malizia, 1969, Applicability and limitations in the use of national input–output tables for regional studies, Papers of the Regional Science Association, 23, 65–77.

[16] Czamanski, S., 1971, Some empirical evidence of the strengths of linkages between groups of related industries in urban-regional complexes, Papers of the Regional Science Association, 27, 137–150.

[17] Davis, H. C., 1967, A Multiregional Input–Output Model of the Western States Emphasizing Heavy Water-Using Sectors (unpublished Ph.D. dissertation), Berkeley, University of California.

[18] Davis, H. C., 1969, Interregional production and water resource dependencies among the western states, Western Economic Journal, VII, 27–39.

[19] Dorfman, R., 1954, The nature and significance of input–output, The Review of Economics and Statistics, XXXVI, 121–133.

[20] Edelstein, R. H., 1968, Methodology of Regional and Subregional Input–Output Studies, Cambridge, Harvard Economic Research Project, Report 8 to Economic Development Administration.

[21] Faucett Associates, Inc., 1963 Interregional Commodity Trade Flows, Lexington, Mass., D. C. Heath & Co., to be published.

[22] Fox, K. A., 1953, A spatial equilibrium model of the livestock-feed economy in the United States, Econometrica, XXI, 547–566.

[23] Ghosh, A., 1964, Experiments With Input–Output Models, Cambridge, Cambridge University Press.

[24] Ghosh, A. and A. Chakravarti, 1970, The Problem of Location of an Industrial Complex, in: A. P. Carter and A. Brody, eds., Contributions to Input–Output Analysis, Amsterdam, North-Holland Publishing Company, 164–179.

[25] Greytak, D., 1969, An Interregional Interindustry Impact Model, in: C. L. Leven, ed., Development Benefits of Water Resource Investments, Washington, U.S. Army Engineer Institute for Water Resources, Ch. 6, 154–216 and Appendices.

[26] Greytak, D., 1970, Regional impact of interregional trade in input–output analysis, Papers of the Regional Science Association, 25, 203–217.

[27] Hansen, W. L., R. T. Robson and C. M. Tiebout, 1961, Markets for California Products, An Analysis of the Sources of Demand, Sacramento, California Economic Development Agency.

[28] Harris, Jr., C. C., 1970, A multiregional, multi-industry forecasting model, Papers of the Regional Science Association, 25, 169–180.

[29] Hartwick, J. M., 1969, Regional Analysis by Means of Interregional Input–Output Models with Applications to Eastern Canada (unpublished Ph.D. dissertation), Baltimore, Johns Hopkins University.

[30] Hartwick, J. M., 1971, Notes on the isard and chenery-moses interregional input–output models, Journal of Regional Science, 11, 73–86.

[31] Heady, E. O. and H. O. Carter, 1959, Input–output models as techniques in the analysis of interregional competition, Journal of Farm Economics, XLI, 978–991.

[32] Henderson, J. M., 1958, The Efficiency of the Coal Industry, Cambridge, Harvard University Press.

[33] Henderson, J. M. and A. O. Krueger, 1965, National Growth and Economic Change in the Upper Midwest, Minneapolis, University of Minnesota Press.

[34] Hoover, E. M., 1971, An Introduction to Regional Economics, New York, Alfred A. Knopf.

[35] Ireri, D. and H. O. Carter, 1970, California-Arizona economic interdependence and water transfer patterns, Berkeley, California Agricultural Experiment Station and Giannini Foundation of Agricultural Economics, Research Report 313.

[36] Isard, W., 1951, Interregional and regional input–output analysis. A model of a space economy, The Review of Economics and Statistics, XXXIII, 318–328.

[37] Isard, W., 1953, Some Empirical Results and Problems of Regional Input–Output Analysis, in W. Leontief *et al.*, eds., Studies in the Structure of the American Economy, New York, Oxford University Press, 116–181.

[38] Isard, W., 1953, Regional commodity balances and interregional commodity flows, American Economic Review, XLIII, 167–180.

[39] Isard, W. and R. F. Kuenne, 1953, The impact of steel upon the greater New York-Philadelphia industrial region, The Review of Economics and Statistics, XXXV, 289–301.

[40] Isard, W. and M. J. Peck, 1954, Location theory and international and inter-regional trade theory, Quarterly Journal of Economics, LXVIII, 97–114.

[41] Isard, W., 1954, Location theory and trade theory: short-run analysis, Quarterly Journal of Economics, LXVIII, 305–320.

[42] Isard, W., 1956, Location and the Space-Economy, New York, Technology Press of MIT and John Wiley & Sons, Inc.

[43] Isard, W., 1958, Interregional linear programming: an elementary presentation and a general model, Journal of Regional Science, I, 1–59.

[44] Isard, W., 1960, Methods of Regional Analysis: an Introduction to the Regional Science, New York, Technology Press of MIT and John Wiley and Sons, Inc.

[45] Lee, T. H., D. P. Lewis and J. R. Moore, Multiregion intersectoral flow analysis, Journal of Regional Science, 11, 33–56.

[46] Lee, T. H., D. P. Lewis and J. R. Moore, Regional and interregional inter-sectoral flow analysis: an application to the Tennessee economy, Knoxville, University of Tennessee Press, to be published.

[47] Leontief, W., 1951, The Structure of the American Economy, 1919–1939, New York, Oxford University Press.

[48] Leontief, W., 1953, Interregional Trade, in: W. Leontief, ed., Studies in the Structure of the American Economy, New York, Oxford University Press, 93–115.

[49] Leontief, W. with the collaboration of A. Strout, 1963, Multiregional Input–Output Analysis, in: Tibor Barna, ed., Structural Interdependence and Economic Development, London, St. Martin's Press, 119–150.

[50] Leontief, W., A. Morgan, K. Polenske, D. Simpson and E. Tower, 1965, The economic impact - industrial and regional - of an arms cut, The Review of Economics and Statistics, XLVII, 217–241.

[51] Leontief, W., 1967, Prepared Statement to the Joint Economic Committee, in:

Economic Effect of Vietnam Spending, Vol. 1, Washington, Government Printing Office, 242–252.

[52] Leontief, W., 1970, Environmental repercussions and the economic structure: an input–output approach, The Review of Economics and Statistics, LII, 262–271.

[53] Leven, C. L., ed., 1969, Development Benefits of Water Resource Investments, Washington, U.S. Army Engineer Institute for Water Resources, 2 volumes.

[54] Martin, W. E. and H. O. Carter, 1962, A California Interindustry Analysis Emphasizing Agriculture, Berkeley, California Agricultural Experimental Station and Giannini Foundation of Agricultural Economics.

[55] Metzler, L. A., 1950, A multiple-region theory of income and trade, Econometrica, XVIII, 329–354.

[56] Meyer, J. R., 1963, Regional economics: a survey of techniques applicable to regional economics, American Economic Review, LIII, 19–54.

[57] Middelhoek, A. J., 1970, Tests of the Marginal Stability of Input–Output Coefficients, in: A. P. Carter and A. Brody, eds., Applications of Input–Output Analysis, Amsterdam, North-Holland Publishing Company, 261–279.

[58] Miernyk, W. H., 1965, The Elements of Input–Output Analysis, New York, Random House.

[59] Miernyk, W. H., K. L. Shellhammer, D. M. Brown, R. L. Coccari, C. J. Gallagher, and W. H. Wineman, 1970, Simulating Regional Economic Development, Lexington, Mass., D. C. Heath and Company.

[60] Miernyk, W. H., Regional and Interregional Input–Output Models: a Reappraisal, in: M. Perlman, B. Chinitz and C. Leven, eds., Spatial, Regional and Population Economics: Essays in Honor of Edgar M. Hoover, New York, Gordon and Breach, to be published.

[61] Miller, R. E., 1966, Interregional feedback effects in input–output models: some preliminary results, Proceedings of the Regional Science Association, 17, 105–125.

[62] Miller, R. E., 1969, Interregional feedbacks in input–output models: some experimental results, Western Economic Journal, VII, 41–50.

[63] Ministry of International Trade and Industry, 1970, The Interregional Input–Output Table of Japan, Tokyo.

[64] Moore, F. T., 1955, Regional economic reaction paths, American Economic Review, XLV, 133–148.

[65] Moore, F. T. and J. W. Petersen, 1955, Regional analysis: an interindustry model of Utah, The Review of Economics and Statistics, XXXVIII, 368–383.

[66] Moses, L. N., 1952, Regional Input–Output: a Method of Analyzing Regional Interdepence, unpublished Ph.D. thesis, Cambridge, Harvard University.

[67] Moses, L. N., 1955, The stability of interregional trading patterns and input–output analysis, American Economic Review, XLV, 803–832.

[68] Moses, L. N., 1960, A general equilibrium model of production, interregional trade and location of industry, The Review of Economics and Statistics, XLII, 373–397.

[69] National Bureau of Economic Research, 1965, Input–Output Analysis: an Appraisal, Princeton, Princeton University Press.

[70] Ohlin, B. G., 1933, International and Interregional Trade, Harvard Economic Studies, XXXIX, Cambridge, Harvard University Press.

[71] Polenske, K. R., 1966, A Case Study of Transportation Models Used in Multiregional Analysis, unpublished Ph.D. dissertation, Cambridge, Harvard University.

[72] Polenske, K. R., 1969, Shifts in the Regional and Industrial Impact of Federal

Government Spending, EDA Report no. 2 (revised), Harvard Economic Research Project.

[73] Polenske, K. R., 1970, Empirical Implementation of a Multiregional Input–Output Gravity Trade Model, in: A. P. Carter and A. Brody, eds., Applications of Input–Output Analysis, Amsterdam, North-Holland Publishing Company, 143–163.

[74] Polenske, K. R., 1970, A Multiregional Input–Output Model for the United States, Cambridge, Harvard Economic Research Project, Report 21 (revised Dec., 1970).

[75] Polenske, K. R., An Empirical Test of Interregional Input–Output Models: Estimation of 1963 Japanese Production, Cambridge, Harvard Economic Research Project (mimeo) undated.

[76] Riefler, R. F. and C. M. Tiebout, 1970, Interregional input–output: an empirical California-Washington model, Journal of Regional Science, X, 135–152.

[77] Riefler, R. F., 1966, Interregional Input–Output: Washington and California, unpublished Ph.D. dissertation, Seattle, University of Washington.

[78] Shaffer, W. A. and K. Chu, 1969, Nonsurvey techniques for constructing regional interindustry models, Papers of the Regional Science Association, 23, 83–101.

[79] Siebert, H., 1969, Regional Economic Growth: Theory and Policy, Scranton, Pa., International Textbook Co.

[80] Spiegelman, R. G., 1968, A Study of Industry Location Using Multiple Regression Techniques, Agricultural Economic Report no. 140, Economic Research Service, U.S. Department of Agriculture.

[81] Stillson, R., 1970, Regional Trade and Structure Model for a Pollution Abatement Study, Proceedings, Fourth Annual Symposium on Water Resources Research, Columbus, Ohio State University.

[82] Suzuki, K., 1971, Observations on the stability of the structure of the interregional flow of goods, Journal of Regional Science, 11, 187–209.

[83] Tiebout, C. M., 1957, Regional and interregional input–output models: an appraisal, Southern Economic Journal, XXIV, 140–147.

[84] Tiebout, C. M., 1969, An empirical regional input–output projection model: the state of Washington, 1980, The Review of Economics and Statistics, LI, 334–340.

[85] Tilanus, C. B., 1967, Marginal versus average input coefficients in input–output forecasting, Quarterly Journal of Economics, 81, 140–145.

[86] Udis, B., ed., 1968, An Interindustry Analysis of the Colorado River Basin in 1960 with Projections to 1980 and 2010, Boulder, Bureau of Economic Research, University of Colorado.

[87] U.S. Department of Commerce, Office of Business Economics, 1965, the transactions table of the 1958 input–output study and revised direct and total requirements data, Survey of Current Business, 45, 33–49.

[88] U.S. Bureau of the Census, 1966, 1963 Census of Transportation, III, Commodity Transportation Survey, Washington, Government Printing Office.

[89] U.S. Department of Commerce, Office of Business Economics, 1969, Input–Output Structure of the U.S. Economy: 1963, 1, Transactions Data for Detailed Industries, Washington, Government Printing Office.

[90] U.S. Department of Commerce, Office of Business Economics, 1969, Input–Output structure of the U.S. economy: 1963, Survey of Current Business, 49, 16–47.

[91] U.S. Department of Commerce, Office of Business Economics, 1971, Toward Development of a National Regional Impact Evaluation System and the Upper Licking Area Pilot Study, Staff Paper in Economics and Statistics, no. 18.

[92] Vaccara, B. N., 1970, Changes Over Time in Input–Output Coefficients for the United States, in: A. P. Carter and A. Brody, eds., Applications of Input–Output Analysis, Amsterdam, North-Holland Publishing Company, 238–260.

[93] Wonnacott, R. J., 1961, Canadian-American Dependence, Amsterdam, North-Holland Publishing Company.

CHAPTER 9

An analysis of United States commodity freight shipments

KAREN R. POLENSKE*

Massachusetts Institute of Technology

1. Introduction

As efforts are being made to understand and solve some of the current economic problems of the United States, the need for a comprehensive and systematic analysis of these problems at a regional level becomes increasingly evident. The impact of almost all changes in the economic conditions of the country varies significantly among different regions. A dock-workers' strike on the West Coast, for example, creates bottle necks at those ports, but it also can have tremendous adverse repercussions on workers, consumers, and industries located within that region, as well as in other regions of the country.

Although the preceding statements seem obvious and beyond dispute, the investigation of many important economic issues, such as transportation strikes, the energy and environmental crises, and inflation, is often conducted at a national, rather than at the frequently more relevant regional, level. The national studies that have been made and are being made can therefore be misleading, or inapplicable, or, if a regional analysis is made, it generally has been an extremely limited study. Part of the reason for the neglect of the regional or multiregional studies is that tools for both types

* I am deeply grateful for the assistance received from Mary M. Shirley, Kathryn L. Norris, Margaret Feiger, and particularly from John A. Makdisi in doing the calculations for this paper. The results presented are preliminary and are based upon research that was done for the Office of Systems Analysis and Information of the U.S. Department of Transportation under contract #DOT-OS-10222. I take full responsibility for the conclusions, which are not necessarily those of the sponsoring agency.

of studies have been developed so slowly and that detailed regional statistics have seldom been readily available. The concern of the present paper is to present a discussion of the application of a new analytical tool, the multiregional input–output model, to investigate the transportation requirements in different regions of the United States.

2. The general framework

A national input–output model provides a completely consistent framework within which the interdependence of the transportation sector with the rest of the economy can be described and analyzed. A multiregional input–output model provides a basis for consistent estimates of transportation requirements by industry and region, and all the many interactions between changes in the rest of the economy and transportation can be studied in considerable industrial and regional detail. Whenever changes in one sector of the economy greatly affect another sector, an economic analysis of only the one industry or region usually fails to account for the entire impact of a given change. The complex linkages between transportation and other industries can be observed in most day-to-day economic activity. Now, however, it is becoming more and more obvious that changes in one region of the economy will have both direct and indirect effects not only on that region, but on other regions, as well; and it is, in fact, almost impossible to analyze any regional economic issue without giving specific consideration to transportation. On the other hand, in the United States, most of the general conclusions made about transportation at the national level have almost no relevance if applied to a particular region.

For these reasons, the analysis of transportation presented in this paper has been based upon a multiregional input–output (MRIO) model. It is both a comprehensive and a multi-purpose tool. On the basis of this preliminary study, the model appears to have a great potential for aiding in systematic studies of regional economic policies in general and of transportation policy in particular. Most previous regional economic analyses were restricted to the study of a single region at a time. Generally, only the direct effect of a given variation in economic activity was measured, and only the net inflow or outflow of a commodity was established. In contrast to these previous studies, the use of the MRIO model has four advantages: (1) indirect, as well as direct, repercussions can be measured; (2) gross, rather than just net, shipment of commodities to and from each region can be estimated; (3) all analyses can be made providing considerable industrial and regional detail while maintaining an internal consistency of all calculations; (4) the framework can be used to make analyses of the industrial and regional impact of economic policy decisions for the nation as a whole, and at the same time, economic analysts in each region or group of regions can use the basic results of the calculations to provide controls in their own investigations of economic problems particular to the region or group of regions under study.

3. The specific model employed

From 1967 to 1970, under a contract between the Economic Development Administration of the U.S. Department of Commerce and the Harvard Economic Research Project, a complete multiregional input–output table was assembled for the United States for 1963, and supplemental historical state final demand estimates were made for 1947 and 1958. The six major components of final demand were also projected to 1970 and 1980. From 1971 to 1972, the multiregional input–output research was continued under a contract at Harvard University with the Office of Systems Analysis and Information of the U.S. Department of Transportation.[1]

All of the multiregional statistics were assembled according to the 87-industry classification scheme of the Bureau of Economic Analysis (formerly the Office of Business Economics) for 51 regions (50 states plus the District of Columbia) whenever feasible and have been made consistent with the published national input–output tables. The seven sets of data available from the multiregional study are listed in table 1.

For the determination of interregional shipments among the states, three fixed trade coefficient models have been tested within the multiregional input–output framework: point estimate gravity, column coefficient, and row coefficient.[2] The first implementation of the model has been made using the column coefficient model, for which only a limited amount of actual

[1] As of July 1, 1972, the multiregional research project has been moved to the Department of Urban Studies and Planning at the Massachusetts Institute of Technology.

[2] The comparisons of the three models are given in a paper written by Polenske [5]. The gravity model was originally described in a paper written by Leontief and Strout entitled "Multiregional Input–Output Analysis" [2, ch. 7]. The first empirical testing of the complete multiregional input–output model for the United States is discussed in a report by Polenske [6], prepared for the Economic Development Administration of the U.S. Department of Commerce, and a complete and updated specification of the MRIO model is now available in a report written by Polenske *et al.* for the Office of Systems Analysis and Information of the U.S. Department of Transportation [7].

Table 1

Multiregional input–output data for the United States [1]

Name of matrix	Matrix dimension [2]	Years		
1. Final demands				
(6 matrices for each year)	88×53	1947	1958	1963
2. Payrolls, employment, and outputs [3]				
Payrolls	88×53	1947	1958	1963
Employment	88×53	1947	1958	1963
Outputs	88×53	1947	1958	1963
3. Projected final demands [3]				
(6 matrices for each year)	88×53		1970	1980
4. Regional input–output tables				
(44 matrices)	87×87			1963
5. Interregional trade flows				
(61 matrices)	45×45			1963
6. Projected outputs	80×45		1970	1980
7. Projected interregional trade flows (61 matrices for each year)	45×45		1970	1980

[1] All data listed in this table are available on computer tapes from the National Technical Information Service, Washington, D.C.

[2] The matrix dimensions include row and column sums.

[3] These data were assembled for the study by Jack Faucett Associates, Inc., under a subcontract with the Harvard Economic Research Project.

regional data is needed, namely: base-year technical coefficients, a_{ij}^h, base-year trade coefficients, c_i^{gh}, and a set of final demands, y_i^h, for the given year. When the model is implemented, the outputs, x_i^{go}, and the inter-regional trade flows, x_i^{gh}, are determined for all regions and industries in the economy.[3]

4. The empirical results

Because a general overview of the regional material was impossible to obtain from the extremely detailed 44-region, 79-industry data, the multiregional model was also implemented at a 9-region, 10-industry level of aggregation. The regional aggregation system for the nine census regions is given in the

[3] The i designates the producing industry, j the purchasing industry, g the shipping region, and h the receiving region. The o indicates summation over all regions.

appendix, table A1, and the industrial aggregation system is given in table A2. The ten industries were chosen to highlight those industries that are of the greatest importance to the transportation of commodities in the United States; therefore, the livestock, mining, and transportation equipment industries were kept separate. The nine census regions in some ways distort the importance of transportation among areas of the country, because such a large percentage of the total production and consumption is situated within Region 2, Middle Atlantic, and Region 3, East North Central. As shown in table 2, these two regions produced over 50 % of the products of Industry 7, Transportation equipment and ordnance, Industry 8, Other manufacturing industries, and Industry 9, Machinery and equipment, and over 35 % of the products of the remaining manufacturing and service industries. These are, however, all industries that transport commodities of high value but relatively low tonnage. Nevertheless, for high-tonnage commodities, such as Industry 1, Livestock, almost 20 % of the production is concentrated in the East North Central region, while 30 % is produced in the West North Central region. For Industry 2, Other agriculture, the corresponding percentages are 18 and 23. Mining is highly

Table 2

Regional distribution of 1963 production (per cent)

	1 New England	2 Middle Atlantic	3 East North Central	4 West North Central	5 South Atlantic	6 East South Central	7 West South Central	8 Mountain	9 Pacific	10 Total
1 Livestock	2	7	19	30	9	7	10	8	9	100
2 Other agriculture	1	5	18	23	13	8	12	6	13	100
3 Mining	2	9	9	7	8	5	38	13	8	100
4 Construction	5	14	17	7	13	5	10	6	21	100
5 Food, tobacco	3	16	20	15	16	7	8	3	12	100
6 Fabrics, textile products	9	33	6	2	36	8	3	0	4	100
7 Transportation equipment, ordnance	4	12	47	8	6	2	4	1	16	100
8 Manufactured products	6	23	28	5	10	5	10	2	11	100
9 Machinery, equipment	10	27	36	6	5	3	3	1	10	100
10 Services	6	24	20	8	12	4	8	4	14	100
11 Industry total	6	21	23	8	12	5	8	3	13	100

concentrated in one region, with 38 % of the total production occurring in Region 7, West South Central. Given the location of the automobile industry, it is not surprising that the East North Central region alone produced 47 % of the output of Industry 7, Transportation equipment.

Of the nine regions, three are relatively small consumers, as well as producers, as shown in table 3. They are: Region 1, New England, Region 6, East South Central, and Region 8, Mountain. In general, the regional consumption of all products is considerably more dispersed than the production, which naturally leads to the need for the goods to be transported from the place of production to the place of consumption. Only eight of the ten industries have commodities that are transported by the normal modes of transportation. Industry 4, Construction, and Industry 10, Services, are therefore not shown in the bar graphs that will now be discussed.

Fig. 1, which shows the percentage of production shipped out of each region, indicates that the regional dependency on trade to provide a market for production is in general 50 % or less. Of the total production of livestock in Region 2, Middle Atlantic, for example, 46 % is shipped to other regions, the remaining 54 % being consumed within the region. Of the total

Table 3

Regional distribution of 1963 consumption (per cent)

	1 New England	2 Middle Atlantic	3 East North Central	4 West North Central	5 South Atlantic	6 East South Central	7 West South Central	8 Mountain	9 Pacific	10 Total
1 Livestock	3	10	18	28	9	6	9	7	10	100
2 Other agriculture	3	10	19	17	16	7	11	5	12	100
3 Mining	2	16	19	6	8	4	27	7	11	100
4 Construction	5	14	17	7	13	5	10	6	21	100
5 Food, tobacco	6	21	19	9	13	5	9	4	14	100
6 Fabrics, textile products	7	28	15	5	22	6	5	2	9	100

7 Transportation
  equipment,
  ordnance
	6	15	31	9	10	3	6	3	17	100

8 Manufactured products	6	21	25	7	12	5	8	3	13	100
9 Machinery, equipment	7	24	25	7	10	4	6	3	14	100
10 Services	6	24	20	8	12	4	8	4	14	100
11 Industry total	6	21	21	8	12	5	8	4	14	100

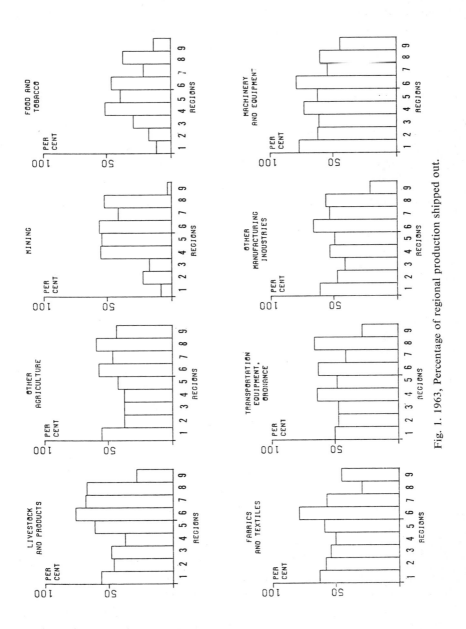

Fig. 1. 1963, Percentage of regional production shipped out.

goods produced in each region, the percentage that is shipped out of the region to other regions varies considerably from industry to industry. In each of the nine regions, considerably less than 50 % of the products of Industry 5, Food and tobacco, is shipped out of the region. (The only exception is Region 4, West North Central, where 51 % is shipped out.) Obviously, bread, milk, and many other food products are produced and consumed locally, even if the region is reduced to that of a metropolitan area. For five of the nine regions, mineral products are also mainly consumed within the region where they are produced. Here, the expense of shipping heavy commodities long distances is a factor contributing to the location of the consuming industries. For crops, six of the nine regions ship less than 50 % of the output to other regions. Again, the weight, and in the case of fruits and vegetables, the perishability, of the commodity are factors contributing to the lack of long-distance transport of the products. Of the remaining five industries, Industry 9, Machinery and equipment, is the one where in all except the Pacific region 50 % or more of the products are shipped outside the region. As the industry is defined for this analysis, it contains a diverse array of establishments, producing everything from farm machinery to household appliances to medical and scientific instruments. One final observation should be made about the information presented in fig. 1. For each industry, the Pacific region, number 9, has a very low percentage of regional production shipped out compared with the other regions, showing a high dependency on its own production.

The geographic isolation of the Pacific region is indicated also by the bar graphs in fig. 2. These graphs show the percentage of regional consumption that is shipped into each region. For example, 64 % of the consumption of livestock in New England is supplied from outside the region, with the remaining 36 % being shipped from within the New England region. The bar graphs thus indicate the dependency of the regions upon other regions to provide needed inputs and to satisfy final demand. The taller the bar, the more dependent the region is upon other regions; the shorter the bar, the closer the region comes to satisfying its intermediate and final consumers with its own production. Small producing regions, such as the Mountain region, show a high dependency on other regions for all products except mining. Similarly, the West North Central region has a low dependency on trade to supply its needs for raw materials, while a large amount of its demand for manufactured and finished products is fulfilled by goods shipped from outside the region. On the other hand, a large producing region, such as the East North Central, shows a low dependency on other regions as sources of supply.

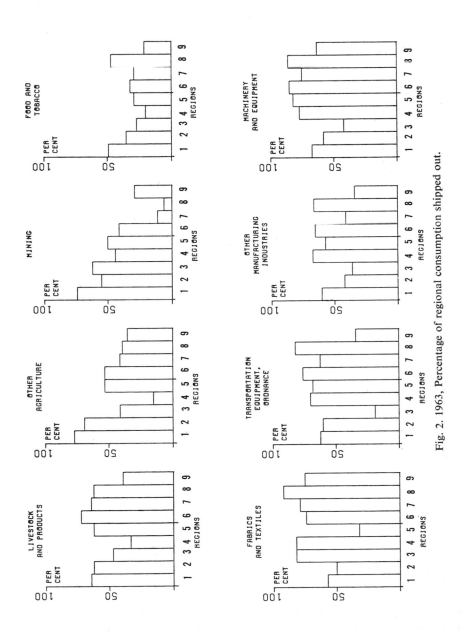

Fig. 2. 1963, Percentage of regional consumption shipped out.

Table 4
Column percentage distribution; 1963 column coefficient interregional shipments (tonnage)

Industry 1 — Livestock

	1	2	3	4	5	6	7	8	9
1	19	10			02				
2	47	28			19	06	02		
3	20	26	50	13	30	32	12	03	04
4	02	05	28	60	09	32	38	28	06
5	07	18	06		19	05	03	01	01
6	02	06	06	02	10	12	11	03	02
7	01	04	05	11	08	09	16	09	04
8			03	10	01	02	13	20	11
9	02	03	01	04	02	01	06	38	72

Industry 2 — Other agriculture

	1	2	3	4	5	6	7	8	9
1	13	06	01		02				
2	39	31	04	01	15	03	01		
3	13	24	55	07	30	37	10	03	01
4	01	02	21	71	04	17	30	09	06
5	19	18	06	01	28	08	03	01	01
6	02	01	01	01	07	12	03		
7	03	03	02	02	07	12	39	04	04
8	01	02	02	05	01	03	04	36	24
9	09	13	09	12	06	08	11	47	62

Industry 3 — Mining

	1	2	3	4	5	6	7	8	9
1	72								
2	10	67	02		08	01			
3		02	57	06	02	03			
4	01	02	07	77	01	01	01	01	
5	10	13	10	01	76	08			
6	02	02	05	01	07	74	01		
7	05	14	15	11	07	12	95	03	03
8			04	04			02	95	07
9						01		01	89

Industry 5 — Food, tobacco

	1	2	3	4	5	6	7	8	9
1	59	02							
2	20	74	04	01	08	01	01	01	01
3	08	09	76	08	09	15	05	04	02
4	07	06	11	81	05	08	10	05	03
5	02	05	02	01	63	02	01	01	01
6	01	01	02	01	11	64	05	01	
7	01	01	02	03	02	08	76	06	01
8	01	01	02	02	01		01	62	05
9	01	02	02	03	02	01	02	19	87

Industry 6 — Textile products

	1	2	3	4	5	6	7	8	9
1	31	11	05	02	07	04	02	08	03
2	34	45	35	20	21	19	18	28	16
3	02	05	19	16	02	03	04	08	07
4	01		02	11		01	03	04	01
5	27	31	29	25	59	52	30	16	37
6	04	06	06	04	10	15	06	07	02
7			02	20	01	04	24	05	03
8								08	
9	01	01	02	02		01	13	15	31

Industry 7 — Transportation equipment

	1	2	3	4	5	6	7	8	9
1	07	05	02		03		01		01
2	29	30	13	08	16	07	03	01	04
3	51	46	79	68	48	40	35	27	41
4	02	04	04	17	01	16	30	26	02
5	05	12	01	01	28	20	04		
6	02	01	01	01	02	12	02	01	01
7			01	02		02	21	06	
8	02							04	
9	03	01		02	02	02	03	34	50

Table 4 (continued)

	Industry 8 Manufactured products										Industry 9 Machinery, equipment								
	1	2	3	4	5	6	7	8	9		1	2	3	4	5	6	7	8	9
1	39	04	01	01	01	01				1	32	11	06	05	09	04	05	04	04
2	22	59	08	02	11	03	01	01	01	2	29	35	20	14	24	19	20	19	16
3	02	08	73	20	06	15	04	04	01	3	28	41	60	45	37	47	34	30	30
4			04	58		07	03	03		4	03	04	05	22	06	09	08	12	07
5	03	07	04	02	51	07	02	01		5	03	03	03	02	14	06	03	04	03
6	01	01	03	02	07	49	04	01		6	02	02	02	03	05	10	03	02	02
7	31	17	04	07	23	17	82	07	01	7		01	01	03	01	03	16	04	02
8			01	05			01	64	09	8			01	01			02	07	02
9	01	03	01	03	01	01	02	18	87	9	03	03	03	04	04	03	09	17	33

Tables 4 and 5 give the 1963 percentage distribution of region-to-region shipments for each of the eight commodities that are transported. The first is for the tonnage and the second is for the value flows. For both tables, the sum of each column adds to 100 %, except for rounding errors. The 1963 interregional trade flows were first estimated in terms of tons and then a set of regional prices was assembled to convert the tonnage flows to values. Each of the two sets of estimates was initially made at the 44-region level for the 61 commodities that are transported. These data were then aggregated to 9 regions and 10 industries for use in calculations made for this paper. The same type of data is available for 1970 and 1980.

For three of the eight industries, the percentage of intraregional shipments (goods produced and consumed within the same region) for the tonnage data is always equal to or less than the corresponding percentage for the value flows. The industries are: Industry 1, Livestock and products; Industry 2, Other agriculture; and Industry 7, Transportation equipment and ordnance. These are all industries dominated by high-weight commodities. The reverse is true, however, for Industry 3, Mining, another industry with high-weight commodities. For this industry, none of the intraregional tonnage percentages are larger than the corresponding value percentage. This provides an example where aggregation of commodities is causing distortion in the analysis, because IO-8, Crude petroleum and natural gas, represents more than one-half of the total production of the mining sector and has a substantially different distribution of interregional shipments from that of the other mining industries.

The analysis at the 9-region and 10-industry level indicates that the West South Central and Pacific regions may be interesting ones to investigate in additional detail. In the first case, the region appears to have a phenomenal rate of growth; in the second case, the region would be interesting to study

Table 5

Column percentage distribution, 1963 column coefficient interregional shipments (value)

	Industry 1 Livestock									Industry 2 Other agriculture								
	1	2	3	4	5	6	7	8	9	1	2	3	4	5	6	7	8	9
1	36	11			02					23	04	01		01				
2	39	38	01		16	05	02			19	31	02		05	01			
3	10	15	53	09	20	27	07	02	05	08	16	59	03	15	18	05	01	01
4	02	03	21	67	07	24	28	22	08	02	02	16	85	04	10	23	08	06
5	10	23	09	01	38	07	04	01	03	26	24	07	01	47	06	02	01	01
6	02	06	07	02	09	28	10	04	04	08	04	03	01	15	47	06	01	01
7	01	03	05	11	06	07	36	10	07	05	05	03	02	10	13	59	05	09
8			03	09	01	02	10	38	11	02	03	03	03	01	02	02	61	17
9	01	01		02	01		02	23	61	07	11	06	05	03	03	03	24	65

	Industry 3 Mining									Industry 5 Food, tobacco								
	1	2	3	4	5	6	7	8	9	1	2	3	4	5	6	7	8	9
1	26									51	01							
2	30	45	02		11	01			01	17	65	03	01	06		01	01	01
3	03	03	38	11	02	04				09	10	73	08	07	11	05	04	04
4	01	03	15	56	01	01	01	01		11	08	11	80	05	08	12	09	04
5	14	09	07	02	50	08	01	01	05	07	12	06	05	71	06	06	03	05
6	04	04	04	01	11	59	02			02	02	03	02	08	68	05	04	01
7	21	33	26	21	22	24	89	03	05	01	01	01	02	01	06	71	08	01
8		04	07	09	02	03	06	94	18	01	01	01	01			01	53	04
9					01				71	01	01	01	02	01		01	19	79

	Industry 6 Textile products									Industry 7 Transportation equipment								
	1	2	3	4	5	6	7	8	9	1	2	3	4	5	6	7	8	9
1	43	12	04	02	04	03	02	06	02	38	05	01	01	05	01	02	01	02
2	29	50	41	31	15	19	31	29	28	16	40	07	06	11	04	03	01	03
3	02	03	18	10	01	03	06	11	08	32	38	81	46	39	32	24	21	21
4			02	18		01	05	03	01	01	04	04	30	01	14	22	21	03
5	22	27	25	23	68	44	21	17	29	03	10	01	01	32	16	03		01
6	04	07	06	05	09	26	06	07	02	02	01	01	01	03	24	02	02	01
7	01		02	06	01	03	21	05	04			01	06	01	04	38	07	02
8								08		03			02	01		01	18	01
9	01	01	02	03	01	02	10	15	25	04	02	03	08	07	05	06	29	66

Table 5 (continued)

	Industry 8 Manufactured products										Industry 9 Machinery, equipment								
	1	2	3	4	5	6	7	8	9		1	2	3	4	5	6	7	8	9
1	40	07	03	03	04	02	02	02	02	1	33	13	06	06	11	06	06	05	05
2	30	58	15	08	19	09	06	06	08	2	32	42	22	16	25	21	18	17	18
3	08	15	64	35	14	22	13	15	10	3	22	31	58	40	30	34	27	23	23
4	01	01	04	33	01	05	05	06	02	4	03	03	04	23	05	07	06	12	06
5	07	09	05	04	43	11	05	02	03	5	03	03	03	02	18	09	03	05	04
6	02	02	03	04	08	35	06	03	01	6	01	02	02	02	05	15	03	03	02
7	09	06	04	07	09	14	59	11	03	7		01	01	05	02	04	25	06	03
8		01	03	01		02	34	05		8				01			01	14	02
9	02	01	02	03	02	01	03	20	66	9	05	04	03	05	04	03	10	17	37

at a more disaggregated level because of its relative geographic isolation from the rest of the nation. The small number of transportation flows that do occur may therefore be easier to evaluate for this region.

A considerable amount of transportation information is obviously available from the MRIO calculations and can be used to undertake a comprehensive analysis of this important sector of the American economy. As mentioned earlier, the 1970 and 1980 projections of the interregional trade flows are available for 61 industries and for 44 regions. (Plans are being made to extend the data base to the state level within the coming year.) The results presented in this paper are only a representative sample of the enormous quantities of value and tonnage flow data that are now available from the MRIO model for the United States. The estimates are preliminary and are therefore subject to revision.

5. Conclusion

One of the major advantages of using an MRIO framework for the analysis of transportation is the assurance that the commodity trade flows are internally consistent, that they can be used in conjunction with other information for a regional economy, such as technology and employment data, and that they are consistent with national aggregates for each commodity. A consistent, integrated approach to transportation analysis is useful for transportation policy decision makers who can analyze the direct and indirect effects that changes in the transportation sector or other sectors of the economy in one region of the United States will have upon transportation in all regions of the country. The present model and information, however, is only a small beginning in this direction.

Two basic needs exist for expanding the present study. One is to extend the transportation data base by including statistics on mode of transport, on regional variations in the transportation margins applied to the commodities produced by the input–output industries, and on regional transportation investment. The other is to extend the theoretical work on the model and to develop supplemental models for transportation to provide a more complete analysis. The transportation flows, for example, need to be analyzed by mode of transportation. This may require the development of a supplemental modal-split model that can be linked into the basic MRIO framework. In addition, the MRIO model needs to be extended into a dynamic framework where current and future commodity transportation can be examined while accounting for changes in the economy over time. The static fixed coefficient models rely upon a basic assumption that neither the technology nor the trade coefficients change from those of the base period. Even this rather restrictive assumption, however, can be relaxed if projections of the coefficients are available. At the national level, for example, the technical input–output coefficients have been projected to 1970 and 1980, and it will hopefully be just a matter of time before similar projections are made of regional technical coefficients. Although no projections have been made of the trade coefficients, additional in-depth study of commodity transportation would make it possible to alter the regional trade coefficients. In addition, a dynamic framework would take explicit account of capital investment in the economy.

Because fewer data are required and because cross-hauls are explicitly estimated, the fixed coefficient models are superior to models that minimize transportation costs or maximize regional outputs. Transportation models that have cost minimization as their objective function must often be extensively refined to make them applicable for estimating interregional trade flows where cross-hauling occurs among regions. Cross-hauling, for example, accounted for some of the unreasonable results reported by Moses [3] in his linear programming model for the United States. As more transportation and other regional data become available, additional testing of alternative transportation models should be done, along the lines of the studies included in Parts II and III of this volume, to determine the conditions under which the various models operate most satisfactorily for policy purposes.

As stated earlier, the MRIO methodology provides four important advantages over most other regional study techniques in terms of the amount and consistency of regional and industrial detail supplied in the results and the use of the model and calculations by policy makers. Results of implementing the MRIO model will therefore be important for policy makers, in general, and for transportation policy makers, in particular.

Appendix

Table A1

Regional classification

	Regions		States		Regions		States
9 [1]	44	51	Name	9 [1]	44	51	Name
	1	18	Maine		24	16	Kentucky
	2	44	Vermont		25	41	Tennessee
		⎧20	Massachusetts	6	26	1	Alabama
1	3	⎨38	Rhode Island		27	23	Mississippi
		⎩28	New Hampshire				
		6	Connecticut		28	3	Arkansas
					29	17	Louisiana
	4	31	New York	7	30	35	Oklahoma
2	5	⎧37	Pennsylvania		31	42	Texas
		⎩29	New Jersey				
					32	25	Montana
	6	⎧21	Michigan		33	11	Idaho
		⎩34	Ohio		34	49	Wyoming
3	7	⎧13	Indiana		35	5	Colorado
		⎩12	Illinois	8	36	30	New Mexico
	8	48	Wisconsin		37	2	Arizona
					38	43	Utah
	9	22	Minnesota		39	27	Nevada
	10	14	Iowa				
	11	24	Missouri		40	46	Washington
4	12	33	North Dakota		41	36	Oregon
	13	40	South Dakota	9	42	4	California
	14	26	Nebraska		43	50	Alaska
	15	15	Kansas		44	51	Hawaii
	16	⎧7	Delaware				
		⎩19	Maryland				
	17	8	District of Columbia				
	18	45	Virginia				
5	19	47	West Virginia				
	20	32	North Carolina				
	21	39	South Carolina				
	22	10	Georgia				
	23	9	Florida				

[1] The names of the 9 census regions are: 1, New England; 2, Middle Atlantic; 3, East North Central; 4, West North Central; 5, South Atlantic; 6, East South Central; 7, West South Central; 8, Mountain; 9, Pacific.

Table A2

Multiregional input–output industry classification

Industry no.		Industry title	Industry no.		Industry title	Industry no.		Industry title
MRIO	OBE		MRIO	OBE		MRIO	OBE	
10	79		10	79		10	79	
1	1	Livestock, prdts.	8	31 31	Petroleum, related inds.	7	61 61	Other transport. equip.
2	2	Other agriculture prdts.	8	32 32	Rubber, misc. plastics	9	62 62	Profess., scien. instru.
10	3	Forestry, fisheries	8	33 33	Leather tanning, prdts.	9	63 63	Medical, photo. equip.
10	4	Agri., forest., fish. serv.	8	34 34	Footwear, leather prdts.	9	64 64	Misc. manufacturing
3	5	Iron, ferrous ores mining	8	35 35	Glass, glass prdts.	10	65 65	Transport., warehousing
3	6	Nonferrous ores mining	8	36 36	Stone, clay prdts.	10	66 66	Communica., exc. brdcast.
3	7	Coal mining	8	37 37	Primary iron, steel mfr.	10	67 67	Radio, TV broadcasting
3	8	Crude petrol., natural gas	8	38 38	Primary nonferrous mfr.	10	68 68	Elec., gas, water, san. ser.
3	9	Stone, clay mining	8	39 39	Metal containers	10	69 69	Wholesale, retail trade
3	10	Chem., fert. min. mining	8	40 40	Fabricated metal prdts.	10	70 70	Finance, insurance
4	11	New construction	8	41 41	Screw mach. prdts., etc.	10	71 71	Real estate, rental
4	12	Maint., repair constr.	8	42 42	Other fab. metal prdts.	10	72 72	Hotels, personal serv.
7	13	Ordnance, accessories	9	43 43	Engines, turbines	10	73 73	Business services
5	14	Food, kindred prdts.	9	44 44	Farm mach., equip.	10	74 74	Research, development
5	15	Tobacco manufactures	9	45 45	Construc. mach., equip.	10	75 75	Auto. repair, services
6	16	Fabrics	9	46 46	Material handling mach.	10	76 76	Amusements
6	17	Textile products	9	47 47	Metalworking machinery	10	77 77	Med., educ. services
6	18	Apparel	9	48 48	Special mach., equip.	10	78 78	Federal govt. enterprise
6	19	Misc. textile prdts.	9	49 49	General mach., equip.	10	79 79	State, local govt. ent.
8	20	Lumber, wood prdts.	9	50 50	Machine shop prdts.	11	80 80	Directly allocated imports
8	21	Wooden containers	9	51 51	Office, comput. machines	12	81 80	Transferred imports
8	22	Household furniture	9	52 52	Service ind. machines	13	82 89	Value added (row)
8	23	Other furniture	9	53 53	Elect. transmiss. equip.			Final demand (column)
8	24	Paper, allied prdts.	9	54 54	Household appliances	14	83	Transfers-in (row)
8	25	Paperboard containers	9	55 55	Electric lighting equip.			Transfers-out (column)
8	26	Printing, publishing	9	56 56	Radio, TV, etc., equip.	15	84	Inventory depletion
8	27	Chemicals, select. prdts.	9	57 57	Electronic components	16	85 83	Scrap production
8	28	Plastics, synthetics	9	58 58	Misc. electrical mach.	17	86 83	Scrap purchases
8	29	Drugs, cosmetics	7	59 59	Motor vehicles, equip.	18	87	Regional total production
8	30	Paint, allied prdts.	7	60 60	Aircraft, parts			

References

[1] Chenery, H., 1953, Regional Analysis, in: H. Chenery and P. Clark, eds., The Structure and Growth of the Italian Economy, U.S. Mutual Security Agency, Rome.

[2] Leontief, W. and A. Strout, 1963, Multiregional Input–Output Analysis, in: T. Barna, ed., Structural Interdependence and Economic Development, New York, St. Martin's Press, Inc.

[3] Moses, L. N., 1960, A general equilibrium model of production, interregional trade, and location of industry, Review of Economics and Statistics, 42, 209–224.

[4] Moses, L. N., 1955, The stability of interregional trading patterns and input–output analysis, American Economic Review, 45, 803–832.

[5] Polenske, K. R., 1970, An empirical test of interregional input–output models: estimation of 1963 Japanese production, American Economic Review, 60, 76–82.

[6] Polenske, K. R., 1970, A Multiregional Input–Output Model for the United States, EDA Report No. 21, prepared for the Economic Development Administration, U.S. Department of Commerce.

[7] Polenske, K. R., C. W. Anderson and M. M. Shirley, 1972, A Guide for Users of the United States Multiregional Input–Output Model, Prepared for the Office of Systems Analysis and Information, U.S. Department of Transportation.

CHAPTER 10

Linkages between industries in urban-regional complexes

STAN CZAMANSKI

Cornell University

1. The problem of interindustry relations in regional studies

The empirical question most frequently faced in regional analysis springs from the policy objective to invigorate or "rehabilitate" the local economy and start a growth process. In an often small and, as a rule, open regional economy, a major breakthrough can result only from the introduction of new productive activities. Both location and development theory support the view that the attractiveness of a region and the pull that it exercises upon industries looking for suitable locations are a function not only of geographical and socio-economic factors taken in isolation but of a complex interplay of external economies characteristic of a prior industrial agglomeration. Accordingly, a group of industries complementary to one another, characteristic of an industrial complex, forms the most propitious background for initiating self-supporting growth processes. Under modern conditions, the strength and variety of forward and backward interindustry links generates economies of scale and agglomeration which are the basis of regional growth and development.

The problem can also be viewed in a slightly different way. The importance of a new industry to a depressed region resides not only in the volume of new employment and income that it generates but very often primarily in its indirect impact, the strength of which can be effectively measured with the help of input–output analysis. A common feature of depressed regions is the general weakness of multiplier effects generated in their economies, due mainly to the size of leakages present. The absence of substantial indirect effects ordinarily accompanying new investments constitutes one of the greatest obstacles to efforts aimed at invigorating the economies of depressed regions, and makes the process at best a slow and expensive one.

Yet, the introduction of new industries progressively reduces leakages and reinforces the indirect impact of new activities until a point is reached when, in a group of related industries linked by flows of goods and services, the multiplier effects become significantly stronger, signalling a qualitative as well as a quantitative change.

Analytically, it is important first to assess the overall ability of a regional economy to generate multiplier effects. Second, from among all the sectors of which a regional economy is comprised, those forming an industrial cluster with strong internal and relatively weak external flows have to be identified [11]. More specifically, the analysis would have to be applied to a substantial number of existing industrial complexes in order to study the patterns of clusters existing under various circumstances. Third, the often advanced hypothesis that in an urban agglomeration the various ancillary links with suppliers of technical, commercial, or financial services take precedence over links based on flows of raw materials, basic production ingredients, or outputs would have to be tested. If vindicated, it would mean that in a metropolitan agglomeration industrial complexes based on technical affinity among plants are relatively rare and that economies of urbanization are more important than those due to localization.[1]

The research reported here falls into two distinct parts. The first, described in the following section, examines the methodology of adjusting various existing regional input–output tables so as to make them amenable to comparative analysis. In the second, presented in sect. 3, a model for identifying clusters of interrelated industries has been developed and tested on a selected sample of regional interindustry tables. In sect. 4 some tentative conclusions are submitted.

2. Divergences between regional input–output tables

The first problem to be faced in any attempt to ascertain empirically which industries form interrelated clusters subject to important external economies is the choice of a set of appropriate regional interindustry accounts. The main difficulty encountered here derives from the profound dissimilarities between available regional input–output tables, due both to substantive

---

[1] External economies, as opposed to economies of scale, are customarily classified into economies of agglomeration resulting from spatial concentration of like plants and into economies of urbanization resulting from agglomeration of unlike activities. Together they are referred to as economies of spatial juxtaposition.

differences in the industrial structure of the regions considered and to diverging methods of constructing the accounts.

The substantive differences in production functions, reflecting variations in technology, in industrial mix, and in the structure and relative importance of foreign trade, are of major interest. These phenomena are, however, usually obscured by methodological differences in the construction of input–output tables which result in tables differing in size, in the degree of aggregation and system of sectoring, in the treatment of intermediaries or, more generally, in the routing and pricing methods employed. Foreign trade is an especially sensitive issue because of its importance in open economies and the notorious lack of reliable data on interregional flows. In addition, the dates of construction of the tables are often several years apart which further impairs their value. Whether on the other hand differences in the relative prices of inputs between regions within a country as economically integrated as the United States are important is not intuitively obvious.

The methods of ensuring an acceptable degree of conformity among regional input–output tables, constructed at different times, for different purposes, and by different teams of economists are far from reliable and have not been sufficiently tested. Fortunately, the problem is similar to the by now familiar issue of using national input–output coefficients in regional studies.

The first part of the research reported here is an attempt at a rigorous determination of the feasibility of using surrogate coefficients and by the same token of the inherent divergences between various input–output tables.[2] Its specific major objectives were:

(1) To develop and test a model for adjusting national input–output coefficients for regional uses so as to eliminate all or part of the differences due to (i) changes in the relative level of prices over time, (ii) degree of fabrication, (iii) composition of demand, (iv) industry mix, (v) structure of imports.

(2) To determine which sectors could be handled by short-cut methods without destroying the analytic and forecasting value of the input–output table and which sectors would have to be covered by a field study.

(3) To analyze the probable errors introduced by the use of the model and compare these with savings in cost and time.

A case study approach was used in attempting to reconstruct the State of Washington Input–Output table for 1963 with the help of national input–output coefficients and such information as is readily available from

---

[2] For details see [12].

regional income and product accounts. The results were compared with the Washington State table based on direct data [1].

The first task was to develop surrogate regional input–output coefficients using as the only source of information regional income and product accounts disaggregated by sectors. This amounts to the knowledge of the bill of goods and of the row and column totals and is by itself insufficient for reconstructing the intersectoral flows. The problem has too many degrees of freedom. In order to reach a solution, an additional source of information is required, the most readily available and frequently used being the national table of technical input–output coefficients. In order to yield the regional row and column totals when multiplied by total regional output, the national coefficients have to be adjusted by making the following assumptions:

(1) Price differences operate uniformly along rows; whenever there is a difference in the average prices of the products of a sector it is charged in the same proportion to all users.

(2) Whenever there is substitution of one product for another due to differences in demand or industry mix it affects all users to the same extent.

(3) Wherever there is a change in the degree of fabrication it uniformly affects all productive processes.

The corollary of the last two assumptions is that differences in selling patterns and/or differences in technology operate uniformly along rows and columns, respectively.

In order to explain the model,[3] the following definitions are introduced:

A = national (1958) input–output coefficients matrix.

B = regional (Washington State 1963) input–output coefficients matrix.

x = regional vector of gross outputs by sector.

t = regional vector of intermediate outputs (row totals).

z = regional vector of intermediate inputs (column totals).

G = grouping matrix.

G_w = weight matrix, where $g_{w.ij} = 0, 1, w_{ij}$;

$$0 \leqq g_{w.ij} \leqq 1 \quad \text{and} \quad \sum_{i=1}^{n} g_{w.ij} = 1;$$

p = vector of price ratios 1963/1958;

i = identity vector.

---

[3] The model is an adaptation of a model presented by Richard Stone and Alan Brown [18, 19] and used by them in order to adjust for changes in national input–output tables over time. For a later, different approach see Fontela, E. *et al.* [13].

Capital letters refer to matrices.

Lower case letters refer to vectors.

Capped letters refer to diagonal matrices obtained from vectors.

Superscripts: T = transpose

r = regional

-1 = inverse or, in case of a diagonal matrix, another diagonal matrix whose non-zero elements are reciprocals of the original matrix.

Subscripts: 1, 2, 3 ... n refer to successive estimates.

The equation numbers and steps in the computer program are synonymous.

First, the national matrix was adjusted for differences in relative price levels between 1958 and 1963, and both were reduced to the same dimensions.

$$A_1 = \hat{p}A\hat{p}^{-1}; \tag{1}$$

$$A_2 = GA_1 G_W^T; \tag{2}$$

$$B_1 = G'BG_w^{r.T}. \tag{3}$$

Next, it is obviously true that

$$t_2 = A_2 x; \tag{4}$$

where t_2 is an estimate of the known t.

Ordinarily $t_2 \neq t$, however,

$$\hat{t}\hat{t}_2^{-1}\hat{t}_2 = \hat{t}\hat{t}_2^{-1}A_2\hat{x}; \tag{5}$$

Hence,

$$\hat{t} = \hat{t}\hat{t}_2^{-1}A_2\hat{x}; \tag{6}$$

$$A_3 = \hat{t}\hat{t}_2^{-1}A_2; \tag{7}$$

is an improved estimate of B adjusted for row totals, but not for column totals. Now,

$$z_3 = x^T A_3^T i; \tag{8}$$

$$\hat{z}\hat{z}_3^{-1}\hat{z}_3 = \hat{z}\hat{z}_3^{-1}\hat{x}A_3^T; \tag{9}$$

$$z = \hat{x}(A_3\hat{z}\hat{z}_3^{-1})^T i; \tag{10}$$

and

$$A_4 = A_3\hat{z}\hat{z}_3^{-1}; \tag{11}$$

is a new improved estimate of B now adjusted for column totals but no longer for row totals. One can use, however, A_4 in eq. (4) and obtain A_5 in eq. (7) which then can be used in eq. (8) and so on. In the corresponding computer program this forms a loop.

The only remaining problem is to find out whether the process converges, at what speed, and whether the limit towards which it converges is the *B* matrix of true regional coefficients.

The above model was used for testing six different cases in order to isolate the effects of (1) degree of aggregation (size of the matrix of coefficients), (2) differences in the relative level of prices between 1958 and 1963, and (3) differences in the relative size and structure of Washington State and U.S. imports. More specifically, the following cases were studied:

Case I: Both the U.S. and the 54×54 Washington State input–output coefficients matrices were aggregated to size 43×43 by the use of appropriate grouping and weighting matrices in steps (2) and (3) of the program. The relative importance of the various sectors in the national and Washington State economy provided the respective weights. No adjustments were made for differences and changes in the relative price levels, i.e. step (1) of the program was omitted.

Case II: Repeated Case I except that both the U.S. and Washington State matrices were aggregated to size 36×36.

Case III: Both matrices were aggregated to size 43×43. The U.S. matrix was adjusted for changes in the relative price levels between 1958–1963. This was accomplished in step (7).

Case IV: Repeated Case III except that both the U.S. and Washington State matrices were aggregated to size 36×36.

Case V: Both matrices were aggregated to size 36×36. The Washington State matrix was adjusted by including domestic imports in the appropriate sectors. The input–output coefficients obtained by applying the model to the U.S. input–output matrix were compared with Washington State coefficients, which included inputs per dollar of output imported from the rest of the U.S., as well as those obtained from other industries in the State.

Case VI: Repeated Case V except the U.S. matrix was adjusted for changes in the relative price levels between 1958–1963.

In order to assess the validity of the results, the absolute deviations between the Washington State coefficients estimated from national coefficients with the help of the model and the 'true' coefficients were calculated. These deviations were transformed into percentages, and the mean, standard deviation, and distribution by deciles of errors were derived. More formally, the program covered the following steps:

$$D_1 = B_1 - A_4; \tag{12}$$

$$d^*_{1.ij} = \left[\frac{d_{1.ij}}{b_{1.ij}} \right]; \qquad \text{where } b_{ij} \neq 0. \tag{13}$$

$$\text{Mean of } D_1^* = \frac{\sum_i \sum_j d_{1.ij}^*}{m}. \tag{14}$$

$$\text{Standard deviation of } D_1^* = \sqrt{\frac{\sum_i \sum_j d_{1.ij}^{*2}}{m} - \left(\frac{\sum_i \sum_j d_{1.ij}^*}{m}\right)^2}; \tag{15}$$

where

D_1 = matrix of absolute deviations between the calculated and real coefficients.

D_1^* = matrix of deviations between the calculated and real coefficients expressed as percentages of the real coefficients.

$d_{1.ij}$ = elements of the D_1 matrix.

b_{ij} = elements of the B matrix.

$d_{1.ij}^*$ = elements of the D_1^* matrix.

m = number of entries in the D_1^* matrix.

These calculations were repeated after each iteration of the model. Together with the distribution of percentage deviations by deciles they enable a crude assessment of the relative value of the various approaches and hypotheses tested. The major drawback, however, appears to be the way in which the deviations have been implicitly weighted. Notice that a deviation from a small 'true' coefficient affects the end result far more than an equal deviation from a large coefficient. Weighting the deviations by the absolute size of the flows is of no analytic interest since these flows would refer to one particular region only and would not necessarily help to test the basic assumptions of the method used. Obviously, size of flows and of sectors varies greatly from one region to another.

In order to overcome this deficiency at least partly, the information theory approach was also used for measuring the accuracy of input–output coefficients [20, 21]. The estimated Washington State Input–Output table (A_n) was treated as a forecast of the 'true' table (B), the information content of which was defined as

$$I(B : A_n) = \sum_i \sum_j \left| b_{ij} \log_2 \frac{b_{ij}}{a_{n.ij}} \right|; \tag{16}$$

where each estimate is weighted by the 'true' coefficient, b_{ij}.

The case study involved the use of the following sources of data:

United States Input–Output Coefficients Table, 1958, which is a 77×77 matrix. This table was enlarged to an 89×89 table by including additional information provided by the Office of Business Economics [17]. More specifically, three sectors were expanded: (1) Food and kindred products, to nine separate sectors; (2) Primary nonferrous metals manufacturing, to three sectors; (3) Electric, gas, water, and sanitary services, also to three sectors.

Washington State Input–Output Tables for 1963, which included a gross flows table and a 54 × 54 table of coefficients.

An adjusted Washington State Input–Output Technical Coefficients Table for 1963 was calculated by reducing the Washington State Gross Flows Table to size 46 × 46, adding inputs from the U.S. by receiving sectors and converting the resulting flow table into a technical coefficients table.

Wholesale price indexes for 89 sectors showing average changes from 1958 to 1963, [2, 8].

Sales, receipts, value-added, and value of shipments data for the U.S. and Washington State which were used to calculate the weights needed for aggregating coefficients, as elements of the weighting matrices [3–7].

Six different cases were considered and are summarized in the following table. The results were obtained after ten iterations of the process. The striking fact is that the process converges extremely rapidly. As a matter of fact, the differences in the results obtained after ten iterations and those obtained after the first iteration were never nearer than in fourth or fifth decimal place. In most cases, there were no differences whatsoever.

The results gave rise to different interpretations depending on whether one considered the mean percentage errors or the 'I' values. The two almost invariably deviated from one another. The mean percentage errors, however, were implicitly weighted inversely to the size of the coefficients. Hence, the analysis was based mainly on the 'I' values.

The first six cases summarized in table 1 show very wide deviations between the estimates and the real matrix. Whichever way one looks at them, they seem to exceed by far any tolerance limits. The adjustment for domestic imports has clearly increased the errors and diminished the value of the estimates. This rather surprising result seems to have something to do with the differences in routing used in the U.S. and Washington tables.

On purely theoretical grounds one would expect the greatest deviations to occur in sectors strongly affected by (1) differences in routing practices, (2) fundamental differences in natural conditions, and (3) sectors in which the regional economy is highly specialized.

Differences in the routing practices would be particularly significant in the tertiary sectors. The errors in the seven tertiary sectors, Communications, Electric companies, Gas companies, Water services, Wholesale services, Wholesale and retail trade, Finance and insurance, Real estate,

Table 1

Deviations between estimated and 'true' regional input–output coefficients

Case	I	II	III	IV	V	VI	VII [1]
Matrix size	43×43	36×36	43×43	36×36	36×36	36×36	28×28
Price adjustments	No	No	Yes	Yes	No	Yes	No
Domestic imports adjustments	No	No	No	No	Yes	Yes	No
Mean percentage error of coefficients	58.65	71.73	59.03	69.92	80.81	79.20	38.93
Standard deviation of percentage error	2.211	3.716	2.202	3.378	6.314	6.177	2.160
'I' values [2]	9.085	6.279	9.266	6.408	54.169	54.262	0.779

[1] Repeats II after removing 'problem' sectors (1, 2, 3, 4, 8, 14, 16, 24).

[2] $I(B_1 : A_{10}) = \sum_i \sum_j \left| b_{ij} \log_2 \frac{b_{ij}}{a_{n \cdot ij}} \right|$;

Business services, and Personal services, were particularly large. The grouping of the seven tertiary sectors into two considerably improved the results[4]. Of the six cases examined, Case II, in which both matrices had been aggregated to order 36×36 through grouping of the tertiary sectors and without adjustments for prices or domestic imports, yielded the best results.

Primary activities, which on theoretical grounds were expected to yield poor results, were represented by four sectors: Agricultural crops, Livestock products, Forestry and fishing, and Mining. The errors in these sectors were over two standard deviations larger than the mean error of the whole array. It can be safely assumed that these high errors can be largely explained by the wide range of activities grouped together. Agricultural crops in Washington State, for example, would include different activities from the U.S. average. This will be even more true of Mining, Livestock products, or Forestry and fishing. Many types of mining included in the U.S. sector do not exist in Washington State.

The last group of sectors in which large deviations were expected to occur were those in which the regional economy is highly specialized. Measuring the degree of specialization by location quotients[5] it was found that six out

[4] Compare Case I to II and III to IV, which are otherwise identical.

[5] The location quotients were compiled by taking the ratio

$$L = \frac{E_{ir}}{E_r} : \frac{E_{i \cdot us}}{E_{us}} ;$$

where L = location quotient, E_{ir} = employment in industry i in Washington, 1963, E_r = total employment in Washington State, 1963, $E_{i \cdot us}$ = employment in industry i in U.S., 1963, and E_{us} = total employment in the U.S., 1963.

of the thirty-six sectors had location quotients of 2.0 or more:

(3)	Forestry and fishing	3.1
(8)	Canning and preserving	2.5
(14)	Lumber and wood products	5.1
(16)	Paper products	2.0
(24)	Non-ferrous metals manufacturing	2.4
(31)	Aerospace industry	7.7

Of the six sectors, Forestry and fishing, a primary industry, has been explained above, while Aerospace industry is a case apart. It seems that sectors in which the regional economy is highly specialized have a different technology from the national average and their input–output coefficients cannot be estimated by short-cut methods. This is not true, however, for the Aerospace industry. In this case, the coefficients estimated on the basis of the U.S. table were quite close to actual. This is undoubtedly due to the fact that Aerospace industry in Washington State forms an important part of the national total and, hence, does influence the structure of national coefficients. In fact, on the basis of employment it would appear that 11 % of the U.S. Aerospace industry is concentrated in this state.

By removing eight sectors (four primary industries and four industries in which Washington State is specialized) from the 36×36 table, a considerable decrease in the 'I' value was achieved, which becomes 0.799 after removing the eight sectors, certainly an acceptable level of error by any standard.

It appears, thus, that while national input–output tables cannot be used for purposes of regional studies without considerable adjustment, acceptable results for purposes of interregional comparison can be achieved by the methods tried on the Washington State table, provided that (1) tertiary sectors are reduced to one or two by aggregation; and (2) field surveys are used in order to obtain coefficients of (a) primary industries, and (b) industries in which the regional economy is specialized.

3. Characteristics of industrial complexes

An industrial complex is usually defined as a set of activities with total output above a certain minimum size, occurring at a given location, and belonging to a subsystem subject to important production, marketing, or other interrelations. The extent of relative 'closeness' of a local economy, or conversely its dependence upon exports and imports, can be simply measured with the help of the following index:

$$S = \sum_i \sum_j x_{ij} / \sum_i X_i;$$

where S = index of relative 'closeness' of the regional economy; x_{ij} = flow of goods and services in dollars from industry i to industry j, both located in the study region; and X_i = total output of industry i.

Alternatively, one could use value added rather than flows, although the results are slightly different.

$$U = \sum_j V_j / \sum_i X_i;$$

where V_j = value added (primary inputs) in industry j.

Other indexes could measure the dependence of the regional economy upon particular types of imports or take into account differences in price levels. Such synthetic measures fail, however, to account explicitly for the important indirect and induced effects that are at the heart of a growing agglomeration. This failure and their generality make them devoid of analytic and policy applications.

The alternative approach described below starts by identifying industries belonging to a subgroup with closer links among themselves than with the rest of the local economy [11]. Two industries, k and l, may be operationally defined as 'forming' an industrial complex if they are connected by strong flows of goods or services. Four coefficients may describe this type of relationship:

$$a_{kl} = \frac{x_{kl}}{X_l}; \qquad a_{lk} = \frac{x_{lk}}{X_k}; \qquad b_{kl} = \frac{x_{kl}}{X_k}; \qquad b_{lk} = \frac{x_{lk}}{X_l}.$$

An 'a' coefficient exceeding a certain cut-off point ($a_{kl} \geqq a^*$) indicates a dependent industry, while a large 'b' coefficient ($b_{kl} \geqq b^*$) indicates a complementary industry. An example of a dependent industry may be a plant producing glue out of waste products of a fish processing plant, while an example of a complementary industry may be a plant producing, say, windshields for a car factory, with the relationship being important in terms of the supplying unit.

Far more significant analytically are the more typical indirect links. Two industries, k and l, may be members of an industrial complex in the absence of direct links. For example, an oil refinery and a pharmaceutical plant may both belong to a petro-chemical complex even though they may not trade with one another. The link in this important case is established through other activities of the complex. More generally, two industries, k

and *l*, may be considered to be members of a complex if their trading patterns with suppliers or purchasers involve the same group of industries. This type of link is revealed by correlation analysis.

Specifically, four coefficients of correlation describe the similarity between the input–output structures of two industries:

$$r(a_{ik} \cdot a_{il}), \quad r(b_{ki} \cdot b_{li}), \quad r(a_{ik} \cdot b_{li}), \quad r(b_{ki} \cdot a_{il}).$$

A high $r(a_{ik} \cdot a_{il})$ coefficient indicates that the two industries, *k* and *l*, have similar input structures or draw their supplies from the same producers. A high $r(b_{ki} \cdot b_{li})$ coefficient signifies that the two industries, *k* and *l*, supply their products to a similar set of users. A high $r(a_{ik} \cdot b_{li})$ coefficient implies that the supplier of *k* industry are users of the products of *l*. Finally, a high $r(b_{ki} \cdot a_{il})$ coefficient points towards a reverse relationship between *k* and *l*, namely the users of the products of *k* are suppliers of *l*. Provision has to be made to eliminate similarities based on high import and export content of the two industries, undifferentiated by region and sector or origin or destination.

The formal model for studying the interindustry linkages consists of the following major steps:

(1) A set of four zero order correlation coefficients of the form

$$r(a_{ik} \cdot a_{il}), \quad r(b_{ki} \cdot b_{li}), \quad r(a_{ik} \cdot b_{li}), \quad r(b_{ki} \cdot a_{il}); \qquad (i = 1, \ldots, n);$$

is derived for all possible pairs of industries included in the interindustry flow table examined.

(2) A symmetric intercorrelation matrix *R* is set up by selecting the highest of the four coefficients[6], or

$$r_{lk} = r_{kl} = \max \left[r(a_{ik} \cdot a_{il}), r(b_{ki} \cdot b_{li}), r(a_{ik} \cdot b_{li}), r(b_{ki} \cdot a_{il}) \right];$$

[6] Two additional approaches might be considered. The weaker involves the use of pooled coefficients of correlation in the construction of the matrix, whose entries become:

$$\rho_{ij} = \frac{(n_1-3)z_1' + (n_2-3)z_2' + (n_3-3)z_3' + (n_4-3)z_4'}{\sqrt{(n_1-3) + (n_2-3) + (n_3-3) + (n_4-3)}};$$

where $z' = \frac{1}{2} \log_e 1 + r/(1-r)$. The somewhat stronger alternative applied involved constructing an *R* matrix in which in addition each coefficient is set equal to zero, or $r_{lk} = r_{kl} = 0$; whenever

$$t \leqq t_{.05}; \text{ and where}$$

$$t = \frac{r}{s_r}; \text{ and } s_r = \frac{1-r^2}{n-2}.$$

Furthermore, one could also examine four separate matrices of coefficients of correlation, or construct an *R* matrix by selecting the smallest of the four coefficients describing the relations between any pair of industries.

It appears that generally an examination of intercorrelation matrices R set up by selecting the highest of the four zero order correlation coefficients is most fruitful. The entries in the R matrix help to identify affinities between pairs of industries based on their links with a subgroup forming a hypothetical complex.

More formally, the first two steps can be summarized as follows: Given an $n \times n$ matrix of input–output flows expressed in dollars

$$
X = \begin{bmatrix} x_{11} & x_{12} \ldots x_{1n} \\ x_{21} & x_{22} \ldots x_{2n} \\ \vdots \\ x_{n1} & x_{n2} \ldots x_{nn} \end{bmatrix}.
$$

an $n \times 4n$ matrix of zero order correlation coefficients is derived

$$
r = [r(a_{ik} \cdot a_{il}) \mid r(b_{ki} \cdot b_{li}) \mid r(a_{ik} \cdot b_{li}) \mid r(b_{ki} \cdot a_{il})].
$$

Each entry in the first sub-matrix is a measure of the degree of affinity between any two industries k and l on the basis of similarity in their buying patterns. Each entry in the second sub-matrix is a measure of the degree of affinity between any two industries k and l on the basis of similarity in their selling patterns. The entries in the third and fourth sub-matrices measure the degree of affinity between pairs of industries by correlating the suppliers of the one with customers of the other. Each complete row of the matrix is interpretable as a description of an industry in terms of $4n$ characteristics, each of which measures its affinity to other industries in terms of various relations to the remaining sectors in the system.

Next an $n \times n$ covariance matrix is formed

$$
K = E[(r - \bar{r})(r - \bar{r})^T];
$$

Here the matrix of deviations is post multiplied by its transpose, since the purpose of this step is to compare pairwise industries on the basis of their characteristics, with the final objective of reducing the number of industries while maximizing total variance.

The covariance matrix is transformed into an $n \times n$ correlation matrix

$$
R = D\left(\frac{1}{\delta_i}\right) KD\left(\frac{1}{\delta_i}\right);
$$

where D = diagonal matrix of standard deviations of the variates (r's).

(3) In order to eliminate similarities based on high import and export contents, all industries are removed from the matrix for which both

$$\frac{m_i}{x_i} \geqq \alpha^*; \quad \text{and} \quad \frac{e_i}{x_i} \geqq \beta^*;$$

where m_i = total imports of industry i; e_i = total exports of industry i; and α^*, β^* = constants determined by an interative process and finally set, in one empirical study, at $\alpha^* = \beta^* = 0.30$. The removed industries are those having relatively weak links with the regional economy. Any similarities in trading patterns of such industries revealed by correlation analysis are thus deemed to be spurious, based solely on ancillary inputs and outputs.

(4) In order to identify, from the set of all industries, the subgroup belonging to a complex, an iterative process is applied. For this purpose all industries having a null column or a null row vector (or all k industries for which $r_{ik} = r_{ki} = 0$; $(i = 1, \ldots, n)$ for all $i \neq j$) are removed from the R matrix, and the whole process repeated until no more null vectors are left.

(5) The relative strength of the links binding the remaining industries together is assessed with the help of eigenvalues of the R matrix, computed as:

$$(Ra - Ia\lambda) = 0;$$

$$(R - I\lambda)a = 0;$$

$$|R - I\lambda| = 0;$$

where a = eigenvector, or characteristic vector, and λ = eigenvalue, or characteristic root. The ratios of the characteristic roots to the trace of the R matrix define an index of association

$$C_n = \frac{\lambda_n}{\text{tr } R} \times 100.$$

This provides an aggregate measure of the strength of the ties connecting the industries remaining in the R matrix — a large C_1 indicating the existence of an industrial complex, and a fairly large C_1 and C_2 pointing towards the existence of two identifiable complexes.

The eigenvalues, λ_i, are interpretable as variances along a particular dimension, and determine the degree of affinity of industries forming a subsystem because the elements of the eigenvectors were standardized by setting $a_i^T a_i = 1$.

The above model has been tested by applying it to input–output tables of the United States, Philadelphia SMSA, Washington State, West Virginia, and Nova Scotia. Two of the regions examined, namely Philadelphia and Washington State, were selected because they represent highly industrialized economies comprised of groups of industries expected to meet the criteria of industrial complexes. Two others, namely West Virginia and Nova Scotia, were selected for the opposite reason, as extremely 'open' economies with scant manufacturing activity. The input–output table of the United States was studied in order to gain some insights into the clustering of industries in a complex economy and in the absence of spatial juxtaposition.

The five tables used in the study differed greatly in size, methods of classification of sectors, criteria used for routing and valuation, and date of construction. The United States economy was studied with the help of the 1958 (77 × 77) input–output table enlarged to 89 × 89 by expanding three sectors on the basis of additional information: (1) food and kindred products to nine separate industries; (2) primary nonferrous metals manufacturing to three industries; and (3) electric, gas and sanitary services also to three industries. The 1963 (85 × 85) input–output table for the United States became available recently, but preliminary tests showed that as far as the model reported here is concerned no significantly different results are forthcoming. The 1959 Philadelphia SMSA table (89 × 89) was derived by aggregating the original 496 × 496 matrix [14], the 89 sectors being identical with those appearing in the United States table. The 1963 Washington State table (54 × 54) [1], differs in several respects from the United States and reduced Philadelphia tables, but was made comparable by aggregation to size 43 × 43, 36 × 36, and 31 × 31. The West Virginia table (48 × 48) is highly disaggregated with respect to primary industries [16]. Attempts to reduce its size in order to make it comparable to the other regional tables yielded a 23 × 23 matrix. The 1960 Nova Scotia table (58 × 58) is based on a different industrial classification [15]. Only 28 sectors proved roughly comparable to those used in the United States and Philadelphia studies.

The large differences in classification precluded a direct comparison of the eigenvalues and indexes of association derived with the help of the original tables, while aggregation by methods described in sect. 2 resulted in tables too small for analysis. The sectors in the aggregated tables were frequently comprised of such heterogeneous activities that flows between them reflected the accidents of presence or absence of certain plants rather than technical affinity. On the basis of a careful perusal of the results, it appears that valid conclusions cannot be based on tables comprised of less than 50–60 sectors.

While methods of sectoring or grouping of plants affect interregional comparisons, the treatment of vertical integration, either physical or institutional, is likely to assume even greater importance. The lack of evidence of flows internal to a plant might lead to surprising conclusions. For example, the important aerospace complex in Washington State does not stand out as a cluster of interlinked activities, because the bulk of the flows of inputs and outputs either take place within the complex itself or between it and the rest of the world.

The indexes of association derived with the help of the model for the five regions analyzed are summarized in table 2.

Table 2

Values of the indexes of association

$$C_n = \frac{\lambda_n}{\mathrm{tr}\ R} \times 100$$

Region		Size of the R Matrix							
		89×89	58×58	54×54	48×48	43×43	36×36	31×31	28×28	23×23
United States	C_1	23.86				35.88	44.46	43.49		
	C_2	11.99				11.57	12.72	13.36		
	C_3	7.27				8.23	8.11	8.45		
Philadelphia	C_1	25.85				38.94	44.36	43.74		
SMSA	C_2	12.84				13.10	14.29	14.57		
	C_3	9.61				11.79	10.86	10.37		
Washington	C_1			40.25		43.49	46.12	47.83		
State	C_2			10.36		11.60	11.32	12.59		
	C_3			8.98		10.00	9.13	9.74		
West	C_1				28.75					74.20
Virginia	C_2				12.22					13.43
	C_3				8.90					6.71
Nova	C_1		31.51						52.38	
Scotia	C_2		14.36						16.00	
	C_3		10.75						12.02	

Several aspects of the results deserve attention. First, the values of the indexes increase consistently and significantly with increasing aggregation (and decreasing size of the tables). This was to be expected, but the strength of the effect makes interregional comparisons based on tables of different dimensions impossible. Notice that in the Philadelphia SMSA table a reduction from 89×89 to 43×43 increased C_1 by more than one-half, while a reduction of the West Virginia table from 48×48 to 23×23 almost tripled the value of C_1.

Second, interregional comparisons may have to encompass more than the first three eigenvectors. The relatively low values of C_1 in the case of Philadelphia, and even more so in the case of the United States, result from substantial clustering along other dimensions as well, whereas in the case of Washington State and West Virginia the first three eigenvalues are the only substantial ones. While this is precisely the phenomenon the index of association is designed to measure, a consideration of a profile based on all eigenvalues may be more relevant for other purposes.

In spite of these limitations certain tentative conclusions can be drawn on the basis of the indexes of association. Within the roughly comparable size range of 89×89 to 48×48, the United States, Philadelphia SMSA, and Washington State tables show a distinctly higher degree of association than West Virginia and Nova Scotia.[7] The contrast would be even sharper were it not for the fact that in the latter two cases the service sectors have been far more disaggregated than in the former.

While the indexes of association provide a crude measure of the degree of clustering along some dimensions and an indication of the formation, in the regional economy, of industrial groupings based on direct and indirect intersectoral flows, interesting insights can be gained by studying the composition of eigenvectors. The sectors associated with the highest values in the first three eigenvectors are listed in table 3.[8]

The relatively large United States table displays some features clearly related to the size and complexity of the economy. The first two eigenvectors are headed, in terms of associated values, by industries belonging to a metal complex, with the second showing a more pronounced orientation towards machinery and equipment-producing industries. The third vector has few large entries, but those most prominent seem associated with chemicals, drugs, and photographic equipment.

The Philadelphia SMSA and Washington State tables are most interesting. The first eigenvector of the Philadelphia table is characterized by strong ties among the industries it encompasses. It contains mostly metal fabricating and machinery and equipment-producing industries. Rather surprisingly, it also contains the wholesale and retail trade sector, which, at variance with the national economy, forms part of the first eigenvector of every regional table examined. The second eigenvector seems to combine elements of

---

[7] This becomes even more evident when the absolute values of the first eigenvalues are considered, namely 21.21, 23.02 and 21.68 for the United States, Philadelphia SMSA, and Washington State, respectively, as against 13.79 and 17.95 for West Virginia and Nova Scotia.

[8] The cut-off points were chosen so as to exclude sectors contributing little to total variance along each particular dimension.

Table 3

Industries associated with largest values in eigenvectors

First eigenvector			Second eigenvector			Third eigenvector		
No.	Industry	Value	No.	Industry	Value	No.	Industry	Value

United States 89 × 89 matrix

$C_1 = 23.86$ $C_2 = 11.99$ $C_3 = 7.27$

No.	Industry	Value	No.	Industry	Value	No.	Industry	Value
54	Farm machinery & equipment	0.1748	51	Stampings, screw machine products and bolts	0.1843	73	Optical, ophthalmic & photographic equipment	0.1802
5	Iron & ferroalloy ores mining	0.1690	52	Other fabricated metal products	0.1784	36	Plastics and synthetic materials	0.1703
52	Other fabricated metal products	0.1681	55	Construction, mining & oil field machinery	0.1744	37	Drugs, cleaning & toilet preparations	0.1578
50	Heating, plumbing & structural metal products	0.1651	45	Primary iron & steel manufacturing	0.1683	38	Paints & allied products	0.1567
51	Stampings, screw machine products and bolts	0.1643	59	General industrial machinery & equipment	0.1643			
65	Electric lighting & wiring equipment	0.1637	57	Metal working machinery & equipment	0.1550			
71	Other transportation equipment	0.1546	50	Heating, plumbing & structural metal products	0.1537			
58	Special industrial machinery & equipment	0.1534	56	Materials handling machinery & equipment	0.1520			
49	Metal containers	0.1527						

two complexes: an urban-oriented, mainly food-processing, group of industries, and some services. Despite the fact that some of the sectors represented are often found in harbor-based industrial complexes, the group as a whole seems clearly to be oriented toward the agglomeration of consumers and the large market of Philadelphia and its hinterland. The third eigenvector is composed entirely of services, many of which are typically found in large metropolitan areas.

The Washington State table displays a different, but not less intriguing, pattern. The sectors associated with the first eigenvector do not fall clearly into any one category, although typically urban services are very promenent.

Table 4

	First eigenvector			Second eigenvector			Third eigenvector	
No.	Industry	Value	No.	Industry	Value	No.	Industry	Value
	Philadelphia SMSA 89 × 89 matrix							
	$C_1 = 25.85$			$C_2 = 12.84$			$C_3 = 9.61$	
81	Wholesale & retail trade	0.2109	19	Sugar	0.2058	76	Other communications	0.1967
54	Farm machinery & equipment	0.2086	17	Grain mill products	0.2016	82	Finance and insurance	0.1947
62	Service industries machines	0.2072	33	Paperboard containers & boxes	0.1932	78	Electric utilities	0.1893
52	Other fabricated metal products	0.2043	76	Other communications	0.1848	85	Business services	0.1865
50	Heating, plumbing & structural metal products	0.2032	3	Forestry & fishery products	0.1828	83	Real estate & rental	0.1592
57	Metal working machinery & equipment	0.1951	21	Beverage industries	0.1816	87	Automobile repair service	0.1575
58	Special industry machinery & equipment	0.1940	2	Other agricultural products	0.1756	79	Gas utilities	0.1554
49	Metal containers	0.1938	34	Printing & publishing	0.1734	84	Hotels, personal & repair services	0.1534
31	Other furniture & fixtures	0.1927	22	Miscellaneous food & kindred products	0.1695			
45	Primary iron & steel manufacturing	0.1899	82	Finance & insurance	0.1692			
51	Stampings, screw machine products and bolts	0.1883	4	Agriculture forestry & fishing products	0.1588			
53	Engines and turbines	0.1858	1	Livestock & livestock products	0.1570			
64	Household appliances	0.1813	14	Meat products	0.1570			
56	Materials handling machinery and equipment	0.1747	37	Drugs, cleaning and toilet preparations	0.1562			
59	General industry machinery & equipment	0.1740	84	Hotels, personal & repair services	0.1558			
60	Machine shop products	0.1687	20	Confectionery & related products	0.1535			

Table 4 (continued)

| First eigenvector | | | Second eigenvector | | | Third eigenvector | | |
No.	Industry	Value	No.	Industry	Value	No.	Industry	Value
	Philadelphia SMSA 89×89 Matrix							
	$C_1 = 25.85$			$C_2 = 12.84$			$C_3 = 9.61$	
69	Motor vehicles & equipment	0.1644	78	Electric utilities	0.1532			
30	Household furniture	0.1637	85	Business services	0.1521			
55	Construction, mining & oil machinery	0.1511	18	Bakery products	0.1501			

Table 5

| First eigenvector | | | Second eigenvector | | | Third eigenvector | | |
No.	Industry	Value	No.	Industry	Value	No.	Industry	Value
	Washington State 54×54 matrix							
	$C_1 = 40.25$			$C_2 = 10.36$			$C_3 = 8.98$	
47	Communications	0.2295	17	Sawmills	0.3418	11	Other foods	0.3334
52	Real estate	0.2033	15	Forestry	0.3392	2	Vegetables	0.3294
30	Iron & steel	0.1994	18	Plywood	0.3335	8	Canning & preserving	0.3009
53	Business services	0.1968	21	Pulp mills	0.3146	5	Fishing	0.2501
49	Wholesale & retail	0.1966	19	Other wood products	0.2965	28	Glass & stone	0.2441
19	Other wood products	0.1874	22	Paper mills	0.2474	34	'Light' metal products	0.2417
54	Personal services	0.1863	16	Logging	0.2175	23	Paper board mills	0.2343
24	Printing & publishing	0.1807				9	Grain mill products	0.2079
33	'Heavy' metal products	0.1788				21	Pulp mills	0.2028
37	Nonelectric industrial equipment	0.1780						
45	Gas companies	0.1769						
20	Furniture & fixtures	0.1745						
48	Construction	0.1729						
50	Finance	0.1706						
43	All transportation	0.1694						
14	Mining	0.1693						
51	Insurance	0.1677						
46	Water services	0.1658						
17	Sawmills	0.1650						

Table 6

First eigenvector			Second eigenvector			Third eigenvector		
No.	Industry	Value	No.	Industry	Value	No.	Industry	Value

West Virginia 48 × 48 matrix

$C_1 = 28.75$ $C_2 = 12.22$ $C_3 = 8.90$

No.	Industry	Value	No.	Industry	Value	No.	Industry	Value
31	Retail gasoline service stations	0.2666	30	Retail food stores	0.2698	35	Insurance agents & brokers	0.2440
41	All other services	0.2467	10	Food & kindred products (dairies)	0.2662	38	Hotels & other lodging places	0.1791
38	Hotels & other lodging places	0.2387	9	Food & kindred products (meats g.n.e.c.)	0.2598	31	Retail gasoline service stations	0.1727
43	Trucking & warehousing	0.2292	32	All other retail	0.1981	45	Communications	0.1634
8	Special trades contractors	0.2267	12	Food & kindred products (beverages)	0.1910	33	Banking	0.1577
32	All other retail	0.2118	39	Medical & legal services	0.1870	39	Medical & legal services	0.1519
33	Banking	0.2044	33	Banking	0.1510	32	All other retail	0.1494
34	Other finance	0.2019	1	Agriculture	0.1381	46	Electric companies & systems	0.1369
45	Communications	0.1979	37	All other finance, insurance & real estate	0.1368	41	All other services	0.1302
35	Insurance agents and brokers	0.1925	13	Apparel & accessories	0.1015	24	Electrical machinery and apparatus	0.1291
29	Wholesale trade	0.1894				34	Other finance	0.1053
48	Water & sanitary services	0.1852						
28	Eating & drinking establishments	0.1705						

The second and third eigenvectors, on the other hand, are composed of industries with obvious technical links. Thus, the second subsystem clearly revolves around wood products, while the third has at its core food products and packaging materials. Both might properly be termed industrial complexes. The strong links between the components of the latter two groups are noticeable. The pattern displayed in the Washington State table may point towards the conclusion that in a regional economy the links due to spatial juxtaposition take precedence over those due to technical affinity. The latter make their appearance only after the former have been accounted for and their effects removed.

Table 7

First eigenvector			Second eigenvector			Third eigenvector		
No.	Industry	Value	No.	Industry	Value	No.	Industry	Value
			Nova Scotia 58 × 58 matrix					
	$C_1 = 31.51$			$C_2 = 14.36$			$C_3 = 10.75$	
51	Wholesale & retail trade	0.2475	9	Poultry processors	0.3742	24	Sawmills & other wood products	0.3135
31	Iron foundries, metal rolling stock	0.2349	10	Dairy factories	0.3609	25	Miscellaneous wood industries	0.2253
7	Quarries & sand-pits	0.2163	14	Feed manufacturers	0.3485	30	Iron & steel mills	0.2041
50	Gas & water systems	0.2073	8	Meat products	0.3211	39	Clay & concrete	0.2030
38	Electric wire, cable & batteries	0.2046	22	Cordage, canvas cloth mills, etc.	0.2944			
54	Finance, insurance & real estate	0.2012	2	Forestry	0.2571			
39	Clay & concrete	0.1998	1	Agriculture	0.2196			
47	Transportation	0.1981						
25	Miscellaneous wood industries	0.1979						
22	Cordage, canvas, cloth mills, etc.	0.1964						
48	Radio broadcasting, telephone & telegraph	0.1960						
52	Automobile operation	0.1920						
30	Iron & steel mills	0.1872						
46	Nonresidential construction	0.1855						
12	Secondary fishery, (all other) i.e. not shellfish	0.1833						

The remaining two regional economies are characterized by a rather weak manufacturing base. The 48 × 48 West Virginia table groups primarily services in all three eigenvectors. The links displayed are anyway weak, and their appearance may be due to the fact that these sectors have been disaggregated to a much greater extent than in the other tables.

An examination of the Nova Scotia table shows again that the grouping of activities associated with the highest values in the first eigenvector is typical of regional, especially of urban, agglomerations. It seems to vindicate the hypothesis that in an urban-industrial complex the exchange of goods and services between unrelated industries exceeds in volume that between technically related ones. Indirectly this supports the thesis that for plants attracted to urban agglomerations the very existence, rather than the nature of the numerous and manifold links, is a prime consideration [9, 10]. Industries associated with the highest elements in the second eigenvector, on the other hand, seem to be technically related to one another and, with one exception, related to food processing. The links among industries entering the third eigenvector are less obvious, although the few on top of the list are all based on local extractive activities.

4. Some tentative conclusions

Recapitulating the main tentative findings, it appears that multivariate analysis may be a useful tool for analyzing linkages existing in regional economies. The sample of input–output tables so far examined was far too small for any regularities to emerge. Nonetheless, the pervasiveness of links based on spatial proximity rather than technical affinity in the first subsystems falls in line with theoretical considerations and deserves careful attention.

Yet, even aside from the uncertainties surrounding any conclusions that might be drawn from an inadequate sample, the study revealed some serious methodological limitations inherent in any attempts at interregional comparisons without considerable adjustments of input–output tables based on different sectoring and methods of construction. In addition to the constraints imposed by the fixed coefficients production function underlying any input–output analysis, the results in the absence of at least partial direct, specially constructed field surveys seem to depend to a rather high extent upon accidents of an industrial classification developed with other objectives in mind. The results so far derived seem also to indicate that the frequent use of small, highly aggregated input–output tables for regional studies limits their usefulness. As far as multivariate analysis is concerned, the highest possible degree of detail would be required. Some of these difficulties appear to have been successfully avoided in the next, more extensive stage of the research now under way.

The practical significance of the research for decision making and policy formulation derives primarily from the at least partly vindicated hypothesis that identifiable clusters of interlinked activities might account for a substantial part of total multiplier effects capable of being generated in a region. Hence, an important additional criterion in selecting industries deserving support from the point of view of regional development would be their belonging to complexes linked by intersectoral flows. Evaluation of industries on the basis of their individual characteristics, such as high employment/investment or output/capital ratio, may be improved by considering their contribution towards increasing multiplier effects in the local economy and the attractiveness of the region (increased externalities) to other activities.

The findings of the research may play an even more important role in formulating regional plans and long-run development policies. The idea that promotion of clusters of interrelated industries rather than of scattered individual plants may be more efficient in invigorating the economies of stagnating or declining regions has been gaining ground recently. The feasibility of this bolder and more ambitious approach hinges upon the identification of the smallest possible meaningful clusters of industries. A related but so far not yet fully explored issue is the possibility of introducing partial complexes into a remote, depressed region. A more rigorous analysis of this important policy problem involves the explicit examination of the effects of distance upon interindustry flows and above all upon the more elusive and difficult to quantify role played by externalities.

Finally, the results of the research stress the role of service activities, especially wholesaling and retailing, in urban complexes. This reopens the familiar question with respect to developing nations, raised by Hirschman, of investing in infrastructure vs. productive activities. On the basis of the preliminary results reported above, the issue seems to acquire a new significance in regional planning, with the notion of infrastructure extended to encompass some of the most typical urban activities.

References

[1] Bourque, P. J. *et al.*, 1966, The Washington Interindustry Study for 1963, University of Washington.

[2] Bureau of Budget, Committee Staff, Subcommittee on Economic Statistics of the Joint Economic Committee and Office of Statistical Standards, Consumer Price Index for Urban Wage Earners and Clerical Workers, Economic Indicators, Suppl., 1964, 91.

[3] Bureau of Business, U.S. Department of Commerce, Census of Business: 1963, Selected Services, Vol. 7, Area Statistics, Part 3, Table 7, Section 49, Washington: U.S. Government Printing Office, 1966, 5.

[4] Bureau of the Census, 1963, Census of Manufacturers, Vol. III, Area Statistics, Section 48, Table 6, Washington: U.S. Government Printing Office, 1966, 11–12.

[5] Bureau of the Census, 1963, Census of Mineral Industries: Washington Area Statistics MIC 63 (2), Section 46, Washington: U.S. Government Printing Office, 1962, 4–5.

[6] Bureau of the Census, Census of Population: 1960, Characteristics of the Population, Vol. I, Washington, Part 49, Table 62, Washington: U.S. Government Printing Office, 1962, 114–115.

[7] Bureau of the Census, U.S. Department of Commerce, U.S. Census of Agriculture: 1959, Final Report, Counties, Vol. 1, State Table, 17, Washington: U.S. Government Printing Office, 42.

[8] Bureau of Labor Statistics, U.S. Department of Labor, Wholesale Prices and Price Indexes — 1963, Bulletin No. 1513 (June 1966).

[9] Czamanski, S., 1965, A Model of Urban Growth, Papers of the Regional Science Association, XIII, 177–200.

[10] Czamanski, S., 1965, Industrial Location and Urban Growth, The Town Planning Review (Liverpool), XXXVI, no. 3, 165–180.

[11] Czamanski, S., 1971, Some Empirical Evidence of the Strengths of Linkages Between Groups of Related Industries in Urban-Regional Complexes, Papers, Regional Science Association, Vol. XXVII, 137–150.

[12] Czamanski, S. with E. Malizia, 1969, Applicability and Limitations in the Use of National Input–Output Tables for Regional Studies, Papers, Regional Science Association, Vol. XXIII, 65–77.

[13] Fontela, E. et al., 1970, Forecasting Technical Coefficients and Changes in Relative Prices, in: A. P. Carter and A. Brody eds., Applications of Input–Output Analysis, Amsterdam: North-Holland Publishing Company, 331–346.

[14] Isard, W., T. W. Langford, Jr. and E. Romanoff, 1966, Philadelphia Region Input–Output Study, Department of Regional Science, University of Pennsylvania, and Regional Science Research Institute.

[15] Levitt, K., 1969, A Macro-Economic Analysis of the Structure of the Atlantic Provinces (mimeo).

[16] Miernyk, W. H. et al., 1970, Simulating Regional Economic Development, Lexington Books.

[17] Office of Business Economics, U.S. Department of Commerce, Survey of Current Business, Vol. 45, no. 9 (1965), 33–49; Vol. 46, no. 4 (1966), 14–17.

[18] Stone, R., 1966, Mathematics in the Social Sciences and Other Essays, Chapman & Hall, 243–244.

[19] Stone, R. and A. Brown, 1965, Behavioral and Technical Change in Economic Models, in: E. A. G. Robinson ed., Problems in Economic Development, London and New York: Macmillan and Co., 433–436.

[20] Theil, H., 1967, Economics and Information Theory, Amsterdam: North-Holland Publishing Company.

[21] Tilanus, C. B. and H. Theil, 1964, The Information Approach to the Evaluation of Input–Output Forecasts, Econometric Institute of the Netherlands School of Economics.

CHAPTER 11

Application of a turnpike theorem to planning for efficient accumulation: an example for Japan*

JINKICHI TSUKUI[1]

Osaka University

1. Introduction

Among various types of turnpike theorems, those given by McKenzie and the author are for a computable dynamic Leontief model and therefore have some relevance to actual planning. There have not yet been any attempts at empirical application, however. Criticism of such attempts is mainly directed at two characteristics of the model: that it is a rigid type of planning model with constant technological coefficients, and that it is a closed system. Our opinion with respect to the first point is that a planning model — even if it is rigid type of model — may be useful in any type of economy as a tool for the analysis of the possibility for economic growth. An efficient path of economic growth found by using a planning model may be useful as a guidepost from which one may judge the efficiency of the actual growth path. With respect to the second point, we shall show that some flexibility is possible. When labor is not a scarce factor of production, the labor sector can be removed from the model, while final demand can be represented by a linear (not necessarily homogeneous) function of income. Our fundamental assumption in this respect is that the effect of technological progress appears in the reduction of labor input coefficients, while input–out-

* A major portion of this paper appeared in Econometrica, vol. 36, 1968 and is reprinted here with the permission of the publisher.

[1] The author is grateful to the referees for their valuable comments. The computations in this paper were performed while the author was visiting the Harvard Economic Research Project. He is grateful to Professor Wassily W. Leontief for his encouragement and valuable suggestions. The preliminary result of computation was reported at the Rochester Conference on Mathematical Models of Economic Growth in July, 1964. Thanks are due to Professor Lionel W. McKenzie and the other participants of the conference for their valuable comments.

put and stock-flow matrices remain invariant, and as a result, labor is not a scarce factor for the Japanese economy in our planning period. While (disguised) unemployment exists, the per capita productivity of an economy can grow with invariant input–output technology by continuous accumulation of capital. Moreover, when we consider the fact that the input–output and stock flow coefficients of Japan and of an advanced economy, say the U.S., are very similar[2] (despite the great difference in their average labor productivities — about one to six in 1955), our assumption may be thought reasonable as a first approximation to reality.

Our study may be thought of as simply a pilot study in the field of application of recent theoretical achievements. It also has another feature, however, that is rather theoretical: that is, the investigation of the characteristics of the efficient growth-path and the Leontief trajectory. We found from theoretical analysis of our computational results that, in general, the dynamic Leontief system is relatively, completely unstable, and that the catenary movement of the efficient path toward the turnpike is generally a prominent feature even in a short term (several years) program.

2. The model

Our model is a linear programming version of the dynamic Leontief system. Let $x(t)$ be an n-dimensional vector of output levels in period t; A an n by n input–output matrix; and B an n by n stock-flow matrix. Let $c(t)$ be an n-dimensional vector of consumption in period t. Let $e(t)$ and $m(t)$ be an n-dimensional vector of exports and of competitive imports in period t, respectively. Then, we have the following inequality in every period:

$$(I-A+B)x(t)-Bx(t+1) \geqslant c(t)+e(t)-m(t), \quad x(t) \geqslant 0$$
$$(t = 0, 1, 2, \ldots), \quad (1)$$

where I is a unit matrix of rank n, and $x(0)$ is given by the initial conditions.

We shall now assume that the final demand is expressed as a function of income $y : c(t)+e(t)-m(t) = f(y(t))$. Making the Taylor expansion of $f(y(t))$ in the neighborhood of the initial income $y(0)$, and neglecting the terms with derivatives of higher order, we obtain from (1)

$$(I-A+B)x(t)-Bx(t+1) \geqslant f(y(0))+d(y(t)-y(0)) \text{ for } x(t) \geqslant 0$$
$$(t = 0, 1, 2, \ldots), \quad (2)$$

---

[2] See for example [1].

where d is an n-dimensional vector of the first order derivatives, $d = f'(y(0))$.

The next step is to derive a closed system from (2) so that the turnpike theory is applicable. Let v be an n-dimensional vector of value added ratios; then the income $y(t)$ is given by

$$y(t) = vx(t). \tag{3}$$

The stationary state, in which a final demand $f(\bar{y})$ is constantly reproduced every period, is represented by

$$(I-A)\bar{x} = f(\bar{y}) = f(y(0)) + d(\bar{y}-y(0)). \tag{4}$$

The output level $\bar{x}$ is obtained from

$$\bar{x} = (I-A-dv)^{-1}(f(y(0))-dy(0)), \tag{5}$$

since $\bar{y} = v\bar{x}$ by (3). Then, we obtain from (2) and (4) the following closed system:

$$(I-\bar{A}+B)z(t) - Bz(t+1) \geqslant 0, \quad z(t) \geqslant -\bar{x} \quad (t = 0, 1, 2, \ldots), \tag{6}$$

where $z(t) = x(t)-\bar{x}$ and $\bar{A} = A+dv$.

Now, let the planning periods be 1 to T. Let $p(\geqslant 0)$ be an n-dimensional vector of valuation prices for the stocks in period T. The programming problem for the system (6) is given by

Maximize $p(I-\bar{A}+B)z(T)$ subject to

$$(I-\bar{A}+B)z(t) - Bz(t+1) \geqslant 0 \qquad (t = 0, 1, \ldots, T-1), \tag{7}$$

$$z(t) \geqslant 0^3 \qquad\qquad\qquad (t = 0, 1, \ldots, T),$$

where $z(0)$ is given by the initial conditions.

If the matrices $\bar{A}$ and B satisfy certain conditions, there exists a unique positive characteristic vector z^* (the Neumann output vector) which corresponds to the Frobenius root γ of the positive matrix $(I-\bar{A})^{-1}B$. As is well known, the half line $\{\lambda z^*|\lambda \geqslant 0\}$ in the n-dimensional output space R^n is referred to as the Neumann output ray (the turnpike), and $1/\gamma$, as the Neumann growth rate.

A fundamental problem with (7) concerns the arbitrariness in the establishment of the price vector p. Any particular choice of p implies a value judgement. The turnpike theorem is important in this respect, since it tells us the way to escape the vexing problem of value judgements.

---

[3] In our particular problem, $x(t) \geq 0$ is insured by this constraint, since a positive $\bar{x}$ was obtained by (5) as shown in table 1.

According to the turnpike theorem, all efficient paths of $z(t)$ (which are the solutions to the programming problem (7)) approach the turnpike and spend most of the planning periods in its neighborhood no matter what the price vector p and the initial output $z(0)$ may be. (The two commodity case is illustrated in fig. 1.) Therefore, the wisest course for a planning agency is to abstain from worrying about the choice of p and to plan to

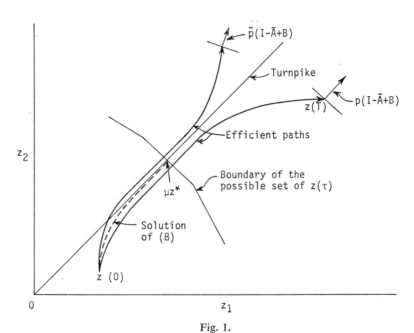

Fig. 1.

lead the economy efficiently toward the turnpike in the beginning, say, in period 1 to τ, and then to keep it growing along the turnpike as shown by the dotted line in fig. 1. By doing so, we can approximate any efficient paths for any $p(\geqslant 0)$ during most of the planning periods except those near the end. This can be done by solving the following programming problem:

Maximize μ subject to

$$(I-\bar{A}+B)z(t)-Bz(t+1) \geqslant 0 \qquad (t = 0, 1, \ldots, \tau-2),$$
$$(I-\bar{A}+B)z(\tau-1)-\mu Bz^* \geqslant 0, \qquad\qquad\qquad (8)$$
$$z(t) \geqslant 0 \qquad (t = 0, 1, \ldots, \tau-1),$$

where z^* is the normalized Neumann output vector: $\sum_i z_i^* = 1$. Our object is to compute this solution for the Japanese economy.

3. Data and computation

The year 1955 was chosen as the base year, since this was the latest year for which we could obtain both input–output and stock-flow tables. The number of the industrial sectors was limited to twelve because of lack of information of capital coefficients. The planning period was tentatively set at five years (i.e., $\tau = 5$) which might seem to be insufficiently short. The computational result, however, showed that it was sufficient for our particular problem, since the solution to (8) reached the turnpike in the third year (see sect. 4 and table 3).

The preparation of data was carried out in the following way.

Input-Output Matrix: In our model, each input coefficient a_{ij} must be the sum of a current input coefficient a_{ij}^1 and an input coefficient a_{ij}^2 for the maintenance of fixed capital. The former was computed through aggregation from the 124-order flow table of 1955. To compute the latter, let δ_j be the depreciation per unit output in the jth industry, and θ_i the depreciation rate of the ith good (allowed by tax law). Then, we have $a_{ij}^2 = \delta_j \theta_i b_{ij}^1 / \sum_i \theta_i b_{ij}^1$ $(i, j = 1, \ldots, 12)$, where b_{ij}^1 is the ith component of the jth column of the matrix of fixed capital coefficients in 1955. Table 4 shows the matrix A thus obtained.

Stock-Flow Matrix: Each of our stock-flow coefficients b_{ij} must be the sum of a fixed capital coefficient b_{ij}^1 and an inventory coefficient b_{ij}^2. The former was obtained from the table "The Average Fixed Capital by Industry and Industries of Origin for 1955 in 1955 Price," in [2]. For the estimation of the latter coefficient, we used the inventory figures by industry given in "Industry Statistics, Census of Manufactures, 1955" from the Ministry of International Trade and Industry.[4] From these figures, we could obtain for each industry the inventories of energy b_{9j}^2 and of raw materials $\sum_{i \neq j, 9} b_{ij}^2$ necessary for the production of a unit output.[5] The latter inventory was then distributed to respective industrial sectors according to the relative magnitude of current input coefficients:

$$b_{ij}^2 = \left(\sum_{i \neq j, 9} b_{ij}^2 \right) a_{ij}^1 / \sum_{i \neq j, 9} a_{ij}, \qquad i \neq j, 9.$$

Table 5 shows the stock-flow matrix B thus obtained.

---

[4] For agriculture and service, an average inventory figure of manufactures was used, since the data were not available for these two sectors.

[5] We assumed that these inventories were normally necessary amounts in each industry in 1955. The ninth sector is the energy industry.

Final Demand Function $f(y)$ and $\bar{x}$: In our model all investment is in productive capital. Therefore, consumption must include not only consumption by usual definition, but also all social investment, such as the construction of new houses, etc. According to this definition, the final demand vectors of 1951 and 1955 were obtained in 1955 prices from the flow tables of these two years. Then d was estimated by

$$d = f'(y(1955)) = [f(y(1955)) - f(y(1951))]/[y(1955) - y(1951)].$$

Then $\bar{x}$ was computed by (5). Finally, $f(\bar{y})$ was obtained by (4). These results are shown in table 1.

Table 1

Industry	d	$f(\bar{y})^*$	$\bar{x}^*$
1 Agriculture and foods	0.169170	1315.6	2325.3
2 Textile and leather	0.088544	169.3	393.3
3 Lumber and products	0.005991	28.2	220.1
4 Paper, printing, misc.	0.034714	81.1	290.4
5 Chemical	0.022802	3.2	194.3
6 Mining and metal	0.012079	118.5	489.9
7 Machinery	0.013481	31.2	120.0
8 Transportation equipment	0.024015	−16.8	21.6
9 Energy	0.009677	63.6	247.0
10 Construction	0.069427	113.5	251.9
11 Transport	0.051167	133.7	238.3
12 Service and trade	0.370746	1135.8	1617.4
Total	0.871813	3176.9 $(\bar{y})$	6409.5

* Unit: one billion yen.

Computation of z^*: Let $(I - \bar{A})^{-1} B = D$. Let $(\gamma_1, \ldots, \gamma_n)$ be the characteristic roots of D, and $(h_1, \ldots, h_n)$, the corresponding (normalized) characteristic vectors. The general solution to the system of difference equation $s(t+1) = Ds(t)$ is given in the form:

$$s(t) = \gamma_1^t \varepsilon_1 h_1 + \gamma_2^t \varepsilon_2 h_2 + \ldots + \gamma_n^t \varepsilon_n h_n, \tag{9}$$

where $\varepsilon_1, \ldots, \varepsilon_n$ are determined by the initial conditions. Since D is a positive matrix, there exists the Frobenius root, say γ_1, such that $\gamma_1 > |\gamma_i|$ $(i = 2, \ldots, n)$. Therefore, for any $s(0) \geqslant 0$, we find from (9) that

$$\lim_{t \to \infty} \frac{s(t)}{|s(t)|} = \lim_{t \to \infty} \frac{D^t s(0)}{|D^t s(0)|} = \frac{h_1}{|h_1|} = z^*,$$

and

$$\lim_{t \to \infty} \frac{|s(t+1)|}{|s(t)|} = \lim_{t \to \infty} \frac{|D^{t+1}s(0)|}{|D^t s(0)|} = \gamma_1,$$

since $\varepsilon_1 > 0$ for any $s(0) \geqslant 0$. Using these two relations, we have estimated z^* and γ_1 with respect to D^{50} and D^{51} (table 2). We found in our computation that every column vector of D^t converged very rapidly to the Neumann output vector. The estimates of z^* and γ_1 by D^8 and D^9 were the same as those by D^{50} and D^{51} to the fifth digit.

Table 2

$1/\gamma_1 = 0.127960$

$$z^* = \begin{bmatrix} 0.167714 \\ 0.088900 \\ 0.049601 \\ 0.051682 \\ 0.042398 \\ 0.108051 \\ 0.040493 \\ 0.021907 \\ 0.037745 \\ 0.102925 \\ 0.042092 \\ 0.246492 \end{bmatrix}$$

After the preparation of these data the solution to (8) was computed with Program LP/90 by CEIR. The efficient path of output levels $(x(t)$'s) were then obtained from the definition: $x(t) = z(t) + \bar{x}$.

In table 3 these $x(t)$'s are shown in the form of production-indices with 1955 output of each industry equal to 100. In the same table, the shadow prices of the products in every period, which are the dual solution to the original problem (8), are also shown.

4. Theoretical analysis of the computational results

Let us first study the following equality system with respect to the constraints in (8):

$$z(t+1) = (I + D^{-1})z(t), \tag{10}$$

Table 3

Production indices — actual and computed
(1955 output equals 100)

Industry	Year	1956	1957	1958	1959	1960
1 Agriculture and foods		99.0	105.7	112.8	120.8	129.8
					(115.8)*	
2 Textile and leather		97.0	107.1	117.7	129.7	143.2
		(120.2)	(133.0)	(119.4)	(138.8)	
3 Lumber and products		106.7	122.0	134.1	147.8	163.2
					(122.4)	
4 Paper, printing, misc.		102.9	113.3	123.9	135.9	149.3
					(172.1)	
5 Chemical		102.3	112.8	123.9	136.4	150.5
		(120.8)	(142.0)	(147.3)	(164.1)	
6 Mining and metal		97.0	111.9	122.9	135.4	149.5
		(120.9)	(136.8)	(129.5)	(167.2)	
7 Machinery		89.0	116.0	128.4	142.5	158.2
		(110.7)	(136.9)	(162.3)	(250.6)	
8 Transportation equipment		90.8	100.9	113.0	126.7	142.2
					(234.4)	
9 Energy		141.8	114.7	125.0	136.6	149.7
					(170.2)	
10 Construction		109.3	135.4	150.3	167.1	186.2
					(173.4)	
11 Transport		103.5	113.5	124.1	136.0	149.5
					(152.6)	
12 Service and trade		102.4	112.5	122.6	134.0	146.8
					(158.9)	
Total output		102.1	112.4	122.6	135.0	146.9
					(155.3)	

* Figures in parentheses show the actual values.

where $D = (I - \bar{A})^{-1}B$. As is well known, a path of $z(t)$ which satisfies (10) is called a Leontief trajectory.

Now, let $(\lambda_1, \ldots, \lambda_n)$ be the characteristic roots of $(I + D^{-1})$, and $(h_1, \ldots, h_n)$ the corresponding characteristic vectors. Then, $\lambda_i = 1 + (1/\gamma_i)$ $(i = 1, \ldots, n)$. Clearly, λ_1 is the Neumann growth factor, and h_1, the Neumann output vector.

The general solution to (10) is given in the form

$$z(t) = \lambda_1^t \varepsilon_1 h_1 + \sum_{i \in I} \lambda_i^t \varepsilon_i h_i + \sum_{i \in J} \lambda_i^t \varepsilon_i h_i, \tag{11}$$

Table 3 (continued)

Shadow prices (Machine output)

Industry no. Year	1956	1957	1958	1959	1960
1	0	0.32706	0.68582	0.68508	0.61618
2	0	0.65689	0.65306	0.68087	0.60543
3	0	0.53333	0.69154	0.64750	0.57357
4	0	0.72752	0.67760	0.66380	0.58612
5	0	1.36817	0.72218	0.70380	0.62299
6	0	2.21552	0.69518	0.68348	0.60644
7	0	0.81924	0.89148	0.69667	0.61428
8	0	0.84424	0.83650	0.71038	0.62221
9	29.32626	0	0.77547	0.82066	0.69093
10	0.80127	0.89208	0.73000	0.65659	0.58387
11	0	0.07024	0.98014	0.92260	0.81579
12	0	0.33547	0.75466	0.68222	0.60694

where the subscripts $(2, \ldots, n)$ are divided into two groups, I and J, such that $|\lambda_i| < \lambda_1$ for any $i \in I$ and $|\lambda_i| > \lambda_1$ for any $i \in J$.

Now, according to the turnpike theorem, an efficient path of $z(t)$ which is the solution to (8) must satisfy (10) in the neighborhood of the turnpike except for certain periods at the beginning and at the end of the entire period. Therefore, if neither I nor J is an empty set, the following results will be obtained from our computations:

(a) In the initial periods, the efficient path of $z(t)$ is led to a point in the sub-space $R(h_1, h_i | i \in I)$ spanned by the vectors h_1 and h_i's $(i \in I)$. Therefore, disposal of products occurs in these periods.

(b) Thereafter, the efficient path follows the Leontief trajectory started from the above point, and in the terminal periods, it is led to the turnpike. Disposal of products occurs again in these periods.

The theoretical grounds of these expectations are as follows: the value losses are smaller when we lead $z(t)$ in (8) to a point in $R(h_1, h_i | i \in I)$ rather than to the turnpike. A Leontief trajectory, starting from a point in $R(h_1, h_i | i \in I)$, is relatively stable with respect to the turnpike, and thus approaches it relatively with the lapse of time. Therefore, remembering that there is no value loss on the Leontief trajectory, the value losses as a whole will be smaller if we first lead $z(t)$ to a point in $R(h_1, h_i | i \in I) - (a)-$then lead it to follow the Leontief trajectory started from that point, and finally, to the turnpike $-$(b).

Contrary to this theoretical expectation, our computational result shows that (b) does not occur, although (a) does, since the disposal of products only occurs in the initial periods (in periods 1 and 2). This is seen from the fact that the shadow price vectors in periods 1 (1956) and 2 (1957) contain zero components, but those in latter periods do not as shown in table 3. This can occur only if I is an empty set, i.e., $R(h_1, h_i | i \in I) = R(h_1)$. The following theorem is useful to confirm the emptiness of I; that is, $|\lambda_i| > \lambda_1$ $(i = 2, \ldots, n)$.

Relative instability theorem: The balanced growth in (10) is relatively; completely unstable, that is $|\lambda_i| > \lambda_i(i = 2, \ldots, n)$, if and only if there exists a (finite) positive integer m such that $(I + D^{-1})^{-m} > 0$.

Proof: The proof is similar to that of the author's relative stability theorem.

By computing $(I + D^{-1})^{-1}$ and $(I + D^{-1})^{-2}$, we found that although the former matrix contains seventeen negative components, the latter contains no non-positive component; that is, $(I + D^{-1})^{-2} > 0$ as shown in table 6. This implies, by the above theorem, that $|\lambda_i| > \lambda_1(i = 2, \ldots, n)$. Therefore, our expectation of the emptiness of I is shown to be correct.

Professor Leontief once computed the characteristic roots of matrix D using U.S. data. In this computation he chose several matrices of different ranks obtained by changing the level of aggregation. In every case, however, he found that $|\lambda_i| > \lambda_1$ $(i = 2, \ldots, n)$.

It would be rash to draw a general conclusion from these few examples for Japan and the United States. We suspect, however, that the balanced growth in the dynamic Leontief system (10) is, relatively, completely unstable in most cases under a common industrial classification. In our computation, relatively large components of the stock-flow matrix B are those of 6th, 7th, 10th, and 12th rows in every column. This implies that the absolute value of $|B|$ is relatively small, and thus the absolute value of every component of B^{-1} is relatively large — i.e., most components are far larger than unity. Hence, the characteristics of matrix $(I + D^{-1})$ will be similar to those of matrix D^{-1} which is the inverse of positive matrix D (here we must remember that the balanced growth in the system $z(t+1) = D^{-1}z(t)$ is, relatively, completely unstable). The general resolution of this problem, however, depends on further investigation.

5. Comparison of actual and computed values

The 1959 actual value of output of every industry was computed through aggregation from the 35-order input–output table of 1959 in 1955 prices. This was the latest year for which we could obtain an input–output table. For Industries 2, 5, 6, and 7, we estimated the respective values of outputs in intermediate years by interpolation using the production indices (fig. 2). Although this procedure may produce some errors in estimation — since the production indices are computed by using, as the weights in aggregation,

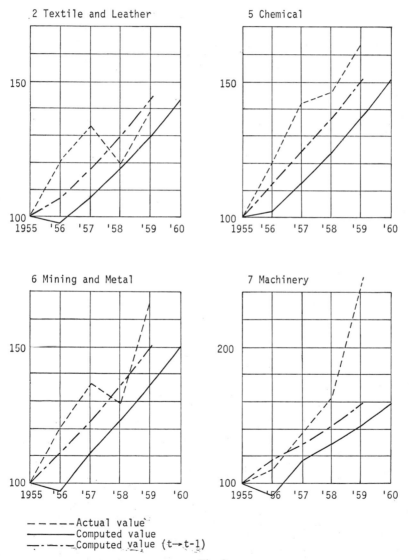

Fig. 2.

Table 4

1955 Input–Output matrix A

Industry	1	2	3	4	5	6	7	8	9	10	11	12	f(y('55))	Invest.	Total output
1 Agriculture and foods	*36963	7613	511	482	4999	193	47	28	70	830	64	6468	**2302.5	**119.7	**4630.9
2 Textile and leather	451	48141	386	2430	1537	642	470	792	223	252	502	434	685.9	57.1	1638.1
3 Lumber and products	609	269	39081	5592	735	898	784	3393	1684	15638	682	1344	63.2	7.2	802.7
4 Paper, printing, misc.	786	2570	660	34297	789	866	1614	339	612	1089	926	4055	283.6	5.4	954.9
5 Chemical	3053	3474	1159	4754	23780	1237	1991	7860	1294	1096	900	1584	136.2	9.8	748.1
6 Miming and metal	885	421	1595	3163	4344	38618	32638	27481	1906	29417	1260	735	188.9	102.3	1916.0
7 Machinery	654	1062	523	964	1497	1858	16082	16370	2894	4297	784	664	108.9	143.0	638.0
8 Transportation equipment	456	37	174	42	107	141	110	4156	167	733	4861	703	123.3	105.4	353.7
9 Energy	1078	1856	1208	3121	8261	6482	1771	2064	15013	770	12897	1188	120.0	-1.2	718.7
10 Construction	1147	861	1009	964	1511	919	988	509	7486	563	9631	3464	518.6	407.5	1349.9
11 Transport	898	611	486	1131	2045	1702	956	1187	3423	3185	13399	918	432.1	5.3	777.7
12 Service and trade	4844	4414	2654	8420	10400	2975	6238	5513	2588	4941	10004	14540	3298.6	40.8	4791.6
Non-competing imports	*1116	9083	37	2995	4986	397	63	0	15514	0	0	23			
Value added	47060	19590	50517	31647	35009	43053	36270	30308	47127	37188	44092	63881			

* Coefficient units: 10⁻⁵.

** Final demand and total output units: 1 billion yen.

Table 5

1955 Stock-flow matrix *B*

Industry	1	2	3	4	5	6	7	8	9	10	11	12
1 Agriculture and foods	*8892	3370	199	73	2005	141	16	0	14	82	13	647
2 Textile and leather	160	2350	150	241	615	506	188	198	28	30	64	65
3 Lumber and products	158	147	772	1079	374	569	408	961	320	1622	257	380
4 Paper, printing, misc.	151	1142	262	1770	321	485	611	85	97	111	90	426
5 Chemical	587	1538	449	639	5908	851	768	2036	195	111	90	159
6 Mining and metal	218	226	685	388	1831	3299	12618	7238	390	3030	424	463
7 Machinery	5498	9078	4921	5885	14597	11602	16379	16737	46668	1459	7741	5952
8 Transportation equipment	2838	202	1159	189	602	783	721	2234	1127	1452	47615	1933
9 Energy	207	824	473	702	3302	4530	674	537	334	74	1286	119
10 Construction	40143	6648	19609	4597	12699	9932	10125	13486	102393	1237	203395	62491
11 Transport	266	110	75	73	174	141	172	141	571	30	669	113
12 Service and trade	2641	1643	1221	1110	2754	2156	2508	2431	8473	711	15713	1726
Total	61759	27276	29974	16745	45181	34995	45188	46084	160609	9349	277356	74472

* Coefficient units: 10^{-5}.

Table 6

Matrix $(I+D^{-1})^{-1}$

Industry no.	1	2	3	4	5	6	7	8	9	10	11	12
1	*2435	950	629	312	1020	548	801	829	3210	192	5657	1682
2	751	713	389	232	551	412	522	538	1925	116	3400	969
3	360	—58	312	150	—54	1	—58	97	1012	210	2342	833
4	415	324	235	359	282	242	350	283	1096	72	1855	585
5	365	309	191	154	879	223	267	436	726	59	1491	372
6	596	15	477	91	290	498	1976	1339	2510	397	4391	1348
7	60	610	231	404	886	672	1114	1194	3464	24	—1375	23
8	118	—32	42	—12	—22	21	—15	137	—298	131	4137	—17
9	242	189	168	143	545	629	250	238	631	46	1214	306
10	851	—670	510	—351	—941	—750	—1020	—737	2668	—356	6783	2641
11	375	119	187	81	203	152	228	234	1010	45	1807	519
12	2188	907	1084	597	1423	1015	1518	1569	6046	353	10651	2735

Matrix $(I+D^{-1})^{-2}$

Industry no.	1	2	3	4	5	6	7	8	9	10	11	12
1	*1458	652	637	356	992	730	921	951	3369	207	5865	1587
2	710	332	344	196	527	408	518	529	1833	115	3175	849
3	412	136	194	93	228	184	205	220	986	52	1901	523
4	409	193	201	120	305	238	307	311	1082	67	1824	494
5	337	164	163	95	281	188	249	265	849	57	1552	396
6	789	379	426	255	654	534	701	736	2566	131	3819	1006
7	218	203	160	136	405	366	384	381	887	76	1351	283
8	185	39	85	26	60	37	80	87	453	17	910	257
9	278	123	147	79	224	171	285	265	784	61	1342	365
10	933	323	395	208	537	448	391	419	1925	118	3795	1025
11	341	150	163	92	249	196	239	246	868	53	1507	402
12	1979	884	953	541	1472	1153	1416	1454	5095	313	8820	2352

* Figure units: 10^{-4}.

value added contrary to the output — these errors seem not to be so large as to make our comparison of actual and computed values meaningless.

A significant point which we can notice from fig. 2 and table 3 is that the actual values are larger than the computed, except for Industries 1 and 3. This will be explained mainly by a rapid growth and a high rate of investment in periods 1956 to 1959 (except 1958)[6]. The interesting thing, however, is the adjustment of output levels to the turnpike which occurred in 1958. We can also notice that the discrepancies between the computed and the actual values become very small[7] if we compare the former in a year with the latter in the previous year (see the chain lines in fig. 2). This way of comparison is appropriate since, in our computation, the stock–flow matrix B is estimated under the assumption of normal rates of utilization of productive capacities.[8] Thus the output levels can be increased without new additions to capital equipment until the full capacity levels are attained. The change of output level from 1955 to 1956 is very small in every industry, and the computed output levels in 1957 are, undoubtedly, attainable in 1956 (see table 3). In this respect we shall also mention that, in our model, the unused products in periods 1 and 2 are assumed to be disposed of − see the shadow prices in table 3 − and therefore the inclusion of stock activities in the model will increase somewhat the computed values.

After due consideration of this sort, however, and of the higher investment rate in 1956 and successive years, we may still conclude from our computational results that, from 1955 to 1959 (and, probably, in successive years), the Japanese economy has grown with a very high efficiency that would be difficult to attain even under intensive central planning.

6. Concluding remarks

Compared to many remarkable achievements in the theoretical field of multisectoral analysis of economic growth in recent years, few empirical applications have been attempted. Undoubtedly, one of the main difficulties in their application concerns the availability of necessary data, especially those of stocks. Such data as input–output and stock-flow tables in advanced economies are very useful for the generalization of our type of analysis to include the problem of technological progress. At the present stage, however,

[6] The rates of investment for fixed capital in periods 1955 to 1959 are as follows: 11.2 % (1955), 14.5 % (1956), 14.5 % (1957), 14.6 % (1958), 16.5 % (1959).

[7] The exceptions are Industries 7 and 8. The domestic production of consumers' durable goods of reliable quality started in 1955 − T.V. sets, washing machines, and electric refrigerators in Industry 7, and automobiles in Industry 8. Since then, demand for these products has increased explosively. This increase of demands was so rapid that our simple extrapolation of the past trend has produced underestimations for the output levels of Industries 7 and 8.

[8] The base year rates of capacity utilization are assumed to be normal. They are about 0.75 in every industry.

there is the further, very difficult problem concerning the comparability of the tables of different countries, even if they are available. Another possible way to obtain the information about new technologies may, perhaps, be from technical data.

We hope that the necessary data becomes available in the near future so that a more detailed analysis of economic growth will be possible.

Further development of the model: addendum

The model presented in this paper has, recently, been generalized in many respects by Professors Y. Murakami, K. Tokoyama, and the author under a project of the Economic Planning Agency of the Japanese Government.

As the first generalization, the final demand function $f(y)$ was allowed to be a non-linear function of income y. As an example, the following type of piece-wise linear function was built in the model [2].

$$f(y) = \bar{c} + c^1 y^1 + c^2 y^2$$
$$y = y^1 + y^2$$
$$y^2 = 0 \quad \text{if} \quad y \leqq \bar{y}$$
$$y^1 = \bar{y} \quad \text{if} \quad y > \bar{y},$$

where $\bar{c}$, c^1 and c^2 are constant non-negative vectors.

It is shown in this particular case that the two different turnpikes — each corresponding to one of the two different marginal consumption coefficients: c^1 and c^2 — are asymptotically connected by a full capacity path and produce a new bent-turnpike, and that every optimal path spends most of the programming period in the neighborhood of this bent-turnpike [4].

As the second generalization, the possibility of technological change was introduced into the model by assuming that the input–output and the stock-flow matrices (A and B) are both variables of time t written as A^t and B^t [3].

The similar generalization was attained by assuming the existence of two different technologies or two different set of matrices (A, B) and (A^N, B^N), – the former representing the technology used at present and the latter, the possible new one [7]. In parallel with new technology, both the labor constraint and the research and development activity which would affect the efficiency of labor were introduced into the model [7]. With this type of generalized model, we could not only find an optimal path of accumulation, but also an optimal sequence of technological change (or switching) among industries — from the present technology to the possible new one.

Along with these generalizations of the so-called final state turnpike model, the consumption turnpike model [6] was built and tested based on the consumption turnpike theory [5]. The main finding in this case is that, under a certain restriction on technological possibility, the optimal path is rather stable or invariable with respect to the change of time discount rate of future consumption [6].

In addition to these major improvements, several minor improvements were added to the model, such as the introduction of stock activity and the endogenous treatment of import–export activity.

A large scale model of 56 industrial sectors was recently tested in the Economic Planning Agency. An interesting finding in this testing is that the system is still relatively completely unstable, that is, the absolute values of all 55 characteristic roots $\lambda_2, \lambda_3, \ldots, \lambda_{55}$ of the matrix $(I+B^{-1}(I-\bar{A}))$ are greater than the Von Neumann (turnpike) growth factor λ_1.

It may be said in conclusion that the turnpike model is more flexible than expected in looking at the basic model presented in this paper. Even the environmental constraints and the pollution control processes are going to be built in the model in the recent work of the Economic Planning Agency.

References

[1] Chenery, H. B., and T. Watanabe, 1958, International Comparisons of the Structure of Production, Econometrica, vol. 26, no. 4, 1958, pp. 487–521.

[2] Council For Industry Planning, 1958, Capital Structure of the Japanese Economy, Tokyo.

[3] Murakami, Y., K. Tokoyama and J. Tsukui, 1969, Efficient path of accumulation and the turnpike of the Japanese economy, A. P. Carter and A. Brody (eds.), Application of Input–Output Analysis, Amsterdam: North-Holland Publishing Company.

[4] Tsukui, J., 1972, Optimal path in a non-linear dynamic input–output system — A generalization of the turnpike model, A. Brody and A. P. Carter (eds.), Input–Output Techniques, Amsterdam: North-Holland Publishing Company.

[5] Tsukui, J., 1967, The consumption and the output turnpike theorems in a Von Neumann type of model — a finite term problem, The Review of Economic Studies, 34, No. 1.

[6] Tsukui, J. and Y. Murakami, 1971, Change of time discount rate and stability of optimal growth path, mimeographed paper presented at the Fifth International Conference on Input–Output Techniques, Geneva.

[7] Tsukui, J. and Y. Nakamura, 1972, Optimal program of structural change, mimeographed paper presented at the Rokko Conference, Kobe, Japan.

PART II

LINEAR PLANNING MODELS OVER SPACE AND TIME

A. SPATIAL PROGRAMMING MODELS

CHAPTER 12

Optimal transportation patterns of single commodities in capacitated networks

L. J. KING, E. CASETTI and C. C. KISSLING*

1. Introduction

Studies of the flows and movements of persons and goods continue to provide an important avenue of research for economic geographers whose concern is with the spatial organization of economic activity. Until recently, most of the studies completed along these lines emphasized descriptions of the existing trade and flow patterns, witness for example, the works of Ullman [18] and Taaffe [17]. By contrast, some more recent studies, also by geographers, have been normative in character and at least suggestive of bases for particular planning programs. Examples of this 'new' concern on the part of economic geographers are provided by Morrill and Garrison's study of wheat trade in the United States [14], Casetti's analysis of the Canadian iron and steel industry [3], Gould and Leinbach's study of the optimal organization of hospital service areas [8], and Gauthier's study of commodity flow patterns in Brazil [7].

This present paper, in its emphases, accords well with this new interest in economic geography. The two analyses reported on in the paper were concerned with the determination of optimal transportation patterns for particular commodities on networks having capacity constraints. The first problem involved the transportation patterns of bituminous coal throughout the Great Lakes region in the United States, while the second focussed on the movements of certain perishable fruits throughout New

* McMaster University, Hamilton, Ontario; The Ohio State University, Columbus, Ohio; and The University of Canterbury, Christchurch, New Zealand.

Zealand.[1] In both cases, the problem as noted above, was to determine optimal transportation patterns and this was achieved using the particular form of network flow analysis presented by Fulkerson [6] in his Out-of-Kilter Algorithm (hereafter referred to as OKA). The results of the two studies were intended to provide the bases for planning programs but for reasons that are elaborated upon later, these applications of the results were not pursued very far.

The first main section of this paper presents a brief review of the OKA. The two analyses are then reported on in detail and this involves also a discussion of certain modifications of the OKA which were demanded by the problems at hand. Finally, an attempt is made to evaluate the usefulness of the findings and to comment on possible extensions of the work.

2. The Out – of – Kilter Algorithm and the modelling of commodity flows

The Out-of-Kilter Algorithm involves a form of network flow analysis. As developed by Fulkerson [6] the algorithm is particularly suited to solving a sequence of flow problems which differ only slightly from each other. The optimal flows solution of each problem in such a sequence initiates the computation for the following problem, and as a result the solution time of each successive problem is only a small fraction of the time that would be required to solve it separately. For each successive problem only the information concerning the differences of that problem from the preceding one need be provided.

Basically, there are two types of situations that can be handled by the OKA model. In the context of commodity flow studies, the first type of problem would assume that a commodity in question is required in specified amounts at a set of destination nodes; that the commodity is available at a set of origin nodes; that for each origin there is a maximum amount of the commodity that it can provide; that the sum of the maximum amounts available at the set of origins exceeds the sum of the amounts required at

---

[1] These analyses have already been reported on separately elsewhere, namely in King *et al.* [10] and Sinclair and Kissling [16]. Grateful acknowledgement is made of the permissions granted by our earlier co-authors and the editors of Economic Geography and The New Zealand Geographical Society to reproduce in this paper extensive sections of these two earlier publications. Both studies made use of the Rand Corporation computer program for the OKA algorithm; Dr. H. Gauthier of Ohio State University kindly made available his copy of this program.

the set of destinations; and finally, that the origins and the destinations are embedded in a network which includes also nodes that are neither origins nor destinations, has pairs of nodes connected by one or more directed arcs (each admitting a flow in one direction only), and has specified for each arc a transportation cost, an upper capacity, and a lower capacity.

The second type of problem differs from the first in that it involves only nodes that are either origins or destinations and only arcs connecting origins to destinations. That is to say, intermediate nodes and the related transportation arcs are not considered.

In both problems, the aim is to determine a set of flows through the arcs that involves a minimum total cost; that makes available at the various destinations the amounts required there; that involves shipments from the various origins equal to or smaller than the amounts of the commodity available; and that does not violate the capacity limitations on the transportation arcs. In fact, by identifying optimal flows, the solutions to these problems indirectly determine which origins ship to capacity, which ones export less than they have available, and which ones, if any, are 'inactive'.

The second type of problem is a special case of the first and, therefore, no generality is lost by discussing the application of the OKA to the first type of problem.

In order to determine by the OKA the set of minimal cost flows that satisfy the demands and yet do not violate the various capacity constraints of such network problems, it is necessary to reformulate the problems as follows. Two new nodes are added and called the *dummy destination* and the *dummy origin*. Each destination is connected to the dummy destination by a directed arc which is given a cost of zero, an unlimited upper capacity, and a lower capacity equal to the amount of the commodity required at the destination. The dummy origin, in turn, is connected to all the origins by directed arcs which have zero transportation costs, upper capacities equal to the maximum amounts that the origins can provide, and lower capacities of zeros. Associated with each of the other arcs in the network there will be given the cost of one unit of flow along the arc, an upper bound on the amount of flow along the arc, and a lower bound on the amount of flow along the arc. In the case of arcs connecting origins to destinations the upper bounds are set also at an arbitrary large number which is the computational equivalent of unlimited upper capacity. An arc connecting the dummy destination to the dummy origin with zero costs, unlimited upper capacity, and zero lower capacity 'closes' the network. Consequently, the original problem involving the determination of the optimal flows from a set of origins to a set of destinations is translated into a problem of determining a set of optimal circular flows. The lower bound on each destination-dummy destination arc ensures that the destination receives an inflow equal to its demand. The upper bound on each dummy origin-origin arc guarantees that no origin has an outflow greater than the amount of the commodity available there. The arcs linking destinations to the dummy destination and the dummy origin to the origins carry zero costs and consequently do not influence the optimal flows within the original network. Hence, the solution to the reformulated problem is also an optimal solution for the original problem.

The OKA solution yields the flows that minimize total cost defined as $\sum_{ij} c_{ij} x_{ij}$ for all i and j, where c_{ij} is the transportation cost on the i-jth arc. The solution is subject to the constraints, $l_{ij} \leqq x_{ij} \leqq u_{ij}$ for all i and j, where l_{ij} and u_{ij} are the lower and upper capacities of the i-jth arc, and $\sum_j x_{ji} - \sum_j x_{ij} = 0$ for all i, which establishes the circulation principle that what flows into a node must also leave it. The solution gives 'net arc costs' which are the overall costs to the system of one unit of flow on any arc in question. It also provides 'node prices' which in effect are shadow prices for a unit of the flow commodity at the different nodes.

In the applications of the OKA which are presented in the next section of this paper, some modification of the basic model discussed above was necessitated by the requirement that storage be allowed at certain nodes. This modification is discussed at the appropriate point in the following section.

3. *Bituminous coal flows in the Great Lakes region*

3.1.

The study area included the bituminous coal producing areas and the coal receiving centers of the midwest and Great Lakes region of the United States and Canada. The area extended from southern Kentucky to the northernmost extension of the Great Lakes, and roughly from Harrisburg, Pennsylvania in the east to Minneapolis-St. Paul in the west. The major coal receiving centers on the Atlantic seaboard were excluded.

The major generalized rail-routes included the routeways from western Pennsylvania to the southern shores of Lake Erie (the Baltimore and Ohio, and Bessemer and Lake Erie lines); northern West Virginia to the southern shores of Lake Erie (the Baltimore and Ohio line); central West Virginia to the southern shores of Lake Erie (the Chesapeake and Ohio, and New

York Central lines): southern West Virginia and Kentucky to the southern shores of Lake Erie (the Norfolk and Western, and Louisville and Nashville lines); southern Illinois to the Chicago area (the Illinois Central line); and finally, Kentucky and southern Indiana to the Chicago area (the Chicago and Eastern Illinois line).

The major Great Lakes movements of coal originated in the eastern sections of the region. Mayer [13] showed, in fact, that this eastern dominance allows the midwestern mines to dominate coal markets in the lakes area only as far north as Milwaukee.

In the study, some 104 transportation routes for which rates were readily available, were considered. This set of routes excluded barge movements for which no rates were available, and it considered lake movements only in combination with rail shipments. That is to say, the 104 routes or transportation arcs were either rail links or rail–lake routes.

For the analysis, each coal producing area or coal receiving center was treated as a node. In the case of the coal producing areas, the regional groupings given in the Keystone Manual (1968) were used to define the nodes. These coal districts corresponded in most cases with the rate districts used by the railroads serving the areas, and for any one such district the railroads charge a single rate for all coal shipments originating at points within the district.[2]

The node identified with each coal producing region was the major transportation center within the region. The productive capacity of each node was defined as the sum of the bituminous coal shipments for 1963 from the counties included in the region, as published in the Census of Mineral Industries [4, p. 43]. No attempt was made to differentiate the coal produced according to its grade. For the later testing of the model, only 15 composite nodes were used to represent the coal-mining districts (table 1).

There are two points which should be noted with respect to this aggregation. First, the three nodes of Clearfield, Broadtop, and Blossburg in central Pennsylvania were excluded from the analysis since these centers were too far away from any other production center to be grouped with it, and transportation rates were not available for them. Second, Pittsburgh's own demand for coal was subtracted from the coal capacity for Pittsburgh and only the balance entered the transportation network.

Two major sources of coal demand were considered, thermal-electric generating plants, and the coking ovens of the steel industry. Together these

---

[2] The coal producing regions in Illinois and Indiana were modified somewhat from their definition in the Keystone Manual for closer correspondence with the rate groups.

Table 1

Aggregated coal nodes

Node	Capacity (1000 tons)
C1 Butler (includes Freeport)	8 941
C2 Pittsburgh	392
C3 Connellsville (includes Somerset)	12 882
C4 Moundsville	6 644
C5 Fairmont (includes Preston, Randolph)	24 233
C6 Kanawha (includes Nicholas)	31 950
C7 Pocahontas (includes Logan Williamson, Raleigh)	76 569
C8 East Kentucky (includes Elkorn, Hazard, Harlan, Middlesboro)	22 016
C9 Ohio 8 (includes Leetonia, Cambridge)	26 444
C10 Middle (Ohio)	5 427
C11 South Ohio	2 832
C12 Princeton (includes West Kentucky, Boonville)	32 697
C13 Terre Haute (includes Danville, Sullivan)	1 992
C14 Belleville (includes Centralia, Southern Illinois)	10 718
C15 Peoria (includes Springfield, La Salle)	7 891

two sets of customers used approximately three-quarters of the coal consumed in the region.[3] Only utility plants with an installed capacity greater than 100 000 kW were considered; for these plants data were available from the National Coal Association [15, pp. 3–41] on their locations and the amounts of coal used in 1966. Data on the Canadian utilities were provided by Beier and Heskett [2]. A total of 139 utility plants were covered by the study.

The coking ovens, as listed by the American Iron and Steel Institute [1] were found at 21 different locations in the study area and all of these were

---

[3] See, U.S. Bureau of Mines. Minerals Yearbook, 1966. Vol. II, Fuels. Washington: Government Printing Office, 1967, p. 620.

included. The amounts of coal used at these locations were estimated as follows. The number of ovens per location was known; the capacity of ovens at the different locations was assumed uniform and hence an average production level per oven per year could be obtained by dividing total annual regional coke production by the total number of ovens — this yielded a level of 4500 tons of coke; it was assumed that the weight of coke produced at each oven was three-fourths the weight of the coal charge and thus, annual coal demand per oven should be around 6000 tons; finally, annual coal demand per coking oven center was obtained by multiplying this level of 6000 tons by the number of ovens at the center.

The utility plants and coking-oven centers were first aggregated into 82 receiving nodes. Small receivers were grouped with large ones so long as there were no marked differences in the coal transportation rates applicable to the centers in question. These 82 nodes then were aggregated further into the 19 major centers listed in table 2.

Table 2

Coal receiving nodes

		Demand (1000 tons)
R1	Toronto	3532
R2	Buffalo	3021
R3	Detroit	9935
R4	Milwaukee	2802
R5	Green Bay	938
R6	Duluth	1026
R7	Chicago	35 297
R8	Toledo	2054
R9	Cleveland	5106
R10	Cincinnati	3119
R11	Youngstown	2012
R12	Steubenville	3083
R13	Beverly, Ohio	2485
R14	Cheshire, Ohio	5685
R15	Dayton	2314
R16	Canton	186
R17	Erie	658
R18	Dunkirk, New York	1367
R19	Rochester	679

As regards transportation rates, the study used volume and trainload rates which apply to most major coal shipments. In a few cases, carload rates had to be used. For each route, the lowest rate for coal shipments was applied. This ensured a consistent basis for the application of rates although it was not completely realistic since all shipments did not meet the volume or trainload requirements for the lowest rates. The rail rates used were those which were in effect between September 1, 1962 and August 19, 1967.[4]

A few characteristics of the rate structure for coal shipments are worth stressing in the context of this study. First, the rates reflect competition and are not related simply to distance of haul. The volume and unit train rates, especially, have been established consistent with the particular marketing strategies of the companies involved. Second, in the case of volume rates particularly, there are a number of attached conditions regarding minimum trainloads, annual volumes, and in some cases, demurrage charges, which affect the utilization of the service. Finally, rates for rail-hauls to the lake ports are differentiated according to the ultimate destination of the coal. For example, the rate for coal shipments from Connellsville to the port of Conneaut, assuming the coal ultimately goes to Buffalo by lake vessels, was higher than the corresponding rates for Toronto and Green Bay as final destinations, but lower than those for Detroit and Milwaukee as final destinations. This third feature of the rate structure was an overriding consideration in structuring the coal network flow problem. As was noted in the above section, the model can be structured in terms of origins, desti-nations, and intermediate nodes. But in this analysis intermediate nodes such as the lake ports hardly warranted consideration as such, and the network was best handled as a set of only origins and destinations. The costs on the connecting cars represented the sum of the special rail rates and the estimated lake carrier rates. One problem with this approach was that the model solution could result in a port capacity being violated. However, this can be taken care of in the model as will be noted later.

The charges for coal hauling via lake carriers are contractual agreements, and there were no published rates. One piece of available information was that an 83 ¢ per ton lakecarrier charge was included in a rail-lake combined rate offered to Duluth. This was probably an unusually low vessel charge, but it was used as the basis for estimating lake carrier costs as a direct function of distance (table 3). Dumping charges which were levied at some ports were not taken into account in these estimates.

---

[4] The rate information was generously provided by officers of the Bessemer and Lake Erie Railroad, Pittsburgh, and the Elgin, Joliet, and Eastern Railroad, Chicago. The rail rates used are at ex parte 223 level. This level was in effect between September 1, 1962 and August 19, 1967, and was used because most published rates were at this ex parte level.

Table 3

Estimated lake carrier charges (¢ per ton)

Destinations	Chicago	Ports Conneaut	Ashtabula	Lorain	Sandusky	Toledo
Duluth		83	83	83	83	83
Milwaukee	60	110	110	110	100	100
Green Bay	70	100	100	100	90	90
Detroit		40	40	40	30	30
Toronto		60	60	70	70	70
Buffalo		35				
Toledo		35		30	30	

3.2. Selected solutions to the model of coal shipments

The coal flow problem was first solved as a single regimen problem without the possibility of seasonal storage at the Great Lakes ports. The problem was then reformulated as a spatial-temporal transportation network problem and solved for three different levels of storage costs.

The results for a single regimen transportation system, which is simply the summer regimen operated on a year-long basis, are shown in table 4.

Table 4

Least-cost allocation of coal flows, single regimen (millions of tons)

Nodes*	C1	C2	C3	C4	C5	C6	C7	C8	C9	C10	C11	C12	C13	C14	C15
R1	3.03														
R2	3.02														
R3									9.94						
R4													0.05		2.75
R5									0.94						
R6	1.03														
R7												29.22	0.94		5.14
R8	1.36								0.37	0.32					
R9										5.11					
R10								3.12							
R11		0.39							1.62						
R12									3.08						
R13									2.48						
R14						2.85						2.83			
R15					2.31										
R16									0.19						
R17						0.66									
R18					1.37										
R19									0.68						

Identifying codes are given in tables 1–2.

Four coal nodes (Butler, Pittsburgh, Middle, and South Ohio) operated at full capacity, whereas four others (Connellsville, Moundsville, Pocahontas, and Belleville) were completely inactive. Coal nodes in the mid-continent section (Princeton, Terre Haute, Belleville, and Peoria) served only the Chicago and Milwaukee nodes, whereas coal producing nodes in the eastern section were able to capture the remainder of the lake coal markets. This finding was in accord with Mayer's results noted earlier.

It was possible to perform a variety of sensitivity analyses on the model by changing transportation costs and deleting different nodes. These results, however, are not reported here but instead attention is given to the problem of storage and seasonal regimens and the modifications which these features require in the model.

Coal flows in the Great Lakes area take place under two distinct regimens, the first corresponding to the months when the lakes are navigable (summer regimen), and the second to those when the lakes are not navigable (winter regimen). During the summer the coal moves through a network which includes railroad and lake routes, but in winter only the more costly railroad network is available. The existence of two transportation regimens involving higher costs for the winter makes it convenient in many cases to collect coal at storage points, either at the destinations where coal received in the summer is reserved for winter use, or at the origins or lake ports where coal mined in the winter is stored for shipment during the summer. If optimal coal flows were to be determined in a network which involved two regimens and the possibility of storage, then a spatial-temporal transportation or transhipment format had to be adopted. Kriebel [12] and King and Henry [11] have also discussed the general problem of intertemporal optimal flows.

Storage was viewed as a flow through time and was handled in a manner identical to flows through space. The points in time were identified as nodes, and storage costs and capacities were associated with the flows through time. Since flows through space and flows through time were expressed in mathematically identical terms, they could in fact be handled simultaneously.

Again, data considerations precluded the analysis of the intertemporal situation as one involving transhipments through intermediate nodes. As was noted earlier, volume rail rates for the movement of coal to lake ports differed only according to the ultimate destination of coal and it was not possible, therefore, to consider intermediate nodes and associated transportation routes. This was unfortunate since large amounts of coal are stored, in fact, at the Great Lakes ports.

In the analysis, each node was separated into a winter node and a summer node and the supplies at the coal origins and the demands at the destinations were divided equally between these winter and summer nodes. The possibility of storage was allowed by placing an arc between the winter and summer nodes at each origin or destination.

The rate on each arc that involved a lake shipment was doubled for the winter period. Rates on all-rail shipments remained the same during the winter. The solution for 50 ¢ per ton storage charges is presented in table 5. Storage of coal received in the summer took place at Toronto (1 766 000 tons), Buffalo (1 510 000 tons), Detroit (4 967 000 tons), and Duluth (513 000 tons), and there was no storage at any of the origins.

Table 5

Least-cost allocation of coal flows* for dual regimen, 50 ¢ storage costs (millions of tons)

Nodes	C1	C2	C3	C4	C5	C6	C7	C8	C9	C10	C11	C12	C13	C14	C15
R1	3.53														
R2	0.94			2.08											
R3									9.93				0.50		0.90
R4													(0.50)		(0.90)
R5					1.15 (1.15)					0.16		0.31			(0.47)
R6			1.03												
R7												14.07 (15.08)			3.04 (2.57)
R8	(1.03)			1.03											
R9										2.55 (2.55)					
R10									1.56 (1.56)						
R11	(1.01)	0.20	0.74							0.07					
R12										1.54 (1.54)					
R13										1.24 (1.24)					
R14					1.43 (1.43)							1.42 (1.42)			
R15															
R16										0.09 (0.09)					
R17	(0.33)					0.33									
R18			(0.68)	0.68											
R19			(0.34)							0.34					

* Figures n parentheses are winter shipments; others are summer shipments.

Apparently, some of the origin nodes which had more favorable rates were able to ship during the summer an entire year's supply of coal to receiving nodes where coal was then stored for the winter. During the winter, the producing nodes served a different set of receiving nodes. Accordingly, some nodes were active only during the summer and others shipped less coal during the winter than they shipped during the summer. For example, Butler shipped its entire summer production to Toronto and Buffalo, and during the winter shipped to Toledo, Youngstown, and Erie. During the summer, Toledo was supplied from Moundsville, while Youngstown received coal from Pittsburgh, Connellsville, and Ohio 8, and Erie was supplied from Kanawha.

When storage costs were lowered to 25 ¢ per ton the storage at destinations remained the same. One instance of storage at an origin occurred: Butler stored 2 633 000 tons of winter coal for summer use. This allowed Butler to expand its dominance of the lake coal market, controlling all supplies to Buffalo and part of the supply to Detroit (table 6).

As a further sensitivity test of the model another variation on storage cost was considered. At 10 ¢ per ton storage costs even more coal was stored at Butler and some coal was also stored at another origin, Middle (150 000 tons). As a result, Middle increased its summer shipments to Green Bay at the expense of Princeton.

The analysis of coal flows in the Great Lakes region in the manner outlined above, did yield significant insights into the spatial organization of this particular transportation system. The study, of course, was not without its limitations and three of these in particular are worth noting since the analysis reported on in the next section of the paper tackled at least two of these issues directly.

First, the point has been made that the storage question could not be treated adequately in view of data limitations. By contrast, in the fruit distribution problem discussed below, the data were such that intermediate nodes could indeed be considered as storage points and had this been possible in the coal problem the results would have been even more meaningful. Second, variations in haulage rates other than on the storage arcs in the model would have emphasized further how sensitive flow patterns are to transportation costs. Rate structures do not simply reflect distance of haul. Rather they reflect competition and the marketing strategies of the companies involved. Where volume rates apply there are often the attached conditions regarding minimum train-loads, annual volumes, and demurrage charges, which reflect the utilization of the service. In a situation such as this, where many firms independently make decisions on levels of service

Table 6

Least-cost allocation of coal flows* for dual regimen, 25 ¢ storage costs (millions of tons)

Nodes	C1	C2	C3	C4	C5	C6	C7	C8	C9	C10	C11	C12	C13	C14	C15
R1	3.53														
R2	3.02														
R3	0.55								9.38						
R4													0.50 (0.50)		0.90 (0.90)
R5										0.16					(0.47)
R6			1.03									0.31			
R7												14.67 (15.08)	(2.57)		3.04
R8	(1.03)			1.03											
R9															
R10								1.56 (1.56)	2.55 (2.55)						
R11	(0.81)	0.20 (0.20)	0.19						0.62						
R12									1.54 (1.54)						
R13									1.24 (1.24)						
R14							1.43 (1.43)		1.42 (1.42)						
R15						1.15 (1.15)									
R16									0.09 (0.09)						
R17							0.33 (0.33)								
R18				(0.68)	0.68										
R19				(0.34)					0.34						

* Figures in parentheses are winter shipments; others are summer shipments.

to be offered, it is perhaps not surprising that transportation researchers find considerable difficulty in ascertaining actual freight rate agreements, for in a highly competitive market, small shifts in rates may induce considerable changes in actual flow patterns. Finally, related to the previous point is the obvious fact that the study ignored company organization and hence both the analysis and the results were too aggregated to be of immediate use to any one company or organization. This generalization was, of course, intentional and in no way does it detract from the potential value of such modelling and analysis to any one decision-making unit.

4. Fruit distribution in New Zealand

Calculation of system-wide transportation efficiency in terms of minimal total transportation costs naturally is of great interest to an agency which has complete responsibility for distribution of the commodity involved. The New Zealand Apple and Pear Marketing Board is one such agency which is responsible for the orderly marketing of all orchardist's fruit that has been inspected and accepted by the Department of Agriculture. The Board must ensure that local market requirements are supplied with acceptable quality fruit over as long a period of each year as is possible, and must also arrange in advance of the harvesting season the shipping program for overseas exports. About 75 % of New Zealand's annual crop comes from two regions and harvesting extends over a period of approximately four months, the peaks differing for each district. Hence, for this perishable commodity, cool-storage space is required along with a complex marketing framework to ensure adequate supply at the large number of markets throughout New Zealand.

The formulation of this problem in a way that could be handled by the OKA involved the following considerations. Fruit moves from individual orchards to a series of inspection depots located in the fruitgrowing districts. There are 12 of these in the system and each one was represented by a node in the network. Once accepted, the fruit passes to a cool-store either for long-term or short-term storage. Each of the 18 cool-stores in the system was represented by two nodes in the model, one to represent the entry to a cool-store and the other the exit. The connecting arc capacity parameters defined the cool-store capacity. From the cool-stores, 29 local markets and nine export ports are served. Again, each of these involved a node except that in order to define export port loading capacities, the port nodes were doubled, as in the case of the cool-stores, with each connecting arc defining port handling capacity. Receipts at depot nodes for the time period under consideration (a week), were entered by setting the upper and lower capacities equal to the requisite amount on the dummy arcs connecting them from the supply node. Likewise, weekly demands by local merchants and/or export ports were entered in the model by setting the upper and lower capacities of the dummy arcs leading from these nodes to the final demand node. An arc from the final demand node to the supply node completed the network in circulation form as required by the algorithm.

To ensure that the conservation of flow constraints were met and to permit the storage of excess supply over demand, additional dummy arcs connected each cool-store directly with the final demand node. Any flow over these arcs would be equivalent to the amount of fruit left in the cool-store in question. Fruit could also be moved between cool-stores. For each successive time period (week), in addition to supplies of new fruit entering the system through the depots, fruit being held in storage had also to be re-entered into the system and made available to serve the new local market or export port demands. This was accomplished by setting the upper and lower capacities on the dummy arcs connecting the supply node directly to each cool-store, equal to the amounts being held in each store from the previous week. The complete fruit distribution network then, was represented by 88 nodes and 320 arcs.

This network representation could be used to evaluate alternative or competing modifications to the fruit distribution system, in terms of how such changes would influence the total system operations. For example, cool-storage capacity might be varied, transportation costs might be reduced over particular arcs, managerial decisions might be made to reserve cool-store space for expected late season requirements, or export flows might be channelled through a limited number of ports. One such sensitivity analysis is illustrated in table 7 where the total distribution costs are given for different configurations of port loadings. The three port configuration was clearly superior whether or not any restrictions were placed on storage.

Table 7

Evaluation of alternative export fruit distribution programs

	Total distribution costs (dollars)[a]	
	Restriction on storage[b]	No storage restrictions
Two port loading[c]	461 521.286	460 520.236
Three port loading[d]	442 034.082	441 760.408
All ports	500 974.125	499 568.549

[a] Representing the costs incurred in moving fruit from depots, through cool-stores, to ports, and onto export vessels.

[b] For demonstration purposes cool-storage space in some areas was arbitrarily reserved for local fruit.

[c] Export fruit was only permitted to move through the ports of Nelson and Napier.

[d] Export fruit was only permitted to move through the ports of Nelson, Napier and Auckland.

The Apple and Pear Marketing Board in New Zealand is never certain as to the amount of fruit it will be required to market during a season until this fruit is actually received. As such its planned distribution or cool-storage program can only be viewed as a guideline. When it is appreciated that the total fruit crop may increase by as much as 10 % given favorable conditions during critical growth periods, and that such seasonal fluctuations are common and can have serious effects on the timing of overseas shipping requirements, then the value of having an analytical framework such as the one reviewed here is immense. While the model does not produce an optimal network configuration, it does produce optimal movement patterns through any given network configuration and helps pinpoint bottlenecks which impede efficient movement of the commodity.

It should be noted, however, that the approach outlined above is partial in the sense that whilst the flow patterns solved for each week are optimal, the total year's pattern may not be so. The location of final markets for instance does not necessarily influence where fruit which must be stored for several weeks, as opposed to being chilled, would be held. For this purpose, the model tends to select cool-stores adjacent to depots for any surplus receipts assuming the stores are not already full. These cool-stores may not prove to be the optimal choices if final market demand is not located close by. Overall, it could well be cheaper to pay slightly more for transportation initially, and to transport fruit to more distant cool-stores which hold promise of being located closer to the points where the fruit is finally demanded. Unfortunately, these future demand patterns are not 'known' to the model when it calculates weekly flows.

A possible solution to the above difficulty would involve a network formulation that solves both for the annual pattern and the weekly flows. This would require not only considerable duplication of the nodes in the network but also the use of estimates of fruit receipts at individual depots and sales at the local markets for the year in question. Such a formulation of the model has not yet been attempted.

5. Conclusion

The studies reviewed above have emphasized the application of the 'Out-of-Kilter Algorithm' in the determination of optimal least cost flow patterns, and with reference to selected real-world data have illustrated some of the sensitivity analyses that can be performed on the model. It is its capability of indicating system-wide impacts of any changes in the structure of a transportation system, for example in the originating and terminating nodes as illustrated in the Great Lakes coal flow model and also in intermediate handling points as in the fruit distribution model, that makes the use of the OKA of such value in providing a base for informed decision making.

The further application of the algorithm to a wide range of comparable problems in transportation flow analysis is obviously possible.[5]

It is worth stressing also that the OKA algorithm appears flexible and powerful enough to handle problems that are somewhat more complex than the ones outlined in this paper. For example, it appears well suited for the approximate solution of problems involving non-linear separable cost functions such as could be the case if the transportation cost c_{ij} on a link in the network were an increasing function of the flow x_{ij} on that link.[6] Then in order to make the non-linearity amenable to treatment using the OKA algorithm, a piecewise linear approximation of the function $c_{ij}(x_{ij})$ would be selected. The two nodes in question would then be connected by as many links as there are linear segments in the approximation. Each of these links would have a lower capacity of zero, an upper capacity equal to the upper threshold (x'_{ij}) of that particular linear segment, and a cost equal to the 'slope' of the corresponding linear segment. Assuming aggregate costs were to be minimized in the solution, then flows through one of the links would occur only if the capacities of the lower cost links were exceeded.

References

[1] American Iron and Steel Institute, 1964, Directory of Iron and Steel Works in the United States and Canada, New York.

[2] Beier, F. J. and J. L. Heskett, 1966, A Major Market for U.S. Bituminous Coal in Canada, Cambridge: Harvard Business School.

[3] Casetti, E., 1966, Optimal location of steel mills serving the Quebec and Southern Ontario steel market, The Canadian Geographer, 10, 27–39.

[4] Census of Mineral Industries, 1963, Summary and Industry Statistics, vol. 1, Washington D.C.: Govt. Printing Office.

[5] Charnes, A. and W. W. Cooper, 1962, Management Models and Industrial Applications of Linear Programming, vol. 1, 1961, New York: Wiley.

[6] Fulkerson, D. R., 1961, An out-of-kilter method for minimal cost flow problems, Journal Soc. Indust. Appl. Mathematics, 9, 18–27.

[5] For example, one of the authors, Dr. Kissling, has been associated with a study which uses the algorithm in evaluating future flow patterns of containerized freight from New Zealand ports.

[6] See, for example, Hadley [9, pp. 104 ff.] and Charnes and Cooper [5, pp. 326 ff.].

[7] Gauthier, H. L., 1968, Least cost flows in a capacitated network: a Brazilian example, in: F. Horton (ed.), Geographic Studies of Urban Transportation and Network Analysis, Evanston: Northwestern University Press, 102–127.

[8] Gould, P. R. and T. R. Leinbach, 1966, An approach to the geographical assignment of hospital services, Tijdschrift voor Economische en Sociale Geografie 57, 203–206.

[9] Hadley, G., 1964, Non Linear and Dynamic Programming, Reading, Mass.: Addison-Wesley.

[10] King, L., E. Casetti, J. Odland and K. Semple, 1971, Optimal transportation patterns of coal in the Great Lakes region, Economic Geography 47, 401–413.

[11] King, R. A. and W. R. Henry, 1959, Transportation models in studies of interregional competition, Journal of Farm Economics 41, 997–1011.

[12] Kriebel, C. H., 1961, Warehousing with transhipment under seasonal demand, Journal of Regional Science 3, 57–69.

[13] Mayer, R., 1964, Competition in the Midwestern Coal Industry, Cambridge: Harvard University Press.

[14] Morrill, R. L. and W. L. Garrison, 1960, Projections of interregional trade in wheat and flour, Economic Geography 36, 116–126.

[15] National Coal Association, 1967, Steam Electric Plant Factors 1966, Washington D.C.: Division of Economics and Statistics.

[16] Sinclair, J. G. and C. C. Kissling, 1971, A network analysis approach to fruit distribution planning, Proc. Sixth N.Z. Geography Conference, Christchurch, 131–136.

[17] Taaffe, E. J., 1959, Trends in airline passenger traffic: a geographic case study, Annals, Assoc. of American Geographers, 49, 393–408.

[18] Ullman, E. L., 1957, American Commodity Flow: A Geographic Interpretation of Rail and Water Traffic based on Principles of Spatial Interchange, Seattle: Univ. of Washington Press.

CHAPTER 13

An application of a multi-commodity transportation model to the U. S. feed grain economy*

L. J. GUEDRY

Louisiana State University

1. Introduction

This study is concerned with a price and allocation analysis of the U.S. feed grain economy. Its general objective is to examine the feed grain (corn, oats, barley and grain sorghum) sector within the framework of a spatial price equilibrium system and to use the information generated as a basis for 'description' and 'prescription'. In particular, the objectives were to estimate (i) surplus and deficit regions for each feed grain and the amount by which it is surplus or deficit; (ii) the direction and magnitude of the flows between each possible pair of regions for each feed grain that will maximize the net returns of each source and minimize total transport costs; (iii) a set of regional price differentials for each feed grain consistent with the optimum flow patterns; (iv) the optimum storage location of each feed grain under conditions of equilibrium; (v) the aggregate net trade of each feed grain and the total transportation cost involved in the distributing process; and (vi) to use this information to evaluate the performance of the pricing and allocation mechanisms and processes for this sector.

2. The economic environment

The demand for feed grains is more or less dispersed over the entire United States, although their production is located primarily in what is generally called the Corn Belt and its peripheral states. In the aggregate, production

---

* The study reported in this chapter is contained in Guedry and Judge [3] and was directed at an analysis of the 1961–62 marketing year for feed grains.

of the feed grains, corn, oats, barley and grain sorghum, had increased over the past 30 years from a low of 44.2 million tons in 1934 to a high 155.6 million tons in 1960; this increase occurred mainly over the past decade. Total utilization of feed grains followed the same general pattern as production, but the major components of demand varied. Livestock feed demand generally increased; food, industry, and seed demand remained relatively stable; and export demand was irregular, with a substantial increase in 1958, '59, '60 and '61. However, the increase in demand was not large enough to offset the increase in production. As a result, surpluses increased substantially, particularly since 1952, to a high of 84.7 million tons in 1960.

During the previous decade, corn prices trended downward since 1951, when the average price was $ 1.66 per bushel, the low being approximately $ 1.00 per bushel in 1960. Average prices of oats and barley were more stable, although there was a range of about 10 cents per bushel since 1950. Grain sorghum prices had followed a pattern similar to corn prices, ranging from a high of $ 2.82 per cwt in 1952 to a low of approximately $ 1.50 per cwt in 1960.

Since the 1930's, government programs have been in existence for one or more of the feed grains. The types of programs applied varied, but in general they can be classified as storage, allotment, or price support, either alone or in combination. The Emergency Feed Grain program for 1961, Public Law 87–5, was a voluntary acreage allotment program with price supports.

3. The model

3.1.

For purposes of model construction the feed grain sector is characterized as follows: There are many regions trading corn, oats, barley and grain sorghum, all of which are assumed to be homogenous. Every region is assumed to be a single and distinct market for each grain, and each possible pair of these markets is separated by a transportation cost per physical unit of these respective commodities. Regional demands and supplies for the marketing year are taken as given; the regional demands are equal to or less than the total supply for that year. Within this context the following restrictive and expository assumptions are made:

(1) Perfectly competitive behavior is assumed for all participants.

(2) The supply and demand regions are assumed to be represented by

a fixed point, and interregional flows take place at zero costs.

(3) The transportation rates connecting the regions are not affected by volume, and the grain flows among regions are not limited by governmental or other obstructions.

(4) There is homogeneity among feed grains for feeding purposes; therefore, producers are indifferent to the source or type of feed grain they use.

(5) Supply and demand are assumed to be correctly reported in data references for the marketing year 1961–62.

Notation:

In the formal presentation of the model the following notation is used.

Let:

k represent the commodities; corn, oats, barley, and grain sorghum ($k = 1, 2, 3, 4$)

m represent the commercial, feed and export types of demands ($m = 1, 2, 3$)

i, j represent the region ($i, j = 1, 2, \ldots, 42$)

x_{ij}^{km} represent the number of corn equivalents per cwt shipped from region i to region j for the kth commodity and mth type demand.

t_{ij}^{km} represent the cost of shipment from region i to region j for the kth commodity and mth type of demand.

x_i^k represent the supply of commodity k in region i.

y_j^{km} represent the requirement of commodity k for the mth demand in region j.

v_j^{km} represent the value of product k for the mth demand in region j.

u_i^{km} represent the value of product k for the mth demand in region i.

TC represent the total cost of all shipments.

S represent the results obtained from all shipments.

3.2. The mathematical programming specification

In order to derive the minimum cost flows of feed grains among regions and to estimate the set of geographical prices consistent with these flows the following joint or multi-commodity transportation model is used:[1]

Determine a set of x_{ij}^{km} which minimizes

$$TC = \sum_{m=1}^{3} \sum_{k=1}^{4} \sum_{i=1}^{42} \sum_{j=1}^{42} t_{ij}^{km} x_{ij}^{km} \tag{1}$$

[1] For a discussion of the conceptual framework for this model see [1], [2], [4], [7], [8], [9] and [10].

subject to

$$\sum_{m=1}^{3} \sum_{i=1}^{42} x_{ij}^{km} = x_i^k \tag{2}$$

$$\sum_{m=1}^{3} \sum_{i=1}^{42} x_{ij}^{km} = y_j^{km} \tag{3}$$

such that

$$\sum_{m=1}^{3} \sum_{k=1}^{4} \sum_{j=1}^{42} x_{ij}^{km} = \sum_{m=1}^{3} \sum_{k=1}^{4} \sum_{i=1}^{42} x_{ij}^{km} \tag{4}$$

and

$$x_{ij}^{km} \geqq 0 \qquad \text{for all } i, j, k \text{ and } m. \tag{5}$$

The dual problem is:

To maximize

$$S = \sum_{m=1}^{3} \sum_{k=1}^{4} \sum_{j=1}^{42} y_j^{km} v_j^{km} - \sum_{k=1}^{4} \sum_{i=1}^{42} x_i^k u_i^k \tag{6}$$

subject to

$$v_j^{km} - u_i^{km} \leqq t_{ij}^{km} \tag{7}$$

$$u_i^k, v_j^k \geqq 0. \tag{8}$$

Eq. (7) may be rewritten as

$$v_j^{km} \leqq u_i^{km} + t_{ij}^{km}. \tag{9}$$

The restriction reflected by eq. (7) implies that the value of any commodity for a particular type of demand in a deficit region must be less than or equal to the value of that commodity, for that particular type of demand, in the shipping region, plus transportation cost. Eq. (9) holds as an equality for regions between which flows take place. The optimum set of u_i^{km} and v_j^{km} estimates the price differentials for the original formulation and provides two additional types of information. The u_i^{km} gives the comparative advantages of the surplus regions and the price differentials at the deficit regions consistent with the minimum cost allocation are given by v_j^{km}.

4. Empirical data used in the model

4.1. Regional demarcation

The area under investigation in this study was the continental limits of the United States. A state was taken as the regional unit with the exception of the New England states,[2] Maryland and Delaware. Production and consumption in these two groups of states was sufficiently small to justify grouping them together to form two regions, leaving 42 regions to be considered in the study.[3] One city within each region, located near its center of producing, consuming or exporting area was selected as the basing point.

4.2. Regional demands

The demands to be considered in the model are annual demands which were obtained for various secondary data sources. The demands for feed grains were divided into three categories: commercial, export, and feed demands. Commercial and export demands are specific in nature; that is, they must be satisfied by the individual grain demanded. The feed demand, however, is not specific and can be satisfied by any one of the feed grains. That is, for use as feed the grains are directly substitutable for one another. However, if the grains are to be directly substitutable for one another, some standard measurement must be employed so that a bushel of corn can be substituted for a bushel of oats directly in the model. Therefore, in order that this might be done, both the demands and supplies were placed on a corn equivalent per hundredweight basis (c.e. cwt.) based on protein content.[4]

The commercial demand includes seed, food and industrial uses of feed grains. Secondary data sources [5], [6] and [12] were used to determine the percentage of total commercial demand for each region and grain, excluding grain sorghum. For grain sorghum all industrial use was allocated to Texas. Seed use of grain sorghum was allocated to the other regions by the percentage each region's production was of the total production. No food use for grain sorghum was assumed in the study.

Export demands were taken from published data, [14], on shipments from inspected areas and ports. These data included approximately 90 % of all grain exported from the U.S.

Feed demand as used in this study specifies livestock feeding requirements. To incorporate all livestock feed demands into one aggregate feed

---

[2] The New England states, as used here, include Vermont, New Hampshire, Maine, Massachusetts, Connecticut and Rhode Island.

[3] All other regions were confined to state boundaries.

[4] To obtain c.e. cwt. protein basis, corn was let to represent 1.00 protein content and the others as follows: Oats 0.9, barley 0.9, and grain sorghum 0.95. The following weights were used: corn and grain sorghum 56 lb/bu., oats 32 lb/bu. and barley 48 lb/bu.

demand, the animal unit standard was used.[5] The number of animal units in each region then formed the basis for determining regional feed demands, [17]. A minimum corn requirement was placed on feed demand for poultry. In specifying the minimum, it was assumed that at least 20 % of the poultry feed requirements must be satisfied by corn. Twenty percent of each region's feed demand for poultry was allocated to the commercial demand for corn and subtracted from the total feed demand in each region, [19].

4.3. Regional supply

The total available supply of feed grains were determined on the basis of the following information: (1) production of feed grains for the year, (2) beginning stocks of feed grains as of October 1 and (3) ending stocks of feed grains as of September 31, [11], [20]. In the analysis, total supply was determined by adding production to the difference between beginning and ending stocks. In the information available on each of the feed grains, there was a small quantity of unallocated stocks to avoid divulging individual operations. To allocate these data, the following procedure was used: For corn, oats and barley, the unallocated proportion was distributed to the unallocated regions by using the percentage of total production for these combined regions. Grain sorghum had to be handled differently: one-fourth was allocated to Louisiana and one-fourth to Illinois, and the remaining one-half was then prorated to the unallocated regions on the basis of each region's percentage of total stocks of the other three feed grains.

4.4. Transportation costs

An estimated transport cost function, based on published rail freight rates, the ICC's carload waybill studies, and truck and water transport rates relevant to private grain companies, provided the basis for most rates utilized in the analysis. The following linear regression equation was estimated using the above information:

$$Y = 0.0526 \, X + 7.796; \quad R^2 = 0.96,$$

where Y represents the transport rate in cents per hundredweight and X rep-

---

[5] Conversion into animal units of the different kinds of livestock was done by weighting the number of each kind of livestock by a factor, the amount of feed consumed per head per year by this particular kind of livestock, divided by the amount consumed by one average milk cow in the United States.

resents the miles. The equation was initially formulated as a truck transport function for shipments east and southeast, applicable to distances up to 800 or 900 miles. The cost of truck transport, at the time of the study had been found to be lower generally than other shipment costs for movements up to about 1200 miles, except where combined truck and barge movement was possible, or where rail rates were low. In each case the minimum truck, barge or rail rates were used in the analysis.

5. *Empirical results from model application*

The output obtained from the analysis is fairly large and to conserve space only a summary of the optimum flow patterns for each grain will be presented.[6] However, the price differentials will be presented for both the domestic and export market.

5.1. *Optimum geographical flows and price differentials*

Tables 1 and 2 present the equilibrium regional price differentials for domestic and export demands, respectively, derived from the solution of the model for each of the feed grains. Illinois was taken as the base region for corn, oats and barley, while Texas was taken as the base region for grain sorghum. These estimated price differentials provide two types of information. First, they show the comparative advantage or disadvantage of a surplus region. For example, a corn price differential of 7.84 ¢ per bushel in Ohio means that Ohio has a comparative advantage by this amount over Illinois in the sale of corn. In this case, the advantage was possibly due to Ohio's proximity to the deficit East Coast states. Second, the differentials reflect the proposition that the price in a deficit region should be higher than the price in the supplying region by the amount of the transport cost, and that the difference in price between two regions in which shipments do not take place must be equal to or less than the relevant transport cost. For example, a corn price differential of 33.97 ¢ per bushel in New England reflects that the price in New England should be 33.97 ¢ per bushel higher than in Illinois. The resulting regional price differentials are the competitive equilibrium values that would result if the surplus regions sold their excess supplies to the deficit regions and to the export points at the maximum possible gain.

---

[6] For complete results, see Guedry and Judge, [3], pp. 15–38.

Table 1

Estimated regional domestic price differentials by feed grains

Region	Corn	Oats	Barley	Grain sorghum
			(cents per bushel)	
1 New England	33.97	19.41	18.33	
2 New York	23.80	13.60	18.67	
3 New Jersey	27.16	15.52	9.41	
4 Pennsylvania	24.28	13.87	6.94	
5 Ohio	7.84	4.48	−1.08	
6 Indiana	4.03	2.30	−4.54	8.57
7 Illinois	0	0	0	4.54
8 Michigan	5.82	3.33	−1.18	
9 Wisconsin	4.93	2.82	5.69	
10 Minnesota	−9.63	−5.50	−14.66	
11 Iowa	−10.28	−5.87	−9.24	−5.74
12 Missouri	2.13	1.22	−7.90	6.66
13 North Dakota	−0.92	−0.53	−14.66	
14 South Dakota	−11.82	−6.75	−15.89	−7.28
15 Nebraska	−10.95	−6.27	−16.15	−6.41
16 Kansas	−6.69	−4.38	−20.13	−5.99
17 Delaware & Maryland	25.65	14.66	8.11	
18 Virginia	22.79	13.02	5.66	27.33
19 West Virginia	18.87	10.78	2.30	
20 North Carolina	23.63	13.50	6.38	28.17
21 South Carolina	23.27	13.30	6.07	27.81
22 Georgia	21.76	12.43	4.78	26.30
23 Florida	35.12	20.06		39.65
24 Kentucky	11.76	6.72	−3.79	16.16
25 Tennessee	14.20	8.11	−1.70	18.73
26 Alabama	20.25	11.57	3.48	24.22
27 Mississippi	12.15	6.94	−3.46	16.69
28 Arkansas	8.65	4.94	−6.55	13.19
29 Louisiana	15.79	9.02	−0.34	20.33
30 Oklahoma	−0.20	−2.06	−17.09	0.78
31 Texas	−1.99	−2.26	−6.00	0
32 Montana	11.62	6.64	−3.91	
33 Idaho	16.86	9.63	0.58	21.39
34 Wyoming	11.54	6.59	−3.98	
35 Colorado	6.61	3.78	−8.21	11.14
36 New Mexico	−4.70	−3.79	−19.55	−2.10
37 Arizona	13.08	7.47	−2.66	17.61
38 Utah	20.36	11.63	3.58	24.89
39 Nevada	20.36	11.63	3.58	
40 Washington	33.86	19.34	15.14	
41 Oregon	32.99	18.85	14.40	38.52
42 California	33.86	19.34	15.14	38.39

Table 2

Estimated regional export price differentials by feed grain

	Region	Corn	Oats	Barley	Grain sorghum
				(cents per bushel)	
1	Boston, Mass.	21.84		21.96	
2	New York, N.Y.	19.32		16.27	
4	Philadelphia, Pa.	20.16		13.99	
5	Toledo, Ohio	12.24		6.67	
7	Chicago, Ill.	5.49	5.46	1.46	
9 & 10	Duluth-Superior	1.65	1.73	−3.50	
17	Baltimore, Md.	18.48		13.22	31.64
18	Norfolk, Va.	18.48		11.69	
26	Mobile, Ala.	12.35	7.70	2.98	19.07
29	New Orleans, La.	11.12	7.70	2.98	19.07
31	Galveston, Tex.	9.05		3.67	22.09
31	Corpus Christi, Tex.				21.39
40	Seattle, Wash.	32.99		18.89	40.74
41	Portland, Ore.	32.99		20.81	49.34
42	San Francisco, Calif.	32.99		23.93	33.90

In addition it was possible, in general, to estimate the total amount of feed grain to be allocated and at what minimum cost. These results by grain and demand along with the totals are given in table 3. A total amount of 3 028 995 000 c.e. cwt of feed grain was allocated at an estimated total cost of $ 371,605,493. It must be remembered, however, that the estimated total cost of shipments refer to only the movement of feed grains from surplus to deficit regions; intraregional shipments were assumed to have a zero transportation cost. The quantity of feed grains moving in interregional shipments totaled 891 876 000 c.e. cwt, and the remaining 2 137 119 000 c.e. cwt was utilized within individual producing regions.

The type of results obtained for each feed grain can be indicated by a discussion of the general regional consumption patterns which exist for each and the results generated from the model. This discussion will be presented by grain in the following order: corn, oats, barley and grain sorghum.

Corn: Corn is the feed grain with the largest production. As feed for livestock, it is consumed primarily in the large beef and hog producing states of the Corn Belt, with the largest consumption in Illinois and Iowa. From the joint feed grain analysis, the following patterns of shipments of corn for livestock feed is estimated to exist: with the notable exception of Iowa, the corn-belt states east of the Mississippi River supply the eastern

Table 3

Quantities of feed grains shipped to each demand and total cost of each shipment

Feed grain	Commercial demand		Export demand		Feed demand		Total	
	Quantity shipped	Transport cost	Quantity shipped	Transport cost	Quantity shipped	Transport cost	Quantity shipped	Transport cost
			(1000 c.e. cwt.)					
Corn	55 398	$ 20,031,514	227 938	$ 78,354,932	466 387	$ 217,614,950	749 723	$ 316,001.396
Oats	2132	401 604	6 766	1 506 422	7 089	2 249 423	15 987	4 157 449
Barley	29 708	12 335 074	37 457	12 063 476	1 480	375 180	68 645	24 773 730
Grain sorghum	50	28 227	51 942	24 362 762	5 529	2 281 929	57 521	26 672 918
Total	87 288	$ 32,796,419	324 103	$ 116,287,592	480 485	$ 222,521,482	891 876	$ 371,605,493

and southeastern states. The Corn-Belt states west of the Mississippi River generally ship to the western half of the country.

The same general pattern of shipments appears to exist in satisfying commercial demand throughout the country. The largest consumption of corn for this purpose is in the two Corn-Belt states of Illinois and Iowa. Corn is also the feed grain exported in the largest quantity. In 1961–62, the United States shipped to other countries somewhere in the neighborhood of 407 million bushels. Of this total, the Gulf ports exported about 52 %; Great Lakes ports, 22 %; Atlantic ports, 25 %; and West Coast ports, 1 %. These ports are generally supplied by Iowa, Illinois and South Dakota.

Table 3 shows the estimated quantity of corn shipped to meet each type of demand greatly exceeded that of the other three grains. Corn was estimated to provide the largest interregional movement to satisfy feed demand and also the largest quantity of feed grain shipped to meet any demand. In shipments to meet commercial demand, 55 398 000 c.e. cwt of corn moved in interregional trade at a total cost of $ 20,031,514. Nebraska was the dividing point of estimated shipments east and west. States east of Nebraska shipped to the eastern and southeastern states in commercial marketing channels, while states west of and including Nebraska shipped to the western states. The dividing point for the eastern and western interregional movements of corn in the feed market was located in Nebraska and South Dakota. Again corn shipments were the largest of any of the estimated grain flows, with 466 387 000 c.e. cwt at a cost of $ 217,614,950. The quantity of corn moving in export trade totaled 277 938 000 c.e. cwt at a cost of $ 78,354,932. It was estimated that states east of South Dakota all shipped to the East Coast ports, while South Dakota shipped to the three West Coast ports. In the optimum flows Illinois does not ship corn to New Orleans for export, which is contrary to the actual flow pattern. The reason for this is that the transportation cost that was used made it more efficient for Illinois to ship its surplus elsewhere.

An estimated set of price differentials consistent with the estimated optimum flows of corn are given in tables 1 and 2. The differentials given in table 2 are consistent with both the commercial and the feed demand flows, since the transportation costs are the same. Those given in table 2 are consistent with the flows in export channels; they differ from commercial and feed differentials because the transportation rates are lower for grain moving to ports of exit. To facilitate the interpretation of the estimated price differentials, table 4 gives the surplus and deficit regions for corn. There are 25 deficit, 12 surplus and 5 self-sustaining regions for corn. This added information makes it possible to assess the economic significance

Table 4

Surplus and deficit regions by feed grains

Region	Corn	Oats	Barley	Grain sorghum
			(1000 c.e. cwt)	
1 New England	−47 861		−604	
2 New York	−25 255		−2 110	
3 New Jersey	−13 899			
4 Pennsylvania	−42 744		1 889	
5 Ohio	34 306		204	
6 Indiana	82 892		755	
7 Illinois	147 830		−5 679	
8 Michigan	21 039		46	
9 Wisconsin	−21 119	−2 905	−26 205	
10 Minnesota	55 897	2 905	−1 609	
11 Iowa	145 208	120	83	
12 Missouri	−8 551	−3 162	−116	
13 North Dakota			22 124	
14 South Dakota	43 923		4 004	
15 Nebraska	117 055		1 574	12 701
16 Kansas	40 491	3 162	9 401	19 009
17 Delaware & Maryland	−34 181		−180	−60
18 Virginia	−45 283			
19 West Virginia	−7 043			
20 North Carolina	−27 281			
21 South Carolina	−6 081			
22 Georgia	−57 892			
23 Florida	−14 046			
24 Kentucky	−17 959			
25 Tennessee	−22 693			
26 Alabama	−50 086	−6	−11	−1 460
27 Mississippi	−31 206			
28 Arkansas	−44 065	−291		
29 Louisiana	−110 025	−5 882	−963	−8 841
30 Oklahoma	2 013	291	704	
31 Texas	14 291	5 768	−1 733	−11 351
32 Montana			6 643	
33 Idaho			3 390	
34 Wyoming	−230		−1 574	
35 Colorado				−4 133
36 New Mexico	251			1 446
37 Arizona			2 802	
38 Utah	−5 380			
39 Nevada	−1 064			
40 Washington	−4 449		−2 662	−290
41 Oregon	−7 245		−5 833	−4 220
42 California	−59 558		−4 340	−2 801

of price differentials as explained at the beginning of this section. With Illinois as the base, the domestic price differentials range from a low of − 11.82 ε per bushel in South Dakota to a high of 35.12 ε per bushel in Florida. This range is consistent with the estimated flow patterns, since the longest shipment from Illinois eastward would be to Florida. Nebraska is used as the dividing point for shipments westward placing South Dakota as one of the westward supply points.

In general, the export differentials are lower than the domestic differentials. The exceptions are shipments to ports of exit in Texas, Ohio and Illinois. They exist because of the additional distance involved in shipping to these ports in relation to the basing points in the states for commercial and feed demands. In each case these regions have a surplus supply of corn, but their export points receive shipments from surplus regions outside their own regional boundaries. Such shipments may occur if the combined cost of shipping to these ports from other surplus regions is less than it would be for each of these regions to satisfy its own export demand and let the regions shipping to the ports satisfy the deficit regions to which they shipped their surplus.

Oats: A set of optimum flows similar to that for corn was also generated for oats, barley and grain sorghum. However, for the purposes of this presentation, only a discussion of these in relation to tables 1, 2, 3 and 4 will be considered. As indicated by table 3, 15 987 000 c.e. cwt of oats moved in interregional trade at a cost of $ 4,157,449. The largest quantity of oats moving in interregional trade was in the feed marketing channels. Even so, only three shipments were estimated to go into the feed marketing channels and all of them were eastward. The commercial and export demand flow patterns were similar to that for feed. Only four export shipments were estimated to occur: Iowa shipping to the ports of New Orleans and Mobile, and Minnesota and Illinois shipping to ports within their regional boundaries.

Price differentials consistent with domestic and export flows and the surplus and deficit regions for oats appear in tables 1, 2 and 4, respectively. Five deficit, 5 surplus and 32 self-sustaining regions were estimated to exist for oats. The domestic price differentials ranged from a low of −6.75 ε per bushel in South Dakota to a high of 20.06 ε per bushel in Florida. Except for Illinois, the price differentials for exports were lower than the domestic differentials. Illinois had a higher export differential because the basing point for domestic demand was taken as Decatur, Illinois while the port of exit was taken as Chicago.

Barley: The optimum flow patterns for barley represented a movement of 68 645 000 c.e. cwt in interregional trade with an attendant cost of $ 24,773,730, table 3. Commercial and export marketing channels handled most of the interregional movement of barley. All but one shipment (from Nebraska to Wyoming) moved to the commercial demand regions of Wisconsin and New York. Neighboring regions satisfied the export demand, except for the Gulf ports which were supplied primarily by Kansas. Only one shipment was made to meet feed demand, between Nebraska and Wyoming.

Tables 1, 2 and 4 present corresponding price differentials and surplus and deficit regions for barley. It was estimated that for barley there were 14 deficit, 13 surplus and 15 self-sustaining regions. With Illinois as the base, the estimated domestic price differentials ranged from a low of −20.13 *e* per bushel in Kansas to a high of 18.67 in New York. Most of the export price differentials were larger than the corresponding domestic price differentials.

Grain sorghum: Optimum flow patterns for grain sorghum show an estimated 57 521 000 c.e. cwt moving in interregional trade at a cost of $ 26,672,918, table 3. The largest quantity was estimated to move in export marketing channels to the West Coast and Gulf ports. One shipment was estimated to move eastward to Baltimore, Maryland. The geographical dividing point for export shipment channels was Kansas. Only two shipments were estimated to occur in the feed and commercial marketing channels. In both of these channels, it was estimated that grain sorghum moved from Kansas and New Mexico to Colorado and California, respectively.

Price differentials and surplus and deficit regions corresponding to the optimum flow patterns for grain sorghum are given in tables 1, 2 and 4, respectively. There were estimated to be 8 deficit, 3 surplus and 31 self-sustaining regions for grain sorghum. The domestic price differentials range from a low of −7.28 *e* per bushel in South Dakota to a high of 39.65 *e* per bushel in Florida. Corresponding regional export price differentials were generally lower than domestic differentials, except for Texas, which is the base region, and Oregon.

6. Policy implications

The regional pricing information consistent with the flow solutions obtained from the analysis provides one basis for analyzing the price support rates established for the four feed grains. For purposes of this investigation, the estimated domestic price differentials were compared to the actual support price differentials for each grain.[7]

The support price differentials were calculated by using published support rates, table 5. County support rates of the basing points were taken as the support prices for the region. The comparison of the support price differentials with the estimated differentials (table 1) showed that the actual support differentials were generally lower for each grain than those estimated by the model, particularly at the upper levels of the price surface. For example, the high point of the surface estimated by the model was 35.12 ¢ per bushel for corn in Florida; that determined from the actual price supports is 15.00 ¢ per bushel in New England. The same situation appeared in the upper level for each grain; as one moves in all directions from the major producing area, difference between the estimated and loan rate price differentials widens. These results suggest that factors other than transportation costs and the competitive behavior of the participants in the market, as in the model, must have been used in their derivation. Models of the nature presented in this study coupled with regional knowledge of the grain can give perspective to price support determination. They can supply information about competitive price differentials which reflect the locational advantages in production of the various feed grains. This information could be used in establishing new support rates or in determining the economic implications of those now in existence.

If, for example, the competitive price differentials calculated by the model were used as the actual support prices it might be expected that there would be some shift in the areas producing feed grains. Those surplus regions having comparative advantage in the production of each grain would be expected to increase their production, since this competitive advantage would be reflected in the support price they would receive. However, it must be cautioned that factors other than transportation cost enter into the producers' decisions and must be considered when such implications are drawn from the analysis.

[7] In the study on which this chapter is based this comparison was made using the results generated by a modified version of the model presented here. In that analysis the regional supply was increased to include total available supply in the region, ending stocks plus production and regional demands were increased by including a minimum storage requirement of 20 % of the commercial and feed demands. An examination of the results from that analysis shows that the only changes in the case of corn, oats and barley were at the extremes and with respect to slight level changes in the surface. However, considerable change was noted in the structure of the price differentials estimated for grain sorghum, to the extent that in the modified model the low points became high points on the surface. For detailed results, see Guedry and Judge [3], pp. 31–51.

Table 5

Actual regional price support differentials for feed grains in 1961 [a]

Region[b]	Corn[c]	Oats[d]	Barley[e]	Grain sorghum[f]
		(cents per bushel)		
1 New England	15.00	10.00	5.00	
2 New York	11.00	9.00	5.00	
3 New Jersey	12.00	10.00	5.00	
4 Pennsylvania	11.00	9.00	5.00	9.00
5 Ohio	2.00	4.00	−5.00	0
6 Indiana	0	1.00	−4.00	0
7 Illinois	0	0	0	−2.00
8 Michigan	2.00	2.00	−4.00	−5.00
9 Wisconsin	1.00	2.00	4.00	−5.00
10 Minnesota	−9.00	−7.00	−5.00	−5.00
11 Iowa	−8.00	−2.00	−3.00	0
12 Missouri	1.00	3.00	0	6.00
13 North Dakota	−13.00	−9.00	−7.00	−13.00
14 South Dakota	−12.00	−8.00	−7.00	−3.00
15 Nebraska	−6.00	−3.00	−13.00	2.00
16 Kansas	−2.00	2.00	−5.00	−6.00
17 Delaware & Maryland	10.00	9.00	5.00	
18 Virginia	10.00	9.00	5.00	9.00
19 West Virginia	10.00	10.00	2.00	
20 North Carolina	8.00	10.00	5.00	9.00
21 South Carolina	7.00	10.00	5.00	9.00
22 Georgia	6.00	10.00	4.00	9.00
23 Florida	6.00	14.00	4.00	6.00
24 Kentucky	3.00	10.00	−1.00	6.00
25 Tennessee	7.00	10.00	2.00	6.00
26 Alabama	6.00	10.00	1.00	6.00
27 Mississippi	4.00	9.00	1.00	6.00
28 Arkansas	4.00	7.00	−6.00	0
29 Louisiana	4.00	9.00	−8.00	6.00
30 Oklahoma	5.00	6.00	−6.00	−1.00
31 Texas	6.00	8.00	5.00	0
32 Montana	1.00	−7.00	−26.00	
33 Idaho	8.00	1.00	−16.00	−8.00
34 Wyoming	1.00	−1.00	−24.00	−8.00
35 Colorado	1.00	2.00	−14.00	−8.00
36 New Mexico	10.00	9.00	−4.00	0
37 Arizona	13.00	15.00	3.00	19.00
38 Utah	13.00	9.00	−14.00	−8.00
39 Nevada	14.00	12.00	−9.00	−3.00
40 Washington	8.00	7.00	6.00	0
41 Oregon	10.00	6.00	2.00	0
42 California	13.00	10.00	5.00	22.00

Results from the model can also be used by the Commodity Credit Corporation (CCC) to evaluate their operations in feed grains. The results contain information which would allow an evaluation of whether or not present and future storage facilities are located in the most advantageous positions. In particular, some insight is given to where the sale of stock held by the CCC should be made to attain the highest return, given existing facilities at the same time taking into account where the sales would best facilitate the existing feed grain program.

The application of the linear transportation model to the feed grain economy demonstrates the adaptability of the model to the multi-commodity problem. Used in this way, it allows a more realistic analysis of the pricing and allocation system for products which are substitutes and for which the rate of substitution can be specified. The usefulness of this model could be improved by incorporating into the regional demand structure more refined estimates of the location of storage facilities and their capacities. In addition, the model results could be made more useful to those decision makers who are concerned with daily decisions in the market by providing a time dimension to the model. That is, conduct the analysis of a marketing year by incorporating in the model regional demand and supply data on a monthly or quarterly basis. Such an analysis would provide pricing and allocation information at regular intervals throughout the marketing year giving a basis for evaluating market decisions by producers, firms and the government on a short run basis.

References

[1] Dorfman, R., P. A. Samuelson and R. M. Solow, 1958, Linear Programming and Economic Analysis, New York: McGraw-Hill.

Notes from table 5.

[a] U.S.D.A., Grain Price Support Supplement to Handbook 14-G.R., Bulletin 1, Supplement 2, Washington, D. C., Commodity Credit Corporation, Commodity Stabilization Service, 1961 (Reprinted from The Federal Register).

[b] The basing point for corn, oats, and barley is Illinois and for grain sorghum is Texas.

[c] Supports for number 3 graded corn.

[d] Supports for number 3 graded oats.

[e] Supports for number 2 or better graded barley.

[f] Supports for Classes I to IV inclusive, grading number 2 or better and containing not in excess of 13 % moisture.

[2] Enke, S., 1951, Equilibrium among spatially separated markets: solution by electric analogue, Econometrica XIX.

[3] Guedry, L. J. and G. G. Judge, 1965, The Spatial Structure of the Feed Grain Economy, AERR-78, Department of Agricultural Economics, University of Illinois.

[4] Heady, E. O. and W. Candler, 1958, Linear Programming Methods, Ames, Iowa: The Iowa State University Press.

[5] Hieronymus, T. A. and G. G. Judge, 1962, Interregional Analysis of the Corn Sector. AERR-55, University of Illinois, Department of Agricultural Economics.

[6] Jennings, R., 1954, Feed Consumed by Livestock, Supply and Disposition of Feeds, 1949–50, Statistical Bulletin No. 145, U.S.D.A.

[7] Judge, G. G., 1956, A Spatial Equilibrium Model for Eggs, Bulletin 318, Storrs Connecticut Agricultural Experiment Station.

[8] Judge, G. G. and T. D. Wallace, 1959, Spatial Price Equilibrium Analysis of the Livestock Economy, Technical Bulletin TB-78, Oklahoma State University, Department of Agricultural Economics.

[9] Samuelson, P. A., 1952, Spatial price equilibrium and linear programming, American Economic Review, XLII.

[10] Takayama, T. and G. G. Judge, 1971, Spatial and Temporal Price and Allocation Models, Amsterdam: North-Holland Publishing Company.

[11] U.S.D.A., 1963, Crop Production 1963 Annual Summary, Washington, D.C., Statistical Reporting Service, Crop Reporting Board.

[12] U.S.D.A., 1962, Feed Situation (1963 Outlook Issue), Washington, D.C., Economic Research Service.

[13] U.S.D.A., 1963, Feed Situation (1964 Outlook Issue), Washington, D.C., Economic Research Service.

[14] U.S.D.A., 1962, Grain Marketing News, Washington, D. C., Agricultural Marketing Service.

[15] U.S.D.A., 1961, Grain Price Support Supplement to Handbook 14-G.R., Bulletin 1, Supplement 2, Washington, D.C., Commodity Credit Corporation, Commodity Stabilization Service (reprinted from the Federal Register).

[16] U.S.D.A., 1961, Grain Transportation in the North Central Region, Marketing Research Report No. 490, Washington, D.C., Agricultural Marketing Service, Transportation and Facilities Research Division.

[17] U.S.D.A., 1963, Livestock-Feed Relationships 1909–1963, Statistical Bulletin No. 337, Washington, D.C., Economic Research Service.

[18] U.S.D.A., 1963, Livestock and Meat Statistics 1962, Statistical Bulletin No. 333, Washington, D.C., Agricultural Marketing Service, Statistical Reporting Service, Economic Research Service.

[19] U.S.D.A., 1963, Poultry and Egg Situation, Washington, D.C., Economic Research Service.

[20] U.S.D.A., 1962, Stocks of Grains in All Positions, Washington, D.C., Agricultural Marketing Service, Crop Reporting Board.

[21] U.S.D.A., 1963, Supplement for 1962 to Dairy Statistics, Statistical Bulletin No. 303, Washington, D.C., Economic Research Service.

[22] U.S.D.A., 1964, Supplement for 1963 to Grain and Feed Statistics, Statistical Bulletin No. 159, Washington, D.C., Economic Research Service, Economic and Statistical Analysis Division.

CHAPTER 14

A spatial analysis of the U. S. livestock economy*

G. G. JUDGE, J. HAVLICEK and R. L. RIZEK**

1. Introduction

The purpose of this study is to analyze, within the context of an inter-regional activity analysis model, the optimum location of livestock slaughter and the corresponding optimum geographical flows and prices of livestock and meat.

The livestock sector is dynamic in nature since the transportation systems, technology of livestock slaughter and production, consumer meat preferences and the geographical distribution of population has changed and is changing rapidly over time. Thus, this industry where plans are being drawn and executed, provides an excellent research base for spatial price and allocation problems. The time frame considered in this article means that its purpose is to some extent expository. However, it is of relevance in this collection since it reflects how spatial models and methods have been and can be applied and the results used for decision and planning purposes.

2. The economic environment and problem specification

The general problem underlying this analysis has the following characteristics: we are given in each of n regions of the U.S. economy a known non-negative quantity of a particular type of livestock for some time period t. This primary or intermediate product passes through a processing plant and by this production activity is converted to a final commodity (beef). The

---

* Some of the material contained in this chapter was first published in [4] and [10].
** University of Illinois at Urbana-Champaign, Purdue University, and Agricultural Research Services, USDA.

rate at which the primary or intermediate product may be transformed into a final consumable product is known for each region, product, and time period. A non-negative quantity of the final product is consumed in each of the n regions, and the regional consumption is assumed known for some time period t. Each region has some non-negative capacity for processing the primary and intermediate product or, alternatively, the production of the final commodity, and these capacities are known and fixed for any time period t. Thus, each slaughtering plant is assumed to be an immobile primary commodity. Each region has a unit processing cost for converting the primary or intermediate commodity into a final commodity, and these costs or cost differentials are known for time period t.

The primary and final commodities are assumed mobile and all possible pairs of regions are separated by a transportation cost per physical unit for each type of product, from region i to j are known for time period t. It is further assumed that when the total regional supplies of primary or intermediate product livestock is converted into the final commodity beef, the resulting total potential supply of the final commodity is equal to or greater than the total consumption. For processing and consumption purposes, each product is assumed homogeneous and thus processing firms and consumers are indifferent as to their source of supply. It is further assumed that the commodities are traded in competitive markets.

Given this economic environment for a multi-region industry, the problem within a planning, evaluation and decision context is to determine the level and location of livestock slaughter and the volume and direction of slaughter cattle and beef flows which will maximize returns to each supplier and minimize the costs to consumers. This means that we seek the pricing and allocation solution at time t which will minimize the aggregate slaughter and transportation costs.

3. The formal model

3.1. Notation

As a basis for specifying the model in mathematical form, let:

i, j denote the regions; $i, j = 1, 2, \ldots, n$.

s_i^δ denote the quantity of the primary or intermediate product available in region i (quantity available before inshipments and outshipments).

y_i^k denote the demand for the kth type of final commodity in region i.

x_{ij}^{δ} denote the quantity of the primary or intermediate product shipped from region i to j to be used in producing the final commodity.

x_{ij}^{k} denote the quantity of the final product shipped between regions i and j.

c_{i}^{k} denote the unit cost of processing the final commodity in region i.

t_{ij}^{δ} denote the unit transport costs for a shipment of the primary or intermediate commodity from region i to j.

t_{ij}^{k} denote the unit transport cost for a shipment of the final commodity from region i to j.

α_{i}^{qk} denote the rate at which the qth (constant proportion at all output levels) type of product is converted per unit of process into the mth type of product in region i; $q = \delta, m$.

s_{i}^{m} denote the capacity of the mth processing plant in region i.

x_{i}^{k} denote the level of production of the final product in region i.

e_{i}^{q} denote net availability (amount remaining after imports, exports, and use) in region i; $q = k, l, r$.

3.2. *The mathematical model*

Since we wish to determine the production and allocation solution that will minimize the total transportation and plant costs, we may, using the above definitions, express the constrained extremum problem as: To maximize

$$f(X) = -\sum_{i}\sum_{j} t_{ij}^{k} x_{ij}^{k} - \sum_{i}\sum_{j} t_{ij}^{\delta} x_{ij}^{\delta} - \sum_{i} c_{i}^{k} x_{i}^{k} \tag{1}$$

subject to

$$e_{i}^{k} = -y_{i}^{k} + \sum_{j} x_{ji}^{k} \geqq 0. \tag{2}$$

The shipment of beef to region i from itself and other regions is equal to or greater than the demand in region i.

$$e_{i}^{\delta} = s_{i}^{\delta} - \sum_{j} (x_{ij}^{\delta} - x_{ji}^{\delta}) - \alpha_{i}^{\delta k} x_{i}^{k} \geqq 0. \tag{3}$$

The quantity of the slaughter cattle used in processing when producing the final commodity beef in the ith region, plus inshipment of the product into the ith region, minus outshipments of the slaughter cattle from the ith region, must be equal to or less than the native availability of the product in the ith region.

$$e_{i}^{m} = s_{i}^{m} - \alpha_{i}^{mk} x_{i}^{k} \geqq 0. \tag{4}$$

The quantity of slaughter cattle processed by the processing plants in region i is equal to or less than capacity.

$$e^{ik} = x_i^k - \sum_j x_{ij}^k \geqq 0. \tag{5}$$

The amount of beef region i ships to itself and other regions is equal to or less than the amount produced by the plants in region i [5].

Finally, all producing and flow variables are constrained to be non-negative.

$$x_i^k, x_{ij}^\delta, x_{ij}^k \geqq 0. \tag{6}$$

As developed in Takayama and Judge [11, pp. 68–71], in order to derive an efficient production and allocation program, regional values and rents must be such that:

(a) Profits are zero on all production and flow processes actually used and no process may show a positive profit. Thus, the values (prices) for two regions can differ at most by the transport cost per unit and flows only take place when this value differential is equal to the transport cost.

(b) Values of the slaughter cattle may exceed zero only if their regional net availability e_i^δ is equal to zero.

(c) Rents on processing plants and fixed regional demands may exceed zero only if the capacities in each case are fully utilized.

The dual formulation for this type of model and the corresponding primal-dual programming tableau is given in Takayama and Judge [11, pp. 71–76].

4. The data

The U.S. economy has been partitioned into 26 regions which are identified in figs. 1 and 2. The slaughter cattle-beef subsector of the livestock industry reflects the commodity space for the analysis. The calendar year 1960 is the time period considered. The estimated regional consumption of beef and the production of cattle for this time period are given in table 1. Each region is assumed to have processing facilities for converting slaughter cattle to beef and the estimated total regional annual capacities of these slaughtering plants are given in table 1. The rate at which cattle are converted to beef is assumed to be the same in each region, and this technical coefficient (dressing percentage) was estimated at 0.573. The total regional supply of cattle when converted to beef is assumed to be equal to the total regional

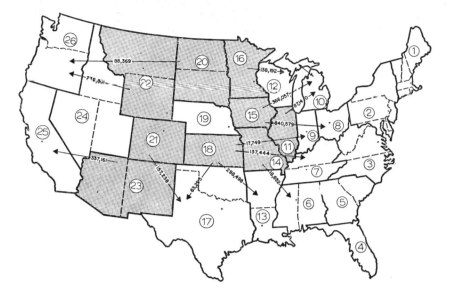

Fig. 1. Optimum shipment pattern of slaughter cattle for 26 regions of the U.S. using estimated slaughter capacities, jointly determined model (1000 pounds), 1960.

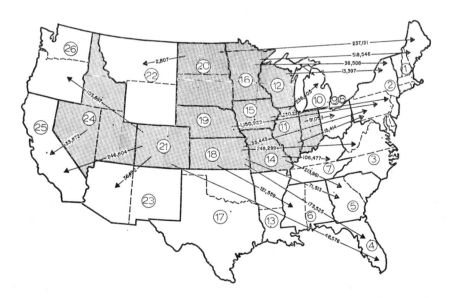

Fig. 2. Optimum shipment pattern of beef for 26 regions of the U.S. using estimated slaughter capacities, jointly determined model (1000 pounds), 1960.

Table 1

Regional estimates of slaughter cattle production, beef consumption, slaughter capacity, and costs, 1960

Region[a]	Slaughter cattle production (live weight)[b]	Beef consumption (dressed weight)[c]	Slaughter capacity (live weight)[d]	Labor costs for slaughtering[d]
	(Thous. lb)	(Thous. lb)	(Thous. lb)	(¢ per 100 lb)
1	149 913	841 637	502 704	0.30
2	875 177	3 001 461	2 794 019	0.28
3	520 317	546 441	700 920	0.19
4	143 197	304 153	449 070	0.19
5	99 155	342 290	737 683	0.21
6	281 671	292 498	574 166	0.21
7	412 570	353 050	1 053 420	0.27
8	588 737	900 051	1 642 874	0.29
9	745 559	424 908	901 627	0.30
10	408 643	730 239	861 840	0.28
11	2 159 185	935 463	2 072 045	0.32
12	498 099	351 198	1 213 899	0.32
13	192 808	281 518	499 701	0.20
14	1 270 807	398 193	1 254 155	0.31
15	3 789 796	229 914	2 583 160	0.33
16	1 621 086	294 584	1 482 894	0.38
17	1 860 991	1 192 712	3 058 282	0.25
18	1 978 551	189 139	1 461 567	0.28
19	2 214 325	117 883	2 448 835	0.32
20	689 994	104 733	601 625	0.30
21	1 216 031	171 119	1 058 793	0.31
22	402 338	96 514	163 537	0.26
23	670 703	227 612	333 542	0.26
24	375 847	181 488	664 501	0.29
25	1 879 717	1 550 747	2 892 311	0.34
26	285 777	455 115	1 056 808	0.30
Total	25 330 994	14 514 660	33 063 978	–

[a] The states in each region are shown in figs. 1 and 2.

[b] For a discussion of assumptions and procedures for developing these estimates see Havlicek *et al.* [2].

[c] For a discussion of the development of these alternative regional consumption estimates see Judge *et al.* [3].

[d] For a discussion of the basis for these estimates see Rizek *et al.* [9].

consumption of beef. Thus, eqs. (2) and (3) of the model appear as equalities.

Regional slaughtering costs as reflected by differences in labor costs are given in table 1. Transport costs between each pair of regions were estimated from transportation cost functions generated for both cattle and beef.[1] Given these specifications and the set of basic data (restrictions), the programming model involves 72 equations and 1326 activities.

5. The results

The sets of interregional flows of slaughter cattle and beef consistent with the model and basic data previously specified are given in figs. 1 and 2. The shaded areas in fig. 1 reflect regions in which supplies of slaughter cattle exceeded slaughter capacity[2], while the shaded areas of fig. 2 represent regions in which the supply of slaughtered cattle (carcass beef) exceeds the demand for beef. The arrows indicate the direction of flows and the numbers within the line segments indicate the size of shipments.

Under the optimum solution, total annual slaughter cattle shipments were estimated at 2.8 billion pounds (11 % of the total supply of slaughter cattle), with an accompanying transportation bill of $ 30.1 million. Of the 9 regions shipping to other regions, Iowa had the largest excess supply of slaughter cattle (1.2 billion pounds). In most cases, slaughter cattle from the surplus regions were shipped to the closest region with excess slaughter capacity, because net transportation costs are higher for slaughter cattle than for carcass beef. Thus, for example, the regions on the East Coast did not receive any shipments and slaughtered only their own production.

Under the optimum solution 4.98 billion pounds (approximately 33.5 % of the total beef supply) of carcass beef moved in interregional trade at a corresponding total cost of $ 98 million. The dominant surplus areas of carcass beef were the Corn Belt (Iowa and Nebraska accounted for approximately 50 % of the total surplus) and Northern Plain States, while the East Coast was the dominant deficit area.

The optimum level of regional slaughter generated by the analysis is given in table 2. In comparison with actual slaughter (also given in table 2) under the optimum solution, 13 regions would have increased their slaughter. In region 2 (New York, Pennsylvania, New Jersey, Delaware, Maryland), the optimum level of slaughter was about 1.2 billion pounds less than the

---

[1] For the functions underlying these transport rates, see [2] and [3].

[2] An exception to this identification is the region represented by Nebraska, which exported cattle although slaughter capacity was not fully utilized.

Table 2

Regional estimates of the optimal level of cattle slaughter, price differentials, and rents, and actual cattle slaughter, 1960

Region	Actual (live weight)[a]		Slaughter	Excess capacity	Optimally determined		Rent per 100 lb. (live basis)
	Slaughter	Estimated excess capacity			Price differentials per 100 lb		
					Carcass weight	Live weight	
	(Mil. lb.)	(Mil. lb.)	(Mil. lb.)	(Mil. lb.)	(Dollars)	(Dollars)	(Dollars)
1	207.2	295.5	149.9	352.8	2.78	1.35	
2	2096.1	697.9	875.2	1918.8	2.56	1.23	
3	358.0	342.9	520.3	180.6	2.52	1.21	
4	281.2	167.9	143.2	305.9	2.71	1.31	
5	335.2	402.5	99.2	638.5	2.17	1.01	
6	432.9	141.3	298.3	275.8	1.92	0.86	
7	513.2	540.2	430.3	623.1	1.76	0.77	
8	1165.1	477.8	1429.3	213.6	1.76	0.77	
9	650.3	251.3	883.0	18.6	1.34	0.53	

10	731.9	129.9	801.8	0	1.80	0.72	0.07
11	1483.1	588.9	2072.0	0	1.02	0.07	0.28
12	1040.6	173.3	636.3	577.6	0.90	0.28	
13	246.3	253.4	491.3	8.4	1.64	0.70	
14	1105.1	149.1	1254.2	0	0.72	−0.03	0.20
15	2667.7	−84.5	2583.3	0	0.59	−0.32	0.42
16	1492.5	−9.6	1482.9	0	0.52	−0.29	0.35
17	1598.6	1459.7	2081.5	976.8	1.45	0.59	
18	1159.5	302.1	1461.6	0	0.56	−0.30	0.38
19	2204.9	243.9	2214.4	234.5	0.42	0	
20	463.7	137.9	601.6	0	0.11	−0.38	0.20
21	1079.9	−21.1	1058.8	0	0	−0.61	0.37
22	121.0	42.5	163.5	0	1.42	−0.39	0.97
23	203.7	129.8	333.5	0	1.90	0.05	0.80
24	446.8	217.7	375.8	288.7	1.17	0.43	
25	2540.6	351.7	2216.9	675.4	2.45	1.17	
26	705.9	350.9	612.9	443.9	2.44	1.16	
Total	25 331.0	7848.1	25 331.0	7733.0			

[a] For a discussion of the development of these data see Rizek *et al.* [9].

amount of actual slaughter. In only ten regions was all of the slaughtering capacity used (table 2).

Internal prices consistent with the optimum flow patterns and regional livestock slaughter are given in table 2. The differential regional values for carcass beef are derived relative to Colorado as the base region. These values indicate the comparative price advantage which surplus regions have relative to Colorado and the delivered price differentials which deficit regions have relative to the base region. These results indicate, for example, that carcass beef is worth $ 1.02 more per 100 pounds in Illinois, and $ 1.34 more per 100 pounds in Indiana than in Colorado because of their proximity to the deficit regions of the East. Alternatively, carcass beef is worth $ 1.76 more in deficit New England than in Illinois. The surplus regions with the greatest comparative price disadvantage are Nebraska, North and South Dakota, and Colorado. The value of slaughter cattle was highest in the Northeast.

In 10 of the 26 regions, slaughter capacity was completely utilized. Therefore, a rent may accrue to the plants in these locations. The internal rents consistent with the price and allocation solution are also given in table 2. These rents, which are a function of both location and quality (costs), varied from a low of 7 ¢ per 100 pounds of slaughter cattle in Michigan to a high of 97 ¢ per 100 pounds in Montana and Wyoming. One reason for the high rent accruing in Montana and Wyoming is that slaughter capacity is so restrictive that this region must export cattle and then import carcass beef. The rents that accrue to regions where capacity is exhausted give an indication of the relative profitability of increasing slaughter capacity in each of the particular regions.

Comparable analyses performed for the calendar years 1955 yielded similar optimum flows of slaughter cattle and beef.[3] The percent that flows were of total cattle production decreased slightly from an estimated 12 % in 1955 to 11 % in 1960 while the flows of beef increased from 31 % of total beef production in 1955 to 33.5 % in 1960. All regions except North and South Dakota increased consumption from 1955 to 1960 with the largest increases occurring on the East and West coasts. Fifteen regions, located mainly in the East, decreased slaughter cattle production between 1955 and 1960 while increases occurred in the Western part of the Corn Belt and adjacent regions. Nineteen out of 26 regions increased their cattle slaughtering capacities between 1955 and 1960 with Iowa and Nebraska having the greatest increases and Illinois exhibiting the largest reduction.

---

[3] The details of the analyses for 1955 are developed in [4] and [10].

Several major changes occurred when slaughter capacities were assumed to increase to a level 1000 pounds less than slaughter cattle production in regions which had deficit capacity in 1955 and 1960.[4] Except for Minnesota and North and South Dakota, which continued to ship small amounts of slaughter cattle in 1955, slaughter took place at the point of production. Over 40 % of the total beef supply was estimated to move interregionally in each of these two years. The analyses suggest that a considerable gain in efficiency would be realized through reduced transportation costs by locating slaughter in the areas of production. For example, total transportation costs were reduced $ 4.1 and $ 7.1 million in 1955 and 1960, respectively. These suggested changes are right in line with what has happened in the last decade. Changes in equilibrium prices of cattle and beef were minor in most cases, but analyses suggested that part of the reduced transportation costs associated with locating slaughter at the point of production would be passed on to producers of slaughter cattle. In general, equilibrium prices, of slaughter cattle of dominant producing regions were increased relative to the base region. Also, beef consumers especially those in regions where the demand for beef exceeded slaughter capacity would stand to benefit from lower beef prices.

6. *Implications of the results*

The results of the analysis for slaughter cattle and beef reflect the fact that slaughtering plants will probably continue to be located at the points of production, and that under the cost structures considered, the dominant producing regions will continue to slaughter at or near capacity levels, even though slaughtering costs are lower in other regions such as the Southeast. A factor not considered in this analysis, which would tend to strengthen this conclusion, is that plants in the Corn Belt and other dominant producing regions tend to have larger rated capacities because of the high density of livestock production. In view of the economies of scale depicted by Logan and King [7] and others, the regional differentials in labor slaughtering costs would be reduced between the Corn Belt and regions in the Southeast, thus giving further emphasis to slaughtering at the point of production. Areas of consideration for both producers of slaughter cattle and the meatpacking industry are the possible changes in their markets as slaughter capacity is increased in the major production areas. If consumers in

[4] See [10] for details.

different sections of the country actually prefer different types of beef (i.e., carcass weight, grade, etc.), producers and meat packers in certain pivotal regions may need to change their product to meet the type of demand for their new markets.

The results of the analysis substantiate the conclusion of considerable excess slaughter capacity in the meat packing industry. The estimates of optimal level and location of slaughter indicate that the major portion of the excess slaughter capacity exists in the regions on the East and West Coasts. The estimated rents that accrue in the regions where slaughter capacity is completely utilized give a measure of the economic incentive for expanding plant capacity in these regions, and the estimates of opportunity costs that result for regions where slaughter capacity is not completely utilized indicate how much transportation costs or slaughtering costs would have to be reduced before these regions would increase their level of slaughter. The structure of the model and the results of the analysis point up the role of and the great need for accurate projections on regional production and consumption in reaching decisions about future changes in the location and capacity of livestock slaughter facilities.

7. Concluding remarks

The model as formulated will handle a multi-region, multi-final product industry using intermediate or primary commodities as inputs in either single-product or multi-product processing plants which have fixed capacities and are geographically distributed over n regions in some predetermined manner. The level and location of primary and intermediate commodity processing and the volume and direction of primary and intermediate commodity flows, which will maximize returns to each supplier and minimize the costs to consumers, may be determined and the impacts of changes in location of production, processing capacity, demand, wages, etc. may be evaluated. The model could be extended to include the activities reflecting the production and flow of intermediate products. If processing costs (c_i^k) differed between regions, then the restrictions on plant capacity could be omitted and the model could be used to determine the ideal long-run level and location of processing activities. If the regional prices of final commodities are assumed to be known, then the same model could be employed with the modification that $(c_i^k + t_{ij}^k)$ would be replaced by $(p_i^k - c_i^k - t_{ij}^k)$ in the objective function. If desired, restrictions could be specified for the flows of one or more commodities between regions, then the cost of this rigidity to resource owners could be assessed (this is the same type of rigidity as assuming plant location and capacity as given).

Alternative models have been proposed by King [5] and Rhody [9] as a basis for analyzing problems of determining the processing and final and primary commodity flows simultaneously. However, the transshipment model [7] proposed by King, and the method of reduced matrices [1] proposed by Rhody, handle problems involving only one primary and final commodity. Thus, the transshipment and reduced matrices models are too restrictive for many problems which need to consider a mult-product commodity space and multi-product processing plants.

For analyses of this type, data underlying regional demands, supplies and plant costs and capacities remain as an effective restriction that the investigator must face. Also to evaluate the performance of a subsector of an economy more and better data must be made available on actual geographical flows and prices. Until these data are available, it is very difficult if not impossible to check the realism of the model results or gauge the performance of the economic system.

References

[1] Dwyer, P. S. and B. A. Galler, 1957, The method of reduced matrices for a general transportation problem, Journal of Associated Computing Mach.

[2] Havlicek, J., R. L. Rizek and G. G. Judge, Spatial Analyses of the Flows of Slaughter Livestock in 1955 and 1960, S. Dakota State University, North Central Regional Bulletin.

[3] Judge, G. G., J. Havlicek and R. L. Rizek, Spatial Analyses of the Meat Marketing Sector in 1955 and 1960, S. Dakota State University, North Central Regional Bulletin.

[4] Judge, G. G., J. Havlicek, and R. L. Rizek, 1965, An interregional model: its formulation and application to the livestock industry, Agricultural Economics Research XVII, no. 1, 1–9.

[5] King, G. A. and S. H. Logan, 1964, Optimum location, number, size of processing plants with raw product and final product shipments, Journal of Farm Economics 46, 94–108.

[6] Kuhn, H. and A. Tucker, 1951, Non-linear programming, Second Berkeley Symposium Proceedings, J. Neyman, ed., University of California Press 481–492.

[7] Logan, S. H. and G. A. King, 1962, Economies of scale in slaughter plants, Giannini Foundation Research Report 260, University of California.

[8] Orden, A., 1956, The transshipment problem, Management Science 2, 277–85.

[9] Rhody, D. H., 1963, Interregional competitive position of the hog-pork industry in the southeast United States, unpublished Ph. D. thesis, Iowa State University.

[10] Rizek, R. L., G. G. Judge and J. Havlicek, 1965, Joint Spatial Analysis of Regional Slaughter and the Flows and Pricing of Livestock and Meat, South Dakota State University, North Central Regional Publication.

[11] Takayama, T. and G. G. Judge, 1971, Spatial and Temporal Price and Allocation Models, Amsterdam: (North-Holland Publishing Company).

CHAPTER 15

An interregional analysis of the United States soybean industry

J. V. LEUNIS and R. J. VANDENBORRE

Katholieke Universiteit te Leuven

1. Introduction

1.1. Major objective

The economic activity of the soybean processing industry takes place in a space-time continuum. Within this space-time framework, major changes such as technology of production and transportation, supply and demand conditions, transport rate structure have occurred in the basic locational determinants of the industry, [3]. In this context, the major objective of this study is to develop and analyze for the marketing years 1967–68 and 1975–76 a spatial model of the U.S. soybean processing industry where regional soybean supplies and regional processing capacities are given and where regional final product demands, the location and level of processing and the interregional shipments of raw and final products are jointly determined.

1.2. Specific objectives

Through the application of a linear activity analysis model, and under given sets of constraints, we seek to:

(1) Develop, for the marketing years 1967–68 and 1975–76, estimates of regional soybean availabilities and regional estimates of high protein feeds (other than soybean meal), to specify crushing processes and transfer functions, and to estimate regional demands for soybean meal and oil.

(2) Incorporate into the basic interregional activity analysis model the main characteristics of the processing-in-transit privilege system and to develop in this manner a theoretical model approximating the real world soybean processing industry.

(3) Develop and analyse for the same time periods a spatial model of the soybean processing industry where regional soybean supplies and regional processing capacities are given and where regional final product demands, the location and level of processing and the interregional shipments of raw and final products are jointly determined.

1.3. Information output and uses

The direct solution of the programming problem provides the following information: (i) the location of soybean processing; (ii) the shipments of soybean meal and oil; (iii) the shipments of soybeans; (iv) the equilibrium prices of meal and oil. The dual solution provides information concerning: (i) the imputed prices of the factors of production consistent with equilibrium flows; (ii) the cost associated with introducing activities not in the solution.

2. The economic model

2.1. The economic environment

The location of the soybean processing plants in various regions in the United States depends on a set of interdependent relationships in the feed-livestock and fats and oils economies. At the level of the processing industry, these relationship involve regional demands for soybean meal and oil; production functions for the final products meal and oil; regional availability of factors of production and transportation costs functions for final products and raw materials which tie regions together in a spatial equilibrium sense. At this point, it is necessary to incorporate these factors in a simplified model representing the location economics of the soybean processing industry. We will proceed under the following assumptions:

(1) the U.S. economy can be partitioned into different industries; the soybean processing industry is the subject of analysis;

(2) a known non-negative quantity of soybeans is given for the n regions of the multi-regional soybean industry. The regional supply of soybeans is assumed to be given for a particular marketing year. The regional availability of soybeans is assumed to be equal to the regional production of soybeans adjusted for changes in stocks, for use of soybeans for seed and other farm uses.

(3) it is assumed that only one production process is available by which soybeans are converted into the final products meal and oil. The rate

at which soybeans may be transformed into a consumable product is constant for all levels of production and is the same for any time period in each region. The conversion rates are the same for all regions. Given the same technology, this implies also that all plants are equally efficient in extracting oil and meal.

(4) the final products, meal and oil, are consumed in non-negative quantity in each of the *n* regions; the regional demands for meal and oil are represented by known linear price dependent functions;

(5) each region has some non-negative capacity for processing soybeans and these capacities are known for any time period;

(6) in each region, a base point has been selected at which the supply of soybeans, the demand for the final products as well as the processing capacity is assumed to be concentrated;

(7) processing costs per unit are known in time period *t* for each region and they may differ among regions. Costs of processing (costs other than the prices paid for the acquisition of soybeans) were specified for each region on the basis of empirical data available for five different plant sizes in the State of Illinois. The cost of processing differs among regions because of regional differences in the average size of processing plants and regional differences in the price of important inputs more in particular, in the wage levels.

(8) all possible pairs of regions are separated by a transportation cost per unit of soybeans and final products and these transportation costs are known for time period *t*. The unit transfer costs are independent of the flow volume;

(9) processing of soybeans and consumption of the final products, meal and oil, are assumed homogeneous and thus processing firms and consumers are indifferent about the source of supply, i.e., competitive behavior is stipulated for all participants in the industry;

(10) finally, it is assumed that all commodities are traded in competitive markets.

2.2. *Notation*

The following notation will be used:

i, j denote the regions: $i, j = 1, 2, \ldots, n$;

p_i^0 denote the quantity of soybeans supplied in region i (quantity available before inshipments and outshipments);

d_i^m denote the demand for the mth type of final product in region i, for $m = 1$ soybean meal, $m = 2$ soybean oil;

x_{ij}^0 denote the quantity of soybeans shipped from region i to region j under non-transit rate;

$x_{ij.k}^{00}$ denote the quantity of soybeans shipped from region i to region j under transit rate; the equivalent amount of meal must be shipped to region k;

x_{ij}^m denote the quantity of the mth final product shipped from region i to region j, for $m = 1$ shipment of meal under non-transit rate, $m = 2$ shipment of oil;

$x_{ij.k}^{11}$ denote the quantity of soybean meal shipped from region i to region j under transit rate; the equivalent amount of soybeans must have been shipped in from region k;

s_j^0 denote the level of crushing soybeans in region j;

$$(s_j^0 = \sum_i x_{ij}^0 + \sum_i \sum_k x_{ij.k}^{00}).$$

c_i denote the unit processing cost in region i;

t_{ij}^0 denote the unit non-transit transfer cost for a shipment of soybeans from region i to region j;

$t_{ij.k}^{00}$ denote the unit transit transfer cost for a shipment of soybeans from region i to region j; the equivalent amount of meal $(x_{jk.i}^{11})$ of the flow $x_{ij.k}^{00}$ must be shipped to region k;

t_{ij}^m denote the unit transfer cost for a shipment of the mth final product from region i to region j; for $m = 1$ non-transit transfer rate on meal, $m = 2$ transfer rate on oil;

$t_{ij.k}^{11}$ denote the unit transit transfer cost for a shipment of meal from region i to region j; the corresponding flow $(x_{ij.k}^{11})$ is the equivalent of the inbound flow $(x_{ki.j}^{00})$;

P_{ij}^m the net price for the mth final product to a processing plant in region i for a shipment (non-transit) to region j,

$$P_{ij}^m = P_{jj}^m - t_{ij}^m;$$

$P_{ij.k}^{11}$ the net price for soybean meal to a processing plant in region i for a shipment under transit to region j,

$$P_{ij.k}^{11} = P_{jj}^1 - t_{ij.k}^{11};$$

a^{0m} denote the rate at which soybeans are converted into meal (a^{01}) and into oil (a^{02}).

r_i denote the crushing capacity in region i.

2.3. Mathematical model[1]

Given the restrictive and expository assumption and using the foregoing definitions and notations, the constrained extremum problem may be expressed as follows:

To maximize:

$$F = \sum_i \sum_j \sum_m P_{ij}^m x_{ij}^m + \sum_j \sum_k \sum_i P_{jk.i} - \sum_i c_i s_i^0 - \sum_i \sum_j t_{ij}^0 x_{ij}^0$$
$$- \sum_i \sum_j \sum_k t_{ij.k}^{00} x_{ij.k}^{00} \quad (1)$$

subject to

$$\sum_j x_{ij}^1 + \sum_j \sum_k x_{ij.k}^{11} - a_i^{01} s_i^0 \leqslant 0$$

$$\sum_j x_{ij}^2 - a_i^{02} s_i^0 \leqslant 0. \quad (2)$$

The final product shipment, meal and oil, of the *i*th region to itself and other regions cannot exceed the meal equivalent respectively oil equivalent of the soybeans processed in region *i*.

$$\sum_j (x_{ij}^0 - x_{ji}^0) + \sum_j \sum_k (x_{ij.k}^{00} - x_{ji.k}^{00}) + s_i^0 \leqslant p_i^0. \quad (3)$$

The quantity of soybeans processed in the *i*th region cannot exceed the quantity of soybeans available in region *i*.

$$s_i^0 \leqslant r_i^0. \quad (4)$$

The quantity of soybeans processed in region *i* is less than or equal to the available regional processing capacity.

$$- \sum_j x_{ji}^1 - \sum_j \sum_k x_{ji.k}^{11} \leqslant - d_i^1$$

$$- \sum_j x_{ji}^2 \leqslant - d_i^2. \quad (5)$$

The shipment of meal respectively oil to region *i* from itself and other regions must fulfill the demand in region *i*.

$$a^{01} x_{ij.k}^{00} - x_{jk.i}^{11} = 0. \quad (6)$$

For the transit rate to be applicable, a specified technical relationship between the flows of soybeans and the equivalent flow of soybean meal must exist.

$$x_{ij}^m, x_{ij}^0, x_{ij,k}^{11}, x_{ij,k}^{00}, s_i^0 \geqslant 0. \quad (7)$$

[1] The basic references for this section are Beckman and Marschak [1], Judge *et al.* [2], Rizek *et al.* [5], Schrader and King [6], and Takayama and Judge [7, 8].

All choice variables have to be non-negative.

If the system (1) through (7) is defined as the primal problem, then the corresponding dual (counterpart of the production and flow solution) may be defined as follows:

To minimize:

$$G = -[\sum_m \sum_i d_i^m u_i^m - \sum_i r_i u_i^r - \sum_i p_i^0 u_i^0]. \tag{8}$$

If the u_i^q are interpreted as internal prices and rents, then the dual objective function (8) may be interpreted as to minimize the cost of the predetermined quantities of the final products meal and oil to regional consumers or to maximize the returns to the soybean growers and to the processing plant owners.

Subject to

$$u_i^m - u_j^m \geqslant p_{ij}^m \qquad \text{for non-transit flows} \tag{9}$$

$$u_i^m - u_j^m - u_i^t \geqslant p_{ij.k}^m \qquad \text{for transit flows}$$

$$\sum_m a_i^{0m} u_i^m + u_i^0 + u_i^r \geqslant -c_i \tag{10}$$

$$u_i^0 - u_j^0 \geqslant -t_{ij}^0 \qquad \text{for non transit flows} \tag{11}$$

$$u_i^0 - u_j^0 + a_j^{01} u_j^t \geqslant -t_{ij.k}^{00} \qquad \text{for transit flows.}$$

The u_i^q may be interpreted as follows:[2]

- $u_k^m \ldots u_n^m$ are prices imputed to meal $(m = 1)$ and oil $(m = 2)$ in the respective regions.

  In the final solution these correspond exactly to the prices used in the objective function.
- $u_m^0 \ldots u_p^0$ are prices imputed to soybeans delivered at the processing plants.
- $u_a^r \ldots u_s^r$ are prices imputed to the processing plants.

  As soybeans and processing capacities are fixed the prices are rents.
- $u_r^d \ldots u_w^d$ represent the difference between the prices appearing in the objective function and the prices imputed to meal respectively oil in the supply regions. As price dependent demand functions are used, these imputed prices approach zero as the equilibrium solution is approached.
- $u_v^t \ldots u_z^t$ are dual prices arising out of the possibility of transit shipments.

Accordingly, the constraints of the dual problems have the following economic interpretations:

[2] For a tableau representation, see Takayama and Judge [8].

(9) The difference in value for final product m in the demand region j and the supply region i must be equal to or less than the transportation cost. This must hold for the non-transit flows. For the transit flows, the difference must be equal to or less than $(t_{ij.k}^{11}+u_i^t)$.

(10) The value of soybeans in the ith region after crushing $(a_i^{01}u_i^1 + a_i^{02}u_i^2)$ is equal to or less than the value of soybeans in region i (u_i) plus the internal rent that may accrue to the soybean processing plant in region i (u_i^r) plus the unit cost of processing in region i.

(11) The difference in value of soybeans between region i and region j is equal to or less than the transportation cost. This must hold for the non-transit flows. For the transit flows the differences must be equal to or less than $(t_{ij.k}^{00}+a_j^{01} u_j^t)$.

The system of inequalities (9), (10) and (11) spells out the profit conditions of equilibrium in a competitive industry, i.e., no activity $(x_{ij}^0; x_{ij.k}^{00}, x_{ij}^m, x_{ij.k}^{11}, s_i^0)$, may permit a positive profit and for those activities which operate at positive levels profit must be zero. Therefore, for (1) to be a maximum, the internal prices and rents must satisfy conditions (9) through (11).

The solution of the problem is then obtained by assuming a set of prices for soybean meal and oil, maximizing the value of the final products minus the combined processing cost and cost of transportation of soybeans and final products subject to given sets of constraints and then using an iterative procedure to bring prices and quantities in equilibrium. The problem as structured has postulated that all the regional demands for meal, respectively oil, must be fulfilled.

2.4. Variations to the basic mathematical model

2.4.1. Model I and model II

The mathematical model thus far discussed incorporates the transit privilege system and in this way approximates closely the real world soybean economy. However, data problems and restrictions imposed by computer facilities do not permit us to consider the transit system for the location analysis of the soybean processing industry as a whole.

Accordingly, to investigate the locational pattern of the soybean processing industry within the continental United States, with due consideration to the export sector of the industry, some modifications must be made to the basic model. For model I, the following modifications are necessary: (i) the flows-under-transit for soybeans $(x_{ij.k}^{00})$ and for meal $(x_{ij.k}^{11})$ must be removed, i.e., a basically point-to-point mileage rate structure is assumed to exist only; (ii) the set of constraints (6) imposing the necessary relationship between the inbound weight of soybeans and the outbound weight of meal under the transit privilege system must also be removed.

In model II, it is assumed that the supply of the processing capacity in each region where processing is appropriate is infinitely elastic, i.e., the regional processing capacities are assumed to be non-limiting. In this way, insight in the changes that may occur over time in the different locational aspects of the industry may be obtained. Therefore, besides the two modifications discussed with respect to model I, it becomes necessary to remove in addition the set of constraints (4) restricting the regional crush to the regional processing capacity in each region.

2.4.2. Model III

The impact of a change in the rate structure from transit to non-transit will be investigated for the state of Illinois so as to provide information about the flexibility of the locational aspects of the U.S. industry as a whole with respect to changes in the rate structure.

Hereto, the state of Illinois is divided into 9 subregions with given regional supplies and crushing capacities. The regional demands for Illinois beans, meal and oil are determined in model I. The internal Illinois oil and meal demands are divided on the basis of the livestock animal units and population. The same transfer functions as in model I are used with transit rates specified where appropriate. The analysis relates also to the marketing year 1967–68.

Given the nature of the model, the net prices of the final products do not appear in the objective function and are replaced by the transportation cost on the final products, i.e., the problem changes from a problem of maximizing the returns to the soybean processing industry to a problem of minimizing the combined costs of processing and transportation. Other modifications must be made accordingly (Judge *et al.* [2]).

3. Data

3.1. Regional demarcation

For the analysis in model I and II the continental U.S. was partitioned into 20 geographically contiguous regions. Furthermore, two export regions have been included: region XXI representing Canada, W. Europe and Japan; region XXII representing other destinations of U.S. exports.

The regional demarcation for model III is given in table 2.

Table 1

Regional demarcation — model I and model II

Region	States	Basepoint
I	New York, Vermont, New Hampshire, Maine Massachusetts, Connecticut, Rhode Island, Pennsylvania, New Jersey	Albany (N.Y.)
II	Delaware, Maryland, Virginia, W. Virginia	Richmond (Va)
III	N. Carolina, S. Carolina	Columbia (S. Car.)
IV	Alabama, Georgia, Florida	Atlanta (Ga)
V	Kentucky, Tennessee	Chattanooga
VI	Ohio, Michigan	Columbia (Ohio)
VII	Indiana	Indianapolis
VIII	Illinois	Decatur
IX	Louisiana, Mississippi	Jackson (Miss.)
X	Arkansas	Little Rock
XI	Missouri	Jefferson City
XII	Iowa	Des Moines
XIII	Minnesota, Wisconsin	Minneapolis (Minn.)
XIV	N. Dakota, S. Dakota	Bismarck (N. Dak.)
XV	Nebraska, Kansas	Kansas City (Kan.)
XVI	Texas, Oklahoma	Dallas (Tex.)
XVII	Arizona, New Mexico	Phoenix (Ar.)
XVIII	Montana, Idaho, Wyoming, Utah, Colorado	Denver (Col.)
XIX	Washington, Oregon	Portland (Ore.)
XX	California, Nevada	San Francisco (Cal.)
XXI	Western Europe, Canada, Japan	
XXII	Rest of the world	

Table 2

Regional demarcation — model III

Subregions	Districts	Basepoint
I	North East	Chicago
II	North West	Dixon
III	West	Quincy
IV	Central	Decatur
V	East	Champaign
VI	East Southeast	Effingham
VII	West Southwest	Litchfield
VIII	South West	Carbondale
IX	South East	Harrisburg
X	region I — model I	
XI	regions XXI — model I	

Source: Reporting districts as used by the Illinois Department of Agriculture for subregions I to IX.

3.2. Regional availability of factors of production and processing costs

The more important data have been summarized in table 3 and table 4. A word of explanation with respect to the derivation of regional processing costs may be needed. As noted earlier, the long run average cost curve was derived for region VIII. Given the average plant size for each region, an 'unadjusted' processing cost is immediately determined. The adjusted regional processing cost equals the unadjusted cost minus the unadjusted labor share plus the labor share (30%) adjusted for regional wage differences.

Table 3

Processing capacity — processing cost — soybean availability (models I and II)

Region	Processing capacity (1000 m.t.)	Average plant size (1000 m.t.)	Adjusted processing cost ($/m.t.)	Soybeans availability 1967–68 (1000 m.t.)	Soybeans availability 1975–76 (1000 m.t.)
I	–	–	5.04	42	30
II	602.8	301.4	4.97	439	365
III	739.2	103.7	5.43	1273	1362
IV	851.1	141.8	5.29	723	1199
V	1582.1	289.1	4.84	975	1643
VI	1031.1	206.2	5.42	1496	1915
VII	1336.6	334.2	5.07	1739	2100
VIII	285.3	306.1	5.11	4589	4853
IX	1202.9	150.0	5.26	2009	4620
X	1614.8	245.5	4.65	2315	3184
XI	747.4	249.1	5.08	1843	2841
XII	2916.0	208.3	5.26	2946	3709
XIII	1568.5	196.4	5.22	1419	2850
XIV	–	–	5.02	208	520
XV	886.5	126.6	5.67	809	1597
XVI	65.5	62.7	5.97	261	440
XVII	–	–	–	–	–
XVIII	–	–	–	–	–
XIX	–	–	–	–	–
XX	49.1	49.1	6.40	–	–
XXI			4.61		
XXII			5.30		

Source: Estimated from information provided by the industry.

Table 4

Processing capacity — processing cost — soybean availability (model III)

Subregion (model III)	Processing capacity (1000 m.t.)	Average plant size (1000 m.t.)	Adjusted processing cost ($/m.t.)	Soybeans availability 1967–68 (1000 m.t.)
I	452.8	226.40	5.24	183
II	–	–	–	138
III	471.9	235.95	5.23	144
IV	1737.6	347.50	4.99	321
V	1145.7	381.90	4.91	396
VI	–	–	–	388
VII	450.1	450.10	4.77	412
VIII	–	–	–	169
IX	–	–	–	147
X	–	–	–	
XI				

Source: Estimated from information provided by the industry.

3.3. Regional demand relations

The two stage least squares estimates of the domestic aggregated demand equations for soybean meal and soybean oil are as follows[3]:

$$Y_1 = -7311.7160 + 379.2545X_4 - 22.9656Y_2 - 1.00120X_2$$
$$\ 8.67 \qquad\qquad 1.52 \qquad\qquad 2.44$$

$$+ 91.2311X_3 + 18.8465X_1 \qquad R^2 = 0.99202 \qquad\qquad (1)$$
$$\ 2.97 \qquad\ \ 3.12$$

$$Y_3 = -2668.191 - 2.5889Y_4 + 23.2031X_5 + 2.2828X_6 - 0.0067X_7$$
$$\ 2.34 \qquad\ \ 9.23 \qquad\ \ 1.67 \qquad\ \ 0.15 \qquad (2)$$
$$R^2 = 0.97160$$

where:

Y_1 = domestic consumption of soybean meal in 1000 metric tons,
X_1 = time (1 to 16 years),
Y_2 = price of soybean meal, Decatur Illinois, in dollars per metric ton,
X_2 = other high protein feed in 1000 metric tons,
X_3 = high protein animal units in million units,

[3] For the basic specification of the relationships see Vandenborre [9].

X_4 = U.S. livestock price index,
Y_3 = domestic consumption of soybean oil in 1000 metric tons,
Y_4 = crude soybean oil price in dollars per metric ton, midwestern mills,
X_5 = U.S. population in millions,
X_6 = crude soybean oil price in dollars per metric ton, midwestern mills,
X_7 = production plus starting stocks of butter and lard in the United
States in 1000 metric tons.

Ideally, market demand relations should be derived for each individual region. However, because there are no adequate data on many of the variables involved, a statistical technique was used to estimate the regional demand relations from the aggregate domestic demand for meal and oil, respectively.

If e.g. the aggregate demand relation for meal is:

$$Y_1 = a_1 + a_2 X_1 + a_3 Y_2 + a_4 X_2 + a_5 X_3 + a_6 X_4 \qquad (3)$$

the demand for meal in region i may be written as:

$$Y_{1i} = a_1(X_{3i}/X_3) + a_2(X_{3i}/X_3)X_1 + a_3(X_{3i}/X_3)Y_2 + a_4 X_{2i} + a_5 X_{3i}$$
$$+ a_6(X_{3i}/X_3)X_4. \qquad (4)$$

Since the X variables are fixed for the given marketing year, their respective effects can be included in the constant term and we get:

$$Y_{1i} = A_i + B_i Y_2, \text{ where (only } B_i \text{ needs clarification)}$$
$$B_i = a_3(X_{3i}/X_3)$$

The regional demands for oil can likewise be derived. All regional demand functions for oil and meal are presented in table 6. The fixed demands for model III (derived from model I) are presented in table 7.

The regional number of high protein consuming animal units is an important factor in the regional demand equation for meal. The same holds with respect to population in the regional oil demand equations. The soybean industry primarily sells however directly to other industries. These industries therefore are the intermediate demand determining factors for the soybean industry and they determine the locational aspects of the demand facing the soybean industry. For the method used to derive the regional demand for meal to be justified, a close locational relationship between the geographic dispersion of the high protein animal units and the geographic dispersion of the feed-mix industry must exist. A similar relationship must hold between the U.S. population and the industries manufacturing soybean oil.

Table 5

Relative distribution of value added in the respective industries and of HPAU and population (1963)

	U.S. 1 000 000 $ total val. add. numbers	North East	East North Central	West North Central	South Atlantic	East South Central	West South Central	West
Feed-mix ind.	930	11.7	26.9	17.8	12.7	9.3	9.0	12.5
HPAU (× 1 000 000)	149	9.1	19.6	29.7	15.1	8.0	8.5	10.0
Shortening and cooking oils	265	18.1	36.0	3.3	8.1	8.1	15.5	10.9
Paints and allied products	1112	27.9	34.8	6.8	7.4	4.3	6.0	12.8
Population (× 1 000 000)	190.7	24.8	19.8	8.3	14.8	6.7	9.6	16.0

Source: 1963 Census of Manufacturers; for data on value added HPAU, own estimates (1964). Population: Statistical Abstract of the United States, 1967.

Table 6

Regional demands for soybean meal and soybean oil – model I and model II

	Soybean meal				Soybean oil			
	1967–1968		1975–1976		1967–1968		1975–1976	
Regions	Intercept	Price SM	Intercept	Price SM	Intercept	Price SO	Intercept	Price SO
I	1091.846	2.1175	826.278	1.6535	641.443	0.6402	710.995	0.6212
II	447.114	0.9301	461.704	0.8405	148.882	0.1486	172.416	0.1507
III	723.940	1.0610	1096.255	1.2745	100.638	0.1004	113.167	0.0989
IV	1279.543	1.9750	2120.716	2.5054	182.342	0.1820	224.260	0.1960
V	360.376	0.7050	209.818	0.5534	94.933	0.0948	103.390	0.0904
VI	719.074	1.2424	508.164	0.9002	249.004	0.2485	276.992	0.2421
VII	592.132	0.9898	534.716	0.8129	65.882	0.0658	72.284	0.0632
VIII	815.683	1.4353	843.014	1.3182	143.435	0.1432	158.196	0.1382
IX	446.074	0.6453	620.659	0.7257	78.851	0.0787	89.763	0.0784
X	452.236	0.6820	907.942	1.0380	26.456	0.0264	29.329	0.0256
XI	387.086	0.9691	344.205	0.8520	60.953	0.0608	65.175	0.0570
XII	1580.986	2.4113	1743.799	2.2690	37.610	0.0375	37.623	0.0329
XIII	1142.239	2.1035	1250.062	1.9635	104.011	0.1038	113.167	0.0989
XIV	403.867	0.6958	523.400	0.6177	18.416	0.0184	18.367	0.0161
XV	689.736	1.5869	1147.945	1.8854	50.579	0.0505	52.732	0.0461
XVI	562.767	1.1184	712.201	1.1482	175.339	0.1750	202.337	0.1768
XVII	39.556	0.1056	123.393	0.1768	34.756	0.0347	44.733	0.0391
XVIII	187.302	0.5190	319.811	0.6086	63.287	0.0632	72.581	0.0634
XIX	145.475	0.3812	166.811	0.3820	66.141	0.0660	74.063	0.0647
XX	638.495	1.2906	938.817	1.4491	250.818	0.2504	330.909	0.2892

Source: Leunis [3].

Table 7

Regional demand for soybean meal and soybean oil — model III (m.t.)

Subregion	Meal	Oil
I	81 924	77 097
II	186 956	8 066
III	93 128	2 965
IV	65 820	7 116
V	44 113	4 982
VI	58 818	3 321
VII	97 329	6 879
VIII	41 312	5 693
IX	30 809	2 491

Source: Leunis, [3].

The results of table 5 point toward such a close spatial relationship.[4]

Export demands for meal and oil are specified for Canada, Western Europe and Japan. The export demands from other countries have largely been determined on the basis of the development of meal and oil exports to these countries during the last decade[5].

The two stage least squares estimate of the export demand for soybean meal of Canada, Western Europe and Japan is:

$$Y_5 = -2495.140 + 224.1887X_1 - 5.4078Y_2 - 7.7336Y_4$$
$$ 4.54 0.41 1.40$$

$$+48.7865 \quad X_8 R^2 = 0.94887 (5)$$
$$2.32$$

where Y_5 = exports of soybean meal under all forms to Canada, Western Europe and Japan, and X_8 = EEC and Canada price index of prices of cattle, hogs and fluid milk, 1958 = 100. The other variables were identified previously.

The two stage least squares estimate of the export demand for soybean oil is:

$$Y_6 = 298.1204 + 55.07626X_1 - 1.9149Y_4 - 0.1307X_9$$
$$ 3.97 1.71 1.47$$

$$+6.3153X_8 R^2 = 0.93350 (6)$$
$$1.48$$

[4] Modified coefficients of localization were computed to investigate the respective spatial relationships. For more detail see Leunis [3].

[5] See Leunis [3].

where Y_6 = exports of soybean oil under all forms to Canada, Western Europe and Japan, and X_9 = Canadian, Western European, Japanese and most important exporters' (outside of the United States) production of food fats and oils (except butter and lard) in 1000 metric tons oil equivalent. The other variables were identified previously.

3.4. Transfer costs

Each region is assumed to be a point market with regional supply of raw material and final product, regional demand and regional processing to be located in the base point. Transfer costs between regions have been calculated for soybeans, meal and oil on the basis of the distance between their respective base points. Intraregional transportation costs are assumed to be zero.

Transfer cost functions are estimated for railroad transportation. Actual barge rates are given between pairs of points. Between each pair of points, the least cost transportation mode and corresponding transfer cost is selected. Combination rates for barge-truck are included in particular cases. Ocean freight rates for soybeans, meal and oil are specified between ports at the Great Lakes, the Atlantic Coast, the Gulf Coast, and Europe (Rotterdam) and Japan. For each region the least cost export route is chosen.[6]

The transit privilege system constitutes an important aspect of transportation in the soybean sector.

Transit privilege may be defined as "the privilege of stopping a shipment en route to enable some process or operation to be performed on the article, and of reshipping to final destination at the through rate applicable from the original shipping point to destination", (Locklin [4]; Leunis [3]).

4. Empirical results[7]

Because of space limitations the detailed results will only be given for model I in tables 8 through 11. As they are sufficiently self explanatory, emphasis in the discussion of the results will primarily be upon the changes occurring in model II with respect to model I. The major conclusions to be drawn from the analyses in model III will also briefly be summarized.

---

[6] For more detail on the rates of transportation see Leunis [3].

[7] All empirical results are presented in 1000 metric tons rounded to the nearest ton; this may result in some rounding errors.

Table 8

Supplies, price differentials, optimum levels of crushings and flows of soybeans, 1967–68

Destination	Origins and quantities of shipments (1000 metric tons).												Supply of soybeans	Optimum processing demand	V^j [b]
	I	III	V	VI	VII	VIII	IX	X	XI	XII	XIV	XVI			
II		18											439	457	10.16
IV		124	4										723	851	4.92
XIII[a]													1419	1419	2.46
XV[a]													809	809	1.34
XX[a]													–	–	27.29
XXI	42	391		465		1914	1518	1305	1281	285	208	195	–	7603	12.42
XXII					402	377							–	779	12.42
Supply	42	1273	975	1496	1738	4588	2009	2315	1843	2946	208	261	23 085		
Processing	–	739	972	1031	1336	2298	492	1010	562	2661	–	66		23 085	
U^i [b]	–1.05	2.80	3.40	–1.24	–1.90	1.43	4.58	4.13	1.16	0	–2.85	–2.41			

Supply: 23 085 metric tons

Total

Shipments: 8 528 462 metric tons

[a] Received no shipments of soybeans from other regions. Crush composed of soybeans grown in the region.
[b] The U^i and V^j are in terms of dollars per metric ton of beans.

Table 9

Excess demands and supplies, optimum flows and price differentials of soybean meal, 1967–68

Origins	I	II[a]	III	IV	IX[a]	XIV	XVI	XVII	XVIII	XIX	XX	XXI	XXII	Excess supplies	U^i[b]
V			41	432										473	3.43
VI	260													260	3.84
VII	554													554	2.40
VIII	137											600	394	1131	1.10
X							410							410	4.21
XI									139					139	1.22
XII						180		29		20	501			731	0
XIII						160								160	2.29
XV										84				84	2.20
Excess demand	951	0	41	432	0	340	410	29	139	105	501	600	394	3942	
V^j[b]	12.49	9.47	9.18	6.48	4.69	11.88	10.72	16.50	14.20	27.28	27.28	12.80			

Destinations (1000 metric tons)

Total shipments: 3 942 196 metric tons

[a] Received no shipments of soybean meal from other regions. Crush fulfilled regional demand.
[b] The U^i and V^j are in terms of dollars per metric ton of meal.

Table 10

Excess demands and supplies, optimum flows and price differentials of soybean oil, 1967–68

Origins	Destinations (1000 metric tons)												Excess supplies	U^i [b]
	I	II	IV[a]	VI	XIV	XVI	XVII	XVIII	XIX	XX	XXI[b]	XXII		
III												48	48	6.12
V		41										52	93	1.36
VII	182												182	3.75
VIII	287												287	2.27
IX												22	22	4.77
X						132						24	157	0.92
XI	27			22									49	0.04
XII	25				15				32	202		165	439	0
XIII												165	165	3.35
XV							28	52	21				101	0
Excess demands	521	41	0	22	15	132	28	52	53	202	0	465	1542	
V^j [b]	17.13	13.13	4.484	10.41	9.79	9.74	22.66	9.90	22.66	22.66	17.05	21.05		

Total
shipments: 1 542 069 metric tons

[a] Received no shipments of soybean oil from other regions. Crush fulfilled regional demand.
[b] The U^i and V^j are in terms of dollars per metric ton of oil.

4.1. Estimated flows

In table 8 the optimal soybean flows for model I are presented. The following major conclusions may be drawn:

(1) the total number of soybeans shipped during the marketing year 1967–68 amounts to 8.5 million metric tons; this amount increases to 14 million metric tons in model II largely because of assumed increased soybean production in 1975–76.

(2) soybean flows among regions within the United States are minimal; this conclusion holds also for model II.

(3) major changes may however be expected in the composition of the more important exporting regions.

The optimal meal flows are presented in table 9. The major conclusions of model I are:

(1) The total amount of soybean meal entering interregional trade during the marketing year 1967–68 is over 3 900 000 metric tons; this amount increases by approximately 25 % in model II.

(2) the dependence of the United States upon foreign demand for soybean meal, already important in 1967–68, is increasing.

(3) the number of regions exporting soybean meal is shown to increase considerably by 1975.

In table 10 the corresponding soybean oil flows are presented. Major conclusions with respect to the oil flows are: (a) the total amount of soybean oil entering interregional trade, 1 542 069 metric ton in 1967–68, increases with approximately 800 000 metric tons in 1975–76, i.e. an increase of more than 50 %; (b) this increase must almost completely be absorbed by region XXII; (c) the dependence of U.S. processors upon foreign countries for the sale of oil increases over time.

4.2. Estimated regional crush

The optimal levels of regional crush as determined in model I as well as the existing excess capacity are reported in table 11. The regional crush of model II is given for purpose of comparison.

4.3 Price differentials and rents

The set of price differentials consistent with the optimal flow pattern of soybeans, soybean meal and soybean oil are presented in the last row and column in tables 8 through 10.

Table 11

Optimum crush, 1967–1968 and 1975–1976

Region	1967–1968			1975–1976
	Crushing (1000 m.t.)	Excess capacity (1000 m.t.)	Capacity utilized (%)	Crushing (1000 m.t.)
I	–	–	–	30
II	457	145	76	365
III	739	–	100	1362
IV	851	–	100	2368
V	972	610	61	475
VI	1031	–	100	1915
VII	1337	–	100	2100
VIII	2298	1987	54	1752
IX	492	711	41	718
X	1010	605	63	1399
XI	562	186	75	700
XII	2661	255	91	3010
XIII	1419	150	90	1491
XIV	–	–	–	520
XV	809	77	91	1597
XVI	66	–	100	494
XVII	–	–	–	–
XVIII	–	–	–	–
XIX	–	–	–	–
XX	–	49	0	–

Region XII was chosen as the base region and the price differentials are computed relative to the base region. For the surplus regions the price differentials indicate the comparative advantage of each region relative to the base region. In the case of deficit regions the price differentials indicate the delivered price differentials relative to the base region.

The estimated price differentials in model I (and in model II) suggest that in general soybean meal and oil prices will be highest in the Mountain states and on the West Coast. Other regions with high relative prices are the export regions and the regions on the East Coast. The prices will generally be lowest in the Midwestern states.

The pattern of comparative advantage of the important surplus regions of soybeans, as indicated by the price differentials in the last row of table 8, is largely the same in model II. The same is also true for the pattern of delivered prices. However it must be pointed out that several regions become self-sufficient in soybeans in 1975–76: they are generally characterized by higher price levels relative to the base region during the marketing year 1975–76.

Relatively important changes in the pattern of comparative advantage of the surplus regions of soybean meal occur between 1967–68 and 1975–76. The comparative advantages of regions V, VI and XIII decrease considerably.

The general pattern of delivered price differentials for the deficit regions in 1967–68 is largely repeated in 1975–76. However, region XIV deviates rather extensively from its delivered price level in 1967–1968 whereas region III, by becoming a surplus region in 1975–1976, is characterized by an important decrease of its price differential relative to the base region.

The relatively advantageous position of region VII (Indiana) and region VIII (Illinois) as oil producing regions in model I has deteriorated considerably in the analysis of model II.

Minor changes have occurred in the set of price differentials for the deficit regions indicating that the pattern of regional price differences in 1975–1976 will be very close to the 1967–68 pattern. The deficit regions with the highest delivered prices are located along both the East and West Coasts of the U.S.

A byproduct of the analysis are the 'rents' for additional soybean crushing capacity that are consistent with the price and allocation solution. The regions to which crushing rents accrued and the amount of rent in dollars per metric ton are:

Region III:	5.43 dollars/m.t.
Region IV:	0.76 dollars/m.t.
Region VI:	5.98 dollars/m.t.
Region VII:	4.67 dollars/m.t.
Region XVI:	11.97 dollars/m.t.

In eleven of the sixteen regions growing soybeans, the production of soybeans exceeded the available regional processing capacities. In region IV, the total regional soybean crushing capacity is utilized by importing soybeans from the adjacent regions III and V. Accordingly, since costs must be incurred in importing the soybeans, the rent for region IV is low relative to the rents accrued to regions III, VI, VII and XVI.

4.4. Major results of model III

The major results may be briefly summarized as follows:

(1) Over 55 % of all soybean movement makes use of the processing-

in-transit privilege. Because of the necessary weight relationships between the inbound tonnage (of soybeans) and the outbound tonnage (of soybean meal) of each pair of transit flows at the transit point, it follows that also over 55 % of all meal is shipped under the transit rate structure.

(2) The elimination of the processing-in-transit privilege and of the corresponding transit rates resulted in an optimum flow pattern, which is considerably different from the optimum flow pattern before the elimination.

(3) The elimination of the transit system affects the regional level of processing. One region may considerably increase its processing at the expense of another.

(4) The elimination of the transit system may also greatly affect the total cost of processing and transportation associated with the optimum levels of regional processing and the corresponding optimum flow pattern. Whereas the processing cost is somewhat lower after eliminating the processing-in-transit privilege system, the transportation cost increases considerably. The total effect of the elimination of the transit system, with no change in the basic railroad rates, is therefore an approximate 5 % increase from the combined processing and transportation cost.

(5) A comparison of the sets of price differentials for soybeans shows that the comparative advantage of those regions shipping soybeans only under the transit system decreases considerably after elimination of this rate structure.

(6) With respect to the meal flows those regions whose regional demands are completely fulfilled by inshipments under the transit system are characterized by a large increase in the delivered prices when the transit system is eliminated.

5. Concluding remarks

5.1. Policy and methodological implications

If the levels of regional processing as determined in model II may be interpreted to be equal to the future optimum required regional crushing capacities, then important changes must take place in the soybean crushing industry within the next decade.

The estimated price differentials in model I and model II suggest that in general soybean meal and oil prices will be highest in the Mountain states and on the West Coast. Other regions with high relative prices are the export regions and the regions on the East Coast. The prices will generally be lowest in the Midwestern states.

The analyses of model III indicate that the elimination of transit privilege system may have considerable influence upon the levels of regional processing, the flow pattern of the commodities in question and the corresponding spatial price pattern.

From a methodological point of view, a major result of this study is that the applicability of the linear activity analysis model in a large empirical analysis is shown. The consideration of the processing-in-transit privilege also shows that the basic linear activity analysis model can be extended to include more realistically the particular characteristics of the sector studied. Although the results obtained are largely conditioned by the data available, it may be concluded that the interregional activity analysis model represents a major tool of analysis in actual business problems.

5.2. *Things this study did not do, and opportunities for additional work*

The locational influences with which this analysis has been concerned are essentially those that affect the choice of an area or a region, i.e., the meaning of location in a wider sense. The choice of a site within a region, or location in the narrower sense, has not been considered. The choice for each individual plant within a region would require local study and would constitute a second stage in the present investigation.

The economic feasibility of replacing plants at less than optimal locations by plants at optimal locations is also not covered in the analysis. To provide a sound judgment about the replacement problem, a detailed study for each individual plant is necessary. Advantages associated with moving to an optimal location must be weighted against the cost of moving.

The actual level of processing in region VIII (Illinois) during the last several marketing years is considerably larger than the estimated level of processing in model I.

This deviation may partially be explained by two characteristics which are inherent to the type of model used in this analysis: (1) the choice of a base point in each region in which all economic activity is assumed to be concentrated and (2) between each pair of base points, the cheapest mode of transportation is selected. Accordingly, in adopting the cheap barge transportation, the advantageous position of Illinois with respect to the export markets may therefore have been given too much emphasis. Research on the impact of using a more differentiated set of modes of transportation upon the level of processing in region VIII could throw more light on this question.

Second existing firms may be processing at margins only covering variable costs. The testing of the hypothesis that the Illinois soybean industry at the present time may be largely operating on the basis of its average variable cost may be another direction in which further research may lead.

References

[1] Beckmann, J. and T. Marschak, 1955, An activity analysis approach to locations theory, Kyklos VIII, 125–145.

[2] Judge, G. G., J. Havlicek and R. L. Rizek, 1965, An interregional model: its formulation and application to the livestock industry, Agricultural Economic Research XVIII, no 1.

[3] Leunis, J. V., 1968, A spatial analysis of the United States soybean industry, unpublished Ph. D. thesis, University of Illinois.

[4] Locklin, D. P., 1966, Economics of Transportation, Homewood, Ill., R. D., 6th ed.

[5] Rizek, R. L., G. G. Judge and J. Havlicek, 1965, Spatial structure of the livestock economy, North Central Regional Research Bull. No. 163.

[6] Schrader, L. F. and G. A. King, 1962, Regional location of beef cattle feeding, Journal of Farm Economics XLIV, no 1, 64–81.

[7] Takayama, T. and G. G. Judge, 1964, An interregional activity analysis model for the agricultural sector, Journal of Farm Economics 46, 2.

[8] Takayama T. and G. G. Judge, 1971, Spatial and Temporal Price and Allocation Models, Amsterdam: North-Holland Publishing Company.

[9] Vandenborre, R. J., 1967, An econometric analysis of the markets for soybean oil and soybean meal, University of Illinois, Agricultural Experiment Station, Bulletin 723.

CHAPTER 16

Pricing and allocation models applied to problems of interregional trade and location of industries

H. E. BUCHHOLZ

Institut für landwirtschaftliche Marktforschung, Braunschweig

1. Introduction

Activity analysis and computer technology opened the road to explicit recognition of spatial and temporal dimensions in economic analysis. The resulting impetus is observed both in theoretical and empirical economic research. Volume I of Takayama and Judge [11] documents the theoretical breakthrough that was realized in an astonishingly short time span. Empirical research work did not follow suit at an equal path. With reference to a particular research area this paper points out some of the empirical research efforts in the field of interregional trade and location of industries. The examples are taken from agricultural commodity markets. The objectives of these studies refer to some very real agricultural policy problems mostly in connection with the question of locational adjustment in the process of European economic integration and the resulting changes in interregional competition.

2. Conceptual premises

From the broad range of models available only two types have found wider application in empirical research. These are (1) the linear distribution model (classical transportation model) and (2) the linear model of production and allocation. Obviously the conceptual simplicity of the former and its clear cut interpretation have facilitated its acceptance as a new tool of economic investigation. The distribution model has taken a firm place in lectures and textbooks of operations research and it can be assumed that it is also being used as a decision making aid to the management of large business firms. Such applications are however rarely published. Therefore, the economic literature only shows some studies of a more expository nature. To be named here are a study of long distance hauling of milk [5], a transportation model of the German sugar industry [3], an interregional activity analysis model of the German paper industry [7] and of the cement industry of North-Rhine-Westfalia [12].

Quite often the reduction of a problem to the dimensions of a pure distribution problem means to neglect important aspects of the analysis. This then would call for the application of the more ambitious spatial activity analysis models. The number of studies that have actually used this model approach is, however, rather limited and moreover the few studies known never went beyond the linear model of production and allocation. That is, single- or multi-product spatial price equilibrium models so far have not been used for practical purposes.

These remarks are made with respect to the situation in West Germany but the state of affairs in other West European countries is largely similar. The reasons for this may be found in the rather stringent assumptions required to develop operational models and also in the considerably large research effort that must be made before meaningful solutions are gained.

With respect to the model assumptions it should only be mentioned here that models of interregional trade and price equilibrium in general are working on the assumption of perfect competition in the respective commodity markets. The possibility of recognising other forms of market behavior such as monopolistic supply exists [11, p. 208 ff.]. The difficulty is, however, that cases of pure monopoly are not frequently encountered in reality and that mixed elements of market behavior are hard to treat methodologically.

The assumption of perfect competition which implies among others profit maximization, homogeneity of product, free access to markets, perfect market knowledge, etc. is most approximately fulfilled on the supply side of agricultural commodity markets. This explains the predominance of agricultural studies in this field. Agricultural markets also show a number of further specific traits that are in line with the more detailed assumptions of regional activity analysis models (cf. [11], p. 65 ff., p. 86 ff.).

In case the model assumptions with respect to a specific study are considered to be tolerable then the actual analysis is still subject to a number of restrictions that are in general not easily overcome. The most serious of these are to be found in the availability and comparability of data on the required regional level. In this context the decision of the regional decomposition of a given total area is in itself a difficult problem. Ideally the regional demarcation should be done following subject matter considerations. In practice, however, the investigator is mostly forced to accept the existing administrative boundaries. Only when the statistical data base on a lower regional level is sufficiently good then larger regions may be synthezised which do not follow state lines. In many cases the required data are, however, simply not available and approximations of one form or another have to be used. This of course requires great skills and should not be undertaken without excellent subject matter knowledge. A great number of problems that are tailor-made for the application of activity analysis methods originated from the formation of the European Economic Community. The practical difficulties of such analyses are, however, enormously enhanced by national differences in the statistical concepts, different socio-economic structures, monetary systems and also by language handicaps. For all these reasons such studies more and more go beyond the capacities of a single researcher or even single institutions and should be pursued with the cooperation of a number of study groups.

3. Analyses of commodity flows

3.1. Sugar

Sugar production in the EEC countries is rather heavily concentrated in particular regions. The question of how distribution costs enter into the price calculations, the level of transport costs and the distances to consumption regions, therefore, are of importance for the competitive position of producers. An assessment of the actual competitive situation of the producing regions under the provisions of CAP therefore was of considerable interest. Such a study was made as early as 1964 [8]. The study was designed to analyse the effects of transport cost differences for the producing regions of the EEC. The analysis was made with data of production and distribution of sugar during the campaign years 1959/60 and 1961/62. The method used was the linear distribution model, with the total area of the EEC partitioned into 61 producer and 119 consumer regions.

From the model solution some valuable insights could be deduced both for the transition period and the final stage of the common market. It was shown that during the transition period, that is, as long as the common price level was not achieved, some production regions with relatively low price levels would have locational advantages over neighbouring regions in countries with a higher sugar price level in the pre-common market era.

They would, however, gain from this situation only as long as world market prices were higher than the target price in the exporting region. With respect to the final stage of the common sugar market characterised by a unique loco plant price in all regions such disturbances of the competitive position of producing regions were shown to disappear. Assuming equal freight rates throughout the community the study implied that the dismissal of the national import regulations would yield but little changes in the inter-regional transport flows of sugar. Most of the producing regions have at their traditional markets locational advantages over competitors who by the new market regulations gained free access to these markets. Although the results as an ex ante projection of the future market structure certainly facilitated decisions to introduce the common sugar policy, the full bearing of the study could not be checked later on since quota regulations were introduced in the common sugar market.

3.2. Grain

A model of interregional grain flows in the EEC was formulated with the objective to check the regional grain price structure of the EEC grain policy [9]. The analysis was based on a linear distribution model with 165 intra EEC regions and 21 trading points for third countries. Minimum transport cost solutions were arrived at separately for wheat and for barley. The model results were used to discuss the problem of the regional deter-mination of intervention prices for grain, the impact of the level of export restrictions on the commodity flows and the competitive position of distant production areas such as Southern Germany. In a subsequent study the same model was used in an analysis of the grain storage capacities in the EEC [10]. In this study the optimum grain flows for the year 1965 and the prospective changes that resulted from a projection of the optimum flows for 1970 were, among other factors, utilized to find criteria for the determina-tion of the future regional grain storage capacities.

3.3. Eggs

The egg market in the EEC is characterised by increasing supplies and stiff competition among member states. A study was designed to analyse the competitive situation of the egg producing regions within the community [6]. Special emphasis was placed on the question of which changes in the competitive position of producing regions occurred as a consequence of the CAP and whether such changes are still to be expected in the future. A number of alternative models were formulated to answer particular questions.

First the minimum cost linear distribution model was used to determine optimum transport flows between surplus and deficit regions. This model abstracts from important market conditions and contains only distances and regional quantity balances. Thus it permits one to analyse the role of transport costs in the determination of commodity flows among regions with given production and consumption structures. Three variations of the linear distribution model with differences in the regional demarcation were solved in order to investigate consequences that follow from the larger uniform market area of the common market.

The next step of the analysis used the regional activity analysis model of production and allocation. The objective was to recognize the element of space not only in egg distribution but also on the production side. Egg production activities were formulated that allowed the incorporation into the model of the locational effects of the regional factors of production such as feed and laying hens as well as those of regional differences in feeding efficiency. Again, three alternative model specifications were formulated. The most comprehensive of these reflects on the supply side the regional production capacities, costs of production, and restrictions on the growth of capacities. The production costs were determined by feeding costs, replacement and feeding efficiency. On the distribution side the model contains regional sales capacities, direct marketing costs, packing-, handling- and interregional transport costs.

The results from all model solutions showed a relatively close correspondence of the actual interregional trade flows and the optimum flows. The activity analysis model solutions confirmed the hypothesis that, mainly on the grounds of higher efficiency of production in the traditional egg surplus regions, a shift of the regional production pattern that would increase production in the deficit regions is not to be expected. In the long run, however, such shifts could not be excluded. That is, the model did not account for changes of internal or external economies in the production, handling and distribution of eggs.

3.4. Poultry

A study of regional competition in the EEC broiler market was based on the regional availability of feed grain as the most important input factor [1]. The objective was to quantify locational advantages or disadvantages for production regions taking into account feed grain availabilities and the demand potential of consumer markets. The model was also used to test the impact of changes in the EEC grain policies and changes in freight rates. The emphasis of the study was put on a particular region of West Germany — the state of North-Rhine-Westfalia — and problems of sales policy for producers in this region are discussed in the light of the model results. The methodological approach consisted of a linear distribution model which was solved separately for the minimum transport costs of (a) feed grains and (b) broilers as the final product. The total area of the EEC was partitioned into 22 regions and data from 1966 and 1967 were used. The model commodity flows were largely in line with real world observations. The study concludes that in the broiler market regional efficiency of production and distribution methods is more significant than the factor location as expressed by transport cost differences.

3.5. Pork

To explain regional price differences in the market for pork in the Federal Republic of Germany a linear distribution model with 32 surplus and 34 deficit regions was developed [14]. Imports of pork from France, The Netherlands and Belgium were admitted on the level of actual imports in 1967. The price differentials obtained from the model showed a similar pattern — increasing from the north to the south — but the absolute differences were considerably less than among observed prices. This was taken as an indication that the quality of the product as well as efficiency of the distribution system could be improved in a number of regions, especially in Southern Germany.

4. Analyses of location of industries

4.1. Egg packing plants

The problem of optimal size and location of processing plants for agricultural raw products was analysed in a study of the structure of egg packing plants in the Federal Republic of Germany [13]. A detailed structural survey showed that the analysis could be restricted to medium and large size packing plants. For these, first the long run cost curve of the industry was determined. Then a linear distribution model was used to find the optimal location of egg packing plants. The model minimized processing costs and transport costs from processing plants to the large urban consumption centers. Regional processing capacities and consumer demand were the restrictions of the model. Different specifications of the capacity restrictions were used in order to arrive at a solution with optimal capacity levels in the processing plants. The final version of the model contained 81 processing locations and 9 urban consumption regions. The optimum solution for this model indicated that 42 processing locations and 115 processing plants would be sufficient to supply the urban consumption centers at least processing and distribution cost. This compares with 169 actual locations and 517 medium and large processing plants in 1969.

4.2. Dairies

The problem of location of milk processing plants was investigated using a linear activity analysis model with spatial and temporal elements [2]. The emphasis of the model focused heavily on the management aspects of such firms. The restrictions of the model, therefore, included liquidity-, capacity-, raw product-, sales-, financial- and definitional restrictions. The analysis was considered as a pilot study to test and to improve the methodological approach for the solution of such problems. Therefore, the model included only seven existent processing firms (dairies) in a single milk production area and their respective sales regions. The time horizon used in the analysis was nine planning periods. The outcome of the model confirmed a strong tendency for concentration in the milk processing industry. The optimum solution for the last period showed that only one firm could handle all processing. Because of the rather specific assumptions made for the individual firms it was not possible to generalize the results for other regions.

4.3. Research in progress

The above stated examples of empirical analyses of commodity flows were largely restricted to more or less homogeneous products or products with a comparatively low degree of interdependence of the production processes. Studies of more complex commodity markets have not yet been completed. Some work in this direction is, however, in progress.

Of the commodity markets within the EEC especially the feed-livestock sector is of interest and attempts are currently being made to work out an integrated interregional model covering the countries of the community in total. Since these efforts are still at the very beginning, and considering also the aforementioned difficulties of such 'inter'national studies it may take some time before first results can possibly be reported.

From another quite ambitious research project results are expected to be available sooner. The study in question is a joint research effort among the West German agricultural economics departments and other research institutes to establish a sector model for German agriculture [4]. The core of the analysis will be an interregional activity analysis model which includes agricultural production, the agricultural labor market, and the marketing of agricultural products. The model is to be run on several levels of regional aggregation. Regional submodels are worked out by regional research teams. The submodels are then coordinated and aggregated in the total model. In each case the following four steps will be taken:

(1) Computation of complete regional balances.
(2) Determination of factors of regional competition.
(3) Comparative static analyses.
(4) Conversion to models of dynamic coupling.

The overall objective is to work out quantitatively a long run development scheme for West German agriculture. For this purpose, projections are intended for the years 1975, 1980 and 1985.

References

[1] Alvensleben, R. v., 1970, Standorte der Junghühnermast in der EWG, Bonner Hefte für Marktforschung, 2.

[2] Grosskopf, W., 1971, Bestimmung der optimalen Größen und Standorte von Verarbeitungsbetrieben landwirtschaftlicher Produkte, Agrarwirtschaft, 45.

[3] Gülicher, H., 1964, Ein ökonometrisches Programmierungsmodell zur Bestimmung der transportkostenminimalen Lieferströme der westdeutschen Weißzuckerindustrie 1955, Zeitschrift für die gesamte Staatswissenschaft 120, 435–463.

[4] Henrichsmeyer, W. and H. de Haen, 1972, Zur Konzeption des Schwerpunktprogramms der Deutschen Forschungsgemeinschaft "Konkurrenzvergleich landwirtschaftlicher Standorte", Agrarwirtschaft 21, 141–152.

[5] Joksch, H. C., 1960, Der Milch-Fernversand in Nordrhein-Westfalen, Zeitschrift für die gesamte Staatswissenschaft 116, 469–494.

[6] Kersten, L., 1971, Die interregionale Wettbewerbsfähigkeit der Eiererzeugung in der EWG, Landbauforschung Völkenrode, 10.

[7] König, H. and R. Thoss, 1965, Der optimale Standort der Industrie: Ein interregionales Programmierungsmodell für die westdeutsche Papierindustrie, Zeitschrift für die gesamte Staatswissenschaft 121, 385–432.

[8] Richter, W., 1965, Die standortbedingte Wettbewerbslage der Zuckererzeuger zu den Zuckerverbrauchsgebieten in der Europäischen Wirtschaftsgemeinschaft, Diss.

Gießen 1965, Veröffentlicht als Heft 38 der Schriftenreihe der Wirtschaftlichen Vereinigung Zucker e.V.

[9] Strecker, O., R. v. Alvensleben and F. Hottelmann, 1968, Zur regionalen Preisabstufung auf dem Getreidemarkt der EWG, Agrarwirtschaft 17, 93 ff.

[10] Strecker, O., W. Schopen, F. Hottelmann and M. v. Oppen, 1968, Getreidelager in der Europäischen Wirtschaftsgemeinschaft, Teil I. Kommission der Europäischen Gemeinschaften, Hausmitteilungen über Landwirtschaft 28.

[11] Takayama, T. and G. G. Judge, 1971, Spatial and Temporal Price and Allocation Models, Amsterdam, North-Holland Publishing Company.

[12] Thül, R., 1968, Ein interregionales Programmierungsmodell der westf. Zementindustrie. Schriften zur angewandten Wirtschaftsforschung, 13 (Mohr [Seilbeck], Tübingen).

[13] Weichelt, A., 1973, Die Bestimmung optimaler Branchenstrukturen bei Be- und Verarbeitungsbetrieben landwirtschaftlicher Produkte, dargestellt am Beispiel von Eierpackstellen, Institut für landw. Marktforschung, Braunschweig-Völkenrode.

[14] Willers, B. and R. v. Alvensleben, 1969, Die regionalen Erzeugerpreisunterschiede bei Schlachtschweinen in der Bundesrepublik Deutschland, Agrarwirtschaft 18, 295–302.

CHAPTER 17

Experiences with multi-commodity models in regional analysis

G. WEINSCHENCK, W. HENRICHSMEYER and C. H. HANF*

1. Introduction

Application of process analysis models at the early stage of its development concentrated mainly around optimization problems on the level of the single farm, but has been expanded to the consideration of farm groups, regions and the total agricultural sector subdivided in regions during the last years. All these investigations have it in common that they consider aggregates of farms instead of single farms as decision making units. They differ with respect to the consideration or neglection of space and the kind of inter-dependencies between the decision making units which are taken into account explicitly. Both differences are strongly connected with the percentage of the production potential of the total agricultural sector, which is considered in the model. Hence, they form a sound base for the separation of farm group models, regional models and interregional models which is not quite clear in literature.

Farm group models. Farm group models consider one or more aggregates of farms as decision making units each of them consisting of a certain number of single farms. Interdependencies which might exist between the decision making units are neglected. Hence, there are only two kinds of production factors:

(a) Factors which are fixed on the level of the decision making units: They are assumed to be perfectly mobile between the single farms of each aggregate.

(b) Factors which are variable: They can be bought by all decision making

---

* Universität Stuttgart-Hohenheim, Universität Bonn, Universität Stuttgart-Hohenheim.

aggregates at given prices, which may or may not differ between the aggregates, and which are assumed to be independent from demand.

Products can be sold by all aggregates at given prices which may or may not differ between the decision making aggregates but which are independent of the volume of production.

Regional models. Regional models consider explicitly the interdependencies, which result from the competition for the use of factors whose regional supply is limited. They consist of aggregates of farms as decision making units like the farm group models, but consider three types of factors of production:

(a) Factors which are fixed at the level of the decision making units: They are assumed to be mobile between the single farms of each aggregate.

(b) Factors which are fixed at the regional level: They are mobile between the decision making units of the region. Two kinds may be distinguished: (i) factors whose maximum amount is given in the region; for example, land, water, etc.; (ii) factors (intermediate goods), which are produced on the farms in the region and for which no imports and exports are assumed.

(c) Factors which are variable: They can be bought by all decision making units at given prices which are independent of the demand like in the farm group models.

Products are sold at given prices which are independent of the volume of production like in the farm group models.

Interregional models. Interregional models consider explicitly the interdependencies between the decision making units which result from the competition on common markets.

Factors whose supply is limited on the national level or is subject to a given price supply function may or may not be distinguished in terms of the three groups of production factors in the regional models. Space is usually considered explicitly in this type of model.

2. Farm group models

Experiences gained by application of farm group models is limited to (a) results of models analysing the principal reasons for errors in aggregated models, their degree and possibilities to avoid them; (b) experiences gained with models investigating the geographical structure of production or used in regional planning under conditions which one might neglect interdependencies between enterprises.

Table 1 shows the structure and objectives of some models which have been applied in these fields.

2.1. Analysis of the main reasons for errors

The main reasons for errors are the aggregation procedure and incomplete statistical information. Ideal requirements are known in both cases.[3] But it is also known that they cannot be met, at least not simultaneously. Aggregates for which reasonable statistical information exist do not meet the requirements for error free aggregation and vice versa separation of farm groups which is likely to be free of aggregation error does not meet minimum requirements for statistical information.

Any result in the direction of the quantification of errors and experiment with pragmatic ways to reduce them has, of course, a special bias or aggregation error from the circumstances of the case under investigation. Therefore, one has to keep in mind that the 'insight' gained from the studies mentioned in table 1 has a West-German bias and allows generalization only with great caution.

Incomplete information on technical data leads to simulation or data creating techniques[4] which depend on the special case and do not allow discussion under general aspects.

Incomplete information on behavioural functions leads to inaccurate or wrong results in dynamic process analysis models which aim at ex ante or ex post prediction of real development. It leads also to irrelevant results in static models which aim at the determination of optimal solutions. The latter aspect has been studied by Golter [6] with respect to the individual opportunity costs of family labour on the farm.

Golter [6] — model I, table 1 — who investigated the aggregation problem and the relation between actual and optimal farm organization in a case study of 53 farms between 1956 and 1963 has shown the difference between the labour capacity of the aggregated farm group and the 'utilizable' labour (table 2). The labour capacity of the farm group is calculated as sum of available labour capacities of the single farms wherever 'utilizable' labour is calculated as the sum of the labour input in the optimum solutions of the single farms. The aggregation error can be diminished by reducing the input of the 'surplus factor' in the aggregate in certain ranges. Golter [6] has shown that in his case study.

Subtraction of the labour surplus (difference between available labour and utilizable labour) did reduce the aggregation error but did not avoid

---

[3] See Day [4], Lee [14], Miller [15], Weinschenck [18] and Weinschenck *et al.* [19].

[4] Data creating techniques have been specially developed in the fodderlivestock economy in which statistical information is specially incomplete though it plays a major role in German agriculture. See Bauersachs [1] and Henrichsmeyer [12].

Table 1

Structure of farm group models

Sources	Objective	Structure	Given are (exogen. variables)	To be determined (endogen. variables)
Golter, Friedrich, Beitrag zur Untersuchung des Aggregationsproblems und des Verhältnisses von tatsächlicher zu optimaler Betriebsorganisation, Dissertation, Stuttgart-Hohenheim, December 1966	Comparison of the development of actual and optimal farm organization from 1956–1963 in a sample of 53 farms quantification of the aggregation error	Static process analysis model of single farms and aggregates according to natural conditions and factor relations on different levels	(a) prices and behaviour (b) technical coefficients (c) capacities (1) of land according to crop rotation rules and existing possibilities of expansion (2) of labour according to actual development (3) of buildings according to existing space subject to increase by investments	(a) production structure of single farm and aggregate at different levels of aggregation (b) normative price supply function of milk at different levels of aggregation (c) determination of the aggregation error at different levels of aggregation
Dietrich, Fritz, Die Behandlung des Aggregationsfehlers bei der Ableitung gemeinsamer Preis-Angebotsfunktionen für Betriebsgruppen, Dissertation, Stuttgart-Hohenheim, Braunschweig-Völkenrode, March, 1970	Determination of a normative price-supply function for milk free of aggregation error from a sample of 126 farms similar natural conditions of different levels of aggregation	Static process analysis models with parametric variation of milk price for different levels of aggregation	(a) price and behaviour restriction from land and labour (b) existing buildings (c) technical coefficients	normative price supply function of milk at different levels of aggregation error at different levels of aggregation
Sauer, Dieter, Regionales Modell der landwirtschaftlichen Produktion in Niedersachsen, Sonderheft der Agrarwirtschaft Nr. 37	Explication of the production structure of 'Niedersachsen' (Lower-Saxony) by a process	Static process analysis model of Niedersachsen subdivided in 8 regions with 5 size groups at a given region	as model I but (a) special land restriction varying between size groups according to statistical	production structure at a given point in time

Author / reference	Objective	Model	Assumptions	Results
Hörner, Karl-Otto, Zur Analyse des Angebotsverhaltens von Betriebsgruppen und geschlossenen Regionen mit Prozeqanalysemodellen, Stuttgart-Hohenheim, February 1973.	Examination of the predictive value of static and recursive process analysis models of a farm sample for the change of the corresponding regional production structure	Static and recursive process analysis models of farm groups representative for the county under investigation	(f) restriction for buildings according to the number of animals at 1959/60 (a) prices and behaviour (b) technical coefficients (c) land restrictions according to crop rotation rules (d) number of workers according to actual development (e) existing buildings at t_0 but no investment restrictions (f) parts of the farm organization (livestock, hogs) in various model types	(a) production in the farm groups (b) marginal value of restriction under (f) and relation between this value and actual change of production (c) relation between actual development in the region and estimated development in the models of the farm groups
De Haen, Hartwig, Dynamisches Regionalmodell der Produktion und Investition für die Landwirtschaft Niedersachsen von 1949 bis 1965, Dissertation, Göttingen, October 1970	Export prognosis or explanation of the development of production and investments in Niedersachsen from 1949–1965	Recursive process analysis, model of Niedersachsen subdivided in 4 regions and 2 size groups at a given region	(a) prices behaviour (b) land restrictions allowing to variations over time corresponding to observed changes (c) labour capacity according to observed (and interpolated) actual changes (d) investment restrictions for buildings and machinery corresponding to observed changes (e) technical coefficients	Development of production and investment between 1949 and 1965

Table 2

Overestimation of utilizable labour capacity in the aggregates of model I

	Spring labour	Labour during grain harvest	Labour during harvest time of root crops	Labour in the rest of the year
	Utilizable labour in per cent of total available labour			
Group I Rhine Valley	90	98	71	72
Group II Neckar Valley	93	88	73	62

it completely because the assumption of perfect mobility does imply the assumption that labour with relatively low productivity on some of the single farms of an aggregate will be redistributed if this is profitable from the "bird's eye view of the general manager of the group farm". Whether such a redistribution is profitable depends on the price relations. Therefore the price relations influence direction and degree of the estimation error with respect to the volume of a given product in any given case. Dieterich [5] – model IV, table 1 – has shown this in a special case (see fig. 1).

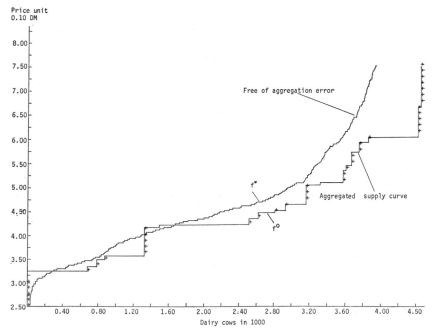

Fig. 1. Price supply functions for dairy cows in model IV.

2.2. Farm group models in regional analysis

2.2.1.

Following the definition at the beginning of this paper, the use of farm group models in regional analysis means that the production and input structure of a given region is analyzed in the framework of a model which consists of a given number of independent farm aggregates representing the production potential of the region. Prices are given or determined outside the model by price expectation functions.

Static models of this kind have only limited value because of their sensitivity to some kinds of aggregation errors. Sauer − model III, table 1 − has shown that the description or explanation of the structure of production of a region at a given point in time requires the introduction of restrictions which limit most of the endogenous variables directly or indirectly and more or less artificially at their observed values.

This corresponds to the introduction of behavioural restrictions in dynamic models, which aim at the description of the regional development of production though it can be justified with better arguments in the latter case.

In introducing behavioural restrictions in dynamic models (recursive programming models), one can distinguish two concepts: (a) the 'naive' approach which is based on the observation that changes in the structure of regional production occur slowly but usually in the 'right' direction; (b) the sophisticated approach which is based on the introduction of behavioural functions[5] (investment functions and (or) consumption functions or both) in order to explain the observed rate of change.

2.2.2. The naive recursive approach

Hörner [13] who wanted to analyse the possibilities to describe and predict the development of agricultural production of a county in Southern Germany between 1950–1968 by farm group models has mainly used the naive approach. His model includes five independent farm groups, each of them representing one size group of the region. Hörner [13] derives the behaviour restrictions which limit the maximum yearly rate of change from time series.[6] Starting from a model version without any behavioural restrictions he has introduced successively restrictions for the most important products and compared his results with the actual development.

[5] See Heidhues [9].
[6] He used the average rate of change of the three years with the largest change in animal production and the average yearly rate of change of the whole period in crop production where he was faced with incomplete time series.

Table 3

Estimation errors with different restrictions of the naive type in a recursive farm group model

No.	Restrictions for	Total cattle[1]			Dairy cows			Bulls for fattening			Pork and farrows (sows)			Pork			Farrows (sows)		
		A	B	C	A	B	C	A[2]	B	C	A	B	C	A	B	C	A	B	C
1	No	39	0	–	43	0	44	–	–	–	239	100	25	423	50	25	238	100	–
2	Pork	36	0	–	31	0	43	–[2]	–	–	230	100		73	0		295	100	
3	Pork and farrows (sows)	13	6	31	12	50	38	72	13	19	29	94	31	35	50	31	31	94	38
4	Pork, farrows, dairy cows and beef	13	0	25	14	0	19	10	0	31	38	100	25	30	56	38	43	100	25
5	All activities	12	0	13	12	0	25	6	13	25	20	94	25	26	25	31	24	94	19
6	All activities but decreased net return expectations[3]	6	0	6	6	0	25	6	38	25	14	94	25	29	13	50	14	6	19

[1] In labour units.

[2] Estimation = 0 in most cases.

[3] For pork = 10 %. Farrow = 28 %. Potatoes = 40 %.

A: Average deviation: $1/n \sum_{t=1}^{n} \Delta x_t / x_{bt} \cdot \Delta x_t$ = absolute difference between observed and calculated value at t; x_{bt} = observed value at t. B: Overestimations in per cent of total observations. C: Estimated changes between periods in wrong directions.

Some of the results for one farm group which are representative for the results of the 4 other groups are shown in table 3. They are in accordance with conclusions one can draw from theoretical reflections.

(a) The estimation error for one product which might be reduced by a special direct restriction will be transferred to other products with similar input structure unless the profitability of corresponding products is very low. (See pork and farrow production in version 1 and 2, table 3.)

(b) The estimation error of aggregates of related processes is in most cases smaller than the estimation error of the single components of the aggregate. Hence, one is not likely to achieve improved results in respect to the single components by introducing restrictions to aggregates, like cattle, etc.

(c) Revision of the assumptions on price expectations or (and) technical coefficients might improve the accordance of estimates and observations if the output of a product is overestimated resp. underestimated in most cases. If this is true in all cases, the introduction of stronger restrictions will have similar effects.

Hörner [13] − model IV, table 1 − has tested the correlation between the observed output of production at $t+1$ and the shadow price of a restriction which fixes the production at the observed value at t using linear regression with the time and the shadow price as independent variables.

Estimation results were satisfying considering closeness of estimates to observations but the interpretation of regression coefficients was difficult because of the high correlation of the shadow price with the trend variable. This was probably the reason, that Hörner [13] did not use these results to revise the restrictions which he had estimated from time series.

2.2.3. The recursive approach on the basis of behaviour functions

Investment functions or consumption functions are available for the whole sector, if at all, but their estimation at the level of regions or farm groups is limited by incomplete statistical information which is difficult to overcome in most cases.

Even if one succeeds in realistic guesses the restrictions derived from behaviour functions restrict only the variability of rather complex aggregates like total investment or available labour. The allocation of these pseudo-fixed factors to competing processes is left to the rationality of the model. Hence, the results are sensible to all the errors mentioned above, specially if the competing processes have similar input structures or require only inputs of fixed factors in a small degree.

Consequently, one would assume that it is rather difficult to analyse the observed development in a region without using at least some 'naive' restrictions. De Haen's experiment of an ex post prognosis of the agricultural development from 1949–1965 in Niedersachsen (Lower Saxony) confirms this assumption [7] – model V, table 1.

De Haen [7] succeeded in the computation of a time path for the most important variables which corresponds rather well to the actual development. But in order to arrive there – very likely after many experiments with unfortunately unknown though probably interesting results – he had to introduce many direct restrictions from the observations of the corresponding periods which limits the degree of freedom of his major variables even more as the naive approach would have done. One becomes aware of the limitations of the predictive value which result from this procedure if one takes a closer look at the formidable task of generating exogenous variables.

The model can endogenously determine the time paths of the following variables: (a) the level of production, factor use and investment within the boundaries of the exogenously determined restraints; (b) movement of labour out of agriculture within the maximum restrictions; (c) capital formation out of own income and borrowed money. The results show that the computed changes of production and investment as well as of labour mobility are determined to a large extent by the exogenous restraints, which correspond more or less directly to the actual observation in the relevant periods.

3. Regional models

3.1.

Problems which can be handled by static regional models defined above have the following structure:

(1) There exist one or more factors which are mobile between the farms of the region and of which the maximum regional supply is given.

(2) There exist at least two different farm groups which compete for the use of the regional fixed factors. Each of these farm groups is characterized as usual by technical coefficients and capacities of factors fixed on the farm level.

(3) Prices or price expectations of products and variable factors are given. The problem is to determine the optimal organization of each farm group with special reference to the optimal allocation of the factors fixed on the regional level.

3.2. A static problem

The problem of optimal allocation of water to different farm groups in semi-arid areas is of the nature to be handled in the framework of a static regional model. Behbehani and Hanf investigated this problem in a case study for a region in the Iran [2, 3, 8].

The whole region was subdivided in one water supplying and six water consuming subregions. The consuming regions are characterized by different production functions depending on soil quality, by different costs and losses for the transportation of water from the point of supply, by a given labour capacity fixed on the level of subregions, and by a given land capacity which is not fully used at present. Because the natural water supply differs extremely from year to year a stochastic dynamic model was used to determine the optimal strategies of storing.

This approach leads to a table which contains optimal strategies of storing depending on the water supply of a given year and the amount of water stored from the previous year (see table 4).

Table 4

Optimal strategies of water storing

Riverwater in year t in mill. m^3	Amount of water available in the storage in mill. m^3, stored in year $t-1$										
	0	11	22	33	44	55	65	76	87	98	109
	Amount of water to be stored for use in $t+1$ in mill. m^3										
153											
174										11	22
196								11	22	33	44
218						11	22	33	44	44	55
240				11	22	33	44	44	55	65	76
262		11	22	33	44	44	55	65	76	87	98
283	22	33	44	44	55	65	76	87	98	98	109
305	44	44	55	65	76	87	98	98	109[a]	109	109

[a] Capacity of the storage fully used.

The determination of the economic effects of water storage has to take into account two facts concerning existing water supply. Firstly, only the distribution function of water is known in fall at the time of cultivation of winter crops (wheat, barley). No or almost no correlation exists between the available water in October and the available water during the following vegetation period. Secondly, the available amount of water is known with high probability in April before cultivation of the spring crops (cotton, vegetables).

Hence a two-stage linear programming model was used to enclose the uncertainty at the beginning of the vegetation period as well as the possibilities for adjusting during the vegetation period. As basic plans in autumn such plans have been used which were optimal in respect to the Bayes-criterion.

3.3. A regional development model

Problems of a nature which can be handled advantageously by static regional models are rare in Western Germany. Land is the only factor which is fixed at the regional level and which might be considered as mobile between farms.

The problem of optimal allocation of land to farms with homogenous production functions under static conditions is equivalent to the problem of optimal farm size and does not need a simultaneous consideration of farms or farm groups. This would become necessary only if there exist long run differences in the production functions or in the objective functions in regions with homogenous quality of land. However, this would be an exceptional case under West German conditions if it exists at all. Therefore, the problem of interdependencies between farms with respect to land use arises only if one investigates the structural development. Hence, the application of regional models is more or less restricted to structural regional development problems. Experiences are rare, however, since the state of arts is still in the developing stage at present. At present, two corresponding case studies are being carried out at the University of Hohenheim.

4. Interregional models

Application of interregional models as defined above requires the existence of a multiregional market for all or at least for some agricultural products. In addition, it must be possible to separate this market from the rest of the world without violating reality too strongly. This requirement may cause some difficulties in studies which are restricted to Western Germany because of its close economic links with the countries of the Common Market. Nevertheless, the studies which are reported below had to be restricted to the 'region' Federal Republic of Western Germany for many apparent reasons of methodical, statistical and organizational nature.

4.1. The Hohenheim model [7]

The Hohenheim research project was carried out by a small research group. Therefore, it was concerned mainly with methodological aspect, especially with the investigation of the possibilities and limitations arising in the application of an interregional model to problems in Western Germany.

The rather rough assumptions with respect to the trade relations of Western Germany with the rest of the world can be seen from the following scheme of exogenously and endogenously determined variables:

Exogenously determined variables	*Endogenously determined variables*
All products	
Technical coefficients	Equilibrium prices of factors fixed on the regional or the national level
Price of variable production factors	
Capacity of fixed factors	
Potatoes, sugar-beets, milk	
Demand for human nutrition and industrial processing	Product prices
	Volume of production (final demand, balance of foreign trade, agricultural input)
Balance of foreign trade	
Grain, beef and veal	
Product prices	Volume of production
Demand for human nutrition and industrial processing	Balance of trade
Pork	
Demand for human nutrition	Product prices
Balance of trade	
(Volume of production = demand + balance of trade)	

The main point of this approach lies in the *interregional* interdependencies. Hence, the primary purpose of this investigation has to be seen in the analysis of the consequences on regional agricultural production which result from changes in the domestic demand for agricultural products, from technical progress and from the changes of opportunity costs for agricultural resources (mainly labour) in a growing economy.

The investigation started out with the development of a static interregional multiproduct process-analysis model to be used for various

---

[7] The different aspects of this research project are described more extensively in the following publications and reports: Bauersachs [1] and Henrichsmeyer [11].

purposes: for interregional balancing of supply and demand, using the model in the sense of an interregional input–output model; for the analysis of the interregional competitive position of various branches of production and groups of farms, derived from the analysis of dual variables; for the analysis of the consequences of various sets of assumptions by comparative static analysis.

4.2. *The structure of the model*

The formal structure of a multi-product interregional activity analysis model is described by Takayama and Judge [17]. Therefore it may be sufficient to outline the empirical specification of the model, which depends mainly on the structure of agriculture and economy in Western Germany:

(a) Many interdependencies exist between the diverse branches of production within single farms, resulting from natural conditions and (small) farm size. This requires the construction of a rather comprehensive production model for each group of farms. Each model contains the main production alternatives and quite a number of constraints, especially for labour, crop rotation, feed balances, and intermediate products.

(b) The given structure with respect to farm size requires the consideration of different groups of farms within regions. Up to four groups of farms according to farm size have been distinguished.

(c) A wide range of differing natural conditions and a scattered distribution of the centers of industrial activity and consumption makes it necessary to distinguish a rather large number of production regions and consumption regions.

Taking this into consideration, the model has the following structure. The production model consists of 32 regions and 4 groups of farms within each region. For each farm group a production model is formulated, which contains 30 to 50 production processes and 20 to 25 restraints on the group level. The production models for the farm groups and regions are interconnected in two ways. Firstly, by the competition for production factors which are fixed on the regional or national level and by the intra- and interregional exchange of intermediate products (fodder, feed grain, cattle). These interdependencies are considered by introducing regional and national constraints and intra- and inter-regional exchange activities. Secondly, they are interconnected by the competition in the demand for the final commodities. Final demand is assumed to be given for all products, which have no fixed administered prices. On the national level final demand is fixed by overall restraints, on the regional level it is attached to the 14 demand regions. Interregional exchange of final goods is determined in an iterative procedure by application of transportation models (because of limited computer capacities).[8]

4.3. The application of the model and results

It does not seem to be very fruitful to describe the results in terms of numerical figures model by model, because this would not mean very much to the reader, who may be unfamiliar with the specific problems and circumstances. Therefore, we will only summarize empirical experiences as far as they are helpful for future research, especially for the DFG-project outlined in the following chapter. It has proven to be expedient to work the model in these stages: (1) to describe consistently the actual regional structure of agricultural production and the interregional exchange patterns with the interregional activity analysis model, (2) to analyse systematically the interregional competitive position of various branches of production and groups of farms by analysing the dual solutions and only on the basis of this information, and (3) to compute 'optimal' production structures for various sets of assumptions.

A few comments will be given to each of these stages.

In the first step an interregional input–output balancing systems is established within the framework of an interregional activity process analysis model in order to describe the actual regional distribution of production and of factor use and the interregional exchange for a given base year (1965) as close to reality as possible based on the existing data. It has proven that this step is a necessary supposition for an effective application of the models. Some advantages ought to be mentioned: the consistency of scattered data can be examined and some data can be derived from a complete balancing system. Data gaps can be identified and a coordinated approach for data gathering and scientific case-studies can be developed. A flexible concept with respect to the data base of the model can be developed. For the first versions of the model some basis information and a large number of assumptions are used. Step by step new information is incorporated as it becomes available.

The consistent input–output description for the base year forms the basis for the interpretation of the computed 'optimal' solutions and projections.

---

[8] The details of the iterative procedure are described by Henrichsmeyer [10]. The general rules for the iterative procedure, which have to be considered, are rather complicated. But for the specific conditions the procedure is rather efficient, because the structure of interregional exchange of a number of products is rather constant (for example the trade of feed grain is determined mainly by imports from the harbours of the North Sea).

The objective of the second step has been to quantify the influence of numerous factors (exogenous variables and parameters) which determine the competitive position of regions and groups of farms. This analysis is based on a systematic analysis of the dual solution of the model. The starting point for this analysis is an inversion of the input–output balancing model. In this case the level of activities has been fixed to the level actually reached in the base year.

The resulting dual variables are used as follows:

(1) A comparison of computed shadow prices with observed market prices allows a further check of the model assumptions besides the check of physical balances in stage one. In most cases a rather plausible relation between shadow prices and actual prices of products and factors resulted.

(2) The dual values for restraints which determine the level of activities show the economic incentives to extend or decrease activities. Additionally they give some insight into the causing factors which determine the change of the production and marketing structure and some information on the sensitivity of the production organization. This approach to sensitivity analysis has been extended in further computations in which the restrictions have been released systematically.

(3) To develop a decentralized information system.

The identification of the influence of the different factors on the shadow prices is rather difficult, because of the structure of the model. Therefore, the impact of single location factors has been analysed systematically following von Thünens approach of isolating abstraction. Then step by step other differentiating factors have been introduced. In this way it has been possible to get a good insight into the economic interdependencies of a complex model.[9]

In the third step the model was used for comparative static analysis. Basis and point of reference for these comparisons was the model for the base year 1965. Some calculations were based on data relating to the year 1965.

With this model these problems were investigated: the effects of mechanization and change of farm size on the regional labour supply of the agricultural sector; the effects of the squeeze between the slowly increasing demand for agricultural goods and the rapidly rising productivity of agricultural production on the land use in marginal regions; the adjustment of agricultural production if alternative assumptions were made about the opportunity costs of agricultural labour.

----

[9] See Henrichsmeyer [11].

Furthermore, model calculations were carried out to get an impression about the likely adjustments to conditions which are assumed to be relevant at a certain future period. Therefore, the values of the exogenous variables and the technical coefficients were projected for the year 1980. In the following, some results of this long run version of the model are reported.

For a wide range of assumptions grain production will be extended to its maximum share in the rotation in most of the areas, especially production of wheat and barley for brewery purposes. Sugar beet production shows a tendency of concentration in areas with favourable natural conditions (the existing production quotas were neglected in the model). Potato production shrinks rapidly and is concentrated in regions with sandy soil and good marketing conditions. Fodder crops are generally reduced, only fodder maize is extended in certain areas.

The delimitation of marginal areas in which agricultural production is bounded depends mainly on the level of prices of grain and livestock products. If the deflated grain price is assumed to be constant fallowness will be restricted to limited areas. The grain acreage will decrease in a greater extent only if the deflated grain price will be reduced by about 15 to 20 % assuming all other prices remaining at the price level of 1965. Under these conditions the level of the meat prices determines whether this land is taken out of production or used for extensive forms of cattle production.

Supply of beef was another central problem analysed with this model. The total number of milk cows was limited by the demand of milk. The results of the calculations indicate a possible concentration of milk production in areas with a large share of grassland and low opportunity costs of labour. Meat production was relatively elastic with respect to the meat prices. Three steps of the price-supply function for meat can be distinguished: at relative low prices only male calves are fattened, then at somewhat higher prices female calves are fattened, too. Finally, when a certain price limit is passed the production of single suckled calves becomes profitable.

4.4. *The DFG-project*

The DFG-project is based on the experiences gained by the Hohenheim model. The methodological concept corresponds to a great extent with the approach developed there. However, while methodological questions were the basic objectives of the Hohenheim model, the DFG-project aims mainly on empirical results which can be used as a base for policy decisions and which allow to derive fruitful information for agricultural advisers and farmers.

4.4.1. Methodological concept

The three stages of analysis, which have been distinguished for the Hohen-heim model, form the basis for the research concept of the DFG-project: (1) Interregional balancing, (2) analysis of dual variables, and (3) comparative static analysis under long run aspects (1980 and 1985).

In a fourth stage it is planned to analyse the adjustment process of agricultural production over time. This will be performed by a specific way of dynamically coupling interregional activity models over successive time periods. The objective of this analysis is not to determine an efficient production structure, but possible and probable time paths of the agricultural sector.

For the analysis of this question, the interregional activity analysis model has to be extended. Behaviour functions have to be introduced with respect to consumption, the speed of change of production and investment processes, etc., and investment and financing will be considered explicitly by introduction of financing and investment activities and restraints. This part will be based on experiences gained with the regional and farm group models, which have been described above.

4.4.2. Research plan

Various research groups contribute to this project. Each group has to investigate certain problem areas like the demarcation of regions, definition of production processes and their coefficients, determination of production capacities, specification of transportation and processing activities, estimation of regional demand functions, estimation of consumption functions for the groups of farms and specification of investment and financing activities and the determination of import and export function.

Special investigations on a regional level are: gathering and preparation of regional data, computation of partial models on the regional level and the interpretation of the results of the interregional model with respect to their region.

The research work is coordinated by a central group, which is responsible for the methodological concept, for the coordination of information and for the computation of the interregional model.

5. Implications of the results for planning and decision making

Experiences discussed are based on static and recursive farm group models, on static regional models and on an interregional model of Western Germany. The experiences gained by application of these models which are distinguished by the interdependences between the decision making units taken into account can be summarized as follows.

Farm group models have turned out to be useful helps in quantifying aggregation errors and in determining pragmatic ways to reduce them. Any result in this direction has a special bias from the circumstances of the case under investigation. Therefore, such case studies ought to be carried out before starting larger and more complicated research projects.

The application of recursive farm group models for analysing and predicting the development path of farm groups or regions is limited by the lack of information on behaviour of farmers. It is probably rather difficult to analyse the observed development without using at least some 'naive' flexibility constraints of the behaviour function type which restrict the variability of rather complex aggregates like total investment or available labour.

Problems of the nature to be handled advantageously by static regional models are rare in Western Germany since land is the only factor which is fixed at the regional level and which might be considered mobile between farms. Therefore, the application of static regional models may be restricted more or less to problems like the optimal allocation of water in semi-arid areas to different farm groups.

The problem of interdependencies between farms with respect to land use arises only if one investigates the structural development of a region. Recursive linear programming models can be used in this case. Though no experiences exist at present one can assume that the statistical determination of flexibility constraints for production, labour and land transfer will cause many difficulties since these changes are not independent.

Experiences indicate that interregional equilibrium models can provide useful information for the formulation of a regional agricultural policy by a central government, though one is faced with similar sources of error as in regional or farm group models. One of the major problems in Western Europe is due to the statistical and computational difficulties to include all countries of the Common Market in one model. The use of import and export functions for the E.E.C. countries and the rest of the world might be one way to overcome these difficulties in national models.

References

[1] Bauersachs, Fr., 1972, Quantitative Untersuchungen zum langfristigen räumlichen Gleichgewicht der landwirtschaftlichen Produktion in der Bundesrepublik Deutschland, Sonderheft der Agrarwirtschaft 47.

[2] Behbehani, E., 1972, Möglichkeiten zur Steigerung der landwirtschaftlichen Einkommen in dem Bewässerungsgebiet Varamin in Persien, Diss. Hohenheim.

[3] Behbehani, E. and C. H. Hanf, 1972, Zur Berücksichtigung wechselnder Bewässerungsbedingungen in der Planung — Eine Fallstudie an Hand des Bewässerungsgebietes Varamin im Iran, unpubl. paper, University of Stuttgart-Hohenheim.

[4] Day, R. H., 1963, On aggregating linear models of production, J. of Farm Economics 45, 797–813.

[5] Dietrich, F., 1970, Die Behandlung des Aggregationsfehlers bei der Ableitung gemeinsamer Preis-Angebotsfunktionen für Betriebsgruppen, Diss. Hohenheim und Braunschweig.

[6] Golter, Fr., 1966, Beitrag zur Untersuchung des Aggregationsproblems und des Verhältnisses von tatsächlicher zu optimaler Betriebsorganisation, Diss. Hohenheim.

[7] De Haen, H., 1970, Dynamisches Regionalmodell der Produktion und Investition für die Landwirtschaft Niedersachsen von 1949 bis 1965, Diss. Göttingen.

[8] Hanf, C. H. and E. Behbehani, 1971, Optimale Strategien zur Speicherung von Wasser bei starken jährlichen Unterschieden im Wasseranfall, Zeitschrift für Bewässerungswirtschaft, 1, 23–37.

[9] Heidhues, T., 1966, A recursive programming model of farm growth in northern Germany, J. of Farm Economics 48, 668–684.

[10] Henrichsmeyer, W., 1966, Das sektorale und regionale Gleichgewicht der landwirtschaftlichen Produktion, Hannover und Berlin.

[11] Henrichsmeyer, W., 1970, Wachstum und struktureller Wandel der westdeutschen Landwirtschaft, Habilitationsarbeit Hohenheim, 2. Teil.

[12] Henrichsmeyer, W. and H. de Haen, 1972, Zur Konzeption des Schwerpunktprogrammes der Deutschen Forschungsgemeinschaft "Konkurrenzvergleich landwirtschaftlicher Standorte", in: Agrarwirtschaft, 1972, p. 141 ff.

[13] Hörner, K. O., 1973, Zur Analyse des Angebotsverhaltens von Betriebsgruppen und geschlossenen Regionen mit Prozessanalysmodellen, Diss. Hohenheim.

[14] Lee, J. E., 1966, The Minimum Sufficient Condition for Exact Aggregation in Linear Models. A Non Mathematical Exposition, United States Department of Agriculture, Production and Resource Response Group, Working Material, Washington D.C.

[15] Miller, T., 1966, Sufficient conditions for exact aggregation in linear models, Agricultural Economics Research, 18, 52–57.

[16] Sauer, D., Regionales Modell der landwirtschaftlichen Produktion in Niedersachsen, Sonderheft der Agrarwirtschaft 37.

[17] Takayama, T. and G. G. Judge, 1971, Spatial and Temporal Price and Allocation Models, Amsterdam: North-Holland Publishing Co.

[18] Weinschenck, G., 1969, Marktwirtschaft und Betriebswirtschaft, in: Landwirtschaftliche Marktforschung in Deutschland, München, Basel, Wien: pp. 51–84.

[19] Weinschenck, G., W. Henrichsmeyer and F. Aldinger, The theory of spatial equilibrium and optimal location in agriculture: a survey, Review of Marketing and Agricultural Economics 37, 1, 3–70.

B. SPATIAL AND/OR TEMPORAL PROGRAMMING MODELS

CHAPTER 18

Recursive programming models: a brief introduction

RICHARD H. DAY

University of Wisconsin

1. Introduction [1]

1.1.

A Recursive Programming (RP) Model is a sequence of constrained optimization problems in which one or more objective functions, constraint or limitation coefficients of a given problem depend functionally on the optimal primal and/or dual solution vectors of one or more problems earlier in the sequence. The recursive dependence of the coefficients on preceding solutions is determined by a set of feedback functions or, more generally, by a feedback operator. In some applications the feedback component is itself an optimization problem.

1.2.

RP models arise in at least three broad areas of study: (1) *economic simulation* in which the behavior of an economic unit, or group of economic units is studied by computer simulation using an RP model; (2) *economic theory* in which RP models are studied analytically to obtain the logical implications of specific assumptions of economic behavior; and (3) *computational algorithms* for static and dynamic optimization problems in which a complex optimization problem is decomposed into a sequence of simpler, approximate or local optimization problems with feedback.

---

[1] For general introductory material see Day and Heiden [6], Day *et al.* [4], and Day and Kennedy [7]. My first attempt at developing the method is in Day [2].

1.3.

In the three immediately succeeding chapters of this book the use of RP models to study industrial and agricultural development is illustrated with models of the U.S. and Japanese steel industries (chs. 19 and 20) and farming in the Indian Punjab (ch. 21). These models, like others of the family to which they belong, are constructed according to the paradigm of a decision maker who proceeds according to a succession of behaviorally conditioned, suboptimizing decisions. The underlying premise is that decisions in farming or industry are based on explicit maximizing plans, drawn up by decision makers who constrain themselves by behavioral rules that afford protection from errors of estimation and forecasting, and that these maximizing plans roll: period after period they are drawn up anew on the basis of current information. Besides corresponding reasonably well to introspection and direct observation of others, this premise seems supported, at least in part, by the simulation results. A concise survey of these and other models, results and their evaluation will be found in Day and Nelson [8].

1.4.

There are many models belonging to the RP class and exemplifying the paradigm just given that would be of considerable interest. Some of these yet to be constructed models might possess superior explanatory power, they might make possible improved projection and they could be amenable to policy repercussion studies of wider usefulness. These new models would include alternative ways of representing uncertainty avoiding behavior, more sophisticated investment relations and price forecasts, oligopolistic and monopolistic strategies and so forth. Some of us are working along these lines already. A particularly important direction of generalization would arise as models of individual sectors are 'closed' at least in part, by imbedding them in a multi-sector framework. This 'dynamic coupling' would lead to models of great complexity. Both simulation and analysis for such models would be formidable tasks. Nonetheless their systematic construction and evaluation would yield many new insights into the dynamic properties of decentralized economies.

1.5.

It should be emphasized that the models under consideration here do not necessarily (and do not usually) incorporate intertemporally optimal strategies in the optimal control or dynamic programming manner. They are meant instead to model behavior in situations that are (or are thought to be) too complicated for dynamic optimization over extended time horizons. The principle of recursive, short horizon or myopic optimization (as opposed to long horizon, intertemporal optimization) goes back at least to Cournot who based his theory of duopolistic competition on it. The 'cobweb model' developed about half a century ago is the purely competitive analog of the Cournot approach and may be easily generalized to obtain a highly instructive family of RP models of individual economic sectors. Examples of this kind form the body of the present chapter. Application of the principle to growth theory was initiated by Leontief [12]. Mathematical treatments of the principle in a similar context are available in Day [3], Beals and Koopmans [1], Goldman [11] and in Day and Fan [5]. The extension of the recursive programming point of view to general equilibrium constitutes the frontier of the subject so far as economic theory goes, just as multisector RP models are the frontier so far as simulation studies are concerned.

1.6.

The paradigm of a behaviorally conditioned, suboptimizing economic decision maker is also a good description of certain algorithms for computing solutions to complicated optimization problems. Some, indeed, many of these algorithms are developed by decomposing the original problem into a simpler problem (or set of simpler problems) and a feedback rule that describes how the simple problem (each of the simpler problems) should be modified on the basis of past solutions, so that when it is (they are) solved by a known, convenient, economical method the solution will be closer to the optimum of the original complicated problem than before. One may think of the original complicated problem as an 'environment', the simplified optimization problem as a decision maker's suboptimizing tactic, and the feedback rule as a means of using past decisions and feedback from the 'environment' to obtain a new decision problem. The sequence of 'decisions' as a whole must converge to the desired optimum if the algorithm is to be a useful one, but in general, one can only approximate the desired solution in this way. The degree of approximation depends on the planner's computing budget and how efficient the algorithm is.

1.7.

The close parallel between the process of optimizing and the behavior of suboptimizing decision makers is evident in the above description. This parallel is reflected in the fact that mathematical models of both can be represented by members of the RP family. It suggests that practical planning tools designed to optimize the planner's objective function will have, at least in some cases, an RP structure. Practical planning, however, especially in extremely complex situations, often proceeds by attempting to project the likely response by the numerous decision makers in the economy to a few discrete changes in some controls. In this case, the simulation models described in sect. 1.3 may also be found to provide practical means of aiding planning when economic details at the individual sector or region are desired.

1.8.

In the remainder of this paper we turn from general considerations to the analysis of two heuristic, generalized cobweb models designed to illustrate some of the properties shared by many recursive programming models, whether they be designed for simulation, economic theory or planning purposes. The properties to which I especially want to draw attention are (1) the multi-phase nature of solutions and (2) the possible convergence under some conditions to efficacious equilibria. It should be understood that the models themselves are neither empirically satisfactory nor theoretically complete. They should, however, suggest the richness and flexibility of the approach.

2. A generalized cobweb model[2]

2.1.

Imagine an economic sector — which we shall hereafter call 'agriculture' — comprised of a set of similar firms or 'farms', each of which produces two homogeneous commodities and uses two resources: one a fixed factor, say 'land', and the second a financial composite of all variable factors, say 'working capital'. Suppose each firm decides its production levels and resource allocation by maximizing its expected gross short-run profits subject to the limitations imposed by its current supplies of land and working capital.

---

[2] This section is based on Day and Tinney [9]. For details see that reference.

2.2.

Let $x_1(t)$, $x_2(t)$ be the amounts, measured in area units, to be produced of each of the two commodities; let $\hat{z}_1(t)$ and $\hat{z}_2(t)$ be the gross unit profits per area unit anticipated for the two commodities at the end of period t. Let c_1 and c_2 be the unit working-capital requirements of the two commodities; and finally, let l and $k(t)$ be the current supplies of land and working capital available for production at the beginning of year t. If we assume that c_1 and c_2 are independent from x_1 and x_2 (constant costs), then the decision problem of each firm at the beginning of period t can be represented by the linear-programming problem:

$$\pi(t) = \max_{x_1, x_2} \left[\hat{z}_1(t)x_1 + \hat{z}_2(t)x_2 \right] \tag{1}$$

subject to

$$x_1 + x_2 \leqq l \tag{2}$$

$$c_1 x_1 + c_2 x_2 \leqq k(t)$$

$$x_1, x_2 \geqq 0. \tag{3}$$

Assume also (for simplicity) that no borrowing or lending of money and that no sales or purchases of land can occur.

If each decision maker expects the same output prices, possesses the same unit costs and possesses initial endowments of land and working capital in the same proportions, then the single linear programming problem (1)–(3) can be used to represent the sum of the decisions of all firms in the industry simply by letting l and $k(t)$ be the aggregate amounts of resources available to the industry. Then the 'optimal' solution of (1)–(3), say $x_1(t)$ and $x_2(t)$, will give the total supply, in area units, of each commodity in year t. In other words, given the data $\hat{z}_j(t)$, $c_i(t)$, l, $k(t)$, $i = 1, 2$, $t = 1, \ldots$ the behavior of 'agriculture' is described by the sequence of linear programmes (1)–(3).

2.3.

The expected marginal-net-revenue values of the two factors land and working capital are given by the solution values $r_1(t)$ and $r_2(t)$ of the dual to (1)–(3), which is

$$\rho(t) = \min_{r_1, r_2} \left[l r_1 + k(t) r_2 \right] \tag{4}$$

subject to

$$r_1 + c_1 r_2 \geq \hat{z}_1(t) \tag{5}$$

$$r_1 + c_2 r_2 \geq \hat{z}_2(t)$$

$$r_1, r_2 \geq 0. \tag{6}$$

2.4.

We retain here the original cobweb assumption that producers are 'naive' price forecasters and use the last received price as their forecast of its immediate future value. Let $p_i(t)$ be the price received at the 'market' *at the end of year t*. Then

$$\hat{z}_i(t) = p_i(t-1) - c_i, \ i = 1, 2. \tag{7}$$

Without borrowing or lending the supply of working capital must be limited to the past year's sales minus payments for overhead (say h). This amount, by our linear-programming definition of supply, must be for agriculture as a whole

$$k(t) = \sum_i p_i(t-1) x_i(t-1) - h, \tag{8}$$

where we have assumed total overhead paid by the industry (consumption, taxes, etc.) to be a constant amount from year to year.

2.5.

We now imagine that after commodities are produced they are 'trucked to and bartered' in a perfectly competitive market that brings about a temporary equilibrium at which the existing supply is sold at a uniform price. Consequently, the price received for each commodity is a function of the amounts of both supplied. For simplicity we assume linear demand functions with no 'cross change' terms and augmented by nonnegativity conditions:

$$p_i(t) = \max \ \{0, a_i + b_i x_i(t)\}, \ i = 1, 2. \tag{9}$$

2.6.

The system (1)–(9) is an RP model. The dual linear programming problems (1)–(6) describe the optimization component. The functions (8)–(9) together with the definition (7) describe the feedback component. It is a closed, discrete time, dynamic system of which one may ask such questions as: Do equilibria exist? Are they stable? Do cycles occur? Are they stable?

Can growth occur? The answers to such standard questions depend on several theoretical facts which we now review.

2.7. Existence of solutions

2.7.1. Feasibility
The dual linear programmes at any time t are dual feasible so long as

$$\sum_i \max \{0, a_i + b_i x_i(t-1)\} x_i(t-1) \geq h. \tag{10}$$

This will always be the case if $h = 0$. If $h > 0$ it may happen this condition is violated. The system then becomes infeasible at time t, and is inviable thereafter.

The meaning of condition (10) is clear. If total revenue in the preceding year is insufficient to cover overhead, then no surplus remains to finance the current period's production. The system goes bankrupt and the industry collapses unless a subsidy is injected from some external source.

2.7.2. Ex ante optimality
So long as each dual programme in the sequence is feasible in the above sense, then optimal solution values $x_1(t)$, $x_2(t)$, $r_1(t)$, $r_2(t)$ exist at each time t. When this occurs $\pi(t) = \rho(t)$ by the duality theorem of linear programming.

It is very important to emphasize that the 'solution' values $x_1(t)$, $r_1(t)$, ... describe and do not prescribe behavior in our model world. That is, these values are not necessarily optimal ex post. For the industry as a whole the actual optimum is the monopoly solution given by the quadratic programming problem that arises when a perfect knowledge of the demand curves (9) is accounted for by the decision makers. The dynamic process defined by (1)–(9) can generate such a point only by accident, and even if attained, it is not a position of rest. Our decision makers − ignorant as they are of the position of the demand curves − will plough their profits back into production and move away from this monopolistically optimum point. For well known reasons, the monopoly solution is not a realistic one with large numbers of competitors so we do not consider it further.

2.8. Phase structure of solutions

2.8.1. Corner solutions and the existence of phases
If the solution of the problem at the time t is unique it lies on a 'corner' of the feasible region for that period. If there is more than one solution,

then corner solutions are among them. Consequently, a solution at any time t can be represented by a set of equated constraints that give the algebraic description of the corner. Because of the recursive character of the sequence of programmes, these sets of equated constraints identify difference equations that describe the behavior of the production variables and marginal values for a given period of time. Since these sets may change from time to time, the system as a whole is a multiple-phase system.

The importance of this latter fact lies in its making possible a complete analysis of the behavior of the system as a whole using the conventional tools of dynamic analysis. Questions concerning growth, cycles and equilibrium consequently boil down to an analysis of the conditions for the occurrence of specific phases (sets of difference equations) and the dynamic properties of each phase.

2.9.

By examining the corner-solution possibilities we find the following six cases:

Phase 0 (Null Phase): nothing produced, no imputed value.
Phase $1l$: fixed factor constraint equated, the first commodity produced.
Phase $2l$: fixed factor constraint equated, the second commodity produced.
Phase $1k$: financial constraint equated, the first commodity produced.
Phase $2k$: financial constraint equated, the second commodity produced.
Phase $12kl$: both constraints equated, both commodities produced.

To each of these corners corresponds a set of equations:
Phase 0:
$$x_1(t) = 0$$
$$x_2(t) = 0$$
$$r_1(t) = 0$$
$$r_2(t) = 0$$

Phase $1l$:
$$x_1(t) = l; \qquad\qquad\qquad x_2(t) = 0$$
$$r_1(t) = a_1 + b_1 x_1(t-1) - c_1 \qquad r_2(t) = 0$$

Phase $2l$:
$$x_2(t) = l; \qquad\qquad\qquad x_1(t) = 0$$
$$r_1(t) = a_2 + b_2 x_2(t-1) - c_2 \qquad r_2(t) = 0$$

Phase 1k:

$$x_1(t) = 1/c_1[\sum_i \{a_i + b_i x_i(t-1)\}x_i(t-1) - h]; \qquad x_2(t) = 0$$

$$r_2(t) = 1/c_1[a_1 + b_1 x_1(t-1) - c_1]; \qquad r_1(t) = 0$$

Phase 2k:

$$x_2(t) = 1/c_2[\sum_i \{a_i + b_i x_i(t-1)\}x_i(t-1) - h]; \qquad x_1(t) = 0$$

$$r_2(t) = 1/c_2[a_2 + b_2 x_2(t-1) - c_2]; \qquad r_1(t) = 0$$

Phase 12kl:

$$\begin{bmatrix} x_1(t) \\ x_2(t) \end{bmatrix} = \left(\frac{1}{c_1 - c_2}\right) \begin{bmatrix} -c_2 & 1 \\ c_1 & -1 \end{bmatrix} \begin{bmatrix} l \\ \sum_i \{a_i + b_i x_i(t-1)\}x_i(t-1) - h \end{bmatrix}$$

$$\begin{bmatrix} r_1(t) \\ r_2(t) \end{bmatrix} = \left(\frac{1}{c_1 - c_2}\right) \begin{bmatrix} -c_2 & c_1 \\ 1 & -1 \end{bmatrix} \begin{bmatrix} a_1 + b_1 x_1(t-1) - c_1 \\ a_2 + b_2 x_2(t-1) - c_2 \end{bmatrix}$$

2.10.

Which phase holds in a given time period depends on the solution in the preceding time period and the relative 'positions' of constraints and objective functions which that preceding solution brings about. A complete analysis of the several possibilities has been given in Day and Tinney [9]. Various possibilities are shown to occur, including phase and production periodicity, convergence to a stationary state and so on. In order to give the reader an idea of the richness of results possible even in such a simple, heuristic RP model we reproduce one particularly appealing example.

2.11. *Production in Wisconsia*

In this example, we apply the model to describe economic development in a small fictional region of Wisconsia. Starting with a small initial amount of production in the 'capital-saving' commodity 2 ($c_1 > c_2$ here) and none of the 'capital-intensive' commodity 1, the system grows for several periods in phase 2k. That is, farmers continue to specialize in commodity 2, using all of their working capital in its production. After a time, however, they become sufficiently well endowed with capital to allow some production of the capital-intensive commodity 1. As revenue grows, this more profitable commodity drives out its competitor and the region shifts into its specialization, a situation described by phase 1*l*, which is an equilibrium phase describing a stationary state. Suppose now that the capital-intensive commodity is 'milk' and the capital-saving commodity is 'wheat', and that time is measured in decades. Development begins in 1830 at *t* = 0. The development of the wheat economy by the 'Great Rebellion' period makes Wisconsia a dominant wheat producer. After that time it begins rapidly to develop its dairy industry, which, shortly after the turn of the century, dominates the agricultural scene. This parable is curiously and instructively like the facts.[3]

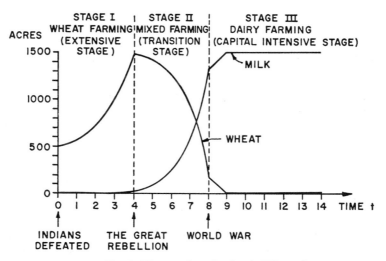

Fig. 1. History of production in Wisconsia.

2.12.

The phase progression 2*k*–12*kl*–1*l*, which is illustrated graphically in fig. 1, is reminiscent of the stage theories of the 'stage makers'. The econometric history of our model passed through three distinct stages: a land surplus, primary food production stage, a developed, mixed farming stage, and a capital intensive farming stage. But this particular result was achieved not through some immutable ordering of the stages of growth, but through a particular, logically arbitrary configuration of parameters and initial conditions. With other configurations of the data many other phase evolutions are possible, even in this little model.

[3] Day and Tinney [9], p. 103.

2.13.

It is also worth noting that the drive to partial equilibrium is, in the special example shown, characterized by a maximal growth of 'working capital' invested in the sector and a maximal rate of decline in consumer prices. At the final, partial equilibrium[4] the market is cleared, zero profits prevail, and consumers obtain their produce at the minimum price compatible with producer equilibrium: Pareto optimality prevails.

3. A 'multi-regional' model[5]

3.1.

The model we have just outlined can be generalized slightly to introduce in the simplest possible terms the application of Recursive Programming to multi-regional economics. We do this now by developing a discrete version of von Thünen's spatial economy. In von Thünen's world, 'industry' with its market for agricultural produce is located in the center of an agricultural area which is called 'The Town'. In our version, farms are located in three concentric ring-like regions around The Town. The distance from the center of any farm to The Town is, say d_j for a farm in the jth ring, $j = 1, 2, 3$.

3.2.

Each farm's decision is represented by primal and dual l.p. models exactly like (1)–(6) in sects. 2.2–2.3, except that when transport cost is added to production cost, unit cost differs from region to region. Hence, let c_{ij} be the total unit cost of production and transportation for the ith commodity in the jth zone. Then

$$c_{ij} = c_i + \tau_i d_j, \qquad i = 1, 2 \text{ and } j = 1, 2, 3, \qquad (11)$$

where c_i is the amount of working capital required to produce one unit of the ith commodity, where τ_i is the cost of transporting one unit of the ith commodity one distance unit and where d_j, as noted above, is the distance of the jth region from the center.

---

[4] Since these are models of an individual economic sector, the equilibria discussed, as in the usual single good supply-demand theory, or in the Cournot duopoly model, are partial economic equilibria.

[5] This section is based on Day and Tinney [10]. For details see that reference.

When we assume that within each region farms are identical and can not borrow or lend and when we assume that each farmer must use only his own initial endowment of land, then production in von Thünen's discrete isolated state can be represented by the sequence of linear programming problems

$$\pi(t) = \max_{x_{ij}} \sum_j \sum_i \hat{z}_{ij}(t) x_{ij} \tag{1'}$$

subject to the land and working capital constraints

$$\sum_{i=1}^{2} x_{ij} \leq l_j, \qquad j = 1, 2, 3 \tag{2'}$$

$$\sum_{i=1}^{2} c_{ij} x_{ij} \leq k_j(t), \qquad j = 1, 2, 3 \tag{3'}$$

$$x_{ij} \geq 0$$

where x_{ij} is the amount of crop i to be produced in region j, where $k_j(t)$ is the amount of working capital available to farms at the beginning of period t; and where l_j is the total amount of land in region j. We denote an optimal solution of (1')–(3') as $x_{ij}(t)$, $i = 1, 2, j = 1, 2, 3$.

3.3.

The 'dual' of the program describes the marginal returns to the factors (land and working capital) in each region.

$$\pi(t) = \min \sum_j \{l_j r_{1j} + k_j(t) r_{kj}\} \tag{4'}$$

subject to

$$r_{1j} + c_{ij} r_{kj} \geq \hat{z}_{ij}(t), \qquad i = 1, 2; \quad j = 1, 2, 3. \tag{5'-6'}$$

$$r_{1j}, r_{kj} \geq 0, \qquad j = 1, 2, 3.$$

The solution values of these dual problems (when they exist) are denoted $r_{1j}(t)$, $r_{kj}(t)$, $j = 1, 2, 3$. Of course these 'dual variables', 'shadow prices', or 'marginal values' depend on expected unit profits which differ (except at equilibrium) from expost or received profits.

3.4.

Now assume, as before, a naive price forecast, and denote $p_i(t)$ as the price received in The Town at the close of the tth production period. Then expected returns per unit of area are

$$\hat{z}_{ij}(t) = p_i(t-1) - c_{ij}, \qquad i = 1, 2; \quad j = 1, 2, 3 \tag{7'}$$

where for simplicity input costs are assumed constant and c_{ij} comes from (11). The working capital constraints for each region are, under our assumptions, the same as before. We have

$$k_j(t) = \sum_i p_i(t-1) x_{ij}(t-1) - h_j, \qquad j = 1, 2, 3. \tag{8'}$$

Likewise, the 'actual' prices received by farmers upon 'trucking to and bartering' their produce in The Town's market are

$$p_i(t) = \max \{0, a_i + \sum_k b_{ik} \sum_j x_{kj}(t)\}, \qquad i = 1, 2 \tag{9'}$$

where, of course, $\sum_j x_{k_j}(t)$ is the total production of crop k, $k = 1, 2$.

3.5.

The system $(1')$–$(9')$ is an RP model, in which $(1')$–$(6')$ describe the optimization component and $(7')$–$(9')$ the feedback component. The sets of equated constraints that can be satisfied during any period are — for a given region — six in number. They are indeed exactly Phases 0, $1l$, $2l$, $1k$, $2k$, $12kl$ of sect. 2.9. Because any of the six could, under suitable initial conditions and parameters, hold at a given time in each of the regions there are $6^3 = 216$ district potential phases. A complete theoretical analysis is possible in principle though tedious. A computational example is sufficient to illustrate the possible results.

3.6.

The simulation begins with an initial distribution of production in which each region produces some of both commodities. Commodity 1 is relatively capital intensive and relatively costly to transport. It should be expected, therefore, that with the passage of time the area close to The Town will specialize in the first commodity and the more remote area will specialize in the second transportation saving commodity. That is precisely what comes to pass as is shown in fig. 2. In the first region the output of commodity 1 rises and the output of commodity 2 falls steadily until the eleventh period when the region completely specializes in commodity 1. Production of this transportation costly commodity also rises in the second region but instead of driving out the second commodity it shares more or less evenly the land resources with the second commodity. Throughout the drive towards partial equilibrium it is a zone of 'mixed' farming. In the remotest region 3 oscillations of diminishing magnitude and duration occur. By the thirty-seventh period partial equilibrium occurs and only the transportation saving commodity is produced here. At its final resting place in this example, the model produces two farming regions of complete specialization separated by a zone of mixed farming.

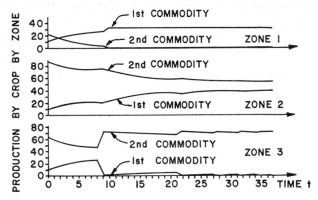

Fig. 2. Time paths of output by zone.

3.7.

The behavior of production in the third region is of special interest. It seems to be upset by progress in the other, more advantageously located rings. That is, farmers in this region are led away from their final solution place, but by smaller and smaller amounts, as their supply of working capital diminishes and they must successively save on variable costs. Even so, at the final, partial equilibrium (in this example) they generate a small surplus of working capital. This could be spent on consumption or hoarded. It is a kind of 'tax' above direct cost the farmer in his role as landlord can extract from the consumers. Profit ratios have shifted because of transportation costs so that the second commodity has a slight edge. Of course, when equilibrium is finally reached, land rent as given by the dual, falls progressively from the closest to the furthest zone from The Town. Because it is a scarce resource, even in the remotest region, land retains a rent. This result is strikingly different from the Ricardian 'no-rent' situation von Thünen obtained for the remotest regions and brings up an aspect of the dynamic model not anticipated by von Thünen: The final resting place (if it exists) and the evolution toward it depend on all the parameters in the model and may work itself out in a great variety of ways.

4. *Summary, qualifications and conclusions*

4.1.

By using the cobweb principle and replacing the supply curve by a linear programming model of production we obtained a highly stylized but not wholly unrealistic model of an individual economic sector. Then, by assuming several distinct cost situations, we obtained a dynamic analog of von Thünen's simple spatial economy. These could in principle be analyzed completely for conditions under which stationary states or cycles of any order existed. More important, though, were the results that (1) solutions are in general multi-phase — they satisfy different sets of dynamic equations at various times during the course of their evolution; and (2) among the possible solutions of a given system are sometimes ones that exhibit an optimality property — they converge to some desirable state. Of course, the latter result is not obtained in general, but it is an important fact that when it comes to pass it is so as much because of the environment and environmental feedback as because of the specific optimizing tactic. *This illustrates the principle upon which decentralized control and indirect policies are based: a change in a decision maker's environment may be one way to bring about improved overall performance.*

4.2.

For purely theoretical or heuristic purposes it can be a great convenience and can do no harm to assume that a group of decision makers comprising an industrial sector or a farming region are identical or sufficiently similar to allow for exact aggregation. This was done in the examples of sects. 2 and 3 above. However, when we carry over this practice to simulation — as we must when we wish to describe or project the actual behavior of anywhere from a hundred or so (e.g., the steel industry) to several thousands or even hundreds of thousands of individuals (as in farming), a question of theoretical interest and practical consequence arises: How far does the behavior of a single (or a few) optimizing model(s) depart from the 'true' behavior of a large number of optimizing individuals? An answer to this question goes well beyond the scope of this brief introduction, and so far as I know has not yet been found. Any claims in this field must be qualified in recognition of this serious deficiency.

4.3.

Nonetheless it seems clear that recursive programming offers an attractive approach for modelling economic behavior. First, the paradigm of the decision maker which it reflects seems true-to-life, much more so than the economic man of complete knowledge and infinite wisdom required to apply conventional programming and optimal control models. Second, in spite of the complexities and rich possibilities of their potential behaviors, such models are amenable to exact, theoretical analysis. Progress in this direction should become more rapid when the general approach receives the attention it deserves. Third, it offers a way to incorporate intra-industrial and intraregional details in quantitative simulation models, and since the successful implementation of policies and programs often depends on an understanding of and ability to influence such details, this would seem to be a strong point in its favor.

References

[1] Beals, R. and T. Koopmans, 1969, Maximizing stationary utility in a constant technology, SIAM Journal of Applied Mathematics, 1001–1015.

[2] Day, R. H., 1963, Recursive Programming and Production Response, Amsterdam: North-Holland Publishing Company.

[3] Day, R. H., 1969, Flexible utility and myopic expectations in economic growth, Oxford Economic Papers, 21, 299–311.

[4] Day R. H., M. Abe, W. Tabb and C. Tsao, 1970. Recursive programming models of industrial development and technological change, A. P. Carter and A. Brody (eds.), Input–Output Techniques, vol. 1: Contributions to Input–Output Analysis, Amsterdam: North-Holland Publishing Company.

[5] Day, R. H. and Y. Fan, 1971, Myopic optimizing, economic growth and the golden rule, SSRI Workshop Paper # 7021.

[6] Day R. H. and E. Heiden, 1969, Recursive programming models for policy formulation, Vincent P. Rock (ed.), Policy Makers and Model Builders, Gordon and Breach, Science Publishers, 319–355.

[7] Day, R. H. and P. E. Kennedy, 1970, Recursive decision systems, Econometrica 38, 666–681.

[8] Day, R. H. and J. Nelson, 1973, A class of dynamic models for describing and projecting industrial development, Journal of Econometrics, 1: 2.

[9] Day, R. H. and E. H. Tinney, 1969a, Cycles, phases, and growth in a generalized cobweb theory, Economic Journal 79, 92–108.

[10] Day, R. H. and E. H. Tunney, 1969b, A dynamic Von Thünen model, Geographical Analysis 1, 137–151.

[11] Goldman, S., 1968, Optimal growth and continual planning revision, Review of Economic Studies, 145–154.

[12] Leontief, W., 1958, Theoretical note on time-preference, productivity of capital, stagnation and economic growth, American Economic Review, 105–111.

CHAPTER 19

Dynamic microeconomic models of production, investment and technological change of the U.S. and Japanese iron and steel industries*

MASATOSHI A. ABE

Marquette University

1. Introduction

The purpose of this paper is to provide an improved understanding of the many forces that determine the development of industries, particularly changes in production, investment and technology through time.

Although a microeconomic approach to productivity, investment and technological change was proposed and tested by Salter [18], this field was not taken up by many economists. This is probably due to a Schumpeterian tradition which had sought to explain productivity and technological change by exogenous forces acting on the economic system. A fundamental relation among productivity, investment, technological change, economic and non-economic activities has been neglected.

Our approach is to use a recursive linear programming (RLP) to analyze this relation. We will explain the behavior of the U.S. and Japanese iron and steel industries for the periods of 1947 to 1966 for the U.S. and of 1950 to 1967 for Japan, using a recursive linear programming model of production, investment and technological change.

With reference to the behavior of the U.S. iron and steel industry in the 19th century, Peter Temin [22, p. 15] stated, "The permanent and cumulative forces at work upon the iron and steel industry may be separated into those deriving from the demand side of Marshall's scissors and those originating on the supply side. Forces impinging on the iron and steel industry

* This paper reports work conducted as part of a project entitled 'Recursive Programming Models of Industrial and Agricultural Development', directed by Richard H. Day, University of Wisconsin, through a grant from the National Science Foundation. I am very grateful to Dr. Day for his continuous help and encouragement in completion of this work.

from the demand side may be expected to be characteristic of the American economy as a whole, while forces that operate through their influence on the supply side of iron and steel may be expected to be more characteristic of the industry itself."

A strong influence has been exerted upon the iron and steel industries by the growth of economies which produced an ever-increasing demand for better quality iron and steel. The most pervasive force on the supply side of the iron and steel industries is the advancement of technology of iron and steel-making. Progress in technology has modernized iron and steel production facilities to widen its product lines and to improve product quality. The history of the iron and steel industries is thus the result of a combination of forces. But above all, two gradual and cumulative trends — advancing technology and a growing demand for iron and steel — have shaped the industry as it is today.

The RLP model used here represents these interacting forces of supply and demand. On the supply side it models decision making in the steel industry in a way characterized by limited rationality.[1] It assumes (1) that economic decisions are made more or less independently of any direct consideration of intertemporal efficiency, (2) that current behavior of the industry is guided by maximizing a certain objective criterion subject to various constraints, (3) that current plans are based on imperfect information, and (4) that the time path of the industry is possibly a suboptimal one. Specifically, the model allows for choices among technically feasible and commercially available techniques of production, and choices involving investment in capital equipment which these techniques utilize.

On the demand side, the model assesses the effect of the external economy by sales forecasting, and thus links the industry with the rest of the economy.

The model as a whole is used to simulate the actual decision making pattern followed by the two industries.

In what follows, recursive programming method in relation to industrial development is briefly explained.[2] Then the major components of recursive linear programming are explained, followed by discussion of its operation and of evaluation of the results of its simulation run of the U.S. and Japanese industries.

---

[1] There is a difference in the degree in 'limited rationality' between the Japanese and the American iron and steel industries as their different industrial development patterns show. As our model simulation will show later, Japan's development follows more closely the path of our 'rationality' than the U.S.

[2] For more detailed analysis of recursive programming method and applications, see Day [9, 10].

2. *Industrial development and recursive programming*

Recursive programming is a recent addition to the inventory of economic models. It appears to be especially suitable for simulating the microeconomic aspects of industrial development.

One of the most remarkable features of industries in the developed countries is that rapid changes in technology have occurred, accompanied by large investments and accumulations of capital. One major production method has been replaced by another as newer cost reducing techniques became available. The industries have responded to a change in relative factor prices by substituting the relatively cheaper factor for the more expansive factor. The substitution also has taken place among production processes which were within the realm of possibilities prescribed by the existing technology of production. Over the periods, however, technology of production has changed, partly due to improving technical knowledge and partly to changing factor prices. With the technical knowledge and factor prices ruling at certain periods of time, a given technique was most appropriate and was adopted by entrepreneurs building new plants or replacing existing ones. But even before a dominant part of an industry was equipped with this technique changes in either technical knowledge or factor prices occurred and a different technique became appropriate. Progress of technical knowledge, and changing factor prices, were continuous processes in time and together gave rise to a stream of new techniques.[3]

Against this stream of new techniques entrepreneurs have most of the time responded rather slowly because of unfamiliarity, the length of the time required to learn a new technique, 'fear' of future more efficient techniques, or uncertainty about future demand.

The fate of a particular production technique, therefore, should be understood in the context of dynamic forces such as changes in technical structure, productivity, demand composition, factor prices and capitalized value of investment goods and limited rational behavior on the part of entrepreneurs.

Thus, in order to explain the production and investment of industries through time, we would need a model that reflects the fact that entrepreneurial decisions are conditioned by an interaction among technological, economic and non-economic factors. In other words, decisions about selecting techniques are shared by several managers who make their decisions more or less independently of any explicit considerations of inter-

---

[3] For more detailed discussion on relationships between investment and technical change, see Salter [18, pp. 5–7].

temporal efficiency. They pursue objectives of local efficiency in a general environment about which they are partially if not almost wholly ignorant. For these reasons a model should be able to simulate the microeconomic decision making environment and the decision making process itself. For this purpose a recursive programming is very well suited.

Specifically our recursive linear programming model consists of the following four major components: (1) A process analysis representation of the industries, (2) sales forecasting, (3) production planning, and (4) investment adjustment rules. They are explained in the following sections.

3. Process analysis[4]

In process analysis the iron and steel industry is treated as one wholly integrated plant containing all phases of the production process of iron and steel; from the production of coke through the production of iron and steel to rolling and finishing of steel. Each of these stages is connected by input–output relationships. Each stage consists of a set of production activities which produce, in most cases, identical goods and thus compete with each other in securing inputs required. With the use of process analysis, therefore, input requirements of each activity are specified and alternative production activities and resource constraints are identified. Since the composition of input material requirement is not the same among the set of competing production activities, the plant has a range of choice regarding which types of inputs and so which activities to use.

Process analysis is presented in a matrix form. This matrix, called the technology matrix, is a schematic presentation of production with all available production activities and constraints. Each production activity is represented in a vector in which inputs appear as positive elements and output as negative elements. The input coefficients show the amount required to produce a unit of the output of an activity.

It should be kept in mind that the technology matrix represents a 'state of production'. Technology presented in the matrix reflects the technological state of the period and the place of concern. Different matrices will be used when our time of concern is shifted to some other period. In this paper two

---

[4] As for the process analysis of the U.S. iron and steel industry, see Fabian [11] and Tsao and Day [21].

different matrices are used for 1947–1966 for U.S. and for 1950 to 1967 for Japan to reflect technological innovation that had taken place during these periods.

4. Sales forecasting and production planning

A representation of the input–output structure of iron and steel production is discussed in process analysis. We now estimate an econometric model of the effects on the expected demand for iron and steel of economic activity in the rest of the macroeconomy. And thus sets the stage for modelling the investment decision in the next section.

Roughly speaking, if demand for the products of the industry is strong the industry will respond by increasing its production capacity. And if demand is moderate, it will be reflected in changes in the industry's rate of operation. A smaller change in demand will be 'contained' in inventory changes. In order to determine its strategy, i.e., to expand its capacity, production rate or inventory, the industry has to diagnose the external environment. An assessment of the expected level of an economic activity constitutes a source of information on which the industry bases its decisions. Therefore, forecasting is a first order of business in the operation of the industry.

According to demand theory,[5] sales of final products are explained in terms of the level of activity of consuming industries and the price of substitutes for domestic steel. Thus in general:

$$S_{it} = f_i(A^*_{it}, L^1_{it}, \ldots, L^r_{it}, K_{it}, D_{it})$$

where

S_{it} = sales of the ith products in the tth period.
A^*_{it} = anticipated activity level of industries consuming the ith good at tth period.
$L^1_{it}, \ldots, L^r_{it}$ = relative prices of substitute goods to the ith good at tth period.
K_{it} = inventory of the ith good at tth period.
D_{it} = dummy variable representing an exogenous shock.

Steel products to be considered for sales are: For the U.S.: (a) for carbon steels: (1) total carbon steel hot rolled, (2) rails, joint bars and tie plate

---

[5] For more detailed discussion of steel shipments, see Higgins [12].

bars, (3) bars, (4) wire reds, (5) plates, (6) sheets and strips, (7) structural shapes, (8) tin mill products, (9) skelp; and (b) for special steel: (1) total special steel hot rolled, (2) bars, (3) wire rods, (4) plates, (5) sheets and strips, (6) structural shapes.

As for Japanese steel products, the following eight products are considered; for carbon steel: (1) rail, (2) shapes, (3) bars, (4) steel pipes, (5) wire rods, (6) plates, (7) sheets and (8) tin plate.

In order to obtain a direct relationship of demand for steel products, it is necessary to consider the level of activities of several industries which use steel products. To represent the activity level of industries, we have used a combined index of the activity level of steel consuming industries by taking a weighted average of Federal Reserve Board's production indexes of the consuming industries with the weight being their shares of GNP.

Anticipated activity level is derived from the actual levels as follows:

$$A_{it}^* = \alpha_1 A_{it-1} + \alpha_2 A_{it-2}: \quad \text{where } \alpha_1 > 0, \ \alpha_2 > 0.$$

For a long run substitution effect the following two year lagged price ratios were used.

$$L_1(t) = \frac{\text{Price of a steel product } (t)}{\text{Price of aluminum } (t)} : \quad L_2(t) = \frac{\text{Price of a steel product } (t)}{\text{Price of concrete } (t)}$$

and so on.

For both industries, aluminum is used as a substitute for tin mill products; plastics and aluminum for sheets and strip; concrete and nonferrous metal for plates, structural shapes and rails.

We can observe that there seems to exist a definite pattern in buying behavior during or around the period of strikes or periods threatened by strikes. As the possibility of strikes can be foreseen, shipments increase immediately before the anticipated strike. The following dummy variables are used: $D_{it} = 1$ for years before threatened work stoppage; $D_{it} = 0$ for other years. For Japan, a strong labor union is not organized on an industry basis and labor disputes are mostly on a company basis. Hence, this 'exogenous shock' is not considered for Japan. The final form used for estimation is:

$$S_{it} = \alpha_{i0} + \alpha_{i1} A_{it-1} + \alpha_{i2} A_{it-2} + \alpha_{i3} K_{it-1} + \alpha_{i4} L_{it-1} + \alpha_{i5} L_{it-2} + \alpha_{i6} D_{it}$$

where i stands for each final steel product, and $\alpha_0, \alpha_1, \alpha_2, \alpha_3, \alpha_4, \alpha_5$ and α_6 are to be estimated.

5. *Production planning*

This section discusses a simple production planning model of the industry based on the estimates of future sales discussed in the previous section, and formulates a model to explain actual production adjustments of the industry.

The following behavioral assumptions and identities are used in order to derive production equations of the industry,

$$P_t + V_{t-1} = S_t + V_t.$$

This is an identity stating that P_t, planned production and V_{t-1}, inventory at the end of period $t-1$ are equal to S_t, planned sales plus V_t, planned inventory at the end of the period T. The above identity can be written as:

$$P_t = S_t + V_t - V_{t-1}.$$

Now the quantity $V_t - V_{t-1}$ represents the planned change in inventory.

In order to explain planned level of inventory various behavioral assumptions can be postulated. The inventory adjustment equation used in this paper is:

$$V_t - V_{t-1} = c(S_t - S_{t-1})$$

where c is a constant.

Our production relation, therefore, can be written as:

$$P_t = S_t + c(S_t - S_{t-1}) \quad \text{or} \quad P_t = (1+c)S_t - cS_{t-1}.$$

Now assuming that planned production differs from actual production only by stochastic elements, e_t's which are assumed serially uncorrelated, our production relation of the industry is written as:

$$P_t = (1+c)S_t - cS_{t-1} + e_t.$$

In estimating the above equation dummy variable representing labor dispute is added: $D_t = -1$ for one year of labor dispute, $D_t = 0$ for other years.

The final form used for estimation is:

$$P_{it} = \alpha_{i0} + \alpha_{i1} S_t - \alpha_{i2} S_{t-1} + \alpha_{i3} D_t$$

where i stands for each final steel product, and α_0, α_1, α_2, and α_3 are to be estimated.

6. Investment activities and constraints

In this section we consider a set of investment activities that allow capacity to be expanded at the beginning of each production period. In this paper the selection of investment activities is explained by investment costs based on a payout principle and production costs, and the level of investment activities is explained by a behaviour assumption called the maximum potential growth principle.[6]

The following investment activities are considered for U.S.: investment in (1) beehive coke ovens, (2) byproduct coke ovens, (3) blast furnaces, (4) Bessemer converters, (5) open hearth furnaces, (6) the conversion of open hearth into open hearth with oxygen lancing, (7) electric furnaces, (8) basic oxygen furnaces. As for Japan: (1) blast furnaces, (2) open hearth furnaces, (3) electric furnaces, (4) basic oxygen furnaces.

The payout principle: There are several criteria which have been proposed for evaluating the profitability of investment projects. The most popular and simple criterion will be the payout principle. It says that no investment will be undertaken unless it is expected to generate profits that will return the initial capital outlays within a certain period of time, say, three, five or ten years. The formula used for calculating investment costs is:

$$I = K[(1/T) - (1/M)]$$

where I is investment cost, K initial capital outlay, T the payout period, M an economic life of a project.

The maximum potential growth principle: The payout principle says that a project can be selected for investment on the basis of its ability to return the initial cost and the project can theoretically be carried out until its annual cash flow is equal to its investment cost. In the world of uncertainty, however, certain investment projects do not take place or are not carried out far enough even though they 'pay for themselves'. We believe that this is due to the fact that investment in capacity is constrained by two essentially different behavioral considerations: the first is a resistance in adopting new techniques because of the time required to learn their use and apply them most efficiently to existing firms. The second is unwillingness to expand capacity excessively in any one year purely on capitalized values and cost differentials because of future superior innovations. We represent the first by a set of behavioral adoption constraints and the second by a set of behavioral adjustment constraints.

---

[6] For more detailed discussion of investment activities and constraints, see Day *et al.* [9].

Algebraically, the adoption constraint is expressed as:

$$y_{ij}(t) \leqq \mu_{ij} K_{ij}(t-1)$$

where j indicates a stage of production (coking, pig iron making, steel refining, etc.) and i indicates a type of equipment (Bessemer, open hearth, etc.) $y_{ij}(t)$ represents investment in the ith capacity of jth stage at t, μ_{ij} adoption coefficient, and the investment adjustment constraint is expressed as:

$$y_{ij}(t) = \alpha_{ij}[\overline{K}_{ij}(t) - K_{ij}(t-1)] \tag{1}$$

where $y_{ij}(t)$ represents investment in the ith capacity of the jth stage at time t, α_{ij} adjustment coefficient, $\overline{K}_{ij}(t)$ is the estimate at year t of desirable ith capacity of the jth stage if all of the jth stage output were produced by the ith capacity, $K_{ij}(t-1)$ actual ith capacity of the jth stage at time $t-1$. α_{ij} should be positive, and its value should be between 0 and 1 if investment follows the maximum potential adjustment path.

$\overline{K}_{ij}(t)$ is estimated as

$$\overline{K}_{ij}(t) = \pi_{ij} \overline{D}_j(t) \tag{2}$$

where $\overline{D}_j(t)$ is the forecasted demand of the output of the jth stage, and π_{ij} represents the proportion of the desired jth stage capacity to be held in the ith capital good. Our model purports to derive explicitly a degree of excess capacity for each of capital goods used in the industry.

$\overline{D}_j(t)$ is estimated from the results of forecast of the previous section. That is

$$\overline{D}_j(t) = b_j \sum_k S_k(t) \tag{3}$$

where $S_k(t)$ represents the forecasted level of the kth product, for example, steel plate, and b_j is the capital coefficient of jth process. (b_j is known from the technology matrix.)

Substituting (2) into (1) we get

$$y_{ij}(t) = \alpha_{ij} \pi_{ij} \overline{D}_j(t) - \alpha_{ij} K_{ij}(t-1). \tag{4}$$

Having first estimated $\overline{D}_j(t)$ in the first step, (4) is used to estimate α_{ij} and π_{ij} in the second step.

Note that because under conditions of declining demand the right side of (1) could be negative and since investment is by nature a non-negative variable this equation should be augmented to preclude negativity. This is done by rewriting

$$y_{ij}(t) = \max\{0, \alpha_{ij}[K_{ij}(t) - K_{ij}(t-1)]\}. \tag{5}$$

The adoption constraint is usually effective or equated in the early stage of development and the adjustment constraint limits investment in later stages of development. When these two constraints are combined we obtain s-shaped curves often observed in development process of technique. Algebraically we can write this:

$$y_{ij}(t) \leqq \min \{\mu_{ij} K_{ij}(t-1), \max \{0, \alpha_{ij}[K_{ij}(t)-K_{ij}(t-1)]\}\}. \tag{6}$$

This states that investment in a given capacity must always equal or lie below the minimum of the adoption of adjustment constraints.

The form the investment will take is shown in fig. 1.

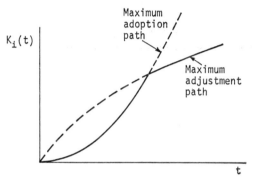

Fig. 1. Path of maximum potential growth.

The maximum potential growth path, however, need not be followed if a given technique becomes relatively expensive, i.e., will not pay for itself during the payout period. Then the model will not predict as much investment as the maximal potential growth principle will allow. This could occur because of input price changes or because of the adoption of a still newer more efficient technique. But in no case can it exceed the bounds set by the maximum potential growth. It is most likely that investment proceeds along the maximum adoption path, but later in its process after switching from adoption path to adjustment path, it will taper off from the maximum adjustment path. However, the question of whether or not the maximum potential growth is followed can be answered only by the simulation of a complete model which will be presented in the next section.

7. Simulation of model

We are now in a position to explore the behavior of the industry over time. In the simulation of recursive programming model all model components discussed before — process analysis, sales forecast, production planning, and investment decision — are all put together. The model is schematically represented in matrix form in table 1, and its flow chart is given in fig. 2.

Table 1

Matrix of model

Type of constraints	Activities			RHS
	Production	Investment	Purchasing	
Cost	$c_1, c_2, \ldots$	$\phi_1, \phi_2, \ldots$	$r_1, r_2, \ldots$	
Primary inputs	A	0	$-I$	0
Purchased inputs	0	0	I	V
Intermediate products	G	0	0	0
Final products	$-H$	0	0	Production decision rules
Investment	I	$-I$	0	K
Investment constraints	0	I	0	Investment decision rules

The structural relations of the model in algebraic forms are presented as follows:

Cost Objective:

$$\pi(t) = \sum_i r_i(t)u_i(t) + \sum_j \phi_j(t)y_j(t)$$

i for all purchasing activities of primary inputs, $u_i(t)$ is the level of purchasing activity of the ith primary input in year t, $r_i(t)$ is the observed price paid for the ith primary input in year t, $\phi_j(t)$ is the investment cost of the jth capital good in year t, $y_j(t)$ is the level of investment in the jth capital good in year t.

Primary Input Constraints:
$\sum_j a_{ij} x_j(t) - u_i(t) \leq 0$; i for all primary inputs and j for all production activities; where a_{ij} is the input–output coefficient for the ith primary input in the jth activity.

Purchased Input Balances:
$u_i(t) - v_i^o(t) \leq 0$; i for all primary inputs, $v_i^o(t)$ is the observed utilization of the ith primary input in year t.

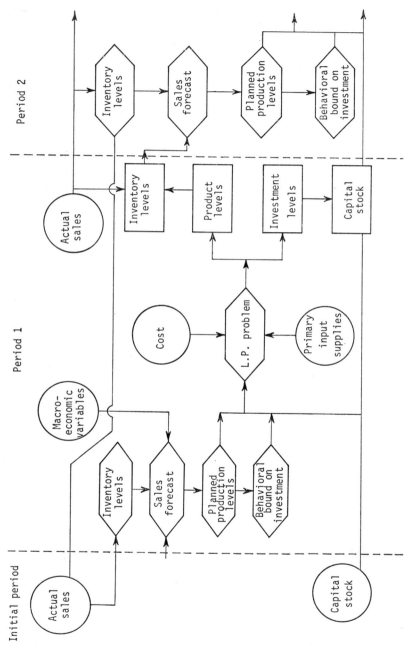

Fig. 2. Schematic representation of recursive programming model (decision rule or forecast equations are represented by hexagonal boxes, endogenous variables by rectangular boxes, and exogenous variables by circles).

Intermediate Product Balances:

$\sum_j g_{ij} x_j(t) \leqq 0$; i for all intermediate products, j for all production activities; where g_{ij} is the input–output coefficient for the ith intermediate product in the jth activity.

Final Product Constraints:

$\sum_j h_{ij} x_j(t) \leqq -s_i(t)$; i for all final products, j for all production activities; where $s_i(t)$ is the predicted production of the ith final product in year t.

Capacity Constraints:

$\sum_j b_{ij} x_j(t) - \sum_k y_{ik}(t) \leqq (1-\delta_i) K_i(t-1)$; i for all capital goods, j for all production activities, k for all investment activities; where b_{ij} is the input–output coefficient of the ith capital good in the jth activity, $K_i(t-1)$ is the capacity of the ith capital good in year $(t-1)$, and δ_i is depreciation rate for the ith capital good. Except for beehive and Bessemer capacities where 5 % depreciation is imposed, $\delta_i = 0$ is assumed for all other furnaces, the assumption being that all capacities are maintained over time.

Behavioral Investment Constraints:

$\sum_k y_{ik}(t) \leqq \min \{\mu_i K_i(t-1), \max \{0, \alpha_i[K(t)-K_i(t-1)]\}\}$; i for all capital goods, k for all investment activities; where μ_i and α_i are the adoption and adjustment coefficients, respectively, for the ith capital good.

Then recursive programming will be to minimize the above cost function subject to the above six sets of constraints.

Operationally a recursive programming model involves a series of interdependent linear programming problems which are solved sequentially. The model takes the solution values of decision variables in one period and considers these to be part of the given environment in which decisions are made in subsequent periods. Thus the entire model is run by (1) giving the initial period's condition; (2) solving the first period's linear programming problem; (3) updating the endogenous and exogenous constraints, variables and cost parameters; (4) solving the succeeding linear programming problem, and so on. The model determines 'automatically' production and investment levels for each period over a number of periods.

8. Testing of the model

The merit of the recursive programming model can be evaluated on two counts. We can examine first how well the model predicts the investment pattern of the industries over years, and secondly how closely the model follows the pattern of investment behavior that was postulated to be followed by the industries. The second point will be to see if the model chooses the phases that prior hypothesis would lead us to believe it would.

As for the first point, the predicted capacity levels are compared with the actual levels. The results are presented in tables 3 and 4 and figs. 3 and 4.

To help answer the second point, prior and posterior phases are presented in table 2.

Table 2

Prior and posterior phases of investment activities

	Prior Phases		Posterior Phases	
	Adoption	Adjustment	Adoption	Adjustment
U.S.				
Byproduct		1947–59		1947, 48
				1951, 56
Blast furnace		1947–59		1947–66
Open Hearth without O_2		1947–53		
Open Hearth with O_2	1954–57	1958, 60		1960–63
		1961, 62		1965
Electric Furnace	1947–53	1954, 57	1948, 50	1957, 65
		1958, 59		1966
Basic Oxygen	1955–66		1961–66	
Japan				
Blast Furnace	1950–67		1951–66	
			except 58, 61	
Open Hearth	1950–60	1961–65	1955–56	
			1958–64	
Electric Furnace		1958–62		1952–63
				1967
Basic Oxygen	1957–67		1957–66	

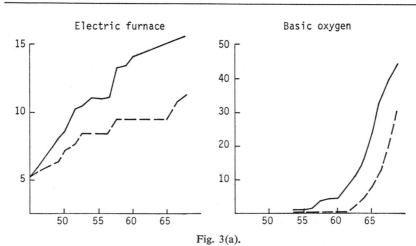

Fig. 3(a).

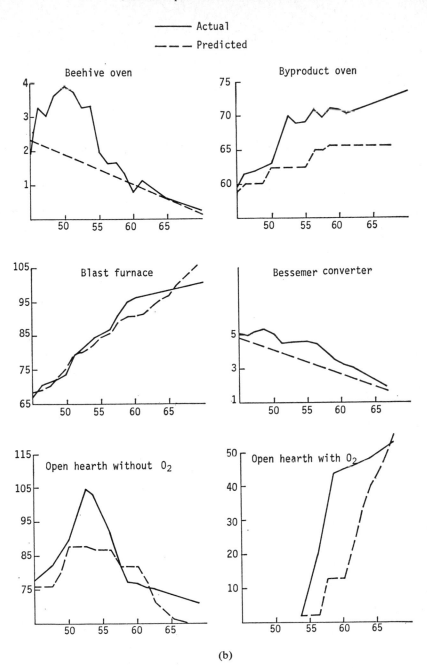

Fig. 3. Comparison of actual and predicted capacities; U.S. – actual; - - - predicted.

Table 3

Comparison of actual and predicted capacities: U.S. (millions of N.T.)

	Beehive Oven		Byproduct Oven		Blast Furnace	
	Actual	Simulation	Actual	Simulation	Actual	Simulation
1947	2.806	2.381	59.699	58.901	67.439	67.713
1948	3.343	2.262	61.573	60.243	70.562	69.883
1949	3.186	2.149	62.283	60.243	71.560	70.959
1950	3.691	2.041	62.570	60.243	72.472	73.383
1951	3.862	1.939	63.198	62.819	73.782	76.438
1952	3.802	1.842	67.379	62.819	79.380	79.009
1953	3.310	1.750	69.980	62.819	82.001	81.221
1954	3.308	1.663	69.377	62.819	83.971	82.853
1955	2.092	1.579	69.416	62.819	85.485	84.862
1956	1.746	1.500	71.225	65.084	86.818	86.881
1957	1.746	1.425	70.453	65.084	91.000	90.978
1958	1.391	1.357	71.708	65.226	94.635	91.311
1959	0.877	1.286	71.433	65.226	96.521	91.311
1960	1.061	1.222	70.821	65.226	97.003	92.008
1961	0.901	1.161	71.175	65.226	97.488	93.971
1962	0.766	1.103	71.531	65.226	97.975	95.838
1963	0.651	1.048	71.889	65.226	98.464	97.238
1964	0.553	0.995	72.248	65.226	98.956	99.448
1965	0.469	0.946	72.609	65.226	99.451	103.090
1966	0.398	0.898	72.972	65.226	99.948	106.727

	Bessemer		O-H without O_2		O-H with O_2	
	Actual	Simulation	Actual	Simulation	Actual	Simulation
1947	5.226	4.896	83.611	81.010		
1948	5.191	4.631	84.817	81.010		
1949	5.537	4.418	86.984	81.010		
1950	5.621	4.197	91.054	84.799		
1951	5.381	3.987	94.974	93.551		
1952	4.637	3.788	102.678	93.551		
1953	4.787	3.599	109.095	93.551		
1954	4.787	3.419	107.522	92.195	2.712	2.712
1955	4.787	3.248	101.984	92.195	10.383	2.712
1956	4.505	3.086	95.698	92.195	21.214	2.712
1957	4.027	2.932	88.227	87.000	34.095	13.102
1958	3.577	2.785	82.419	87.000	44.109	13.102
1959	3.398	2.646	82.289	87.000	44.333	13.102
1960	3.226	2.514	81.415	81.802	45.840	23.497
1961	3.064	2.388	80.544	76.969	47.347	33.163
1962	2.910	2.269	79.676	73.439	48.854	40.222
1963	2.764	2.156	78.811	71.159	50.361	44.781
1964	2.625	2.048	77.950	68.745	51.868	49.609
1965	2.493	1.946	77.092	65.655	53.375	55.788
1966	2.368	1.849	76.237	65.655	54.882	55.788

Table 3 (continued)

	Electric Furnace		Basic Oxygen	
	Actual	Simulation	Actual	Simulation
1947	5.397	5.333		
1948	6.113	5.900		
1949	6.871	5.932		
1950	7.555	6.620		
1951	8.233	7.362		
1952	10.232	7.889		
1953	10.449	8.574		
1954	10.807	8.574	0.540	0.000
1955	10.719	8.574	0.540	0.000
1956	11.502	8.574	1.350	0.000
1957	13.313	9.728	3.580	0.000
1958	13.495	9.728	4.157	0.000
1959	14.396	9.728	4.653	0.000
1960	14.468	9.728	7.500	0.000
1961	14.540	9.728	10.800	2.156
1962	14.613	9.728	15.265	4.510
1963	14.686	9.728	23.040	7.940
1964	14.759	9.728	33.890	12.937
1965	14.833	10.851	39.515	20.218
1966	14.907	11.954	44.015	30.827

Source of data: American Iron and Steel Institute, American Statistical Report, various years. All figures are at the end of the year capacity. Except for BOF, figures for the year 1960–1966, are extrapolated in linear trend. Capacities for BOF are taken from L-D Newsletter, Kaiser Engineers. They include Keldo capacities, also. In the case of conversion of the open hearth with oxygen lancing, the following method was used:

Let K_1, K_2 and K be capacity of O-H without O_2, O-H with O_2 and all of O-H, respectively. Then $K(t) = K_1(t) + K_2(t)$. Let d_1 and d_2 be depreciation rules for O-H without O_2 and O-H with O_2 and y be capacity converted from O-H without O_2 into O-H with O_2. Then

$$K_1(t) = (1-d_1)K_1(t-1) - y(t) \tag{1}$$

$$K_2(t) = (1-d_2)K_2(t-1) + 1.42\, y(t). \tag{2}$$

It was assumed that by the conversion the capacity of O-H is increased by 42%. Assuming for simplicity $d_1 = d_2 = 0$, we have after adding (1) and (2):

$$K(t) = K(t-1) + 0.42 y(t).$$

Thus

$$y(t) = \frac{1}{0.42} [K(t) - K(t-1)].$$

Table 4

Comparisons of actual and predicted capacities: Japan (millions of N.T.)

	Blast Furnace		Open Hearth	
	Predicted	Actual	Predicted	Actual
1950	5.450	5.450	7.176	7.176
1951	5.450	5.450	7.176	7.013
1952	6.159	5.558	7.176	7.405
1953	6.960	5.374	7.176	7.565
1954	7.875	5.560	7.610	7.704
1955	8.578	7.715	8.038	7.814
1956	9.733	7.720	8.730	8.967
1957	11.038	7.785	9.469	9.930
1958	12.513	8.149	10.119	9.436
1959	12.513	10.121	10.953	12.312
1960	14.399	11.630	11.856	15.228
1961	16.527	15.059	12.821	16.971
1962	18.932	17.387	13.853	14.926
1963	18.932	20.589	14.955	17.447
1964	22.003	23.211	16.134	18.650
1965	25.473	27.001	17.394	17.154
1966	29.394	31.589	17.394	16.068
1967	33.825	44.080	17.394	13.721

	Electric Furnace		Basic Oxygen	
	Predicted	Actual	Predicted	Actual
1950	3.668	3.874		
1951	3.668	4.080		
1952	3.668	4.001		
1953	3.792	3.800		
1954	3.991	3.751		
1955	4.203	3.518		
1956	4.557	4.751		
1957	4.952	5.985	0.909	0.909
1958	5.048	6.113	0.909	1.389
1959	5.616	6.883	1.363	1.430
1960	5.640	8.123	2.083	4.843
1961	6.581	8.641	3.085	7.285
1962	7.853	10.162	4.636	10.984
1963	9.474	10.885	6.967	13.399
1964	10.439	11.346	10.471	17.531
1965	10.439	11.357	15.737	24.745
1966	10.439	10.987	23.652	29.912
1967	10.439	11.313	34.502	53.433

Source of data: The Japan Iron and Steel Federation, Statistical Yearbook, various years. All figures are at the end of the year capacity. For some years published capacity figures are smaller than production figures. In this case production figures are substituted for capacity figures.

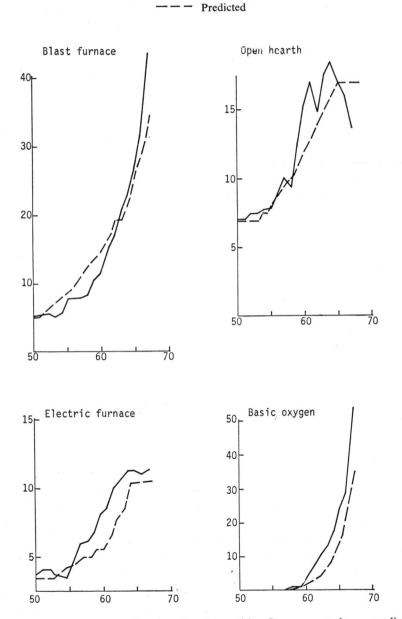

Fig. 4. Comparison of actual and predicted capacities; Japan. – actual; - - - predicted.

In general, as figs. 3 and 4 show, our results for the U.S. are not as accurate as the results for Japan. This is also true of the phase structure as demonstrated by table 2 where most of the U.S. processes exhibited posterior phases which are different from prior phases. For many years the maximum potential growth path was not followed in the U.S. When a model errs in predicting investment activities by falling short of the prior maximum path, the errors accumulate over years and distort the pattern of our predicted capacity levels.

The prior phases for the U.S. byproduct, open hearth without oxygen lancing, and electric furnace processes are not followed from 1952 to 1955, The model failed to predict investment for these processes, while, in fact, the industry kept expanding their capacities during this period. It is during this period that the U.S. steel industry experienced a wide fluctuation in steel production and shipment. The years 1951, 1953 and 1955 were expansion years, while 1952 and 1954 are years of recession. Having failed in forecasting accurately the fluctuating pattern of demand for steel products for these years, the model grossly underestimated demand for steel. According to our forecasts, the level of total steel output data did not return to the 1951 level until 1956. This is one of the main reasons that our prior phases are not followed for these processes, and hence the predicted capacity levels are distorted.

For the U.S. blast furnaces our prior phase was followed and hence prediction followed the actual investment very closely.

Prediction for the U.S. open hearth with oxygen lancing and the basic oxygen processes have very similar patterns. The prior adoption phases were not followed in an early period. For the basic oxygen process this is due to most of the early basic oxygen converters being operated at such a small scale that large steelmakers were not anxious to introduce this process until large scale operation of this process was proven technologically and economically feasible. One of the reasons for failure of the model to predict early posterior phase for the open hearth with oxygen lancing is that only the conversion of the open hearth process was considered. If an investment activity for the open hearth with oxygen lancing had been included in the model, the posterior phase might have been predicted.

Although the model missed the actual initial conversion date, the model did show that the conversion of the open hearths into the open hearths with oxygen lancing was more economical than scrapping the old open hearths and replacing them by the basic oxygen converters. The expansion of the open hearth capacity even after the introduction of the more efficient basic oxygen process may be explained by this conversion process.

The predictions for the Japanese industry are better than for the U.S. for phases and investment levels. In the case of the Japanese open hearth process, a wrong phase change was predicted. This is due to the use of the officially announced open hearth capacity data, while, in fact, the Japanese steelmakers have limited considerably the use of the open hearth to avoid over-production of steel. For the other Japanese processes, prior phases are, for most cases, followed rather closely and the predicted capacity level is close to the actual one.

9. Concluding remarks

Our major concern of this paper was to analyze the behavior of industry over time. For this we were interested in forces that determined the development of the industries. In order to evaluate our effort the results for the investment activity were reported. The basic assumptions of our model were: (1) economic decisions were made more or less independently of any direct consideration of intertemporal efficiency; (2) current behavior of the industry is guided by maximizing a certain objective function subject to various constraints; and (3) current plans are based on imperfect information.

More specific to our model, the investment activity is critically dependent upon several model components: Iron and steelmaking technology was represented by input–output technique. Production levels were planned to meet forecasted sales plus incremental changes in inventory stocks. Cost minimizing behavior of the industry was assumed. The payout principle and the maximum potential growth principle were postulated to explain the investment behavior. Furthermore the maximum potential growth was based on sales forecasts.

A slight mistake in any of these would affect the prediction of the investment activity. Hence it is very difficult to pinpoint the causes of our prediction errors. If the prediction of investment is the only concern of this paper, it is of interest to assume, for example, that the industry had perfect forecasts, and hence to use the actual sales for predicting our investment activities. Recalling that our investment predictions were affected by poor sales forecasts, it would be an instructive way of testing our investment hypotheses.

However, our major concern was to analyze the investment activity in the context of such dynamic factors as input price changes, changes in demand composition, improvement in technical knowledge, capitalized value of investment goods and limited rational behavior on the part of the decision maker of the industry. To my knowledge no other model has attempted to explain investment of the steel industry with the same degree of complexity as our model.

Comparing our results for the U.S. and the Japanese industries, we noted that our predictions for Japan were more accurate than for the U.S. But recalling that during the periods of our concern the Japanese iron and steel industry has made rapid growth while the U.S. counterpart was slow in progress, our model, though it assumes limited rationality on the part of decision makers, was more successful in explaining the behavior of a decision maker who followed more closely the path of "rationality" as evidenced by the case of Japan.

Poor results for the U.S. iron and steel industry may seem to render inconclusive our hypotheses of the payout principle and the maximum potential growth principle, but future research on sales forecasting and production decisions can improve the prediction of investment levels.

References

[1] Abe, M. A., 1970, Dynamic microeconomic models of production, investment and technological change of the U.S. and Japanese iron and steel industries, unpublished Ph.D. dissertation, University of Wisconsin, Madison.
[2] American Iron and Steel Institute, Annual Statistical Report, each year, New York.
[3] The Bank of Japan, The Monthly Statistics of Japan, Tokyo, Japan.
[4] Bashforth, G., 1957, The Manufacturing of Iron and Steel, vols. I, II and III, 2nd ed., London: Chapman and Hall.
[5] Battelle Memorial Institute, 1964, Final Report on Technical and Economic Analysis of the Impact of Recent Developments in Steelmaking Practices on the Supplying Industries, Columbus, Ohio.
[6] The British Iron and Steel Institute, 1963, The Iron and Steel Industry of Japan, Report of the Delegation from the British Iron and Steel, Institute, London: William Lee and Co.
[7] Case, S., D. Moore, C. Sims and R. Lund, 1954, Comparative Economics of Open Hearth and Electric Furnaces for Production of Low Carbon Steel, Columbus, Ohio: Battelle Memorial Institute.
[8] Chenery, H., 1952, Overcapacity and the accelerator principle, Econometrica, 1–28.
[9] Day, R. H., M. Abe, W. Tabb and C. Tsao, 1969, Recursive programming models of industrial development and technological change, A. P. Carter and A. Brody (eds.) Contributions to Input–Output Analysis, Amsterdam: North-Holland Publishing Co., pp. 99–118.
[10] Day, R. and C. Kennedy, 1970, Recursive decision systems: an existence analysis, Econometrica, 666–681.
[11] Fabian, T., 1963, Process Analysis of U.S. Iron and Steel Industry, A. Manne and H. Markowitz (eds.) Studies in Process Analysis, New York: Wiley and Sons.

[12] Higgins, C., 1968, An econometric description of the U.S. iron and steel industry, unpublished Ph.D. thesis, University of Pennsylvania.

[13] The Japan Iron and Steel Federation, Statistical Yearbook, each year, Tokyo, Japan.

[14] The Japan Iron and Steel Federation, Summary of Iron and Steel Statistics (Testuko Tokei Yoran), each year, Tokyo, Japan.

[15] Johnston, J., 1961, An econometric study of the production decision, Quarterly Journal of Economics.

[16] Koizumi, S. and C. Higgins, 1965, An econometric study of the U.S. iron and steel industry, Discussion paper no. 13, Economics Research Service Unit, University of Pennsylvania.

[17] Ono, K. and H. Namba, 1955, The growth of iron and steel industry in Japan and the problem of raw materials, Kyoto University Economic Review.

[18] Salter, W., 1966, Productivity and Technical Change, 2nd ed., Cambridge University Press.

[19] Smith, V., 1961, Investment and Production, Harvard University Press.

[20] Tabb, W., 1963, A recursive programming model of resource allocation and technological change in the U.S. bituminous coal industry, unpublished Ph.D. dissertation, University of Wisconsin.

[21] Tsao, C. and R. Day, 1971, A process analysis model of the U.S. steel industry, Management Science, B588–B608.

[22] Temin, P., 1964, Iron and Steel in 19th Century America, An Economic Inquiry, the M.I.T. Press.

[23] U.S. Congress, 1963, Steel Prices, Unit Costs, Profits and Foreign Competition, Hearing Before Joint Economic Committee.

[24] Watanabe, T. and S. Kinoshita, 1966, An Econometric Model of the Japanese Steel Industry, draft, the Ministry of Industry and Trade, Japan.

CHAPTER 20

An interregional recursive programming model of the U. S. iron and steel industry

JON P. NELSON

Pennsylvania State University

1. Introduction

Few industries attract as much attention from the economic analyst as the U.S. iron and steel industry. From the standpoint of systematic modeling along structure, conduct, and performance lines, virtually every aspect of the industry has been examined and reexamined.[1] Econometric studies of costs and prices, investment and output have appeared with a frequency only surpassed by the studies of cost or production functions for electric power. Such experimental replication is not always viewed favorably by the economist. Another article on steel industry economics must therefore make some advance indication of its alleged contribution to knowledge.

To begin, few models of industrial systems have attempted to integrate in any substantial manner, elements of both structure and conduct. We have, on the one hand, structuralistic theories and indices which "postulate a syllogistic premise–conclusion relationship between structure and (performance)", Markham [22, p. 102].[2] It is easy to demonstrate, however, that by simply changing the assumptions about the rivals' behavior, oligopoly models of, say, the Cournot phylum will predict quite different performance. Behavioralists, on the other hand, have often been too willing to view conduct as a polyglot which can only be described but not analyzed or to abandon the fundamental duality that exists between decision rules and procedures and explicit optimizing of the neo-classical vein (Day [9, p. 463]). Decision rules are viewed as somehow devoid of past history and, as a consequence, the notion of equilibrium is entirely subordinate to the

---

[1] See, for example, Adams [2] and Weiss [38].

[2] Further discussion of the structure — conduct debate may be found in Baldwin [4], Scherer [30], and in the papers by McKie, Phillips, and Bain in [21].

behavioral mechanisms. One can argue, as Cyert and March do in their illuminating work [8, pp. 15–16], that behavioralistic theories and models are designed to answer a different set of questions relative to conventional theories. There is great truth in this position and we shall return to it at the end of this paper.

The model presented here attempts to integrate the partially conflicting viewpoints represented by these two schools of analysis. First, we view decision making under uncertainty as necessarily guided by rough, even crude, rules of thumb. We argue that these rules may be quite consistent with so-called rational behavior when the right constraints have been designated and when mechanisms are postulated that allow the decision maker in question to alter the rule or otherwise switch the procedures employed. Second, dynamic, adaptive decision making involves sequential feedback of past experience and information as a guide in determining the present structure of decision making. The information obtained through feedback is necessarily of a local rather than a global nature. Third, the behavioral aspects of decision making — rules of thumb and feedback — are embedded in an explicit optimizing framework. In our case, this structure can be summarized in two words: technology and location. By technology, we mean the actual process of production, including the actual or potential techniques employed. The locational structure in part follows from the technology employed but is viewed here as an added dimension in the range of choice involved with industrial production, investment, and technological change.

The coupling of conduct and structure can thus result in (1) different performance depending upon the decision rules selected and their estimated parameters and (2) the decision rules themselves may have an additional feedback effect on the structure of the industry in question. However, these questions do not alter the basic incarnations of neo-classical theory. The goals and objectives of the decision maker are still crucial assumptions. The constrained optimization problem is still guided by marginal conditions of one sort or another. What the model attempts to do is present not just the substance of choice within a given structural framework, but also present in a limited fashion, the process of production and decision making.

The paper is divided into four parts. Part one briefly analyzes the technological and locational structure of the U.S. steel industry from 1947 to 1967. Part two describes the primal recursive programming problem along with the behavioral and feedback relationships. In part three, we present some graphical results based on empirical implementation of the model and propose inference tests for the results based on information theoretic concepts. Part four summarizes our findings and makes some suggestions for further research.

2. The structure of decision making in the steel industry

2.1. Technology

The technology of steel production is best characterized as process oriented.[3] At each stage in production, the product must be passed on to the next productive unit so that the output of each stage is an intermediate product to be used in another stage or a final product. The boundaries of each stage are thus defined in terms of a major output; all other outputs for a given stage are termed byproducts. The amount of product that can pass through each stage is limited by the capacity of the productive unit(s) for that stage. Within each stage, there are one or more activities which utilize the same or alternative productive capacities and which, according to our definition, result in the same intermediate or final product. For a given time period, the decision maker must then select the set of activities to be used within each stage and the sequence of activities to be used over all stages. His focus is thus on alternative methods of production (processes) such as furnaces, mills, and ovens.

The question of technical efficiency — the 'how' problem of resource allocation — is thus explicitly represented in a process analysis model. In neo-classical analysis, the choice problem is to determine the relative amounts of various inputs to be hired or purchased. When summarized in a production function, the theory presupposes that the optimal set of technical production processes has already been determined [6, p. 271], [11, pp. 201–203], [40, pp. 97–99]. In process analysis, the firm can only vary the relative quantities of inputs employed indirectly through substitution among the methods of production available to it. Each activity then designates one of the decision variables in the production plan.

Representing the production process by fixed input proportions for alternative activities is in some cases a simplification justifiable on operational grounds. However, under normal short-run economic conditions, many steel production processes are used within fairly limited ranges and can be represented realistically by a select few activities with fixed technological coefficients. Thus, in the range in which the economy normally

[3] Earlier process analysis studies of iron and steel, include Fabian [12], Kendrick [19], and Trozzo [36]. See also [5].

operates, and taking into account the administrative costs associated with change, the production functions behave as if they were linear and homogeneous. Be that as it may, our interest is still in representing the decision process as well as its substantive structure.

This point may be illustrated as follows: Table 1 shows for each major type of steelmaking furnace (steel ingot stage), the current scrap proportion, and the maximum and minimum proportions which would be technically feasible. Technically feasible is used here to mean that the extremes could be used without introducing intolerable technical problems. It ignores the fact that the use of maximum or minimum proportions would undoubtedly increase operating costs under most conditions. For example, production time and fuel consumption tend to increase as scrap replaces hot metal. Actual scrap utilization as a percentage of total metallics for 1947 to 1967 shows [28] that the range of scrap utilization in a given furnace is small; say, four or five percent at the most. Total scrap utilization in the steel industry is much more heavily influenced by shifts in the relative use of alternative production processes. For example, the share of a raw steel

Table 1

Technically feasible maximums and minimums in scrap proportion of total metallics

Type of furnace	Scrap as a percent of total metallics used[a]		
	Actual in 1967	Technically feasible maximum	Technically feasible minimum
Steelmaking (all types)	43	72	19
Open hearth	41	80[c]	20[e]
Cold metal shops	80[b]	80[c]	20[e]
Hot metal shops	40[b]	80[c]	20[e]
Electric	98	99	70 (or less)[f]
B.O.F.	29	50 (or more)[d]	0
Bessemer	5	20	0

[a] Total metallics is pig iron plus scrap.

[b] Estimated.

[c] The maximum could be pushed to 100 % scrap but cost and quality control problems make this practice impractical as too much carbon is removed and melt time is excessively long.

[d] Maximum proportion may be increased by preheating of scrap.

[e] Furnace reactions are considered excessively violent below 20–30 % scrap charged.

[f] Estimates are that this ratio could be pushed as low as 50 %. Sources: Nelson [28] and U.S. Dept. of Commerce [37].

production accounted for by the open hearth furnace fell from 86.4 % in 1961 to 36.6 % in 1970 while the proportional share of the basic oxygen furnace rose from 4.0 % to 48.2 % (Nelson, [28]). As a result, scrap utilization has declined.

These shifts in process utilization represent both technical and technological change. Changes in relative prices for scrap and hot metal (and other inputs) cause substitution among the various activities, while embodied and disembodied technological change shift the entire production function or, more accurately, segments of the production function. To the extent that technological change is market determined, attempting to separate the individual effects of technical and technological change is nebulous. We can, however, directly account for the effect of technological change on the decision variables by: (1) introducing new activities in the technological matrix and require capital investment in the productive capacity associated with the new activities; and (2) changing the technological coefficients of existing activities to represent learning by doing, more effective organization, etc.

To return to our choice problem, the decision maker must now select among (1) old techniques with fixed coefficients, (2) old techniques with revised coefficients, and (3) new techniques with associated investment requirements. Moreover, our emphasis here on the scrap-pig iron trade-off at the ingot stage is not by accident. The proportion of pig iron used has a direct influence on the material, labor, and capital requirements at the blast furnace stage, coking, sintering, and other prior production stages. Our description of the choice problem in terms of investment and production activities thus concentrates on the ingot, pig iron, and coking stages. We ignore other new developments such as continuous casting, vacuum degassing, beneficiation of ores, direct reduction of ores, high-speed rolling mills, and computerization of controls for all phases of steelmaking. These developments are not beyond the scope of our model. However, we have chosen to emphasize yet another dimension of steel economics; the spatial location of production and investment.

2.2. Location

Economic activity takes place in a time–space continuum but Anglo-Saxon economists since Marshall have emphasized the temporal element in their analysis; implicitly assuming that all factors of production, commodities, and consumers are concentrated at a single point in space, and that problems of transportation and location can therefore be ignored. For certain manufactured commodities, however, transportation costs and location take on added significance in the decision making process, especially where the product is: (1) standardized; (2) low in value relative to weight; and (3) produced with marginal cost low relative to total unit cost at less than capacity operation. Production in these industries typically occurs in geographically segmented markets. For example, the number of theoretical steel markets is approximately six, since 80 % of all primary iron and steel products (SIC 3312) were shipped less than 395 miles in 1963 [39, p. 25].[4]

Steel is a classic example of a transport oriented industry.[5] The choice of location of new investment is heavily influenced by both changes in the composition of demand and technological change, as well as shifts in relative prices for substitutable inputs or for the same input in different geographic locations. Technological change may, for example, reduce the weight (and locational pull) of certain raw materials consumed, alter the durability and weight of the final product, or shift the location of consuming industries. Over the last half century, the steel industry has undergone a historic long term shift among the following production sites: (a) coal-oriented production sites, typified by Pittsburgh; (b) coal and ore oriented sites (Cleveland, Buffalo); (c) urban market sites (Detroit, Chicago); and (d) coastal sites (Baltimore, Houston). Tables 2 and 3 indicate the effect of the changes

Table 2

Average percent of steel capacity, by region

Region name	1947–54	1955–60	1961–67	Change 1947–54 to 1961–67
New York	4.88	5.18	5.42	0.54
Eastern	15.13	15.93	14.96	(0.17)
Pittsburgh-Youngstown	38.77	34.83	32.14	(6.36)
Cleveland-Detroit	9.27	10.63	12.20	2.93
Chicago-Gary	21.35	21.86	22.42	1.07
Southern	3.96	4.13	4.20	0.24
Texas	0.95	1.62	1.97	1.02
Western	2.70	2.78	3.12	0.42
California	2.97	3.03	3.30	0.33

Source: Nelson [28].

[4] Contrary to popular opinion, the steel industry is not highly concentrated unless account is taken of product or geographic differences among the major firms. Geographic concentration is discussed in detail in Nelson [27].

[5] Studies of the location of the steel industry or of particular producing regions have been numerous. See especially Isard and Capron [17] and Isard [18].

Table 3

Average percent of steel ingot production, by region

Region name	1947–54	1955–60	1961–67	Change 1947–54 to 1961–67
New York	5.16	5.34	5.22	0.06
Eastern	14.52	16.05	15.53	1.01
Pittsburgh-Youngstown	38.39	33.50	30.77	(7.62)
Cleveland-Detroit	9.33	10.76	12.58	3.25
Chicago-Gary	21.81	22.77	23.38	1.57
Southern	4.09	3.89	4.14	0.05
Texas	0.98	1.66	1.97	0.99
Western	2.70	2.78	2.71	0.01
California	3.01	3.24	3.70	0.69

Source: Nelson [28].

since 1947 on steel ingot capacity and production at nine different steel producing regions. One can impute a proportional effect on the resource demands (raw materials, labor, capital, transportation) associated with steel production at these different locations.

In contrast to some industries, the effects of technological innovation and other changes on the location of steel production have generally been of modest proportions and severe employment dislocations have been avoided. The same cannot be said to be true of the dislocations caused by imported steel. Steel imports rose from 4.7 % of apparent consumption in 1961 to 16.7 % in 1968, then receded to 13.8 % in 1970 under voluntary restraint agreements on imports. Estimates are that the 18 million tons of steel products imported during 1968 were equivalent to employment opportunities in the basic steel industry of 108 000 jobs and in supporting industries of another 22 000 jobs [3, p. 8].[6] The causes of increased imports are complex and varied and we can mention the following factors as being of some importance: (1) differences in wage levels and productivity; (2) governmental policies; (3) international exchange rates; (4) pricing policies; and (5) technological progressiveness and overall efficiency. In addition, the degree of import substitution has varied considerably among regional markets in the United States. In the Southern, Southwestern, and Western

[6] Economic analysis of the steel import problem may be found in Molz [24], Rippe [29], Shorrocks [31] and Thorn [34].

markets, imports in 1968 accounted for 19.0, 32.7 and 28.3 % of apparent consumption, respectively [3, p. 66]. To many observers, it is exactly these areas that the steel industry has been laggard in constructing new facilities even when account is taken of economies of scale. As a result, the cost of meeting import competition is higher than it would otherwise be if production facilities were optimally located.

In the past, formal collusion in the form of the basing point system more likely than not retarded the adjustment of productive capacity to regional growth in demand. Today, inertia in the form of fixed capital and the bottleneck or rounding-out problems created by vertical integration no doubt account for some of the slowness in adjustment. However, tacit collusion should not be ruled out although a behavioral mechanism facilitating coordination has not been identified.

This completes our brief survey of the economic environment of steel industry and we turn now to an attempt to incorporate aspects of both structure and behavioral mechanisms in a formal recursive programming model.

3. An interregional recursive programming model

3.1. The primal problem

Beginning with Beckmann and Marschak [7], a considerable amount of effort has been devoted to the spatial theory of the firm and industrial economy using interregional linear programming (ILP). However, empirical implementation of such models has remained almost solely the province of the agricultural economist. With the exception of Marschak's study of petroleum refining [23], spatial programming models of U.S. manufacturing and extractive industries have been limited to simpler Hitchcock–Koopmans transportation problems. The interesting empirical questions associated with such activities as production, inventorying, investment and technological change have been ignored in the ILP-spatial context. To a large extent, this deficiency has been due to the lack of an analytical framework that describes the temporal element of these decisions. Here, we formulate an ILP model suitable for positive, descriptive analysis of interregional production and investment behavior *over and through time*. Like other recursive programming (RP) models, our analysis contains four basic assumptions about the nature of decision-making activity. These assumptions are:

(1) An explicit hypothesis about short-run optimizing behavior.

(2) A time horizon that is short relative to the economic process as a whole.

(3) A process analysis description of the technological structure of the industry being studied.

(4) A set of behavioral or frictional constraints and feedback relationships that reflect incomplete knowledge, uncertainty, and myopia in the investment process.

We begin here by presenting the primal problem incorporating these four components.

Consider a multiregional industry composed of j regionally distributed firms who independently obtain raw material (variable) inputs from i regional 'pools' and sell final products at k regional markets. There are n regional production activities with constant coefficients of the form, a_{jj}^{mn}. The superscript m may be any of the $m = 1, \ldots, K$ mobile variable inputs; $m = K+1, \ldots, L$ immobile capital goods (primary capacities); $m = L+1, \ldots, \bar{L}$ immobile intermediate products; or $m = \bar{L}+1, \ldots, M$ mobile final products.

Transportation or purchasing activities connect the producing regions to the raw material and final product consuming regions. The f.o.b. values and transportation charges for variable inputs are given exogenously and the objective function parameters for these commodities are stated in delivered terms (t_{ij}^m = f.o.b. price plus transport cost for variable input m, i to j). The transportation activities for final products contain only the exogenously determined transportation charges (t_{jk}^m = transport cost on final product m, j to k). No predetermined distribution pattern is imposed on the model for either raw materials or final products shipments.

The quantity of raw material available in each supply region, q_i^m, is specified exogenously in each time period. The quantity of each final product required in each consuming region, $\hat{s}_k^m$, is determined by a behavioral, sales forecasting relationship. Each producing region has a limited amount of each type of primary capacity, c_j^m, but the stock available in any given time period is determined by the depreciated stock of the preceding period plus the optimal level of investment in the current period. The cost and constraints on investment in each time period are examined below and may be considered endogenous.

The primal problem consists of four activity sets (purchases, production, investment, sales) subject to eight constraint sets. The endogenous parameters in each time period are

c_j^m = quantity of primary capacity m available in producing region $j (m = K+1, \ldots, L)$.

θ_j^m = annual dollar cost of one unit of primary capacity m in region $j (m = K+1, \ldots, L)$.

$\bar{y}_j^m$ = maximum level of investment in primary capacity m in region $j (m = K+1, \ldots, L)$.

$\hat{s}_k^m$ = expected level of final demand for final product m in region $k (m = \bar{L}+1, \ldots, M)$.

The decision or activity variables are

x_j^n = level of production activity n in region $j (n = 1, \ldots, S)$.

x_{ij}^m, x_{jk}^m = flow of variable input m from region i to region $j (m = 1, \ldots, K)$, and flow of final product m from region j to region k ($m = \bar{L}+1, \ldots, M$), respectively.

y_j^m = level of investment in primary capacity m in region $j (m = K+1, \ldots, L)$.

We first summarize and interpret the cost minimizing primal problem and then examine the behavioral-feedback relationships. The primal problem is

$$\rho^*(t) = \min_{x(t), y(t)} \left[\sum_i \sum_j \sum_{m=1}^{K} t_{ij}^m(t) x_{ij}^m(t) + \sum_j \sum_k \sum_{m=\bar{L}+1}^{M} t_{jk}^m(t) x_{jk}^m(t) \right.$$
$$\left. + \sum_j \sum_{m=K+1}^{L} \theta_j^m(t) y_j^m(t) \right] \quad (1)$$

subject to

$$\sum_j x_{ij}^m(t) \leq q_i^m(t) \qquad \text{for all } i (m = 1, \ldots, K) \qquad (2)$$

$$-\sum_i x_{ij}^m(t) - \sum_{n=P+1}^{S} a_{jj}^{mn}(t) x_j^n(t) + \sum_{n=1}^{P} a_{jj}^{mn}(t) x_j^n(t) \leq 0$$
$$\text{for all } j (m = 1, \ldots, K) \quad (3)$$

$$\sum_{n=1}^{P} x_j^n(t) - y_j^m(t) \leq c_j^m(t-1)$$
$$\text{for all } j (m = K+1, \ldots, L) \quad (4)$$

$$y_j^m(t) \leq \bar{y}_j^m(t) \qquad \text{for all } j (m = K+1, \ldots, L) \qquad (5)$$

$$-\sum_{n=P+1}^{S} x_j^n(t) + \sum_{n=1}^{P} a_{jj}^{mn}(t) x_j^n(t) \leq 0$$
$$\text{for all } j (m = L+1, \ldots, \bar{L}) \quad (6)$$

$$-\sum_{n=P+1}^{S} x_j^n(t) + \sum_k x_{jk}^m(t) \leqq 0$$

$$\text{for all } j(m = \bar{L}+1, \ldots, M) \quad (7)$$

$$-\sum_j x_{jk}^m(t) \leqq -\hat{s}_k^m(t)$$

$$\text{for all } k(m = \bar{L}+1, \ldots, M) \quad (8)$$

and the requirement that all activity levels are non-negative.

Inequality (2) is an industry constraint on the use of each supply region's variable input. While the supply available to an individual producing region is virtually unlimited, the interaction of firms with each other, and with other sectors of the economy, limits each raw material supply in the aggregate. Inequality (3) is a material or interstage balance equation on variable inputs by individual producing regions. More explicitly, (3) can be rewritten as

$$\sum_{n=1}^{P} a_{jj}^{mn}(t)x_j^m(t) \leqq \sum_i x_{ij}^m(t) + \sum_{n=P+1}^{S} a_{jj}^{mn}(t)x_j^n(t)$$

where the first term is the total amount of the mth variable input required in production (activities $n = 1, \ldots, P$), the second term is the total amount purchased, and the third term is the total amount produced as a byproduct (activities $n = P+1, \ldots, S$).

Inequality (4) is the usual constraint on production due to a fixed productive capacity but capacity available at the beginning of time period t may be augmented through investment. Inequality (5) is the maximum amount of investment that can take place in each capacity in each region during the current period. Inequalities (6) and (7) are, respectively, interstage balance equations on intermediate products and final products. Inequality (8) states that the total amount supplied by all producing regions of the mth final product must at least equal the amount required by each consuming region.

Finally, eq. (1) states the objective, namely, the minimization of the sum of delivered costs of variable inputs, transportation costs on final products, and the cost of investment in new capacity. The logical structure of the model requires then that Inequality (8) will always be equated or tight. The costs of using each production activity do not appear directly in the primal objective function; imputed values on intermediate and final products are determined in the dual problem.

3.2. Behavioral-feedback relationships

We have argued above that industrial performance hinges, in part, on how firms react in a behavioral sense to uncertainty. Cyert and March, for example, suggest that firms avoid the need for anticipating distant events by using decision rules that emphasize short-run reaction to short-run feedback [8, p. 119]. By proceeding sequentially, decision makers obviate the need to precisely predict the future and may resolve any conflict among goals by attending to different goals at different times. Observable behavior may as a result neither follow intertemporally optimal time paths nor necessarily be guided by decision procedures which constitute optimal strategies in the dynamic programming sense. Various rules-of-thumb such as the target rate of return and the payoff period are managerial tools for accommodating the effects of contingencies including oligopolistic interdependencies. We assume that the decision maker in question will pursue objectives of local efficiency in a global environment about which he is partially ignorant and that, moreover, the set of feasible alternatives currently available to him depend in part on the sequence of already executed decisions as well as his interaction with other decision makers.

Consider now the nature of investment decisions within the context of a process industry (e.g., iron and steel). Interdependencies exist between investment projects because the product flows from one productive unit to another in a series of stages (coke, pig iron, ingot, semifinished and finished products). Alternative activities and alternative processes are available for the production of the same commodity (Bessemer, open hearth, electric and basic oxygen steelmaking furnaces). New technology is periodically introduced and capital has a long physical life. Product demand, in the case of steel, may fluctuate substantially. The change over to new technology will typically be a slow and continuous process through time, dependent on improving technical knowledge and changing factor prices. The analysis of technical and technological change must take place within a framework which is intermediate between long- and short-period frameworks and draw upon elements of both.

New capacity will be added in our model where it yields the greatest return per dollar of annual cost where annual project benefits are the dual imputed values of each capacity in each region [16, pp. 110–111]. The marginal cost of investment must now be considered. As a hedge against uncertainty, decision makers frequently employ one form or another of the payoff period. We hypothesize that annual investment costs are determined by a specific payoff concept, the cash-flow payoff period.

Assume the project under consideration will produce a known uniform flow of annual benefits over its life, call the annual benefits per unit of capacity, $r_j^m(t)$. If the original investment outlay per unit is $\gamma(t)$, assuming straight line depreciation, the cash-flow payoff period, τ_j^m, is expressed as

$$\tau_j^m = \frac{\gamma_j^m(t)}{r_j^m(t) + [\gamma_j^m(t)/L_j^m]} \tag{9}$$

where I_j^m represents the depreciation life of the project in years. At equilibrium, annual earnings per unit will equal annual cost per unit, $\theta_j^m(t)$. Thus, if $r_j^m(t) = \theta_j^m(t)$, then

$$\theta_j^m(t) = \gamma_j^m(t)\left(\frac{1}{\tau_j^{m*}} - \frac{1}{L_j^m}\right) \tag{10}$$

becomes the behavioral expression used to determine the endogenous parameter $\theta_j^m(t)$ in eq. (1) and τ_j^{m*} may be interpreted as the equilibrium payoff period $(\tau_j^{m*} \leqq L_j^m)$. Observed values for τ_j^{m*} are then used to calculate the marginal cost of investment. Typically, management will specify the maximum payoff period they are willing to consider and this process may be considered quasi-dynamic as new conditions force a reappraisal of the investment program [32, p. 222].

Budgetary controls also enter the investment process. The parameter $\bar{y}_j^m(t)$ in inequality (5) rations the amount of capital that can be spent on each type of capacity. Such spending constraints may be externally imposed by the capital market or internally imposed due to risk and uncertainty and managerial preferences regarding control and autonomy. The exact source of the upper bounds will not concern us here. Rather, we shall specify a functional form to capture the process of adoption and diffusion of innovation over a fairly long period of time.

During the initial or adoption phase, production capacities are frequently observed to follow geometric growth curves. The rate of uncertainty reduction (diffusion) depends on the size of the required investment, the expected profitability of the new process, and the proportion of firms which have successfully used the innovation. As a surrogate for the proportion of successful firms, we hypothesize that the willingness or potential to invest is some proportion of previous exposure, where the latter is measured by the stock in current use. Thus

$$\bar{y}_j^m(t) = \mu_j^m c_j^m(t-1) \qquad \text{for all } j, t; \quad m = K+1, \ldots, L, \tag{11}$$

and, μ_j^m, we shall call the adoption coefficient. Substituting eq. (11) in constraint (5) and ignoring depreciation, we have

$$c_j^m(t) \leqq (1 + \mu_j^m)c_j^m(t-1) \tag{12}$$

since

$$y_j^m(t) = c_j^m(t) - c_j^m(t-1).$$

Assuming the upper bound on investment is actually attained in each and every period during the adoption phase, we can solve the following expression for the adoption coefficient

$$c_j^m(t) = (1+\mu_j^m)^t c_j^m(0). \tag{13}$$

After some point in time, the rate of growth of capacity is frequently observed to decline continuously. During this adjustment phase, the upper bound on investment is determined by expected profitability and considerations of expected demand expressed by a flexible accelerator relationship

$$\bar{y}_j^m(t) = \alpha_j^m[\hat{c}_j^m(t) - c_j^m(t-1)]$$
$$\text{for all } j, t; m = K+1, \ldots, L, \tag{14}$$

where α_j^m is the adjustment coefficient and $\hat{c}_j^m(t)$ is the desired level of capacity. The specification of the desired level of capacity is based on the expected level of sales of the final products and the current 'capital potential' of the mth primary capacity. By assumption, each capacity can be used in only one production stage. Capital potential is based on the amount of the mth capacity required if the entire output of the respective stage were produced with it and no other capacity. Thus

$$\hat{c}_j^m(t) = F_c[\hat{s}_j^m(t)] \qquad \text{for all } j, t; \quad m = K+1, \ldots, L, \tag{15}$$

where $\hat{s}_j^m(t)$ is the expected level of sales and the functions F_c are weighted averages of the sales forecasts of final commodities in which the weights depend on the input–output coefficients of the various production stages.

The RHS of (14) should be augmented to preclude negativity under conditions of declining demand. When combined with eq. (11), we have the following expression for the 'maximum potential level of investment'.

$$\bar{y}_j^m(t) = \min \left[\mu_j^m c_j^m(t-1), \max \{0, \alpha_j^m[\hat{c}_j^m(t) - c_j^m(t-1)]\} \right]$$
$$\text{for all } j, t; m = K+1, \ldots, L. \tag{16}$$

If constraint (5) is always binding, the adoption and adjustment phases given by (16) will trace out the well-known sigmoid growth curve.[7] A final or obsolescence phase may be represented by a constant percentage rate of physical depreciation. Primary capacity currently available is then given by the usual identity

$$c_j^m(t) \equiv y_j^{m*}(t) + (1-\delta_j^m) c_j^m(t-1)$$
$$\text{for all } j, t; m = K+1, \ldots, L. \tag{17}$$

---

[7] For similar treatment of diffusion as a two-phase process, see Griliches [14], p. 515n.

where δ_j^m is a percentage rate of depreciation, and $y_j^{m*}(t)$ is the optimal (model predicted) level of investment in the current period, which may, of course, be zero. Eqs. (16) and (17) may, thus, be used to represent the full range of nonlinear growth of technology.

Our final relationship is for expected demand or sales. Let a short run sales forecast for time t to be given by

$$\hat{s}_k^m(t) = F_s[s_k^m(t-1), \ldots, s_k^m(0); z(t), \ldots, z(0)]$$

$$\text{for all } k, t; \; m = \bar{L}+1, \ldots, M, \quad (18)$$

where the set of variables, $z(t)$, are exogenous (output and price indices, dummy variables for strikes and import substitution).

The complete interregional recursive programming model consists of (1) through (8), (10), (13), and (15) through (18). Solution then requires estimation of the parameters in the standard interregional LP model and those parameters contained in the hypothesized behavioral relationships. Operationally, of course, a model will be tailored to the industry it represents. The dual to the primal is presented and described in Nelson [25], [28].

4. Estimation and inference

4.1. Estimation

Operationally, a recursive programming model consists of a series of inter-dependent mathematical programming problems which are formulated and solved sequentially. The model takes the solution (optimal) values of decision variables in one period and considers those to be part of the environment in which decisions are made in subsequent periods. Once the technological, behavioral, and feedback relationships have been estimated or solved for, the entire model is run by (1) taking the initial period's conditions as given; (2) solving the first period's linear programming problem; (3) updating the endogenous and exogenous parameters; (4) solving the succeeding period's linear programming problem, and so on.

The model presented above was applied to the U.S. iron and steel industry for the period 1947–67. Basic data sources are found in Nelson [28]. The geographic model structure consisted of ten coal supply regions, six iron ore supply regions, nine steel producing regions, and fifteen steel consuming regions. Fourteen variable inputs were included; two types of coal, three types of iron ore, two grades of scrap, limestone, labor, natural gas, fuel oil, oxygen, electrodes, and purchased electricity. Twenty production activities were included for each producing region, resulting in five intermediate products, seven byproducts, and one aggregate final product. Ten different primary capacities were included and investment was possible in eight of these. In all, each period's linear programming problem contained approximately 390 rows and 490 columns, exclusive of slack variables. Of course, many of the latter are purchasing or transportation activities with only two coefficients, plus one and minus one.

Technological change is incorporated in three ways. First, for entirely new production processes (basic oxygen furnace), new regional production activities are entered exogenously at the year of adoption and initial and subsequent levels of investment are predicted. Second, for modification of old processes (oxygen lancing in the open hearth furnace), new production activities are entered exogenously and the investment activities include coefficients reflecting conversion.[8] Third, all other technological coefficients were periodically updated reflecting disembodied technological change.

4.2. Inference

Figs. 1 and 2 present the actual and predicted levels of aggregate basic oxygen furnace (BOF) and open hearth furnace (OHF) capacity. Figs. 3 and 4 present similar results for regional BOF and OHF capacity.[9]

For regional capacities, the graphs would appear to indicate generally satisfactory results with the exception of the Pittsburgh-Youngstown region. While graphical results give us some indication of the relative success of the model, more formal tests are urgently needed. We turn briefly to two nonparametric inference tests based on information theoretic concepts. These tests have been extensively developed by Theil [33].[10]

The first test is on the model's ability to explain the proportional shares of certain observable capital capacity data at the steel ingot stage. The second test is on the qualitative change in the level of production at the ingot stage. We regard the model predicted relative shares of the four steelmaking furnace capacities as a prior (indirect) message where the l shares to be predicted are, say, $\rho_1^*, \ldots, \rho_l^*$ where $\rho_l^* \varepsilon [0, 1]$ and $\sum_l \rho_l = 1$.

---

[8] This activity adds positive coefficients to inequality (4) reflecting disinvestment in technology of the old vintage. Investment is based on a one-period time horizon; multiperiod models are currently being developed.

[9] A more extensive presentation and analysis of the results may be found in Nelson [28].

[10] Richard Day and I have further developed information theoretic tests in [10].

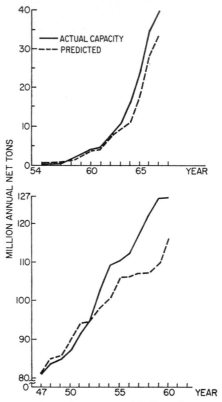

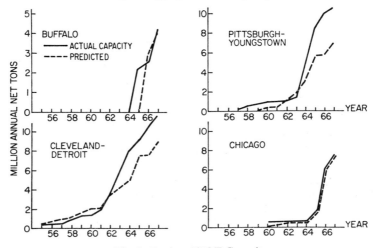

Fig. 1. Aggregate BOF Capacity.

Fig. 2. Aggregate OHF Capacity.

Fig. 3. Regional BOF Capacity.

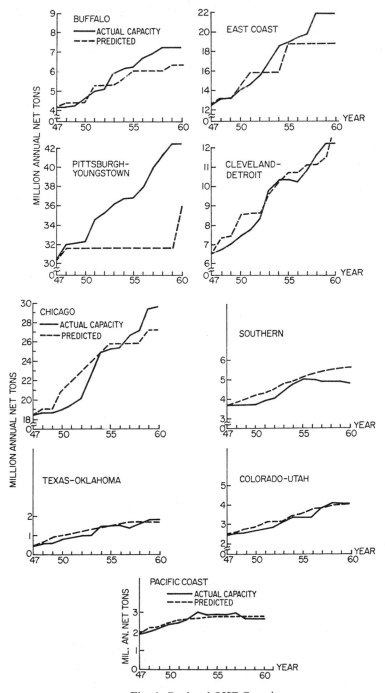

Fig. 4. Regional OHF Capacity.

The observed or realized share, $\rho_1^0, \ldots, \rho_l^0$ form a posterior message. A measure of the information inaccuracy of the predictions with respect to the realizations in a given year is

$$I(\rho^0 : \rho^*) = \sum_l \rho_l^0 \log (p_l^0/\rho_l^*) = \sum_l \rho_l^0[h(\rho_l^0) - h(\rho_l^*)] \qquad (19)$$

where, say, $h(\rho) = -\log (\rho)$. Thus, $I(\rho^0 : \rho^*)$ is ". . . the difference between the expected information prior to the message evaluated at the probabilities which are now known to be true and the expected information in the new situation". (Tilanus and Theil [35, p. 849]). It is the information inaccuracy of the predictions given the realizations. Since the entropy or expected information of a distribution, $H = \sum_l \rho_l h(\rho_l)$, is a function of both equality among the possible outcomes and the number of outcomes, it follows that: (1) errors in predicting less important shares are weighted less heavily than the same relative error in larger shares; and (2) an increase in the number of shares to be predicted will, ceteris paribus, increase the information inaccuracy. If (19) takes a 'large' value, this indicates that the posterior message differs substantially from the prior message and the model predictions (goodness of fit) are poor. If, on the other hand, the information inaccuracy is 'small', the model results may be considered accurate.

The norms, large and small, can only be evaluated here relative to some other alternative model. An appropriate alternative is a one-period, no-change extrapolation forecast. This naive model amounts to replacing ρ_l^* in (19) by $\rho_l^0(t-1)$ and recomputing I [33, p. 38]. A comparison of the information inaccuracy in the two models can then be made.

The relative information inaccuracy is defined as

$$R(\rho^0 : \rho^*) = I(\rho^0 : \rho^*)/H(\rho^0) \qquad (20)$$

which is an indication of what proportion of the total expected information content of the model has been lost in a given year. Since the information content is essentially additive, the average values of I and R can also be computed.

The expected information content of the observations on the four types of steelmaking furnaces is given in column (1) of table 4. It is evident that this value has been increasing over time as new technologies are introduced and begin to replace old techniques. Columns (2) and (3) present, respectively, the information and relative information inaccuracy for the RP model. Columns (4) and (5) present the same data for the naive extrapolation model. The mean values of I and R indicate that the two models perform about equally well on the average. This is not surprising; relative shares in

Table 4

Information analysis of model predictions of relative capacity levels

Year	Observed data (1) Expected information content	RP model (2) Information inaccuracy (bits)	RP model (3) Relative information inaccuracy	Naive model (4) Information inaccuracy (bits)	Naive model (5) Relative information inaccuracy
1947	0.323	0	0		
1948	0.331	0	0	0	0
1949	0.347	0	0	0	0
1950	0.373	0.002	0.005	0.001	0.003
1951	0.392	0.001	0.003	0	0
1952	0.402	0.001	0.002	0	0
1953	0.440	0.004	0.009	0.001	0.002
1954	0.426	0.001	0.002	0	0
1955	0.470	0	0	−0.006	−0.013
1956	0.463	0	0	0	0
1957	0.478	0.001	0.002	0.001	0.002
1958	0.545	0.001	0.002	0.005	0.009
1959	0.588	−0.001	−0.002	0.004	0.007
1960	0.651	0.001	0.002	0.003	0.005
1961	0.671	0.006	0.009	0.001	0.001
1962	0.751	0.009	0.012	0.006	0.008
1963	0.816	0.009	0.011	0.004	0.005
1964	0.919	0.016	0.017	0.011	0.012
1965	1.033	0.022	0.021	0.013	0.013
1966	1.137	0.017	0.015	0.011	0.010
1967	1.179	0.019	0.016	0.002	0.002
Simple average		0.005	0.006	0.003	0.005

any economic system rarely change drastically from one year to the next (recall our discussion of scrap utilization). Naive one-period models should perform well in this context. However, if we were to use a RP model to predict performance, say, five years hence, we would want the model to perform at least as well as a naive model on a year-to-year basis.

The second test of model performance is for qualitative changes in the level of production at the steel ingot stage.[11] To simplify matters, we ignore

[11] The results analyzed here are for a static interregional LP model which excluded the investment activities and other behavioral relationships.

'no-change' definitions and indicate an 'increase' in a production level by the index 1 and a 'decrease' by 2. For S time periods, we let f_{ij} be the relative frequency of all cases in which the model predicts a Type i change in a given production level and realizations are that there actually was a Type j change, where i and j take the two values just mentioned. For any intermediate or final product level, the f's form a 2×2 array

| Prediction: | Realization: | | Marginal |
	increase	decrease	
increase	f_{11}	f_{12}	$f_{1.}$
decrease	f_{21}	f_{22}	$f_{2.}$
Marginal	$f_{.1}$	$f_{.2}$	1.0

where the marginal frequencies, $f_{i.}$ and $f_{.j}$, measure the total frequency of Type i forecasts and Type j realizations, respectively. The correct qualitative forecasts are given by the diagonal frequencies. A measure of the information content of the predictions with respect to the realizations is given by [33, p. 30]

$$C = \frac{1}{f_{i.}} \sum_{j=1}^{2} f_{ij} \log \frac{f_{ij}}{f_{i.}f_{.j}}. \qquad (21)$$

The expected value of C is

$$\hat{C} = \sum_{i=1}^{2} f_{i.} \frac{1}{f_{i.}} \sum_{j=1}^{2} f_{ij} \log \frac{f_{ij}}{f_{i.}f_{.j}} = \sum_{i=1}^{2} \sum_{j=1}^{2} f_{ij} \log \frac{f_{ij}}{f_{i.}f_{.j}}. \qquad (22)$$

The above measures may also be applied to naive model forecasts as well. The larger the value of C or $\hat{C}$, the more accurate the model predictions in either case.

Table 5 presents the information content and its expected value for the output of the four types of steelmaking furnaces along with the proportion of current predictions in each case (diagonal sum $f_{11}+f_{22}$). Here, it is evident that the RP model performs considerably better than the one-period naive model. The weighted averages for the four statistics are calculated by using the relative output of each furnace type over the entire study period, 1947–67. The weighted average information expectation, which is zero if the messages sent and received are stochastically independent, is 0.667 for the RP model and only 0.035 for the naive model.

Table 5

Information analysis of model predictions of qualitative production level changes

Variable and model	(1) Correct predictions (%)	Information content		(4) Information expectation (bits)
		(2) Increase (bits)	(3) Decrease (bits)	
Bessemer				
RP	0.842	1.655	0.060	0.312
Naive	(0.500)	(0.049)	(0.011)	(0.024)
Open Hearth				
RP	0.947	0.594	0.923	0.750
Naive	(0.389)	(0.037)	(0.036)	(0.036)
Electric				
RP	0.842	0.115	0.718	0.274
Naive	(0.444)	(0.022)	(0.101)	(0.048)
BOF				
RP	1.000	0	5.144	0
Naive	(1.000)	(0)	(5.144)	(0)
Wt. average	0.940	0.554	1.090	0.667
	(0.426)	(0.034)	(0.285)	(0.035)

5. *Conclusions and suggestions for further research*

5.1. *The dual variables*

The results of the model appear to be generally satisfactory as a positive description of reality. However, there is some tendency to underpredict the level of investment in the Pittsburgh-Youngstown region and to over-predict the level of investment in the southern and western producing regions. These results tend to confirm earlier suspicions concerning optimal location in the steel industry. Excess capacity in the industry is reflected in the changing advantages of different technologies and different geographic regions as well as the traditional concern with restricted output due to market power. Even so, the results strongly suggest that excess capacity is to be found largely in one geographical region. Further analysis of the model would permit quantitative estimation of the cost saving that would result from relocation of productive capacity along optimal lines.

The primal results are of course mirrored in the shadow prices generated by the dual problem. Table 6 presents the shadow prices for the BOF in the nine geographic steel producing regions along with the annual investment charge derived from eq. $(10)^{12}$. These values would permit a ranking of potential additions to capacity by geographic regions. The greatest advantage lies in expansion in the four southern and western producing regions. Several major steel companies have recently indicated interest in expansion on the Gulf Coast [1]. If and when the steel import problem is resolved, further locational shifts seem likely.

Table 6

Regional shadow prices, basic oxygen furnace ($/net ton)

Year	Buffalo	East Coast	Pitts-burgh–Youngs-town	Cleve-land–Detroit	Chicago	Southern	Texas-Okla-homa	Colora-do–Utah	Pacific Coast	Annual Invest-ment Cost
					Geographic producing region [a]					
1967	$2.345	$2.751	$2.345	$2.345	$2.464	$3.942	$5.431	$5.674	$12.552	$2.345
6	2.376	2.856	2.248	1.545	2.446	4.584	5.627	4.909	14.751	2.248
5	2.176	3.156	3.191	2.176	3.696	10.613	8.854	5.746	16.695	2.176
4	2.914	3.020	2.698	2.115	3.563	7.199	7.721	4.191	15.906	2.115
3	2.455	2.988	3.180	2.068	2.996	6.177	5.448	0.0	10.783	2.068
2	2.168	3.019	3.128	2.917	4.582	8.615	10.446	2.659	14.745	2.104
1	2.451	2.420	1.275	1.612	2.088	4.817	6.043	9.391	19.795	2.088
0	2.054	2.042	2.344	2.089	2.054	7.844	0.0	2.054	4.537	2.054
1959	1.983	1.983	1.983	3.525	2.762	8.961	1.983	11.319	21.262	1.983
8	2.638	2.638	2.638	4.326	4.652	8.426	2.638	8.815	21.655	2.638
7	3.893	2.546	2.546	3.893	4.036	12.935	17.400	20.373	28.245	2.546
6	2.634	2.420	3.423	3.626	4.841	11.807	15.443	14.616	22.759	2.420
5	6.142	4.878	3.598	7.179	9.053	14.616	13.804	22.236	27.135	2.344

[a] Underlining indicates initial year of actual adoption in each geographic region.

5.2. Suggestions for further research

Sufficiently honed, the model could be used as a management tool for optimal location of new capacity on both a technological and geographical basis. In addition, the impact on supporting industries and resources could

[12] Annual investment costs per unit of capacity are based on a five to seven year payoff period and an eighteen to twenty year depreciation life. Initial construction costs were obtained from some twenty-five engineering reports (See Nelson [28, pp. 377–392]).

be estimated, again on a specific product and locational basis. This information would also be of potential use by public decision makers in formulating adaptive policy as a result of anticipated changes in resource use. An interregional recursive programming model thus seems potentially useful both for private and public policy making.

An extension of the model would make it even more useful in both realms. Economists have come to realize that economic activity must follow fundamental physical laws, in particular, the First and Second Laws of Thermodynamics.[13] The First Law requires that economic models recognize the interdependencies among potential pollutants as we have emphasized the interdependence among production, investment, etc. The Second Law states that waste is an inevitable product of economic activity and ceteris paribus increases in greater proportion than the intensity of such activity; hence, entropic behavioral constraints must be considered. By closing the model, to account for residual byproducts (effluents), additional activities can be added which require treatment and disposal of the residuals, where treatment would include recycling of wastes. In the absence of inventory costs, the economist must essentially force the model to utilize non-economic goods in order for treatment and disposal to take place. Formulating the appropriate constraints on effluent use is an interesting exercise in itself since treatment and disposal activities contribute nothing toward meeting the final demand constraints. Appropriate environmental standards can then be imposed on alternative forms and quantities of waste. The dual variable associated with a standard can be interpreted as an effluent charge. But more importantly, the dual variables can be transposed for internal use in selecting appropriate treatment and disposal activities and associated investment levels for new or old technology. A closed model thus represents a complete description of economic activity, including the output and opportunity cost associated with residual byproducts. Recursive programming methodology would also require an investigation of any behavioral considerations associated with waste treatment and disposal, both in the private and public realms.

---

[13] See, especially, Georgeseu-Roegen [13] and Kneese *et al.* [20]. The structure of a closed model and associated behavioral relationships is developed further in [26].

References

[1] A Steelmaker Casts an Eye to the Gulf, Business Week, July 25, 1970, p. 22.

[2] W. Adams, ed., 1971, The Structure of American Industry, 4th ed., New York: Macmillan, ch. 3.

[3] American Iron and Steel Institute, 1970, Steel Imports — A National Concern, Washington, D.C., July.

[4] W. L. Baldwin, 1969, The feedback effect of business conduct on industry structure, Journal of Law and Economics 12, April, 123–153.

[5] Battelle Memorial Institute, 1964, Final Report on Technical and Economic Analysis of the Impact of Recent Developments in Steelmaking Practices on the Supplying Industries, Columbus, Ohio, October 30.

[6] W. J. Baumol, 1965, Economic Theory and Operations Analysis, 2nd ed., Englewood Cliffs: Prentice-Hall.

[7] M. Beckmann and T. Marschak, 1955, An activity analysis approach to location theory, Kyklos 8, 125–141.

[8] R. M. Cyert and J. G. March, 1963, A Behavioral Theory of the Firm, Englewood Cliffs: Prentice-Hall.

[9] R. H. Day, 1964, Review of [8], in Econometrica 32, 461–465.

[10] R. H. Day and J. P. Nelson, 1973, A class of dynamic models for describing and projecting industrial development, Journal of Econometrics, 1: 2.

[11] R. Dorfman, P. A. Samuelson and R. M. Solow, 1958, Linear Programming and Economic Analysis, New York: McGraw-Hill.

[12] T. Fabian, 1963, Process Analysis of the U.S. Iron and Steel Industry, in: A. S. Manne and H. M. Markowitz, eds., Studies in Process Analysis, New York: John Wiley, ch. 9.

[13] N. Georgeseu-Roegen, 1971, The Entropy Law and Economic Process, Cambridge: Harvard University Press.

[14] Z. Griliches, 1957, Hybrid corn: an exploration in the economics of technological change, Econometrica 25, 501–522.

[15] G. Hadley, 1962, Linear Programming, Reading: Addison-Wesley.

[16] A. P. Hurter, Jr. and L. N. Moses, 1964, Regional investment and interregional programming, Papers, Regional Science Association 13, 105–119.

[17] W. Isard and W. M. Capron, 1949, The future locational pattern of iron and steel production in the United States, Journal of Political Economy 57, 118–133.

[18] W. Isard, 1948, Some locational factors in the iron and steel industry since the early nineteenth century, Journal of Political Economy 56, 203–217.

[19] D. A. Kendrick, 1967, Programming Investment in the Process Industries, Cambridge: The M.I.T. Press.

[20] A. V. Kneese, R. V. Ayres and R. C. D'Arge, 1970, Economics and the Environment, Baltimore: Resources for the Future.

[21] J. W. Markham and G. F. Papanek, eds., 1970, Industrial Organization and Economic Development, Boston: Houghton Mifflin.

[22] J. W. Markham, 1970, Structure versus conduct in antitrust, in: W. Sichel, ed., Antitrust Policy and Economic Welfare, Ann Arbor: The University of Michigan, Bureau of Business Research, ch. 5.

[23] T. Marschak, 1963, A spatial model of U.S. petroleum refining, in: A. S. Manne and H. M. Markowitz, eds., Studies in Process Analysis, New York: John Wiley, ch. 5.

[24] F. L. Molz, 1970, The political economy of steel import quotas, Journal of Economic Issues 4, June-September, 60–76.

[25] J. P. Nelson, 1971, An interregional recursive programs model of production, investment, and technological change, Journal of Regional Science 11, April, 33–47.

[26] J. P. Nelson, 1972, Residuals, materials balance, and interregional competition, unpublished paper

[27] J. P. Nelson, 1972, Regional concentration in the steel industry, Northeast Regional Science Review 2, Spring, 218–25.

[28] J. P. Nelson, 1970, An interregional recursive programming model of the U.S. iron and steel industry, unpublished Ph.D. dissertation, University of Wisconsin.

[29] R. D. Rippe, 1970, Wages, prices, and imports in the American steel industry, Review of Economics and Statistics 52, February, 34–46.

[30] F. M. Scherer, 1970, Industrial Market Structure and Economic Performance, Chicago: Rand McNally, ch. 1.

[31] A. F. Shorrocks, 1971, Measuring the imaginary: The employment effect of imported steel, Industrial and Labor Relations Review 24, 203–215.

[32] V. L. Smith, 1966, Investment and Production, Cambridge: Harvard University Press.

[33] H. Theil, 1967, Economics and Information Theory, Amsterdam: North-Holland.

[34] R. S. Thorn, 1968, Steel imports, labor productivity, and cost competitiveness, Western Economic Journal 6, December, 375–384.

[35] C. B. Tilanus and H. Theil, 1965, The information approach to the evaluation of input–output forecasts, Econometrica 33, October, 847–862.

[36] C. L. Trozzo, 1966, The technical efficiency of the location of integrated blast furnace capacity, unpublished Ph.D. dissertation, Harvard University.

[37] U.S. Department of Commerce, 1966, Business and Defense Services Administration, Iron and Steel Scrap Consumption Problems, Washington, D.C.: U.S. Government Printing Office.

[38] L. W. Weiss, 1971, Case Studies in American Industry, 2nd ed., New York: John Wiley, ch. 4.

[39] L. W. Weiss, 1968, The geographical size of markets in manufacturing, unpublished paper

[40] Y. L. Wu and C. W. Kwang, 1960, An analytical and graphical analysis of marginal analysis and mathematical programming in the theory of the firm, in: K. E. Boulding and W. A. Spivey, eds., Linear Programming and the Theory of the Firm, New York: Macmillan, ch. 4.

CHAPTER 21

Recursive programming models of agricultural development*

INDERJIT SINGH

Ohio State University

1. The green revolution: its scope and analysis

1.1. Introduction

The importance of a developing agriculture in an overall strategy of economic development derives from the fact that few nations have achieved high per capita incomes without first achieving substantial gains in agricultural productivity. This is especially true of the developing countries today. Even where the exploitation of natural resources such as petroleum or minerals has been possible in some low-income countries, the increases in per capita income have been confined to a very small segment of the total population. Such development, tied through export dependence to a developing country (often a previous colonial power) has led to social, cultural and economic dualism, and where these gains have not been accompanied by improvements in agricultural productivity, neither the income nor the lives of a majority of the people have been improved.

Economic growth depends upon the performance of the agricultural sector because in developing countries with per capita incomes of less than $ 300, 40–80 % of the total labor force and between 30–60 of the total GNP are accounted for by agriculture. In addition the non-agricultural sectors have to depend upon rural labor and capital resources for their growth in the early stages and these are not forthcoming unless agricultural

* This paper is a revised version of an earlier paper, Singh [41] and draws heavily on three previous papers, Singh and Day [44, 45], and Day and Singh [9], and the author's dissertation, Singh [42]. The work reported here is part of a continuing collaborative effort with Professor R. H. Day to whom my personal debt is immeasurable. Errors that remain, however, are my sole responsibility.

productivity and efficiency increase substantially. Furthermore, almost 70–80 % of the manufacturing industries in many developing countries are either based on raw materials from agriculture or produce materials for use in farm production. Low rates of growth of income and production in agriculture can seriously retard the growth of the non-agricultural sectors.

The importance of agricultural development is further enhanced by the dynamics of demography in the developing countries. Rates of population growth of 2–3 % or more are nearly double the rates that prevailed in Western Europe and Japan during their early stages of development.

The crucial question therefore is whether agricultural output and productivity can increase rapidly enough to meet the needs of the expanding population as well as satisfying the requirements of growth. It has been calculated that the supply of agricultural products must increase by 4 % or more per annum in developing countries in order to meet the expanding domestic demand from population growth and income increases if major price inflation disruptive to growth is to be avoided. In some countries even larger gains are needed to provide more nutritionally adequate diets [47]. Agricultural output growth rates of 4–5 % per annum are more than twice as high as those achieved in most developed countries for a period of a decade or longer. Can these rates be achieved?

The answer to this question in the first half of the decade of the sixties was negative. This pessimism reflected in part the poor performance of the agricultural sectors in the developing countries in the previous decade, but also partly the view, then widely held, that decision makers, especially peasants in the developing countries were tradition bound, "non-rational", "uneconomic" men limited by cultural and institutional restraints to any but insignificant responses to economic and market incentives designed to improve their lot.

This extreme pessimism seems to have been exaggerated in the light of the evidence. In 34 of the 54 developing countries agricultural output expanded 3 % or more per year; while 17 had growth rates of 4 % or more, demonstrating substantial progress.[1] What is more this rate of growth has accelerated recently in many developing countries. The most recent breakthroughs described as "the green revolution", and associated mainly with

[1] Thus between 1950–68 annual growth rates exceeded 4 % for such diverse countries as Costa Rica (4.2), Guatemala (5.0), Mexico (5.1), Nicaragua (5.9), Ecuador (6.0), Venezuela (5.1), Greece (4.6), Yugoslavia (4.6), Cyprus (4.9), Israel (9.3), Malaysia (4.1), Taiwan (4.4), Thailand (4.5), Senegal (4.3), and Sudan (4.1) [47, p. 11]. In addition, regional development in West Pakistan, South Brazil, several states in India, Philippines and Taiwan has matched these growth rates.

vast improvements in the biological conditions of production have substantially changed the outlook for overall economic development in the
1970's.

Until recently it was strongly felt that custom, tradition and authority
were the major sources of the allocative and distributive directives in peasant
agriculture, and that these constraints limited drastically both the use of
traditional economic tools as well as market incentives to transform the
sector. Recent empirical studies have, however, shown that agricultural
production in peasant and traditional agriculture in specific L.D.C.'s is
responsive to economic incentives, especially when factors such as subsistence, adjustment lags due to uncertainty, quasi-fixity of capital stocks
and the state of the arts and knowledge are accounted for.[2] What these
studies demonstrate is that models based on the assumption of rational
economic behavior and using the standard tools of economic analysis can
be used effectively to explain, understand, predict and plan the process of
agricultural transformation in these developing countries.

It is the purpose of this paper to show how one such tool − recursive
programming − can be used to generate the past development of the agricultural sector in a selected region in a manner that can allow us to understand the process of transformation. Sect. 1 of this paper briefly describes
the importance of incorporating details we consider strategic to this transformation process, details without which such a model could not be
operationally useful; sect. 2 presents the various components of the programming model designed to effectively incorporate these details; sect. 3 presents
briefly the empirical results obtained for the Indian Punjab from 1952–65
for which the model was used to describe and understand its recent agricultural transformation. The paper concludes briefly with some of the data
requirements and several possible policy applications for the model.

1.2. Details strategic to the analysis of modern agricultural transformation in the LDC's

In order to analyze and understand the recent experience of agricultural
development in the LDC's, certain elements need to be incorporated. A
brief examination shows that modern agricultural transformation in the
LDC's has been mainly carried out in an environment in which (1) decision

---

[2] This latter view starting mainly with the pioneering work of Schultz [40] and the
alternative views are presented in Wharton [49] where a series of articles on both sides
of this controversy are available.

making occurs at the farm level and involves firm-household units;[3] (2) technological elements, both biological and mechanical have been critical to the transformation process; (3) government participation either directly through the allocation of scarce resources or indirectly through established markets has substantially directed ('distorted') and channeled the development process; and (4) the development of the agricultural sector has had important implications for development elsewhere in the economy and vice versa. These facts define the environment within which modern agricultural transformation is taking place. This environment impinges so critically on the developmental process that we must attempt to incorporate these elements explicitly in our analysis.

1.2.1. Farm-household interdependence and farm-level decision making

Agricultural production in the LDC's, apart from commercialized plantation type production, is mainly carried out on privately owned and operated farms. There are several recognized elements of farm level decision making and production response that studies of agricultural development do not incorporate or incorporate unsatisfactorily. These were emphasized by Day [4] and include: (1) the interdependence of outputs using common inputs (i.e., the multiproduct nature of the agricultural production firm); (2) changes in both acreage and yield components in field crop production; (3) the relative interaction of input and output prices; (4) the rate of investment in factors fixed in the short run; (5) uncertainty and adjustment over time; (6) planned or programmed policy actions.

In addition, the interdependence of firm-household decisions and the special importance of subsistence production to the analysis of developing agriculture needs to be emphasized. The farm combines two fundamental units of microeconomic analysis — the household and the firm. Some attention has been given to the resulting interdependence in the economic analysis of developed agriculture, Heady *et al.* [15], Day [5], Day and Heidhues [8], Heidhues [16, 17]. But while this interdependence is clearly of the essence in the analysis of developing agriculture, and defines the point of departure between the study of development in 'traditional' and 'modernized' agriculture, scant attention has been paid to its implications.[4]

---

[3] Usually also under a regime of private ownership. Agricultural progress under state ownership has had a dismal record, and where partially successful has relied on decentralized decision making and economic incentives rather than centralized allocative and distributive mechanisms.

[4] The exceptions have been Nakajima [33–36] and Mellor [27, 28] who have both contributed significantly to a clearer theoretical understanding of this interdependence.

The most important implication is that developing agriculture is often characterized by subsistence production where (i) the farm-household depends upon the farm-firm for its main items of consumption so that production is mainly carried out to meet these needs and not for the market and (ii) the farm-firm relies upon the household for its needs of labor and other production inputs. As a direct result of this, the response to market incentives is modified considerably as household consumption requirements act as a constraint on both the product mix as well as the marketed surplus.

The choices between leisure and income (amount of family labor offered for work), between present and future income (consumption and saving) and between retained and marketed output (amount of total income converted to monetary income) that the *household* makes, effects the choices between technologies (labor vs. capital intensive), between production and investment outlays (variable and quasi-fixed inputs), between subsistence and commercial outputs (outputs for consumption and outputs for sales), and between owned and commercial inputs ('traditional' and 'modern') that the *firm* makes. This interdependence makes it difficult to differentiate the activities of the farm-household from the farm-firm. Consequently, all economic activities of the firm-household have to be treated in an integrated framework.[5]

Furthermore, the real differences in the economic behavior of farmers in developing agriculture arise not from any lack of rationality but from differences in their means and the environment in which they arrive at their decisions. In this context we wish to emphasize the importance of uncertainty, learning and adoption and multiple goals that often define the environment of decision making in developing agriculture.

That farming is a highly uncertain business is obvious even to a casual observer. That the degree of uncertainty is greater in developing agriculture due to a greater degree of dependence upon the environment, fewer means to control or circumvent it, greater disaster in case of failure, and the greater rate of innovation and change may not be so obvious. Accounting for uncertainty in some way is an imperative both for the farmer, and the economist if he is to understand the farmer's decisions. However, these are unlikely

---

[5] Consideration of these factors suggests that there are great similarities between the traditional farm and the traditional "household" of economic analysis. Both the household and the traditional farmer get incomes by utilizing their labor, both aim at the maximization of their utilities which are the function of income (and all goods) and the quantity of labor (or leisure). The essential difference is in their income equations; the income equation of the traditional farmer contains the production function, while that of the household does not.

to take the form of Monte Carlo or other sophisticated rules currently in vogue among economic analysts. They are more likely to come closer to the rules of thumb procedures summarized as strategies of cautious optimizing, examples of which include the chance-constrained models of Charnes and Cooper [2], the focus-loss principle of Shackle [38], the behavioral bounds of Cyert and March [3], the safety-first principle of Roy [37] and the flexibility constraints of Henderson [18] and Day [4, 5].

The breakdown of age-old practices and habits takes time, partly because the supply of new inputs and their distribution must go through a development of their own, and partly because adjustments to profitable opportunities occur with a lag. These external constraints on input supplies and internal constraints due to the learning process and lagged adjustments assure that the impact of new technologies, following their introduction, will be distributed over time. These facts about learning and adoption behavior should clearly be incorporated in any analysis of development.

There is a growing realization that economic decision making involves a multiplicity of goals and that single criteria like profit maximization are inadequate in describing the decision process. Furthermore, all goals do not have an equal priority and are often ranked according to a set of preferences. This has a very special significance for peasant agriculture where food requirements to meet basic survival needs or safety criteria may be placed ahead of profit maximization. Such ordering of goals, evident even in the most advanced industrial organizations should also be included in the analysis if possible.

1.2.2. Technology and technological change

The most strategic role in the modern transformation of traditional agriculture is assigned to technological change. The neoclassical theory of the firm is primarily based on twice differentiable production functions which assume a single output and represent a given technology. Technology in agriculture is really characterized by multiple outputs, and during periods of transition (which are the main focus of our interest), by multiple technologies. Activity analysis as developed by Koopmans [25], Leontief *et al.* [26] and applied by many investigators allows us to represent all three of these characteristics in great detail providing a means of identifying and measuring technology.

Anyone who had directly observed traditional agricultural production is impressed by the fact that it is a complex phenomenon with hundreds of tasks, being performed by many possible combinations, requiring detailed knowledge of soils, topography, climate and an ability to distribute a variety of scarce resources over time, and crop use. These choices are increased when technological change occurs. The most important components of technological change that need to be quantitatively analyzed include new material inputs (water, inorganic fertilizers, herbicides, pesticides, fungicides), new outputs (new crops, improved varieties), new implements and power sources (steel implements, powered implements, and electric and diesel engines as sources of power) and new cultural practices (multiple cropping, new tasks such as transplanting, contour or row planting, deep furrowing and terracing). All these involve in a fundamental way the factor–product, factor–factor- and product–product relationships. Only by representing major technological alternatives in an activity analysis framework can we expect to effectively understand and analyze the many choices describing the transition from traditional to modern agriculture.

1.2.3. Government policy actions and intersectoral linkages
While keeping our focus primarily on the farm sector we recognize that government policy actions can alter the environment of farm decision making and that important intersectoral linkages exist.

We view government policies as affecting the farm sector through (i) a direct control of scarce economic and physical resources for allocative or distributive purposes, (ii) existing markets by subsidizing or supporting input and/or output prices and (iii) changes in the social infrastructure that reduce the cost of farm production or increase (in quantity and quality) the resource endowments of the farm sector.

In explicitly accounting for government policy actions, policies are seen either as affecting (i) the payoffs (opportunities) or their expectations or (ii) the resource endowments (constraints) facing decision makers in the farm sector.[6] Although this allows most policy actions to be effectively treated, the real problem is to translate the effects of a specific policy on specific payoffs and endowments in order to realize their quantitative dimension, a no mean task in itself.

We have mentioned the external constraints imposed by the limited availability of non-farm inputs such as implements, farm machinery, fuels and fertilizers, indicating that the development of the agricultural and other

---

[6] Policies can also affect the farm sector through their impact on non-farm commodity and factor markets and the development of the non-farm infrastructure. Part of this impact is captured through linkages with the non-farm sector, but their detailed treatment will have to await a more general multi-sectoral model of development, a task towards which the current farm sector model is an important and necessary step.

sectors is interdependent.[7] The most important intersectoral linkages include (i) the demand for farm outputs by the non-farm and export sectors which affect the prices of farm outputs and which act as a constraint upon the expansion of farm output, as well as convert the potential demand for non-farm inputs into actual demand by providing the markets for commercial sales; (ii) the supply of non-farm inputs such as fuels, fertilizers and machinery whose availability and supply price crucially determine their adoption; (iii) opportunities for non-farm employment that compete for labor as well as provide supplementary income transfers to the agricultural sector; (iv) opportunities for non-farm investments that compete for capital (private and public) and may restrict the flow of credit to the farm sector; and (v) the demand for non-farm consumer goods on part of the farm sector; that given its size and contribution to employment and output, provide the main markets for the expansion of the non-farm sector in most LDC's given the inelasticity of the export markets.

Some of these linkages occur indirectly through market prices and some occur directly through physical and behavioral limitations on the use and availability of resources. Hence even in models whose primary focus is on the development and planning within the farm sector these linkages must be accounted for.

2. A recursive programming model of agricultural development

2.1.

Since the details to be incorporated are so complex and the variety of their applications, at least in principle, unlimited, it is most difficult to construct a general model that would apply to all types of agricultural transformations underway in the LDC's.

In order to make our model concrete we discuss its application in terms of a given region — the Indian Punjab — that has recently experienced a vast agricultural transformation evidenced by high rates of growth of output, and a rapid transition from subsistence to commercial production.[8]

---

[7] This interdependence has been continually emphasized (see Johnston and Mellor [23] and Johnston and Kilby [22]) and is the primary focus of the general systems simulation approach to agricultural sector analysis developed by Johnson and his associates [20].

[8] This region has experienced growth rates in excess of 5 % per annum. See Hendrix and Giri [19], Kahlon *et al.* [24].

This will also enable us to discuss the model results and their implications in more specific terms. However, it is our contention that the methodology can be easily modified for application elsewhere, since the basic theory and components remain unchanged, only their explicit specification and the data used for estimation vary.

2.2. The model[9]

The Punjab model is made up of six basic components. These are (1) an annual objective function measuring the expected revenues from crop sales, the costs of purchased and hired inputs and an investment charge for resource augmenting investment decisions; (2) a technology matrix representing the input–output structure of home and cash consumption, farm production, investment, sales, purchase and financial activities; (3) a 'technical' constraint structure representing regional resource and financial limitations; (4) a 'behavioral' constraint structure representing adaptive, 'safety-first' limitations for protection against mistakes of cropping and investment choices, and representing drags on investment due to 'learning' and 'unwillingness to change'; (5) a set of feedback functions that relate the parameters of the current programming problem to previous decisions, giving the model its dynamic character; and (6) exogenously given input and output prices, regional supplies of land and labour resources and exogenously estimated subsistence and cash consumption requirements.

The model can be succinctly summarized by the following system of equations:

$$\text{Max } \Pi(t) = \sum_j a_j X_j(t) \tag{1}$$

subject to

$$\sum_j b_{ij} X_j \leqq C_i(t) \tag{2}$$

where

$$C_i(t) = g_i(X_j^*(t-1), C_i(t-1), Z(t)) \tag{3}$$

$$j = 1, \ldots, n, \quad i = 1, \ldots, m, \quad t = 1, \ldots, \theta.$$

$X_j(t)$ is a vector of farm-household activities that include production (land preparation, planting, cultivating, fertilizing, harvesting, processing and transportation of final and intermediate outputs of field crops in two crop-

---

[9] For the general methodology of recursive linear programming models see Day [5, 7]; for its application to regional agriculture see Day [4, 5] and T. Heidhues [16, 17]. For a theoretical statement and validation of the model in this study see Day and Singh [9]. For a detailed exposition of all the model components see Singh [42].

ping seasons), purchase (of variable inputs such as fuel, fertilizers, hired labour, improved seeds, feeds, concentrates and government controlled canal water), sales (of final outputs after harvest), financial (saving, borrowing and debt repayment), investment (land improvement and purchase of capital goods such as tractors, tubewells, threshers, harvesters and cane crushers) and household (subsistence consumption of food and fodder, commercial consumption and labour supplying on and off farms) activities.[10]

Eq. (1) measures the expected net cash returns to fixed farm resources for each year. The $a_j(t)$ coefficient is the expected price per quintal of the appropriate cash crop when j is a sales activity;[11] the current variable cost of the appropriate production input when j is a purchase activity; the nominal rate of interest when j is a borrowing activity; the average regional time deposit rate when j is a saving activity and an investment charge estimated on a straight-line depreciation basis when j is an investment activity (i.e., $a_j(t) = p_j(t)/L_j$ where $p_j(t)$ is the current purchase price and L_j the use life of the jth investment good).

Components of mechanical technology are incorporated by a set of intermediate production activities that allow alternative mechanical ways of performing a task.[12] The biological components of technology are incorporated by another set of intermediate activities that allow for crop fertilization at various levels of nutrient use. The choice among these components depends upon their relative costs, the rate of adoption and the availability of non-farm inputs.

The objective function is maximized period after period subject to the constraints appropriate for each period.

Farmers' choice activity levels are constrained by resource, financial, subsistence, and behavioral limitations. These are represented at the regional level by a system of inequalities (2) for each crop year.

[10] Activities are assumed to be linear, finite in number and their levels $X_j, j \in X$ are measured for the regional aggregate. Constraining factors are identified by an index $i \in Y$. The technical coefficients $b_{ij}, i \in Y, j \in X$ are assumed constant over time and all technology is assumed to be embodied.

[11] The sales activity payoff coefficients are assumed to be lagged values for simplicity. More complete price expectation models have also been investigated. See Mudahar [30] and Muller [31].

[12] The use of these intermediate production activities allows us to analyze the mechanical components of technological change that include new power sources and implements being adopted in the region. For a detailed task by task breakdown of the mechanical components of technology in the Punjab see Singh *et al.* [46] and for an exposition of how to incorporate them into programming models see Day [5] and Singh [42].

Briefly (i) resource constraints include constraints on family and wage labour, on non-farm purchased inputs, on animal draft and machine capacities, and on fixed regional resources of irrigable, rain-fed and canal irrigable area for two cropping seasons; (ii) financial constraints include a constraint on working capital availability and on the amounts of short-term borrowing at various interest rates; (iii) subsistence constraints include constraints on crop outputs expressed as lower bounds on the amounts of farm outputs required for household consumption and maintenance (family labour being treated as a fixed resource with zero reservation price) and on the amount of fodder required for maintaining and using draft animals;[13] and (iv) behavioral constraints include crop flexibility constraints that place lower and upper bounds on individual crop acreages in any given year,[14] and adoption constraints that place upper bounds on the adoption of new technologies or crop varieties that describe an S-shaped diffusion path over time and account for adaptive and adjustment lags due to learning, experience and exposure. These prevent new technologies from being fully adopted immediately upon their introduction if they are profitable.[15]

Since agricultural production depends critically on the timing of operations, the supplies of labour, animal draft and machine capacities are considered during seven periods in the cropping season to account for seasonality.

The inclusion of feedback functions by a system of equations (3) 'outside' the optimizing model is what distinguishes recursive from ordinary

[13] Both household food consumption and fodder consumption by draft animals are considered as annual costs of maintenance for owned resources that are essentially fixed in the short run. These subsistence requirements are a first order objective before farmers begin to minimize short run cash costs. For a more complete exposition see Day and Singh [9]. For an alternative treatment of family labour and the use of step functions to represent demand and supply schedule constraints in large l.p. models, see Duloy and Norton [11] and Goreux *et al.* [12].

[14] For a use of flexibility constraints see Day [5], Henderson [18], Schaller [39], Heidhues [16] and Singh [42]. For their theoretical justification and implications see Day [6] and Day *et al.* [7]. The consumption-flexibility constraints provide the model with a set of inequalities that restrict the range of cropping patterns to ones that (1) provide farm outputs for household consumption, (2) provide sufficient fodder for the farmers' draft animals and (3) do not permit 'unreasonably' large acreages for 'unusually' profitable crops on the basis of one year's information. See Gotsch [13] for a similar use in a model of W. Pakistan agriculture, and Miller [29] for an evaluation of alternative formulations.

[15] Such adoption paths are not peculiar to agriculture but are also evident in industrial investment behavior. See Day *et al.* [7].

linear programming problems and links the problem from one year to the next. These generally depend upon the vector of past solutions X^* $(t-1)$, previous constraint levels $C_i(t-1)$ and exogenously given data $Z(t)$. The elements of explicit feedback incorporated in the model are: (1) the adaptive flexibility and adoption and adjustment constraints that define producers adjustments and response to risk, uncertainty and learning over time and which depend upon the previous year's activity levels; (2) machine and power capacity constraints that depend on past investment levels; (3) cash availability in its dependence on past sales; and (4) credit limits in their dependence on current debts and assets which in turn depend on past borrowing and debt repayment activities.[16]

The remainder of the constraint coefficients depend on exogenous data. The availability of regional land, labor and animal draft resources are estimated exogenously from census data and projected by means of their time trends.

2.3. Model summary

The principles which we assume reflect farmers' decision making in our model can be summarized as follows:

(1) Farmers first determine subsistence needs;

(2) Their willingness to adopt new practices is related to exposure and this can be measured by the current amount of production already involving the new practice;

(3) Farmers also limit investments in given capital goods according to a flexible accelerator type of bound to limit risks of investing 'too much';

(4) Farmers attempt to distribute marketing risk by choosing a 'portfolio' of crops. Changes in the 'portfolio' are limited by 'rule of thumb' percentages that approximate more sophisticated risk programming models;

(5) Farmers' cash consumption depends on cash income;

(6) Anticipated prices are based on recent market experience;

(7) Given these considerations, farmers allocate their resources so as to maximize anticipated net cash returns from farming.

The model is computed by setting up and solving a linear programming problem (1)–(2) for a given initial year. The optimal solution vector and the resource constraint vector are then used to estimate a new set of con-

---

[16] The explicit form of the feedback function depends upon the constraint being considered. See Singh [42] for details.

straints using the feedback functions (3) and exogenous data on regional land and labour supplies. Using exogenously estimated input and output prices, (1)–(2) are again set up and a new linear programming problem is solved for the next year. The complete model consists of a sequence of linear programs; the parameters of each member in the sequence depends on the solutions to the preceding problem in the sequence and on various exogenous data. Such a model is an open recursive linear programming model, Day [5, ch. III]. It describes the aggregate farm decisions by sequence of 'rolling plan' or 'recursive programs' rather than by optimal trajectories computed from a long horizon, dynamic programming model.

3. Model results and possible applications

3.1. Model results: Central Punjab (1952–1965)

We use this model to estimate resource use, production patterns, technological change, factor productivity and factor proportions for the Central Punjab for the years 1952–65. How well the model performs depends upon its ability to capture the historical trends for these variables over the period for which the model was estimated. Detailed data of the sort needed to test such complex models is usually not available, nor do we have a complete theory for their evaluation.[17] However, a detailed comparison of the model estimates for crop acreages suggested that the model represented the economic history of the region fairly well. A complete analysis of the model evaluation is contained in Day and Singh [9]. We now turn our attention briefly to some of the specific model results and policy and analytic applications of this and similar models.

Some of the model results for the Central Punjab from 1952–1965 are displayed in figs. 1–6.

Fig. 1 shows the observed and predicted cropping pattern for the four most important crops in the region. Besides being able to predict crop acreages, the advantages of a model that is able to simultaneously account for multiple outputs in a double cropping system is clearly demonstrated

---

[17] Even for simply dynamic models for which the structural and econometric specifications are fully known evaluation criteria have not been fully developed (see Dhrymes *et al.* [10]). For dynamic simulation models of the type used in this study, for which the structural and econometric specifications violate many of the assumptions of classical statistical inference, even greater insurmountable problems to evaluation exist. See Johnson and Rausser [21] for a discussion of the pertinent issues in model evaluation.

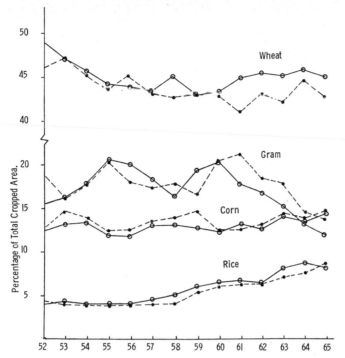

Fig. 1. Observed and predicted cropping patterns in Central Punjab (1952–1965). –, observed; - - -, predicted. Source: Singh [42], table 37.

by its ability to capture the time path of a complex cropping pattern with reasonable accuracy.[18] The main prediction errors arise from the wheat-gram combination which is difficult to predict as well as observe because a wheat-gram mixture is often planted to unirrigated acreages in the rabi season. If the rainfall is adequate the wheat requiring more water is allowed to grow, while if it is inadequate, the gram is allowed to mature to harvest.

The most important aspect of the model (if we can attest to its ability to predict observed behavior) is its capability in augmenting our understanding of the transformation process, given the observed values of the exogenous data (input and output prices and regional supplies of land and labor), by presenting a detailed quantitative chronicle of farm activities and their outcomes as they may have occurred, even where regional data are unavailable.[19]

[18] The model included ten major crops besides fodder crops in a double cropping system.

[19] Such a detailed chronicle which captures the main features of the agricultural transformation in the Punjab is provided in Singh and Day [44].

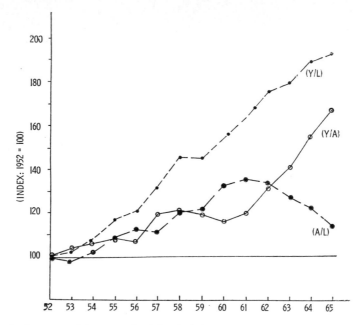

Fig. 2. Aggregate labour productivity (Y/L), output per acre (Y/A), and land-labour ratio (A/L) in Central Punjab (1952–65). Source: Singh and Day [44], tables 30, 31; model results.

Following Hayami and Ruttan [14] in fig. 2 we illustrate the growth of aggregate labour productivity (Y/L) predicted by the model, by decomposing it into two components, the aggregate output per acre (Y/A) and the land–labour ratio (A/L) to account for different 'types' of technological change. It is apparent that the Punjab experienced both biological (labour intensive or land-saving) and mechanical (labour saving) innovations over the period, the former associated with an increase in (Y/A) and the latter with (Y/L). The major change has been in the adoption of the green revolution package, but this has also been accompanied by the adoption of labour saving task specific mechanization. The decline in the land–labour ratio after 1960 is directly correlated with the adoption of new varieties and increased yields per acre thus leading to an increase in the demand for labour at a rate faster than its reduction through mechanization.

After 1960 the major source of increase in land productivity involved biological innovations as shown by the indices of modern and traditional variable inputs in fig. 3. The modern non-farm inputs such as new seeds and fertilizers along with fuel and tubewell delivered water increased very rapidly, while the most important traditional inputs — labour and animal

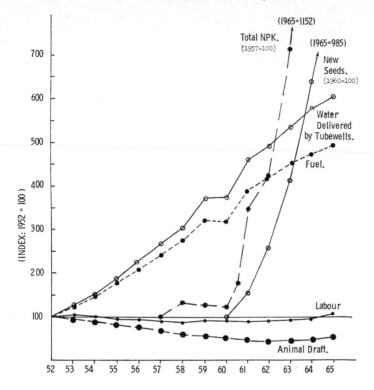

Fig. 3. Modern and traditional input use in Central Punjab (1952–65). Source: Singh and Day [44], tables 3, 8, 11, 16; model results.

draft — declined or remained relatively unchanged. These model results correctly predict the rapid adoption of the biological 'green revolution' inputs as well as the changing composition of farm inputs.

The process of task specific mechanization as predicted by the model is illustrated in fig. 4 which shows the increase in the proportions of irrigation planting and cultivation and land preparation that have been mechanized. Most other tasks continued to be dominated by traditional technologies, including harvesting in spite of the increase in the demand for labour during the harvesting period occasioned by increased output.

Furthermore, model predictions show that in spite of a labour surplus environment (in an aggregate annual sense) the time structure of the demand for annual labour and its changing pattern over time is such that serious seasonal scarcities and surpluses can occur. This is illustrated in fig. 5 which shows seasonal labour use during the winter harvest (April 16–30) and the period just prior to it (March 16–April 15), and labour use

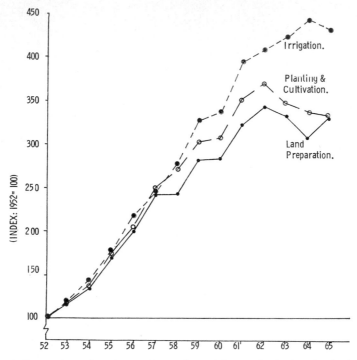

Fig. 4. Proportion of various tasks performed by mechanical technologies in Central Punjab (1952–65). Source: Singh and Day [44], tables 5, 6, 8; model results.

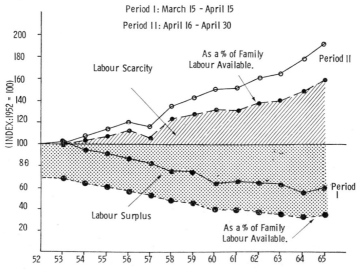

Fig. 5. Seasonal labour use in Central Punjab (1952–65). Source: Singh and Day [44], tables 23, 25; model results.

as a percentage of available family labour, with increasing scarcity in the former and increasing surplus in the latter period.

The large changes in the composition and structure of inputs have not in general been accompanied by large changes in the composition of outputs as suggested by the fairly stable cropping pattern (fig. 1), although improved varieties have started to displace indigenous ones. However, the model predicts increasing commercialization of farm production as shown in fig. 6. On the output side outlays on non-farm inputs as a percentage of total production outlays have increased. A substantial part of this increase has been due to the purchase of nutrients.

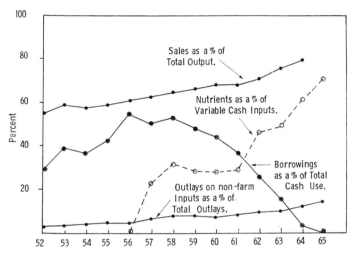

Fig. 6. Commercialization of the farm sector in Central Punjab (1952–65). Source: Singh and Day [44], tables 15, 28, 29; model results.

An interesting reversal of this increased dependence of the farm sector predicted by the model, is the decline after 1958 in borrowings to meet cash requirements. This is due primarily to the increased output and sales that have allowed farmers to meet their debt obligations and become relatively independent of external financing. The model predicts this trend much earlier than it actually occurred, but that it did occur can be attested to by the rapid rise in rural deposits in the region after 1965.

Thus the model is able to predict in detail the main features of the agricultural transformation that occurred in the Punjab, and which has included (i) a rapid growth in output and productivity, (ii) a rapid adoption of the 'green revolution' package (new seeds, fertilizers and water), (iii) task specific mechanization in an apparently aggregate labour surplus environment, (iv) a structural change in the demand for and the composition of inputs, and (v) an increasing commercialization of farm production through forward (output) and backward (input) linkages with the non-farm sector.

3.2. Some model applications

The model's ability to capture in a detailed quantitative manner an economic chronicle of resource use factor productivities and factor proportions is its most important although by no means only application. The large variety of model applications can be grouped into three classes (i) static, (ii) comparative static, and (iii) dynamic.

3.2.1. Static applications
The possible static applications of the model encompass all those that are possible with one period linear programming models and include (a) price and cost parametrics, (b) resource parametrics, and (c) matrix coefficient parametrics. Thus, for example, the model consisting of the l.p. problem specified by (1) and (2) for any given year '*t*' could be used to analyze the impact of changing the price of any given output parametrically to trace the ceteris paribus *supply response*; or the cost of a specific input can be varied parametrically to trace the ceteris paribus *derived demand* for that input. Similarly varying a set of product prices relative to others traces a *production frontier*, while varying resource costs can allow us to trace *short-term factor substitution* possibilities. Another way of tracing the demand for a resource is to vary its availability (right-hand side parametrics), allowing the solutions to the dual (shadow prices) to trace its opportunity cost.

Matrix coefficient variations can also be used to trace the impact of changes in the structure of the model. An important application of this is to trace the impact of yield variations due to weather, taking a range of expected yields, a range of expected outcomes could provide a confidence interval to the model predictions that would be very useful for planning and projecting regional development.

3.2.2. Comparative-static applications
The recursive nature of the model allows us to extend the range of static applications already discussed to a number of selected years providing a comparative-static framework. Thus, for example, it becomes possible not only to trace the short-run derived demand and supply response schedules, but also to approximate shifts in these schedules between any two time periods within the model. Thus shifts in the demand for inputs and the

supply of outputs over time can be traced quite easily, extending considerably the range of parametric results.[20]

3.2.3. Dynamic applications

Since the recursive nature of the model also allows us to capture the dynamic path of economic outcomes its most useful applications are dynamic. Three broad sets of dynamic applications can be identified: (a) simulating economic history, (b) simulating policy alternatives, and (c) projection and forecasting.

The model's ability to simulate the economic history of regional development has already been discussed. This ability allows us to obtain useful insights into the dynamics of transformation and learn how it took place, what the major constraints were during the period and what structural changes were brought about.

Alternatively, instead of using historical price and resource data and historical initial conditions, the impact of alternative policy choices or initial conditions can be simulated. Thus, for example, the impact of changing prices, resource availabilities and alternative technologies can be easily traced over time by changing the exogenous data or the behavioral parameters in the model. These dynamic simulations are particularly useful in tracing alternative historical paths to analyze, ceteris paribus, the changes in specific policies.[21]

Furthermore, by projecting exogenous data, conditional forecasts of the model can be obtained by projecting it into the future. The variety of policy issues that can be tackled and their validity will depend partly upon the reliability of the forecast on the endogenous data and partly on the ability to directly relate specific policy actions explicitly to farm payoffs and opportunities incorporated in the model.

3.3. Conclusions

We conclude by emphasizing the great flexibility of recursive programming models of regional agricultural development. As analytic tools they allow us to capture explicitly and often in great detail those elements that are

[20] Static and comparative-static experiments and their results for the current model are given in Singh and Day [45] in great detail. Also see Singh and Ahn [43] for similar applications to a r.l.p model of the wheat region in Southern Brazil.

[21] For a detailed exercise in dynamic simulation to analyze the impact of support price programs and subsidized credit on regional income growth and distribution using an r.l.p. framework, see Ahn and Singh [1].

crucial to our understanding of, and planning for, modern agricultural change. Their usefulness as analytic and policy tools, however, is often limited by the availability of data in sufficient quantity and quality to allow their construction and estimation. Data requirements would include a fairly detailed knowledge of the mechanical and biological technologies, time series on input and output prices, regional land and labour estimates and if the model is to be tested rigorously, regional data on crop acreages and production.

Given these data needs, it is apparent that such detailed dynamic micro-economic models have to await the development of good statistical reporting and should not be used in the first stages of analysis. However, data of good quality are becoming increasingly available in the LDC's, while the interest and growing need for sophisticated models of this nature will facilitate and can direct such data gathering activities. In spite of data and validation problems, such dynamic models should find increasing application in the near future.

References

[1] Ahn, C. Y. and I. J. Singh, 1972, Distribution of farm incomes under alternative policy regimes: a dynamic analysis of recent developments in southern Brazil (1960–70), a paper presented at the seminar on Applied Welfare Economics at the Annual Meetings of the American Agricultural Economics Association, Gainesville, Florida.

[2] Charnes, A. and W. W. Cooper, 1959, Chance constrained programming, Management Science 6, 73–79.

[3] Cyert, H. and M. March, 1969, The Behavioural Theory of the Finn, New York: Prentice Hall.

[4] Day, R. H., 1962, An approach to production response, Agricultural Economics Research 14, 134–148.

[5] Day, R. H., 1963, Recursive Programming and Production Response, Amsterdam: North-Holland Publishing Company.

[6] Day, R. H., 1971, Rational choice and economic behavior, Theory and Decision, 1, no. 3, 229–251.

[7] Day, R. H., in collaboration with M. Abe, W. K. Tabb and C. Tsao, 1969, Recursive programming models of industrial development and technological change in: Contributions to Input–Output Analysis, A. P. Carter and A. Brody, eds., 99–118, Amsterdam: North-Holland Publishing Company.

[8] Day, R. H. and T. Heidhues, 1966, Towards a microeconomic model of agricultural production and development, Farm and Market Workshop Paper No. 6702, Social Systems Research Institute, University of Wisconsin.

[9] Day, R. H. and I. J. Singh, 1972, A dynamic microeconometric model of agricultural development, Paper No. 7135, Social Systems Research Institute, University of Wisconsin.

[10] Dhrymes, P. J., et al., 1972, Criteria for evaluation of econometric models, Economic and Social Measurement, 1, 259–290.

[11] Duloy, J. and R. D. Norton, 1971, A programming model of the agricultural sector in Mexico, Development Research Center, IBRD. A paper presented at a Conference on Agricultural Sector Analysis and Programming, Ames, Iowa: Iowa State University.

[12] Goreux, L., R. Vawrs and A. Condos, 1971, A programming model of the Ivory Coast, Development Research Center, IBRD.

[13] Gotsch, C., 1971, A programming approach to some agricultural policy problems in West Pakistan, in: Studies in Development Planning, H. P. Chenery, ed., Cambridge: Harvard University.

[14] Hayami, Y. and V. W. Ruttan, 1970, Factor prices and technical change in agricultural development: The United States and Japan, 1880–1960, J.P.E., 78, no. 5: 1115–1141.

[15] Heady, E. O., W. B. Back and E. A. Peterson, 1953, Interdependence between the farm business and the farm household with implications for economic efficiency, Research Bulletin No. 398, Agricultural Experiment Station, Iowa State College.

[16] Heidhues, T., 1966, A recursive programming model of farm growth in Northern Germany, Journal of Farm Economics 48, 668–684.

[17] Heidhues, T., 1969, Recursive programming in agricultural applications, A. P. Carter and A. Brody eds., Input–Output Techniques (in honour of Wassily Leontief), Vol. I: Contributions to Input–Output Analysis, Amsterdam: North-Holland Publishing Company.

[18] Henderson, J. M., 1969, The utilization of agricultural land: a theoretical and empirical inquiry, The Review of Economics and Statistics, XLI, no. 3, 242–259.

[19] Hendrix, W. E. and R. Giri, 1969, Approaches to agricultural development in India 1949 to 1965: progress, regional differences and associated factors, U.S.D.A., Economic Research Service and Directorate of Economics and Statistics, Ministry of Food, Agriculture and Community Development and Cooperation, Government of India.

[20] Johnson, G. L., *et al.*, 1971, A Generalized Simulation Approach to Agricultural Sector Analysis: with Reference to Nigeria, Michigan State University, East Lansing.

[21] Johnson, S. R. and G. C. Rausser, 1972, Notes on verification problems for systems models, a paper presented at the A.D.C. Conference on General Systems Analysis Approach to Agricultural Sector Analysis at Airlee, W. Virginia.

[22] Johnston, B. F. and P. Kilby, 1972, Interrelations between agricultural and industrial growth, a paper presented at the International Economic Association Conference on the Place of Agriculture in the Development of Underdeveloped Countries, Bad Godesberg, West Germany.

[23] Johnston, B. F. and J. W. Mellor, 1961, The role of agriculture in economic development, American Economic Review.

[24] Kahlon, A. S., *et al.*, 1966, The Dynamics of Punjab Agriculture, Department of Economics and Sociology, Punjab Agricultural University, Ludhiana, India.

[25] Koopmans, T. C., ed., 1951, Activity Analysis of Production and Allocation, New York: John Wiley and Sons, Inc.

[26] Leontief, W., *et al.*, 1953, Studies in the Structure of the American Economy, Oxford Economic Press.

[27] Mellor, J. W., 1965a, The subsistence farmer in traditional economies, Paper presented at the A.D.C. Seminar on Subsistence and Peasant Economies, East-West Center, Honolulu, Hawaii.

[28] Mellor, J. W., May 1965, Towards a theory of agricultural development, paper prepared for SSRC Symposium on Agriculture and Development, University of Chicago.

[29] Miller, T. A., 1972, Evaluation of alternative flexibility restraint procedures for recursive programming models used for prediction, A.J.A.E. 54, 1.

[30] Mudahar, M. S., 1971, A dynamic microeconomic analysis of the agricultural sector: The Punjab, a paper presented at the Fifth International Conference on Input–Output Techniques, Geneva, Switzerland.

[31] Muller, G. P., 1970, Forecasting and rolling plans for competitive supply with production lags, QME 7052, Social Systems Research Institute, University of Wisconsin.

[32] Myrdal, G., 1968, Asian Drama: An Inquiry into the Poverty of Nations, New York: Twentieth Century Fund.

[33] Nakajima, C., 1957a, Overemployment and theory of the family farm, Osaka Daigaku Keisaigaku.

[34] Nakajima, C., 1957b, Equilibrium theory of family farms, Osaka Daigaku Keisaigaku.

[35] Nakajima, C., 1965, The subsistence farmer in commercial economies, paper presented at the A.D.C. Seminar on Subsistence and Peasant Economies, East-West Center, Honolulu, Hawaii.

[36] Nakajima, C., 1970, Subsistence and commercial family farms: some theoretical models of subjective equilibrium, in: C. R. Wharton Jr., ed., Subsistence Agriculture and Economic Development, Chicago: Aldine Publishing Company.

[37] Roy, A. D., 1952, Safety first and the holding of assets, Econometrica 20, 431–448.

[38] Shackle, G. L. S., 1958, Time in Economics, Amsterdam: North-Holland Publishing Company.

[39] Schaller, W. N., 1968, A national model of agricultural production response, Agricultural Economic Research, U.S.D.A., E.R.S., Vol. 20 (2).

[40] Schultz, T. W., 1964, Transforming Traditional Agriculture, New Haven: Yale University Press.

[41] Singh, I. J., 1968, Recursive programming models of agricultural development, Systems Formulation and Methodology Paper No. 6836, Social Systems Research Institute, University of Wisconsin.

[42] Singh, I. J., 1971, A recursive programming model of traditional agriculture in transition: a case study of the Punjab, India, Ph.D. Dissertation, University of Wisconsin.

[43] Singh, I. J. and C. Y. Ahn, 1972, Employment and capital-labour substitution in South Brazilian agriculture, Occasional Paper No. 72, Department of Agricultural Economics and Rural Sociology, Ohio State University.

[44] Singh, I. J. and R. H. Day, 1972a, A microeconometric chronicle of the green revolution, paper no. 7133, Social Systems Research Institute, University of Wisconsin.

[45] Singh, I. J. and R. H. Day, 1972b, Capital-labour utilization and substitution in Punjab agriculture, paper No. 7134, Social Systems Research Institute, University of Wisconsin.

[46] Singh, I. J., R. H. Day and S. S. Johl, 1968, Field crop technology in Punjab, India, Social Systems Research Institute, University of Wisconsin, Madison.

[47] U.S.D.A., 1970, Economic progress of agriculture in developing nations 1950–68, Foreign Agriculture Economic Report No. 59, Economic Research Service, U.S. Department of Agriculture.

[48] Wharton, Jr., C. R., 1963, The economic meaning of subsistence, Malayan Economic Review VIII (2).

[49] Wharton, Jr., C. R., ed., 1970, Subsistence Agriculture and Economic Development, Chicago: Aldine Publishing Company.

PART III

NON-LINEAR MODELS OVER SPACE AND TIME

A. SPATIAL PROGRAMMING MODELS

CHAPTER 22

Spatial equilibrium analysis of livestock products in Eastern Japan

KOZO SASAKI

Obihiro Chikusan University

1. Introduction

This chapter presents a review of empirical applications by Sasaki [1–3] of the Takayama–Judge model [4, 5] to the spatial equilibrium analysis of three important commodities in Eastern Japan's agriculture. The commodities considered are milk, hogs and poultry, demand for which has been sharply increasing and is expected to continue to expand in the future. The following analyses are done for the purpose of interregional adjustment as to the production, transportation, and marketing of various farm products.

Any algorithm for quadratic programming could be applied to solve a spatial equilibrium problem of this type. Among other things, those algorithms by Wolfe [9], and by Takayama and Judge prove to be efficient. In addition, separable programming (see [10]) is recognized as an efficient and useful tool that is applicable to a single commodity case.

Agricultural regions are roughly grouped into two parts, Eastern Japan and Western Japan. The former regions which are dealt with in the analyses form a wide market and appear rather independent of the latter regions as far as the three commodities are concerned. Major agricultural regions and their basing cities involved in the models are indicated in fig. 1.

2. Milk: whole milk, 1964–65

2.1.

The principal objective of this study is to find out the competitive pattern of the whole milk market in Eastern Japan at the farm-plant level for the

Fig. 1. The agricultural regions investigated in Eastern Japan. Names in parentheses indicate basing cities. In region 14, either a or b is used corresponding to particular problems. Hokkaido District: 1. Central Hokkaido (Sapporo), 2. Northern Hokkaido (Kitami), 3. Southern Hokkaido (Hakodate), 4. Eastern Hokkaido (Obihiro). Tohoku District: 5. Aomori (Aomori), 6. Iwate (Morioka), 7. Miyagi (Sendai), 8. Akita (Akita), 9. Yamagata (Yamagata), 10. Fukushima (Fukushima). Kanto District: 11. Ibaragi (Mito), 12. Tochigi (Utsunomiya), 13. Gunma (Maebashi), 14. Saitama (a. Urawa, b. Omiya), 15. Chiba (Chiba), 16. Tokyo (Tokyo), 17. Kanagawa (Yokohama). Tosan District: 18. Yamanashi (Kofu), 19. Nagano (Matsumoto). Hokuriku District: 20. Niigata (Niigata).

interregional adjustment of milk utilization and transportation. The whole milk market is defined in two ways; i.e., fluid and manufacturing milk markets which deal with a single homogeneous product, respectively. A spatial equilibrium model is applied to the two markets, separately for the convenience of analysis. Data used in this analysis are the 1964–65 average. The results obtained show that prices of fluid and manufacturing milk are high in and around large consumption regions and become gradually lower as they get farther from consumption centers. Price differentials among regions are on the decrease in both fluid and manufacturing milk markets. It is found that interregional flows of milk are required to be cut down to some extent and are particularly restricted in the manufacturing milk market. It implies that manufacturing milk is centered excessively in large consumption regions. The conception is that it is at present disadvantageous to put into operation the long-distance transportation of whole milk from the Hokkaido district to the Kanto district.

2.2. Problem

This study chiefly attempts to determine rational utilization and transportation of whole milk as well as optimum price levels in major regions of Eastern Japan in 1964–65. Problems of where to haul and how to utilize fresh whole milk produced on farms are given much attention because they affect, more or less, farm and consumer prices of milk in various regions. Along with a tendency toward expanded market area and regional specialization of milk production, longer hauls of whole milk have become a problem of growing importance. It is now discussed extensively as an interregional competition problem. As a matter of fact, the whole milk market in Eastern Japan faces such important problems as reduction of price differentials among regions at the farm-plant level in marketing channels, choice of transport routes and estimation of optimum shipments, establishment of appropriate milk utilization for each region, etc.. These problems can really be treated in the framework of spatial equilibrium analysis.

The Kanto and Tohoku districts actually form a wide market in which a good deal of whole milk is transported for long distances. Hokkaido appears to remain an isolated market shipping no portions of milk production except for occasional shipments in small amounts for experimental purposes. Improvements in transportation facilities and regional specialization of milk production, however, would sooner or later permit the expansion of the distance of milk shipments and set up an interregional shipment network combining the conventional market area with Hokkaido. It still seems significant, at the present time, to determine objectively the spatial equilibrium of the whole milk market east of the Kanto district, which includes Hokkaido, and to examine the possibilities and limitations of long-distance transportation. Attention is also focused on the possibility of shipping whole milk from the large production area, Hokkaido, to the major consumption area, Kanto. It is certainly very important to see whether the existing price mechanism operates effectively and what adjustments may be needed in the whole milk market.

2.3. Model

The Takayama-Judge model that is adopted in approaching the spatial equilibrium problem raised in this section was first adapted by West and Brandow [8] to the spatial equilibrium analysis of the dairy industry in the Northeastern and North Central regions, U.S.A.. Many important conclusions were explicitly drawn by them for price and marketing policy in the dairy industry though the model was applied in a somewhat restrictive manner. In the following analysis, however, it is directly applied to the actual problem under consideration in order to derive a lot of empirical implications.

The market area consists of three districts; i.e., Hokkaido, Tokohu and Kanto. Of the two models constructed in the analysis, the model for the fluid milk market consists of the ten major regions with data available. They are Central Hokkaido, Miyagi, Fukushima, Ibaragi, Tochigi, Gunma, Saitama, Chiba, Tokyo and Kanagawa. The model for the manufacturing milk market is composed of the following eight major regions; Central Hokkaido, Northern Hokkaido, Southern Hokkaido, Eastern Hokkaido, Iwate, Gunma, Chiba and Tokyo.

There are few empirical analyses of demand and supply for whole milk. Since there is practically no evidence on price elasticities of demand and supply, regional demand and supply functions have to be estimated directly from empirical data. For the sake of simplicity, supply is assumed fixed and the demand function is estimated for each region as a linear equation in demand and price from 1961–65 data by the least squares method. The average 1964–65 data on demand, supply, net exports and prices of whole milk for fluid and manufacturing uses are given the lower rows of tables 3 and 4.

Current levels of demand shown in these tables were derived from demand functions, evaluating regional prices at the average 1964–65 levels. On the other hand, supply is obtained either by deducting net import from demand or by adding net export to demand, because supply is equal to demand minus net import and is equivalent to demand plus net export. The average 1964–65 levels of demand are somewhat underestimated for most regions since demand of whole milk has been markedly increasing in recent years throughout the country. Therefore, regional supply computed from regional demand and net export is also underestimated. The net export for each region comprises its individual net exports to all regions. Approximate quantities exported or imported for different uses from one region to another are calculated in the following manner; i.e., individual flows of whole milk between any pair of regions investigated in the models are divided into two parts in proportion to current levels of demand for fluid and manufacturing milk at import regions. Both current imports from and exports to regions outside the market area are maintained at existing levels. In table 4, supply of manufacturing milk in Tokyo amounts to 60 528 tons. It is mostly composed of imports from Saitama, Tochigi, Ibaragi, Kanagawa and Fukushima which are eliminated from the model. Most of these regions have no price data needed for estimating regional demand functions. Milk consumed at farm-households and fed to calves are eliminated from the model. The model constructed under the above conditions is a familiar case, which may be easily visualized.

Whole milk is usually transported by a tank lorry. Unit transport costs are calculated according to freight rates of a 10-ton tank lorry and distances between basing point cities. They are taken equal between the same two cities despite different directions of transportation and set to be zero

Table 1

Unit transport costs among regions in the fluid milk market, 1964–65 (t_{ij}).
Yen per kg. of fluid milk

Region i \ Region j	1	2	3	4	5	6	7	8	9	10
1 Central Hokkaido (Sapporo)	0									
2 Miyagi (Sendai)	9.2	0								
3 Fukushima (Fukushima)	10.1	1.3	0							
4 Ibaragi (Mito)	11.9	3.2	2.6	0						
5 Tochigi (Utsunomiya)	11.9	3.2	2.4	1.6	0					
6 Gunma (Maebashi)	13.7	5.1	4.2	3.0	2.4	0				
7 Saitama (Urawa)	12.9	4.2	3.3	2.0	1.4	1.5	0			
8 Chiba (Chiba)	13.5	4.8	4.0	2.3	2.1	2.3	1.1	0		
9 Tokyo (Tokyo)	13.1	4.5	3.6	1.9	1.7	1.8	0.6	0.8	0	
10 Kanagawa (Yokohama)	13.4	4.8	3.9	2.2	2.1	2.1	1.0	1.2	0.7	0

Table 2
Unit transport costs among regions in the manufacturing milk market, 1964–65 (t_{ij}).
Yen per kg. of manufacturing milk

Region i \ Region j	1	2	3	4	5	6	7	8
1 Central Hokkaido (Sapporo)	0							
2 Northern Hokkaido (Kitami)	4.1	0						
3 Southern Hokkaido (Hakodate)	3.7	7.3	0					
4 Eastern Hokkaido (Obihiro)	3.5	2.4	6.7	0				
5 Iwate (Morioka)	7.2	10.8	4.1	10.1	0			
6 Gunma (Maebashi)	13.7	17.3	10.6	16.6	7.0	0		
7 Chiba (Chiba)	13.5	17.1	10.3	16.4	6.9	2.3	0	
8 Tokyo (Tokyo)	13.1	16.7	10.0	16.1	6.5	1.8	0.8	0

within one region. Information on unit transport costs among regions is given for both fluid and manufacturing milk markets in tables 1 and 2, respectively. Prices and transport costs are all expressed in terms of 1965 yen.

2.4. Results and their implications

The spatial equilibrium solution for each of fluid and manufacturing milk markets is determined under particular conditions of regional demand and supply, and unit transport costs among regions. Competitive equilibrium solutions are shown in tables 3 and 4 for regional demands, net exports, prices and interregional flows of whole milk. They are mentioned in upper rows as compared with current levels of those variables in lower rows in the two tables.

In the fluid milk market, interregional price differentials tend to decrease slightly. The price level in the Kanto district is evidently higher than the Tohoku and Hokkaido districts. Moreover, prices remain at high levels in the big cities and decline with distance from those cities. Farmers received price increases in Miyagi, Gunma, Saitama, Chiba and Kanagawa, but decreases in Fukushima, Ibaragi, Tochigi and Tokyo. In the latter regions, consumer prices of milk may be expected to decline, reflecting lower prices received by farmers. As for the interregional transportation, effective transport routes for whole milk are considerably simplified in equilibrium, though they are rather complex in actuality. Tokyo and Kanagawa are characterized as import regions. Of the other eight regions, Fukushima changes from an export region to an independent region with no interregional

Table 3

The spatial equilibrium solution and current data for the fluid milk market, the 1964–65 average

Origin \ Destination	1	2	3	4	5	6	7	8	9	10	Supply x_i	Net export	Price p_i
1 Central Hokkaido	35,362								0		35,362	0	37.0
	35,257								0,105		35,362	0,105	37.0
2 Miyagi		27,144	0				0	0	0	4,170	31,314	4,170	35.4
		27,768	1,913				0,229	0,020	1,149	0,235	31,314	3,546	35.2
3 Fukushima			33,505	0	0	0	0		0		33,505	0	36.4
			27,799	0,825	0,706	0,228	0,921		3,026		33,505	3,768	37.4
4 Ibaraki				22,909	0	0	0	0	21,087	8,371	52,367	29,458	38.0
				19,377	0,944	0	0,391	15,867	15,578	0,210	52,367	32,165	39.3
5 Tochigi					22,112	0	0	0	52,666	0	74,778	52,666	38.2
					17,975	3,619	13,783	1,131	32,491	5,779	74,778	55,153	39.8
6 Gunma						25,664	0	0	45,860	0	71,524	45,860	38.1
						22,933	3,000	0,142	33,508	11,941	71,524	44,744	37.6
7 Saitama							54,189	0	39,912	0	94,101	39,912	39.3
							36,899	0,251	49,167	7,784	94,101	38,878	37.7
8 Chiba								82,183	42,077	0	124,260	42,077	39.1
								66,675	46,179	11,406	124,260	40,174	38.7
9 Tokyo			0						19,364		19,364	−201,602	39.9
			25						19,364		19,364	−193,348	40.6
10 Kanagawa									0	79,404	79,404	−12,541	40.2
									12,145	67,234	79,404	−25,185	39.0
Demand y_i	35,362	27,144	33,505	22,909	22,112	25,664	54,189	82,183	220,966	91,945	615,979	0	
	35,257	27,768	39,737	20,202	19,625	26,780	55,223	84,086	212,712	104,589	615,979	0	

Quantities are stated in tons and prices are expressed in yen per kg. The upper figures indicate the equilibrium solution and the lower figures represent current data.

Table 4

The spatial equilibrium solution and current data for the manufacturing milk market, the 1964–65 average

Origin \ Destination	1	2	3	4	5	6	7	8	Supply x_i	Net export	Price p_i
1 Central Hokkaido	65,443							0	65,443	−1,166	35.0
	65,354							0,089	65,443	−14,793	32.4
2 Northern Hokkaido	0	189,721						0	189,721	0	31.3
	12,449	177,203						0,069	189,721	11,662	31.9
3 Southern Hokkaido	1,166		61,402	0					62,568	1,166	32.0
	1,975		58,536	2,057					62,568	4,032	33.2
4 Eastern Hokkaido	0	0		177,744					177,744	0	32.6
	0,458	0,856		176,430					177,744	−0,743	32.5
5 Iwate					86,213				86,213	0	31.9
					86,210				86,213	3	31.9
6 Gunma						24,049	0	7,912	31,961	7,912	33.3
						16,863	0,043	15,055	31,961	15,098	—
7 Chiba							14,435	8,929	23,364	8,929	34.3
							13,227	10,137	23,364	10,094	36.7
8 Tokyo								60,528	60,528	−16,841	35.1
								60,528	60,528	−25,353	30.6
Demand y_i	66,609	189,721	61,402	177,744	86,213	24,049	14,435	77,369	697,542	0	
	80,236	178,059	58,536	178,487	86,210	16,863	13,270	85,881	697,542	0	

Quantities are stated in tons and prices are expressed in yen per kg. The upper figures indicate the equilibrium solution and the lower figures represent current data.

Basic data on quantities are from: Seinyu Inyogyunyu Nyuseihin no Seisan Shohi ni kansuru Tokei (Statistics on Production and Consumption of Whole Milk, Fluid Milk and Manufactured Milk Products), The Ministry of Agriculture and Forestry, Japan, 1961–65. Price data are from: Noson Bukka Chingin Tokei (Statistics of Prices and Wages in Rural Areas), The Ministry of Agriculture and Forestry, Japan, 1961–65.

trade, and Central Hokkaido is compelled on a commercial basis to stop exporting to Tokyo. The other six regions remain export regions. Fluid milk imported to Tokyo from Ibaragi, Tochigi and Gunma increases greatly while imports to Tokyo become zero from Central Hokkaido, Miyagi, Fukushima and Kanagawa, and decrease appreciably from Saitama and Chiba. Imports to Kanagawa come from Miyagi and Ibaragi instead of Tochigi, Gunma, Saitama and Chiba. Net import increases slightly in Tokyo, but is reduced by half in Kanagawa.

On the other hand, price differentials among regions are also reduced in the manufacturing milk market. Equilibrium prices of manufacturing milk settle at high levels in such regions as Tokyo, Chiba and Central Hokkaido. Current price for the average 1964–65 is not available in Gunma. Production and processing of manufacturing milk are concentrated in Hokkaido. Interregional shipments as a whole show a marked decline. Exports to Tokyo and Sapporo are reduced by large amounts. It is also pointed out that manufacturing milk centered excessively on Tokyo, judging from the fact that the prevailing price in Tokyo was the lowest of all. As Tokyo has plenty of manufacturing milk available, the large bulk of fluid-eligible milk imported to Tokyo should be converted from manufacturing uses to fluid use.

In order to realize the shipment of whole milk from Hokkaido to Tokyo, current unit transport costs have to be reduced to half or so, with other things being equal. Equilibrium prices are 399 yen per 10 kg of fluid milk in Tokyo, 313 yen for whole milk in Northern Hokkaido, and 326 yen in Eastern Hokkaido. Price differentials are 86 yen between Tokyo and Northern Hokkaido and 73 yen between Tokyo and Eastern Hokkaido while the corresponding unit transport costs are 167 yen and 161 yen. Means of milk transportation, traffic network and supply conditions in major production areas may be considerably improved in the near future, so that there is a strong possibility of the long-distance transportation of milk from Hokkaido to metropolitan areas.

2.5. Possible extensions of the analysis

A wide range of empirical data and analyses of demand, supply and transportation cost conditions are generally required to achieve an effective spatial equilibrium analysis. Because of the lack of information on demand and supply conditions, regional demand functions were estimated for fluid and manufacturing milk, separately, in this analysis on the assumption that supply is fixed for every region. This assumption may be permissible in the short-run analysis. It is important, however, to estimate regional supply functions in an attempt to determine optimum levels of production as well as consumption in respective regions. Demand and supply functions should generally be estimated by the simultaneous-equation approach. It is of great necessity to examine efficient means of milk transportation and to obtain accurate information on unit transport costs among regions.

3. Hogs, 1966

3.1.

This analysis attempts to determine equilibrium solutions in regional prices, production, disposition and interregional shipments of hogs in order to investigate optimum levels of farmers' received prices and efficient patterns for planned production and shipment under existing circumstances in various regions. It is of great advantage to hog raising farmers to set and stabilize the standard level of hog prices subject to short-run fluctuations. It is interesting to inquire into the trend toward regional specialization of hog production and processing. There are no marked differences between equilibrium solutions and actual results in regional demand and supply levels, and in intra-regional shipments of live hogs. Interregional shipments, however, differ substantially between both cases. Effective transport routes are remarkably simplified in such a way that transportation is carried out among fewer regions on a larger scale.

3.2. Problem

With increasing demand for meat, pork production has been sharply rising both absolutely and relatively. In fact, it accounted for 55 % of the total livestock meat production in carcass weight in 1964, 63 % in 1965, and 77 % in 1966. In addition, pork production accounted for 54 % of all livestock and poultry meat production in 1965 and 63 % in 1966. It is obvious that hog raising is a very important enterprise in the meat-livestock production.

The major concern with regard to the hog raising problem centers around efficient production and transportation as well as optimum pricing of live hogs in the whole market area in question. Such a subject may be handled as a typical spatial equilibrium problem. The spatial equilibrium model mentioned before is straightforward applied here to the hog raising industry, in which each region possesses its particular demand and supply functions.

Seasonal and annual changes together with geographic differences in hog prices necessitate planned production and transportation of hogs for each region, keeping the balance with other regions. In spite of the fact that interregional shipments of hog carcasses have been markedly increasing, the efficient shipment of live hogs remains an important subject to be settled at the farm-packing-plant level among various regions. The proportion of interregional shipments to total shipments of live hogs in number of head has been declining, but still accounts for one fifth in the whole country; i.e., 26 % in 1963, 24 % in 1964, 20 % in 1965 and in 1966, and 21 % in 1967.

It is said that hog production and processing tend to be more specialized by certain regions or to be substantially concentrated in specific regions in view of more specialized and larger-scale hog raising, establishment of central wholesale market of meat and so on. It will be worthwhile, therefore, to examine the regional specialization phenomena in hog production and disposition by the spatial equilibrium analysis. It is also interesting to raise the interregional adjustment problem in the lines of working off the discrepancy between equilibrium solutions and actual results.

3.3. Model

The market area considered in the model covers nineteen regions in five districts; i.e., Hokkaido, Tohoku, Kanto, Tosan and Hokuriku. The four regions of Hokkaido are unified into a single region because of the lack of data on interregional shipments of live hogs within Hokkaido. Therefore, the model really comprises sixteen regions, which are mentioned in the tables below.

The number of hogs slaughtered in this market area accounts for 65 % of the total slaughter in the country in 1966. Supply of live hogs forms 64 % of the total supply. It follows, then, that only one percent of live hogs is imported into the market area from outside. The market area concerned is a major production and processing area on a nation-wide scale. It has little trade relations with other regions excluded from the model.

Regional demand and supply functions are derived on the basis of the price elasticities of demand and supply that were estimated on a national level by Yuize [6] and by Yuize and Fujiwara [7]. The average value of -1.451 is obtained for the demand elasticity of pork at the wholesale level. Supply elasticity of pork is 0.349 at the wholesale level. Each demand and supply function is approximated by a linear equation relating quantity demanded or supplied with price. Regional demand is represented by the number of hogs slaughtered in an individual region. Supply is regionally

Table 5

Unit transport costs among regions, 1966 (t_{ij}). 1000 yen per head of hog

Region i \ Region j	1	2	3	4	5	6	7	8	9	10	11	12	13	14	15	16
1 Hokkaido (Sapporo)	0															
2 Aomori (Aomori)	0.505	0														
3 Iwate (Morioka)	0.731	0.289	0													
4 Miyagi (Sendai)	0.934	0.492	0.266	0												
5 Akita (Akita)	0.711	0.269	0.207	0.367	0											
6 Yamagata (Yamagata)	0.945	0.503	0.336	0.118	0.297	0										
7 Fukushima (Fukushima)	1.022	0.579	0.354	0.140	0.397	0.154	0									
8 Ibaragi (Mito)	1.206	0.764	0.538	0.335	0.606	0.371	0.272	0								
9 Tochigi (Utsunomiya)	1.204	0.761	0.535	0.332	0.578	0.343	0.244	0.168	0							
10 Gunma (Maebashi)	1.385	0.942	0.716	0.513	0.759	0.511	0.425	0.311	0.244	0						
11 Saitama (Omiya)	1.292	0.849	0.629	0.419	0.666	0.431	0.331	0.207	0.140	0.147	0					
12 Chiba (Chiba)	1.365	0.922	0.696	0.493	0.739	0.504	0.405	0.237	0.229	0.230	0.126	0				
13 Tokyo (Tokyo)	1.325	0.833	0.656	0.453	0.699	0.465	0.365	0.201	0.182	0.189	0.070	0.082	0			
14 Kanagawa (Yokohama)	1.357	0.915	0.688	0.485	0.731	0.497	0.397	0.229	0.218	0.224	0.111	0.126	0.070	0		
15 Niigata (Niigata)	1.084	0.571	0.506	0.310	0.365	0.240	0.266	0.540	0.492	0.311	0.399	0.472	0.433	0.465	0	
16 Nagano (Matsumoto)	1.573	1.131	0.883	0.680	0.632	0.692	0.592	0.465	0.432	0.252	0.324	0.394	0.349	0.366	0.348	0

equivalent to demand plus net export in the whole country. However, net exports for individual regions are calculated within the market area concerned in this case. As a result, current supplies for Tokyo and Kanagawa in table 6 are greater than the actual ones by 25 % and 10 %, respectively. Supplies in both cases consist of intra-regional production and imports from outside the market area. Current supply for Nagano in table 6 is less than the actual one by 3 %. It implies that 3 % of the actual supply was exported out of the market area and is eliminated from the model. Price is expressed in terms of 1000 yen per head of hog whose weight is 90 kg on the average. The analytical model constructed under conditions of linear demand and supply functions, and of given unit transport costs is the typical one that was illustrated by Takayama and Judge [4].

The use of trucks has become very popular in hog transportation. A 10-ton truck is usually loaded with about 60 head of hogs. Transport costs per head of hog are shown in table 5. They are based on truck freight rate, distances traveled and number of hogs loaded.

3.4. Results and their implications

Equilibrium values of the various variables are shown in upper rows in contrast to actual results in lower rows in table 6. Price differentials among regions are reduced. Price remains at a high level in the Kanto district, and it falls in regions farther from that area. Low price regions are concentrated in the Tohoku and Hokkaido districts. As for current prices, the highest is 2168 yen per 10 kg in live weight for Tokyo and the lowest is 1695 yen for Yamagata. With regard to equilibrium prices, the highest is 1949 yen for Kanagawa and the lowest is 1847 yen for Aomori. The difference between highest and lowest prices is 473 yen in actuality, but it is reduced to 102 yen in equilibrium.

As the equilibrium is achieved, the highest price under actual conditions falls by 10 % while the lowest price rises by 9 %. Regional prices are equalized at the level of about 1900 yen. Price declines appreciably in the consumption centers such as Tokyo, Saitama, Kanagawa, Gunma and Nagano. It rises to some extent, however, in such production regions as Yamagata, Akita, Miyagi, Fukushima, Iwate and Tochigi through the inter-regional competition of hog production. Price levels are rather stable in Hokkaido, Aomori and Ibaragi.

With a decline in price, hog disposition increases considerably in the five regions of the Kanto and Tosan districts, particularly in Tokyo. Production decreases slightly in those regions, reflecting the inelastic supply of hogs.

Tabl┤

The spatial equilibrium solutior

Destination / Origin	1	2	3	4	5	6	7	8	9
1 Hokkaido	404.638 404.257								
2 Aomori		185.912 183.339	0 5.847					0 0.320	
3 Iwate			155.588 162.985	0 0.749					
4 Miyagi				186.947 205.467				0 1.245	0 0.53
5 Akita	0 1.173	0 1.515			112.261 130.876	0 0.275			
6 Yamagata				0 0.012		156.012 187.718	0 1.602		
7 Fukushima				0 0.466			157.651 172.231	0 0.246	0 3.4┃
8 Ibaragi							951.540 924.213		
9 Tochigi								0 33.815	177.9┤ 196.2┤
10 Gunma								0 0.224	
11 Saitama									
12 Chiba									
13 Tokyo									
14 Kanagawa									
15 Niigata								0 1.016	
16 Nagano									
Demand y_i	404.638 404.257	185.912 184.512	155.588 170.347	186.947 206.694	112.261 130.876	156.012 187.993	157.651 173.833	951.540 961.079	177.9┤ 200.1┤

Quantities: 1000 head; prices: 1000 yen. The upper figures indicate the equilibrium solution and the low┤ ones represent actual results. Source: Nikuchiku no Fukenbetsu Shukkatosu Kentoshiryo (Survey Interregional Shipments of Meat-Livestock), Noson Bukka Chingin Tokei (Statistics of Prices and Wag┤ in Rural Areas), The Ministry of Agriculture and Forestry, Japan, 1966.

nd actual results for hogs, 1966

10	11	12	13	14	15	16	Supply x_i	Net export	Head p_i	10 kg
			0				404.638	0	16.675	1.853
			0.474				404.731	0.474	16.686	1.854
0	61.151		0	0			247.063	61.151	16.626	1.847
15.530	7.225		32.794	2.460			247.515	63.003	16.713	1.857
0	0		62.983	0			218.571	62.983	16.853	1.873
1.963	2.641		45.573	0.200			214.111	43.764	15.903	1.767
0	0		67.220	0			254.167	67.220	17.056	1.895
1.182	23.536		11.778	4.712			248.458	41.764	16.002	1.778
	0		51.322	0			163.583	51.322	16.810	1.868
	12.206		4.253	7.875			158.173	27.297	15.309	1.701
	39.973		32.000	0			227.985	71.973	17.044	1.894
	6.112		11.688	11.890			219.022	31.029	15.255	1.695
0	0		116.161	0	0		273.812	116.161	17.144	1.905
0.021	13.802		47.417	30.105	0.112		267.814	93.981	16.110	1.790
	0	0	169.725	72.074			1193.339	241.799	17.308	1.923
	41.802	66.785	153.603	4.093			1190.496	229.417	17.190	1.910
0	107.771		0	0			285.704	107.771	17.335	1.926
3.171	30.676		14.279	0.086			278.263	78.075	16.101	1.789
0.308	0		0	0			490.308	— 17.338	17.387	1.932
71.536	20.152		0.851	0.450			493.213	— 2.303	17.685	1.965
	476.664		0	0			476.664	—208.895	17.475	1.942
	451.509		27.408	3.883			482.800	—168.352	18.135	2.015
	0	587.616	25.042	0			612.658	25.042	17.427	1.936
	11.932	540.013	39.996	16.093			608.034	1.236	17.055	1.895
			287.313				287.313	—592.426	17.509	1.945
			297.991				297.991	—467.663	19.512	2.168
			0	395.349			395.349	—110.739	17.537	1.949
			3.278	395.929			399.207	— 87.334	18.036	2.004
7.338	0		67.973	0	256.236	0	341.547	85.311	17.076	1.897
2.109	25.259		37.240	0.668	270.801	0.061	337.154	66.241	16.461	1.829
0			0	38.665		232.829	271.494	38.665	17.201	1.911
0.004	4.300		37.031	8.097		224.491	273.923	49.371	17.649	1.961
7.646	685.559	587.616	879.739	506.088	256.236	232.829	6144.195	0		
5.516	651.152	606.798	765.654	486.541	270.913	224.552	6120.905	0		

Consequently, net imports of the four regions in the Kanto district are expanded and net export of Nagano is reduced. In such regions as Yamagata, Akita, Miyagi, Fukushima, Iwate and Tochigi, hog production expands by 2 to 4 % and disposition shows a substantial reduction with a rise in price. Net exports of these regions are expanded. Similar phenomena are observed in Ibaragi, Chiba and Niigata. Hokkaido changes from a surplus region to an independent market.

The interregional adjustment of hog shipment is a concern of great importance. The consolidation of conventional transport routes and dispersed shipments is needed so that hogs are shipped among fewer regions in a larger quantity. It is necessary that Aomori and Tochigi should ship exclusively to Saitama, and that Iwate, Miyagi, Akita, Fukushima and Chiba should give priority to shipping to Tokyo. Yamagata should ship to both Saitama and Tokyo, Ibaragi to both Tokyo and Kanagawa, Niigata to both Tokyo and Gunma, respectively. Nagano is required to expand its shipment to Kanagawa.

Consequently, hog production increases in the Tohoku district, but decreases in the Kanto district where consumption centers are located. On the demand side, the Kanto district enhances its position in the relative importance in slaughtering and processing hogs while the Tohoku district declines in the relative status. The total quantity in the market area is slightly greater in equilibrium than the actual situation.

3.5. Possible extensions of the analysis

Regional demand and supply functions used in the model are based on the price elasticities of demand and supply of pork at the wholesale level, which were estimated on a nation-wide scale. Each of both demand and supply elasticities is taken equal among regions. It would be necessary, therefore, to estimate regional demand and supply elasticities or functions at the farm-plant level or to derive them from those elasticities or functions at the wholesale level. Demand and supply elasticities or functions should be regionally estimated in view of the regional variation in production and consumption structures. Moreover, it is useful to take account of possible changes in the regional demand and supply conditions of hogs and in the transport cost conditions among regions. It is also interesting to analyze the spatial equilibrium of the hog raising industry in the long run as well as in the short run.

4. Broilers, 1966

4.1.

Spatial equilibrium patterns of the broiler industry are ascertained to serve the practical purpose of interregional adjustment, by comparing the results obtained on the basis of upper and lower limits of demand elasticities. The price elasticity of demand appears rather elastic, but it is not definitely obtained for broilers. However, the range in which the price elasticity falls is approximately determined from empirical evidence. Results yielded from the analysis indicate that the equilibrium total quantity is little different from the actual one, and that price levels decline in general while price differentials among regions are slightly on the decrease. Both the number of effective transport routes and total interregional shipments of live broilers are considerably reduced, reflecting the principle of local processing and carcass transportation of broilers. Spatial equilibrium solutions based on the two different elasticities of demand have many points in common. It would be concluded, therefore, that the equilibrium solution is little susceptible to influences from a small error in the elasticity of demand or supply of broilers in view of relatively inelastic features on the supply side.

4.2. Problem

Broiler production has been expanding at a rapid rate since the late 1950's with increased demand for meat. Poultry meat now ranks second in carcass weight next to pork in the meat production, and broilers amount to 70 % of the total poultry meat production. Besides, the total number of broilers raised in the whole country has increased at the rate of 22 % on the annual average in 1964–69. The number of broiler raising farms has decreased at the average annual rate of 3 %. Accordingly, the number of birds raised per farm shows an increase at the average rate of 26 % annually. This reveals partly the tendency toward more specialized broiler raising on a larger scale.

Broiler raising is a relatively new industry that undergoes various changes in technological and institutional conditions. It is a matter of interest, therefore, to see how producers and processors adjust themselves to changing economic environments. In the past, broilers used to be transported alive from production areas to consumption centers. With the establishment of processing facilities in production areas, shipments of live broilers among regions have been greatly reduced, and a large portion of broilers have been immediately processed at local packing plants. Even at the stage that broiler shipment in processed form is highly developed, interregional adjustment will be needed at the farm-plant level in production, processing and shipments if there exist marked differences in regional prices of live broilers.

Since broiler raisers concern themselves about where and how much to produce, and how far and how much to ship, a spatial equilibrium problem would necessarily be raised at the farm-plant level. Spatial equilibrium analysis is attempted to examine optimum price levels as well as rational geographic distribution of production and processing for a wide market area including four districts. In the derivation of regional demand functions from a price elasticity on a national level, it is difficult to obtain a definite value for the elasticity. Therefore, sensitivity analysis is made of the spatial equilibrium with different values for the demand elasticity.

4.3. Model

The market area consists of seventeen major regions in the four districts of Hokkaido, Tohoku, Kanto and Tosan. Hokkaido is taken as a single market on account of the lack of data, so that the model is actually composed of fourteen regions. This is a large market area in the country, handling a little more than 30 % of the total quantity that amounts to 131 million birds in 1966. The total quantity is rapidly increasing over time, 172 million birds in 1967 and 229 million birds in 1968. The ratios of exports and imports made by the market area concerned are also practically equal in 1967 and 1968, and remain at 1966 level. Hence, the market area proves independent from outside areas.

As for the shipment of live broilers, intra-regional shipments occupy a large portion of the nation's supply. The ratio of interregional shipments has been gradually declining throughout the country and range from 18 % in 1966 to 15 % in 1967 and to 13 % in 1968. It implies the difficulty of hauling live broilers longer distances.

Current prices, demands, supplies and interregional shipments as of 1966 are summarized in table 7. Demand and supply functions by regions are derived from those current prices, demand and supply levels, and price elasticities of demand and supply. Prices are those received by farmers, and they are expressed in terms of yen per bird. A bird's weight is 1.24 kg on the average in this market area. The average live weight is less than the national average of 1.34 kg.

Two sets of regional demand functions are derived corresponding to upper and lower limits of price elasticity of poultry-meat demand at the

Table 7

Actual results for broilers, 1966

Destination / Origin	1	2	3	4	5	6	7	8	9	10	11	12	13	14	Supply x_i	Net export	Price per Bird p_i	Price per 10 kg
1 Hokkaido	1863														1863	0	288.2	2324
2 Aomori		388													388	− 313	250.1	2017
3 Iwate		313	1293	424											2030	737	242.8	1958
4 Miyagi				1352	41										1393	− 383	234.0	1887
5 Fukushima					1904		180		171		25				2280	321	253.8	2047
6 Ibaragi					14	3294			613	252	936				5109	1588	242.4	1955
7 Tochigi						215	3033	52	628		99				4027	814	224.1	1807
8 Gunma						12		2535	161		231				2939	352	230.8	1861
9 Saitama									3310						3310	−4392	222.3	1793
10 Chiba									302	4556	335				5193	385	242.3	1954
11 Tokyo									775		373				1148	−1669	227.2	1832
12 Kanagawa									191		97	1554			1842	288	228.8	1845
13 Yamanashi									962		661		3440	6	5069	1629	234.9	1894
14 Nagano									589		60			4518	5167	643	228.3	1841
Demand y_i	1863	701	1293	1776	1959	3521	3213	2587	7702	4808	2817	1554	3440	4524	41758	0		

Quantities: 1000 birds; prices: yen. Source: Shokucho Ryutsu Tokei (Statistics of Poultry Marketing), Noson Bukka Chingin Tokei (Statistics of Prices and Wages in Rural Areas), The Ministry of Agriculture and Forestry, Japan, 1966.

wholesale level. The upper and lower limits of demand elasticities are −3.246 and −2.137, respectively, which are obtained from the estimates given by Yuize [6]. The supply elasticity is taken as 0.701 that was determined for the wholesale level by Yuize and Fujiwara [7]. The analytical model constructed under different sets of regional demand and supply functions, and of particular unit transport costs is illustrated in fig. 2.

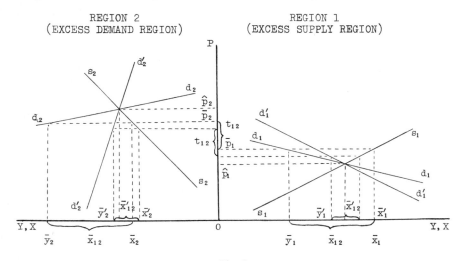

Fig. 2.

Medium-size trucks are used as a means of broiler transportation among regions. A 5-ton truck, say, is usually loaded with 1500 birds. Unit transport costs are evaluated to take into account shrinkage and loss of weight in broiler transportation, as shown in table 8.

4.4. Results and their implications

Spatial equilibria of the broiler industry are shown in table 9. Equilibrium solutions obtained for the demand elasticities of −3.246 and −2.137 are indicated in the upper and lower rows, respectively. High price regions, such as Hokkaido, Fukushima, Aomori, Iwate and Ibaragi, show a decrease in price. In addition, such low price regions as Saitama, Tochigi, Tokyo and Kanagawa indicate an increase in price. Thus, price differentials among regions have been reduced, with prices settling in the range from 1780 to 2230 yen per 10 kg. Price is relatively higher in the Hokkaido and Tohoku districts, and is lower in the Tosan district and in certain regions in the Kanto district.

Table 8

Units transport costs among regions, 1966 (t_{ij}). Yen per bird of broiler

Region i \ Region j	1	2	3	4	5	6	7	8	9	10	11	12	13	14
1 Hokkaido (Sapporo)	0													
2 Aomori (Aomori)	29.0	0												
3 Iwate (Morioka)	40.3	14.3	0											
4 Miyagi (Sendai)	50.6	24.5	13.2	0										
5 Fukushima (Fukushima)	55.0	28.9	17.6	6.8	0									
6 Ibaragi (Mito)	64.1	38.0	26.7	16.7	13.4	0								
7 Tochigi (Utsunomiya)	63.8	37.8	26.4	16.5	12.0	8.2	0							
8 Gunma (Maebashi)	70.0	44.1	32.8	22.6	18.1	11.2	9.2	0						
9 Saitama (Omiya)	68.3	42.2	31.1	20.9	16.5	10.1	6.8	7.2	0					
10 Chiba (Chiba)	72.1	45.8	34.7	24.5	20.1	11.8	11.2	11.5	6.1	0				
11 Tokyo (Tokyo)	70.0	43.8	32.8	22.6	18.1	9.8	8.9	9.2	3.5	4.0	0			
12 Kanagawa (Yokohama)	71.6	45.5	34.2	24.2	19.8	11.2	10.7	10.9	5.4	6.1	3.5	0		
13 Yamanashi (Kofu)	76.6	50.5	39.1	28.9	24.8	18.1	15.6	13.7	11.2	13.7	11.5	9.8	0	
14 Nagano (Matsumoto)	79.3	53.5	42.2	32.0	27.5	20.6	18.7	12.3	15.9	20.1	17.9	16.5	9.5	0

Table 9

The spatial equilibrium solutions for broilers, 1966

Origin \ Destination	1	2	3	4	5	6	7	8	9	10	11	12	13	14	Supply x_i	Net export	Bird p_i	10 kg
1 Hokkaido	1812														1812	− 289	276.9	2233
	1799														1799	− 257	274.2	2211
2 Aomori		389													389	− 305	250.9	2023
		386													386	− 326	248.2	2002
3 Iwate	289	305	1400												1994	594	236.6	1908
	257	326	1394												1977	583	233.9	1886
4 Miyagi				1441											1441	− 57	245.3	1978
				1445											1445	− 128	246.4	1987
5 Fukushima					2193										2193	− 112	240.0	1935
				7	2186										2193	7	240.0	1935
6 Ibaragi				57	112	4171					567				4907	736	228.6	1844
				121		3914			23		864				4922	1008	229.7	1852
7 Tochigi							2938		1163						4101	1163	230.0	1855
							3009		1101						4110	1101	230.7	1860
8 Gunma								2616	317						2933	317	230.0	1855
								2598	338						2936	338	230.3	1857
9 Saitama									3462						3462	−2610	236.8	1910
									3469						3469	−3104	237.5	1915
10 Chiba										5120					5120	0	237.5	1915
										5093					5093	0	235.6	1900
11 Tokyo											1187				1187	−1179	238.4	1923
											1191				1191	−1298	239.5	1931
12 Kanagawa											458	1419			1877	458	234.9	1894
											434	1449			1883	434	236.0	1903
13 Yamanashi									752				4105		4857	752	220.9	1781
									1014				3855		4869	1014	221.6	1787
14 Nagano									378		154			4613	5145	532	226.9	1830
									628					4535	5163	628	228.0	1839
Demand y_i	2101	694	1400	1498	2305	4171	2938	2616	6072	5120	2366	1419	4105	4613	41418	0		
	2056	712	1394	1573	2186	3914	3009	2598	6573	5093	2489	1449	3855	4535	41436	0		

Quantities: 1000 birds; prices: yen. The upper and lower figures indicate the equilibrium solution in the case that demand elasticity is taken as −3.246 and −2.137, respectively.

Demand increases in Hokkaido by 10 to 13 %, and in Tohoku by 2 to 3 % with a fall in price. It also increases in the low price regions, Tosan, by 5 to 9 % with a further decline in price. Demand decreases by 4 to 6 % in other low price regions, Kanto, where price goes up slightly. Supply decreases in Hokkaido, Tohoku and Tosan by small percentages, 3 %, 1 %, and 2 %, respectively. It increases in Kanto by less than 1 %. Both production and processing of broilers are still highly concentrated in Kanto and Tosan, extending to the surrounding districts, Tohoku and Hokkaido.

Interregional shipments are substantially reduced, reflecting a marked decline in the number of effective transport routes. Most of the interregional transport routes lead to Saitama and Tokyo. A shipment is suggested from Iwate to Hokkaido, but it seems difficult for technical reasons. In that case, production should be increased in Hokkaido. Several unstable results for interregional shipments should in practical terms be interpreted in conjuction with other factors affecting regional demands.

4.5. *Possible extensions of the analysis*

Sensitivity analysis would be of great use in the case of the lack of accurate data. It can also be adopted in the comparative static analysis. The model would need to include the situation of imperfect competition, because the broiler industry is inclined to be rather imperfectly competitive. As longer hauls of live broilers are becoming less, the size of market area covered by the model should be properly determined.

5. Concluding remarks

The primary purpose of these analyses is to determine competitive equilibrium prices as well as optimum production, shipments and consumption for three farm products in various regions of Eastern Japan. In each analysis, price differentials now existing among regions are notably reduced by adjusting regional production and consumption, and interregional shipments. The Takayama and Judge models may likewise be applied to many other farm products such as beef cattle, eggs and crops. Since such farm products as milk, hogs and broilers undergo constant changes in technological and/or institutional conditions, more accurate and detailed data are required to attempt a spatial equilibrium analysis in multi-periods.

References

[1] Sasaki, K., 1969, Higashi-Nihon no Seinyushijo ni Kansuru Chiikikan Kinko (Spatial Equilibrium in Eastern Japan's Milk Market), Nogyo Keizai Kenkyu (Journal of Rural Economics) 41, 106–116.

[2] Sasaki, K., 1970, Higashi-Nihon Yoton no Chiikikan Kinko (Spatial Equilibrium in Eastern Japan's Pork Industry), Nogyo Keizai Kenkyu 42, 11–19.

[3] Sasaki, K., 1971, Buroira Yokei no Chiikikan Kinko (Spatial Equilibrium of the Broiler Industry), Nogyo Keizai Kenkyu 43, 25–32.

[4] Takayama, T. and G. G. Judge, 1964, Spatial equilibrium and quadratic programming, Journal of Farm Economics 46, 67–93.

[5] Takayama, T. and G. G. Judge, 1964, Equilibrium among spatially separated markets: a reformulation, Econometrica 32, 510–524.

[6] Yuize, Y., 1963, Demand for livestock and dairy products in the market survey, Nogyo Sogo Kenkyu (Quarterly Journal of Agricultural Economy) 17, 65–113.

[7] Yuize, Y. and T. Fujiwara, 1968, Short-term econometric model of livestock economy, Nogyo Sogo Kenkyu 22, 37–98.

[8] West, D. A. and G. E. Brandow, 1964, Space-product equilibrium in the dairy industry of the Northeastern and North Central Regions, Journal of Farm Economics 46, 719–731.

[9] Wolfe, P., 1959, The Simplex method for quadratic programming, Econometrica 27, 382–398.

[10] Japan IBM, 1969, MPS Separable Programming, Tokyo.

CHAPTER 23

A positive model of spatial equilibrium with special reference to the broiler markets*

TSOUNG-CHAO LEE and STANLEY K. SEAVER

University of Connecticut

1. Introduction

Spatial equilibrium models are often formulated within the context of normative economics to show how the output at many producing regions "should" flow to many consuming areas if competitive conditions are to be attained and costs minimized. Takayama and Judge [13] derived such a spatial equilibrium quadratic programming model by maximizing the so-called "net social payoff" subject to the given or known regional linear demand and supply functions. Many researchers [7, 8, 15], when applying this model, have estimated demand and supply functions based on methods that are exogenous to the structure of spatial equilibrium. The supply function for each market often is estimated as a single regression equation not only independent of the supply functions in other markets but also independent of the demand function in the same market [15]. Or market supply functions may be estimated by the micro-to-macro build-up approach based upon the linear programming step supply functions [8]. The demand functions are usually constructed [7, 8] from Brandow's demand elasticities or slopes which were estimated in 1961 [1].

However, if one is to produce quantitative statements 'describing' the existing competitive markets and predict the future course of economic variables, a positive model of spatial equilibrium is required. From the positive economics point of view, a spatial equilibrium model is a competitive economic model in which the economic system may be described

* Scientific Contribution No. 512, Storrs (Connecticut) Agricultural Experiment Station, University of Connecticut. This paper is a revision of two previous publications by the authors [10, 11], including 3 SLS and dynamic recursive results which are not published elsewhere.

by a set of simultaneous equations including the aggregate demand for each good by consumers for each market, the aggregate supply of each good by producers for each market, the distribution activities over space, and equilibrium conditions. It is assumed that in each market each consumer acts to maximize his utility, each producer acts to maximize his profit, and perfect competition prevails. In empirical study, one must estimate demand and supply functions within the framework of the spatial equilibrium model[1] in order to achieve consistency and efficiency in estimation. In other words, within the context of econometrics, equilibrium conditions and definitional equations place a restriction on the parameters that are being estimated.

In contrast to the normative spatial equilibrium model, the positive model permits the statistical testing of economic hypotheses. Here the hypothesis refers to a single coefficient of regional demand or supply functions. For many applications we are interested in the reduced form rather than the structural form of the model. The reduced form coefficients of the positive model permit one to study the multiplier effect of a predetermined variable on the jointly determined variables of spatial equilibrium. In the presence of lagged endogenous variables, one may also study the delay multipliers, cumulated multipliers and equilibrium multipliers from the 'final form' of the dynamic model. Other inherent dynamic properties concerning fluctuation and stability of the dynamic system may be studied.

A general simultaneous-equation model of spatial equilibrium will now be presented followed by a specific model of spatial equilibrium with some variations. Emphasis will be placed on the structural change of broiler markets in the aggregate and upon regional interrelationships. There is no intention of studying the broiler industry at the producing or retail firm level.

2. The simultaneous-equation model of spatial equilibrium

Assuming n spatially separated markets or regions, and a single commodity, we hypothesize the linear supply function in the ith region as

$$S_i = \beta_i p_i + b_{i0} z_0 + b_{i1} z_1 + \ldots + b_{ik} z_k + v_i \tag{1}$$

[1] "A most dangerous procedure in estimating parameters in systems of stochastic equations is to fit each equation separately without regard to the fact that the variables involved are, usually, assumed to satisfy, simultaneously, a number of other stochastic relations." [6].

and the linear demand function in the jth region as

$$D_j = \alpha_j p_j + a_{j0} z_0 + a_{j1} z_1 + \ldots + a_{jk} z_k + u_j \qquad (2)$$

where p_i and p_j are prices and z's are the predetermined variables such as income and factor input prices, and u_j and v_i are stochastic variables which may be assumed to have zero means, constant variances over time, and zero autocorrelations, but may not be independent of price. The parameters to be estimated are α_j, β_i, a's and b's. Of course, some of the parameters may be assigned a priori value of zero. There are n supply and n demand equations.

Since spatial equilibrium models consider the interregional flow of commodities, supply of the ith region will be distributed among n regions such that

$$S_i = \sum_{j=1}^{n} x_{ij} \qquad j = 1, 2, \ldots, n \qquad (3)$$

and demand in the jth region will be fulfilled by shipping from n supply regions such that

$$D_j = \sum_{i=1}^{n} x_{ij} \qquad i = 1, 2, \ldots, n \qquad (4)$$

where x_{ij} denotes quantity shipped from ith region to the jth region. There are n equations for each type (3) and (4). A static analysis reveals that before reaching equilibrium, commodity flow is considered possible whenever the price differential in any pair of regions exceeds the transportation costs t_{ij}. Thus, whether the product in the ith region should be sold in the jth region depends on the following per unit loss (or per unit gain):

$$r_{ij} = t_{ij} - (p_j - p_i) \qquad \text{all } i, j. \qquad (5)$$

There are n^2 such definitional equations. Since in the same region the transportation cost is assumed zero, only $n(n-1)$ equations are required to determine $n(n-1)$ interregional flows of commodities.

In a static analysis, the process of restoring equilibrium after an impulse of exogenous changes is that the existence of a profit $(r_{ij} < 0)$ will continue to induce the flow of commodity $(x_{ij} > 0)$ until the changing price structure eliminates profit $(r_{ij} = 0)$. For a pair of regions where the price differential is less than the transportation cost, the non-existence of profit $(r_{ij} > 0)$ will induce no shipment $(x_{ij} = 0)$. Thus for a competitive equilibrium to hold, there must be no profit $(r_{ij} = 0)$ or there must be no flow of commodities $(x_{ij} = 0)$.[2] There are $n(n-1)$ equilibrium conditions.[3]

$$r_{ij} x_{ij} = 0 \qquad \text{for } i \neq j. \tag{6}$$

In total there are $2n+2n^2$ equations with the same number of jointly dependent variables, which specify a complete system of equations.[4]

The model as specified is for a single product but it may be generated into a multi-product case of general equilibrium. Supply and demand functions may be formulated as functions of many commodity prices and some predetermined variables. In estimation, one may use the restricted least-squares to account for Slustky's symmetric or reciprocal integrability conditions in demand functions [4].

In summary, the spatial equilibrium model involves equations for demand and supply (1) and (2), commodity distributions (3) and (4), and equilibrium conditions (6), in which the loss variable (or profit margin) is defined in (5).

3. Identification and estimation of spatial equilibrium model

A necessary condition for the identification of a structural equation is that the number of predetermined variables appearing in the model but outside of the structural equation (K^{**}) be equal to, or greater than, the number of endogenous variables in the structural equation (G^*) minus 1,

---

[2] These two assertions are equivalent to the Kuhn–Tucker conditions of the quadratic programming formulation of spatial equilibrium. See [13].

[3] In practice, because of the error in measurement and imperfect competition, the sample data do not necessarily fulfil this condition, especially in the supply-demand adjustment over space for short periods of time. If we adopt this assumption, we may redefine the per unit loss as

$$r_{ij}^* = (t_{ij}+c_{ij})-(p_j-p_i)+d_{ij} \tag{5a}$$

where c_{ij} denotes opportunity cost defined as the possible profit that the producers would earn if they engaged in other economic activities with the same effort as shipping one unit of the commodity from i to j, and d_{ij} is the possible error in measuring prices. Thus, c_{ij} is due to imperfect competition and d_{ij} to errors of observation which may have zero expectation. The equilibrium condition is then

$$r_{ij}^* x_{ij} = 0. \tag{6a}$$

[4] An augmented model may contain n^2 equations for each set of (5) and (6) including r_{ij}'s, and the demand price p_i may be different from supply price (say p^i). Thus there will be $4n+2n^2$ equations and $4n+2n^2$ variables, and the system is still complete. An abbreviated model may be obtained if eq. (3) and (4) are substituted into eq. (1) and (2). In this case, there will be only $2n^2$ equations and $2n^2$ variables, and the model is still complete. See table 1.

i.e., $K^{**} \geq G^* - 1$. For each equation of (1) or (2) $G^* = 2$, and K^{**} is at least equal to the number of t_{ij}, i.e., $n(n-1)$. Thus $n(n-1) \geq 1$ always holds for $n > 2$. In practice, some of the predetermined variables (z's) may not appear in both demand and supply equations a priori, and the equation will be, in most situations, over-identified (even for the case $n = 1$).

To obtain consistent estimates of the parameters of regional demand and supply that are identifiable in a system of equations, the simultaneous estimation approach should be used. If the system of equations is large, with many markets or products involved, and if available time series data are rather short,[5] principal components of predetermined variables may be used as instrumental variables. For this approach, see Kloek and Mennes [9]. In the following application to broiler markets, the two-stage least-squares (2SLS) and the three-stage least-squares (3SLS) estimators are used.

4. Spatial equilibrium and comparative static analysis

To solve for the reduced form equations, the model may be simplified by equating eqs. (1) and (3), and (2) and (4) to reduce the number of variables and equations to obtain

$$\sum_{j=1}^{n} X_{ij} - \alpha_i p_i = \sum_{m=0}^{k} a_{im} z_m + u_i \qquad \text{all } i \qquad (7)$$

and

$$\sum_{i=1}^{n} X_{ij} - \beta_j p_j = \sum_{m=0}^{k} b_{jm} z_m + v_j \qquad \text{all } j. \qquad (8)$$

Then, eqs. (7) and (8) together with eq. (5) may be expressed by compact matrix notations as

$$\begin{bmatrix} 0 & H & I \\ G & B & 0 \end{bmatrix} \begin{bmatrix} X \\ P \\ R \end{bmatrix} = \begin{bmatrix} T \\ \Gamma Z \end{bmatrix} + \begin{bmatrix} 0 \\ U \end{bmatrix} \qquad (9)$$

and the whole set of eq. (6) may be equivalently expressed as

$$R'X_0 = 0 \qquad (10)$$

---

[5] Difficulties will arise since the estimation method used requires estimates of the moments of reduced form disturbances. The reduced form equation estimation requires that price be regressed on all predetermined variables including all transportation costs. With a large number of regions, multicollinearity may be encountered because of transportation costs.

under the nonnegative conditions

$$X, R, P \geqq 0 \tag{11}$$

where

$$X = (X_0' : X_{00}')'$$
$$= (x_{12} x_{13} \ldots x_{1n} x_{21} x_{23} \ldots x_{2n} \ldots x_{nn-1} : x_{11} x_{22} \ldots x_{nn})'; n \times n$$
$$R = (r_{12} r_{13} \ldots r_{1n} r_{21} r_{23} \ldots r_{2n} \ldots r_{nn-1})'; n(n-1) \times 1$$
$$T = (t_{12} t_{13} \ldots t_{1n} t_{21} t_{23} \ldots t_{2n} \ldots t_{nn-1})'; n(n-1) \times 1$$
$$P = (p_1 p_2 \ldots p_n)'; n \times 1$$
$$Z = (z_1 z_2 \ldots z_k)'; k \times 1$$
$$U = (u_1 u_2 \ldots u_n v_1 v_2 \ldots v_n)'; 2n \times 1$$

B is a $(2n \times n)$ matrix with elements, slopes of demand and supply equations; Γ is a $(2n \times k)$ matrix of the coefficients of predetermined variables a's and b's; G is a $(2n \times n^2)$ matrix with elements 0's and 1's permuting for the distribution of commodities; H is a $(n(n-1) \times n)$ matrix of 0's, 1's and (-1)'s permuting for price differentials; and I is a $(n(n-1) \times n(n-1))$ identity matrix.

The procedure for obtaining a solution when equations have been simultaneously estimated and the predetermined variable z's are given is first to assign $n(n-1)$ variables out of $n(n-1)$ r_{ij}'s and $n(n-1)$ x_{ij}'s with value zero. Next eliminate variables assigned zero from eq. (9) and solve the system for remaining $n + n^2$ variables. Not all $2^{n(n-1)}$ solutions will fulfill the restraints (11), and only the one which satisfis (11) will be chosen.

In practice, the Gauss elimination or pivoting method may be used for solving simultaneous linear equations. Nonnegative restraints are imposed and controlled by choosing the smallest nonnegative pivot ratio as if solving a linear programming problem. Condition (10) will be controlled by watching the counterparts r_{ij} and x_{ij} so that both do not have positive solutions. In simplex algorithm terminology, if r_{ij} is in the basis, do not introduce x_{ij} and vice versa. Thus, the procedure is equivalent to Wolf's quadratic programming algorithm [16], which was also adopted by Takayama and Judge [13]. Thus solving the second degree simultaneous eqs. (1) through (6) is equivalent to solving Takayama and Judge's quadratic spatial equilibrium problem.[6]

---

[6] The exactly identical Takayama–Judge simplex tableau may be obtained if demand and supply prices are independently defined. In this formulation we prefer to have the simplex tableau written in the most compact form and yet contain the necessary information.

When the equilibrium solution is obtained, those variables taking value zero from (10) may be deleted and the set of reduced form equations obtained. If we let asterisks denote the submatrix after the deletion of such $n(n-1)$ variables and the corresponding $n(n-1)$ column of coefficients, then the structural equations associated with an equilibrium solution may be written as

$$\begin{bmatrix} 0 & H & I_* \\ G_* & B & 0 \end{bmatrix} \begin{bmatrix} X_* \\ P \\ R_* \end{bmatrix} = \begin{bmatrix} T \\ \Gamma Z \end{bmatrix} + \begin{bmatrix} 0 \\ U \end{bmatrix}. \qquad (12)$$

The reduced form equations are then

$$\begin{bmatrix} X_* \\ P \\ R_* \end{bmatrix} = \begin{bmatrix} 0 & H & I_* \\ G_* & B & 0 \end{bmatrix}^{-1} \begin{bmatrix} T \\ \Gamma Z \end{bmatrix} + V, \qquad (13)$$

where V is a $((n^2+n)\times 1)$ vector of the reduced form disturbances. Eq. (13) is known only when directions of commodity flows are known, that is, those x_{ij}'s which are zero are known and may be deleted. However, the precise quantity of flow is not necessarily known. Direction of flow is primarily determined by the magnitude of exogenous variables T and Z. Although the quantity of shipment may be different, the direction of shipment may remain unchanged when the exogenous variable falls within certain ranges. This comparative static analysis takes account of the interdependence among regional demand, supply, shipment and prices.

5. Spatial equilibria and dynamic analysis

If the change in z_i or t_{ij} is not infinitesimally small, the direction of commodity flow may change and a new equilibrium must be relocated to determine the flow pattern and the associated new set of reduced form equations.

When the predetermined variables include lagged endogenous variables, the model is dynamic. We may be interested in how the time path of the exogenous variables generates the time path of the endogenous variables. Due to the bilinear equilibrium conditions of the spatial problem, the dynamic model will have special inherent dynamic properties. For each distribution pattern, there is a corresponding reduced form and hence a corresponding 'final form'[7] associated with it. Each 'final form' has its own inherent dynamic properties such as impact and time delayed multipliers.

A set of reduced form equations may be written in the compact matrix notations as

$$y_t = Ay_{t-1} + Bz_t + w_t, \tag{14}$$

where y_t denotes the vector of current endogenous variables, y_{t-1} the vector of lagged endogenous variables, z_t is the vector of predetermined variables, w_t is the vector of disturbances, and A and B are reduced form parameter matrices. The necessary condition for the dynamic system to be stable is that the matrix A^t approaches a null matrix as t increases [5, pp. 376–378]. The matrix A^t will approach a null matrix if the nonzero real latent roots of the matrix A are all less than unity in absolute value. For each pair of conjugate complex roots $a(\cos b \pm i \sin b)$, the real constant a also must be less than unity in absolute value, so that the amplitude a^t of a cycle with a period of $2\pi/b$ will diminish.

The spatial equilibrium is not 'globally stable' since the distribution pattern may change if predetermined variables change in large magnitude. Thus to understand dynamic stability, each of the A matrices relating to different reduced forms should be studied. The time path of an endogenous variable may jump from one distribution pattern to another, where the amplitude of fluctuation is different from that of another distribution pattern.

In the real economy, the exogenous variables will not usually hold constant. The usefulness of a dynamic analysis is to gain insight into the inherent dynamic properties without intervention of exogenous forces.

6. Empirical analysis for broilers

6.1. A model for broilers

Broiler markets, in our analysis, are considered spatially competitive. Broiler production in the southern states has been increasing tremendously since 1957, while the northeast region has changed from a surplus to a deficit area. It is believed that the change is associated with decreasing farm price of broilers and increasing feed price in the northeastern states

---

[7] The 'final form' or 'final equation', or 'separated form' is the transformed reduced form equation in which each endogenous variable appears in a difference equation without any current or lagged values of other endogenous variables [2, p. 180].

relative to that of the southern states. In view of these changes of the broiler economy, the objective is to analyze the effect of a change in feed price in each region on (1) broiler production, (2) price of broilers, (3) shipment of broilers among regions, and (4) derived demand for feed.

Alternative relationships among variables were formulated to estimate supply functions of broilers in the Northeast, the South, and the rest of the United States.[8] In most cases, estimated price coefficients are negative and not significantly different from zero. At the national level, it has been shown that change of broiler supply from the preceding year is positively related to lagged profitability [14, p. 10]. Thus, current supply of broilers is related to the preceding year's supply and profitability. If the spatial flow of broilers is also considered, lagged supply in other regions may also affect current regional supply. In the final analysis, therefore, regional supply is hypothesized as a function of lagged national supply Q_{t-1} and lagged regional profitability R_{it-1}. Hence,

$$S_{it} = b_{i0} + b_{i1} Q_{t-1} + b_{i2} R_{it-1} + v_{it} \qquad (15)$$

where v_{it} is the disturbance term. Lagged regional profitability in this study is defined as the lagged broiler price (p_{it-1}) minus the major cost of production. The major cost is calculated as regional lagged feed price (p_{fit-1}) multiplied by lagged feed per pound of broilers (F_{it-1}).[9] In equation form, the profitability relation is

$$R_{it-1} = p_{it-1} - F_{it-1} p_{fit-1}. \qquad (16)$$

It implies that producers will respond to profitability but are indifferent as to whether the increase in profitability is due to an increase in broiler price or decrease in feed price, or improvement in technology.

On the demand side, aggregate quantity demanded in each region is postulated as a linear function of current broiler price p_{it} and current total

[8] The northeast region consists of New England, Mid-Atlantic states, and Virginia. The southern region includes North Carolina, South Carolina, Georgia, Florida, Alabama, Mississippi, Louisiana, and Arkansas. Hereafter, the North will be region one; the South, two; and the rest of the United States, three.

[9] The cost analysis would be in detail if other costs were included such as chick costs, medication and grower payments. However, from the regional cost advantage point of view, only relative profitability between regions is necessary. Hence, only feed costs are included in the regional profitability function. Other components of total costs vary between regions in almost the same manner as do feed costs. Feed costs represent over 60% of the total cost of a finished bird and are approximately 60% of total costs even after adjusting feed prices for integrated operations.

national disposable income y_t:

$$D_{it} = a_{i0} + a_{i1} p_{it} + a_{i2} y_t + u_{it} \tag{17}$$

where u_{it} is the disturbance term.[10]

The definitional equations include 6 equations of the decomposition of supply and demand into shipments (3) and (4) and 6 equations of the per unit loss (5). The 6 equilibrium conditions are defined to be of type (6). Thus there are in total 18 equations in which 12 equations are linear and 6 equations are bilinear. The simplex tableau for the three-market model is given by table 1.

Table 1

The spatial simplex tableau for the three-market model

	Basis	B_0	1	2	3	4	5	6	7	8	9	10	11	12	13	14	15	16	17	18
			X_{12}	X_{13}	X_{21}	X_{23}	X_{31}	X_{32}	X_{11}	X_{22}	X_{33}	p_1	p_2	p_3	r_{12}	r_{13}	r_{21}	r_{23}	r_{31}	r_{32}
1	13	t_{12}										-1	1		1					
2	14	t_{13}										-1		1		1				
3	15	t_{21}										1	-1				1			
4	16	t_{23}											-1	1				1		
5	17	t_{31}										1		-1					1	
6	18	t_{32}											1	-1						1
7	0	$D_1(z)$			1		1		1			$-\alpha_1$								
8	0	$D_2(z)$	1					1		1			$-\alpha_2$							
9	0	$D_3(z)$		1		1					1			$-\alpha_3$						
10	0	$S_1(z)$	1	1					1			$-\beta_1$								
11	0	$S_2(z)$			1	1				1			$-\beta_2$							
12	0	$S_3(z)$					1	1			1			$-\beta_3$						
13			$x_{ij} = 0$ if $r_{ij} > 0$						$x_{ii} \geqq 0$			$p_i \geqq 0$			$r_{ij} = 0$ if $x_{ij} > 0$					
18																				

[10] Regional disposable income was used in the initial analysis and then deleted in the final analysis because (1) regional disposable income is highly correlated with national disposable income, and (2) if the regional disposable income is used, the reduced form equations suffer from multicollinearity and are very expensive in terms of degrees of freedom.

6.2. The estimated structural equations

Although current regional broiler prices are in fact not used in explaining supply, they are simultaneously determined by the regional demand, shipments, and predetermined quantity of supply in each region. That is, the broiler price that fulfils the demand equation should also fulfil per unit loss eq. (5) which in turn will be considered in the equilibrium condition (6).

Both two-stages least-squares (2SLS) and three-stage least-squares (3SLS) are used in estimating the parameters. In the first stage the regional broiler farm prices are regressed on all the predetermined variables including lagged regional profitabilities, transportation costs of broilers among three regions, lagged national broiler production, and national disposable income to obtain a set of reduced form equations. This is done in order to obtain the 'calculated value' of regional farm prices. The 'calculated' prices are then used in the second stage as regressors,[11] combining other predetermined variables to estimate regional demand and supply functions. The results are given in table 2. The figures in parentheses are standard errors of the coefficients. The *t*-value for the statistical significance tests may be calculated by dividing the estimated coefficient by the standard error. The results show that lagged quantity as well as profitability are very significant variables in explaining current supply at the one percent significance level. In the demand equations, the variables are highly associated; coefficients are significant; and signs are compatible with theory.

The 2SLS is limited since it only considers the excluded predetermined variables but does not make use of the excluded dependent variables such as prices in other regions and shipments among regions. Therefore, the 3SLS method is employed because it consistently and simultaneously estimates the parameters of all structural equations. The results of 2SLS estimation are used in the third stage where the residual covariances of all equations are estimated and inverted to serve as a weight matrix in simultaneous estimation of all structural equations. The empirical results are also given in table 2. It should be noted that the standard errors of coefficients of 3SLS are smaller than those of 2SLS, although the slope coefficients are relatively larger and constant intercepts are smaller. The 3SLS estimates are more significant than 2SLS estimates.

[11] The terms regressand and regressors are used instead of conventional dependent and independent or explanatory variables because (1) our regressors are not necessarily independent but are jointly dependent, and (2) some of the regressors in the second stage estimation are the 'calculated' value of jointly dependent variables. For the distinctions among terms, see Goldberger [5, pp. 213–215].

Table 2

Estimated regional supply and demand relations for broilers, 1956–1967, by two-stage and three-stage least-squares

Region	Supply or demand	Constant term (mil. lb)	National disposable income (bil. $)	Lagged national supply (mil. lb)	Regional farm price	Lagged regional profitability
					(cents per lb)	
		Results from the two-stage least-squares				
North	S_1	536.1950		0.1066		7.1109
		(116.5)		(0.01751)		(6.141)
South	S_2	−1436.6000		0.8879		50.7407
		(241.3)		(0.04114)		(15.08)
Rest of U.S.	S_3	523.4655		0.0909		6.1178
		(137.7)		(0.01927)		(7.104)
North	D_1	902.8352	0.00312356		−31.7407	
		(307.7)	(0.0002761)		(9.195)	
South	D_2	288.2400	0.00173915		−13.5484	
		(123.97)	(0.0001361)		(3.787)	
Rest of U.S.	D_3	1197.217	0.00623560		−44.9175	
		(686.3)	(0.0006882)		(19.29)	
		Results from the three-stage least-squares				
North	S_1	466.1		0.1151		11.65
		(106.7)		(0.0164)		(5.46)
South	S_2	−1520.0		0.8974		59.49
		(216.4)		(0.0380)		(12.75)
Rest of U.S.	S_3	471.4		0.09607		9.76
		(101.7)		(0.0153)		(4.85)
North	D_1	753.4	0.003199		−26.65	
		(197.7)	(0.000209)		(5.90)	
South	D_2	227.1	0.001778		−11.34	
		(85.68)	(0.000108)		(2.58)	
Rest of U.S.	D_3	637.9	0.006658		−28.11	
		(490.4)	(0.000538)		(13.91)	

6.3. The predicted competitive spatial equilibrium

The equilibrium solution[12] for each year is solved when all predetermined variables are given by numerical values. The solutions from the two sets

[12] Equilibrium solutions are computed merely for the purpose of forecasting, and no normative connotation is attached [12, p. 8]. Deviations of the data from equilibrium solutions are only an indication of the goodness-of-fit and not a normative critique of the competitive markets.

of structural equations (2SLS and 3SLS) are both consistent with the fact that in 1956 the northeast region was self-sufficient with essentially no receipts of broilers from the southern states. In 1957 the northeast region became a deficit area and in 1967 approximately 30 percent of the broilers consumed came from the southern states. Comparing the predicted equilibrium and actually measured prices, we find that differences are in general small for both 2SLS and 3SLS results. The equilibrium solutions for both are given in table 3.

Table 3

The equilibrium solutions for broiler markets in 1967

Predetermined variables			Jointly determined variables			
				2SLS	3SLS	Measurements
Q_{t-1}	=	6191	mil. lb	P_1 = 20.61	20.56	¢ per lb
Y_t	= 536815		bil. $	P_2 = 18.96	18.91	,,
t_{12}	=	1.65	¢ per lb	P_3 = 20.26	20.21	,,
t_{21}	=	1.65	,,	X_{11} = 1217.85	1231.81	mil. lb
t_{13}	=	1.51	,,	X_{22} = 964.98	967.09	,,
t_{31}	=	1.51	,,	X_{33} = 1114.92	1111.94	,,
t_{23}	=	1.30	,,	X_{12} = 0	0	,,
t_{32}	=	1.30	,,	X_{13} = 0	0	,,
R_{1t-1}	=	4.56	,,	X_{21} = 707.63	690.83	,,
R_{2t-1}	=	2.59	,,	X_{23} = 2519.69	2531.97	,,
R_{3t-1}	=	4.69	,,	X_{31} = 0	0	,,
				X_{32} = 0	0	,,
				γ_{12} = 3.30	3.30	¢ per lb
				γ_{13} = 1.86	1.86	,,
				γ_{31} = 1.16	1.16	,,
				γ_{32} = 2.60	2.60	,,
				γ_{21} = 0	0	,,
				γ_{23} = 0	0	,,

6.4. The direct effect of price and income on demand and partial elasticities

The conventional way of studying consumer behavior is via the price and income elasticities from demand equations. However, the slope of the demand equation only indicates a direct effect within a single sector of the economy especially when price or quantity is simultaneously determined with other sectors. Thus, elasticities computed from a single structural equation may be considered as 'partial' elasticities.

Ceteris paribus, partial price and income elasticities are evaluated at equilibrium prices and quantities.[13] The results, given in table 4, indicate that elasticities are changing from time to time because of simultaneous shifting of demand and supply. One will also note that the elasticities obtained from 3SLS are in general positively larger than those obtained

Table 4

Estimated 'partial' price and income elasticities for broilers at farm level, by regions, 1956–1967

Year	Price elasticities			Income elasticities		
	North	South	Rest of U.S.	North	South	Rest of U.S.
			Two-stage least-squares			
1956	−1.03	−0.94	−0.81	1.02	1.24	1.09
1957	−0.98	−0.82	−0.71	1.02	1.18	1.05
1958	−0.74	−0.62	−0.56	0.91	1.06	0.96
1959	−0.60	−0.49	−0.45	0.86	1.00	0.92
1960	−0.53	−0.43	−0.40	0.83	0.97	0.90
1961	−0.48	−0.39	−0.36	0.82	0.95	0.89
1962	−0.44	−0.35	−0.33	0.82	0.94	0.88
1963	−0.47	−0.38	−0.35	0.85	0.97	0.91
1964	−0.44	−0.36	−0.33	0.86	0.98	0.92
1965	−0.49	−0.39	−0.36	0.92	1.02	0.96
1966	−0.39	−0.31	−0.29	0.88	0.98	0.93
1967	−0.34	−0.27	−0.25	0.87	0.97	0.92
			Three-stage least-squares			
1956	−0.84	−0.78	−0.49	1.02	1.23	1.12
1957	−0.88	−0.73	−0.47	1.06	1.22	1.12
1958	−0.64	−0.53	−0.35	0.94	1.09	1.04
1959	−0.49	−0.40	−0.28	0.87	1.01	0.99
1960	−0.48	−0.39	−0.27	0.88	1.01	1.00
1961	−0.36	−0.29	−0.21	0.83	0.96	0.96
1962	−0.35	−0.28	−0.20	0.83	0.96	0.96
1963	−0.35	−0.28	−0.20	0.85	0.97	0.97
1964	−0.37	−0.30	−0.21	0.89	1.00	0.99
1965	−0.44	−0.35	−0.23	0.95	1.05	1.02
1966	−0.33	−0.26	−0.18	0.90	1.00	0.99
1967	−0.29	−0.22	−0.16	0.89	0.99	0.98

[13] In most empirical studies the elasticities are evaluated at the average price. Since demand and supply are shifting over time, it is more appropriate to evaluate them at equilibrium prices and quantities.

from 2SLS. This is because the slopes of the structural equations obtained from 3SLS are positively larger than those obtained from 2SLS (see table 2), while the equilibrium solutions are quite close to each other (see table 3). The 2SLS results show that price elasticities in the northeast decreased in absolute figures from 1.03 in 1956 to 0.34 in 1967. Price elasticities in the other regions follow the same pattern.[14] Income elasticities are rather stable changing from 1.02 in 1965 to 0.87 in 1967 in the Northeast. Income elasticities in the southern states are a little higher than in the north.

6.5. *Spatial equilibrium multipliers and 'total' elasticities*

To study the effect of a change in any predetermined variable (say income) on endogenous variables, after taking account of interdependencies among current endogenous variables, requires solving the set of structural equations for reduced form equations. Reduced form coefficients indicate 'total' effect and may be called 'multipliers'. Since the equilibrium solution in 1956 is different from other years in the series, the pattern of the derived reduced form equations for 1956 is different from that of other years. Our interest is in the most current situation and therefore impact multipliers are computed for the shipping pattern of the period 1957 through 1967.

Table 5 shows the equilibrium multipliers derived from 3SLS estimates of structural equations. The multipliers derived from 2SLS estimates are presented in [10, 11] and will not be repeated here. The patterns of multiplier effect for both results are similar except in magnitude. Since supply equations do not depend on current prices the model may be considered a recursive system. The figures in table 5 may be interpreted as follows: if profitability in the northeast region is increased by one cent per 1b, other predetermined variables being constant, supply in the northeast region will increase by 11.65 million pounds. However, this increase in Northeast supply will cause a decrease in supply price of 0.18 cents per pound. The increase in supply and decrease in price in the Northeast will result in a decreased shipment of broilers from the South to the North by 6.95 million pounds. However, the South will increase shipments to the rest of the nation by 4.95 million pounds and increase by 2.0 million pounds the quantity of broilers sold in the South. As a result, the South and the rest of the nation must decrease the

---

[14] The elasticities in 1956 may be compared with the average monthly elasticities for the period 1953–1963 given by Farris and Darley [4]. In making comparison, however, one should bear in mind that their elasticities were converted from flexibilities computed at mean prices and quantities for 1953–1963. In addition, all data were on a per capita basis, and estimates were obtained by single equation ordinary least-squares.

Table 5

Spatial equilibrium multipliers for broilers, 1957–1967 (the 3SLS results)

Total effect of \ On	Lagged profitability			Lagged national supply	National disposable income	Transportation costs			Constant term
	North	South	Rest of U.S.			South to North	South to rest of U.S.	North to rest of U.S.	
P_1	—0.1763	—0.9000	—0.1477	—0.0168	0.0001760	0.5967	—0.4251	0	33.3000
P_2	—0.1763	—0.9000	—0.1477	—0.0168	0.0001760	—0.4032	—0.4252	0	33.2975
P_3	—0.1763	—0.9000	—0.1477	—0.0168	0.0001760	—0.4030	0.5746	0	33.2928
X_{11}	11.6500	0	0	0.1151	0	0	0	0	466.1003
X_{21}	—6.9524	23.9876	3.9354	0.3319	—0.0014925	—15.9011	11.3287	0	—600.1453
X_{22}	1.9987	10.2063	1.6745	0.1902	—0.0002181	4.5720	4.8222	0	—150.4937
X_{23}	4.9537	25.2962	—5.6099	0.3753	0.0017105	11.3291	—16.1509	0	—769.3608
X_{33}	0	0	9.7600	0.0961	0	0	0	0	471.4004
S_1	11.6500	0	0	0.1151	0	0	0	0	466.1003
S_2	0	59.4901	0	0.8974	0	0	0	0	—1519.9998
S_3	0	0	9.7600	0.0961	0	0	0	0	471.4004
D_1	4.6976	23.9876	3.9354	0.4470	—0.0014925	—15.9011	11.3287	0	—134.0450
D_2	1.9987	10.2063	1.6745	0.1902	—0.0002181	4.5720	4.8222	0	—150.4937
D_3	4.9537	25.2962	4.1501	0.4714	0.0017105	11.3291	—16.1509	0	—297.9604

price by 0.18 cents to stimulate more consumption. The consumption will increase by 4.7, 2.0 and 5.0 million pounds for the North, the South, and the rest of the United States, respectively.

For another example look at column two of table 5. If the profitability in the South is increased by one cent with other things being constant, supply in the South will increase by 59.49 million pounds. The increased supply will be distributed over three regions. The increased consumption will be 23.99 million pounds for the North, 10.21 million pounds for the South and 25.30 million pounds for the rest of the U.S. The price for every region will decrease by 0.9 cents per pound.

'Total' elasticities, which take into account the interdependence of current endogenous variables, are evaluated at equilibrium in 1967 (table 6). The results indicate that the lagged supply and disposable income have a larger effect on prices and interregional shipments than lagged profitability and transportation costs. Note that the 'total' income elasticities are smaller than the 'partial' income elasticities.

Table 6

'Total' elasticities, 1967 (the 3SLS results)

Elasticity of	Lagged profitability			Lagged national supply	National disposable income	Transportation costs	
	North	South	Rest of U.S.			South to North	South to rest of U.S.
P_1	−0.0391	−0.1134	−0.0337	−5.0588	4.5953	0.0377	−0.0341
P_2	−0.0425	−0.1253	−0.0366	−5.5002	4.9963	−0.0277	−0.0371
P_3	−0.0398	−0.1153	−0.0343	−5.1464	4.6749	−0.0259	0.0469
X_{11}	0.0431	0	0	0.5785	0	0	0
X_{21}	−0.0459	0.0899	0.0267	2.9744	−1.1598	−0.0299	0.0268
X_{22}	0.0094	0.0273	0.0081	1.2176	−0.1211	0.0065	0.0082
X_{23}	0.0089	0.0259	−0.0104	0.9176	0.3626	0.0058	−0.0105
X_{33}	0	0	0.0412	0.5350	0	0	0
S_1	0.0431	0	0	0.5784	0	0	0
S_2	0	0.0430	0	1.3260	0	0	0
S_3	0	0	0.0412	0.5350	0	0	0
D_1	0.0135	0.0323	0.0096	1.4393	−0.4128	−0.0108	0.0097
D_2	0.0094	0.0273	0.0081	1.2176	−0.1199	0.0061	0.0082
D_3	0.0062	0.0180	0.0053	0.8009	0.2446	0.0040	−0.0073

6.6. The effect of change in feed price on broiler production and its effect on derived demand for feed

Increased profitability may result from either an increase in output price or decrease in input cost. The effect of a change in feed price on broiler production may be evaluated by

$$\frac{\partial S_{it}}{\partial p_{fit-1}} = \frac{\partial S_{it}}{\partial R_{it-1}} \cdot \frac{\partial R_{it-1}}{\partial p_{fit-1}} = -\frac{\partial S_{it}}{\partial R_{it-1}} \cdot F_{it-1}.$$

With 1967 technology, if the feed price decreased by one cent per pound, production in the Northeast will increase 40.6585 million pounds according to 3SLS estimates. Production in the South will increase 242.5204 million pounds, the rest of the U.S. will increase 34.0624 million pounds. Total increase in U.S. broiler production will be 317.2413 million pounds. The increase in feed demanded would be 141.8982, 846.3962 and 118.8778 million pounds for the North, the South, and the rest of the United States, respectively. The elasticities of supply of broilers and derived demand for feed with respect to feed price are identical: −0.17, −0.29, and −0.15 for the North, the South, and the rest of the U.S., respectively. The 2SLS estimates have smaller coefficients for the structural equations and hence the effects of a change in feed price on broiler production and derived demand for feed are also smaller [10].

6.7. The stability of the dynamic spatial equilibrium

The spatial equilibrium model presented is a dynamic recursive model. Regional supplies are functions of lagged national supply (which is equal to national demand) and lagged regional profitability, which is a function of lagged broiler price. Thus given the quantity produced, prices are determined by the demand functions and transportation costs, and generated current prices determine next year's production. The resulting cobweb model involves three markets with one commodity.

As discussed in sect. 5, in order to study the stability of a dynamic system, one needs to examine the matrix of the reduced form coefficients for lagged endogenous variables. For the empirical model, 3SLS results give such a matrix in table 7.

Table 7

The reduced form coefficients for lagged endogenous variables (derived from 3SLS estimates)

Eqs.	P_{1t-1}	P_{2t-1}	P_{3t-1}	X_{11t-1}	X_{21t-1}	X_{22t-1}	X_{23t-1}	X_{33t-1}
P_{1t}	−0.1763	−0.9000	−0.1477	−0.0168	−0.0168	−0.0168	−0.0168	−0.0168
P_{2t}	−0.1763	−0.9000	−0.1477	−0.0168	−0.0168	−0.0168	−0.0168	−0.0168
P_{3t}	−0.1763	−0.9000	−0.1477	−0.0168	−0.0168	−0.0168	−0.0168	−0.0168
X_{11t}	11.6500	0	0	0.1151	0.1151	0.1151	0.1151	0.1151
X_{21t}	−6.9524	23.9876	3.9354	0.3319	0.3319	0.3319	0.3319	0.3319
X_{22t}	1.9984	10.2063	1.6745	0.1902	0.1902	0.1902	0.1902	0.1902
X_{23t}	4.9537	25.2962	−5.6099	0.3753	0.3753	0.3753	0.3753	0.3753
X_{33t}	0	0	9.7600	0.0961	0.0961	0.0961	0.0961	0.0961

If shipments are aggregated into one national supply variable the lumped matrix (for the abbreviated system) is given by

$$
\begin{array}{c}
\quad\quad P_{1t-1} \quad\quad P_{2t-1} \quad\quad P_{3t-1} \quad\quad Q_{t-1} \\
\begin{array}{c} P_{1t} \\ P_{2t} \\ P_{3t} \\ Q_t \end{array}
\begin{bmatrix}
-0.1763 & -0.9000 & -0.1477 & -0.0168 \\
-0.1763 & -0.9000 & -0.1477 & -0.0168 \\
-0.1763 & -0.9000 & -0.1477 & -0.0168 \\
11.6500 & 59.4901 & 9.7600 & 1.1086
\end{bmatrix}
\end{array}
$$

The matrix is singular and has rank 2. The latent roots are found to be -0.0913, 0, 0, 0.2783, in which none is larger than 1 in absolute value. Thus the system is stable. If we raise the power of the matrix, it may be considered as a null matrix when the power is approximately equal to 7.

The 2SLS results also give a similar matrix of the reduced form coefficients for lagged endogenous variables. The matrix is also singular and has rank 2. The nonzero latent roots are -0.0112 and 0.3845, which are also less than one in absolute value. The matrix may be considered as a null matrix when the power is approximately equal to 10. In another model which is not reported here and in which the current regional broiler price is introduced in region 2 only, the matrix of the reduced form coefficients for lagged endogenous variables also has rank 2 with the complex latent roots: $-0.1923 \pm 0.3957 \, i$. The pair of conjugate complex roots may also be written in the following trigonometric expression: $-0.4401(\cos 5.1656 \pm i \sin 5.1656)$. Thus the complex roots introduce a sinusoidal component with period 1.2 years $(2\pi/5.1656)$ and amplitude $(-0.4401)^t$ into the time path of the endogenous variable.

Table 8

Recursive solutions for broilers with all predetermined variables held constant

Year	P_1	P_2	P_3	X_{11}	X_{21}	X_{22}	X_{23}	X_{33}	Q_t
				The 2SLS Results					
1967	20.61	18.96	20.26	1217.85	707.63	964.98	2519.69	1114.92	6525.06
1968	17.26	15.61	16.91	1250.75	780.95	1010.32	2649.66	1135.27	6826.96
1969	16.01	14.36	15.66	1259.14	812.32	1027.29	2698.94	1142.24	6939.91
1970	15.54	13.89	15.19	1262.27	824.05	1033.64	2717.38	1144.84	6982.18
1971	15.37	13.72	15.02	1263.45	828.44	1036.01	2724.28	1145.82	6998.00
1972	15.30	13.65	14.95	1263.89	830.08	1036.90	2726.86	1146.19	7003.91
1973	15.28	13.63	14.93	1264.05	830.70	1037.23	2727.83	1146.32	7006.13
1974	15.27	13.62	14.92	1264.11	831.93	1037.36	2728.19	1146.37	7006.96
1975	15.26	13.61	14.91	1264.14	831.02	1037.40	2728.32	1146.39	7007.27
1976	15.26	13.61	14.91	1264.14	831.05	1037.42	2728.37	1146.40	7007.38
				The 3SLS Results					
1967	20.59	18.94	20.24	1231.81	690.24	966.82	2531.04	1112.13	6532.04
1968	16.29	14.64	15.94	1248.78	787.77	1015.55	2635.24	1128.71	6816.04
1969	16.79	15.14	16.44	1231.41	791.93	1009.93	2635.95	1114.06	6783.28
1970	16.72	15.08	16.38	1233.42	791.45	1010.57	2635.87	1115.75	6783.05
1971	16.73	15.08	16.38	1233.19	791.51	1010.50	2635.88	1115.56	6786.63
1972	16.73	15.08	16.38	1233.21	791.50	1010.50	2635.88	1115.58	6786.68
1973	16.73	15.08	16.38	1233.21	791.50	1010.51	2635.88	1115.58	6786.67
1974	16.73	15.08	16.38	1233.21	791.50	1010.51	2635.88	1115.58	6786.67

An alternative way to determine the stability of the system is to recursively compute successive equilibria by holding other predetermined variables constant. This may be accomplished by recursive quadratic programming iterations. The results, which are given in table 8, agree with the implication of latent roots that the dynamic system converges in approximately 7 to 10 years. For 2SLS results, the dynamic equilibrium prices are 15.26 ε, 13.61 ε and 14.91 ε for the North, the South and the rest of the U.S., respectively. For 3SLS results, the dynamic equilibrium prices are 16.73 ε, 15.08 ε and 16.38 ε, respectively for the North, the South and the rest of the U.S. The results of 3SLS seem to converge faster than 2SLS. This is due to the fact that the structural parameters in 3SLS are positively larger than those of 2SLS. In other words, supply functions have a larger response with respect to lagged profitability in 3SLS results than in 2SLS results. On the other hand, the demand functions are less responsive with respect to price in 3SLS. In any case, the models show that broiler markets are stable as a whole. In the actual markets, demand functions are shifting upward and therefore the actual prices for broilers will be higher than 15 ε.

7. Summary and conclusions

Spatially competitive markets may be positively analyzed. Accepting a certain level of statistical significance, the simultaneously estimated demand and supply functions along with equilibrium conditions describe how interregional competition has developed and therefore provides a basis for forecasting, assuming past structure prevails in the future. In addition, the model provides equilibrium multipliers which answer questions arising from comparative static analysis.

The estimated demand functions for broiler markets are compatible with consumer behavior. Income slowly stimulates consumption in each region. Supply is largely predetermined by the previous year's production with an insignificant amount of adjustment to the previous year's profitability.

The simultaneous shifting of demand and supply has a tendency to decrease equilibrium prices and increase broiler production. In 1967 interregional shipment of broilers equalized farm prices at approximately 19 cents per pound of ready-to-cook broilers in the South, with prices in other regions higher by transportation costs.

Spatial equilibrium multipliers indicate that an increase in consumer income will increase broiler prices. If lagged profitability increases, broiler prices will also increase. The negative effects of the lagged national supply on prices have important implications for broiler supply control.

The forecasted equilibrium solutions from both 2SLS and 3SLS are quite close to the observed values despite the fact that the study is highly aggregated over time and space and does not take into account seasonality and normative aspects of the production process. However, it does give a positive picture of the existing and changing structure of interregional competition in broilers.

References

[1] Brandow, G. E., 1961, Interrelations among demands for farm products and implications for control of market supply, Pennsylvania Agr. Exp. Sta. Bul. 680.

[2] Christ, C. F., 1966, Econometric Models and Methods, New York: John Wiley and Sons, Inc.

[3] Court, R. H., 1967, Utility maximization and the demand for New Zealand meats, Econometrica, 35, 424–446.

[4] Farris, P. L. and R. D. Darley, 1964, Monthly price-quantity relations for broilers at the farm level, Journal of Farm Economics, 46, 849–856.

[5] Goldberger, A. S., 1964, Econometric Theory, New York: John Wiley and Sons, Inc.

[6] Haavelmo, T., 1943, The statistical implications of a system of simultaneous equations, Econometrica, 11, 1–12.

[7] Hall, H. H., E. O. Heady and Y. Plessner, 1968, Quadratic programming solution of competitive equilibrium for U.S. agriculture, American Journal of Agricultural Economics, 50, 536–555.

[8] Hsiao, J. C. and M. W. Kottke, 1968, Spatial equilibrium analysis of the dairy industry in the northeast region, an application of quadratic programming, Connecticut (Storrs) Agr. Exp. Sta. Bul. 405.

[9] Kloek, T. and L. B. M. Mennes, 1960, Simultaneous equations estimation based on principal components of predetermined variables, Econometrica, 28, 45–61.

[10] Lee, T. C. and S. K. Seaver, 1971, A simultaneous-equation model of spatial equilibrium and its application to the broiler markets, American Journal of Agricultural Economics, 53, 63–70.

[11] Lee, T. C. and S. K. Seaver, 1972, A positive spatial equilibrium model of broiler markets: a simultaneous equation approach, Connecticut (Storrs) Agr. Exp. Sta. Bul. 417.

[12] Samuelson, P. A., 1947, Foundations of Economic Analysis, Cambridge: Harvard University Press.

[13] Takayama, T. and G. G. Judge, 1964, Spatial equilibrium and quadratic programming, Journal of Farm Economics, 46, 67–93.

[14] U. S. Department of Agriculture, 1969, Poultry and Egg Situation, ERS, PES-255.

[15] West, D. A. and G. E. Brandow, 1964, Space-product equilibrium in the dairy industry of the northeastern and north central regions, Journal of Farm Economics, 46, 719–731.

[16] Wolfe, P., 1959, The simplex method for quadratic programming, Econometrica, 27, 382–398.

CHAPTER 24

A spatial analysis of EEC trade policies in the market for winter oranges [1]

PINHAS ZUSMAN, ABRAHAM MELAMED and ITZHAK KATZIR

Hebrew University of Jerusalem

1. Introduction

The evolving agricultural trade policy of the European Community (EEC) aims at stabilizing, at high levels, the internal prices of farm products. In this endeavor, there is an increasing reliance on various measures designed to maintain certain 'minimum import prices'.

One such mechanism has been recently applied to imports of fruits and vegetables. A system of 'countervailing charges' or 'compensatory levies', based on a set of 'reference prices', has supplemented the high tariffs already applicable to imports of fruits and vegetables.

The essential feature of this mechanism, which was first envisaged as a short-run stabilization device, is the imposition of countervailing charges as automatic regulator whenever import prices fall below the predetermined reference prices. The system applies at present, with various degrees of effectiveness, to most fruits and vegetables.

The objectives of the present study are to examine the operation and effects of the combined application of high-import duties and a mechanism of reference prices on the market for winter oranges. The analyzed system is complex: There are several exporting and importing regions and two varietal groups of oranges; the incorporation of the reference price mechanism introduces additional complexities which render accepted solution procedures ineffective. It was, therefore, necessary to develop alternative methodological approaches to the analysis of the equilibrium of international trade.[2] Because two varietal groups of oranges were distinguished

---

[1] Based on a study [19] submitted for publication April 11, 1969.

[2] The solution procedure employed in the present analysis is a multiproduct variant of Tramel and Seale's "reactive programming" technique [15].

and one of the study's objectives was to evaluate the welfare implications of the possible EEC policies, it was also necessary to construct the analytical tools that would provide some measures of the changes in the welfare of the trading parties, following the adoption of the various EEC policies. It is believed that, in addition to the specific findings, there is some interest in the method of analysis since it is applicable to trade problems in general and, in particular, to problems involving variable import levies and similar policy measures.

The welfare and trade effects of the EEC tariff policy were studied extensively by Dean and Collins [2, 3]. However, because (until 1965) "the reference prices established . . . have been well below levels at which fresh oranges have been imported into the EEC", [3, p. 24] the operation and effects of the reference price mechanism were disregarded in Dean and Collins' study. Since 1965, levels of orange reference prices have been raised, and the system has become a matter of great concern to exporting countries. It is not unlikely that a policy instrument first designed to prevent temporary disturbances of the market may develop into a principal protective device. In this study we shall, therefore attempt to determine the levels at which reference prices become effective and to evaluate their consequences.

2. The European market for fresh winter oranges

The international market for oranges and tangerines was described by Dean and Collins [2, 3]. The main features of the European market for winter oranges — those marketed during November through May — are presented in table 1.

Except for Lebanon, Turkey, and Egypt, Mediterranean countries deliver a negligible fraction of their total orange exports to non-European markets. Furthermore, winter oranges are imported to Europe almost exclusively from Mediterranean producers. The European-Mediterranean market thus constitutes an almost closed system with rather weak links with the rest of the world.

The crucial importance of the EEC trade policy derives from the fact that imports to its member countries constituted in 1963–64 approximately 65 % of total imports of fresh oranges to European countries.

Eastern Europe, including Yugoslavia, was a relatively small market in 1963–64. However, it is a fast-growing market and may soon become one of the major outlets for Mediterranean exporters. Imports to East European countries are, however, mostly determined by governmental policies and not by the interplay of free-market forces.

Table 1

Exports, imports, and shipments of fresh winter oranges, 1963–64

Exporters	France	West Germany	The Nether lands	Belgium- Luxem- bourg	United Kingdom	Scandi- navia	Switzerland and Austria	East Europe	Non- European countries	Total exports
				(1000 metric tons)						
Italy	*	50		3	1	21	58	11		144
Greece		3					3	40		46
Spain	271	396	105	85	126	91	69	37	1	1.181
Algeria	121	9			7			12		149
Morocco	177	102	44	2	18	6		55	8	412
Tunisia	22					1		1		24
Israel	6	66	24	18	124	83	14	13	18	366
Cyprus		2	2		22		1	16	7	50
Lebanon								14	79	93
Turkey		1					2	6	2	11
Egypt		1						1	3	5
United States [1]	3		17	9		5				34
Total imports	600	630	192	117	298	207	147	206	118	2.515

* Blanks indicate no exports.

[1] Only exports to European countries are listed. Source: (19).

The shipment pattern is a function of supply and demand conditions, relative transportation costs, and tariff policies. Thus, the North African countries rely heavily on the French market because the French government, in the past, has accorded them substantial tariff preferences. However, past trade policies have been changing rapidly in recent years, and major shifts in the pattern of shipments are to be expected. Both demand and supply of winter oranges are predicted to grow rapidly [8], and the equilibrium of trade will be subjected to major displacements.

3. The EEC tariff and reference price policy

3.1. General outlines

The EEC tariff policy with regard to oranges has been characterized by the establishment of a Common External Tariff and the gradual abolition of tariffs and other trade barriers among the member countries.

This policy aims at protecting the Community producers from external competition and encouraging trade within the EEC. After the harmonization process is completed, no import duties will be levied on orange exports originating within the Community, while exports from 'third' countries will be subject to high and uniform tariff rates.

Compared to their 1963–64 levels, tariff rates on imports of fresh oranges to West Germany and Benelux countries will increase by some 30 %, while corresponding rates in France will be lowered by about 35 %. The new Common External Tariff rate will be around 20 %.

The principal beneficiaries of these changes are Italy, a member of the EEC, and Greece, whose association with the Community entitles her to duty-free exports of citrus fruit up to a certain quota.[3]

The system of reference prices and countervailing charges for fruits and vegetables was initiated in 1962 by Regulation 23 of the Council of the European Economic Community [4]. Regulation 100 provided, later in 1962, a procedure for determining reference and entry prices [5].

However, in view of the accumulated experience, Regulation 23 was amended in 1965 by Regulation 65/65/EEC [6]. The revised Article 11 [2] states:

'2. In order to avoid disturbances due to offers from Third countries at abnormal prices, reference prices applicable to the whole Community shall be fixed annually.

'The reference price shall be equal to the arithmetic mean, . . ., of the producer price in each Member State. These producer prices shall correspond to the average of the prices recorded during the three years prior to the date of fixing the reference price for an indigenous product with specified commercial characteristics, on the representative market or markets situated in the production zones, where prices are the lowest . . ..

The reference price shall be fixed for the period of one year. However, in order to take into account seasonal differences of price, each year may be divided into several periods, within which prices remain relatively stable.

'The price on entry of that product shall be fixed on the basis of the lowest price recorded on the representative import markets . . ., less Custom duty arising from application of Article 23 of the Treaty and less other import dues as well as transport charges from those markets to the Community frontier transit points.

'In the case of the price on entry . . . being lower than the reference price, imports of this product from Third countries shall be subject to countervailing duty. However, if imports are made at prices which on entry are lower than the reference price, only from certain countries the countervailing duty shall be limited to imports from those countries.

[3] In 1962 this quota amounted to 22000 metric tons. Over the succeeding five years, the quota was to be increased by 20 % annually (see [1], pp. 208 and 209).

'The amount of the countervailing duty shall be equal to the difference between the reference price and the price on entry. The amount of this duty shall be the same for all Member States and shall be added to the Customs duties in force.'

The 1965–66 season's reference price regulation has established three varietal groups and a method of computing the countervailing charges designed to assure qualitative comparability between the Italian varieties and those of non-EEC countries [7]. Thus, entry prices are obtained by multiplying quoted wholesale or auction prices (net of import duties) by certain "correction coefficients" given in the EEC regulation for specific varietal groups. Countervailing charges are then equated to the difference between entry and reference prices.

3.2. The impact of reference price mechanism — a simplified graphic analysis

Before undertaking a detailed mathematical and quantitative analysis, let us investigate the economic functioning of the reference price mechanism by a simplified graphic analysis. This will help clarify the operation of the system and provide insight into its modus operandi.

To this end, consider an international market consisting of two importing countries, A and B, and a fixed world supply of oranges. Assume that both countries impose an ad valorem tariff but only country A employs a reference price mechanism. Assume, further, that there are no transportation costs,

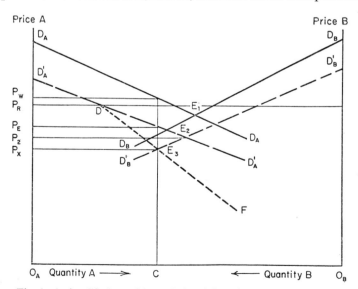

Fig. 1. A simplified graphic analysis of the reference price mechanism.

and competition prevails in all markets. This situation is depicted graphically in fig. 1. $D_A D_A$ and $D_B D_B$ are the demand functions at the wholesale level of country A and country B, respectively. (Note that the quantity demanded by country B is measured from 0_B to the left.) The curves $D'_A D'_A$ and $D'_B D'_B$ are the demand function's net of import duties, and the total fixed supply is represented by the interval $0_A 0_B$.

Under free trade, the world equilibrium is represented by the point E_1. However, once import duties are introduced, the equilibrium point shifts to E_2.

Suppose now that, in addition to import duties, country A puts into effect a 'reference price' mechanism with reference prices set at P_R. To find the new equilibrium point, we construct a new demand function $D'_A DF$ which represents demand behavior in country A net of both import duties and countervailing charges. This is done by connecting all points, under the horizontal line through P_R, whose vertical distance to DD'_A (from below) is equal to the vertical distance between DD'_A and the horizontal line through P_R. The equilibrium point for trade with tariff and a reference price mechanism is then represented by the intersection of $D'_A DF$ and $D'_B D'_B$ at point E_3. In equilibrium, the quantities imported to country A and country B are represented by $0_A C$ and $0_B C$, respectively. Wholesalers in country A pay the price P_W whereas exporters get the price P_X. The difference is made up of an ad valorem tariff, $P_W - P_E$, and a countervailing charge, $P_E - P_X$, which is equal, by the construction of $D'_A DF$, to $P_R - P_E$. P_E thus represents the entry price. As long as the reference price, P_R, is below the price, P_2 — the equilibrium entry price in country A under tariffs alone — the reference price is ineffective.[4] Also, an increase in reference prices above P_2 leads to diversion of trade from country A to country B, increased price within country A and lower prices to exporters and to consumers in country B.

4. The model

4.1.

The model developed in the present analysis is essentially a static model of interregional competition with transportation costs, tariffs, and the peculiar mechanism of reference prices and countervailing charges.

---

[4] This actually was the situation in the early years of the program.

The assumption of competition appears to be, at least approximately, valid because there are numerous buyers and sellers in all markets.

In constructing the model, seven consuming regions, four producing regions, and two varietal groups have been distinguished. The model reflects short-run relationships, because production in each producing region was regarded as fixed. The following consuming and producing regions were distinguished:

Producing regions	*Consuming regions*
1. Italy and Greece	1. Italy and Greece
2. Spain and Portugal	2. Spain and Portugal
3. Northwest Africa	3. Switzerland and Austria
4. Near East	4. Scandinavia
	5. United Kingdom
	6. West Germany and Benelux
	7. France

East European countries, including Yugoslavia, were excluded from the analysis because their imports are determined directly by governments and not by the interplay of market forces. Shipments to these countries were, therefore, naively projected and then subtracted from the producing region's outputs. A similar approach was applied to the rest of the world, which constitutes an insignificant share of total Mediterranean exports.

Domestic consumption in Northwest Africa and the Near East is supplied mostly by oranges not suitable for export. Exports from these regions were, therefore, assumed to be price inelastic.

4.2. Formal statement of the model

Let

x_i^k = quantity of fresh oranges of the kth varietal group supplied by ith producing region;

y_j^k = quantity of fresh oranges of the kth varietal group demanded by the jth consuming region;

x_{ij}^k = shipment of oranges of the kth varietal group from the ith producing region to the jth consuming region;

p_j^k = auction or wholesale price of oranges of the kth varietal group in the jth consuming region;

v_i^k = f.o.b. price of oranges of the kth varietal group in the ith producing region;

R_{ij}^k = countervailing charges levied on oranges of the kth varietal group imported from the ith producing region to the jth consuming region;

A_{jk},

$\quad \alpha_{kk'j}$ = parameters of the demand relations;

$\quad \pi_{ij}$ = tariff plus internal tax rate imposed in the jth consuming region on imports from the ith producing region;

$\quad t_{ij}$ = per unit transportation cost from the ith producing region to the jth consuming region;

$\quad P_{RK}$ = the reference price for the kth orange group,

and

$\quad K_k$ = the correction coefficient applied to the 'quoted' price to obtain the entry price of varietal group k.

4.3. The structural relations

In the following we set forth the structural relations:
(a) Demand relations in consuming regions:[5]

$$y_j^k = A_{jk}(p_j^1)^{\alpha_{k1j}}(p_j^2)^{\alpha_{k2j}} \qquad j = 1, 2, \ldots, 7; \quad k = 1, 2. \tag{1}$$

(b) Shipments balance equations:
(i) Supply

$$x_i^k = \sum_{j=1}^{7} x_{ij}^k \qquad i = 1, 2, 3, 4; \quad k = 1, 2. \tag{2}$$

(ii) Demand

$$y_j^k = \sum_{i=1}^{4} x_{ij}^k \qquad j = 1, 2, \ldots, 7; \quad k = 1, 2. \tag{3}$$

(c) Nonnegative shipments:

$$x_{ij}^k \geq 0 \qquad i = 1, 2, 3, 4; \quad j = 1, 2, \ldots, 7; \quad k = 1, 2. \tag{4}$$

(d) F.o.b. prices in producing countries:

$$v_i^k \geq p_j^k(1 - \pi_{ij}) - t_{ij} - R_{ij}^k \qquad i = 1, 2, 3, 4; \quad j = 1, 2, \ldots, 7; \quad k = 1, 2. \tag{5}$$

Whenever $x_j^k > 0$, the strict equality in eq. (5) holds and, conversely, if the strict inequality in eq. (5) holds, $x_{ij}^k = 0$.

---

[5] The particular functional form of the demand functions (eq. (1)) was selected for computational convenience. The constant elasticity assumption implied by this form was actually retained only at a restricted neighborhood of the project equilibrium. The effect of income is included in the constant A_{jk}. The effect is made explicit in eq. (7).

(e) The reference price mechanism:

$$
R_{ij}^k = \begin{bmatrix} \max\ \{0,\ P_{RK} - K_k \tfrac{1}{2} \sum_{j=6}^{7} p_j^k(1 - \pi_{ij})\} \\ \quad \text{if } i = 2, 3, 4 \quad j = 6, 7 \quad k = 1, 2 \\ 0 \quad \text{otherwise.} \end{bmatrix} \tag{6}
$$

That is, the countervailing charges are calculated as the differences between the average entry prices $(\tfrac{1}{2}\sum_{j=6}^{7} p_j^k[1 - \pi_{ij}])$ and the reference prices P_{RK}.

5. Values of the structural parameters and exogenous variables

5.1. The demand relations

The structure of demand for fresh oranges has been the subject of several studies. Earlier studies were surveyed in Levhari [10] and the more recent estimates of demand elasticities are cited by Wolf [18], and Dean and Collins [2, 3]. Most estimates of the price elasticities of demand for the aggregate of all fresh oranges at the wholesale level are at the range of -0.6 to 1.0. Following Dean and Collins, a uniform price elasticity of -0.8 was adopted in the present study for all consuming countries. A sensitivity

Table 2

Price flexibilities of demand $(\delta_{kk'j})$ [a] for winter oranges, 1963–64 and 1970 projected

Countries	Actual 1963–64 conditions				1970 projected conditions			
	δ_{11}	δ_{12}	δ_{21}	δ_{22}	δ_{11}	δ_{12}	δ_{21}	δ_{22}
Italy and Greece	-0.704	-0.537	-0.662	-0.580	-0.792	-0.458	-0.752	-0.498
Spain and Portugal	-0.810	-0.440	-0.769	-0.481	-0.931	-0.318	-0.889	-0.361
Austria and Switzerland	-0.817	-0.433	-0.776	-0.474	-0.938	-0.312	-0.896	-0.354
Scandinavia	-1.006	-0.244	-0.962	-0.288	-1.087	-0.163	-1.039	-0.211
United Kingdom	-1.053	-0.197	-1.008	-0.242	-1.183	-0.067	-1.130	-0.120
West Germany and Benelux	-0.909	-0.341	-0.867	-0.383	-0.915	-0.335	-0.873	-0.377
France	-0.891	-0.359	-0.849	-0.400	-0.545	-0.705	-0.499	-0.751

[a] $\delta_{kk'j} = \dfrac{\partial p_j^k}{\partial y_j^{k'}} \cdot \dfrac{y_j^{k'}}{p_j^k}$

analysis for other values of the price elasticities within the above-mentioned range was carried out by Dean and Collins. Equilibrium prices were found to be insensitive to these parametric changes.

Without adequate information on prices and quantities by varietal groups in the various consuming regions, it was impossible to estimate the direct and cross-price elasticities of demand as defined in the present study. However, some propositions of the classical theory of consumer behavior and certain estimates obtained by Levhari allowed us to construct the desired estimates.

The detailed estimation method is presented in Zusman *et al.* [19, pp. 9–11].

Demand flexibilities, rather than elasticities, were used in the iterative computations. They were obtained by inverting the matrix of elasticities. Values of the flexibilities for actual 1963–64 and the 1970 projected conditions are presented in table 2.

For the base year, the values of the parameters A_{jk} were obtained by solving eq. (1) for the given quantities, prices, and price elasticities. Consumption and prices of fresh oranges for 1963–64 are presented in table 3 (see also [19], Appendix B).

Since the main analysis of the EEC policy was in terms of 1970 conditions extrapolation of the demand functions was achieved using the formula:

$$A_{jk, 1970} = A_{jk, 1963-64}[(1+\theta_j)(1+\eta_{kj}\varepsilon_j)]^{-6.5} \quad [6] \tag{7}$$

where θ_j is annual rate of population growth in region j and ε_j is annual rate of increase in per capita income in region j. The income elasticities of demand were assumed equal for both varietal groups. They vary between countries and are, on the whole, in the neighbourhood of 1.0.

5.2. 1970 supplies

Projected 1970 supplies by producing countries were obtained by interpolation from 1975 projections of the Food and Agriculture Organization (FAO) of the United Nations, taking into account recent trends in production: 1970 supplies to East European countries and to the rest of the world were projected likewise and subtracted from overall supplies [8]. The varietal composition in 1970 was assumed to resemble that of 1963–64.

---

[6] The exponent 6.5 is equal to the number of years between the 1963–64 season and the 1970 calendar year. The estimation of the A_{jk} and the extrapolation method are identical with the one used by Dean and Collins [7, pp. 7–10].

Table 3

Exports, imports, prices, countervailing charges, and trade flows of winter oranges for actual 1963–64 conditions and for 1970 projected conditions under three alternative tariff and reference-price situations [a]

Exporting countries	Economic situation	Consuming regions							Exporting countries, totals	
		Italy and Greece	Spain and Portugal	Austria and Switzerland	Scandinavia	United Kingdom	West Germany and Benelux	France	Total supply or export	F.o.b. prices
		(1000 metric tons)							(1000 metric tons)	(dollars per metric ton)
Italy and Greece	1963–64 actual [b]	379.3 [c]	—[d]	30.7	10.8	0.5	28.1	—	449.4	149.15
	1970 projected	437.7	—	30.3	10.2	0.5	27.9	—	505.6	104.98
	1970 high reference prices	471.8	—	—	—	—	127.7	—	599.5	179.82
		404.5	—	—	—	—	272.0	—	676.5	128.11
	1970 free trade	425.5	—	—	—	—	174.0	—	599.5	189.05
		433.6	—	—	—	—	242.9	—	676.5	133.76
		536.8	—	—	—	—	62.7	—	599.5	159.00
		423.4	—	—	—	—	253.0	—	676.4	113.66
Spain and Portugal	1963–64 actual [b]	—	305.3	38.0	50.1	69.4	322.9	149.3	935.0	130.06
	1970 projected	—	248.7	31.0	40.9	56.6	263.1	121.7	762.0	91.31
	1970 high reference prices	—	501.2	136.0	—	—	166.3	302.9	1106.4	119.08
		—	250.3	62.0	—	—	—	589.3	901.6	85.35
	1970 free trade	—	603.0	158.7	—	—	100.8	243.9	1106.4	114.54
		—	164.6	43.2	—	—	43.5	650.3	901.6	84.21
		—	379.4	110.7	—	—	268.4	347.9	1106.4	156.00
		—	242.1	83.5	—	—	9.2	566.8	901.6	110.66
North Africa	1963–64 actual [b]	—	—	—	5.9	18.3	126.2	227.9	378.2	157.50
	1970 projected	—	—	—	1.1	6.7	30.8	92.1	130.7	115.00
	1970 high reference prices	—	—	—	22.5	32.3	326.6	—	381.4	117.08
		—	—	—	21.4	8.1	118.1	—	147.6	82.60
	1970 free trade	—	—	—	77.6	23.7	280.1	—	381.4	112.54
		—	—	—	5.7	2.2	139.7	—	147.6	82.23
		—	—	—	3.5	12.1	365.8	—	381.4	154.00
		—	—	—	28.8	13.2	105.5	—	147.5	108.68
Near East	1963–64 actual [b]	—	—	15.5	83.0	146.0	112.8	6.0	363.3	124.00
		—	—	1.5			1.2		2.7	79.52

Note: In each pair of entries the upper figure refers to varietal Group 1 and the lower figure refers to varietal Group 2.

	1	2	3	4	5	6	7
(continued)							
1970 projected	218.3 / 27.8	307.5 / 17.9	144.8 / 1.7	—	—	670.6 / 47.4	106.08 / 71.60
1970 high reference prices	188.0 / 25.0	334.9 / 14.0	147.7 / 8.4	—	—	670.6 / 47.4	101.54 / 71.23
1970 free trade	198.9 / 29.8	289.0 / 17.6	182.7 / —	—	—	670.6 / 47.4	143.00 / 97.67
Total imports (1000 metric tons)							
1963–64 actual [b]	379.3 / 437.7	305.3 / 248.7	84.2 / 62.8	149.8 / 52.2	234.2 / 63.8	590.0 / 323.0	383.2 / 213.8
1970 projected	471.8 / 404.5	501.2 / 250.3	136.0 / 62.10	240.8 / 49.2	339.8 / 26.0	765.4 / 391.8	302.9 / 589.3
1970 high reference prices	425.5 / 433.6	603.0 / 164.6	158.7 / 43.2	265.6 / 30.7	358.6 / 16.2	702.6 / 434.5	243.9 / 650.3
1970 free trade	536.8 / 423.4	379.4 / 242.1	110.7 / 83.5	202.4 / 58.6	301.1 / 30.8	879.6 / 367.7	347.9 / 566.8
Wholesale prices at entry (dollars per metric ton)							
1963–64 actual [b]	149.15 / 104.98	130.06 / 91.31	184.08 / 137.83	180.23 / 135.98	181.20 / 130.16	192.20 / 144.00	186.50 / 142.83
1970 projected	179.82 / 128.11	119.08 / 85.35	162.89 / 124.49	160.17 / 123.62	160.42 / 122.55	206.82 / 155.10	177.30 / 128.68
1970 high reference prices	189.05 / 133.76	114.54 / 84.21	157.73 / 123.20	155.37 / 123.33	155.44 / 122.15	216.05 / 160.75	186.14 / 133.14
1970 free trade	159.00 / 113.66	156.00 / 110.66	180.00 / 134.66	188.00 / 142.68	183.00 / 137.68	186.00 / 140.67	169.00 / 123.66
Countervailing charges (dollars per metric ton)							
1963–64 actual [b]	—	—	—	—	—	—	—
1970 projected	—	—	—	—	—	12.24 / 6.39	12.24 / 6.39
1970 high reference prices	—	—	—	—	—	23.97 / 11.16	23.97 / 11.16
1970 free trade	—	—	—	—	—	—	—

[a] 1970 projected = 1970 conditions with a change to the EEC common tariffs (alternative A for North Africa), tariffs in non-EEC countries at the 1963–64 levels, and reference prices set at $171 and $86 per metric ton (1965–66 levels). 1970 high reference prices = same as in 1970 projected, but reference prices set at $200 and $100 per metric ton. 1970 freed trade = 1970 conditions but with tariffs and reference prices in all countries at zero levels.

[b] Derived on the assumption that the varietal composition of all flows originating in a given country is the same.

[c] The upper figure in each pair of entries refers to varietal Group 1. The lower figure refers to varietal Group 2.

[d] Dashes indicate no trade flow between countries.

[e] Inclusive of import duties and countervailing charges.

5.3. Transportation costs

Transportation costs from producing to consuming regions are presented
in table 4. The figures in the table are based on estimates obtained by Dean
and Collins [3], but some of the original estimates have been modified to
account for changes in geographical reference points.

Table 4

Least-cost transportation costs of oranges from producing to consuming regions

Exporting regions	Importing regions				
	Switzerland and Austria (central point)	Scandinavia (Copenhagen)	United Kingdom (London)	West Germany and Benelux (Hamburg)	France (Marseilles)
	(dollars per metric ton)				
Italy and Greece (Italy)	22 [a]	39	34	27	19
	(0+ 0+22)	(29+10+0)	(24+10+0)	(0+ 0+27) [b]	(0+ 0+19)
Spain and Portugal	24	36	31	30	13
	(0+ 0+24)	(26+10+0)	(21+10+0)	(0+ 0+30) [b]	(0+ 0+13) [c]
Northwest Africa	40	34	29	32	29
	(15+10+15)	(24+10+0)	(19+10+0)	(22+10+ 0)	(19+10+ 0)
Near East (Israel)	40	45	40	43	40
	(20+10+10)	(35+10+0)	(30+10+0)	(33+10+ 0)	(30+10+ 0)

[a] The top number in each cell is the transportation cost. The lower figures in parentheses provide a breakdown
of total costs into sea freight plus unloading from ship plus rail freight, respectively.
[b] For shipments originating in Spain and Italy, the reference point was shifted from Hamburg toward the
sources.
[c] For shipments originating in Spain, the reference point was shifted to the Spanish border.
Source [3, p. 22].

5.4. Tariff and internal tax rates

Combined tariff and internal tax rates in 1963–64 and 1970 projected are
presented in table 5.[7] All values represent ad valorem rates. In a few cases
the actual duties and taxes are in absolute terms. The rates were then
computed using base-year prices. In the non-EEC countries, 1970 rates
are assumed to be at their 1963–64 levels. Table 5 reflects the expected
rise in EEC tariff rates and the preferred position of Italy and Greece.
Because the future of the tariff preferences accorded to North African
exporters is uncertain, the analysis was carried out under two alternative
assumptions: (1) All preferences will be abolished, and (2) imports from
North Africa will enjoy somewhat lower tariffs which will be uniform

---

[7] Only internal taxes imposed at the wholesale level were included.

(8 %) in all of the Community markets. In the present paper we report the findings related to the first alternative only. A full report is given in [19].

Table 5

Combined tariff and internal tax rates on winter oranges in 1963–64 and 1970

Exporting region	Importing region				
	Switzerland and Austria	Scandinavia	United Kingdom	West Germany and Benelux	France
			(per cent)		
Italy and Greece					
1963–64	12.16	5.68	8.94	10.50	16.97
1970	12.16	5.68	8.94	4.19	0
Spain and Portugal					
1963–64	12.16	5.68	8.94	17.13	26.97
1970	12.16	5.68	8.94	22.01	18.60
Northwest Africa					
1963–64	12.16	5.68	8.94	17.13	0
1970: Alternative 1	12.16	5.68	8.94	22.01	18.60
Alternative 2	12.16	5.68	8.94	12.19	8.00
Near East					
1963–64	12.16	5.68	8.94	17.13	26.97
1970	12.16	5.68	8.94	22.01	18.60

Sources: 1963–64: Figures based on information available in [1, Appendix V]. 1970: Figures derived from [3, Appendix A].

5.5. Reference prices

Regulation 156/65/EEC specified the following system of reference prices for 1965 [7].

Varietal group	Reference price (P_{RK})	Correction coefficient (K_k)
$k = 1$	$P_{R1} = 171$	$K_1 = 1.10$
$k = 2$	$P_{R2} = 86$	$K_2 = 0.76$

The analysis was carried out on the assumption that the 1965 reference prices will continue in 1970. However, since the EEC policy is instrumental in raising prices paid to the Italian producers, reference prices, which are based on a moving-average price, are also expected to rise. The effects of higher reference prices were, therefore, investigated also. To this end, reference prices were set at $P_{R1} = \$ 200$ per metric ton and $P_{R2} = \$ 100$ per metric ton.

6. *The solution procedure*

The endogenous variables of the system are the quantities demanded in each consuming region (y_j^k), the interregional shipments (x_{ij}^k), wholesale or auction prices (p_j^k), f.o.b. prices (v_i^k), and the countervailing charges (R_{ij}^k).

The equilibrium values of the endogenous variables may be obtained by solving eqs. (1) through (6). Because some of the conditions are, in effect, strict equalities while others are inequalities and because the set of relations which are equalities can be determined only by solving the equilibrium conditions, the problem of finding a suitable solution procedure assumes primary importance.

Accepted solution procedures have, so far, relied, in various degrees, on the application of some kind of programming technique. However, the algorithms turn out either to be difficult to use because the system is complex, or inappropriate because of some general a priori considerations.[8] A natural solution to the problem may, therefore, be provided by the market mechanism which, in some senses, may be viewed as a computational device. This approach was actually adopted in the present analysis.[9]

The equilibrium values of these variables were obtained by an iterative procedure which is essentially a simulation of the shipment adjustment process taking place in a competitive international market. Accordingly, starting with an arbitrary shipment program satisfying the balance eq. (2) and the non-negativity constraints in eq. (4), f.o.b. prices were computed, using eqs. (1), (3), (5), and (6). The shipping program of each producer was then adjusted by shifting quantities from markets yielding low f.o.b. prices to more remunerative markets. The change in shipments was made proportional to the f.o.b. price differentials, subject to the nonnegative shipment constraints. The process continues until eq. (5) is satisfied at some required degree of accuracy. Provided the demand relations satisfy some mild stability conditions, convergence of the adjustment process may be assured by selecting appropriate adjustment factor. The accuracy required in the present analysis was 1 cent as the maximum f.o.b. price differential among markets to which there were non-zero shipments. The solution

---

[8] See Zusman *et al.* [19, Appendix A].

[9] To our knowledge, the use of this approach was first suggested by Tramel and Seale [16].

procedure described above represents a deviation from some programming procedures hitherto used in solving competitive trade equilibria. For a more detailed discussion see Zusman *et al.* [19, Appendix A].

7. Equilibrium values of prices and quantities in 1970 under three alternative trade policies

7.1. The tested policies

The following trade policies were considered:

(a) *1970 projected.* Tariffs are at the levels cited in table 5 (with Alternative 1 for North Africa), and reference prices are at their 1965 levels ($ 171 per metric ton for Group 1, $ 86 per metric ton for Group 2).

The effects of tariff preferences for North African producers (Alternative 2) were explored separately and are reported in [19].

(b) *1970 high reference prices.* Tariffs are at the levels cited in table 5, but reference prices are raised to $ 200 per metric ton for Group 1, and $ 100 per metric ton for Group 2.

(c) *1970 free trade.* Tariff rates and reference prices are set at zero levels for all importing regions.

The first alternative provides information concerning the equilibrium values of prices and quantities under the 1970 projected supply and demand conditions and trade policies most likely to prevail. However, existing political pressures, coupled with rising producer prices in Italy, may lead to increased reference prices. The effect of such changes is examined in the second alternative. The third alternative is designed to provide a norm of comparison, particularly with reference to welfare implications. It may also provide some indications on the likely changes due to possible relaxations of trade restrictions (for instance, in consequence of agreements achieved in the Kennedy Round negotiations).

7.2. Main findings

7.2.1. Prices

Future developments in supply and demand conditions in conjunction with projected changes in the EEC trade policy are expected to have depressing effects on exporters' f.o.b. prices, except for EEC producers who will benefit substantially from the projected changes. F.o.b. prices to non-EEC producers will fall by some 5–30 %, while f.o.b. prices in Italy and Greece will rise by some 13–20 %.

The contribution of the reference price mechanism to these changes constitutes about one-third of the change as can be judged from the values of the countervailing charges. The effect on wholesale or auction prices is mixed. In all non-EEC consuming regions and in France, prices will fall by 6–15%; in West Germany, Benelux, Italy, and Greece, prices are expected to rise by 4–20%.

The tested increase in reference prices will further lower f.o.b. prices in non-EEC exporting countries by approximately 3–7% and raise f.o.b. prices to EEC producers by some 7%. At these levels, the countervailing charges amount to about 20% of wholesale prices in EEC markets, and reference prices become a major protective mechanism.

The increase in reference prices will also lead to a rise in wholesale or auction prices in all EEC consuming regions. Consequently, trade flows will be diverted to non-EEC consuming regions, thus bringing about a further price decline in these markets.

Trade liberalization tends to reverse these trends. Wholesale prices in non-EEC countries (that actually gain from the high degree of protection in the EEC), will increase under free trade, while an opposite price change is expected to take place in the EEC consuming regions.

As a result of free trade, non-EEC producers will enjoy a substantial increase in their f.o.b. prices at the expense of EEC producers who will face much lower prices.

7.7.2. Trade flows

Supplies of all orange groups in 1970 will rise much above their base-year levels. Most of this increase will be absorbed by a simultaneous growth in demand.

Two profound changes in the pattern of trade flows are expected to take place. First, the termination of trade preferences accorded to North African exporters in the French market will lead to a major diversion of trade. North African oranges will be completely shifted away from the French market, which will be taken over by Spanish oranges exclusively. Since North Africa produced in 1963–64 mostly Group 1 oranges, French consumption also consisted mainly of Group 1 oranges. With Spanish exports dominating the French market in 1970, the composition of French orange consumption will be reversed in favor of Group 2 oranges. Imports of Group 2 oranges to other markets will, consequently, suffer a relative decline. Second, Italian and Greek exporters will concentrate on the German and Benelux markets, refraining from shipping oranges to any other market.

This tendency is bound to lower the sizable present exports from Greece to East European countries.

An increase in reference prices will enhance these trends and will encourage diversion of orange exports, particularly Group 1 oranges, to non-EEC markets. However, a shift to free trade is not expected to modify the predicted changes in the destination of North African, Italian, and Greek exports.

The equilibrium solutions obtained under the various alternative assumptions are sensitive to disturbances. In many cases the f.o.b. prices obtainable from rival markets are very close. For example, the pattern of shipments from the Near East and North Africa could be modified without violating the equilibrium conditions because the differentials of transportation costs from the two regions to various destinations are alike.[10]

Similarly, in the 1970 projected equilibrium, the f.o.b. prices that Spanish exporters could realize by allocating some Group 1 oranges to Scandinavia and the United Kingdom are lower by only $ 4.00 per metric ton than comparable prices actually received in France and West Germany. Such narrow price differentials are hardly discernible by exporters, and deviations from the predicted equilibrium pattern of trade are likely to occur.

Indeed, given the imperfect price information, the presence of product differentiation, and the importance of established trade channels characterizing real markets, one expects actual shipment programs to be more diversified than those predicted by our model. Dean and Collins [3] report similar observations. However, only mild price effects are associated with such deviations.

8. Welfare implications

In analyzing the welfare consequences of the EEC trade policy, three components of the problem are distinguished: (1) producers' income, (2) consumers' surplus, and (3) government revenue.

Because outputs are regarded constant, variation in producers' income represents the corresponding variation in producers' welfare measured in momentary terms. However, in treating consumers' welfare some measure

---

[10] For this reason, the number of nonzero shipments exceeds 20, the number implied by the solution to a transportation cost minimization problem inherent in the equilibrium conditions (see Takayama and Judge [12–14]). It is possible to rearrange the shipments program without violating the equilibrium conditions so that the number of non-zero shipments will be 20.

of consumers' surplus must be adopted. In the present analysis, the aggregate compensating variations are used to measure changes in consumers' welfare.[11] The compensating variation is a particularly convenient measure because it allows a direct application of the 'compensation principle' of welfare economics. The meaning and derivation of this measure deserve a short explanation.

The individual income function, $M^r(p_j^1, \ldots, p_j^n, U_r)$ is defined to be the smallest income required to furnish the rth consumer with a utility level (real income), U_r, in the price configuration $p_j^1, \ldots, p_j^n$. Accordingly, the individual compensating variation (CV_r), associated with the price configuration $\bar{p}_j^1, \ldots, \bar{p}_j^n$ relative to $p_j^1, \ldots, p_j^n$, represents the change in minimal income required to compensate the consumer for the change in prices from $p_j^1, \ldots, p_j^n$ to $\bar{p}_j^1, \ldots, \bar{p}_j^n$; that is,

$$CV_r = M^r(\bar{p}_j^1, \ldots, \bar{p}_j^n, U_r^0) \tag{8}$$

and, assuming independent utilities among individuals, we have for the aggregate:

$$CV = \sum_r CV_r. \tag{9}$$

Now, it has been shown that

$$\frac{\partial M^r}{\partial p_j^k} = y_r^{kc}(p_j^1, \ldots, p_j^n, U_r) \tag{10}$$

$$i = 1, 2, \ldots, n$$

where y_r^{kc} is the compensated demand function of the rth individual for the ith commodity [9, p. 272]. Similarly, the corresponding partial derivative of the aggregate income function, $M = \sum_r M^r$, is the market-compensated demand function.

The demand functions for oranges are dominated by the substitution effects and may be closely approximated by compensated demand functions. The approximation was actually accomplished by imposing symmetric cross-price derivatives in the estimation procedure. However, the symmetry conditions hold only at the 1970 projected equilibrium point, whereas eq. (10) implies symmetry everywhere. This requirement can be satisfied by linearizing our demand functions about the 1970 projected equilibrium

---

[11] For a detailed discussion of the concept, see [17, pp. 395–423], and [11, pp. 83–114].

point. Eq. 1 then becomes:

$$y_j^k = y_j^{kc} = \beta_{jk} + \gamma_{jk1} p_j^1 + \gamma_{jk2} p_j^2$$

$$j = 1, 2, \ldots, 7; \quad k = 1, 2,; \quad \text{with} \quad \gamma_{j12} = \gamma_{j21}.\,^{12}) \tag{11}$$

We now conceive our system as consisting of three commodities: Group 1 oranges, Group 2 oranges, and a composite commodity comprising all other commodities with its price being identically equal to one — that is, the composite commodity serves as a numeraire.

The aggregate income function of the jth consuming region is then quadratic:

$$M_j(p_j^1, p_j^2) = \delta_{0j} + \beta_{j1} p_j^1 + \beta_{j2} p_j^2$$

$$= \tfrac{1}{2}[\gamma_{j11}(p_j^1)^2 + (\gamma_{j12} + \gamma_{j21})p_j^1 p_j^2 + \gamma_{j22}(p_j^2)^2], \tag{12}$$

as can be verified by differentiation M_j with respect to p_j^k;[13] δ_{0j} can be determined from overall consumer expenditures. In the present analysis, however, the value of δ_{0j} is immaterial as we are interested solely in changes in M_j and not in its absolute value.

Evidently, the validity of our analysis is restricted to the neighbourhood of the 1970 projected equilibrium in which eq. (11) is a good approximation. The measures presented in table 6 furnish welfare comparisons between the 1970 projected equilibrium and the other two 1970 equilibria discussed in the preceding section. The 1970 projected equilibrium was thus selected as a base, and the entries in table 6 represent deviations from the 1970 projected welfare measures.

Perhaps the most striking finding of the analysis is the relative insensitivity of the overall welfare measure to considerable variation in trade policies. Thus, if one is willing to adopt the compensation principle, then the gainers from free trade are left with a net gain of a mere $ 5.950 million after having compensated the losers. In view of the overall size of the market (hundreds of millions of dollars), this is a negligible amount.

However, the distribution effects are more substantial. Thus, an increase in reference prices by some 16 % will raise returns to Italian and Greek producers by $ 9.4 million and lower returns to the other exporters by about

---

[12] The coefficients β_{jk} and $\gamma_{jkk'}$, were obtained from the 1970 elasticities and equilibrium prices and quantities by expanding the demand equations in a Taylor expansion about the equilibrium values neglecting the nonlinear terms.

[13] The income function, eq. (2), is in fact the line integral $\int \Sigma_{k=1}^2 y_j^{kc}(p_j^1, p_j^2) dP_j^k$. This is the n commodities generalization ($n = 3$) of the "consumer surplus" measured by the "area under the (compensated) demand curve".

P. Zusman. A. Melamed, I. Katzir

Table 6

Welfare comparisons of high reference prices and free trade relative to 1970 projected conditions winter oranges, 1970 [a]

Country	High reference prices [b]				Free trade			
	Con-sumers' surplus	Govern-ment revenue	Pro-ducers' income	Net gain or loss	Con-sumers' surplus	Govern-ment revenue	Pro-ducers' income	Net gain or loss
				(1000 dollars)				
Italy and Greece	—6494	0	9352	2858	16 392	0	—22 255	—5863
Spain and Portugal	2700	0	—6049	—3349	—21 757	0	63 664	41 907
Switzerland and Austria	821	58	0	879	—2805	—3633	0	—6438
Scandinavia	1233	24	0	1257	—7097	—2535	0	—9632
United Kingdom	1736	0	0	1736	—7601	—5159	0	—12 760
West Germany and Benelux	—9083	5030	0	—4053	22 475	—41 675	0	—19 200
France	—5144	6087	0	943	5582	—31 571	0	—25 989
North Africa	0	0	—1785	—1785	0	0	17 930	17 930
Near East	0	0	—3058	—3058	0	0	25 995	25 995
Total, all countries	—14 231	11 199	—1540	—4572	5189	—84 573	85 334	5950

[a] Entries represent deviations from the 1970 projected equilibrium.

[b] For Group 1 oranges, $200 per metric ton; for Group 2 oranges, $100 per metric ton.

Source: [19].

$ 11 million. The associated losses by EEC consumers are valued at $ 20.7 million, while the increase in government revenues in the EEC countries is $ 11.1 million.

All EEC countries together actually realize a net loss because of higher reference prices, but the loss is negligible ($ 252,000). The principal function of the increase in reference prices is, therefore, to redistribute income from EEC consumers to EEC governments and producers. The cost of this transfer is borne by the non-EEC producers who, consequently, stand to lose about $ 10.9 million, while non-EEC consumers will benefit from increased reference prices.

The distributional effects associated with a move toward free trade are considerable. The resulting net increase in producers' income is $ 85.3 million, while the loss in governments' revenues amounts to $ 84.6 million (of which $ 16 million are derived from countervailing charges). Because the net loss to the Community, due to trade liberalization, adds up to $ 51 million, EEC countries have a strong incentive to retain their protective policy in the orange market. The same conclusions, in essence, were arrived at by Dean and Collins [2, 3].

9. Concluding remarks

The present study is in effect an extension and updating of Dean and Collins' work [2, 3]. In particular, it aims at analyzing the possible effects of the reference-prices and countervailing-charges mechanism, which may evolve into a principal protective device of the EEC agricultural trade policy.

The incorporation of reference prices required a disaggregation of winter oranges into varietal groups and increased considerably the complexity of the system. Consequently, it was necessary to develop appropriate solution procedures and to generalize the concept of consumer surplus to the many-commodities situation. These needs were met by devising a 'market simulating' algorithm and by adopting the changes in aggregate income functions as welfare measures.

Though adding to the complexity of the model and increasing the number of parameters which have to be estimated, the disaggregation provided a more realistic description of the European market for fresh oranges and shed additional light on the shipping patterns.

The projected developments of prices and quantities in the European market tend to substantiate Dean and Collins' findings. In general, consumer and producer prices in the EEC markets are expected to rise, while consumer prices in other importing countries and f.o.b. prices in exporting countries (excluding Italy and Greece) will tend to decline.

The role of the reference-price mechanism in these developments will be significant but not dominant, provided reference prices are retained at their 1965–66 levels. However, an increase of 16 % in reference prices will have adverse effects on producers' income outside the EEC. At these levels, a system of reference prices and countervailing charges constitutes a very effective protective device.

The distributional effects of the EEC protective policy are considerable, with government revenues and producers' gains exceeding consumer losses. The distributional effects of high reference prices are significant, but the net gain to the Community at large is negligible and is achieved at substantial costs to non-EEC producers.

The findings of the present study are derived from a short-run model. In the longer run, the equilibrium values depend critically on the rate at which Italian and Greek producers are capable of expanding orange production relative to the anticipated growth in demand.

All the forecasts derived from the present analysis are conditional on the assumed policy measures, which are subject to constant change. Thus, trade preference previously accorded to North African countries may be modified but not abolished; the United Kingdom may join the EEC; or tariffs may be lowered in some countries in consequence of Kennedy Round negotiations. However, any analysis of the likelihood of such events is beyond the scope of the present study.

References

[1] Commonwealth Economic Committee, 1965, Intelligence Branch, Fruit, no. 15. London: Great Britain Foreign Office.

[2] Dean, G. W. and N. R. Collins, 1966, Trade and welfare effects of EEC tariff policy: a case study of oranges, Journal of Farm Economics, Part I. 48(4), 826–846.

[3] Dean, G. W. and N. R. Collins, 1967, World Trade in Fresh Oranges: An Analysis of the Effect of European Economic Community Tariff Policies, University of California, Giannini Foundation Monograph 18. Berkeley.

[4] European Economic Community, 1962, Regulation No. 23 on the Progressive Establishment of a Common Organization of the Market in Fruit and Vegetables, London: Great Britain Foreign Office.

[5] European Economic Community, 1962, Regulation No. 100: Laying Down Procedures for Giving Effect to Article (11)2 of the Council's Regulations 23 on the Progressive Establishment of a Common Organization of the Market in Fruit and Vegetables, London: Great Britain Foreign Office.

[6] European Economic Community, 1965, Regulation No. 65/65/EEC: To Amend Article 11(2) of Regulation No. 23 on the Progressive Establishment of a Common Organization of the Market in Fruit and Vegetables, London: Great Britain Foreign Office.

[7] European Economic Community, 1965, Regulation No. 156/65 EEC: Fixing Reference Prices for Sweet Oranges, London: Great Britain Foreign Office.

[8] Food and Agriculture Organization of the United Nations, 1967, Agricultural Commodities – Projections for 1975 and 1985, Vol. I: Citrus Fruit, CCP 67/3, Rome.

[9] Karlin, S., 1962, Mathematical Methods and Theory in Games, Programming, and Economics. Vol. I, London: Addison-Wesley Publishing Co.

[10] Levhari, D., 1964, Supply and demand of citrus, in: Y. Mundlak, ed., Long-Term Projections of Supply and Demand for Agricultural Products in Israel, Vol. II, Jerusalem: Faculty of Agriculture, The Hebrew University.

[11] Patinkin, D., 1963, Demand curves and consumer's surplus, in: Carl Christ *et al.*, eds., Measurement in Economics: Studies in Mathematical Economics and Econometrics in Memory of Yehuda Grunfeld, Stanford, California: Stanford University Press.

[12] Takayama, T., 1967, International trade and mathematical programming, The Australian Journal of Agricultural Economics 11(1), 36–48.

[13] Takayama, T. and G. G. Judge, 1964, Equilibrium among spatially separated markets: a reformulation, Econometrica 32(4), 510–524.

[14] Takayama, T. and G. G. Judge, 1971, Spatial and Temporal Price and Allocation Models, Amsterdam: North-Holland Publishing Company.

[15] Tramel, T. E., 1965, Reactive programming – an algorithm for solving spatial equilibrium problems, Mississippi Agric. Exp. Sta., AEC Tech. Pub. 9, State College, Mississippi.

[16] Tramel, T. E. and A. D. Seale, 1963, Reactive Programming Techniques, Appendix A and Appendix B, Interregional Competition Research Method Workshop. North Carolina State College.

[17] Winch, D. M., 1965, Consumer surplus and the compensation principle, American Economic Review, 55(3), 395–423.

[18] Wolf, J., 1965, The citrus economy and the feasibility of international market arrangements, food and agriculture org. of the UN. Monthly Bull. of Agricultural Economics and Statistics, 14(9), 1–15. Rome.

[19] Zusman, P., A. Melamed and K. I. Katzir 1969, Possible Trade and Welfare Effects of EEC Tariff and "Reference Price" Policy on the European-Mediterranean Market for Winter Oranges. University of California, Giannini Foundation Monograph 24, Berkeley.

CHAPTER 25

A spatial price analysis of the world wheat economy: some long-run predictions*

ANDREW SCHMITZ and D. LEE BAWDEN

University of Wisconsin
University of California, Berkeley

1. Introduction

The world wheat economy, which occupies more of the world's cultivated acreage than any other single cereal crop, has undergone dramatic changes in the past 15 years. In the late 1950's and early 1960's, world wheat stocks rose to an unprecedented level, depressing world prices. Then came massive sales of wheat to Communist China and the U.S.S.R., dramatically reducing stocks and increasing prices. In 1967 a new International Cereals Agreement was negotiated, and in 1966–67 the European Economic Community (EEC) began implementing its Common Agricultural Policy (CAP). At this time world wheat prices reached a peak, but by 1969 wheat prices again dropped drastically and surpluses began to accumulate. Concurrently, the major part of the 'Green Revolution' occurred, more than doubling the wheat yields in some Asian countries.

These are some major changes that have caused the recent world wheat market to be relatively unstable; their full effects are not yet felt. The new International Cereals Agreement, the EEC's agricultural policy, and the trading policies of Communist China and the Soviet Union all will have a significant impact on the wheat economy in the future. One purpose of this analysis is to assess this impact on prices, production, and trade flows by country. Another purpose is to measure the likely consequences on the world wheat market of changes in domestic wheat programs and trade policies. Individual countries may alter their domestic wheat programs or

* This study is taken from Andrew Schmitz [23]. We are indebted to Professors R. E. Baldwin, P. Helmberger, and S. Naya and to Miriam Revzan for their comments. We are also indebted to the Canadian Wheat Board, the University of Wisconsin, and the U. S. Department of Agriculture for providing financial assistance.

trade policies to mitigate undesirable consequences for them and to improve their relative position vis-à-vis their competitors. For example, the United States has pursued a policy of gradual abandonment of acreage controls within the constraint of keeping stocks at a reasonable level. In light of the EEC's agricultural policy and the 1967 International Cereals Agreement, can this policy of expanding acreage be continued? What will be the likely consequences if it is? The probable impact on the world wheat economy of this and other policy alternatives will be assessed.

2. Framework of analyses and data inputs

A spatial equilibrium model of production, consumption, prices, and trade is constructed to represent the world wheat economy in 1980. The basic model is that developed by Samuelson in 1952 [20], generalized by Takayama and Judge in 1964 [28–30], and adapted to international trade by Bawden in 1966 [2]. This general model is then adapted to accommodate the peculiarities of the world wheat economy. Its components consist of estimates and projections to 1980 of wheat supply and demand response equations for the wheat trading nations, transfer costs among all countries, and policy parameters. Given these data, the model is solved for equilibrium wheat prices, production, consumption, and trade flows by country, using a quadratic programming algorithm.[1] Strong features of the model are that space (via transfer costs) and alternative policies are explicitly incorporated in the analytical framework. Price is the equilibrating mechanism by which a solution is derived. Since wheat prices are endogenous to the system, each country's wheat exports (imports), production, and consumption are dependent on price and vice versa.

The objective of the study is to *predict* the future wheat situation in each country under alternative economic and policy assumptions. Therefore, the demand and supply equations and transfer costs are estimated and then

---

[1] In the solutions derived, the shipping activity is assumed to be perfectly competitive. If the transfer cost between any two countries exceeds the difference in their equilibrium prices, they will not trade with each other. Conversely, if the difference in their prices exceeds transfer costs, sufficient trade will be induced to alter the prices so that the equilibrium-price difference just equals their mutual transfer costs (after adjusting for import duties and export subsidies). Such conditions are consistent with competitive behavior and the realized objective of every country to sell each product at its maximum price. However, since producer and consumer response within each country is dictated by demand and supply functions, producers do not necessarily maximize profits nor consumers their utility.

projected to represent an arbitrarily selected year in the future — 1980.

To make the analysis manageable, the world is divided into 15 geographic regions. Individual demand equations are estimated for 11 of these: the United States, Canada, Australia, Argentina, Japan, the United Kingdom, Belgium-Luxembourg, the Netherlands, France, Italy, and West Germany (the last 5 are aggregated into one region — the EEC — for policy analysis). These regions include most of the major wheat trading nations of the world; together they accounted for approximately 85 % of total world exports and 25 % of imports during the period 1959–60 to 1963–64.

Except for the United States, supply equations are also estimated for these countries. For reasons presented later, a supply equation cannot be meaningfully estimated for the United States; therefore, its supply is exogenous to the model, and equilibrium solutions are derived under alternative fixed supply levels.

The remainder of the world is separated into four large blocks – Africa, Other Europe (which includes the U.S.S.R.), Other Asia, and Other America. These four geographic divisions are represented not by wheat demand and supply equations but by point estimates of 1980 production and consumption. Most of the countries in these four regions, when viewed separately, have little effect on world trade and pricing of wheat. For the few large producers and consumers, principally the Soviet Union and Communist China, there is insufficient data to estimate demand and supply equations.[2]

Although demand and supply equations for wheat in individual countries have been estimated by a number of researchers, no one study has made estimates for all of the wheat trading countries considered in the present analysis.[3] Nor are the equations in these studies consistent with respect to time, definition of variables, functional form, or data sources. We have, therefore, estimated our own demand and supply functions using ordinary least squares and converting the time series data used to U.S. dollars. In countries where currency devaluation or appreciation has occurred over the estimated time period, it was necessary to select

---

[2] If data were available it would be difficult to estimate supply and demand functions for the Communist countries since prices and the levels set for wheat consumption and production (except for biological factors) are determined by the central planning authorities.

[3] See Allen [1], Bowlen [5], Brandow [7], Candler [8], Cromarty [9], Duloy and Watson [10], Farnsworth and Jones [11], Gruen and others [12], Kahlen [14], Lehfeldt [16], Meinken [17], Oury [19], Schmitz [22], Schultz [24], Vigen [32], Wang [33], Wold and Jureen [35], and Working [36].

a base rate rather than yearly exchange rates for converting time series price data [4]. The year 1965 was chosen because it is a recent year in which exchange rates among the major importers and exporters of wheat did not change. Of the countries included in the analysis, Argentina is the only one experiencing rapid inflation in recent years. Hence, prior to estimation of its demand and supply equations, Argentina's demand prices were deflated by the consumer price index; and prices in the acreage equation were deflated by the cost-of-input index. In both cases 1965 was used as the base year.

Two additional measurement constraints are imposed by the programming algorithm. First, the supply and demand equations must be specified as a function of wheat prices alone. Thus, other independent variables were fixed at a predetermined level, multiplied by their respective coefficients, and added to the constant term. Second, the equations must be in linear form. If nonlinear equations are estimated, they must be approximated linearly. Since the errors introduced by linear approximations may well be as large as those obtained by direct linear estimation, the latter approach was taken.

Wheat is viewed as a homogeneous commodity.[4] Also, separate demand equations were not estimated for the four uses of wheat — food, feed, industrial, and seed — because there is no breakdown by wheat uses for some countries. In many cases aggregation may not be serious since most of the wheat is consumed in the form of bread.

Finally, equations representing the demand for stocks were not estimated. Stocks are exogenous to the model and are either assumed to remain at their past levels or alternative levels are introduced.

2.1. Demand equations

Two types of demand equations were estimated, both at the wholesale level. In one, all four wheat uses were aggregated; in the other, wheat

---

[4] There appears to be a large degree of substitutability among wheats in the manufacture of bread. At least 90% of the wheat traded is used for bread and related bakery products; the remainder is used for highly specialized bakery products, macaroni, and other pastes. It is agreed generally, for example, that the United Kingdom requires high-protein wheat from Canada to combine with its soft wheats. However, it appears that 95% of the flour mix can consist of any combination of wheats, including the Hard Red and Soft Red Winter varieties from the United States. In this study adjustments are made via the transportation cost matrix to allow for differences in wheat quality; therefore, the consequences of viewing wheat as a homogeneous commodity are probably not seriously damaging.

consumed as food was the regressand, and a fixed quantity was added after estimation to represent the other three uses. For the solutions presented in this study, the latter type of equation was used except for Argentina, Italy, and Belgium-Luxembourg where data on demand for wheat as food only were not available.[5]

Table 1 contains the price and income elasticities for this set of equations. Except for Argentina, all the negative price elasticities are less than 0.45; and except for Japan the income elasticities are also negative. Since prices and incomes have been increasing in all countries, the negative income and price elasticities reflect the decline in per capita demand for wheat as food. The one exception is Japan where per capita consumption has increased, and the estimated income elasticity is positive. All of the negative income elasticities are less than 0.40, except for Australia.

Table 1

Price and income elasticities of demand for
wheat as food by country [a]

Country	Price elasticities	Income elasticities
United States	−0.035	−0.347
Canada	−0.256	−0.075
Australia	−0.204	−0.590
Argentina	−1.484	−0.255
Japan	−0.140	+0.352
United Kingdom	−0.285	−0.365
France	−0.112	−0.256
Italy	−0.023	−0.001
Belgium-Luxembourg	−0.079	−0.117
West Germany	−0.412	−0.209
The Netherlands	−0.431	−0.055

[a] Elasticities are computed at the mean value for price and income.

In order to specify quantity solely as a function of price, the population, income, and trend coefficients were multiplied by 1980 values for the variables themselves. The estimated intercept value was then adjusted by these values.

[5] For each equation type, several different combinations of independent variables were used in estimation. Solutions were run using many of these; they are reported in Schmitz [23].

2.2. *Supply equations*

Acreage equations and wheat yields were estimated and projected separately and then combined to form supply equations. This procedure was used because acreage planted and yields are determined largely by different factors.

Two general types of acreage equations were estimated. First, a simple price expectation model was used in which expected price at time t equals price in $t-1$. Secondly, a distributed lag formulation, developed by Koyck [15] and used by Nerlove [18], was used for some countries. For the major exporting countries — Canada, Australia, Argentina, France and Italy — equations were estimated using wheat acreage as the regressand. For the remaining countries, equations were estimated using as a regressand the ratio of wheat acreage to total cultivated acreage available in the region.

Wheat price elasticities with respect to acreage are shown in table 2. Two estimates of the simple lagged model are presented for each country except West Germany; Nerlovian elasticities are shown only for the five countries for which this type of equation was estimated. The elasticities vary considerably, both within and among countries. Considering only those derived from using the simple lagged price expectation model, the range is from 0.089 to 1.527. In four of the nine regions for which two estimates are shown, one elasticity is roughly twice the other.

In general, the elasticities suggest that farmers are more responsive to wheat price changes in Canada, Australia, Argentina, and the Netherlands than in Japan, France, Italy, and West Germany. Belgium-Luxembourg falls somewhere in between, and the United Kingdom is difficult to categorize (though elasticities of three of the four equations estimated for the United Kingdom ranged between 0.30 and 0.55).[6]

The acreage equations are projected to 1980 in a manner similar to demand. Projections are made of all regressors except wheat price, and

---

[6] Unfortunately, studies with which these elasticities can be compared are available for Australia and France only. The wheat price elasticities estimated by Duloy and Watson [10] for Australia are similar to those obtained in this study. Their estimates, using the simple lagged model, range from 0.480 to 0.893. In this study the corresponding elasticities are 0.817 and 0.868. In theAustralian study the short-run elasticities, based on the distributed lag model, range from 0.131 to 0.505; the long-run elasticities range from 0.596 to 7.950. The authors' short-run elasticities are 0.398 and 3.538, respectively. Oury [19] presents four acreage equations for France, but they are not directly comparable with those of the authors because the wheat price is deflated. If deflated prices are used, the results appear to change significantly. The elasticity computed by Oury for deflated wheat prices is 0.631; the undeflated price elasticities calculated by the authors range from 0.051 to 0.214.

Table 2

Wheat price elasticities computed from estimated acreage equations by country [a]

Country	Elasticity		
	Simple lag model	Distributed lag model (Nerlove type)	
		Short run	Long run
Canada	0.863	0.559	1.186
	0.873	0.565	1.354
Australia	0.817	0.398	3.538
	0.868		
Argentina	0.696		
	1.310		
Japan	0.233		
	0.216		
United Kingdom	0.543		
	0.344		
France	0.089	0.051	0.109
	0.214		
Italy	0.219	0.188	0.328
	0.144		
West Germany	0.155		
Belgium-Luxembourg	0.747		
	0.314		
Netherlands	1.527		
	1.040		

[a] The elasticities are computed at the mean values for price and acreage.

each projected regressor is multiplied by the relevant estimated coefficient so that acreage is expressed solely as a function of price.

Yield equations are more difficult to estimate than acreage equations because yield depends principally on biological factors for which data cannot readily be quantified (disease, insects, weather, etc.). Because of the difficulties encountered in estimating wheat yields as a function of such variables, yields were regressed against time and projected to 1980 using the trend coefficient.[7] The results are shown in column 1 of Appendix

[7] In the original study, yields were also estimated using a recent statistical method of analysis developed by Box and Jenkins [6] known as parametric modeling. Some of the results are presented in Schmitz and Watts [21].

table A1.[8] As an alternative, yield equations for Canada, Australia and Argentina were reestimated, deleting one outlying observation in each time series. These estimates, plus the original for the United States, were then used to project yields to 1980 for the other seven regions analyzed. Both the percentage and average increases for the original four countries were applied to the mean yields for each of those countries in order to obtain the 1980 projections. The 'high' and 'low' yields are given in columns 2 and 3, respectively, of Appendix table A1.

The yield projections in Appendix table A1 are multiplied by the 1980 acreage equations to form the 1980 supply equations for each region.

2.3. Export–import gaps

For the regions not represented by estimated demand and supply equations, it is necessary to make consumption and production projections. Actual consumption and production in Other Europe, Other Asia, Africa, and Other America from 1959 to 1965 were regressed against time and projected to 1980 using the time trend coefficient. Thus, for these regions, demand and supply are exogenous. The export–import gap (the difference between projected consumption and production) is given for each region in Appendix table A2. Of the four regions, only Other Europe is projected to be a net wheat exporter.

2.4. Transfer costs

In order to estimate the cost of intercountry transfer, production and consumption points must be specified in each country in addition to the ports through which wheat is shipped. Each country (or group of countries) is represented by one production and one consumption point, chosen to be representative of its major wheat producing and consuming areas. These designations are listed in Appendix table A3.

The cost of transferring wheat from one country to another is an aggregation representing several activities: handling by the grain elevators, loading for transfer to the port, inland transportation, unloading at the port; loading on an ocean-going vessel, ocean transportation, unloading at

---

[8] These results appear to be unsatisfactory. For example, the yield projection for the United States seems to be high relative to that for Canada and Australia. United States yields are projected to exceed Canada's by 12.5 bushels per acre, but there has been an average difference of only 3.1 bushels per acre over the data range. Also, Italy has the lowest past mean yields of the six European regions; but it is projected to have the third highest yield by 1980, nearly 19 bushels per acre above that of France.

the port; and loading for transfer to the consumption center, inland transportation, unloading, and further handling. The total costs of transferring
wheat from the production to consumption centers in Appendix table A3
are given in Appendix table A4.

3. Empirical results

3.1.

Several alternative solutions are now discussed and their consequences
later interpreted. An arbitrarily selected basic solution is first presented.
Several non-policy alternatives (Group I) are then explored in order to
observe the sensitivity of the results (1) to changes in the import–export
gap for the two major world producers, the U.S.S.R. and Communist
China, and (2) to changes in yields for all countries.[9] Finally, some specific
policy alternatives (Group II) are considered relating to United States
acreage allotment and the EEC target price for wheat.[10]

3.2. The basic solution (Model 1)

The underlying supply equations for the basic solution reflect the low-
yield projections in column 3, Appendix table A1. United States acreage
controls are assumed to remain in effect; therefore, the production corresponding to this acreage (1.5 billion bushels) is fixed. A common internal
price for the EEC of $ 2.90 per bushel is assumed.[11] The figures in Appendix

[9] In deriving a single equilibrium solution, only one demand and one supply equation
can be used for each region. Since several were estimated for each region, a choice among
alternative equations has to be made for each solution. The choices were made using both
statistical tests applied to the equations themselves and the 'reasonableness' of the
equilibrium solutions. For a detailed discussion of the equations from which the
solutions were derived and the selection process involved, see Schmitz [23, ch. 8].

[10] Several other policy alternatives were also considered and reported in Schmitz [23].

[11] Also, Canada's supply intercept is decreased by 200 million bushels to allow for
recent Canadian wheat sales to the Soviet Union and Communist China. Correspondingly,
the demand projections for Other Europe and Other Asia are each decreased by 100
million bushels since each is forced to import that amount from Canada. Shipping costs
from Canada to the United Kingdom are reduced by 10 cents per bushel, thus giving
Canadian exports an advantage in the United Kingdom market. Likewise, the cost of
wheat shipments from the United States to Japan is reduced by the same amount. Canada
appears to have an advantage in the United Kingdom market because of its high-protein
spring wheat. (Among the non-Communist countries, the United Kingdom is by far the
largest importer of Canadian wheat.) On the other hand, the Japanese seem to prefer
low-protein wheats, some of which are grown in the United States.

table A2 are used for the exogenous regions, except that the export gap for Other Europe is assumed to be 600 million bushels rather than the projected 762.4 million bushels.[12]

The results are shown in table 3. Producer (origin) prices are less than $ 1.50 per bushel for the four largest wheat exporting countries (United States, Canada, Australia, and Argentina) and less than $ 1.25 per bushel for Canada and Australia. In none of the 11 regions is the producer price above $ 1.80 per bushel, except for the EEC where the target price is $ 2.90 per bushel. In no case is the miller's (destination) price above $ 2.00 per bushel, except for the EEC.

Since total world production equals consumption at the equilibrium prices, both are predicted to be 11.62 billion bushels in 1980, considerably higher than the annual average of 8.90 billion bushels for the crop years 1959/60–1963/64. Production and consumption for Other Asia are fixed at 1.30 billion and 2.97 billion bushels, respectively; for Other Europe, 5.6 billion and 5.0 billion bushels, respectively. The two regions combined produce 6.91 billion bushels (nearly 60 % of the total) and consume 7.79 billion bushels (67 % of the total). The countries for which equations were estimated produce 4.15 billion bushels, which is 36 % of world production. Of this quantity, the United States, the EEC, and Canada (the largest producers in that order) account for 3.38 billion bushels (81 %). Likewise, the countries represented by demand equations consume 2.53 billion bushels, or 22 % of the world total. Of this, the EEC and the United States account for 62 %.

Of the world total of 11.62 billion bushels, 2.62 billion bushels are exported. The exporters in order of importance (in millions of bushels) are: the United States, 880; Canada, 630; Other Europe, 600; Australia, 263; Argentina, 151; and the EEC, 89. The United States and Canada comprise 58 % of the total exports.

On the import side, Other Asia receives 1.66 billion bushels, which is 63 % of the world export total. The United Kingdom and Japan, generally considered to be large importers, account for only 13 %.

3.3. Group I

In this set of results, alternative production and consumption levels are considered for the major wheat trading nations.

---

[12] This change is made to demonstrate that, even with extremely conservative estimates for the U.S.S.R. production, prices for the major exporters (Canada, Australia and the United States) are still below those established by the Cereals Agreement.

Table 3 (Model 1)

1980 predictions; EEC target price of $ 2.90 per bushel — low wheat yields
(prices in United States dollars per bushel; quantities in thousands of bushels)

To \ From	United States	Canada	Australia	Argentina	Japan	United Kingdom	EEC	Other Europe [a]	Other Asia	Africa	Other America
United States	619 635							100 000	779 110		101 260
Canada	207 720				174 155	173 820			181 605		
Australia		99 420							200	262 495	
Argentina			153 725								154 145
Japan				50 000							
United Kingdom						100 000					
EEC							951 290			88 715	
Other Europe [a]								4 900 000	700 005		
Other Asia									1 306 200		
Africa										233 890	
Other America											48 790
Origin price	1.41	1.22	1.22	1.47	1.55	1.62	2.90	1.54	1.79	1.76	1.75
Destination price	1.53	1.44	1.56	1.63	1.68	1.70	2.90	1.62	1.97	1.90	1.84
Consumption	619 635	207 720	99 420	153 725	224 155	273 820	951 290	5 000 000	2 967 120	585 100	534 270
Production	1 500 005	837 300	362 115	307 870	50 000	100 000	1 040 005	5 600 005	1 306 200	233 890	278 860

[a] Includes the U.S.S.R.

3.3.1. Wheat production in the U.S.S.R.

In the basic solution, production in Other Europe (which includes the U.S.S.R.) was fixed at 5.6 billion bushels, and it was noted that the U.S.S.R. is the world's largest single wheat producer. An alternative solution (Model 2, Appendix table A5) shows the impact on 1980 price and trade predictions of a reduction in Other Europe's production from 5.6 billion to 5.2 billion bushels (an extremely conservative estimate, reducing the export–import gap to 200 million bushels from the 600 million bushels in the initial solution). First, this decrease in production increases producer prices in the large exporting regions by approximately 50 cents per bushel, bringing producer prices above $ 1.70 per bushel. Interestingly, 1980 world production is only slightly less than in the initial solution. This is because the endogenous regions increase supply in response to an increase in wheat prices (caused by the reduction in Other Europe's production).[13]

The increase in supply and decrease in demand in Canada, Australia, and Argentina, caused by the above price rise, resulted in a 35 % increase in exports from these regions (from 1.05 billion to 1.42 billion bushels). United States exports increased only 6.1 million bushels, or less than 1 %. Since supply is unresponsive to price, the increase in exports is due solely to the decrease in domestic demand caused by the rise in prices. While the magnitude of trade flows changes from the initial solution, the pattern does not.

3.3.2. Demand in Other Asia

The import–export gap of Other Asia, the largest importing region, had been set at 1.67 billion bushels in the two previous solutions, reflecting recent large shipments of wheat from the United States to India under P.L. 480. In this solution, the gap is set at 1.16 billion bushels to reflect the possibility that P.L. 480 shipments will decline by 1980 (Model 3).

The major results are as follows (for detailed information, see [23]): Producer prices in the regions represented by supply and demand response equations fall below $ 1.50 per bushel (except for the EEC fixed price of $ 2.90); and world production in 1980 is predicted to be 11.13 billion bushels compared with 11.57 billion bushels when Other Asia's demand was set at 2.97 billion bushels. This decrease in world production almost equals the reduction in Other Asia's demand because the drop in price has a

---

[13] The more price elastic supply and the more inelastic demand the greater is the supply forthcoming. It can be shown also that the greater the price elasticities of both the supply and demand equations the smaller is the change in price resulting from an exogenous change in supply.

greater influence on supply response than it has on demand. Price elasticities computed from the estimated demand equations are small; hence, a large increase in demand in other countries does not follow when prices decrease by 65 cents per bushel because of the 500-million-bushel reduction in Other Asia's import–export gap.

In the first alternative solution, Canada exported 835 million bushels; Australia, 350 million bushels; and Argentina, 238 million bushels — a total of 1.42 billion bushels. After the demand decreased to 2.47 billion bushels for Other Asia, exports fell to 955 million bushels — a decrease of 33 percent. While the magnitude of trade flows changes due to a demand decrease in Other Asia, the pattern of trade changes little; Canada now exports to Africa, and Australia discontinues its exports to Other Asia.

3.3.3. The impact of yield changes (Model 4)
The results of using high-yield projections in the supply equations are shown in Appendix table A6. The principal effect is to increase EEC production by 17 % (to 1.21 billion bushels). For the four largest wheat exporting countries, producer prices drop to less than $ 1.10 per bushel and to less than $ 1.00 for Canada and Australia. Prices paid by the millers are not above $ 1.60 per bushel in any region except the EEC where $ 2.90 is paid. In general, prices decrease by 20 cents per bushel when the high rather than low wheat yields are assumed. Interestingly, total world production is the same under both low and high wheat yields. This is because the increase in EEC production is offset by a supply decrease in Canada, Australia, and Argentina due to falling prices.

Wheat-yield increases for the EEC change the world trade flows in the following manner: (1) Total wheat exports from the traditional large exporters decline due to the 170-million-bushel increase in exports from the EEC; (2) Canada's wheat exports to Africa cease and her shipments to the United Kingdom decline since the latter now imports wheat from the EEC which did not occur under low yields; and (3) Australia exports wheat to Other Asia.

3.3.4. Summary of Group I solutions
In addition to the above results, equilibrium solutions were derived under several other consumption and production levels for Other Europe and Other Asia. Also, alternative projections of Japanese demand were used since Japan's current per capita consumption of wheat is the lowest among the countries for which equations were estimated. By 1980 demand could well be above that projected on the basis of past trends.

The 1980 predicted prices, production, consumption, exports, and imports from all the equilibrium solutions computed are briefly summarized in table 4. The prices are for producers in Canada and Australia (which are the same) and for the United States. Corresponding to each of the predicted farm prices are (1) wheat exports for the United States, Canada, and Australia and Argentina combined — the four largest wheat exporters; (2) total 1980 world exports (which equal imports); (3) total 1980 production (which equals consumption); and (4) the export–import gaps for Other Europe and Other Asia.

Table 4

A summary of 1980 predictions for prices, production, consumption, exports, and imports. EEC target price of $ 2.90 per bushel; United States production of 1.5 billion bushels; (prices in United States dollars per bushel; quantities in millions of bushels)

Producer prices		Exports			Total exports = net imports	Total production = consumption	Export–import gap for	
Canada, Australia	United States	United States	Canada	Australia, Argentina			Other Europe [a]	Other Asia
0.87	1.03	876	496	292	2126	11 146	200	−1160
1.00	1.16	877	548	335	2423	11 437	400	−1361
1.09	1.28	879	578	374	2120	11 127	200	−1161
1.22	1.41	880	630	417	2716	11 616	600	−1661
1.35	1.53	882	681	459	2311	11 305	200	−1361
1.48	1.66	883	732	502	2606	11 384	400	−1661
1.52	1.71	884	750	682	2606	11 380	200	−1661
1.74	1.92	886	835	588	2598	11 572	200	−1661
1.84	2.03	888	793	623	2593	11 653	200	−1661
2.03	2.21	890	962	656	2597	11 557	0	−1655

[a] Includes the U.S.S.R.
Source: Computed from equilibrium solutions.

Table 4 indicates that (1) producer prices in Canada and Australia range widely, from 87 cents to $ 2.03 per bushel, while those in the United States vary from $ 1.03 to $ 2.21 per bushel; (2) United States wheat exports vary only slightly, from 876 million to 890 million bushels; (3) Canada's exports reach a high of 962 million bushels from a low of 496 million bushels, while the combined exports for Australia and Argentina vary from 292 million to 656 million bushels; (4) total world exports (equal net imports) range from 2120 million to 2716 million bushels; (5) total world wheat production (equals consumption) remains within a narrow range of 11 127 million to

11 616 million bushels; (6) the export–import gap for Other Europe varies from 600 million bushels to 0; and (7) the corresponding gap for Other Asia varies from −1160 million to −1661 million bushels.

3.4. Group II

This group of solutions explores alternative policies of the United States and the EEC, assuming different yields.

3.4.1. United States Acreage Allotments

To this point no attempt has been made to determine how changes in United States acreage allotments will affect world wheat prices and exports. In the previous solutions, United States production was set at 1.5 billion bushels, corresponding to slightly over 42 million acres and a projected wheat yield of 35 bushels per acre.[14]

In the following two cases, United States sales for commercial markets are set at 1.2 billion (Model 5) and 1.8 billion bushels (Model 6), corresponding to 34.3 million and 51.4 million acres, respectively. Producer prices in the major exporting countries are well above $ 2.00 per bushel when United States production is 1.2 billion bushels. However, when United States production is increased to 1.8 billion bushels, producer prices drop to less than $ 1.65 per bushel. The results show that a drop in production from 1.8 billion to 1.2 billion bushels increases producer prices by approximately 85 cents per bushel.[15]

While producer prices are greatly affected by different acreage control levels, world wheat production is not. The increase in United States production of 600 million bushels (from 1.2 billion to 1.8 billion bushels) increases world production only 70 million bushels. This is similar to the earlier example of varying supply levels in Other Europe. Supply decreases in the endogenous regions by almost the full amount of the increase in United States production because demand in these regions is not greatly affected by price. As a result, exports from the other large exporting countries (Canada and Australia and Argentina) decline by almost the amount of the

---

[14] United States wheat acreage allotments have varied from 43 million acres in 1953 to 68 million acres in 1966; therefore, from an acreage standpoint, 42 million acres is low. However, production has ranged from a low of 1.09 billion bushels in 1962 to a high of 1.50 billion bushels in 1967. Consequently, if yields in the United States did not increase by 1980, the 1.5-billion-bushel estimate is on the high side.

[15] These results can be compared also with those in Appendix Table A5 which are based on the same data, except production in the United States is 1.5 billion bushels.

increase in United States exports — 561 million versus 590 million bushels, respectively. This results in a loss of approximately $ 2.2 billion export revenue for Canada and Australia and Argentina.

The next two solutions (Models 7 and 8) show how overall wheat prices are affected by combinations of change in production and demand in other regions, under two assumed U.S. acreage allotment levels. While production is held at 1.2 billion and 1.8 billion bushels, respectively, the following data changes are made: (1) Other Europe's production is increased from 5.2 billion to 5.7 billion bushels, which is the amount projected in Appendix table A2; (2) the high-yield projections specified previously are used; and (3) Japan's demand intercept is increased by 100 million bushels. These changes significantly affect world wheat prices. With United States production at 1.2 billion bushels (Model 7), producer prices in the major exporting countries decrease from over $ 2.00 per bushel (Model 5) to less than $ 1.70 per bushel (Model 7). The drop is from a high of $ 1.70 per bushel (Model 7) to below 90 cents per bushel (Model 8) when United States production is 1.8 billion bushels along with low wheat yield (Model 8).

Again, total world wheat production is not greatly affected by the increase in United States production from 1.2 billion (Model 7) to 1.8 billion bushels (Model 8), increasing merely from 11.70 billion to 11.77 billion bushels. Furthermore, these figures are only slightly above those when low yields were assumed and Other Europe's production was dropped to 5.2 billion bushels.

3.4.2. EEC target price of $ 3.30 per bushel

By 1980 it is conceivable that wheat in the EEC would be supported above $ 2.90 per bushel (Model 10); hence, a solution was derived using a support price of $ 3.30 per bushel (Model 9). Apart from the change, the results are based on the same data as the basic solution (Appendix table A5). When the price support level is $ 2.90 per bushel, production and consumption in the EEC are 1040 million and 951 million bushels, respectively. At $ 3.30 per bushel, production increases by 46 million bushels and consumption decreases by only 19 million bushels. The pattern of export trade is not changed by the increased support price; and producer prices in the major exporting countries are not greatly affected, showing a decline of only 10 cents per bushel.

3.4.3. Eliminating the EEC target price (Model 10)

To assess the effect of EEC's common agricultural policy with respect to wheat, a solution was derived assuming no internal EEC target price. The results appear in Appendix table A7 and may be compared with the figures in Appendix table A6, since all other data assumptions are the same for both solutions. Thus United States production is set at 1.5 billion bushels, and Other Asia's imports and Other Europe's exports are set at 1160 million and 200 million bushels, respectively.

The prices in the non-EEC countries increase by approximately $ 1.50 per bushel. As a result, the EEC exports only 11.5 million bushels, a considerable drop from previous exports of 262.9 million bushels. Production and exports in non-EEC countries increase to take up most of this decline. EEC wheat shipments to the United Kingdom are replaced by Canadian exports, and those to Africa are replaced by exports from both the United States and Canada.

3.4.4. Summary of Group II solutions

Additional solutions were computed for various combinations of wheat yields, United States allotments, and tariff levels for the EEC. The 1980 predicted prices, production, consumption, exports, and imports using

Table 5

Summary of 1980 predictions for prices, production, consumption, exports, and imports. Alternative levels of EEC target prices and United States acreage controls; (prices in United States dollars per bushel; quantities in millions of bushels)

Producer prices		Exports			Total exports = net imports	Total production = consumption	Export–import gap for	
Canada, Australia	United States	United States	Canada	Australia, Argentina			Other Europe [a]	Other Asia
0.53	0.67	1172	423	180	2738	11 768	700	−1661
1.00	1.16	1177	548	335	2723	10 642	400	−1661
1.04	1.21	878	555	353	2323	11 213	200	−1361
1.20	1.34	880	622	402	2116	11 167	200	−1161
1.27	1.45	881	648	431	2314	11 293	200	−1361
1.35	1.53	1182	681	460	2612	11 603	200	−1661
1.38	1.57	582	694	470	2709	11 702	700	−1661
1.42	1.60	883	708	481	2609	11 581	200	−1661
1.42	1.50	882	708	480	2270	11 243	200	−1161
1.65	1.84	885	801	558	2598	11 560	200	−1661
1.74	1.92	586	835	587	2209	11 198	200	−1161
2.16	2.35	592	1006	694	2581	11 535	200	−1661

[a] Includes the U.S.S.R.
Source: Computed from equilibrium solutions.

alternative EEC target prices and United States acreage allotments are summarized in table 5. Prices given are for producers in Canada and Australia combined and the United States. Also given are (1) wheat exports for the United States, Canada, and Australia and Argentina combined — the four largest wheat exporters; (2) total 1980 wheat exports (which equal net imports); (3) total 1980 production (which equals consumption); and (4) the export–import gaps for Other Europe and Other Asia.

Table 5 shows that (1) producer prices in Canada and Australia range from 53 cents to $ 2.16 per bushel, and those in the United States vary from 67 cents to $ 2.35 per bushel; (2) United States exports vary from a low of 582 million bushels to a high of 1182 million bushels; (3) Canada's exports reach a high of 1006 million bushels from a low of 423 million bushels, while the combined amounts for Australia and Argentina vary from 694 million to 180 million bushels; (4) total world exports (equal to net imports) range from 2709 million to 2116 million bushels; (5) total world wheat production (equal to consumption) increases from a low of 10 642 million bushels to a high of 11 702 million bushels; (6) the export–import gap for Other Europe varies from 200 to 700 million bushels; and (7) the corresponding gap for Other Asia varies from −1161 million to −1661 million bushels.

4. Conclusions and implications

In a study such as this, it is not meaningful merely to present the solution without giving consideration to possible future government policies and changes in technology. Since these are not known, a range of predictions was provided corresponding to a range of policy actions and technological considerations. Although a comparison of any two solutions is important to evaluate isolated effects of a specific policy change, one must examine all solutions together in order to draw conclusions about the future of the world wheat economy.

Because space does not permit an enumeration of conclusions country by country, the focus here will be on the general state of the world wheat economy in the future, particularly with respect to the price level and its implications for future policy.

In 1967 the historic International Wheat Agreements were replaced by the International Cereals Agreement which set minimum and maximum prices (given in table 6) for the major exporting countries. In general, even the minimum prices are above those predicted in the solutions in

Table 6

1967 International Cereals Agreement, minimum and maximum prices

Country	Negotiated prices	
	Minimum	Maximum
	(United States dollars per bushel, f.o.b.)	
Canada	1.596	1.996
United States	1.501	1.901
Australia	1.299	1.699
Argentina	1.530	1.930

Source: Personal communication with J. L. Leibfried, Canadian Wheat Board, Winnipeg, Manitoba.

this study. When the agricultural policy of the EEC is assumed to remain intact, only six of the solutions predict 1980 wheat prices above the minimums set in the 1967 Cereals Agreement.[16] However, these six solutions are based on a most optimistic set of assumptions which, when taken together, are felt by the authors to be unrealistic. First, United States production is set at 1.5 billion bushels in all six solutions. This corresponds to a 42 million-acre allotment in contrast to recent allotments of 50–68 million acres. Second, all six solutions are based on the low-yield projections. In view of recent yield increases in Japan, the United Kingdom, France, Italy, West Germany, Belgium-Luxembourg, and the Netherlands, our low-yield projections appear to understate the production potential in these areas. When high yields were used in the solutions, regardless of what other assumptions were made, prices were below the minimums negotiated under the 1967 agreement in every case. With high yields, the EEC was predicted to be self-sufficient, even in the absence of a common internal tariff. Thus, the EEC countries as a group are likely to be net exporters in 1980 in contrast to net importers during the early 1960's.

A third optimistic assumption in all six solutions is that production in Other Europe will be below that projected on the basis of past data (that is, 5.2 instead of the 5.7 billion bushels shown in Appendix table A2). However, even the 5.7 billion figure may be too low. The average yield for the U.S.S.R., the largest wheat producer in the world, was approximately 14 bushels per acre for the crop years 1959/60–1963/64. This is substantially

[16] The analysis did not include the United Kingdom as a Common Market country; its entry into the Common Market will result in wheat export prices being further depressed.

below that for countries experiencing similar growing conditions, such as Canada. Thus, yields could easily be above those used in the 1980 projections if the U.S.S.R. central planning authorities decided to invest more heavily in agriculture. If yields increased by 3 bushels per acre, production in the U.S.S.R. would increase by approximately 500 million bushels, a magnitude that would depress world wheat prices approximately 60 cents a bushel.

The final reason why world prices in 1980 are likely to be substantially below the 1967 negotiated minimums (given current policies) is that projections for Other Asia are probably too low on the production side and too high on the consumption side. This is because neither the effect on production of new wheat varieties in Asia nor the effect on consumption of greater rice production due to new varieties were taken into account.

According to Willett [34], in 1968–69 these new varieties occupied approximately 7 % of the rice land and 16 % of the wheat area in the less-developed countries of Asia (excluding Communist China). By comparison, in 1967–68 the new rice and wheat varieties accounted for 3 and 11 % of the areas, respectively; in the previous year they accounted for only 1 and 2 %, respectively. Numerous experiments suggest that, when complemented with adequate irrigation and a high level of fertilization, the new rice and wheat varieties have a yield advantage of 30–100 % over traditional varieties grown under similar conditions [34, p. 13].

At the time of our analysis, the above information on the use of new crop varieties in Asia was not available. Production and consumption for Other Asia were projected merely on the basis of data from 1959 to 1966, which showed a gradual decline in total wheat production while consumption increased. Production for Other Asia was projected to be 1.3 billion bushels, which is below that for any year from 1959 to 1966. In view of the recent introduction of these new varieties, this figure appears to be too low. Data indicate that 5.22 million hectares in Asia are currently planted to new wheat varieties [34]. Assume a 50 % increase in yields over the traditional varieties or a 0.5 metric ton per hectare increase. Although the past rate of adoption of the new varieties is greater than 2 million hectares per year, assume that for each year to 1980 only 1 million hectares are seeded to the new varieties. This would result in an increase in production of approximately 310 million bushels. This amount added to the above projections of 1.3 billion bushels gives a total production of 1.6 billion bushels for Other Asia or a reduction in the import gap from 1.7 billion to 1.4 billion bushels.

The corresponding consumption projection from which the import gap was calculated was 3 billion bushels. The reasonableness of this projection depends, among other things, on rice production increases in Asian countries and the degree to which rice will replace wheat as a major food item. The data show that rice acreage in the Asian regions for 1968–69 was 77.3 million hectares, more than twice the wheat acreage [34], and that prior to the new rice varieties yields were 1.6 metric tons per hectare. Assume that by 1980 rice yields of new varieties increase by 50 % and that 2 million hectares are seeded to the new varieties in addition to the 5.22 million hectares of 1968–69. Based on these assumptions, production would be approximately 800 million bushels above that calculated (using 77.3 million hectares and a yield of 1.6 metric tons per hectare). If part of this increase substitutes for wheat consumption, the projected wheat demand of 3 billion bushels is likely biased upward.

Taking into consideration the effect of new varieties on projections of both production and consumption, the authors feel that an import gap of 1.2 billion bushels for Other Asia is probably more realistic than the 1.7 billion originally projected (Appendix table A2). Price levels for solutions based on a 1.2-billion-bushel import gap are 65 cents per bushel below those based on the 1.7 billion figure.

The predictions in this study were completed in 1967 when world wheat prices and exports were substantially above those in the 1950's and early 1960's. Many believed that even the maximum price negotiated under the 1967 Cereals Agreement could be reached without accumulating large surpluses. In the spring of 1970, the world wheat economy presented a different picture. For the first time in history Canadian farmers were paid to take land out of wheat production, and acreage controls were imposed in Australia. Correspondingly, more restrictive controls were adopted in the United States. Still, world wheat prices at times fell below the minimum established by the 1967 Cereals Agreement, even though the Wheat Boards in Canada and Australia and the Commodity Credit Corporation in the United States accumulated large wheat stocks. In Canada, for example, large wheat stocks were accumulated at the farm level.

Our findings indicate that the situation which existed for the later part of the 1960's is not merely a temporary one despite the large wheat sales in 1972 by the United States to the Soviet Union. The major wheat exporting nations will again be confronted with the problem of disposing large wheat surpluses if the large increase in world wheat plantings expected for 1973 continues for two to three years.

Appendix

Table A1
1980 wheat yield projections, by country

Country	1980 projections [a]				
	Inde-pendent	Revised (high)	Revised (low)	Sorenson–Hathaway	Storey
	(1)	(2)	(3)	(4)	(5)
United States	35.81	35.81	35.81		33.84
Canada	23.34	27.73	27.73		30.10
Australia	26.12	23.89	23.89		23.94 [b]
Argentina	34.45	27.05	27.05		22.72 [c]
Japan	33.70	46.56	41.56		40.34
United Kingdom	90.46	72.21	67.21		
France	63.01	51.81	46.81	68.29	
Italy	81.74	47.78	42.78	39.79	
West Germany	70.96	65.40	60.40	61.60	
Belgium-Luxembourg	76.92	75.35	70.35	64.44	
The Netherlands	93.97	84.94	79.74	80.18	

[a] Stated in bushels per acre.
[b] Projection for Oceania.
[c] Projection for Rio de la Plata region.
Sources: Cols. 1, 2, and 3: Calculated. Col. 4 Sorensen [26]. Col. 5: Storey [27].

Table A2
1980 export–import gap for the four exogenous regions

Region	Production	Consumption	Net exports	Net imports
		(million bushels)		
Other Europe [a]	5695.35	4932.98	762.37	
Other Asia	1306.20	2967.12		1660.92
Africa	233.89	585.10		351.21
Other America [b]	278.86	534.27		255.41
Total	7514.30	9022.49	762.37	2267.54

[a] Includes the U.S.S.R.
[b] Excludes the United States and Canada.
Source: Computed from data contained in International Wheat Council, World Wheat Statistics, London, various issues.

Table A3

Wheat production and consumption centers and ports, by geographic regions

Geographic region	Production center	Consumption center	Ports
United States	Kansas City	St. Louis	Gulf
Canada	Regina	Toronto	St. Lawrence Seaway and Vancouver
Australia	Dubbo	Sydney	Eastern Australia
Argentina	Rosario	Buenos Aires	Rio del Plata
Japan	Tokyo	Tokyo	Tokyo and other
United Kingdom	London	London	Great Britain
EEC	Paris	Mannheim	Amsterdam-Antwerp-Hamburg
Other Europe [a]	Kiev	Kiev	Black Sea
Other Asia	Peking	Calcutta	Communist China or India
Africa	Johannesburg	Capetown	Ghana or Nigeria
Other America	Mexico City	Rio de Janeiro	Rio de Janeiro and West Indies

[a] Includes the U.S.S.R.

Table A4

Wheat transportation cost matrix — production to consumption centers

From \ To	United States	Canada	Australia	Argentina	Japan	United Kingdom	EEC	Other Europe [a]	Other Asia	Africa	Other America
					(cents per bushel)						
United States	12.38	22.94	57.65	52.96	59.66	50.62	48.57	66.95	66.36	64.35	52.96
Canada	29.00	21.84	57.71	64.76	46.06	57.87	56.34	67.67	74.81	68.11	64.76
Australia	82.45	99.39	33.40	71.91	68.56	73.10	77.81	67.67	74.81	68.11	64.76
Argentina	59.36	68.50	53.51	16.46	75.63	56.84	60.44	62.98	71.46	66.10	36.63
Japan	59.66	74.14	43.76	69.83	13.60	35.22	51.35	52.56	42.28	41.61	42.51
United Kingdom	50.08	54.15	47.76	64.23	34.68	8.00	26.37	32.90	49.41	40.70	44.72
EEC	49.09	50.09	49.94	50.97	48.32	23.84	14.70	32.17	48.68	39.97	43.99
Other Europe [a]	67.31	65.21	40.99	57.30	53.28	34.16	40.29	8.63	43.24	45.91	55.96
Other Asia	76.27	81.54	39.86	74.96	52.18	50.82	47.59	47.43	18.51	51.21	69.29
Africa	70.18	70.76	39.28	65.53	47.44	47.07	51.86	51.02	52.13	14.43	66.86
Other America	52.96	61.58	47.20	63.04	71.30	59.99	61.43	55.24	64.38	61.03	8.63

[a] Includes the U.S.S.R.

Sources: U. S. Economic Research Service [31]; International Wheat Council [13], 1966; Searle Grain Co., Ltd. [25]; Bjarnason [3].

Note: The matrix is not symmetrical because different points are used to represent production and consumption within most countries. For example, the total cost from Canada to Australia is 57.71 cents per bushel, but from Australia to Canada it is 99.39 cents per bushel. This is because of the greater distance from Dubbo to Toronto than from Regina to Sydney. Also, note that the estimated cost of shipping wheat from the United States to Japan is considerably larger than from Canada to Japan. This is partly because United States shipments from Kansas City to Tokyo are assumed to pass through the gulf ports and partly because costs in the United States prior to ocean shipment are higher than in Canada.

Table A5

1980 predictions; EEC target price of $ 2.90 per bushel; Other Europe's production of 5.2 billion bushels; (prices in United States dollars per bushel; quantities in thousands of bushels)

From \ To	United States	Canada	Australia	Argentina	Japan	United Kingdom	EEC	Other Europe [a]	Other Asia	Africa	Other America
United States	613 540								868 040		18 425
Canada		193 195			169 475	159 930		100 000	405 200		
Australia			94 780						87 675	262 490	
Argentina				153 725							236 980
Japan					50 000						
United Kingdom						100 000					
EEC							951 290			88 715	
Other Europe [a]								4 900 000	300 005		
Other Asia									1 306 200		
Africa										233 890	
Other America											48 790
Origin price	1.92	1.74	1.74	1.98	2.06	2.13	2.02	2.05	2.30	2.27	2.2
Destination price	2.04	1.95	2.07	2.14	2.20	2.21	2.16	2.14	2.48	2.42	2.35
Consumption	613 540	193 195	94 780	153 125	219 475	259 930	951 290	5 000 000	2 967 120	535 095	534 270
Production	1 500 005	1 027 800	444 945	390 705	50 000	100 000	1 040 005	5 200 005	1 306 200	233 890	278 860

[a] Includes the U.S.S.R.

Table A6

1980 predictions; EEC target price of $ 2.90 per bushel, impact of wheat yield changes; (prices in United States dollars per bushel; quantities in thousands of bushels)

To \ From	United States	Canada	Australia	Argentina	Japan	United Kingdom	EEC	Other Europe[a]	Other Asia	Africa	Other America
United States	624 085								714 165		161 750
Canada		217 155			177 195	119 090		100 000	100 000		
Australia			102 805						46 750	152 065	93 655
Argentina				153 725							
Japan					50 000						
United Kingdom						100 000					
EEC						63 765	951 290			199 140	
Other Europe[a]								4 900 000	300 000		
Other Asia									1 306 200		
Africa										233 890	
Other America											48 790
Origin price	1.03	0.85	0.85	1.10	1.21	1.29	2.90	1.16	1.41	1.38	1.38
Destination price	1.16	1.11	1.18	1.26	1.35	1.37	2.90	1.25	1.60	1.53	1.46
Consumption	624 085	217 155	102 805	153 725	227 197	282 855	951 290	5 000 000	2 467 115	585 095	534 270
Production	1 500 000	713 440	301 620	247 380	50 000	100 000	1 214 195	5 200 000	1 306 200	233 890	278 860

[a] Includes the U.S.S.R.

Table A7

1980 predictions barriers to trade excluding the EEC common agricultural policy — high wheat yields.
United States commercial sales of 1.5 billion bushels,
(prices in United States dollars per bushel; quantities in thousands of bushels)

To \ From	United States	Canada	Australia	Argentina	Japan	United Kingdom	EEC	Other Europe[a]	Other Asia	Africa	Other America
United States	620 415								760 915	6 800	111 875
Canada		208 245			174 325	174 330		100 000	100 000	73 400	
Australia			99 590							259 480	
Argentina				153 725							
Japan					50 000						
United Kingdom						100 000					
EEC							1 008 600			11 530	
Other Europe[a]								4 900 000	300 005		
Other Asia									1 306 200		
Africa										233 890	
Other America											48 790
Origin price	1.34	1.20	1.20	1.40	1.53	1.60	1.49	1.47	1.72	1.74	1.68
Destination price	1.47	1.42	1.54	1.57	1.66	1.68	1.63	1.56	1.91	1.88	1.77
Consumption	620 415	208 245	99 590	153.725	224 325	274 300	1 008 600	5 000 000	2 467 120	585 100	537 270
Production	1 500 000	830 300	359 070	297 255	50 000	100 000	1 012 130	5 200 005	1 306 200	233 890	278 860

[a] Includes the U.S.S.R.

References

[1] Allen, G. R., 1954, Wheat farmers and falling prices, Farm Economist, 7, 335–341.

[2] Bawden, D. L., 1966, A spatial price equilibrium model of international trade, Journal of Farm Economics, 48, no. 4, Part 1, 862–874.

[3] Bjarnason, H. F., 1967, An economic analysis of 1980 international trade in feed grains, unpublished Ph.D. dissertation, University of Wisconsin.

[4] Bjarnason, H. F., M. J. McGarry and A. Schmitz, 1969, Converting price series of internationally traded commodities to a common currency prior to estimating national supply and demand equations, American Journal of Agricultural Economics, 51, no. 1, 189–192.

[5] Bowlen, B. J., 1955, The wheat supply function, Journal of Farm Economics, 37, no. 5, 1177–1185.

[6] Box, G. E. P. and G. M. Jenkins, Time Series, Forecasting and Control, San Francisco: Holden-Day, Inc., forthcoming.

[7] Brandow, G. E., Interrelations Among Demand for Farm Products and Implications for Control of Market Supply, Pennsylvania Agricultural Experiment Station Bulletin No. 680, University Park.

[8] Candler, W., 1957, An aggregate supply function for New Zealand wheat, Journal of Farm Economics, 39, no. 5, 1732–1743.

[9] Cromarty, W. A., 1959, An econometric model for U. S. Agriculture, Journal of the American Statistical Association, 54, no. 287, 556–574.

[10] Duloy, J. H. and A. S. Watson, 1964, Supply relationships in the Australian wheat industry: New South Wales, Australian Journal of Agricultural Economics, 8, no. 1, 28–45.

[11] Farnsworth, H. C. and W. O. Jones, 1956, Response of wheat growers to price changes: appropriate or perverse? Economic Journal, 66, no. 20, 271–287.

[12] Gruen, F. H. and others, 1968, Long Term Projections of Agricultural Supply and Demand, Australia, 1965 to 1980, Clayton, Victoria, Australia, Department of Economics, Monash University.

[13] International Wheat Council, World Wheat Statistics, London, various issues.

[14] Kahlen, A. S., 1962, The domestic demand and price structures for different classes of wheat in the United States, unpublished Ph.D. dissertation, Ohio State University.

[15] Koyck, L. M., 1954, Distributed Lags and Investment Analysis, Amsterdam: North-Holland Publishing Company.

[16] Lehfeldt, R. A., 1914, The elasticity of demand for wheat, Economic Journal, 24, 212–217.

[17] Meinken, K. W., 1955, The demand and Price Structure for Wheat, U.S. Department of Agriculture Technical Bulletin No. 1136.

[18] Nerlove, M., 1958, The Dynamics of Supply: Estimation of Farmers' Response to Price, Baltimore: Johns Hopkins Press.

[19] Oury, B., 1963, A tentative production model for wheat and feedgrains in France, unpublished Ph.D. dissertation, University of Wisconsin.

[20] Samuelson, P. A., 1952, Spatial price equilibrium and linear programming, American Economic Review, XLII, no. 3, 283–303.

[21] Schmitz, A. and D. G. Watts, 1970, Forecasting wheat yields: an application of parametric time series modeling, American Journal of Agricultural Economics, 52, no. 2, 247–254.

[22] Schmitz, A., 1968, Canadian wheat acreage response, Canadian Journal of Agricultural Economics, 16, no. 2, 79–86.

[23] Schmitz, A., 1968, An Economic Analysis of the World Wheat Economy in 1980, unpublished Ph.D. dissertation, University of Wisconsin.

[24] Schultz, H. L., 1938, The Theory and Measurement of Demand, Chicago: University of Chicago Press.

[25] Searle Grain Co., Ltd., 1966, United States and Canadian movements of wheat to the European common market, Grain Market Features, XXXV, 3, 4.

[26] Sorenson, V. and D. Hathaway, 1968, The Grain-Livestock Economy and Trade Patterns of the European Economic Community with Projections to 1970 and 1975, East Lansing: Institute of International Agriculture, Michigan State University.

[27] Storey, G., 1966, Long Range Prospects for Canadian Wheat Markets, unpublished Master's thesis, University of Saskatchewan, Canada.

[28] Takayama, T. and G. G. Judge, 1964, Equilibrium among spatially separated markets: a reformulation, Econometrica, 32, no. 4, 510–524.

[29] Takayama, T. and G. G. Judge, 1964, Spatial equilibrium and quadratic programming, Journal of Farm Economics, 46, no. 1, 67–93.

[30] Takayama, T. and G. G. Judge, 1964, An intertemporal price equilibrium model, Journal of Farm Economics, 46, no. 2, 477–484.

[31] U. S. Economic Research Service, Foreign Agricultural Trade of the United States, various issues.

[32] Vigen, J. W., 1965, Analysis of the Demand for Wheat in the European Economic Community with Projections to 1970 and 1975, unpublished Ph.D. dissertation, Ohio State University.

[33] Wang, Y., 1962, The demand and price structure for various classes of wheat, unpublished Ph.D. dissertation, Ohio State University.

[34] Willett, J. W., 1969, The Impact of New Grain Varieties in Asia, U. S. Economic Research Service, Foreign Regional Analysis Division, ERS-Foreign 275.

[35] Wold, H. and L. Jureen, 1953, Demand Analysis: A Study in Econometrics, New York: John Wiley and Sons, Inc.

[36] Working, H., 1917, The elasticities of demand for wheat, Econometrica, 5, no. 2, 184–197.

B. SPATIAL AND/OR
TEMPORAL MODELS

CHAPTER 26

An evaluation of policy alternatives facing Australian banana producers*

J. W. B. GUISE and W. AGGREY-MENSAH

University of New England
Bank of Ghana

1. Introduction

Like many other fruit producers in Australia, banana growers usually receive relatively low net annual incomes. The banana industry regularly encounters periods of glut and low prices followed by periods of shortage and higher prices. While the effects of supply and price instability partly offset each other, there are still considerable fluctuations in growers' incomes and average returns are often insufficient to maintain a satisfactory standard of living.[1]

Massell [10] has discussed the effects of price stabilization through buffer stock schemes on producers' welfare in the context of competitive markets. He concluded that "... producers are more likely to gain the larger the supply variance relative to the demand variance ..." and that "... the likelihood of gain is greater the steeper the supply curve relative to the demand curve ..." [10, p. 293]. While in the past buffer stocks of such a perishable commodity as bananas have been technologically infeasible, Massell's conclusions suggest that such stocks would tend to increase producers' welfare in the Australian context if new technological developments such as have been reported by the C.S.I.R.O. Division of Food Preservation [6] were to make them economically possible.

In the past, lacking such technological developments, the industry has adopted various measures in an attempt to improve the financial position

* The authors gratefully acknowledge financial assistance provided for this project by the Rural Credits Development Fund of the Reserve Bank of Australia.

[1] For example a survey by the Bureau of Agricultural Economics [5] found that approximately 67% of growers received a net annual income from their banana enterprise of less than $ A1000, and approximately 90% received less than $ A2000.

of growers. These have usually taken the form of supply restrictions through marketing quotas (Macfarlane [11]). However, these attempts have been largely unsuccessful, partly because of lack of sufficient support by growers for voluntary restrictions, and partly because of incomplete knowledge of the market.

One of the problems which has received little attention to date, concerns the distribution of the crop. Few studies providing quantitative information on the seasonal behaviour of banana markets have been reported. Van der Meulen [12] concluded that a monthly supply to the Sydney market in excess of 60 000 cases resulted in negative marginal revenues to the industry.

More recently Aggrey-Mensah and Guise [2] analysed the Sydney banana market on a weekly basis, and found strong evidence of complementary seasonality in the supplies of bananas and the estimated demand relationships. Despite this however, they found that the expected weekly supplies to the market, which varied from approximately 20 000 bushels in July (winter) to approximately 40 000 bushels in November and February, gave rise to negative marginal revenues in almost all time periods, these being most marked in the spring season.

These studies indicate that there could be considerable scope for improving growers' returns by rationalizing supply flows to markets. This would involve the introduction of new methods of controlled atmosphere storage and the diversion of part of the present supplies to alternative market outlets either by way of promotion in a competitive market framework, or by deliberate rationalizing action on the part of producers, in a monopolistic market framework. The present study examines these possible ways of improving banana growers' returns by casting the problem into the framework of alternative spatial–temporal price and allocation models of the type developed by Takayama and Judge [13].

It is assumed that given supplies of bananas are expected during each time period of the planning horizon and these are to be allocated among a number of markets distinguished both spatially and temporally. It is also assumed that the demand function for each market in each time period is known, and that there is a constant storage cost for carrying a unit of the commodity between any two consecutive periods. The problem is to determine optimal quantities to be allocated to each market distinguished, the resulting equilibrium prices, and the revenues accruing to producers as a result of implementing each policy alternative.

Two models which represent extremes of market behaviour are discussed, the first involving the assumption of competitive market behaviour on the part of all participants. In terms of the Australian banana industry, the competitive situation is analogous to the existing situation, apart from the introduction of storage possibilities, since the industry is characterized by many small independent producers pursuing their private interests and taking no account of any common objective function to be maximized.

The second model assumes collusive monopolistic behaviour on the part of producers so that their total supplies are allocated among markets in such a way as to maximize their group returns. Such an arrangement could only be effectively implemented through government legislation additional to the present prohibition on imports, and producer organizations have been actively campaigning for such action in recent years, possibly without a clear idea of the effects of long term supply response to increased prices on the continued viability of any such scheme.

Obviously, to be fully appropriate to the Australian situation these models should take account of all spatially and temporally separated local markets for bananas, as well as the spatial separation of producing regions and their varying patterns of production. While in principle this is not difficult, problems of data availability on both the demand and supply sides of the markets limited the feasible analysis to the Sydney market.

Under the existing competitive allocation of supplies, this market handles approximately 30 % of the total annual production, so that an analysis of the effects on producers' revenues of introducing storage possibilities, and an alternative export market outlet for the quantities currently allocated to this market, should be at least indicative of the likely effects on producers' revenues of introducing similar possibilities in respect of all local regional markets. Further gains to producers might be feasible if an optimal allocation of supplies from various locations among the regional markets replaced the existing allocation.

2. Model definition and development

The basic structural forms of the models used in this study are similar to those outlined by Takayama and Judge [13, pp. 333–373] for the situation of pure intertemporal optimization, so consequently the models will not be developed in detail. For the Sydney market weekly demand functions for bananas over an annual time horizon were specified in matrix notation as

$$P_1 = C_1 - Q_1 Y_1 \tag{1}$$

where P_1, C_1 and Y_1 were each (52×1) vectors and Q_1 a (52×52) positive definite diagonal matrix. For the export market where competitive market pricing was assumed to prevail, a constant net return at the point of export of $ 2.00 per bushel case was assumed, this giving rise to the scalar price and quantity vectors, C_2 and Y_2 respectively.

Weekly productions of bananas throughout the year were assumed to be known and represented by the (52×1) vector S_1. Each week's production was assumed to be allocated among three competing alternatives, these being: supply to meet current demand on the Sydney market represented by the vector X_1, supply to storage for export consignment represented by the vector X_2, and supply to storage for later consumption on the Sydney market, represented by the vector X_3. The relationship

$$S_1 \geqq X_1 + X_2 + X_3 \qquad (2)$$

was defined to limit the allocations in each period to the quantities produced in that period.

Similar relationships were defined to limit consumption and storage in each time period. Weekly consumption of bananas in the Sydney market was limited by the relationship

$$Y_1 \leqq X_1 + X_4 \qquad (3)$$

where X_4 represents the vector of quantities moving out of storage for local consumption, and into local consumption in each time period.

Total export consumption of bananas was limited by the relationship

$$Y_2 \leqq \iota' X_2 \qquad (4)$$

where ι was a (52×1) vector of unit elements, while weekly quantities stored for local consumption were limited by the relationship

$$S_2 \leqq X_3 - X_4 + MZ \qquad (5)$$

where S_2 was a (52×1) vector of predetermined storage quantities (all zero in this instance, apart from initial carry in and final carry out quantities which were assumed known), Z was a (51×1) vector of unknown inter-period storage quantities, and M had the structure of M_X as defined by Takayama and Judge [13, p. 337].

Associated with each of the vectors X_1 to X_4, vectors of transfer costs T_1 to T_4 were defined, these representing transport and ripening costs in the case of T_1, transport and export storage costs in the case of T_2, transport and fixed costs of placing the commodity into local storage in the case of T_3, and fixed costs of taking the commodity out of storage plus ripening costs in the case of T_4. In addition, a vector B of weekly storage costs was defined which was associated with the vector Z of storage quantities. No discount vectors were defined because of the very short time horizon involved.

The alternative objective functions defined for the purpose of determining optimum allocations and prices of bananas were first a "net benefit" function similar to that used by Takayama and Judge, which provided competitive market prices and allocations, and second a net revenue maximizing function which provided monopolistic market prices and allocations on the assumption that banana producers formed themselves into a cooperative marketing cartel.

Since actual market behaviour in the past had closely approximated the competitive situation, and the resulting returns to producers had been unsatisfactory, the additional revenue generated by the monopolistic model was intended to indicate the extent to which producers could improve their position by cooperative self-help. As at least a partial protection for consumer welfare, additional constraints were introduced in the monopoly situation to ensure that certain minimum quantities of bananas were supplied to the Sydney market each week and hence that prices did not exceed levels which they had reached previously in times of short supply. These constraints were specified as

$$Y_1 \geqq S_3, \tag{6}$$

where S_3 was the vector of weekly minimum quantities.

Because a system of commission marketing exists for bananas sold at wholesale auction markets in Australia, and the demand functions which were to be utilized in the models had been estimated on the basis of actual wholesale price realizations, it was necessary to adjust the models to allow for this factor, since it was the wholesale price less commission which was the relevant price for producers at each demand point. If δ represents the marketing margin as a proportion of total price then the net demand functions facing banana producers in the Sydney market may be represented as

$$(1-\delta)P_1 = (1-\delta)C_1 - (1-\delta)Q_1 Y_1. \tag{7}$$

Given this specification, the competitive market problem then involved the maximization of the objective function

$$F_c(Y_1, Y_2, X_1, X_2, X_3, X_4, Z)$$
$$= (1-\delta)(C_1' Y_1 - \tfrac{1}{2} Y_1' Q_1 Y_1) + C_2' Y_2 - T_1' X_1 - T_2' X_2 - T_3' X_3$$
$$- T_4' X_4 - B'Z, \tag{8}$$

subject to the constraints (2) to (5) and non-negativity conditions on all variables, while the monopolistic market problem involved the maximization of the objective function

$$F_m(Y_1, Y_2, X_1, X_2, X_3, X_4, Z)$$
$$= (1-\delta)(C_1' Y_1 - Y_1' Q_1 Y_1) + C_2' Y_2 - T_1' X_1 - T_2' X_2 - T_3' X_3$$
$$- T_4' X_4 - B'Z, \quad (9)$$

subject to the constraints (2) to (6) and non-negativity conditions on all variables.

Because the gross wholesale price variables were of considerable interest in this particular problem it was decided to use the duals of each of these two problems in the process of actually estimating the market equilibria. Takayama and Woodland [14] have shown that the dual of the competitive problem may be expressed as

Competitive Dual
Minimize

$$g(P_1, \rho_1, \rho_2, \rho_3, \rho_4) = \tfrac{1}{2}(1-\delta)C_1' Q_1^{-1} C_1 - (1-\delta)C_1' Q_1^{-1} P_1$$
$$+ \tfrac{1}{2}(1-\delta)P_1' Q_1^{-1} P_1 + S_1' \rho_1 - S_2' \rho_2 \quad (10)$$

subject to

(a) $(1-\delta)P_1 - \rho_1 \leqq 0$
(b) $C_2 - \rho_2 \leqq 0$
(c) $\rho_1 - \rho_3 \leqq T_1$
(d) $\imath\rho_2 - \rho_3 \leqq T_2$ (11)
(e) $\rho_4 - \rho_3 \leqq T_3$
(f) $\rho_1 - \rho_4 \leqq T_4$
(g) $M'\rho_4 \leqq B$

and

(h) $\rho_1 \geqq 0, \rho_2 \geqq 0, \rho_3 \geqq 0, \rho_4 \geqq 0, P_1$ unconstrained as to sign;

where ρ_1 is a vector of imputed net prices received at the Sydney market by producers, ρ_2 is the imputed price at which exports would occur, ρ_3 is a vector of imputed supply prices in the banana producing region and ρ_4 is a vector of imputed prices of the commodity in the local storage region.

In the case of the monopolistic model Guise [8, pp. 256–343] has shown that a dual expressed in terms of market prices may be derived, this being

Monopolistic Market Price Dual

Minimize

$$h(P_1, \sigma_1, \sigma_2, \sigma_3, \sigma_4, \sigma_5) = (1-\delta)C_1' Q_1^{-1} C_1 - 2(1-\delta)C_1' Q_1^{-1} P_1$$
$$+ (1-\delta)P_1' Q_1^{-1} P_1 + S_1' \sigma_1 - S_2' \sigma_2 - S_3' \sigma_5 \quad (12)$$

subject to

(a) $2(1-\delta)P_1 - \sigma_1 + \sigma_5 \leqq (1-\delta)C_1$

(b) $\sigma_2 \leqq -C_2$

(c) $\sigma_1 - \sigma_3 \leqq T_1$

(d) $1\sigma_2 - \sigma_3 \leqq T_2$ $\qquad\qquad\qquad\qquad\qquad$ (13)

(e) $\sigma_4 - \sigma_3 \leqq T_3$

(f) $\sigma_1 - \sigma_4 \leqq T_4$

(g) $M'\sigma_4 \leqq B$

and

(h) $\sigma_1 \geqq 0, \sigma_2 \geqq 0, \sigma_3 \geqq 0, \sigma_4 \geqq 0, \sigma_5 \geqq 0$; P_1 unconstrained as to sign;

where σ_1 is a vector of imputed marginal revenues received at the Sydney market by producers, σ_2 is the imputed marginal revenue at which exports would occur, σ_3 is a vector of imputed marginal values of bananas in the producing region, σ_4 is a vector of imputed marginal values of the commodity in the local storage region and σ_5 is a vector of imputed marginal costs associated with the lower limits on weekly supplies to the Sydney market.

3. Data sources

Since detailed information on the quantities and prices of bananas traded on other principal wholesale markets in Australia were not readily available, the study was confined to the Sydney market for which reliable data was available.

Two types of basic data were used: the quantities of bananas consigned to the Sydney wholesale market from New South Wales and Queensland, and the corresponding prices at which wholesalers sold these to retailers. The supply data were computed from records of the Banana Growers Federation Cooperative Limited, New South Wales, while the price data were extracted from the official records of the Division of Marketing and

Agricultural Economics of the New South Wales Department of Agriculture.

A spectral analysis of the weekly quantities of bananas supplied to the Sydney market over the fifteen years 1953 to 1967 had been carried out by Aggrey-Mensah and Tuckwell [3]. This showed that the strong seasonality in supplies resulted in the annual repetition of the same basic pattern, which was evolving slowly through time. For this reason a simple average of each week's supplies during the five years 1963–1967 was used to determine the expected quantities supplied to the Sydney market in both programming models.

Estimates of weekly wholesale demand functions for bananas on the Sydney market were obtained from the study by Aggrey-Mensah and Guise [2]. This study was based on weekly deflated price data for the years 1953 to 1967 and weekly quantities sold in thousands of bushels, the quantities sold being estimated from the quantities supplied by making use of a weighted three week moving average transformation.[2]

Because the price series used in estimating these functions referred to gross wholesale prices, including commission retained by merchants, it was necessary to introduce the modified model forms developed in sect. 2 to correctly generate producers' returns. Further, because the price series had been deflated for the purpose of estimating the regression relationships, corresponding revaluations were necessary to assess current prices and expected income levels for 1969, the year in which the analysis was carried out. As the relative incomes of producers in each situation were unaffected by this transformation, some of the results discussed in sect. 4 are presented in terms of deflated prices.

In addition to data on supplies, and demand functions, the models require the specification of vectors of transport and storage costs. A weighted average of freight costs from the North Coast of New South Wales to Sydney was approximately $A 0.50 per bushel in 1969. A similar cost was assumed to be incurred in moving bananas from the point of production to the point of export. Costs of storage and of ripening were determined

---

[2] This transformation was based on the known technical lag of approximately two weeks between supply by producers and actual auction, which covers the transportation and ripening processes. In addition, Aggrey-Mensah and Tuckwell [3] besides confirming this lag, had noted that the spectrum of prices contained less power than the spectrum of quantities supplied in the high frequency range. This tended to confirm the a priori hypothesis that merchants would attempt, within the very limited technological scope available to them, to smooth out very short term fluctuations in the quantities supplied, when moving fruit onto the auction floor.

by Aggrey-Mensah [1] using synthetic cost analysis. These were based on a survey of Sydney merchants and additional engineering and cost data obtained from a number of sources.

A typical ripening charge was $A 0.25 per bushel case while a typical charge for storage (together with the fixed costs of transferring fruit into and out of storage) was assumed to be $A 0.165 per week.[3] Consequently each element of T_1 was assumed to be $A 0.75, all elements of T_2 and T_3 were assumed to be $A 0.50, and all elements of T_4 were assumed to be $A 0.25, while the elements of B were taken to be $A 0.165. Since these were current prices in 1969 it was necessary to deflate them to make them compatible with the other price data in the models.

In the case of the monopolistic model an additional vector of minimum weekly quantities was also specified for the Sydney market. These quantities were determined in such a way as to ensure that the demand price on the local market would not exceed $A 7.50 per bushel in current (1969) prices in any time period. Equivalent price levels have been exceeded during periods of scarcity of bananas on a number of occasions in the past, but it was considered that this figure represented a reasonable upper bound on prices consistent with the need to consider consumer welfare.

4. Discussion of results

The models outlined in eqs. (10) to (13) were generated for the specific data discussed in sect. 3 and then solved to obtain optimum price and allocation vectors. In addition, to provide a basis for comparison, solutions were obtained in terms of deflated demand and supply prices to the set of demand equations when expected weekly quantities were marketed without the benefit of storage facilities and alternative market outlets. Illustrative summaries of the more important results of these alternative analyses are provided by figs. 1 and 2 which compare respectively weekly quantities marketed and weekly prices obtained.

Considering first the competition alternative with storage facilities, it was found that storage occurred in thirty weeks of the year, the longest continuous period being fourteen weeks during the late summer and fall.

---

[3] Unfortunately it was not feasible to obtain separate estimates of the fixed transfer costs associated with storage, so that consequently the charge overestimates by perhaps 20% the cost of holding fruit after the first week. This would be partly offset by an interest charge on the working capital tied up in the fruit held in storage, which was not allowed for in the original analysis.

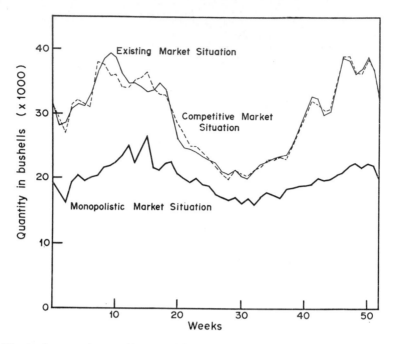

Fig. 1. Comparative weekly quantities of bananas traded on the Sydney wholesale market with different assumptions about market behaviour.

During the remainder of the year storage occurred intermittently, with the marginal cost of storage in the intervening periods (in 1969 prices) ranging from $A 0.03 to $A 0.70 per week. During the weeks when storage occurred the quantities stored were generally small and did not exceed a quarter of the total weekly quantity of fruit supplied to the market. In total only 7 % of the annual supplies were subject to storage.

Comparing the competitive alternative with existing market behaviour it is apparent from fig. 1 that the patterns of distribution are not significantly different. Likewise the demand price pattern in fig. 2 is very similar to that of the existing market situation. At no time did exporting become a viable alternative with competitive market pricing, the marginal cost of exporting (in 1969 prices) varying from $A 0.435 in late summer to $A 2.677 in mid-winter. Total revenue earned by growers from the competitive market with storage situation, measured at the point of supply in 1969 prices, amounted to $A 4.827 million, a figure which represents a net loss of $A 28 000, or approximately a 0.6 % reduction in revenue earned compared with the figure of $A 4.855 million from the existing market situation.

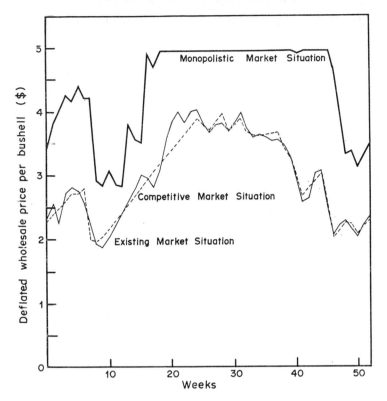

Fig. 2. Comparative weekly prices (deflated) of bananas traded on the Sydney wholesale market with different assumptions about market behaviour.

This somewhat unexpected result, compared with Massell's conclusions [10], arose for four main reasons. First, the cost of storage was relatively high in this situation whereas Massell assumed zero storage cost. Second, a strong covariance existed between shifts in supply and shifts in demand throughout the year and Massell had concluded that this would reduce the benefits of storage compared with the situation of zero covariance with which he was basically concerned. Third, the averaging of five years' data in deriving the expected supplies tended to reduce the variance in supplies which could be expected in a real world single year situation.

Fourth, Massell in his analysis assumed that the slope coefficients of the demand functions for successive time periods were constant, whereas in our situation they were free to vary from period to period. Some elementary graphical analysis will quickly indicate that this can result in losses for producers when storage is speculatively determined in a competitive market situation. Even after making an allowance for the third factor therefore, one could conclude that in the real world situation being analysed, any gains accruing to producers from the introduction of additional storage facilities alone, would be of only minor significance.

Turning to the monopolistic market alternative, it was found that no storage was undertaken for the local market, while approximately 33 % of total supplies were diverted to export markets. This diversion occurred in all weeks of the year, although the actual quantities of bananas involved were considerably reduced in the cooler months. As expected, prices on the Sydney market were substantially higher than those ruling in the other situations.

The constraint imposed upon market prices was effective during the winter months of May to September and again from mid-October to mid-November, making a total of twenty-seven weeks in all. The marginal cost of this restriction to the growers, in 1969 prices, ranged up to $A 2.722 in July, but its total effect on growers' revenue was not dramatic, amounting only to a total cost of $A 66 300, or a little less than 1.4 % of their existing revenue. Such a constraint would be an important determinant of the acceptability of any scheme of supply control to governments and consumers, and the fact that it does not impose a heavy cost on producers should make it generally acceptable to all parties.

The total quantity of bananas sold on the Sydney market fell from 1.540 million bushels under competitive market conditions to 1.031 million bushels under monopolistic conditions but despite this reduction in supplies, returns to producers from the Sydney market, measured in terms of 1969 prices at the point of supply, rose to $A 5.310 million. Total returns to producers including those from export sales increased to $A 6.074 million, this representing an increase of approximately 25 % compared with receipts under existing market conditions.

Since this study was carried out evidence has become available which suggests that a dramatic over supply situation is likely to occur in the world banana market in the medium term future [7]. Consequently, prices received for export bananas in future are likely to be substantially less than the fairly stable levels which have existed in recent years. For this reason two further solutions have been obtained for the monopolistic model using modified assumptions.

In the first case it was assumed that the net return at the point of export fell from $ 2.00 to $ 1.00. In the second case it was assumed that no exports occurred, but that producers continued to supply the Sydney market only up to the stage where their marginal revenue at the point of supply fell to

$A 0.50. This figure was assumed to just cover their marginal costs of harvesting, packing and delivery to the supply point.

In the first instance total producers' revenue in 1969 prices amounted to $A 5.588 million, a 15 % increase over the existing situation, while in the second situation producers' revenue amounted to $A 5.389 million, an 11 % increase over the existing situation. Provided effective market separation could be ensured, alternative uses within Australia should be available for the approximately 400 000 bushels of bananas not sent to the Sydney market in this latter situation. If for example, they were priced at their marginal value of $A 0.50 per bushel, co-operative cattle-fattening enterprises established in each banana producing region by growers would be one possible outlet.

5. Implications for producer policy

The monopolistic model appears to be the logical one for producers to implement in rationalizing market supplies but it carries with it the implicit assumption that growers organize themselves into a producer cartel to exercise market power. In addition to the legislative changes which producers' groups must persuade government to introduce to modify the institutional arrangements in the market, it is necessary that the cooperation of all growers be ensured, since previous schemes aimed at controlled marketing have all failed because of the divergence between individual and group interests.

A consequence of discriminatory pricing schemes such as those envisaged in the monopolistic models discussed in this study is that prices on local wholesale markets would usually be higher than export or alternative use prices. Producers would normally receive a weighted average of these prices for produce sold through the grower-controlled marketing organization. Such a method of payment would tend to encourage some producers to try to by-pass the scheme since the pooled price for all sales would be lower than the price received for local wholesale market sales.

Producers able to sell independently on local markets, and to take advantage of the higher prices ruling there, without having part of their output diverted to lower priced markets, would obviously make greater individual profits. The advantages of selling through the marketing organization would then become less obvious to other producers who would also tend to break away from the scheme, so introducing extensive 'leakage' between markets. This situation has affected all previous attempts to control the supplies of bananas to markets in Australia, as producers can normally sell unhindered on any interstate market of their choice, because of constitutional provisions relating to freedom of interstate commerce (Lewis [9]).

Because complete control of supplies is unlikely to be possible, the successful operation of any new marketing scheme could only be ensured if participants in the scheme were not disadvantaged relative to non-participants. This objective could be achieved in several ways, one of which would be by the introduction of legislation licensing each commercial grower of bananas to grow a specified acreage of bananas, and imposing an annual levy or license fee per acre. The funds so raised would then be used to make up the difference between local wholesale prices and other market prices, so that producers would be paid for all fruit on the basis of prices ruling on the local markets at the time their fruit was sold.[4]

While such a license/levy system has obvious advantages it also has certain theoretical disadvantages since it could encourage inefficient use of resources. Individual producers would tend to substitute non-land inputs for land in order to produce as much as possible from their licensed acreage, and so obtain a greater share of levy funds. Because currently the ratio of non-land to land inputs in the industry seems to be below its optimum level (average yields are less than half those obtained on well-managed plantations), the practical importance of this factor should not be over-stressed.

More important by far in the long term would be the effect on supply of a higher and more stable level of prices. Even with strict limits imposed on acreages of bananas in production through the licensing system, the incentive for improved efficiency of operation on individual plantations could lead to a rapid expansion of supplies. This would tend to increase the quantities that would have to be diverted to alternative markets in order to maintain local wholesale prices at the desired level.

Leverage effects would then compel the marketing organization to increase the annual acreage levy at a rate much more rapid than the rate of expansion of total supplies, because of the low prices at which the additional output could be sold. While the increased levies would tend to stabilize supplies, the benefits to producers of cooperative marketing would tend to be somewhat smaller in the long term than in the short term.

---

[4] The levy to be imposed per acre could be calculated on the basis of the relative proportions of fruit expected to be sold on each market, and the expected differentials between alternative market prices in each week. The levy would require periodic review to allow producers to reap the full benefits of price discrimination, while the licenses would need to be transferable to minimize resource misallocation.

6. Model evaluation and extensions

The results obtained in sect. 4 and the discussion in sect. 5 clearly imply that producers should seriously consider cooperative control of marketing, and some of the possible difficulties which may be encountered by producers in implementing such controls have been outlined. Since consumers as well as producers have an interest in banana markets their welfare also requires consideration in relation to any new marketing arrangements.[5] Although the prices likely to rule under monopolistic management of banana supplies are considerably higher than are expected competitive prices, it is considered that this would have little effect on prices paid by consumers, and hence on consumer welfare.

The reason for this contention is that changes in retail banana prices are not closely related to changes in wholesale prices. For example, in the summer and fall of 1971–72 growers' returns fluctuated between \$A 2.00 and \$A 7.00 per bushel case, but there was little change in the level of retail banana prices over that period. In the 1968–69 and 1969–70 seasons likewise, retail prices remained stable at comparable levels over the summer–fall periods, but wholesale prices diverged markedly. The 1968–69 season was a glut period with very low wholesale prices, while in the 1969–70 season cyclone damage reduced supplies, and wholesale prices similar to the levels which would exist under monopoly control prevailed.

A more important criticism of the models as used in this study is that they are limited by data availability to the analysis of alternative reallocations of only part of the total crop. Theoretically there would be no difficulty in extending the analysis to include a large number of alternative markets for the total Australian banana crop and a number of alternative supply points. While such extensions would obviously result in greater refinement of the solutions and consequently considerably improved planning information (which would be necessary for actual implementation of supply controls) it seems unlikely that they would alter the main conclusion of the existing analysis of policy alternatives.

One further refinement which could also be readily incorporated in the model would be required to establish actual operating policies under a scheme of supply control. The present analysis has proceeded on the assumption that bananas are a homogeneous commodity whereas in practice there are five size grades, and in addition alternative modes of presentation

[5] Berry [4] has shown that welfare comparisons between monopolistic and competitive market situations are by no means straightforward even in relatively uncomplicated situations.

in the market. A detailed analysis of the interactions between quantities and prices of the various grades at different times of the year, on both local wholesale and export markets, would be essential for correct decision making about allocations.

Finally, an important deficiency of the type of model being considered is its abstraction from much of the stochastic element in both demands and supplies through the assumption that demand and supply relations were fixed and known. The formulation of the problem and the method of analysis proceeded under the idealized conditions of certainty or certainty equivalence and this is clearly unsatisfactory in a real market situation characterized by uncertainty and lack of forward information.

Once again in the model context, one could anticipate that taking uncertainty into full account by casting the individual policy alternatives into simulation frameworks would not alter the basic conclusions concerning policy alternatives, but simply refine the solution information for the purpose of actual policy implementation. Because supply normally exceeds local wholesale market requirements in every week under monopolistic assumptions, and demand is generally much less volatile than supply, the effects of uncertainty would in practice be confined mainly to variations in the residual quantities available for disposal in alternative uses. Since export markets usually look for continuity of supply, this may be a further factor influencing producers to consider possible means of local disposal. This alternative would have the advantage that it would prevent Australia from making a direct contribution to the foreseeable difficulties on the world market which have been outlined by the United Nations Food and Agriculture Organization [7].

References

[1] Aggrey-Mensah, W., 1970, A Study of the Sydney Banana Market and of Potential Benefits to Producers of Supply Control, unpublished Ph.D. thesis, University of New England.

[2] Aggrey-Mensah, W. and J. W. B. Guise, 1969, Seasonality in the demand for bananas, Review of Marketing and Agricultural Economics, 37, 181–198.

[3] Aggrey-Mensah, W. and N. E. Tuckwell, 1969, A study of banana supply and price patterns on the Sydney wholesale market. An application of spectral analysis, Australian Journal of Agricultural Economics, 13, 101–117.

[4] Berry, R. A., 1969, A note on welfare comparisons between monopoly and pure competition, Manchester School of Economic and Social Studies, 37, 39–57.

[5] Bureau of Agricultural Economics, 1964, The Australian Banana Industry: An Economic Survey, Canberra: Bureau of Agricultural Economics.

[6] Commonwealth Scientific and Industrial Research Organization, 1966, Annual Report 1965–66: Division of Food Preservation, Ryde: C.S.I.R.O.

[7] Food and Agriculture Organization, 1971, Fourth Session of the Study Group on Bananas, Monthly Bulletin of Agricultural Economics and Statistics, 20(7/8), 9–12.

[8] Guise, J. W. B., 1972, Models of Spatial and Temporal Market Equilibrium, unpublished Ph.D. thesis, University of New England.

[9] Lewis, J. N., 1961, Organised marketing of agricultural products in Australia, Australian Journal of Agricultural Economics, 5, 1–8.

[10] Massell, B.F., 1969, Price stabilization and welfare, Quarterly Journal of Economics, 83, 284–298.

[11] McFarlane, G. C., 1955, Marketing of New South Wales Bananas, Sydney: N.S.W. Department of Agriculture.

[12] Meulen, J. van der, 1958, The demand for bananas in the Sydney wholesale market, Review of Marketing and Agricultural Economics, 26, 157–166.

[13] Takayama, T. and G. G. Judge, 1971, Spatial and Temporal Price and Allocation Models, Amsterdam: North-Holland Publishing Company.

[14] Takayama, T. and A. D. Woodland, 1970, Equivalence of price and quantity formulations of spatial equilibrium: purified duality in quadratic and convex programming, Econometrica, 38, 889–906.

CHAPTER 27

Allocation and pricing of water resources*

J. W. B. GUISE and J. C. FLINN

University of New England
University of Guelph

1. Introduction

As a society expands and increases in affluence there is typically a more than proportional increase in the demand for its natural resources. When the supplies of a resource are limited, as is the case with the regulated supplies of water in many river basins, conflicts eventually emerge between the various users of these supplies. The common strategy adopted by water managers to alleviate or to anticipate these conflicts has been to obtain additional supplies of water, often at high incremental cost, the most popular scheme involving the transfer of surface waters from areas of apparent abundance.

Thus, the water market has tended to become supply orientated. As a result, one alternative rarely considered when there are pressures on existing regulated supplies of water, is the possibility of reallocating water between users within an existing system. Such a review, and the implementation of a revised operating policy, may allow either the postponement of, or a great reduction in, the investment required to meet the planning objective.

There are of course, a variety of complementary and competitive demands for water in a river basin. Some demands for water — for example recreation, transport, hydroelectric power generation, consume little if any water although its location and quality may be changed. Other demands for water, notably agricultural and municipal — industrial use, consume a large proportion of the water supplied. Thus when an authority is planning the pricing and distribution of water, and hence the operating policy of the

* The authors gratefully acknowledge financial assistance for computing which was provided by the Rural Credits Development Fund of the Reserve Bank of Australia.

system, it is necessary to consider both the stock and the flow demands for water, together with the interrelationships between uses which are either complementary or competitive in sequential use through the system.

An operating policy for a river basin is of course only optimal in relation to some planning objective. Rarely, however, are planning objectives explicitly defined for developed river basins, because of the many conflicting goals which may be articulated, and the difficulties encountered in attempting to quantify the substitution possibilities between these goals. Thus it is not surprising that the distribution and pricing policies for water have historically resulted from political, administrative and engineering, as opposed to efficiency considerations.

While it is unlikely that a single policy objective would ever be accepted by all individuals and interest groups competing for water, the important question is whether a particular allocation policy is more desirable in some overall sense than alternative operating policies. One possible objective which has considerable appeal is to maximize the 'social benefit' which may be derived from the supplies of water. While such an objective is commendable, few would suggest that such a complex objective could be quantified.

One economic approximation to social welfare which seems to have some acceptance (Johnson [13]; Winch [25]) is that of maximizing the economic efficiency of the use of a resource in a region. Within such a framework, the dimensions of welfare other than economic efficiency may be incorporated by way of constraints imposed upon the degree of attainment of the desired economic efficiency criterion (Tinbergen [24]). Marglin [19] and Schmid [21] have evaluated the acceptability of the assumptions, and the implications of the use of such an approach in relation to water resources, and found this constrained efficiency approximation to welfare not unduly restrictive.

Economic theory indicates that optimum economic efficiency is approached when a competitive market situation prevails both spatially and temporally. With water resource allocation, a river basin authority is typically the only distributor of surface water, and may also regulate the mining of ground water, so that price cannot be set by free competition between many buyers and many sellers. The competitive market situation may however still be approximated, providing the authority sets its price to each class of customer in each time period, equal to the discounted marginal cost of servicing that customer, and refrains from regulating supplies on the basis of administrative or other non-market considerations (Hirshleifer *et al.* [10]; Krutilla [14]).

While a number of differing types of quantitative model may be suggested, which could approximate such a competitive market solution for the authority in an empirical situation, attention will here be directed to the extensions of Samuelson's [20] interregional competition model developed by Takayama and Judge [22]. Water is a transportable and storable resource subject to competitive demands from groups of users, both between and within regions as well as over time. Hence, if one is prepared to abstract from those aspects of uncertainty not covered by the notion of certainty equivalence (Theil [23]; Malinvaud [18]), these models — designed to establish constrained spatial and temporal market equilibria — are theoretically appropriate. Further, because the demand and the supply schedules generated and encountered by various groups using water can be quantified, these models then provide an efficient means of determining both the equilibrium prices and the quantities of water to be allocated to various users over time.

2. The river basin model

Basically the model has the activity analysis format outlined by Takayama and Judge [22, pp. 399–406] and extended by Guise [7] but because of the special features of the river basin context a number of modifications have necessarily been introduced. For example, the model does not include their intermediate product classification but treats as final products such commodities as hydroelectricity, urban water supplies and rural irrigation water supplies, all of which might be classified as primary commodities in another context. Another feature is the definition of only one process in each region, for producing each final commodity from the primary commodity and resources, so that the special process notation used by Takayama and Judge [22, pp. 275–298] is unnecessary for the present application.

An atypical feature of the activity analysis model is the definition of ground water resource availabilities in terms of bounded functional increasing marginal cost or supply relationships for pumping, rather than as fixed resource quantities, so that the supply function notation used by Takayama and Judge [22, pp. 129–144] is introduced to handle this situation. Further, because of the natural effect of gravity, the mobile primary commodity, surface water, may only be transported between particular regions and then only in one direction. In this respect it is comparable to a commodity storage activity which is feasible in only one time direction.

As Hartman and Seastone [9] have pointed out, an element of complementarity may exist between the various water uses in an upstream region and those in regions further downstream, since a proportion of the water used in producing each final commodity in the upstream region normally becomes available for further productive use downstream. This characteristic has been introduced into the present model, along with additional classes of restrictions not mentioned by Takayama and Judge. These arise because of the introduction of social welfare constraints upon the basic 'economic efficiency' type objective function. These restrictions are designed to take account of the multiple dimensions of social utility associated with the harvesting and management of water resources, and provide specifically for flood control, recreational pursuits, and the minimization of stream pollution.

Because of the special linkages both spatially and temporally in a river basin context, a general multi-dam, multi-ground-water basin model will not be presented. Instead a simple river basin comprising a single main stream, with two dams — referred to respectively as the upstream and downstream dams — will be considered, together with a single ground water basin in the flood plain below the downstream dam. Although specific, this particular framework is sufficient to illustrate the features of, and the principles that apply to, models of a much more general character. In addition, for simplicity only a single region has been specified as demanding each final commodity from each water storage region. This feature, like the basic framework is easily generalized where appropriate.

Notationally then we let

$i = 1, 2, 3$, be the water storage regions where the upstream dam is denoted by $i = 1$, the downstream dam by $i = 2$, and the ground water basin by $i = 3$;

$j = 1, 2, 3$, be the demand regions, where apart from electricity demand, final commodity demands in region $j = 1$, may only be met from supply region $i = 1$, while demands in region $j = 2$ may be met from supply regions $i = 2, 3$. Demand region $j = 3$ is a dummy region to which water is allocated when it passes downstream from storage region $i = 2$;

$k = 1, 2, 3$, be the final commodities demanded, these being electricity, urban water supplies and rural irrigation water supplies. (Obviously supply region $i = 3$ cannot produce hydroelectricity);

$l = 4$, be the primary commodity, stored water;

$m = 5, 6, 7, 8$, be resources, these being respectively electricity generating capacities, filtration plant capacities, irrigation channel capacities, and aquifer sustained yield capacities;

$n = 9, 10, 11, 12$, be 'social resources', these being respectively, irrigation water rights, minimum streamflows, flood protection and aquatic recreation;

$\tau = 1, 2, 3, 4$, be the discrete future time periods identified within the one year planning horizon of the water utility these being identified approximately with the winter, spring, summer and fall seasons respectively.[1, 2]

Using a notation similar to that adopted by Takayama and Judge the various relationships in the model will now be outlined. Because electricity produced is fed into a national grid covering many regions outside the river basin, separate regional demand relationships are not specified for this product. Instead given system prices, representing marginal values to the national grid of a megawatt of electricity produced at each dam in particular time periods, are assumed to be known.[3] These prices are specified by the relationships

$$p_i^k(\tau) = \lambda_{i0}^k(\tau) \qquad \text{for } i = 1, 2; \quad k = 1; \quad \tau = 1, \ldots, 4; \qquad (1)$$

where $p_i^k(\tau)$ is the dollar price of a megawatt of electricity in period τ at powerhouse i ($i = 1, 2$), while $\lambda_{i0}^k(\tau)$ is the marginal value to the national grid of a megawatt of electricity produced at powerhouse i in period τ.

Electricity production is controlled by the relationships

$$y_i^k(\tau) \leqq a_{ii}^{lk}(\tau) x_{ii}^k(\tau) \qquad \text{for } i = 1, 2; \quad k = 1; \quad \tau = 1, \ldots, 4; \qquad (2)$$

where $y_i^k(\tau)$ is the quantity of electricity produced in region i and supplied to the national grid during period τ, $x_{ii}^k(\tau)$ is the quantity of water used in electricity generation in region i to meet demand from the grid during

---

[1] The marked seasonality of both surface water inflows and final commodity demands in most climatic regions where water is a scarce commodity allow a satisfactory analysis to be made with a one year planning horizon. No conceptual problems prevent extension of the planning horizon where this is deemed appropriate.

[2] When $\tau = 0$ it refers to the 'present' time period during which the plan is being formulated and for which data on actual water supplies in storage dams is assumed known. When $\tau = 5$ it refers to the time period just beyond the planning horizon for which certain minimum water supplies in storage dams are assumed to be required.

[3] In a decomposition context (Lasdon [15]) these prices may have been generated within a national planning model for electricity (or energy) supply and demand.

period τ, and $a_{ii}^{lk}(\tau)$ is the input–output coefficient between water used and electricity generated in region i during period τ. The production of electricity in other parts of the national grid is assumed to be managed so that the quantity of electricity produced in the river basin in each time period is fully utilized at the marginal supply price $p_i^k(\tau)$.

Urban water consumption and rural irrigation water consumption in each region and time period are specified by relationships of the form

$$p_j^k(\tau) = \lambda_j^k(\tau) - \omega_j^k(\tau) y_j^k(\tau) \qquad \text{for } j = 1, 2; \quad k = 2, 3; \quad \tau = 1, \ldots, 4; \qquad (3)$$

where $p_j^k(\tau)$ is the product price per acre foot in region j and time period τ while $y_j^k(\tau)$ is the quantity (in acre feet) of the product consumed during period τ in region j. Consumption in each case is controlled by relationships of the form

$$y_j^k(\tau) \leq x_{ij}^k(\tau) \qquad \text{for } i = j = 1; \quad k = 2, 3; \quad \tau = 1, \ldots, 4; \qquad (4)$$

and

$$y_j^k(\tau) \leq \sum_{i=2}^{3} x_{ij}^k(\tau) \qquad \text{for } j = 2; \quad k = 2, 3; \quad \tau = 1, \ldots, 4; \qquad (5)$$

where $x_{ij}^k(\tau)$ is the quantity in acre feet of product k produced in region i and supplied to region j during period τ, the different regional forms arising because both a ground and a surface water storage region can supply these products to demand region 2 but only a surface water storage supplies the other demand region.

Water supplies from the ground water region are specified by the relationships

$$p_i^l(\tau) = v_i^l(\tau) + \sum_{\iota=1}^{\tau} \eta_i^l(\iota) y_i^l(\iota) \qquad \text{for } i = 3; \quad l = 4; \quad \tau = 1, \ldots, 4; \qquad (6)$$

where $p_3^4(\tau)$ is water supply price per acre foot pumped during period τ and $y_3^4(\tau)$ is the quantity of water pumped during period τ.[4] Utilization of ground water is controlled by the relationships

$$y_i^l(\tau) \geq \sum_{k=2}^{3} a_i^{lk}(\tau) x_{ij}^k(\tau) \qquad \text{for } i = 3; \quad j = 2; \quad l = 4; \quad \tau = 1, \ldots, 4; \qquad (7)$$

where the $x_{ij}^k(\tau)$'s are the net (of seepage losses) quantities of water allocated to satisfy each demand in region 2 and the $a_i^{lk}(\tau)$'s are the input–

---

[4] This form of function was adopted because drawdown tends to increase pumping costs in successive seasons throughout the year. Aquifer replenishment is assumed to occur largely in the winter season when the main rains occur and water use tends to be minimized.

output coefficients between the primary commodity in supply region 3 and the primary commodities in demand region 2 during period τ.

Utilization of surface water from storage dams is controlled by the basic production restrictions that water use cannot exceed its availability, which are summarised in the relationships

$$s_i^l(\tau) - \sum_{k=1}^{3} a_i^{lk}(\tau)x_{ij}^k(\tau) - x_{i2}^l(\tau) + x_i^l(\tau-1, \tau) - a_i^{ll}(\tau)x_i^l(\tau, \tau+1) \geq 0,$$

$$\text{for } i = j = 1; \quad l = 4; \quad \tau = 1, \ldots, 4; \quad (8)$$

and

$$s_i^l(\tau) - \sum_{k=1}^{3} a_i^{lk}(\tau)x_{ij}^k(\tau) - x_{i3}^l(\tau) + \sum_{k=1}^{3} a_{1i}^{lk}(\tau)x_{11}^k(\tau) + a_{1i}^{ll}(\tau)x_{1i}^l(\tau) + x_i^l(\tau-1, \tau)$$

$$- a_i^{ll}(\tau)x_i^l(\tau, \tau+1) \geq 0 \qquad \text{for } i = j = 2; \quad l = 4; \quad \tau = 1, \ldots, 4; \quad (9)$$

where $s_i^l(\tau)$ is the expected inflow of water to storage i from sources independent of other storages during period τ, $a_i^{lk}(\tau)$ is the input–output coefficient for the production of commodity k from commodity l in region i during period τ, $x_{i2}^l(\tau)$ and $x_{i3}^l(\tau)$ are quantities of water which flow over dam spillways and are not used for final commodity production in region i during period τ, $x_i^l(\tau-1, \tau)$ is the quantity of water held in storage region i from period $\tau-1$ to period τ this being known when $\tau = 1$ and variable otherwise, $x_i^l(\tau, \tau+1)$ is the quantity of water held in storage region i from period τ to period $\tau+1$, this being specified when $\tau = 4$ but variable otherwise.

The input–output coefficient $a_i^{ll}(\tau)$ makes allowance for evaporation and other losses occurring when water is stored from one time period to the next, while the input–output coefficients $a_{1i}^{lk}(\tau)$ and $a_{1i}^{ll}(\tau)$ define respectively the proportions of water utilized in producing each final commodity in the upstream supply region, and of spillway water losses from the upstream supply region, that contribute to the total inflow to the downstream storage region. It is important to identify these coefficients for through them the policies adopted in upstream supply regions influence the overall availability of the primary commodity in the downstream supply region.[5]

[5] Identification of return flows of saline irrigation water and of treated sewage effluents also permit subsidiary analyses of their ecological effects to be carried out, along lines similar to those followed by Loucks *et al.* [16] or Graves *et al.* [5], to find whether the ecological costs of the proposed optimum policy are excessive. Additional charges per unit of each of these activities could be imposed in the current model by modifying the vector T_1, to be defined later, and then iteratively adjusting these charges until they were equated with the marginal costs of maintaining required water quality standards through treatment of these effluents.

Capacity or resource restrictions affecting the production of each final commodity in each region and the sustained yield of groundwater have the form

$$s_i^m(\tau) - a_i^{mk}(\tau)x_{ij}^k(\tau) \geqq 0 \qquad \text{for } i = j = 1, 2; \quad k = 1, 2, 3; \quad m = k+4;$$
$$\tau = 1, \ldots, 4; \quad (10)$$

and

$$s_i^m - \sum_{\tau=1}^{4} y_i^l(\tau) \geqq 0 \qquad \text{for } i = 3; \quad l = 4; \quad m = 8; \tag{11}$$

except that in (10) when $j = 2, k = 2, m = 6, s_i^m(\tau) - \sum_{i=2}^{3} a_i^{mk}(\tau)x_{ij}^k(\tau) \geqq 0$; where $s_i^m(\tau)$ is the quantity of resource m available in region i during period τ, s_i^m is the sustained yield quantity of groundwater ($m = 8$) available in the aquifer ($i = 3$) to be utilized over the planning horizon ($\tau = 1, \ldots, 4$), and $a_i^{mk}(\tau)$ is the input–output coefficient between resource and product in region i and period τ.

The 'social resource' restrictions are rather more complex and require individual treatment. The provision of certain minimum levels of irrigation water in accordance with specified water rights is allowed for by the relationships

$$s_{ij}^n - \sum_{\tau=1}^{4} x_{ij}^k(\tau) \leqq 0 \qquad \text{for } i = j = 1, 2; \quad k = 3; \quad n = 9; \tag{12}$$

and

$$s_{ij}^n - \sum_{\tau=1}^{4} x_{ij}^k(\tau) \leqq 0 \qquad \text{for } i = 3; \quad j = 2; \quad k = 3; \quad n = 9; \tag{13}$$

where s_{ij}^9 is the aggregate of water rights in region j relating to supply from region i during all four periods of the time horizon. The maintenance of certain minimum stream flows below each dam to protect aquatic life and minimize water pollution involves the relationships

$$s_i^n(\tau) - a_i^{nk}(\tau)x_{ij}^k(\tau) - x_{ih}^l(\tau) \leqq 0$$
$$\text{for } i = j = 1, 2; \quad h = j+1; \quad k = 1; \quad l = 4; \quad n = 10; \text{ and}$$
$$\tau = 1, \ldots, 4; \quad (14)$$

where $s_i^n(\tau)$ defines the minimum total flow required below dam i during period τ, $a_i^{nk}(\tau)$ is the input–output coefficient between electricity production and downstream flow from region i during period τ and $x_{ih}^l(\tau)$ is the quantity of water flowing over the spillway of dam i during period τ and hence directly to the next downstream region.[6]

The remaining restrictions define seasonal maximum and minimum acceptable levels of storage in each dam to ensure a reasonable degree of flood protection in the one case and to provide adequate water for aquatic recreation in the other. They are defined as

$$s_i^n(\tau, \tau+1) - x_i^l(\tau, \tau+1) \geqq 0$$
$$\text{for } i = 1, 2; \quad l = 4; \quad n = 11; \quad \tau = 1, 2, 3; \quad (15)$$

and

$$s_i^n(\tau, \tau+1) - x_i^l(\tau, \tau+1) \leqq 0$$
$$\text{for } i = 1, 2; \quad l = 4; \quad n = 12; \quad \tau = 1, 2, 3; \quad (16)$$

where $s_i^{11}(\tau, \tau+1)$ is the safe seasonal maximum capacity for storage i to carry over to the following period and $s_i^{12}(\tau, \tau+1)$ is the acceptable minimum storage level to carry over to the following period which is compatible with recreational requirements. No relationships are defined for $\tau = 4$ since then carryovers are pre-specified and would naturally be defined so as to be compatible with restrictions of these types.

The only remaining elements of the model requiring definition are the known production and transfer costs per unit of each final commodity which are assumed known and constant and are denoted by $t_{ij}^k(\tau)$ for $i = j = 1, 2$; $k = 1, 2, 3$; and for $i = 3; j = 2; k = 2, 3$; and $\tau = 1, \ldots, 4$; together with the social discount factors which apply to benefits obtainable in each time period these being denoted by $\sigma(\tau)$ for $\tau = 1, 2, 3, 4$; this particular definition being adopted because of the uneven lengths of the time periods. No specific storage costs are imposed per unit of water held in each dam from one time period to the next.

Using this notation and the constraints as defined, the Hotelling [11] type net social benefit function which forms the objective function of the problem may be defined as

$$NSP \equiv \sum_{\tau=1}^{4} \sigma(\tau) \{ \sum_{i=1}^{2} [\lambda_{i0}^1(\tau) y_i^1(\tau) + \sum_{k=2}^{3} [\lambda_i^k(\tau) y_i^k(\tau) - \tfrac{1}{2}\omega_i^k(\tau)(y_i^k(\tau))^2]]$$
$$- v_3^4(\tau) y_3^4(\tau) - \tfrac{1}{2} \sum_{\iota=1}^{\tau} \eta_3^4(\iota) y_3^4(\iota) y_3^4(\tau) - \sum_{i=1}^{2} \sum_{k=1}^{3} t_{ii}^k(\tau) x_{ii}^k(\tau)$$
$$- \sum_{k=2}^{3} t_{32}^k(\tau) x_{32}^k(\tau) \}. \quad (17)$$

[6] This definition is satisfactory while the model is deterministic. If however a sequence of problems were being solved which involved stochastic variation of water inflows the quantities of water going over a spillway while a dam was full would have to be excluded from the relationship, which attempts to provide for a minimum continuous rate of flow.

Formally our problem is to find an optimal solution that maximizes (17) subject to the relevant constraints stipulated by (2), (4), (5), (7) through (16) and non-negativity of the variables.

Assuming that (17) is a concave function and the constraint set satisfies Slater's condition, one may make the routine statement that a solution exists for this problem, and interpret the Kuhn–Tucker optimality conditions derived from the Lagrangean function of this problem as economic equilibrium conditions (see Flinn and Guise [4], ch. 18 of Takayama and Judge [22]).

With this general formulation of an economic model involving efficient pricing and allocation of water over space and time, let us now introduce a hypothetical problem and show how the model can be solved efficiently.

3. Application

An illustrative application of this model was developed for a hypothetical temperate zone river basin by drawing together data from a number of differing sources. Information relating to electricity generation was obtained from the Annual Reports of the Electricity Commission of New South Wales (1967–70) while information relating to urban water requirements was derived using the seasonal relationships presented by Flinn and Guise [4] which were based in part upon the earlier work of Howe and Linaweaver [12]. The data concerned with rural irrigation water requirements were based upon previous work by Flinn [3] while the data used to specify groundwater pumping relationships were based upon unpublished information relating to Arizona. In integrating this information our objective was to arrive at a simplified river basin situation in which the water relationships made sense technically. Our success in achieving this objective may best be judged from the following tables and discussion.

It has been assumed that an appropriate marginal value of electricity is $ 5.00 per megawatt generated at each power station in all seasons of the year. Both generating plants were assumed to be of constant head type and of 300 MW capacity, but the actual operating head of the upstream plant was assumed to be twice that of the downstream plant. It was further assumed that the variable costs of operating the two plants amounted to $ 0.10 per acre foot of water passing through the turbines.

The seasonal demand functions set out in table 1 were assumed to apply in the case of municipal water demands, these relating to cities of 75 000 and 600 000 people respectively, with a somewhat higher proportion of industrial demand in the case of the larger city. Variable costs of production were assumed to amount to $ 50.00 per acre foot of filtered water while filtration plant capacities were assumed to be 50 and 400 acre feet per day respectively, in regions 1 and 2.

Table 1

Assumed regional coefficients for seasonal water demand schedules [a]

	Region 1		Region 2	
Muncicipal demands	$\alpha_1^2(\tau)$	$\beta_1^2(\tau)$	$\alpha_2^2(\tau)$	$\beta_2^2(\tau)$
$\tau = 1$	727.5	200.54	729.5	23.634
$\tau = 2$	423.8	123.89	432.0	15.083
$\tau = 3$	350.6	63.85	356.7	7.855
$\tau = 4$	376.3	89.95	384.4	10.988
Irrigation demands	$\alpha_1^3(\tau)$	$\beta_1^3(\tau)$	$\alpha_2^3(\tau)$	$\beta_2^3(\tau)$
$\tau = 2$	12.0	0.10	12.0	0.035
$\tau = 3$	41.5	0.55	38.2	0.182
$\tau = 4$	12.5	0.08	12.4	0.0285

[a] Based on Flinn and Guise ([4]; pp. 403–405). These coefficients determine prices in dollars per acre foot and quantities in thousands of acre feet.

The seasonal demand functions for irrigation water which are set out in table 1 were assumed to apply in regions 1 and 2 respectively, these relating only to the spring, summer and fall periods, as temperatures rather than water supplies were assumed to limit crop growth in winter. Agriculturalists in region 1 were assumed to own annual water rights amounting to 110 000 acre feet of water while those in region 2 were assumed to have surface water rights amounting to 295 000 acre feet and ground water rights amounting to 120 000 acre feet. Irrigation channel capacities from the two surface supply regions were assumed to be 2000 and 4000 acre feet per day, respectively.

The ground water source was assumed to have a maximum sustainable annual yield of 300 000 acre feet. Because of problems with draw-down as the irrigation season progressed, it was assumed that pumping costs were an increasing function of production throughout the year. With a basic lift of 300′ and a 10′ drawdown over the season, the equations

$$p_3^4(\tau) = 5.730 + (0.000636) \sum_{\iota=1}^{\tau} y_3^4(\iota) \qquad \tau = 1, \ldots, 4; \qquad (18)$$

were synthesized as a basis for determining pumping costs in each season of the year.

Surface water inflows to each dam (excluding those flows moving from the upper to the lower dam) were assumed to represent median flows in the river over a long period of years. Median rather than mean seasonal flows were considered appropriate for planning as the occasional very large flows which inflate the mean tend to be wasted over dam spillways rather than utilized productively. Pollution control in the river was assumed to require minimum daily flows of 1000 acre feet and 2333.3 acre feet respectively, below the upstream and downstream dams.

Flood protection was assumed to be more important in determining maximum storage transfer between winter and spring than later in the year, given the typical spring thaw situation envisaged. Recreational needs were assumed to be satisfied largely during the summer period. Consequently lower bounds on storage were set at fairly high levels for winter–spring, spring–summer and summer–fall transfers but relaxed for fall–winter transfers as water demands from other users remain substantial even after recreational demands decline.

Most of the coefficients used in the model which have not already been discussed are set out in table 2. Those coefficients defined earlier for which values are not indicated took the basic value of unity.

Table 2

Data for river basin model

Electricity generating capacities: (th/ac/ft)

$s_1^5(\tau) = 210, 112.5, 135, 90;$ $\qquad \tau = 1, \ldots, 4.$

$s_2^5(\tau) = 420, 225, 270, 180;$ $\qquad \tau = 1, \ldots, 4.$

Filtration plant capacities: (th/ac/ft)

$s_1^6(\tau) = 7.0, 3.75, 4.5, 3.0;$ $\qquad \tau = 1, \ldots, 4.$

$s_2^6(\tau) = 56.0, 30.0, 36.0, 24.0;$ $\qquad \tau = 1, \ldots, 4.$

Irrigation channel capacities: (th/ac/ft)

$s_1^7(\tau) = -, 150, 180, 120;$ $\qquad \tau = 1, \ldots, 4.$

$s_2^7(\tau) = -, 300, 360, 240;$ $\qquad \tau = 1, \ldots, 4.$

Note that no irrigation is carried out in winter.

Table 2 (continued)

Water inflows to dams: (th/ac/ft)

$s_1^4(\tau) = 490, 210, 60, 39;$ $\tau = 1, \ldots, 4; x_1^4(0, 1) = 200, a_1^{44}(4) \, x_1^4(4, 5) = 204$

$s_2^4(\tau) = 805, 350, 105, 57;$ $\tau - 1, \ldots, 4; x_2^4(0, 1) = 600, a_2^{44}(4) \, x_2^4(4, 5) = 612$

Minimum downstream flows: (th/ac/ft)

$s_1^{10}(\tau) = 140, 75, 90, 60;$ $\tau = 1, \ldots, 4.$

$s_2^{10}(\tau) = 330, 175, 210, 140;$ $\tau = 1, \ldots, 4.$

Seasonal capacities for flood protection: (th/ac/ft)

$s_1^{11}(\tau, \tau+1) = 450, 500, 500;$ $\tau = 1, 2, 3.$

$s_2^{11}(\tau, \tau+1) = 1200, 1300, 1300;$ $\tau = 1, 2, 3.$

Seasonal minimum levels for recreation: (th/ac/ft)

$s_1^{12}(\tau, \tau+1) = 350, 350, 350;$ $\tau = 1, 2, 3.$

$s_2^{12}(\tau, \tau+1) = 800, 800, 800;$ $\tau = 1, 2, 3.$

Variable production and transfer costs: ($/ac/ft)

$t_{ij}^1(\tau) = 0.10, 0.10, 0.10, 0.10;$ $\tau = 1, 2, 3, 4; i = j = 1, 2.$

$t_{ij}^2(\tau) = 50.00, 50.00, 50.00, 50.00;$ $\tau = 1, 2, 3, 4; i = j = 1, 2;$ and $i = 3, j = 2.$

$t_{ij}^3(\tau) = -, 0.50, 0.50, 0.50;$ $\tau = 1, 2, 3, 4; i = j = 1, 2;$ and $i = 3, j = 2.$

Input–output coefficients: $\tau = 1, 2, 3, 4.$

$a_i^{mk}(\tau) \;= 0.2, 0.2, 0.2, 0.2;$ for $m = 4; k = 1; i = 1.$

$\phantom{a_i^{mk}(\tau)} \;= 0.1, 0.1, 0.1, 0.1;$ for $m = 4; k = 1; i = 2.$

$\phantom{a_i^{mk}(\tau)} \;= 1.2, 1.2, 1.2, 1.2;$ for $m = 4, 6; k = 2; i = 1, 2.$

$\phantom{a_i^{mk}(\tau)} \;= -, 1.5, 1.5, 1.5;$ for $m = 4, 7; k = 3; i = 1, 2.$

$\phantom{a_i^{mk}(\tau)} \;= 1.05, 1.05, 1.05, 1.05;$ for $m = 4, 8; k = 2; i = 3.$

$\phantom{a_i^{mk}(\tau)} \;= -, 1.10, 1.10, 1.10;$ for $m = 4, 8; k = 3; i = 3.$

$a_{12}^{mk}(\tau) \;= 0.9, 0.9, 0.9, 0.9;$ for $m = 4; \quad k = 1, 4.$

$\phantom{a_{12}^{mk}(\tau)} \;= 0.6, 0.5, 0.4, 0.5;$ for $m = 4; \quad k = 2.$

$\phantom{a_{12}^{mk}(\tau)} \;= -, 0.1, 0.1, 0.1;$ for $m = 4; \quad k = 2.$

$a_i^{ml}(\tau) \;= 1.01, 1.02, 1.05, 1.02;$ for $m = 4; \quad l = 4; i = 1, 2.$

Table 2 (continued)

One period discount factors

(period $\tau+1$ to period τ) (assumed $\frac{1}{2}\%$ per month)

$\sigma(\tau+1, \tau) = 0.9823, 0.9854, 0.9876$; for $\tau = 1, 2, 3$.

Multi-period discount factors

(period 4 to period τ)

$\sigma(4, \tau) = 0.9569, 0.9742, 0.9876$;   for $\tau = 1, 2, 3$.

---

4. Discussion of results

It will be apparent to readers that the solution obtained for the present model represents only one among many solutions which could be obtained by parametrically varying different coefficients. Obviously, if models of this type were to be used for policy purposes one would be interested in a range of possible solutions at a given point in time as well as for a number of different years over the twenty to fifty year planning horizon of the water reticulation authority. Given the limitations of a single illustrative solution, which are imposed by consideration of the length of this paper, only comments of a general nature will be spelt out.

In table 3 the production and pricing of final products is set out. Given the relatively low profitability of electricity production, only the quantities of water required to maintain downstream flows are used to produce this commodity except in the winter period when water in excess of dam capacities would otherwise accumulate, and in the fall period when some of the water retained in region 1 for recreational purposes over the summer would not otherwise be fully utilized. In region 1 the power plant operates to capacity in period 1, the marginal value of capacity being $ 0.90 per acre foot of water, and some water (21.447 thousand acre feet) is lost over the spillway as it cannot be utilized.

The price of irrigation water rises gradually from season to season (apart from a drop in region 1 during the fall because of the increased availability of water), so as to equate the discounted returns from its use in each period. The price of municipal water rises abruptly in the summer and fall periods because demands would otherwise greatly exceed the capacities of the filtration plants. The differential seasonal pricing which arises naturally

Table 3

Final product solution to river basin planning model

I Electricity production and pricing	Region 1 (1000 MW)	($ per MW)	Region 2 (1000 MW)	($ per MW)
Period 1	42.000	5.000	36.885	5.000
2	15.000	5.000	17.500	5.000
3	18.000	5.000	21.000	5.000
4	13.007	5.000	14.000	5.000
II Municipal water production and pricing	Region 1 (Th/acre/ft)	($ per acre/ft)	Region 2 (Th/acre/ft)	($ per acre/ft)
Period 1	3.377	50.192	28.731	50.480
2	2.987	53.746	25.000	54.925
3	3.750	111.163	34.286	87.386
4	2.500	151.425	22.857	133.246
III Irrigation water production and pricing	Region 1 (Th/acre/ft)	($ per acre/ft)	Region 2 (Th/acre/ft)	($ per acre/ft)
Period 1	–	–	–	–
2	50.580	6.942	184.988	5.525
3	62.422	7.168	178.562	5.702
4	77.976	6.262	231.777	5.794

in this model illustrates the point of the recommendations which Gysi and Loucks [8] made on this question in a recent paper.

Because pumped water can be handled more efficiently by the filtration plant in demand region 2 the municipal supply is drawn from this source in the summer and fall periods when capacity is at a premium. The marginal costs of using surface water were $ 2.596 and $ 9.105 per acre foot in these periods, while in the winter and spring when capacity was not a problem, the marginal costs of using pumped water were $ 5.536 and $ 1.883 per acre foot respectively. The marginal values per acre foot of filtration plant capacity which could be used as a guide to future investment in these facilities are set out in table 4.

Only the minimum aggregate right for pumped irrigation water in region 2 is met, this amount being supplied almost entirely in the fall season. The marginal cost of supplying pumped water in the spring period was $ 0.164 per acre foot. The marginal value of the right to an acre foot of pumped

Table 4

Imputed values in solution to river basin planning model

I Water supply prices	Supply Region 1 ($ per acre/ft)	Supply Region 2 ($ per acre/ft)	Supply Region 3 ($ per acre/ft)
Period 1	0.360	0.400	5.730
2	4.518	3.350	5.730
3	4.677	3.468	5.755
4	4.077	3.530	5.852

II Marginal values of filtration plant capacity	Demand Region 1 ($ per acre/ft)	Demand Region 2 ($ per acre/ft)
Period 1	–	–
2	–	0.754
3	47.448	29.850
4	81.915	73.429

III Marginal values of stream flows	Demand Region 1 ($ per acre/ft)	Demand Region 2 ($ per acre/ft)
Period 1	–	–
2	0.603	2.950
3	0.655	3.068
4	0.000	3.130

water is imputed as $ 1.143, this being the marginal cost incurred by the community to supply an acre foot of pumped water instead of an acre foot of surface water.

The seasonal supply prices imputed to water in each supply region are set out on table 4. In period 1 the marginal value of water in region 2 is only $ 0.40 per acre foot, this being its marginal value for electricity production. The marginal value of water in region 1 is only $ 0.36 in period 1 since the marginal units of water are lost over the spillway and only 90 % of this water reaches region 2 because of seepage losses.

In other periods the supply prices in region 1 are higher than in region 2 since the water has a value in use in demand region 1 *and* part of it finds its way into supply region 2 and is available for further use in demand region 2. The prices in region 3 represent the marginal costs per acre foot of pumped water in each period. These rise as drawdown occurs in successive periods.

The marginal values of stream flows, which represent also the marginal costs of maintaining specified flows in the river so as to combat pollution also appear in table 4. In period 1 (and also period 4, for region 1) flows in excess of the specified minima occur without cost. In later periods the costs of maintaining minimum flows are very much higher for region 2 than for region 1. This occurs because water released from region 1 is used for electricity production and then 90 % of it flows into region 2 where it augments available supplies, while water released from region 2 is used only for electricity production before being lost from profitable use by the reticulation authority.

Storage capacity for flood protection was only limiting between periods 1 and 2 when its imputed cost per acre foot was $ 4.148 in region 1 and $ 2.939 in region 2. Interperiod water storage quantities and surplus capacities are set out in table 5. Only between the summer and fall periods did recreational requirements limit the profitable allocation of water. The marginal cost of the recreational requirement was considerably higher for region 1 than for region 2, the figures being $ 0.895 and $ 0.157 per acre foot respectively. A comparison of these costs with the marginal values of the water for recreational purposes would indicate whether the constraints required modification in a given socio-economic situation.

Table 5
Water storage quantities and surplus capacities in optimal solution

	Supply Region 1 (Th/acre/ft)	Supply Region 2 (Th/acre/ft)
I Inter-period water storage quantities		
Transfer: Period 1 to 2	450.000	1200.000
2 to 3	495.633	1119.185
3 to 4	350.000	800.000
II Inter-period additional capacities for flood protection		
Transfer: Period 1 to 2	0.000	0.000
2 to 3	4.367	180.815
3 to 4	150.000	500.000
III Inter-period additional storage above minimum recreational requirement		
Transfer: Period 1 to 2	100.000	400.000
2 to 3	145.633	319.185
3 to 4	0.000	0.000

5. *Policy implications and extensions*

Spatio-temporal quadratic programming models provide a powerful means of analysing water pricing and allocation decisions for either existing or planned water developments. However, as with any model which must abstract from the real world, the precision and the realism of the solutions generated can be no better than the input data. For the structure and the parameter values of a model of a river basin to sensibly depict the social, economic, biological and physical characteristics of a problem area, detailed data within these various categories must be gathered and integrated for the region of interest. Thus the programming approach provides an efficient nucleus for cooperative research, highlighting the interdependencies and interfaces which exist between the various disciplines that are vital when developing an integrated operating policy for a water resource.

The solution to the programming problem provides two extremely valuable classes of information. First, the optimal distribution of water and the associated prices are defined, providing guidelines for the current operation of the system. Second, shadow prices are generated in relation to those constraints which are effective on the system, providing information for forward planning. For the design engineer, the shadow prices of the physical constraints which are effective provide guidelines to the relative economic returns from investing in new or modifying existing structures. This information, coupled with the cost of providing additional supplies, would indicate the optimal sequence of investment in structures in the basin.

For the social scientist, the shadow prices of institutional constraints enable the economic costs of administrative decisions to be compared with policies based on efficiency criteria alone. In this way, the economic costs of income redistribution policies to various sectors of the economy, supposedly effected through water allocation or pricing policies, could be measured. For example, the case for charging users of irrigation water lower prices for water than alternative users is often argued on the grounds of providing transfer payments to agriculture. Thus, the economic cost of achieving this goal through a water project may be derived and so be available for comparison with the social cost of achieving the same objective through alternative programmes.

In practice, the efficient policy for managing water in a river basin may not generate sufficient revenues to the water agency to leave a surplus for future investment. In consequence, the agency may impose its position as the monopoly supplier, administratively raising prices above the efficient price. In this context, the impact of various pricing policies on the withdrawal and distribution of water and on the financial gains and losses to individual water users and the authority resulting from alternative pricing policies could be predicted.

Possibly a subset of the operating policies which may be efficient for the agency to pursue (in relation to alternative planning objectives) would be deemed socially or politically unacceptable given the historic distribution and/or prices of water. For example, feasible alternative operating policies may require that changes in the supply or prices of water between users may not exceed some proportion of the historic operating policy. Such a policy constraint could be included in the model in a similar fashion to that followed by Louwers *et al.* [17] when evaluating the optimal distribution of milk in the Netherlands.

The analytical model developed was essentially short term in nature, spanning four discrete time periods in a one year planning horizon. However, the model could be extended into a long run adaptive model of a river basin by incorporating the methodology outlined by Takayama and Judge [22, pp. 412–426]. Ideally, the quadratic programming model would be imbedded in a simulation model of the river basin with appropriate feedbacks between the various components of the simulation model. Other major components of the simulation model, which would generate both physical and economic data for the programming model, would include: (a) a hydraulic model of the rainfall-surface-ground-water complex to focus on the supply and the physical constraint side; and (b) an economic, socio-demographic model to focus on the demand and the institutional constraint aspects of the optimising model.[7]

Within this framework the sensitivity of the present and planned allocation, pricing and development policies for water could be identified in relation to those variables which may be stochastic in nature or which may shift over time. For both planned and existing water developments, the integration of optimising and predictive models within an encompassing simulation framework for a river basin would appear to be fruitful in providing a structure within which various scientists and administrators may contribute their individual expertise, in relation to the planning of water resources.

---

[7] In cases of planned rather than existing water resource developments the type of analysis carried out by Dudley *et al.* [1] could be valuable in pinpointing a small number of feasible alternatives for further analysis in a quadratic programming framework.

References

[1] Dudley, N. J., D. T. Howell and W. F. Musgrave, 1972, Irrigation Planning 3: the best size of irrigation area for a reservoir, Water Resources Research, 8, 7–17.

[2] Electricity Commission of New South Wales, 1970, Annual Report for the Year Ending 30th June, 1969, Sydney, New South Wales Government Printer.

[3] Flinn, J. C., 1969, The demand for irrigation water in an intensive irrigation area, Australian Journal of Agricultural Economics, 13, 128–143.

[4] Flinn, J. C. and J. W. B. Guise, 1970, An application of spatial equilibrium analysis to water resource allocation, Water Resources Research, 6, 398–409.

[5] Graves, G. W., G. B. Hatfield and A. B. Whinston, 1969, Water pollution control using by-pass piping, Water Resources Research, 5, 13–47.

[6] Graves, G. W., G. B. Hatfield and A. B. Whinston, 1972, Mathematical programming for regional water quality management, Water Resources Research, 8, 273–290.

[7] Guise, J. W. B., 1972, Models of Spatial and Temporal Market Equilibrium, unpublished Ph.D. thesis, University of New England.

[8] Gysi, M. and D. P. Loucks, 1971, Some long run effects of water pricing policies, Water Resources Research, 7, 1371–1382.

[9] Hartman, L. M. and D. A. Seastone, 1970, Water Transfers: Economic efficiency and Alternative Institutions, Baltimore: The Johns Hopkins Press, for Resources for the Future.

[10] Hirshleifer, J., J. C. De Haven and J. W. Milliman, 1960, Water Supply, Economics, Technology and Policy, Chicago: University of Chicago Press.

[11] Hotelling, H., 1938, The general welfare in relation to problems of taxation and of railway and utility rates, Econometrica, 6, 242–269.

[12] Howe, C. W. and F. P. Linaweaver, 1967, The impact of price on residential water demand and its relation to system design and price structure, Water Resources Research, 3, 13–32.

[13] Johnson, P. R., 1965, The social cost of the tobacco program, Journal of Farm Economics, 47, 242–255.

[14] Krutilla, J. V., 1958, Multiple Purpose River Basin Development, Baltimore: The Johns Hopkins Press.

[15] Lasdon, L. S., 1970, Optimization Theory for Large Systems, New York: Macmillan.

[16] Loucks, D. P., C. S. Revelle and W. R. Lynn, 1967, Linear programming models for water pollution control, Management Science, 14, B166–B181.

[17] Louwers, S. L., J. C. G. Boot and S. Wage, 1963, A quadratic programming approach to the problem of the optimal use of milk in The Netherlands, Journal of Farm Economics, 45, 309–317.

[18] Malinvand, E., 1969, First order certainty equivalence, Econometrica, 37, 706–718.

[19] Marglin, S. A., 1962, Objectives of water resource development: A general statement, in: Design of Water Resource Systems, A. Maass et al., eds., Cambridge: Harvard University Press, 17–87.

[20] Samuelson, P. A., 1952, Spatial price equilibrium and linear programming, American Economic Review, 42, 283–303.

[21] Schmid, A. A., 1967, Non-market values and efficiency of public investments in water resources, American Economic Review, 57, 158–168.

[22] Takayama, T. and G. G. Judge, 1971, Spatial and Temporal Price and Allocation models, Amsterdam: North-Holland Publishing Company.

[23] Theil, H., 1964, Optimal Decision Rules for Government and Industry, Amsterdam: North-Holland Publishing Company.

[24] Tinbergen, J., 1956, Economic Policy: Principles and Design, Amsterdam: North-Holland Publishing Company.

[25] Winch, D. M., 1965, Consumer's surplus and the compensation principle, American Economic Review, 55, 395–423.

CHAPTER 28

Allocation of milk through space and time in a competitively-mixed dairy industry*

MARVIN W. KOTTKE

University of Connecticut

1. Introduction

Two real-world conditions are bothersome in the application of spatial equilibrium models to the dairy industry. They are (1) the multi-dimensional nature of milk allocation, and (2) the diversity of the competitive structure within the dairy industry. Attempts at applying imperfectly competitive conditions in spatial studies have been few.[1] The purpose of this paper is to present a model that deals with multi-dimensions and diversity of competition by supplementing quadratic programming with a set of recursive formulations.[2]

In constructing a dairy allocation model it is useful to divide the annual production and pricing process into stages representing major decision points as milk moves from producers to processors. From a mixture of

---

* Scientific Contribution no. 509, Storrs (Connecticut) Agricultural Experiment Station, University of Connecticut. This paper is a condensation of two previous publications by the author [11, 12].

[1] Empirical applications of spatial equilibrium models using quadratic programming usually have been based on the assumption of perfectly competitive conditions [5, 6, 8]. Maruyama and Fuller [13] proposed an interregional model with varying degrees of competition, but their model was given only a trial empirical test with over-simplified data. Hsiao [7] tried to compare spatial equilibrium solutions under competitive and non-competitive conditions but did not obtain conclusive results for the latter. Whittlesey [18] emphasized the need for "non-competitive equilibrium" studies in a review of supply-demand equilibrium models. More recently, Plessner [14] demonstrated a method of applying imperfectly competitive conditions to a spatial equilibrium study of the apple and pear markets in Israel.

[2] Particular reference is made to the Takayama and Judge [16, 17] formulation which is used in the quadratic programming stage of this multistage model. For a rather extensive bibliography on quadratic programming, see Boot [3].

perfectly competitive, monopolistic and institutional conditions in the over-all market, it is possible to sort out the relevant conditions for each stage.[3] Then the stages are linked with recursive relations to deal with the time dimension, while quadratic and linear programming are used to deal with the spatial dimension.

2. Rationale for a multistage formulation

Separation of the milk allocation problem into stages is based on three considerations. The first is that supply behavior at the farm level is generally conceded as being perfectly competitive, whereas at subsequent levels of allocation, other forms of competitive behavior prevail. Farmers have some individual latitude in varying milk production. They respond recursively to a blend price.[4] Their aggregate response behavior constitutes a supply function for the producers' organization. But such a supply function is relevant only for the case of perfect competition. As pointed out by Baumol [1, pp. 318–319], a supply curve is, strictly speaking, inapplicable to the operations of an imperfectly competitive industry.[5] Accordingly, the part of the problem dealing with producers' supply determination needs to be treated separately as a perfectly competitive activity.

A second consideration is that at the producer-processor level the two major use-allocations of milk (fluid and manufacturing) are subject to different competitive conditions. In fluid milk sheds, institutional regulations

---

[3] If the competitive conditions of the dairy industry were not diverse, but rather purely monopolistic, then one could simply apply the static price-discriminating monopoly model using a quadratic programming formulation. The application would be straight-forward and would simply entail specification of marginal revenue functions in place of demand functions. Of course, the solution would contain equilibrium marginal revenue values instead of equilibrium prices, but discriminatory prices could be derived from the demand functions. Marginal revenue values would differ between areas by no more than transportation costs between areas, but product prices would not be bound by the 'transportation cost' constraint. Unfortunately, while such an application would be straigthforward, it would not be realistic.

[4] Blend price is an average of the fluid milk price and manufacturing milk price weighted by the proportion of milk sold for fluid use to that sold for manufacturing purposes in the total pool of milk in the area. More appropriately, the two kinds of milk are Class I and Class II, which approximately parallel fluid and manufacturing, respectively.

[5] Careful distinction must be made between the supply curve and the marginal cost curve in the case of monopoly. The marginal cost curve is applicable, but it is not a price-quantity supply function as for a perfectly competitive firm.

permit producers' organizations to exercise some degree of control over their sources of milk supply and to operate under an administered price.[6] In contrast, the manufacturing milk supply is subject to national competition so that sources of supply are not controllable. It seems reasonable, therefore, to treat the spatial allocation and pricing of the two uses of milk products separately with imperfectly competitive conditions imposed for fluid milk and perfectly competitive conditions imposed for manufacturing milk. Application of quadratic programming to the manufacturing milk part of the problem is straightforward. Application to the fluid milk part, on the other hand, requires the imposition of additional constraints. Takayama [15] has shown that import quotas, which are a form of supply control, can be incorporated in a quadratic programming formulation. The imposition of minimum prices is less clear, unless prices are set so that price differences between areas equal transportation costs between areas. There is no compelling reason, however, to use quadratic programming for the fluid milk part of the problem. Instead, the quantities of fluid milk demanded at administered prices in each area can be solved separately, and then the sources of supply can be allocated by use of a 'transportation cost-minimizing' linear programming formulation.

A third consideration is that the decision-making process from the producer level to the processor level is not instantaneous and simultaneous. Besides the lagged output responses at the farm level, there are intra-year lags in the allocation of milk and in the determination of the blend price paid to producers. Moreover, there are inter-year changes in demand and supply caused by changes in population, income, technology, and capital investment through time. Dependence on a single quadratic programming model to capture the effects of these recursive and parametric relations would severely strain its capability. Instead, the following multistage formulation, consisting of recursive relations and inter-year parametric relations is presented.[7]

---

[6] This model is oriented primarily toward supply studies and is concerned only with the pricing and allocating activities at the producer-processor level. Market structure at the processor-retailer level is not within the scope of this paper except to the extent that processor demand functions derived from consumer demand functions reflect market structure.

[7] While the model involves a multi-decision-making process, it is unlike Bellman's dynamic programming [2] in that the objective here is not to maximize an objective function over the entire time period. The concept of recursiveness used in this model is similar to that advanced by Day [4].

3. The multistage model

The over-all product allocation process for a single time period, say a year, is separated into five stages which roughly represent the major decision points as milk moves from producers to processors.

3.1. Stage 1. Supply response

At this stage the producers' output response is limited to 'fine tuning' opportunities, principally adjustments in the feeding program.[8] Output in t is recursively related to the blend price in $t-1$ and is written as

$$S_i^t = \alpha_i^t + \beta_i^t B_i^{t-1}, \tag{1}$$

where S_i^t = the total quantity of milk produced in Area i and in year t ($i = 1, 2, \ldots m$ supply areas), α_i^t = the quantity intercept parameter for Area i and year t, β_i^t = the slope parameter for Area i and year t, and B_i^{t-1} = the blend price of milk, i.e., the weighted average price for fluid and manufacturing milk paid to producers in Area i and year $t-1$. For the sake of economy in the use of notation, the superscript t will be omitted hereafter with the understanding that variables and parameters vary by t unless otherwise noted. The solution quantity of milk supply is denoted as $\bar{S}_i$.[9]

3.2. Stage 2. Administration of fluid milk prices

Institutional control of market behavior is introduced at this stage. A milk market administration uses a formula to set the fluid milk price. A general form of the formula is written as

$$P_j = (1+\lambda_j)\bar{P}_j^{t-1}, \tag{2}$$

where P_j = the administered price of fluid milk in Area j and in year t ($j = 1, 2, \ldots n$ demand or destination areas), λ_j = the administrator's

---

[8] Output adjustments due to investment, technological change, and economies of size are introduced by changes of the parameters of the supply function between years.

[9] Solution values of each stage are denoted with a bar over the pertinent variable.

price adjustment coefficient[10], and $\bar{P}_j^{t-1}$ = the administered price of fluid milk in the previous period.

The administrator's formula, in this case, is constructed with the objective of minimizing abnormal surplus or deficit supply situations. This objective is based on a tacit assumption that each area attempts to maintain its proportionate share of the fluid milk market. Needless to say, administrators would like to set the price high enough to assure satisfactory and stable producer income and yet not too high from a competitive standpoint.

3.3. Stage 3. Spatial allocation of fluid milk

At this stage the decision makers are the producers' organization (a cooperative) and the processors. With production of milk under way and with the fluid milk price set, processors then allocate a sufficient quantity of milk to fluid uses to meet retailers' demand, which is derived from consumer demand. The processors' derived demand is written as

$$Q_j = \gamma_j - \delta_j P_j, \tag{3}$$

where Q_j = the quantity of fluid milk demanded in Area j and in year t ($j = 1, 2, \ldots n$ demand areas), γ_j = the quantity intercept parameter for Area j and year t, δ_j = the slope parameter for Area j and year t, and P_j = the demand price of fluid milk in Area j and year t.

By substituting $\bar{P}_j$, the administered price, for P_j in (3), the quantity of fluid milk taken in Area j is obtained. The solution is written as

$$\bar{Q}_j = \gamma_j - \delta_j \bar{P}_j. \tag{4}$$

At this stage the processors also decide on their sources of supply. Processors and producers alike are assumed to be interested in minimizing

[10]
$$\lambda_j = \frac{1}{\varepsilon} \left[\frac{a_i(S_i - S_i^{t-1}) - b_j(\hat{Q}_j - Q_j^{t-1})}{Q_j^{t-1}} \right]$$

where ε = price elasticity of demand for milk, a_i = milk produced in Area i and marketed as fluid milk in Area i as a percent of milk produced in Area i, b_j = fluid milk consumed in Area j as a percent of milk produced in Area j, $\hat{Q}_j$ = the projected consumption (demand) of fluid milk in year t and Area j, and Q_j^{t-1} = the quantity of milk consumed (demanded) in year $t-1$ and Area j. The formula used here is hypothetical. It is only remotely similar to any of the actual Federal Milk Order pricing formulas. Moreover, pricing formulas are not used in some Federal Milk Orders. However, the formula presented in this model essentially accomplishes the objective of an actual administrative pricing policy.

transportation costs. Moreover, the sources of supply are assumed to be restricted by a market order which in effect requires that processors must give priority to local producers.[11]

To solve the spatial allocation problem pertaining to fluid milk, a transportation model is used. The objective is: To minimize

$$C = \sum_{i=1}^{m} \sum_{j=1}^{n} T_{ij} Q_{ij}, \tag{5}$$

subject to

$$\sum_{j=1}^{n} Q_{ij} + E_i = \omega \bar{S}_i \quad (0 < \omega < 1)$$

$$\sum_{i=1}^{m} Q_{ij} = \bar{Q}_j$$

$$Q_{ij}, E_i \geqq 0,$$

where C = total transportation cost for the region in year t, T_{ij} = the unit cost of transporting milk from Area i to Area j, assumed constant over all t, Q_{ij} = quantity of fluid milk transported from Area i to Area j in year t, E_i = excess supply over quantity of fluid milk demanded in Area i in year t (a disposal activity), and ω = maximum proportion of the milk supply available for fluid purposes (to account for seasonal variation of production), assumed to be constant over all areas and all t.[12]

Up to this point the administered prices and the transportation costs have been handled separately. The net price paid to producers for fluid milk involves a deduction for transportation costs as follows:

$$P_i = \bar{P}_j - T_{ij}. \tag{6}$$

3.4. Stage 4. Spatial allocation of manufacturing milk

The supply of milk available for manufacturing milk purposes in a region consists of the excess or residual from Stage 3, any seasonal surpluses produced in peak production periods and the normal imports from outside

[11] In reality, control over sources of supply may be accomplished by requiring differential payments into the local milk pool. For example, if a processor purchases milk from a source outside of the local pool at a lower price, he must pay the difference into the local pool.

[12] The value of ω can be derived from historical patterns of seasonal production and consumption. The usefulness of ω pertains primarily to areas which have deficit supply for the year as a whole but have surplus supply during peak production months.

the region. These supply quantities are expressed as follows:

$$X_i = (1-\omega)\bar{S}_i + \bar{E}_i \tag{7}$$

$$X_r = (1+\mu)\bar{X}_r^{t-1}, \tag{8}$$

where X_i = the quantity of milk available for manufacturing purposes from Area i and in year t ($i = 1, 2, \ldots m$ supply areas), X_r = the quantity of milk available for manufacturing purposes from Area r and in year t ($r = m+1, m+2, \ldots m+p$ of which p are supply areas outside of the region), and μ = an assumed constant annual rate of change in supply for export from areas outside the region.

The processors' derived demand function for manufacturing milk is

$$X_j = \theta_j - \phi_j M_j, \tag{9}$$

where X_j = the quantity of manufacturing milk demanded in Area j and in year t ($j = 1, 2, \ldots n$ demand areas), M_j = the demand price of manufacturing milk in Area j and in year t, θ_j = the quantity intercept of the manufacturing milk demand function for Area j and year t, and ϕ_j = the slope of the manufacturing milk demand function for Area j and year t.

A spatial equilibrium solution for n demand areas and $m+p$ supply areas can be obtained by quadratic programming. In this stage the market forces generate the prices and allocate the supplies. The objective is an equilibrium of demand and supply. The primal of the programming problem for this objective has a quadratic objective function subject to linear constraints. Following Takayama and Judge [16, 17], the problem is made solvable by transforming it into a primal-dual formulation. The objective function in the primal-dual form for the manufacturing milk allocation problem is: To maximize

$$F(M_j, M_i, M_r, X_{ij}, X_{rj}) =$$
$$\sum_j (\theta_j - \phi_j M_j) M_j - \sum_i \sum_j X_{ij} M_i - \sum_r \sum_j X_{rj} M_r - \sum_i \sum_j T_{ij} X_{ij}$$
$$- \sum_r \sum_j T_{rj} X_{rj} \geq 0 \quad (10)$$

subject to

$$M_j - M_i \leq T_{ij}$$
$$M_j - M_r \leq T_{rj}$$
$$\sum_i X_{ij} + \phi_j M_j \geq \theta_j$$

$$\sum_{j} X_{ij} = \bar{X}_i$$

$$\sum_{j} X_{ij} = \bar{X}_r$$

$$M_j, M_i, M_r, X_{ij}, X_{rj} \geqq 0$$

where M_i = the price of manufacturing milk in Area i and in t, M_r = the price of manufacturing milk in Area r and in t, X_{ij} = the quantity of manufacturing milk produced in Area i and marketed in Area j and year t, and X_{rj} = the quantity of manufacturing milk produced in Area r and marketed in Area j and year t.

3.5. Stage 5. Blend price determination

After milk is allocated to its two uses, the producers' cooperative computes the price it pays to member producers. In this model the solution to (10) in Stage 4 and the fluid milk solution in Stage 3 provide the necessary information for computing the blend prices. The computational procedure is written as:

$$B_i = [\sum_{j} \bar{Q}_{ij} \bar{P}_i + \sum_{j} \bar{X}_{ij} \bar{M}_i] \div [\sum_{j} \bar{Q}_{ij} + \sum_{j} \bar{X}_{ij}]. \tag{11}$$

The stages of the model are repeated in the following year with a linkage between Stage 5 in year t and Stage 1 in year $t+1$. The stages can be repeated for as many time periods as appropriate for the problem.

4. Inter-year parameter changes

As the spatial allocation continues from one year to the next, changes in the parameters of the demand and supply functions are introduced. In this model the shifts in demand and supply are assumed to occur independently of the solutions of the endogenous variables.[13] Furthermore, it is assumed that the motion of the forces can be expected to continue unabated for the period from t to $t+n$ where n is a target date within a reasonable range for

---

[13] This is tantamount to saying the forces influencing the parameter shifts are not price dependent in the period under consideration. Of course, price changes do affect the shifts, but they are more likely to result in a distributed lag effect than a current effect. Shifts in demand and supply could be made dependent on endogenous variables in the model; however, the model would then become considerably more cumbersome and the inclusion would not add greatly to its effectiveness.

predictive purposes. Therefore, the entire set of parameters for n years can be specified as given data. The possible sources of parameter data are outlined as follows:

The initial parameters for the fluid milk demand function are $\delta_j = cN_j$ and

$$\gamma_i = N_j Z_j + \delta_j P_j \tag{12}$$

where c = per capita slope coefficient, N_j = population in Area j and year t, and Z_j = per capita consumption of fluid milk in Area j and year t. (Z is a function of income, tastes and preferences.)

The initial parameters for the manufacturing milk demand function are $\phi_j = dN_j$ and

$$\theta_j = N_j U_j + \phi_j M_j \tag{13}$$

where d = per capita slope coefficient, and U_j = per capita consumption of manufacturing milk products in Area j and year t. (U is a function of income, tastes and preferences.)

The initial parameters for the supply function are $\beta_i = hF_i$ and

$$\alpha_i = F_i V_i - \beta_i B_i^{t-1} \tag{14}$$

where h = per dairy farm slope coefficient, F_i = number of dairy farms in Area i in year t, and V_i = milk output per farm in Area i and year t. (V is a function of technological change and investment.)

The changed values of the parameters α_i, β_i, γ_j, δ_j, θ_j, and ϕ_j for subsequent years $(t+1, t+2, \ldots, t+n)$ are obtained by projecting changes in population, income and tastes for demand and number of dairy farms, technology and investment for supply.

5. An empirical application of the model

5.1.

Usefulness of the multistage spatial allocation model hinges primarily on its capability to predict the possible outcome of potential structural changes in an industry. As one of several contributions to the regional 'demand–supply equilibrium' phase of the Northeast Dairy Adjustment project, the model was applied to the Northeast region in 1968 and the results were published in 1971 [12].[14]

[14] The Northeast Dairy Adjustment project was cooperatively conducted by the Economic Research Service, USDA, and the Agricultural Experiment Stations of the Northeastern states.

5.2. The empirical problem

Changes in sources of milk supply and demand, having accelerated in the 1960's, caused concern over the dairy industry's future position in the Northeast economy. Shifting patterns of milk producing areas and urban population centers could seriously disrupt the dairy industry if agricultural areas should become widely dispersed. It appeared that the thrust of urban-industrial expansion had caused some disagglomeration of farming areas in the Northeast [9, 10]. A few scattered farms remaining in an urbanizing area could have two conflicting effects: (1) environmental quality in the form of open space could be preserved, but (2) economic efficiency in assembling and transporting milk could be decreased. At the same time, however, farming areas beyond the reach of urban-industrial expansion could conceivably intensify in dairy production.

5.3. Objectives

The major objective of the study was to examine the on-going inter-area shifting patterns and to estimate the potential near-future outcome of these changes. While the study did not deal directly with spatial density, it was concerned with the broader area-wide dispersions of milk supplies. The analysis was aimed at answering the following questions relative to the potential change in status of Northeastern dairy production in the period 1968–72. Would the excess-fluid milk producing areas continue to meet the deficit areas' demand for milk? Would the producing areas relocate in the face of urban-industrial expansion and concentrate in predominantly agricultural areas? Would the price of milk increase substantially as the supply expansion potential decreased?

5.4. Area demarcation

In designating the areas for the study, the first step taken was to demarcate ten areas based exclusively on state boundaries. Eleven Northeastern states were represented — nine separately and Rhode Island-Massachusetts combined. The second step was to expand the set to twelve Northeastern areas by subdividing and recombining the ten state-designated areas. New York was divided into two subareas; Pennsylvania was divided into three subareas, and Maryland was divided into two subareas. Then Area 8a (southeastern Pennsylvania) was recombined with Area 9 (Delaware) and Area 10b (eastern Maryland). The second set of areas corresponds more

Table 1

Origin and destination shipping points, Northeastern areas

Supply areas	Origin point	Potential destination areas
1	Portland, Me.	1, 2, and 4
2	Concord, N.H.	2, 4, and 5
3	St. Albans, Vt.	1, 2, 3, 4, and 5
4	Boston, Mass.	4, 5, and 6a
5	Hartford, Ct.	4, 5, and 6a
6a	Albany, N.Y.	4, 5, 6a, and 7
6b	Cortland, N.Y.	6a, 6b, and 8c
7	Newark, N.J.	6a, 7, and 8a
8a+ [a]	Reading, Pa.	7, 8a+, 8b, and 10
8b	Pittsburg, Pa.	8a+, 8b, and 10
8c	Towanda, Pa.	6a, 6b, 7, and 8c
10a	Baltimore, Md.	8a+, and 10
11	Petersburg, Va.	10
12	Chicago, Ill. (Midwest)	4, 5, 6a, 6b, 7, 8a+, 8b, 8c, and 10

[a] Area 8a+ includes Area 8a, Area 9 (Delaware) and Area 10b (Eastern Maryland).

Table 2

Inter-area transportation cost, Northeastern areas [a]

Supply areas		Demand areas										
		Me 1	NH 2	Vt 3	M-RI 4	Ct 5	NY 6a	NY 6b	NJ 7	Pa 8a+	Pa 8b	Pa 8c	Md 10
							(dollars)						
1	Me	0	0.18		0.21								
2	NH		0		0.15	0.28							
3	Vt	0.42	0.36	0	0.49	0.51							
4	M-RI				0	0.18	0.34						
5	Ct				0.18	0	0.22						
6a	NY				0.34	0.22	0		0.29				
6b	NY						0.27	0				0.18	
7	NJ						0.29		0	0.23			
8a+	Pa								0.23	0	0.52		0.18
8b	Pa									0.52	0		0.47
8c	Pa						0.44	0.18	0.38			0	
10	Md									0.18			0
11	Va												0.30
12	MW				1.98	1.84	1.64	1.40	1.60	1.45	0.94	1.27	1.38

[a] Based on a rate of $ 0.20 per 100 lb per 100 miles. Sources of data are given in [12].

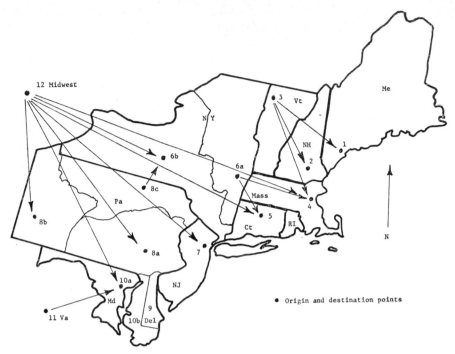

Fig. 1. Projected inter-area shipments of manufacturing milk, Northeastern areas, 1972.

closely to the geographical areas covered by the existing Federal Milk Order markets.

Two areas outside of the region were added as sources of manufacturing milk products. These latter two do not have geographical boundaries but are located in the general vicinities of Virginia and the Lake States Dairy Region.

A listing and description of the areas with their representative shipping points are presented in table 1 and in fig. 1 (which also shows solution shipments). The potential shipping designations can also be seen in the table of inter-area transportation costs (table 2).

5.5. Demand and supply estimates

Operation of the model calls for data prepared on an area basis and for specific dates in time. It was decided to set 1967 as the base year and project the data for five years, 1968 to 1972. Committee members of the Northeast Dairy Adjustment project provided basic data from their respective states for the construction of demand and supply functions.

The procedure used for constructing supply functions was to estimate 'marginal cost per cow' functions from the feed-milk production function used in an earlier phase of the project. Next a projection of cow numbers was made and then the 'marginal cost per cow' function for each state was multiplied by the number of cows to obtain the aggregate supply function for each state and each year. The aggregate supply functions for the initial year are shown in table 3. It was assumed, on the basis of careful estimates, that a constant annual supply of 75.65 million cwt would be available from Area 12 (Midwest) and 4.5 million cwt would be available from Area 11 (Virginia).

Table 3

Milk supply functions, Northeastern states, 1968 [a]

Area		Quantity intercept (α)	Slope coefficient (β)
		(mil. cwt)	
1	Me	5.7840	0.7970
2	NH	3.5828	0.3736
3	Vt	18.0233	2.3153
4	M-RI	7.6017	0.7522
5	Ct	6.3587	0.6126
6a	NY	29.4678	3.3929
6b	NY	72.1453	8.3069
7	NJ	7.9945	0.8974
8a+	Pa	37.2762	4.1061
8b	Pa	17.4289	1.8833
8c	Pa	16.7586	1.8109
10a	Md	11.3700	1.4754

[a] The form of the supply function is

$$S = \alpha + \beta \log (B^{t-1} - k)$$

where the notation is the same as for eq. (1); (k = a constant 3.10 for all areas except 3.2 for Area 2 and 3.30 for Area 8).

Sources of data are given in [12].

The procedure for estimating demand functions involved three steps. First, an estimation of a 'per capita' demand function for each state was made. Second, this was multiplied by population to obtain the aggregate for each state. Third, projections of population, income and tastes and preferences were made. The latter were used to adjust the parameters of each state's demand function for the years 1968–1972. The aggregate demand functions for the initial year are shown in table 4.

Table 4

Milk demand functions, Northeastern states, 1968 [a]

Area		Fluid milk		Manufacturing milk	
		Quantity intercept (γ)	Slope coefficient (δ)	Quantity intercept (θ)	Slope coefficient (ϕ)
		(mil. cwt)			
1	Me	3.5996	0.0945	4.8333	0.5231
2	NH	2.5577	0.0671	3.5291	0.3713
3	Vt	1.5219	0.0401	2.1342	0.2222
4	M-RI	23.6827	0.6078	33.0180	3.3649
5	Ct	11.3469	0.2835	15.6481	1.5698
6a	NY	6.0856	0.1567	8.5051	0.8676
6b	NY	61.5318	1.5844	85.9955	8.7722
7	NJ	26.2606	0.6784	36.7876	3.7558
8a+	Pa	27.9430	0.7253	38.4427	4.0155
8b	Pa	15.0648	0.3917	20.6683	2.1684
8c	Pa	3.0130	0.0783	4.1337	0.4337
10a	Md	13.0204	0.3341	18.0421	1.8495

[a] The demand functions are linear in form as follows:

$$Q = \gamma - \delta P \text{ for fluid milk}$$
$$X = \theta - \phi M \text{ for manufacturing milk}$$

where the notation is the same as for eqs. (3) and (9).
Sources of data are given in [12].

5.6. Parameter shifters

On the supply side, technological change (measured in productivity per cow) and changes in aggregate cow population were used as shifters. On the demand side, changes in income, population and tastes were used as shifters. The composite annual rate of change resulting from a projection of these shifters can probably be best expressed in an average percent change of the intercept parameters. These are shown in table 5. Notice that supply shifted backwards (negatively) for all areas. This was a consequence of projecting a decline in 'cow numbers' which more than offset an increase in 'productivity per cow'.

The shifting pattern of demand over time indicated diversity among areas regarding the direction of projected shifts. The fluid milk demand functions for Maine, Massachusetts, Rhode Island, and Pennsylvania were shifted backward (negatively) as a result of the projections. For all of the other

Table 5

Average annual percent change in the parameters of demand and supply functions for the period 1968–72, Northeastern states [a]

Area		Annual change of supply parameters	Annual change of demand parameters	
			Fluid	Manufacturing
		(percent)		
1	Me	−3.7	−0.5	1.7
2	NH	−2.7	0.7	2.9
3	Vt	−1.7	0.0	2.2
4	M-RI	−4.0	−0.3	1.9
5	Ct	−2.6	0.8	3.0
6a	Ny	−1.2	0.1	2.3
6b	NY	−1.2	0.1	2.3
7	NJ	−8.9	0.7	2.9
8a+	Pa	−1.7	−0.4	1.8
8b	Pa	−1.4	−0.6	1.6
8c	Pa	−1.4	−0.6	1.6
10a	Md	−1.5	1.2	3.3

[a] These rates of change are for the intercept parameters. Rates for the slope parameters are slightly different but show the same variation by areas.

Sources of data are given in [12].

states, except Vermont, the projections resulted in forward (positive) shifts. In contrast, the demand for manufacturing milk shifted forward (positively) for all areas.

5.7. Solutions

Application of the multistage allocation model resulted in a multisolution. There was a solution for each of the five years in the period 1968–1972 and for each year there was a solution for each of the five stages. However, for the sake of brevity, only highlights of the solutions are presented here.

The solutions indicated that the excess-fluid milk producing areas would continue to meet the deficit areas' demand for milk through 1972. It was estimated that fluid uses would account for 67.1 % of the region's milk production in 1968 and continue at about 70 % in 1972. However, several areas within the region would continue to have deficit supplies and depend upon inter-area shipments to meet their area's demand (table 6). In general, the areas which already had a deficit or were near balance would have the

Table 6

Estimated milk supply, intra-area fluid demand and excess-fluid supply, Northeastern areas, 1968 and 1972

Area	1968			1972			Percent change in excess or deficit 1968–72
	Supply of milk	Intra-area demand for fluid milk	Excess or deficit	Supply of milk	Intra-area demand for fluid milk	Excess or deficit	
			(mil. cwt)				
Excess-fluid supply areas							
6a NY	30.53	5.00	25.53	29.52	4.87	24.65	− 3
6b NY	74.64	51.78	22.86	72.21	51.30	20.91	− 9
3 Vt	18.91	1.26	17.65	17.78	1.24	16.54	− 6
8a+ Pa	38.82	23.28	15.54	36.72	22.37	14.35	− 8
8c Pa	17.22	2.54	14.68	16.18	2.45	13.73	− 6
8b Pa	18.07	12.62	5.45	17.21	12.05	5.16	− 5
1 Me	6.16	2.98	3.18	5.37	2.86	2.50	−21
2 NH	3.75	2.12	1.63	3.40	2.14	1.26	−23
10a Md	12.01	10.76	1.25	11.49	10.95	0.54	−57
Deficit fluid supply areas							
7 NJ	8.34	21.88	−13.54	5.92	22.17	−16.95	20
4 M-RI	7.98	19.65	−11.67	6.83	19.05	−12.22	5
5 Ct	6.67	9.33	− 2.66	6.06	9.36	− 3.30	24

greatest relative net change. For example, the deficits of Areas 5 (Ct) and 7 (NJ) would increase about 20 % and the excess supplies of Areas 1 (Me), 2 (NH), and 10a (Md) would decrease over 20 %. On the other hand, the excess supplies of Areas 3 (Vt), 6a (NY), 8b (Pa) and 8c (Pa) would decrease only about 3–6 % according to the solutions. It appeared, therefore, that the latter areas would continue to have ample supplies of fluid milk to meet the deficit areas' demands through 1972.

Would the producing areas relocate in the face of urban-industrial expansion and concentrate in predominantly agricultural areas? The solutions did not, of course, give an explicit answer to this question; however, the solutions can be used to detect whether the projected changes would result in favorable demand-supply conditions for relocation. The solutions showed that Area 3 (Vt) would increase its shipments to Area 4 (M-RI) by 1.35 million cwt (table 7). Area 6a (NY) would increase shipments of fluid milk to Areas 5 (Ct) and 7 (NJ) by 0.57 and 4.06 million cwt, respectively. This implies that Areas 3 (Vt) and 6a (NY) would likely experience

Table 7

Projected changes in spatial allocation of fluid milk between 1968 and 1972, Northeastern areas

Changes in fluid milk supply		Changes in fluid milk demand (mil. cwt)											
Area	quantity (mil. cwt)	Me 1	NH 2	Vt 3	M-RI 4	Ct 5	NY 6a	NY 6b	NJ 7	Pa 8a+	Pa 8b	Pa 8c	Md 10a
1 Me	−0.71	−0.12			−0.59								
2 NH	−0.31		+0.02		−0.33								
3 Vt	+1.33			−0.02	+1.35								
4 M-RI	−1.03				−1.03								
5 Ct	−0.54					−0.54							
6a NY	+4.50					+0.57	−0.13		+4.06				
6b NY	−0.48							−0.48					
7 NJ	−2.18								−2.18				
8a+ Pa	−1.89								−1.59	−0.91			+0.61
8b Pa	−0.57										−0.57		
8c Pa	−0.09											−0.09	
10a Md	−0.42												−0.42
Total	−2.39	−0.12	+0.02	−0.02	−0.60	+0.03	−0.13	−0.48	+0.29	−0.91	−0.57	−0.09	+0.19

Table 8

Projected changes in spatial allocation of manufacturing milk between 1968 and 1972, Northeastern areas

	Changes in manufacturing milk supplied	Changes in manufacturing milk demanded											
Area	quantity	Me 1	NH 2	Vt 3	M-RI 4	Ct 5	NY 6a	NY 6b	NJ 7	Pa 8a+	Pa 8b	Pa 8c	Md 10a
	(mil. cwt)	(mil. cwt)											
1 Me	−0.07	−0.07											
2 NH	−0.04		−0.04										
3 Vt	−2.47	−0.22	−0.10	−0.08	−2.07								
4 M-RI	−0.12				−0.12								
5 Ct	−0.06					−0.06							
6a NY	−5.52				−3.53	−1.59	−0.40						
6b NY	−1.95							−1.95					
7 NJ	−0.24								−0.24				
8a+ Pa	−0.21									−0.21			
8b Pa	−0.28										−0.28		
8c Pa	−0.96							−0.72				−0.24	
10a Md	−0.11												−0.11
11 Va													
12 MW					+3.94	+1.23		−1.08	−1.03	−1.91	−0.92		−0.23
Total	−12.03	−0.29	−0.14	−0.08	−1.78	−0.42	−0.40	−3.75	−1.27	−2.12	−1.20	−0.24	−0.34

conditions favorable for growth of dairy farming, while the negative result for most other areas imply that they could expect further contraction and dispersion. However, one must also examine the manufacturing milk side of the picture before drawing conclusions.

Since the manufacturing milk supply is essentially the residual after fluid demand is met, changes in the allocation of manufacturing milk are usually the converse of changes in fluid milk allocation. The solutions show that this would happen markedly in Areas 3 (Vt) and 6a (NY) and to a lesser extent in the other excess-fluid supply areas (table 8). Vermont's allocation to manufacturing uses would decrease 2.47 million cwt and New York's Area (6a) would decrease 5.52 million cwt. As a consequence, shipments of manufacturing milk products from the Midwest region would shift somewhat from New Jersey, Pennsylvania and New York (6b) to the Massachusetts-Rhode Island and Connecticut areas to replace the reduced shipments from Vermont and New York (6a).

It is of interest to note that the regional manufacturing milk consumption was estimated to decline 12.03 million hundredweight even though a positive shift in manufacturing milk demand was anticipated and applied in the model. This behavior of the model demonstrates that if fluid milk allocation is given preferential treatment, then much of the corrective adjustment in allocation must be accomplished in the manufacturing milk market. Of course, this is precisely the intent of price administration policies which are aimed at price and output stability in the fluid milk market.

The assumption of the outside supply being constant was probably unrealistic. The gap between a growing manufacturing milk demand and a slackening in regional milk output would probably be filled by shipments from outside supply sources. However, such an increase in shipments from outside the Northeast region would not affect the general direction of inter-area changes. The flows of inter-area manufacturing milk shipments are shown in fig. 1 (page 568).

After studying the spatial allocation of both fluid and manufacturing milk, it appears that Areas 3 (Vt), 6a (NY), 6b (NY), 8a+ (Pa), 8b (Pa), and 8c (Pa) could be expected to continue intensive dairy production. Areas 3 (Vt) and 6a (NY) would have the most favorable economic conditions because they would move toward a higher proportion of fluid milk sales. Consequently, blend prices would rise, enhancing the prospects for profits. Moreover, urban-industrial expansion was expected to be slow in these areas (assuming anticipated population growth is an acceptable proxy measure of urban-industrial expansion).

Would the price of milk rise substantially as the supply expansion potential decreased? The solutions presented thus far suggest that the on-going changes in demand and supply were setting the stage for substantial price rises for milk by 1972. Output would be contracting and demand would be remaining fairly stable. A higher proportion of the milk supply would be allocated to fluid uses. More inter-area shipments of fluid milk would be made and, consequently, transportation costs would rise. Therefore, it seemed reasonable to expect the solutions would show a rising time path of milk prices.

For the northeast region as a whole, the blend prices would rise practically constantly at about 1.3 % per year, according to the solution. This is roughly a mirror image of the solution's downward movement (-1.5 % per year) of the Northeast region's milk output. Obviously, these solution-price rises were exclusive of inflationary trends.

Considerable variation in price rise would result among the areas (table 9). Primarily, the results showed that the low-price areas would be 'catching up' somewhat to the high-price areas. Some of the low-price areas would improve the fluid proportion of their milk supply and some would benefit from rising manufacturing milk prices caused by the regional contraction in milk supply. Areas which are expected to have the best prospects for continued intensive dairy farming, such as the Vermont, New York and Pennsylvania areas, would also have the greatest relative increases in blend prices.

Table 9

Percentage changes in estimated milk output and blend milk prices, Northeastern areas, 1968–72

Area		Percent change in estimated milk output (1968–72)	Percent change in estimated blend price (1968–72)
8c	Pa	− 6	+25
6a	NY	− 3	+23
3	Vt	− 6	+18
8b	Pa	− 5	+13
10a	Md	− 4	+13
5	Ct	− 9	+11
6b	NY	− 3	+10
8a+	Pa	− 5	+ 8
1	Me	−13	+ 8
2	NH	− 9	+ 7
4	M-RI	−14	+ 7
7	NJ	−29	+ 5

6. Summary and conclusions

A multistage model was designed to cope with the spatial, temporal, and product-use dimensions of an imperfectly competitive industry. Application of the model to the Northeastern dairy industry traced the effects over time of spatially different shifts in supply and demand. The simulated behavior of price administration and institutional supply control of fluid milk constrained the spatial adjustment of fluid milk production.

The multisolution produced by the model was scanned for information that would answer questions regarding the prospects in the Northeast for (1) an adequate fluid milk supply, (2) a relocation of dairy farming and (3) a substantial rise in the time path of milk prices. The solutions suggested that the region's over-all excess fluid milk supply would decline only slightly (from 79.9 to 67.9 million cwt) between 1968 and 1972. Changes in the spatial allocation of fluid milk indicate that Areas 3 (Vt) and 6a (NY) would expand their allocations to fluid use through shipments to neighboring areas. Basically, the spatial allocations and time paths suggested that the low 'fluid-proportion' areas would tend to 'draw closer' to the high 'fluid-proportion' areas with respect to blend prices.

Supplementing quadratic programming with recursive relations in a multistage formulation, in this case, limits the applicability of the model to the specific industry for which it was designed. As a simulation model, however, it could be used to test a variety of hypotheses and re-applied periodically to update projections for the specific industry. Moreover, the concept of recursiveness in multistages may have general applicability in the design of similar models for other industries.

References

[1] Baumol, W. J., 1965, Economic Theory and Operations Analysis, Englewood Cliffs, New Jersey: Prentice Hall, Inc.
[2] Bellman, R., 1957, Dynamic Programming, Princeton: Princeton University Press.
[3] Boot, J. C. G., 1964, Quadratic Programming, Amsterdam: North-Holland Publishing Company.
[4] Day, R. H., 1961, Recursive Programming and Production Response, Amsterdam: North-Holland Publishing Company.
[5] Engel, N. E., 1967, A Spatial Equilibrium Stochastic Supply: A Study of the Fall Potato Industry, unpublished Ph.D. thesis, University of Connecticut.
[6] Hall, H. H., E. O. Heady and Y. Plessner, 1968, Quadratic programming solution of competitive equilibrium for U. S. agriculture, American Journal of Agricultural Economics, 50, 536–555.

[7] Hsiao, J. C., 1967, A Quadratic Programming Approach to Spatial Equilibrium Analysis of the Dairy Industry in the Northeast Region, unpublished Ph.D. thesis, University of Connecticut.

[8] Hsiao, J. C. and M. W. Kottke, 1968, Spatial Equilibrium Analysis of the Dairy Industry in the Northeast Region — An Application of Quadratic Programming, Storrs (Conn.) Agr. Exp. Sta. Bull. 405.

[9] Kottke, M. W., 1964, Patterns of Dairy Farm Exit and Growth, Storrs (Conn.) Agr. Exp. Sta. Bull. 382.

[10] Kottke, M. W., 1966, Changes in farm density in areas of urban expansion, Journal of Farm Economics, 48, 1290–1296.

[11] Kottke, M. W., 1970, Spatial, Temporal, and Product-use Allocation of Milk in An Imperfectly Competitive Dairy Industry, American Journal of Agricultural Economics, 52, 33–40.

[12] Kottke, M. W., 1971, Projection of Milk Supply, Demand and Price in the Northeast — An Application of A Multistage Allocation Model, Storrs (Conn.) Agr. Exp. Sta. Bull. 416.

[13] Maruyama, Y. and E. I. Fuller, 1965, An Interregional Quadratic Programming Model for Varying Degrees of Competition, Massachusetts Agr. Exp. Sta. Bull. 555.

[14] Plessner, Y., 1971, Computing equilibrium solutions for imperfectly competitive markets, American Journal of Agricultural Economics, 53, 191–196.

[15] Takayama, T. and G. G. Judge, 1964, Spatial equilibrium and quadratic programming, Journal of Farm Economics, 46, 67–93.

[16] Takayama, T., 1966, Spatial Economic Analysis, Armidale, New South Wales: The University of New England.

[17] Takayama, T. and G. G. Judge, 1971, Spatial and Temporal Price and Allocation Models, Amsterdam: North-Holland Publishing Company.

[18] Whittlesey, N. K., 1968, Supply-demand equilibrium models: a critical review, W-54 GP-5 Joint Symposium paper, Fort Collins, Colorado.

CHAPTER 29

Temporal equilibrium analysis of rice and wheat in India *

V. K. PANDEY and T. TAKAYAMA

G. B. Pant University of Agriculture and Technology, India
University of Illinois

1. Introduction

In India, the agricultural revolution during the latter half of the decade of 1960's brought about significant changes on the food front, and more importantly, it held out a great promise for the future. This development calls for a reassessment of the situation with respect to the probable price, production and consumption patterns of the foodgrains over a finite time horizon in the future so that a proper reorientation, if any, of the country's food policy does not remain overdue. With this in view, this study attempts to conduct a temporal equilibrium analysis of the alternative price and output allocation patterns of the two major foodgrains, viz., rice and wheat, over the operative planning period of the Fourth Five Year Plan, i.e., 1969–1974, in India.

The specific objectives laid down for the study, are the following:

(i) To search and develop a suitable temporal price and allocation model that incorporates the demand, supply and price variables together with some additional constraints on prices and land, to provide a temporal solution in terms of optimum consumption, production, year-to-year carry-over quantities, and equilibrium prices along with the requisite imports and exports over time.

(ii) To study the alternative price and output pattern of rice and wheat over a period of five years (1969–74) under the free foodgrains market case.

(iii) To study the alternative price and output pattern of rice and wheat

* We gratefully acknowledge financial support from the Ford Foundation, Office of International Agriculture, and Department of Agricultural Economics, Project #373, of University of Illinois.

over a period of five years (1969–74) when price controls are imposed by government in the foodgrains market.

(iv) To study the policy implications of the results obtained as above in (ii) and (iii).

2. Methodological sketch

2.1.

In order to study the price and quantity flows over time, the temporal price equilibrium model of Takayama and Judge [17] is employed as the basic model in this study. Within the given competitive structure of the economy along with the assumptions underlying demand and supply relations, and the given objective of maximization of some sort of a quasi-welfare function in quadratic form, this model generates the quantities of optimum production, consumption, carry-overs from one period to another, and equilibrium prices over the operative period. Earlier, Pant [14] employed a similar model to conduct spatial and temporal analysis of rice and wheat in India, covering a period of three years (1968–71), by using demand in functional form and supply as fixed point estimates. This study, on the contrary, employs fixed point estimates for demand (for reasons stated later) and lagged price supply functions in the model to generate alternative price-output information over a five year period. It also employs certain modifications so as to enhance the usefulness of the model for policy purposes. The basic model is modified in this study to adjust to the lagged structure of the supply relation, and to accommodate few additional constraints on land and prices (in the form of upper and lower limits imposed externally). Such modifications on the Takayama and Judge model have not been tried before.

2.2. Estimation of parameters

The demand and supply relations, whose parameters form the basic elements of the model, are estimated separately as follows. In case of demand, because of the difficulty in establishing proper functional relationship on the available data which relates to per capita availability and not the actual consumption, projected fixed estimates calculated on the basis of the demand shifters are used in this study in place of the price-dependent demand function. The methodology adopted for demand projections is the same as employed by the National Council of Applied Economic Research [11], and consists of using mainly the coefficients of income elasticity, the likely changes in per capita real income and the expected increase in population over the projected period. However, this study uses its own estimates of expected changes in per capita income and population. The income elasticity coefficients have been borrowed from the work of Ray [15].

In case of supply relations, three years lagged price-dependent supply functions are used in the model. These lagged supply functions have been estimated by first estimating the acreage response functions and then multiplying them by the projected average yields of the respective commodities for each of the time periods under study. For making yield projections, the productivity functions have been estimated separately. The following acreage response function is hypothesized:

$$A(t) = \lambda + \eta_1 P(t-1) + \eta_2 P(t-2) + \eta_3 P(t-3) + \mu R^*(t-1) + \nu W^*(t),$$

where $A(t)$ = area under the crop in period t; $P(t)$ = wholesale price of the crop (12 months post harvest average) in period t; $R^*(t-1)$ = productivity index of crop in period $t-1$ deflated by the combined productivity index of substitute crops in the same period; $W^*(t)$ = pre-sowing period weather index in period t constructed on the basis of rainfall.

The data[1] used in estimating this response function relate to the period 1955–56 to 1968–69. Undeflated prices have been used in the above response functions. In order to avoid the problem of multicollinearity, encountered severely during estimation, the response functions have been estimated by using the Nerlovian expected price [12], $P^*(t)$, constructed as follows:

$$P^*(t) = \tfrac{1}{6}[3P(t-1) + 2P(t-2) + P(t-3)].$$

The following two relations are hypothesized in order to estimate the productivity functions for rice, wheat and their substitute crops:

(i) $R = f(W, T)$
(ii) $R = f(W, F, H)$,

where R is the productivity index of the crop, W is the crop growing period weather index, T is time trend as a proxy variable for technology, F is total fertilizer consumption, and H is area under high yielding varieties.

The data used in the estimation of these relations relate to the period 1955–56 to 1968–69. In projecting the productivity indices and yield per acre during the period under study, a normal growing period weather

---

[1] The data used in estimating the supply response and productivity functions were obtained from various sources listed in references [1, 3–6].

($W = 100$) and Fourth Plan [8] targets for the fertilizer consumption and the area under high yielding varieties have been used.

Lastly, assuming a normal pre-sowing period weather ($W^* = 100$), the acreage response function is converted into the output response function as follows:

$$x(t) = A(t)S(t)$$
$$= \theta(t) + \gamma_1(t)P(t-1) + \gamma_2(t)P(t-2) + \gamma_3(t)P(t-3),$$

where $\theta(t) = [\lambda + \mu R^*(t-1) + vW^*(t)]S(t)$; $\gamma_i(t) = \eta_i S(t)$, for $i = 1, 2, 3$; $S(t)$ = projected average yield in period t; $x(t)$ = supply (planned output) in period t.

Appendix tables A1, A2 and A3 present the estimates of projected demand, acreage response and productivity functions, and supply functions, respectively, used in this study.

2.3. Speculative carry-overs and buffer stock programs

The carry-overs from one period to another (temporal flows) in the storage activities of the temporal price equilibrium model refer to the speculative stocks of the producers and traders, and are functions of the discounted price differential over time and the storage cost. An interest rate of 10%, the usual market rate for most borrowings of the traders, is used in this study as the discount rate. For a speculative grain stocks, the storage cost is a function of quantity stored, since the period of storage (normally less than the difference between the two consecutive production periods) is fixed from the viewpoint of spoilage and storage loss. Since sufficient data on storage cost as a function of quantity stored is not available, average storage costs (rupees 93.00 per ton for rice and rupees 122.00 per ton for wheat, adopted from the study of Kahlon [10]) on the traders godowns are used here.

As regards to the buffer stock program of the government, a beginning was made with a provision for a stock of two million tons in 1968–69, and setting up of a buffer stock of 5 million tons was envisaged for the later periods of the Fourth Plan. Accepting these as the targets for the fixed government's storage activity, this study allocates these targets of food-grains buffer stock between rice and wheat, respectively, for each time period as follows: 0.5 and 1.5 million tons for 1968–69; 1 and 2 million tons for 1969–70; 1 and 3 million tons for 1970–71; and 1 and 4 million tons for 1971–72 and onwards. The allocation of higher proportion to wheat is done for the reason that it would be easier and fair to operate on the stocking of wheat which has shown a greater potential, as compared to rice, for creating surplus in the recent technological breakthrough in Indian agriculture. In view of the availability of scientific storage in the country and the deterioration of grains during storage, it is assumed that the stocks are annually replaced.

2.4. Basic model and its modifications

For the reasons stated earlier, fixed point estimates of demand are used in this study. Also, the estimated supply functions have lagged price structure. Because of these two changes, the matrix "Q" in the quadratic term of the objective function of the original Takayama and Judge temporal price equilibrium model does not remain symmetric and positive definite; instead it becomes asymmetric and positive semi-definite. Therefore, the integrability requirements in the formulation of the quasi-welfare function are not met, and the quantity formulation of the objective function for this study is not possible. However, as suggested by Takayama and Judge [17], the non-integrable case of asymmetry can be handled, and still ensure a competitive solution, by formulating the objective function in terms of net social monetary gains. The maximization of net social revenue, in this case, is surrogate to maximization of net social quasi-welfare function. It has been shown that, although this problem of maximization of net social revenue does not possess the nice property that the feasibility set is non-empty, but, if the problem yields a solution, the solution is a competitive price equilibrium solution [17]. Hence, for the two commodities ($k = 1, 2$) and five time periods ($t = 1, \ldots, 5$), the price formulation of the objective function in terms of the intertemporal net social revenue is attempted for this study as follows:

$$NSR \equiv \sum_{t=1}^{5} \sum_{k=1}^{2} \sigma^{t-1} \rho^k(t) \zeta^k(t) - \sum_{t=1}^{5} \sum_{k=1}^{2} \sigma^{t-1} p^k(t) \xi^k(t)$$

$$- \sum_{i=1}^{3} \sum_{t=1}^{5} \sum_{k=1}^{2} \sigma^{t-1} p^k(t) \gamma_i^k(t) p^k(t-i) - \sum_{t=1}^{5} \sum_{k=1}^{2} \sigma^t b^k(t, t+1) x^k(t, t+1)$$

$$+ \sum_{k=1}^{2} \rho^k(1) x^k(0, 1) - \sum_{k=1}^{2} \sigma^4 \rho^k(5) x^k(5, 6)$$

where $\rho^k(t) p^k(t)$ = market demand price and market price of the kth product at time period t, respectively, $b^k(t, t+1)$, $x^k(t, t+1)$ = storage cost of carrying one unit of product k from t to $t+1$, and the carry-over quantity of the product from t to $t+1$, respectively. $\zeta^k(t)$ = fixed estimates of demand for period t; $\xi^k(t)$ = estimated supply intercept $\theta^k(t)$; for the first period, $\xi^k(1)$ represents fixed supply estimates obtained by using the actual prices of three years prior to $t = 1$ in this model; $\gamma_i^k(t-i) = $ coefficients for $(i = 1, 2, 3)$ of three years lagged prices $p^k(t-1)$, $p^k(t-2)$ and $p^k(t-3)$ in supply function for period t; and $\sigma = 1/1+r$; r being a discount rate.

In order to obtain the set of optimal production, storage, and market prices over time, we have to solve the following typical quadratic programming problem: Maximize NSR defined above subject to the following constraints;

(1) supply feasibility condition:

$$-\xi^k(t)-\sum_{i-1}^{3}\gamma_i^k(t-i)p^k(t-i)+x^k(t) \leqq 0 \text{ for all } k \text{ and } t,$$

(2) no excess demand condition:

$$\zeta^k(t)-\hat{x}^k(t-1, t)+\hat{x}^k(t, t+1)-x^k(t)-x^k(t-1, t)+x^k(t, t+1) \leqq 0$$

for all k and t, and predetermined

$$\hat{x}^k(t-1, t) \equiv 0 \text{ for } t > 1, \text{ and } \hat{x}^k(t, t+1) \equiv 0 \text{ for } t < 5.$$

(3) equilibrium infra temporal price condition:

$$-\rho^k(t)-p^k(t) \leqq 0 \text{ for all } k \text{ and } t,$$

(4) equilibrium inter temporal price condition:

$$\sigma\rho^k(t+1)-\rho^k(t)-\sigma b^k(t, t-1) \leqq 0 \text{ for all } k \text{ and } t,$$

(5) non-negativity condition:

$$x^k(t), x^k(t, t+1), p^k(t), \rho^K(t) \geqq 0 \text{ for all } k \text{ and relevant } t.$$

In this paper the following modifications of the basic model formulated above are attempted: (1) imposition of upper and/or lower bounds on prices, (2) imposition of limit on price differentials between the two products, and (3) imposition of land availability restriction on each product.

When the upper and/or lower limits on prices, $p^{k*}(t)$ and/or $p^{k***}(t)$, are imposed, we incorporate the following additional condition:

$$-p^{k*}(t)+\rho^k(t) \leqq 0 \text{ and/or } p^{k**}(t)-\rho^k(t) \leqq 0 \text{ for some } k \text{ and } t.$$

This, however, tends to generate deficit or surplus in supply over time and render the modified problem infeasible. Thus, we are forced to introduce the following modification of condition (2):

$$\zeta^k(t)-\hat{x}^k(t-1, t)+\hat{x}^k(t, t+1)-x^k(t)-x^k(t-1, t)+x^k(t, t+1)-m^k(t)$$
$$+n^k(t) \leqq 0 \text{ for all } k \text{ and } t,$$

where $m^k(t)$ and $n^k(t)$ are import and export variable respectively.

Price differential constraint, $-d(t)-\rho^1(t)+\rho^2(t) \leq 0$ and $-d(t)-\rho^2(t) +\rho^1(t) \leq 0$ for all t, are introduced to take care of the situation in which product substitution in consumption from one product to the other can take place on the one unit of wheat for one unit of rice basis once the price differential reaches a certain magnitude, $d(t)$. Condition (2) is, accordingly, modified to

$$\zeta^k(t) \cdot \hat{x}^k(t-1, t)+\hat{x}^k(t, t+1)-x^k(t)-x^k(t-1, t)+x^k(t, t+1)-m^k(t)+n^k(t)$$
$$-z^{jk}(t)+z^{kj}(t) \leq 0 \text{ for all } k, jk, \text{ and } t,$$

where $z^{jk}(t)$ and $z^{kj}(t)$ are the quantity of the jth and kth commodity substituted for the kth and jth commodity respectively.

Land constraints are usual linear constraints and will not be discussed here.

3. *Programming sub-models*

The following programming sub-models are specified and the solutions are obtained for various parametric runs of each. Model I specified the basic temporal price equilibrium model. The solutions are obtained under two situations: (i) both with and without land constraint but no fixed government's storage activity − Model I(A), and (ii) with no land constraint but with fixed government's storage activity − Model I(B). The fixed government's storage activity refers to the counter-speculatory buffer stocks, and the targets of storage are incorporated in the fixed demand vector, K, of the model. Further, because of fixed supply for period I (as the use of lagged supply structure in the model requires), a fixed import quota for rice is assumed to cover up the deficit supply of rice in period I. This is required so that the quantity constraint for the initial year is satisfied and the problem becomes feasible.

Model II handles the case when the government's price control policy becomes operative by restricting the domain of price variability over time. The solutions are obtained by imposing the upper and lower price limits for each time period under two situations: (i) with only land constraint − Model II(A), and (ii) with both land constraint and governments' fixed storage activity − Model II(B). However, due to the space limitation, the detailed report of these model results is not given in this paper.[2]

---

[2] For detailed discussions and information, the reader is referred to [13].

Model III deals with the case when the limits on price differential between the two commodities, along with the upper limit on their prices, are
imposed and inter-commodity transfers are allowed in order to cover the
deficit, if any, of one commodity by the surplus, if any, of the other. The
solutions, again, are obtained in two situations: (i) only with land constraint
— Model III(A), and (ii) with both land constraint and fixed government's
storage activity — Model III(B).

4. Discussion on results

Model I(A) relates to the case of free competitive market. The feasible
solution, presented in table 1, is obtained with the initial period import of
1.80 million tons of rice (just enough to cover the deficit in that period).
However, when the land constraint is introduced in the model the problem
becomes infeasible. The land constraint is fixed at 42.7 million hectares
for rice and 18.3 million hectares for wheat, representing 35 % and 15 %,
respectively, for rice and wheat, of the total area expected to be devoted
to foodgrains during the Fourth Plan period. While fixing these limits the
past trend in the area under rice and wheat, and some allowance for the
future shifts in acreage allocation, have been considered. The solution

Table 1

Equilibrium price, optimal production, and intertemporal flows for each period in
Model I(A) [a]. (Price in rupees per metric ton and quantities in thousand metric tons)

Commodities	Period	Equilibrium price $\bar{p}(t)$	Optimal production $\bar{x}(t)$	Intertemporal flows $\bar{x}(t, t+1)$
1. Rice	I	1516.21	41 796	6
	II	1760.83	44 994	
	III	1211.15	48 507	1842
	IV	1425.26	47 853	1523
	V	1660.78	48 107	
2. Wheat	I	134.70	18 527	334
	II	270.18	18 705	53
	III	419.20	19 797	
	IV	0.00	21 912	
	V	0.00	23 349	

[a] Initial period import of rice = 1800 thousand metric tons.

Table 2

Equilibrium price, optimal production, intertemporal flows, and government's fixed storage for each period in Model I(B) [a]. (Price in rupees per metric ton and quantities in thousand metric tons)

Commodities	Period	Equilibrium price $\bar{p}(t)$	Optimal production $\bar{x}(t)$	Inter-temporal flows $\bar{x}(t, t+1)$	Government's fixed storage [b] $g(t, t+1)$
1. Rice	I	1516.21	41 796	6	1000
	II	1760.83	44 994		1000
	III	1211.15	48 507	1842	1000
	IV	1425.26	47 853	1523	1000
	V	1660.78	48 107		1000
2. Wheat	I	660.62	18 527	16	2000
	II	848.68	19 964		3000
	III	660.62	22 201		4000
	IV	0.00	22 307		4000
	V	0.00	23 090		4000

[a] In order to cover up the deficit fixed supply in period I, initial period imports for rice and wheat are, respectively, 2300 and 150 thousand metric tons.

[b] In this model, government's fixed storage in the period 0, which will be carried to period I, i.e., $g(0, I)$, are assumed to be as: 0.50 for rice and 1.5 for wheat. These figures relate to the actual buffer stocks (of 2 million tons) maintained by the government in the year 1968–69.

of Model I(B), which includes fixed government storage, is also feasible only when the land constraint is not introduced in the model, and is presented in table 2.

The results of Model I(A) reveal that, if the supply adjusts itself to market prices while satisfying predetermined demand quantities over time without any government control, the prices would show wide fluctuations from one period to another. The prices of rice would record a much higher level, while the prices of wheat would record a much lower level, as compared to the prices in the period preceding the period of this analysis (1096.81 and 910.93 rupees per ton, respectively, for rice and wheat in the year 1968–69). This behavior of the prices of rice and wheat can be linked with their production pattern. The record success in high yielding varieties of wheat has raised its productivity so much as to create surpluses, whereas the progress in high yielding varieties of rice has not shown much promise so far, and so the country, with the majority of its population eating rice, is still facing a deficit in rice production. The wheat surpluses over time would force the wheat prices down to incredibly low levels, and the rice deficits would force the rice prices to very high levels. The infeasibility of the model I(A) when the land constraint is introduced also indicates that the optimal production of rice would require a considerable rise in the rice prices so as to attract the producers to put more and more land under rice production and, thus, exceed the limits set for rice in the land constraint and making the solution infeasible. From these results, another point may be drawn that the optimal production in Model I(A) would require a drastic shift in the cropping pattern in terms of increased area under rice and, thereby, a reduction in the area under competing crops such as maize, jowar, bajra, sugar cane, etc., under the assumption that there is not much scope for bringing new land under cultivation. Whether this shift in the cropping pattern would be feasible during the operative period of analysis from the viewpoint of the available resources, particularly irrigation water and fertilizer, which are so important in the rice production, and also what impact would such a shift in cropping pattern bring about in the total food economy of the country, are posed as two important questions. Within the scope of this study, however, these questions cannot be answered and are left for further exploration in the broader perspective of the total food economy in future research.

The level of prices and the wide fluctuations in the prices under uncontrolled free operation of the foodgrains market, thus, remains the main focus of this study. The wide fluctuations in the prices may prove to be detrimental to the desired growth and stability of the country's economy, particularly food economy which contributes more than 50 % to the country's net domestic product. Also, a very high level of rice prices would become burdensome to the rice eating majority, and very low level of wheat prices would prove to be a disincentive to the recently rejuvenated hopes of the country's farming community. The results of Model I(B), which includes the government's storage activity for buffer stock operation, do not prove to have any smoothing effect on the price levels and variability, except that the situation with regard to the wheat prices improves somewhat during the first three years.

As an alternative, a system of price control, comprising upper and lower limits on prices, is proposed to be investigated in Models II and III. The policy of price stabilization having in view certain maxima as well as certain minima was recognized as early as the formulation of the First Five Year Plan [7]. However, no attempt was made in this direction until the setting up of Agricultural Price Commission in 1965, on whose recommendation the minimum support prices for important agricultural commodities became the regular feature every year thereafter. But, on the side of maxima, there has been no explicit recognition of maximum price level for agricultural commodities.

In order to make an integrated system of price controls effective in the Model II framework, the government has to take care of the requisite imports and exports generated in the model. This poses an important problem of seeking the opportunities for import of rice and export of wheat in the world food economy, and which would involve obtaining an economically and politically stable solution. However, in the light of the fact that both rice and wheat are staple foods and some degree of substitution is possible in the consumption of the two commodities, the surpluses of wheat (i.e., exports) can be utilized to cover the deficits in rice (i.e., imports). This would save the country from the foreign exchange burden arising from the rice imports and also from the risk of bearing strong competition in the wheat export in the world market. The experience over the recent past has shown that the food deficits in the country have been met largely by wheat imports. Because of the lack of adequate data, no estimate of the extent of possible substitutability of wheat for rice is available. But the high price differential between rice and wheat in the open market prices did force the consumers, in the past, to substitute wheat for rice to some extent.

This idea of transferring wheat surpluses (exports) to cover the rice deficits (imports) is incorporated in the Model III by imposing the maximum limit on the price differential between the two commodities, along with the upper limits on the prices and land constraint (the same as in Model II). These transfers are referred to as inter-commodity transfers in this study. The price differential over time is kept constant, and three parametric runs of the model are made with the three sets of price differentials, i.e., $d(t) = 200$, 300, and 400. The results obtained are presented in tables 7, 8, and 9.

It is observed from the parametric runs of Model III(A) that the price and output pattern, and inter-commodity transfers change significantly with the change in the limit on price differential between the two commodities. Furthermore, the requisite imports are in quite substantial amounts for the first two periods in all three solutions. The solution of Model III(A_2), however, shows less price variability over time in respect to both the commodities. Also, the net social revenue is greater in this case as compared to the other two solutions. Based on these observations, it can be said that the price differential limit of 300 rupees per ton would be a better choice.

Table 7

Equilibrium price, optimal production, intertemporal flows, inter-commodity transfers, and imports for each period when the limit on price differential ($D(t) = 200$ rupees) between the two commodities is imposed along with the upper limit on prices and land constraint in Model III(A_1). (Price in rupees per metric ton and quantities in thousand metric tons)

Commodities	Period	Equilibrium price $\bar{p}(t)$	Optimal production $\bar{x}(t)$	Inter-temporal flows $\bar{x}(t, t+1)$	Inter-commodity transfers $\bar{z}(t)$	Import (+)
1. Rice	I	1093.65	41 796	–	(+) 367	(+) 1427
	II	1126.45	42 714	–	(+) 1542	(+) 743
	III	1160.25	43 494	–	(+) 2955	(+) 30
	IV	838.54	44 440	912	(+) 4583	–
	V	1015.37	43 425	–	(+) 5292	–
2. Wheat	I	893.65	18 527	–	(−) 367	–
	II	926.46	20 522	–	(−) 1542	–
	III	960.25	22 805	–	(−) 2955	–
	IV	638.55	25 343	–	(−) 4583	–
	V	815.37	26 892	–	(−) 5292	–

Table 8

Equilibrium price, optimal production, intertemporal flows, inter-commodity transfers, and imports for each period when the limit on price differential ($D(t) = 300$ rupees) between the two commodities is imposed along with the upper limit on prices and land constraint in Model III(A_2). (Price in rupees per metric ton and quantities in thousand metric tons)

Commodities	Period	Equilibrium price $\bar{p}(t)$	Optimal production $\bar{x}(t)$	Inter-temporal flows $\bar{x}(t, t+1)$	Inter-commodity transfers $\bar{z}(t)$	Import (+)
1. Rice	I	1093.65	41 796	–	(+) 367	(+) 1427
	II	1126.45	42 714	–	(+) 1303	(+) 983
	III	1160.25	43 494	–	(+) 2524	(+) 462
	IV	966.69	44 440	–	(+) 3580	–
	V	1155.36	44 146	–	(+) 5484	–
2. Wheat	I	793.65	18 527	–	(−) 367	–
	II	826.45	20 283	–	(−) 1303	–
	III	860.25	22 374	–	(−) 2524	–
	IV	666.70	24 786	406	(−) 3580	–
	V	855.36	26 768	–	(−) 5484	–

Table 9

Equilibrium price, optimal production, intertemporal flows, inter-commodity transfers, and imports for each period when the limit on price differential $(D(t) = 400$ rupees) between the two commodities is imposed along with the upper limit on prices and land constraint in Model III(A_3). (Price in rupees per metric ton and quantities in thousand metric tons)

Commodities	Period	Equilibrium price $\bar{p}(t)$	Optimal production $\bar{x}(t)$	Inter-temporal flows $\bar{x}(t, t+1)$	Inter-commodity transfers $\bar{z}(t)$	Import $(+)$
1. Rice	I	1093.65	41 796	–	$(+)$ 367	$(+)$ 1427
	II	1126.45	42 714	–	$(+)$ 1063	$(+)$ 1222
	III	1160.25	43 494	–	$(+)$ 2092	$(+)$ 893
	IV	1195.05	44 440	–	$(+)$ 3469	$(+)$ 110
	V	400.00	45 430	–	$(+)$ 4199	–
2. Wheat	I	693.65	18 527	–	$(-)$ 367	–
	II	726.45	20 043	–	$(-)$ 1063	–
	III	760.25	21 942	–	$(-)$ 2092	–
	IV	795.06	24 229	–	$(-)$ 3469	–
	V	0.00	25 889	–	$(-)$ 4199	–

Model III(B), which handles the case of government's storage activities along with the other constraints of that of Model III(A), turns out to be infeasible. The obvious reason for this infeasibility is that there is not enough surplus of these commodities, under the imposed price limits, left out for government's buying and storage. Therefore, the government's storage for buffer stocks, in this case, has to be built up exclusively through the additional imports of both rice and wheat.

5. Conclusions and their policy implications

First, the general conclusion that may be drawn from the above discussion is that, under the assumption of normal weather and projected productivity indices, the deficits in rice would continue to increase over time during the Fourth Plan period, whereas wheat would gradually become the surplus commodity. It may be noted here that the productivity of rice might increase further as the high yielding varieties program of rice gains impetus during this period. Second, the free operation of the foodgrains market would not only cause wide fluctuations in the prices of rice and wheat, but also record the levels of prices such that the rice prices would become burdensome on the consumer's budget and the wheat prices would prove to be a disincentive to the farmers. Further, the infeasibility under land constraint means that the free market solution would require drastic changes in the cropping pattern, and thus, would affect the production of other agricultural commodities.

Third, a well-defined system of integrated price control, keeping in view both maxima and minima, would improve the price and output situation over time and guarantee the solution within the domain prescribed by the land constraints. This solution, of course, would require an acquisition of imports (of rice) and disposal of exports (of wheat) over time by the government in order to make the system of price control effective. Fourth, through another system of price control comprising imposition of maximum limits on the prices and price differentials between the two commodities the substitution of rice demand, in part, by wheat surpluses over time can be enforced in the market. At the most, in this case, if the market itself fails to do it, the government would be required to pick up the wheat surplus from the market at times when the price differential increases beyond the maximum imposed limit, and to distribute the surplus in place of rice to the low income consumers through fair price shops. In fact, there is not much difference between these two systems of price control as both the systems imply, directly or indirectly, imposition of upper and lower limits on the price variability. In the absence of properly estimated demand relationships including cross elasticities for the two commodities, the inter-commodity transfer model suggests an alternative way of handling the commodity substitution problem through a special transfer policy based on revealed market price differential between the pair of commodities.

Fifth, and last, the government's storage programs for building up buffer stocks has to be carried out externally, i.e., outside the market system, through imports. During the initial three periods, there is virtually no scope for building up buffer stocks from the internal market supplies.

It may be drawn from these conclusions that, from the long-run perspective of free functioning of the foodgrains market, greater all out efforts are needed towards increasing the rice productivity. The country might achieve self-sufficiency in terms of the aggregate foodgrains requirement. But, the self-sufficiency in the real terms of a stable foodgrains market operation cannot be had until the situation with regard to rice, which is the major staple food of the people, also improves. Within the scope of this study, the price controls may be suggested as a short term resort to smooth out the price output situation. Quite an effort has been made by the government in this direction in the recent past, but it all centered around only one aspect of the price controls, viz., minimum support prices. Fixation of maximum prices, either directly or indirectly through price differential, needs due consideration to correct lopsidedness in the price policy so as to keep the balance from the producer's as well as consumer's point of view.

Finally, as consummate remarks, two points need to be mentioned here. First, although the procedure of maximization of net social revenue has been employed in obtaining the optimality of the solutions under different alternative sets of conditions, the use of maximized net social revenue as a criterion in evaluating the alternative courses of action is not very much emphasized in this study. In fact, the comparison of two or more Pareto-optimum solutions, each obtained under different sets of conditions, involves rather ethical and economic value judgements and cannot be made just on the basis of the values of the maximized social welfare or social revenue [16]. Second, the results of this analysis are to be viewed in the light of many limitations imposed on this study. The estimations of the parameters of demand and supply relations can be improved still further as more and reliable information is made available. For more comprehensive food and price policy decisions, a detailed study of this kind in the broader perspective of both space and time dimensions and the inclusion of more commodities are needed. The Pant and Takayama paper in this volume is a natural extension of this study. At present a detailed study in optimal spatial and temporal pricing and allocation of wheat in India is under way under the leadership of the senior author of this paper. More detailed investigation into the nature of local, regional, and national markets in relation to the government-operated "fair price shops" is being made in this study as a preliminary step towards attaining the objective of the study stated above.

Appendix

Table A1

Projected population, income, and demand for rice and wheat

Particulars	Projected period				
	1969–70	1970–71	1971–72	1972–73	1973–74
1. Population (million persons)	540	553	567	581	596
2. National income (billion rupees at 1948–49 prices)	173.71	182.40	191.52	201.10	211.15
3. Per capita income (rupees at 1948–49 prices)	321.68	329.83	337.77	346.12	354.27

Table A1 (continued)

Particulars	Projected period				
	1969–70	1970–71	1971–72	1972–73	1973–74
4. Per capita consumption (kilograms per day)					
a. Rice	70.63	71.19	71.73	72.31	72.86
b. Wheat	29.42	30.03	30.64	31.25	31.85
5. Aggregate demand for human consumption (million tons)					
a. Rice	38.14	39.37	40.67	42.01	43.42
b. Wheat	15.89	16.61	17.37	18.16	18.98
6. Aggregate requirement for other purposes (million tons)					
a. Rice	5.45	5.63	5.81	6.01	6.21
b. Wheat	2.27	2.37	2.48	2.60	2.71
7. Total demand (million tons)					
a. Rice	43.59	45.00	46.48	48.02	49.63
b. Wheat	18.16	18.98	19.85	20.76	21.69

Table A2

Estimated acreage response and productivity functions

(1) Acreage response functions

(i) $A_r(t) = 22991.00 + 10.012P^*(t) + 50.244R^*(t-1)$
       (4894.00) (2.130)   (39.946)
       $R^2 = 0.66;$ $d = 0.64;$ $F(2, 11) = 11.04$

(ii) $A_w(t) = 910.00 + 3.835P^*(t) + 42.815R^*(t-1) + 58.022W^*(t)$
       (2202.5) (1.719)   (22.700)   (15.187)
       $R^2 = 0.86;$ $d = 1.40;$ $F(3, 10) = 21.03$

(2) Productivity functions

(i) $R_r = 72.812 + 0.3298W + 1.9597T$
       (20.249) (0.1889)   (0.4523)
       $R^2 = 0.68;$ $d = 2.73;$ $F(2, 10) = 9.47$

(ii) $R_{rs} = 72.962 + 0.2246W + 1.6135T$
       (11.962) (0.1056)   (0.3445)
       $R^2 = 0.66;$ $d = 1.70;$ $F(2, 11) = 10.96$

(iii) $R_w = 76.681 + 0.3110W + 22.2740F + 3.530H$
       (18.913) (0.1845)   (8.7619)   (3.143)
       $R^2 = 0.85;$ $d = 1.90;$ $F(3, 10) = 15.23$

(iv) $R_{ws} = 72.567 + 0.2341W + 1.4904T$
       (11.805) (0.1146)   (0.3377)
       $R^2 = 0.68;$ $d = 2.08;$ $F(2, 10) = 9.75$

Note: Figures in parentheses represent standard error of the coefficients: d is Durbin-Watson statistics; and the subscripts represent the following: r = rice; w = wheat; s = substitute crops.

Table A3

Estimated supply relations for each time period in lagged prices form

For rice:

1. $x(I)$ $= 41796.218$
2. $x(II)$ $= 36812.907 + 5.396p(I)$
3. $x(III)$ $= 33342.012 + 5.471p(II) + 3.648p(I)$
4. $x(IV)$ $= 31806.262 + 5.551p(III) + 3.701p(II) + 1.851p(I)$
5. $x(V)$ $= 32242.111 + 5.626p(IV) + 3.751p(III) + 1.876p(II)$

For wheat:

1. $x(I)$ $= 18527.300$
2. $x(II)$ $= 18382.187 + 2.395p(I)$
3. $x(III)$ $= 18865.019 + 2.588p(II) + 1.726p(I)$
4. $x(IV)$ $= 20117.667 + 2.786p(III) + 1.857p(II) + 0.929p(I)$
5. $x(V)$ $= 22245.941 + 2.983p(IV) + 1.989p(III) + 0.995p(II)$

Note: Roman figures in parentheses refer to each time period (t) under analysis, and relate to years 1969–70 to 1973–74.

References

[1] Cummings, R. W. and R. W. Herdt, 1971, The Future of India's Agriculture: Implications of Green Revolution, unpublished.

[2] Dorn, W. S., 1960, Duality in quadratic programming, Quarterly Journal of Applied Mathematics, 18.

[3] Government of India, Directorate of Economics and Statistics, Agricultural Prices in India.

[4] Government of India, Directorate of Economics and Statistics, Agricultural Situation in India, various issues from year 1950 onwards.

[5] Government of India, 1969, Directorate of Economics and Statistics, Bulletin on Food and Statistics.

[6] Government of India, 1968–69, Directorate of Economics and Statistics, Area, Production and Yield Statistics of Principal Crops.

[7] Government of India, 1953, Planning Commission, First Five Year Plan.

[8] Government of India, 1970, Planning Commission, Fourth Five Year Plan (revised).

[9] Hanson, M. A., 1961, A duality theorem in non-linear programming, The Australian Journal of Statistics, 3.

[10] Kahlon, A. S., 1969, Cost of Storage and Replacement of Buffer Stock in Food-grains, in: Seminar on Foodgrains Buffer Stock in India, Indian Society of Agricultural Economics, Bombay.

[11] National Council of Applied Economic Research, 1962, Long Term Projections of Demand for and Supply of Selected Agricultural Commodities, 1960–61 to 1975–76.

[12] Nerlove, M., 1958, The Dynamics of Supply, Baltimore: The Johns Hopkins Press.

[13] Pandey, V. K., 1971, Intertemporal Pricing and Output Allocation of Major Food

grains in India, Ph.D. thesis, unpublished, University of Illinois at Urbana-Champaign.

[14] Pant, S. P., 1970, An Evaluation of Econometric and Mathematical Programming Models Useful for Planning the Agricultural Sector in India, Ph.D. thesis, unpublished, University of Illinois at Urbana-Champaign.

[15] Ray, S. K., 1969, Demand for Food in India, 1968–69 to 1983–84, mimeographed, USAID, New Delhi.

[16] Samuelson, P. A., 1966, The Collected Scientific Papers of Paul A. Samuelson, Vol. 1, 37–53, Vol. 3, 428–472, Cambridge: MIT Press.

[17] Takayama, T. and G. G. Judge, 1971, Spatial and Temporal Price and Allocation Models, Amsterdam: North-Holland Publishing Company.

CHAPTER 30

An investigation of agricultural planning models; a case study of India's food economy*

S. P. PANT and T. TAKAYAMA

Jawaharlal Nehru Agricultural University,
University of Illinois

1. Introduction

A number of planning models have been worked out or suggested for planning in India. In these efforts the major emphasis has been on macroeconomic planning and general equilibrium [1, 2, 3, 8]. Although the Second Five Year Plan made explicit recognition of the need for "a more studied effort to induce a planned approach to agricultural development", no attempt has so far been made in India to develop formal planning models for the agricultural sector, even though some attractive theoretical and methodological alternatives have been offered [2, 4]. The present study has been undertaken to explore the potential usefulness of certain models in planning the agricultural sector in India. This work is intended to provide a base upon which an overall agricultural development plan can be constructed.

The agricultural planning problem in India is visualized as a complex problem interpenetrating the structural relationships of the general economy from without on the one hand, and spatial and temporal relations from within on the other. The spatial and temporal relationships are really intertwined in any real world economy hence, we have the problem of developing suitable techniques to combine them for efficient planning. Some of the questions asked by the planners to which this study is addressed are:

(1) Given the existing structural relationships in the economy and the anticipated demand rise due to population and income increases, what are the output requirements for different industries and what are the resulting factor requirements?

* We gratefully acknowledge financial support from the USAID, Office of International Agriculture, and Department of Agricultural Economics, Project #373, University of Illinois.

(2) Given optimization of agricultural output as the objective representing the quasi-welfare function in the minds of the decisionmaking authority or a community as a whole and given a competitive economy, what is the production potential in the country and what would be optimum levels of production in each region, their surplus and deficit position, magnitude and direction of flows, and the optimum regional prices over space?

(3) Given an operative planning period and the projected demand and supply relationships, what production and distribution policies over space and time will maximize the social welfare function?

All the information needs listed above cannot obviously be provided by any one model and still be manageable and comprehensible. Hence, the objective of agricultural development planning may most effectively be achieved by empirical application of the following models in the following order on the present day Indian scene:

(i) Input–output analysis model for studying the structural relationships in the economy with special emphasis on the relationships between the agricultural and non-agricultural sectors and projections of output of the various industries especially of the food-grain sub-sector.

(ii) Linear and non-linear activity analysis models to throw light on the spatial relationships in the agricultural sector with the avowed objective of exploring for an answer to the question whether the present day regional agricultural production pattern is out of tune with what optimal, and what resource requirements and price policies be pursued to bridge the gap between the actual and the optimal.

(iii) Temporal-cum-spatial equilibrium model: Here the objective is to develop a suitable model to simultaneously produce a spatial and inter-temporal equilibrium for planning the production, consumption, storage and pricing policies for the major food-grains in India.

2. Structural relationships in the Indian economy

2.1. Leontief input–output analysis

Input–output analysis formed the basis for the India Draft Fourth Five Year Plan. However, since final demands in this analysis are autonomous, their specification in the model is based on assumptions regarding growth of GNP and investment. Altering these assumptions will yield different sectoral output.

The targeted rate of growth envisaged in the Fourth Plan for the period

1965–70 is 7.7 % and for 1970–75 is 7.5 % [6]. Drawing on the past experience, we postulate that these targets, though they may be socially desirable, fall in the realm of infeasibility for the economy. Instead we make three alternative assumptions as shown in table 1.

Table 1

Annual growth rates and estimates of national income

	Estimates of national income (Ro. Th. Million)				1960–65 (Realized)	1965–70 (Realized)	1970–75 (Assumed)
	1960–61	1965–66	1970–71	1975–76			
Fourth Plan	141.4	–	–	–	5.0	7.7	7.5
Model I	141.4	180	252	353	5.0	7.0	7.0
Model II	141.4	180	252	362	5.0	7.0	7.5
Model III	141.4	180	258	362	5.0	7.5	7.0

For each set of hypothesized growth of national income we assume two levels of aggregate investment: (a) as envisaged in the Fourth Plan, and (b) making proportionate adjustment in investment. Assumption (a) explores what happens to the aggregate demand and consequently to the aggregate sectoral production when the economy is forced to the level of investment envisaged in the Plan regardless of the level of likely realizable national income. Assumption (b) is to scale down the investment level proportionately.

The assumptions of no foreign aid beyond 1975–76 and levels of public consumption envisaged in the Plan are accepted. Indirect taxes and miscellaneous receipts and depreciation rates are proportionately adjusted to obtain GDP at market prices. Personal consumption is then derived as a difference between GDP and the projected levels of investment and public consumption.

Based on these assumptions implications of three major alternative courses of development are explored through Models I, II and III and their variants (a) and (b). The alternative courses of development envisaged are presented as under:

Model I(a): Constant annual rate of growth of income with high investment as planned.

Model I(b): Constant annual rate of growth of income with somewhat lower investment.

Model II(a): Rising growth rate with high investment as planned.

Model II(b): Rising growth rate with somewhat lower investment.

Table 2

Projections of domestic output (alternative assumptions)

Items / Sectors	Domestic output 1961	Domestic output 1971 I(a)	Domestic output 1971 I(b)	Domestic output 1971 III(a)	Domestic output 1971 III(b)	Domestic output 1976 I(a)	Domestic output 1976 I(b)	Domestic output 1976 II(a)	Domestic output 1976 II(b)
1. Food grains	3974	6376	6431	6597	6613	8328	8471	8854	8942
2. Other agriculture	2097	3507	3516	3613	3615	4806	4836	4940	4960
3. Animal husbandry	1130	1874	1883	1934	1837	2443	2483	2530	2547
4. Plantations	376	946	926	966	959	1275	1239	1286	1261
Sub-total agriculture	7577	12 703	12 756	13 110	13 024	16 863	17 029	17 610	17 710
5. Food industry	1323	2340	2346	2412	2413	3361	3381	3450	3461
6. Textiles	930	1708	1705	1752	1751	2324	2328	2385	2390
Sub-total agriculture based industries	2253	4048	4051	4164	4164	5685	5709	5835	5851
Total agriculture and agriculture based industries	9830	16 751	16 807	17 274	17 188	22 548	22 738	23 445	23 561
7. Chemical fertilizers	21	185	180	186	185	291	278	293	287
8. Transport and electricity	500	1351	1333	1384	1378	1990	1942	2016	1985
9. Manufacturing, mining and construction	3781	13 001	12 698	13 343	13 242	18 541	18 001	18 674	18 269
Sub-total manufacture	4302	14 537	14 211	14 913	14 805	20 822	20 301	20 983	20 541
Grand total	14 132	31 288	31 018	32 187	21 993	43 370	43 039	44 428	44 102

Model III(a): High growth rate in the first period becoming steady at a lower level in the second period with high investment as planned.

Model III(b): Same with somewhat lower investment.

Having arrived at the aggregate demand we make quantitative allocations by sectors, which are then adjusted for macro projections. The sectoral allocation of the macro estimates of investment is based on derived expansion ratios. Based on these ratios the final allocation of gross capital formation by sectors is derived. The sectoral allocation of export demand and imports is done on the basis of the Plan adjusted to the assumed national income levels.

The interindustry table used in the study is based on a 30 industry table prepared by the Indian Statistical Institute in collaboration with the Perspective Planning Division of the Planning Commission. Since the classification was considered inadequate for our purpose, a reclassification was made and a nine-sector input–output table was compiled so as to be amenable to more intensive analysis of the relation between the agricultural sub-sectors and the non-agricultural sectors (for detailed information, see [5]).

Employing the Leontief inverse matrix, $(I-A)^{-1}$, and the final demand vectors, C's, the alternative estimates, Y's, of domestic output in 1970–71 and 1975–76 calculated by the formula: $Y = (I-A)^{-1}C$ are presented in table 2. Converting the gross values figures into physical quantities at the base level price the domestic output of the foodgrains subsector given by the various models is as in table 3.

Table 3

Domestic foodgrains output projections

1971		1976	
	(mill. tons)		(mill. tons)
Model I(a)	123.0	Model I(a)	140.6
Model I(b)	123.7	Model I(b)	143.0
Model III(a)	126.9	Model II(a)	149.5
Model III(b)	127.1	Model II(b)	151.0

Having derived the foodgrain production estimates from the input–output model, it was considered necessary to test their feasibility in terms of spatial potential and optimality. The significance of this test for planning arises because planned aggregate targets are realised at the innumerable farms spread over space in the country. However, introduction of space in the analysis raises the problems of competitive behaviour arising from the differential resource endowment base, location and transportation. The problem thus takes the form of interregional competition and is analyzed as such. The optimal estimates so derived are then compared with those obtained from input–output analysis model.

2.2. Linear programming analysis

2.2.1.

The planning objective is now extended to explore alternative answers to the basic question of what and where to produce and what resource commitments to make consistent with the optimum growth path of the agricultural sector in India. The activity analysis format was applied to the major foodgrains sector which consists of the rice and wheat crops in India. The objective function to be minimized is the sum of the total costs of production and total transportation costs, and the constraints consist of (1) total land availability, (2) regional upper bounds on acreages for each crop activity, and (3) minimum regional demand restriction for each crop and region.[1]

This model was applied to the 1971 situation specified at the projected level of demand in 1971 and the assumed technology and resource availability. The results of the 1971 model are compared with those of the input–output model.

2.2.2. Producing regions

Producing regions in this study are states or groups of states. Territories excluded in the analysis are the ones classed as "Union Territories" and represent an insignificant proportion of national production of the crops under study. Production of these non-programmed regions has been subtracted from the appropriate demand restraints. The programmed regions are: (1) Assam, (2) Bengal, (3) Orissa, (4) Bihar, (5) Uttar Pradesh, (6) Punjab (including Hariyana), (7) Rajasthan, (8) Madhya Pradesh, (9) Gujrat, (10) Maharashtra, (11) Mysore, (12) Andhra Pradesh, (13) Madras, and (14) Kerala.

2.2.3. Crop acreage restraints

Base period for acreage for each region is 1961–62 to 1965–66, the period covered by the Third Five Year Plan. Thus, crop acreage restraints reflect

---

[1] For a more comprehensive study, it would be desirable to have irrigation and fertilizer constraints. It was not possible to include these in our study due to lack of suitable data.

historical production patterns as they stood in the immediately proceding five-year period. The upper and lower bounds also relate to the maximum and minimum area under these crops in each region during this period.

2.2.4. Crop yields

The base year for crop yields is taken as 1965–66. Since 1965–66 was an extraordinarily bad year, the difficulty was avoided by projecting the crop yields from the previous period and was adjusted suitably to reflect relative mean yields for each region. This was then used as the base year yield.

2.2.5. Production costs

Paucity of regional cost data is the most severe limiting factor in the use of the studies like the one at hand. Price has been used as a proxy variable in place of cost. However, since regional price is a complex of both production and transportation costs, we determine the competitive position of the regions but the spatial flows cannot be determined. Our cost estimates are based on the Farm Management Surveys duly updated and supplemented by the more recent studies.

2.2.6. Transportation data

Transportation activities are specified for each pair of regions in Model I to allow for commodity distribution possibilities and an optimum spatial allocation of production processes while satisfying regional demands for each commodity. Rail rates are assumed to reflect costs of transportation. Within each region a city is designated as the location for export (import) from (to) that region to (from) all other regions. Selection of these center points and in later models selection of a transportation activity, is made on the basis of historic practices.

2.2.7. Consumption demand

Estimates of regional consumption demand were derived by multiplying regional per capita consumption by the regional population. Per capita consumption in this study corresponds to net per capita availability. Figures for these were computed from the data compiled by the Food Grains Policy Committee Report [6].

2.2.8. Model analysis (1970–71)

In this model, our objective was to derive the optimum production pattern and interregional flows as they could be expected in the year 1970–71.

The resulting production pattern is given in table 4. All regions expand

Table 4
Regional production patterns (th. tonnes)*

Region	1962–63 to 1964–65 Average		1970–71	Optimal
	Rice	Wheat	Rice	Wheat
1	1798	3	2030	–
2	5169	30	6116	–
3	4141	7	5148	–
4	4570	455	6605	706
5	3245	3348	1246 [b]	4508
6	561	2994	– [a]	4937
7	109	1020	– [a]	1310
8	3046	2016	4222	3155
9	456	356	– [a]	726
10	1412	403	1671	671
11	1227	95	2067	–
12	4493	5	6107	–
13	3983	–	5030	–
14	1114	–	1320	–
Total	35 324	10 732		
Total production	36 416	10 732		
Import			Nil	1570

[a] Non-programmed regions.
[b] See text.
* One tonne is equivalent to 0.912 tons.

their output of both rice and wheat except region 5 in the case of rice. The results in tables 5 and 6 show that in 1970–71 the country is able to meet its projected demand without imports from the international market. The solution for region 5 reflects the nature of the model as it is constructed. Since we made a provision for imports and no exports the reduced level of output in region 5 implies an excess supply in rice in the country in 1970–71. Major gains in output of rice as revealed by the models occur in regions 4, 11, 12 and 13 and that for wheat in regions 6, 8, 9 and 10.

2.2.9. Flows

No major shift in the direction of flows for rice is foreseeable. Region 1 now is no more an exporter while the deficit of region 10 is now met by region 12 rather than from imports from international market. In the case of wheat, the country is still short in supply though reduced very greatly. However, the major shift is the emergence of region 6 as a substantial supplier.

Table 5

Programmed production, flows and equilibrium prices of rice, Model II (1970–71)

Region	Projected demand (th. tonnes) (1)	Production within region (th. tonnes) (2)	Imports		Exports		Equilibrium price (rs. per tonne) (7)	Production estimates based on assumed growth rates		Col. 2– Col. 9 (10)	Col. 10 as P.C. of Col. 9
			Quantity (th. tonnes) (3)	From region (4)	Quantity (th. tonnes) (5)	To region (6)		Growth rates (8)	Production (9)		
1	2045	2030	15	4	–	–	427	1.0	1909	121	6.3
2	7035	6116	919	3, 4	–	–	408	3.0	6173	– 57	–0.9
3	4270	5148	–	–	878	2	359	4.0	5240	– 92	–1.7
4	4958	6605	–	–	1647	1, 2, 5	349	5.0	6708	–103	–1.5
5	3149	1246 [b]	1903 [b]	4, 8	–	–	403	5.2	4401	– [b]	–
6	– [a]	– [a]	–	–	–	–	–	6.0	793	– [a]	–
7	– [a]	– [a]	–	–	–	–	–	5.8	152	– [a]	–
8	3286	4222	–	–	936	5, 9, 10	354	5.4	4176	46	1.1
9	589	–	589	8	–	–	414	5.4	624	– [a]	–
10	3085	1671	1414	8, 12	–	–	428	3.2	1706	– 35	–2.0
11	2431	2067	364	12	–	–	419	4.0	1973	94	4.8
12	4133	6107	–	–	1974	10, 11, 14	353	2.5	5210	897	17
13	4038	5030	–	–	992	14	391	2.7	4671	359	7
14	2543	1320	1223	12, 13	–	–	463	3.2	1346	– 26	–2

[a] Non-programmed regions (together meet their own demand).
[b] Is proxy quantity representing surplus capacity in the whole country, see text.

Table 6

Programmed production, flows and equilibrium prices of wheat, Model II (1970–71)

Re-gion	Projected demand (th. tonnes)	Production within (th. tonnes) region	Imports		Exports		Equilibrium price (rs. per tonne)
			Quantity (th. tonnes)	From region	Quantity (th. tonnes)	To region	
1	153 [a]	–	153	6, X[1]	–	–	678
2	371 [a]	–	371	X[1]	–	–	600
3	42 [a]	–	42	X[1]	–	–	650
4	1015	706	310	6	–	–	635
5	4532	4508	24	6	–	–	603
6	4166	4937	–	–	771	1, 4, 5, 7, 9	541
7	1627	1310	318	6	–	–	598
8	2191	3155	–	–	964	9, 12	584
9	1700	726	974	6, 8	–	–	644
10	1140	671	469	X[2]	–	–	600
11	300 [a]	–	300	X[3]	–	–	640
12	83 [a]	–	83	8	–	–	664
13	212	–	212	X[3]	–	–	600
14	48	–	48	X[3]	–	–	672

[a] Residual demand after subtracting self supply.

X[1]: Import of wheat into India at Calcutta Port, X[2]: Import of wheat into India at Bombay Port, X[3]: Import of wheat into India at Madras Port.

2.3. Input–output model vs. regional activity analysis

Recapitulating the results of input–output models we note that within the structural relationships of the economy and specified aggregate demands we had found that it was feasible to produce a physical quantity of food-grains ranging from 123 to 127.5 million tons of foodgrains and assuming the proportion of major foodgrains to remain at the 1964–65 level of 57.6 %, the estimated output of rice and wheat in 1970–71 is 71 million tons which is consistent with the output in other sectors of the economy. Since the proportion of rice in the major foodgrains has been remarkably stable ever since 1950–51 and stays around 76 %, we estimate rice production at 54 million tons and wheat at 17 million tons.

The results of our activity analysis model show that for the programmed areas, the optimal production under stipulated conditions is 58 million tons for the major foodgrains, out of which 42 million tons is rice and 16 million is wheat. Adding unused capacity output of region 5 and output of excluded areas the national optimum output of major foodgrains in the year 1970–71 is estimated as 68 million tons. This falls short by about 3 million tons as compared to the input–output analysis results. The obvious conclusion is that agricultural extension programs in the regions need to be pushed further not only to obtain the optimal as suggested by the programming model but to exceed it via yield increase so as to match the achievable potential of the economy as determined by the input–output model.

3. Spatial equilibrium analysis

Development planning involves planning of resource mobilization and allocation for production and planning of distribution and consumption policies. The linkage is provided by the price policies. Having determined the optimal regional production of foodgrains achievable within the structural setup of the Indian economy, we now explore the basis for determining the absolute and relative price levels of interregionally traded agricultural commodities.

3.1. Methods of determining the price level

A continuing search for a suitable price policy capable of reconciling the basic conflict of eliminating distress and providing needed production incentives led to the setting up of the Agricultural Prices Commission in 1965.

The Agricultural Prices Commission considered three criteria to derive appropriate levels of minimum support prices: (1) market prices; (2) intercrop market price ratios; and (3) cost of cultivation.

The market price criterion was dismissed in 1965 due to conditions of scarcity. Inter-crop market price ratios criteria could not be adopted for the obvious reason that they cannot provide a basis for determining their levels initially though the price ratios are required to be such as to promote a balanced growth of all agricultural commodities simultaneously. The Commission was, therefore, in favor of adopting the estimated cost of cultivation as a guiding criterion for determining support prices. Notwithstanding the inherent pitfalls of this method it needs to be recognized that the support price to be effective must bear a reasonable relationship to the long-run market price.

An alternative could be to generate internal prices and rents within the linear activity analysis format to provide a basis for economic decisions regarding efficient production and flow of commodities through a competitive equilibrium price system. However, the assumption of known regional quantities demanded (and therefore prices) is not very realistic. The "equilibrium accounting prices" so obtained are relative prices and do not really represent the price level as such. Given the assumption that competitive market economy is fast emerging in the country it is felt that the quadratic spatial price equilibrium model could be used as a tool to generate rationally informed decisions in determining such prices.

3.2. Method of analysis

Following international trade theorists, let space be formed by discrete sub-spaces called regions. Within the multi-regional economy, there are L_i consumers, each consumer with his own utility function, and H_i producers, each with his production feasibility set. The output of each producer is transportable to all regions by the transportation activity. Let the functions which relate local production and local use to local price be known for each region. Then, given the trade functions and transportation costs, we can determine (1) the absolute price in each region, (2) the quantity of imports or exports for each region, (3) which regions export, import or do neither, (4) the volume and direction of trade between each possible pair of regions.

In this study we assumed a linear price dependent demand function for each region, and fixed supply quantity known in each region. This leads us directly to the quadratic programming formulation developed by Takayama and Judge [7, chs. 8 and 12].[2]

The fixed supply single commodity multi-regional demand model is applied on rice. The reason for adopting the exogenously determined fixed supply is the lack of regional supply response study and the widely varying magnitude and rate of adoption of new technology between regions.[3] For these reasons, it is felt that regional supply functions based on historic prices and production practices may not reflect the current and the near future situation. Instead it is felt that the point estimates based on regional growth rates suitably adjusted to take account of the regional variations in the adoption rate and response coefficients of the new technology may be more reliable. Accordingly, the state growth rates, duly adjusted, were ap-

---

[2] The operational model with regional demand functions and fixed regional supplies used is a special case of the generalized spatial price equilibrium model. For a mathematical formulation and proof how the solution satisfies the conditions of competitive spatial price equilibrium, see Takayama and Judge [7].

[3] For the supply estimation of rice and wheat in India, for a similar purpose to that of this study, readers are referred to ch. 29 of this volume.

plied on the three-year average production of the period 1962–63 to 1964–65. The growth rates used and the production estimates obtained are given in columns 8 and 9 of table 5.

3.3. Estimation of regional demand functions

A systematic analysis of the regional market demand functions in India is almost non-existent, although estimates of the all-India market demand functions have been made by the NCAER and others. Our method has been to estimate the all-India market demand function for rice with per capita consumption as the dependent variable and per capita income and prices as independent variables. Per capita consumption in this study corresponds to net per capita availability and prices are the wholesale prices deflated by the index number of wholesale price of food to eliminate the trend effect and reduce the price series comparable to income series at 1960 61 prices. The estimated equation used is:

$$X = 0.1204 + 0.0019Y - 0.0026p \qquad R^2 = 0.86,$$
$$(0.0004) \quad (0.0013)$$

where X = annual per capita consumption of rice in quintals; Y = per capita real income in rupees; p = wholesale price of rice in rupees.

Having estimated the all-India demand function, we assume that: (i) the form of the equation fitted to the all-India data is applicable to the regions too, and (ii) there is no change in the parameters over time, especially in the short-run. With these assumptions, the regional demand functions for rice are estimated as:

$$x_i = n_i X = n_i(0.1204 + 0.0019Y_i - 0.0026p),$$

where n_i denotes population in region i, and y_i denotes per capita income in rupees in region i.

The regional demand functions so derived were tested for the known quantity demanded and known average wholesale price in the year 1965–66. Adjustments, if necessary, were made using the price elasticity of demand (-0.17). The regional demand functions so derived for the year 1965–66 are given in table 7. These were then advanced to the year 1970–71 by advancing the a_i $(= 0.1204\, n_i)$ at the uniform rate of 3.5 % per year, and are given in the same table.

Table 7

Regional demand functions for rice, 1965–66 and 1970–71

Region	1965–66	1970–717
1	20.67–0.047p	24.54–0.047p
2	71.13–0.157p	84.48–0.157p
3	43.18–0.107p	51.27–0.107p
4	50.14–0.086p	59.53–0.086p
5	31.84–0.069p	37.79–0.069p
6	–	–
7	–	–
8	33.23–0.084p	39.45–0.084p
9	–	–
10	31.21–0.065p	37.06–0.065p
11	24.58–0.041p	29.19–0.041p
12	41.79–0.094p	49.63–0.094p
13	40.82–0.095p	48.48–0.095p
14	25.70–0.057p	30.52–0.057p

3.4. Transportation costs

The regional center points and transportation costs used in this model are the same as those used in the linear activity analysis model. However, in this model all regions do not ship to all other regions as in the previous case. Instead we make use of the information generated by the linear activity analysis model to reduce the size of the programming tableau.

3.5. Model analysis (1970–71)

In this model specification we assume three different states of fixed supply. In Model A ($Q.P.1$), we have the fixed supplies as generated by the linear programming model; in Model B ($Q.P.2$), we substitute the fixed supply generated by the linear programming model in one region (5) by the quantity estimated by the growth rate approach while retaining the L.P. solution output for all other regions; and in Model C ($Q.P.3$), the fixed supplies for all regions are those estimated by the growth rate approach.

Table 8

Results of L.P. and Q.P. models for rice 1970–71. (Prices in Rs. per quintal, quantities in th. tonnes)

Region	Equilibrium prices				Consumption				Regional flows: Import (+), Export (−)		
	L.P.	Q.P. 1	Q.P. 2	Q.P. 3	L.P.	Q.P. 1	Q.P. 2	Q.P. 3	Q.P. 1	Q.P. 2	Q.P. 3
1	42.7	108.5	108.5	134.3	20.4	20.3	20.3	19.1	+14.2 (3, 4)	+15.3 (3, 4)	+13.2 (3, 4)
2	40.8	77.3	69.9	79.6	70.4	75.4	76.5	74.9	− 6.2 (2, 10)	− 5.4 (2)	− 7.3 (2, 11)
3	35.9	72.3	64.9	74.7	42.7	45.3	46.1	45.1	−10.6 (2)	− 9.9 (2)	−11.8 (2)
4	34.9	71.4	64.0	73.7	49.6	55.5	56.1	55.3		− 9.1 (10)	− 9.8 (10, 11)
5	40.3	386.2	60.1	71.0	31.5	12.5	35.0	34.2	−	−	−
6	−	−	−	−	−	−	−	−			
7	−	−	−	−	−	−	−	−			
8	35.4	78.1	63.3	74.3	32.9	34.3	35.5	34.6	− 8.0 (10)	− 6.7 (10)	− 8.2 (10)
9	41.4	−	−	−	−	−	−	−			
10	42.8	85.5	70.7	81.7	30.9	35.4	35.8	33.1	+18.7 (3, 8, 12)	+17.1 (4, 8, 12)	+16.0 (4, 8)
11	41.9	84.6	69.9	87.0	24.3	24.2	27.4	26.7	+ 3.5 (12)	+ 6.7 (12)	+ 6.9 (3, 5)
12	35.3	78.0	63.2	80.8	41.3	44.0	45.4	43.8	−17.0 (10, 11, 14)	−15.7 (10, 11, 14)	− 8.3 (14)
13	39.1	81.8	67.0	84.6	40.4	42.4	43.8	42.1	− 7.9 (14)	− 6.5 (14)	− 4.6 (14)
14	46.3	89.0	74.2	91.8	25.4	26.5	27.4	26.4	+13.3 (12, 13)	+14.2 (12, 13)	+12.9 (12, 13)
Totals					409.8	415.8	449.3	435.2	99.4	106.6	98.0

3.6. Empirical results

Results of the quadratic programming models (table 8) reveal that equilibrium prices given by Model B are lower than those of Model C and that of Model A are intermediate to the two. These three sets of prices provide a range within which the policy maker can operate and coordinate his consumption, storage and shipment policies.

Model A permits minimum consumption, intermediate prices and minimum flows and allows mopping up of surpluses for storage, especially in region 5. Model B allows maximum production and consumption, lowest prices and also maximum flows but no storage. Model C wherein regional fixed supply quantities are specified by growth-rate approach the prices are generally higher, intermediate level of consumption and shipment lower than Model B but with no storage.

4. Spatial and temporal equilibrium analysis

Mobilization and optimum use of resources are the central issues of growth theory and development policy. Since neither desired mobilization nor the desired buildup is instantaneous, planning needs to be a sequential process involving both space and time dimensions. In this section, we develop and work out an intertemporal target planning model for agriculture.

4.1. Problem situation

One outstanding feature of Indian agriculture is that its production is quite vulnerable to irregular and unpredictable weather, causing wide intra- and inter-year price fluctuations. To the extent this price instability induces withholding of resources or distortion of investment in agriculture, it hinders production and sacrifices potential growth.

The basic problem seems to be not that there is no price policy, but that though there does exist a production policy, a price policy and to some extent even a consumption and storage policy. Each one of these bits have stayed disjoint or at best loosely jointed with the whole planning program. It is held here that the theory of intertemporal-spatial equilibrium as developed by Takayama and Judge can be profitably employed to generate information on optimum consumption, production and storage policy consistent with a minimum inter-year price fluctuation under conditions of competitive equilibrium.

4.2. *Economic environment*

The generalized intertemporal spatial equilibrium model is applied on India. The commodity selected is rice. The economic environment is described as follows:

(1) The planning period extends to five years 1966–67 to 1970–71. However, solutions are worked out for the years 1967–68 to 1970–71. This is done because of the extraordinary situation of scarcity during 1965–66 and 1966–67 due to the worst drought in a century.

(2) The country is divided into 6 zones called regions.

(3) Regional demands for rice are given in the form of linear price dependent functions as:

$$y_i(t) = \alpha_i(t) - \beta_i(t) p_i(t).$$

(4) Regional supplies are given as a fixed point estimate for each region for all t.

(5) Government storage policy for the whole planning period is known in the form of a target but annual operational rules are not known.

(6) The storage costs $b(t, t+1)$ for $t = 0, 1, 2, 3, 4, 5$ are known constants.

(7) The upper limit above which no procurement for storage shall be made and a lower limit (a support price) at which all stocks offered will be purchased and stored is fixed by the government in advance, say as a consequence of estimates based on the results of quadratic programming models of the previous section.

(8) The upper limit for the storage capacity and a minimum limit for procurement for storage is fixed in advance.

The planning program then is to derive optimum solutions over time and space for consumption, distribution, prices and storage. Operationally, a version of models developed by Takayama and Judge [7, ch. 18] is employed in this study.[4]

4.3. *Data and analytical procedures*

The method of estimating regional demand functions is the same as in the previous section. The basic demand functions for rice derived for six regions covering the entire country for the year 1965–66 are:

---

[4] For theoretical exposition of over-time allocation problem and quadratic programming formulation of a generalized intertemporal model, see Takayama and Judge [7].

Subregion		α	β
1	(Assam, Bengal, Orissa)	145.43	−0.313
2	(Uttah Pradesh, Bihar)	87.95	−0.155
3	(Punjab, Rajastan)	12.38	−0.028
4	(Madhya Pradesh, Gujarat, Maharashtra)	69.23	−0.150
5	(Mysol, Andra Pradesh)	71.39	−0.131
6	(Madras, Kerala)	72.72	−0.153

Intertemporal regional demand functions were derived on the assumption that the slope of the function holds for the planning period and its functions shift upwards due to shift variables at the uniform rate of 3.5 % per year.

Point estimates of supply were derived by the growth rate approach. The state growth rates used and the production estimates obtained are given in columns 8 and 9 of table 5 while the derived estimates aggregated into six regions are presented in table 9.

Table 9

Regional estimates of fixed supply (th. tonnes)

Region	1962–63 to 1964–65 Average	1967–68	1968–69	1969–70	1970–71
1	11 108	12 159	12 533	12 921	13 322
2	7815	9070	10 061	10 572	11 109
3	1126	1328	1404	1484	1569
4	4458	5118	5361	5615	5882
5	5720	6218	6394	6575	6762
6	5097	5538	5693	5852	6017
All India	36 416	41 795	43 759	45 816	47 969

As for storage, we note that no clear-cut policy has emerged so far. The Plan proposes to build up 'buffer stocks' of six million tons by the end of the Fourth Plan. The questions of composition, location and operating rules for use of such stocks are left unconsidered. To build up an initial working storage policy for our model we distinguish stocks as pipe-line stocks, buffer stocks, and reserve stocks. Pipe-line stocks are just a function of demand, buffer stocks are anti-speculative and are a function of expected imbalance between demand and supply which may be positive or negative and reserve stocks are precautionary in nature and hence are a function of production. Assuming no carry-in for 1967–68 due to the preceding two consecutive bad years and assuming initially that the government plans to spread the building up of stocks evenly over the planning period the allocation of regional stocks is given in table 10.

Table 10

End of the year estimated stock quantities by regions, 1967–68 to 1970–71
(expressed in million tonnes)

Re-gions	1967–68			1968–69			1969–70			1970–71		
	Rice	Wheat	Total	Rice	Wheat	Total	Rice	Wheat	Total	Rice	Wheat	Total
1	0.367	0.013	0.38	0.733	0.022	0.755	1.099	0.031	1.130	1.464	0.036	1.5
2	0.253	0.15	0.403	0.506	0.3	0.806	0.76	0.168	0.168	1.015	0.599	1.614
3	0.025	0.124	0.149	0.052	0.254	0.306	0.079	0.385	0.464	0.106	0.521	0.627
4	0.156	0.076	0.232	0.313	0.153	0.466	0.469	0.228	0.697	0.627	0.307	0.934
5	0.146	0.006	0.152	0.297	0.011	0.308	0.447	0.017	0.464	0.604	0.021	0.625
6	0.178	0.006	0.184	0.349	0.01	0.359	0.521	0.015	0.537	0.684	0.016	0.7
Total	1.125	0.375	1.5	2.25	0.75	3.0	3.375	1.125	4.5	4.5	1.5	6.0

4.4. Programming sub-models

To derive information leading to policy formulation we have specified three sub-models and have obtained solutions for various parametric runs for each. In all models regional demand is represented by a linear price dependent function. Supply is represented by a fixed estimated quantity for all the regions and for all the years. However, model specifications differ in terms of variability in supply and government storage policy.

Model I is our "basic model". Fixed supply in this model is represented by the trend figure. The model has two specifications; (a) without any government storage policy and (b) with a positive government storage policy as developed above.

Model II is designed to test effect of variable supply on prices, and spatial and intertemporal flows both without a government storage policy (II(a)) and with government storage policy (II(b)). Each model has further variants in terms of percentage of variable supply. Variability is assumed from the trend production estimates and is permitted to occur in the end year only (1970–71). Thus, we intend to explore what happens to prices, and spatial and intertemporal flows when difference between previous peak production (1969–70) and the subsequent trough (1970–71) is 5 %, 10 % and 20 % assuming that drought and flood damage is wide-spread and production is affected equally in all the six regions.

In Model III, we study the effect of variable supply in still greater detail. We first classify the fourteen States that comprise our planning area into A, B and C classes based on occurrence of droughts. The area classes are defined as:

Class A: Areas with assured water supply both in volume and spread are grouped in this class. In these areas, production is steadily increasing.

Class B: This group includes areas where supply of water from rainfall or sources of irrigation largely depend on monsoon and is subject to large fluctuations in volume and spread. The whole of region 2, and the States of Madhya Pradesh and Madras are included in this group.

Class C: Group C includes precarious areas with no dependable irrigation and scanty rainfall. We include in this class the States of Rajasthan, Gujrat, Mysore and Maharashtra.

4.5. Crop years

To make a still further rigorous analysis of weather on supply we classify the crop years into 'good', 'average' and 'bad' years. Any particular year is termed 'good', 'average' or 'bad' if weather is good, average or bad in the major rice producing areas.[5]

As for the cycle of good, average and bad years we assume in our analysis that the year 1967–68 was a 'good' year, 1968–69 is treated as 'average' and 1969–70 as 'bad' and 1970–71 again as an 'average' year. Thus, we assume that in a cycle of four years we have one good, one bad and two average years.

From our study of Model II, we note that in the case of supply fluctuating by 5 % the price structure and storage policy stays within manageable limits. The 20 % fluctuating case is ruled out as of rare occurrence. Thus, for further analysis we retain only the case of fixed supply fluctuating 10 % in B and C class areas where the first year (1967–68) is 'good', second is 'average', third is 'bad' and the end year is 'average', again.

4.6. Storage policy Model III

To develop a suitable storage policy in the situation of Model III, we tested four policy measures.

[5] With the elimination of A class areas from this consideration, as they are treated unaffected by weather, a year is defined as 'good' if there is a 10% increase in production in B and C areas; it is 'average' when production in B and C areas is as per trend, and is 'bad' if there is a decrease of 10% or more in these areas.

Model III(b): (1): Situation of Model III but no government storage policy.

Model III(b): (2): Positive government policy but fixed quantities to be stored irrespective of the area and year considerations.

Model III(b) (3): Positive government policy; 50 % of the targeted stock to be stored in the 'good' year and the remaining 50 % is stocked equally in the two 'average' years while no stock procurement is done during the 'bad' year. However, quantities remain the same with regard to the areas.

Model III(b) (4): Same as III(b) (3) with the exceptions that: (1) In class A areas 'average' quantities are stocked irrespective of year class. (2) In B and C areas 50 % of the targeted stock is procured during 'good' years and the other 50 % in two 'average' years while no stock is procured during the 'bad' year.

4.7. Empirical results

The model variants are too numerous to be discussed individually. Instead, we present the results of our "Basic Model" in some detail while that of other models are given in a summary form. Results of Model I(a) and (b) are presented in tables 11 and 12. For the detailed information on Models II and III, the interested reader should refer to [6]. It may be noticed that the equilibrium prices are high in the initial year in both models, I(a) and I(b), due to the assumption of no carry-in. There is a noticeable fall in prices from the initial to the second period after which they get stabilized. In the case of regions 3 and 5, this effect appears in the third rather than the second year.

4.8. Intertemporal flows

The following conclusion can be drawn from the study of the two models:

(1) Given spatial and intertemporal conditions assumed in the model buffer stock policy is effective in stabilizing regional prices over time.

(2) Withholding of stocks from the market, Model I(b) raises the general price level and has three other major effects. (a) Increases the aggregate spatial flow to the extent of 45 % during the entire planning period and hence has its repercussions on the transport system which was assumed not to be a bottleneck in the model. (b) The aggregate community consumption during the planning period increases by about 3.7 million tonnes. (c) The average annual consumption pattern in the regions is affected in accordance to the nature of the regional demand functions and supplies.

Table 11

Regional equilibrium price, optimal consumption, and intertemporal
and spatial flows for each period

Model I(a) [a]

Region	Period	Equilibrium price in Rs. $\bar{p}$	Optimal consumption $\bar{y}$	Govt. policy Gs	Speculator's policy Ss	Import $(+)$ Export $(-)$
1	I	77.74	123.08			1.49 (2) [b]
	II	71.14	125.33	Nil		
	III	71.38	129.21			
	IV	71.62	133.22			
2	I	68.61	78.61			−12.09 (1, 4, 6)
	II	62.00	82.75	Nil	3.77 (2, 3)	− 0.3 (6)
	III	62.25	85.94			−17.1 (4, 6)
	IV	62.49	89.25			14.03 (4, 6)
3	I	68.19	10.45			
	II	68.43	10.87	Nil	2.83 (1, 2)	− 6.0 (4)
	III	59.89	11.56			− 3.27 (4, 5)
	IV	60.13	1.202			− 3.67 (4, 5)
4	I	84.39	51.18			6.3 (2)
	II	67.79	53.61	Nil		6.0 (3)
	III	68.03	56.15			8.74 (2, 3)
	IV	68.27	58.82			8.71 (2, 3)
5	I	79.77	61.81			
	II	80.00	64.31	Nil	0.37 (1, 2)	
	III	72.72	65.75			2.13 (3)
	IV	72.96	67.62			2.94 (3)
6	I	83.17	55.38			4.3 (2)
	II	76.57	56.93	Nil		0.3 (2)
	III	76.81	56.74		2.26 (3, 4)	9.5 (2)
	IV	77.05	62.43			6.05 (2)

[a] Price in Rs. per quintal; quantities in million quintals.
[b] Figures in parentheses show region numbers in the case of last column.

The increase in annual average consumption is in regions 1, 4 and 6 which
are also the importing regions in both models. Incidentally, the three largest
cities of India, Calcutta, Bombay and Madras are also located in region 1,
4 and 6 respectively. The highest increase in annual consumption is shown by
region 4 followed by region 6. The real loser is region 3 where the demand is
least elastic and the region has excess supplies.

Table 12

Regional equilibrium price, optimal consumption, and intertemporal
and spatial flows for each period

Model I(b) [a]

Region	Period	Equilibrium price $\bar{p}$	Optimal consumption $\bar{y}$	Govt. policy Gs	Speculator's policy Ss	Import (+) Export (−)
1	I	90.11	119.20	3.67		1.28 (2)
	II	83.25	126.51	7.34		4.85 (2)
	III	83.49	131.78	11.01		6.24 (2)
	IV	83.73	137.23	14.68		7.68 (2)
2	I	80.98	76.69	2.53		−11.48 (1, 4, 6)
	II	74.12	80.87	5.06	3.74 (2, 3)	−13.47 (1, 4, 6)
	III	74.36	84.06	7.59		−22.87 (1, 4, 6)
	IV	74.60	87.38	10.12		−21.18 (1, 4, 6)
3	I	80.30	10.11	0.25	2.92 (1, 2)	
	II	80.54	10.53	0.50		− 6.17 (4)
	III	72.00	11.22	0.75	1.36 (3, 4)	− 2.0 (5)
	IV	72.24	11.68	1.00		− 5.13 (4, 5)
4	I	96.76	55.63	1.56		6.01 (2)
	II	79.90	66.79	3.12		14.74 (2, 3)
	III	80.14	63.11	4.68		9.41 (2)
	IV	80.38	65.72	6.24		7.57 (2, 3)
5	I	90.91	60.35	1.46	0.37 (1, 2)	
	II	91.15	62.85	2.92		
	III	84.83	66.29	4.38		2.0 (3)
	IV	85.07	68.98	5.84		2.82 (3)
6	I	95.54	57.79	1.78		4.19 (2)
	II	88.68	55.20	3.56		0.05 (2)
	III	88.92	63.96	5.34	2.26 (3, 4)	7.22 (2)
	IV	89.16	66.53	7.12		8.24 (2)

[a] Price in Rs/quintal: quantities in million quintals.
[b] Figures in parentheses are region numbers in the case of the last column.

(3) The targeted quantity of buffer stock of the order of 4.5 million tonnes can be attained if the regional price levels and consumption quantities available in the regions are regarded as reasonable by the policy maker.

(4) To drive the prices lower in the initial year part of the proposed stocks must be built up through imports.

(5) Over and above the government stocks, there was little increase in

the intertemporal flows. The total intertemporal flow attributable to the speculative traders was 9.23 million quintals in the case of Model I(a) and 9.28 million quintals in the case of Model I(b).

Model II(a):

(1) Even without a positive government storage policy, the effect of one bad year out of four raises the equilibrium price in all regions in all periods, even when the drop in fixed regional supplies is only 5 %.

(2) A 10 % drop causes about 8 % rise in equilibrium prices over the 5 % drop but a 20 % drop causes a 20 % rise in average regional equilibrium prices over the prices with a 5 % drop.

(3) The most remarkable effect is on the intertemporal flows as expected. The total intertemporal flow over all periods and all regions for the different models is as:

Models:	I(a)	II(a)	II(a2)	II(a3)
Flows (mill. qtl.):	9.23	32.9	66.2	133.2

Thus, a 5 % drop in supply in one year out of four requires over three times larger intertemporal flow on the speculator's account. Doubling the drop implies doubling the need for such flow. This is both understandable and important from the planning point of view. It is important because it illustrates that given the assumption of short-run interests of the private trade in India, a planned management of stocks is necessary.

Model II(b):

(1) To meet a drop in production in the fourth year in a planned way requires both a drop in consumption and a rise in prices.

(2) Introducing positive government stocking policy raises the general price level more or less uniformly over all regions in all periods as in the case of Model I.

(3) Intertemporal flow is the function of fluctuations in supply. Withdrawing of supplies on government account does not diminish the magnitude of intertemporal flow as government stocks are allowed to flow through the market system over the whole planning period.

Results of Model III:

Comparisons of the results of Model III(b2), III(b3) and III(b4) throw some interesting light on the operational rules for government and speculator intertemporal storage policy. The results reveal that regions 1 and 2 are entirely comprised of A and B class areas, regions 3 and 4 are dominantly C and B while regions 5 and 6 each has as dominant A class areas combined with C and B class areas, respectively. The summary of the results are as follows:

(a) Since production in region 1 is assumed unaffected by drought, there is no observable change in optimal prices, consumptions and import/export quantities as a consequence of varying the government storage policy. But there is a great change in the intertemporal flows. With equal storage policy irrespective of year and area the total intertemporal flow required in the region is 15.3 million quintals as compared to nil in the case of Model III(b3) and 3.3 in the case of Model III(b4).

(b) Region 2 has a fluctuating supply, policy III(b2) increases the price in the second year itself while III(b3) and III(b4) do so in the third year. No change is observable in consumption and export quantities. However, III(b2) requires the highest intertemporal flow of 19.8 million quintals as compared to only 5.2 million quintals in the case of III(b3).

(c) Region 3 has a large precarious area. Prices in the first two years show no observable change between policies. But policy III(b4) shows a remarkable drop in price in the third (bad) and fourth (average) years over III(b2) without affecting total consumption or export quantities.

(d) Region 4 comprises B and C class areas and is a net importer. Policy changes do not seem to affect prices, consumption, and import quantities but there is a substantial increase in intertemporal flows due to III(b3) and III(b4) policies.

(e) Region 5 is a mixed area. However, policy III(b4) has a clear advantage in lowering the level as well as the stability of intertemporal price. It raises the aggregate consumption too.

(f) Region 6 is again a mixed area. Policies III(b3) and III(b4) are almost equally good.

Based on these results we can conclude that storage policies based on the nature of the area and year (alas, if our future environment is perfectly foreseeable!!) are definitely superior as compared to a storage policy that does not take these characteristics into account. The model results could definitely be more conclusive with respect to policies III(b3) and III(b4) if further disaggregation could be made.

5. Concluding remarks

In India, with more than 70 % of the population engaged in agriculture, and agriculture contributing about 50 % of the national income, the key to satisfactory or rapid development of the economy rests crucially on the success of the agricultural or rural developmental policies of the nation and their implementations. The so-called "green revolution" is progressing steadily and future self-sufficiency of India in her foodgrains is in sight.

In sect. 1, the input–output results and national linear programming results were compared giving the rather optimistic conclusion that with a proper interregional allocation mechanism of rice and wheat Indian agriculture is capable of reaching a stage of self-sufficiency in foodgrains in the period 1970–71.

In sect. 2, some unsatisfactory features of the national linear programming models such as predetermined regional demand and supply quantities and program generated solutions for regional prices being impractically departed from actual market prices are pointed out in comparison with the results using the Takayama-Judge type spatial equilibrium models. A new avenue is open for integrated market researchers in pursuing promising research work in the field of commodity market research contributing to the advancement of better understanding and decisionmaking by individual, state or federal decisionmakers.

The challenge is left for sect. 3 where both spatial (interregional) and temporal (storage) aspects of the rice and wheat economy of India are handled by exploiting the quadratic programming methods developed by Takayama and Judge.

The results are quite instructive and useful. One conclusion stands out: that with better knowledge and information on the events in the course of time and in each location, the allocation and pricing work more smoothly. This view is confirmed by the work of Guise and Aggrey-Mensah, ch. 26 of this book. Buffer stock strategies are worked out. However, as is seen in both models and also in Pandey's work in ch. 29 of this book, buffer stock policy at this stage is less expensively executed by importing foodgrains than squeezing them out of the present domestic production.

In India, at this stage of development, interstate flows of agricultural commodities are not systematically and efficiently taking place, and buffer stock policies have not been firmly established. Also, one of Prime Minister Indira Ghandi's major political goals, "eradication of poverty", and its policy implementation through land reform has not been realized yet. However, with the tremendous and conscientious efforts of the Indian government, the Planning Commission, and the Price Commission, the day will come when efficient allocation and pricing of farm commodities and resources will be made through better and more efficient transportation, storage, and marketing systems in the near future. The models developed and the logical pursuance of the objectives put forth in this paper, just to show their potential use, will prove to be operationally effective tools for the decision makers in the mature socialism that Professor Tinbergen (ch. 2 of this book) hopes India will attain.

References

[1] Chenery, H. and J. Sandee, 1960, A Long-Term Planning Model for India, Calcutta.

[2] Eckaus, R. S. and K. S. Parikh, 1968, Planning for Growth, Cambridge: MIT Press.

[3] Mahalanobis, P. C., 1955, Draft plan frame for the second five year plan, Sankhaya, 16.

[4] Manne, A. and A. Ruhdra, 1965, A consistency model of India's fourth plan, Sankhya, Series B, 27, Parts I and II.

[5] Pant, S. P., 1970, An Evaluation of Econometric and Mathematical Programming Models Useful for Planning the Agricultural Sector in India, unpublished Ph.D. Thesis, University of Illinois at Urbana-Champaign.

[6] Planning Commission, Perspective Planning Division, 1964, Notes on Perspective of Development, India: 1960–61 to 1975–76.

[7] Takayama, T. and G. G. Judge, 1971, Spatial and Temporal Price and Allocation Models, Amsterdam: North-Holland Publishing Company.

[8] Tinbergen, J. and H. C. Bos, 1962, Mathematical Model of Economic Growth, New York: McGraw-Hill.

CHAPTER 31

An exact Hume-Ricardo-Marshall model
of international trade*

PAUL A. SAMUELSON

Massachusetts Institute of Technology

1. Introduction

The textbooks and learned journals abound with expositions that involve bits and pieces of Ricardian comparative advantage, Cournot–Marshall partial-equilibrium schedules of supply and demand, incomplete and self-contradictory explanations of the Hume gold-flow mechanism for exchange rate equilibrium. These are generally not integrated with the general equilibrium models of trade associated with work on reciprocal demands and factor-price determination by Mill, Marshall, and Edgeworth; or, in our day, by Ohlin, Viner, Haberler, Lerner, Leontief, Meade, Stolper–Samuelson, McKenzie, and many others. Recently, in connection with the transfer problem, I bridged this gap between partial and general equilibrium (Samuelson [8]).

The present paper will provide needed mathematical foundations for the rigorous partial-equilibrium handling of general equilibrium and will also adjoin to it a much needed explication of the Hume financial mechanism.

Fortunately, neo-classical models of international trade are better than their usual expositions. Thus, when we read about the Hume gold-flow equalisation process, we are likely to read: 'The deficit country loses gold and the surplus country gains it. By the Quantity Theory, this lifts the "general price level" of the receiver and lowers the "price level" of the loser: with the deficit country's prices now relatively lower and the surplus country's prices now higher, the imports of the gainer swell and the imports of

* I owe thanks to the National Science Foundation.

This article appeared in the Journal of International Economics, vol. 1, 1971 and is reprinted here with the permission of the author and the editor of the journal.

the loser fall, thus eventually wiping out the initial deficit and leading to a new equilibrium without gold drain'.

In the quoted passage, a pedantical student might be forgiven for thinking that we are denying that the same good must (transport costs aside) always sell for a common competitive price everywhere in the world (when prices are expressed in comparable foreign-exchange units). And even such a profound scholar as Jacob Viner, after correcting the impression that the Hume adjustment process must rely on price differentials for the same good in different markets, wrongly asserts that it must rely on 'relative variations in the prices of different commodities in the same market, and primarily [on] . . . variations in prices as between export and import commodities'. Since stable equilibrium may result from induced changes in factor prices that change all prices in any market the same way, the reformulation is not correct.[1] In any case, it is a scandal that by this date none of the texts or treatises seem to have set out a mathematically complete explication of the process.

2. Graphical depiction

Fig. 1 presents for a 2-country case, America and England, the partial equilibrium version of international equilibrium. It combines the essence of the Cournot back-to-back diagrams with the Bickerdike version of exchange rate equilibrium, and also provides a classical monetary determination of absolute price levels.[2]

[1] Viner [9] p. 319 contains the quoted words. Related quotations can be found on pp. 292, 293, 305, 318, and elsewhere. That Viner senses the correct doctrine, which involves changes in factor prices, induced by money flows, and having in turn differential effects on costs in the different countries and therefore in their effective sharing of the markets, is shown by the following: It is the relative changes in the *supply* prices [i.e., in the supply schedules] of identical commodities or between different potential sources of supply . . . [which] exercises a significant role in the mechanism of adjustment of international balances. But he nowhere spells out a complete model, and his p. 332 criticism of Yntema for assuming that a balanced money change has effects as much on supply functions as demand functions raises doubt as to whether he had even worked out a consistent Hume model. He was in good company, as one can verify by reading the treatises of Ohlin and Haberler or the standard critiques of the purchasing-power-parity doctrine with their failure to identify clearly its essential grain of truth.

[2] My cited *Festschrift* paper [8] gives references and elucidation of the model, which combines elements from Hume (1749), Cournot [2], Bickerdike [1], and which has been much discussed by Joan Robinson, Haberler, Yntema, and a host of modern writers.

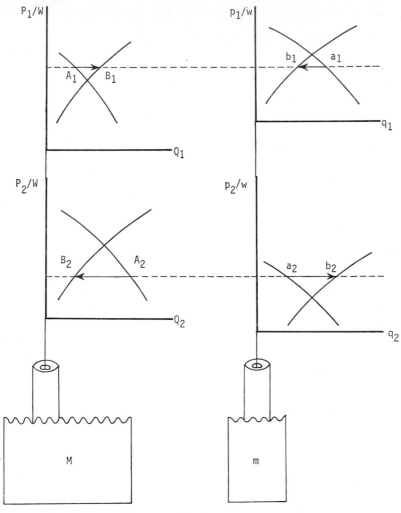

Fig. 1.

The graph can be simply explained. The vertical scales are logarithmic and are aligned so that American prices on the left and British prices on the right are in competitive arbitrage equilibrium along the same horizontal lines (with the ratio of American to British prices exactly equalling the exchange rate). America is shown exporting in equilibrium the first good and importing the second good from Europe, as shown by the matching but opposing export arrows $A_i B_i$ and $a_i b_i$. Because the scales are logarithmic, no simple rectangular areas under $A_i B_i$ and $a_i b_i$ can show the equivalence in equilibrium of value of exports to value of imports, but that is definitely assumed to be realized in the graph. Finally, it will be noted that the axes do not measure price alone but rather price divided by the wage rate. This is for two reasons: first, as will be shown, the curves have an invariance only with respect to such normalized, 'real' prices; second, an increase in the money wage in any country can be shown as a parallel upward shift of all the curves of that country, just as if the vertical axis were made of wire with all the curves soldered to it. Such a differential change in one country's wage relative to the others will thus, the exchange rate being unchanged, definitely shift the schedules compared to each other and lead to a new equilibrium in each market (and of course will upset the posited balance of payments equilibrium). Finally, a shift in the exchange rate, with money wage rates unchanged in each country, will likewise shift one country's curves in a parallel fashion relative to the other country's curves. Thus a depreciation of the dollar relative to the pound would lower *all* the American curves by the same number of inches in comparison with unchanged British curves.

At the bottom of the graph the stock of money of a country is shown as a volume of water upon which the vertical axis and related curves float. This is merely a rendition of Hume's Quantity Theory of Money, which postulates that a doubling of the gold or money supply will ultimately double the wage rate and all prices: with twice the water, the floating axis and curves are shifted upward (reflecting now doubled wage rate in the P/W variables).

We can now simply describe the comparative statics of gold or money changes. Suppose world gold doubles. In equilibrium it will be divided between countries in the same proportions as before. Both tanks of water ultimately have their level raised by the same doubled amount. All curves get shifted upward by the same amount. *The real equilibrium is thus completely unchanged*: all export arrows and amounts are as before, and so are all amounts consumed and produced; all price ratios, P_i/W and p_i/w are as before since both numerators and denominators have doubled with the world doubling of every price and wage; terms of trade, as measured by $P_2/P_1 = p_2/p_1$, are also unchanged. (The fact that total world gold gets redivided among the countries in the same determinate proportions as before constitutes the only meaning to Hume's metaphor that money and water find the same equality of level in all countries. What the determinative proportions of gold between countries are will depend, as Hume knew, on the reserve ratios followed by different countries, their relative sizes, spending habits, and all the other factors that moderns throw into the catch-all of V and Q in the $MV = PQ$ equation of exchange.)

One must realize that the graph depicts only long-run equilibria, not transitional states. Thus, suppose the doubling of world gold first enters Britain from the Indies. Hume would expect this to raise cost levels in Britain, as shown by the upward floating of all her schedules when the water level rises on the right. This will transiently disturb balance of trade equilibrium, Britain's deficit being covered by loss of gold to (North) America. The process comes to an end only when enough water has moved from right to left to lead to proportional wage and price rises all over the world. Either at no instant of time, or for no more than the instants needed for corrective good flows to be initiated, will there be a deviation from equality of prices for the same goods in the different markets. And, as readers of Joan Robinson and Haberler now realize, there is no necessity for the terms of trade to change even during the transition phase between stable equilibria, since it is easy to specify elasticities of the curves which dictate that P_1/P_2 and p_1/p_2 ratios stay the same throughout the relative shifting of the vertical scales and curves!

We may now drop the assumption of a universal gold standard with unchanged exchange rate. Instead imagine that each government sets its own money supply by fiat. Thus, let Britain double her money supply. Such an act would have the same consequences already portrayed for the case where Britain got gold from the Indies provided pounds were readily acceptable in America. But under inconvertibility, where the American authorities set the American money supply in terms of dollars, the initial rise in British money wages and upward shift of her costs and schedules will, in a stable system, cause her to run trade deficits. If these cannot be financed by exporting of pounds (or IOUs), the exchange rate must fall. How far must the pound depreciate when the only permanent change has been a doubling of the English money supply? Obviously the pound must depreciate to exactly half its previous value. For the only way that a doubling of British wages will be compatible with unchanged American wages and with trade equilibrium will be for the upward shift of the right-hand vertical axis and curves to be offset completely by having the vertical axis sink down into the float-cylinder by an equivalent amount: that is the meaning of an exchange rate change in the diagram, and the only way to restore the real equilibrium with all the arrows intact is for the exchange rate to halve when the British fiat money doubles.

This portrays the unshakable nucleus of truth in the purchasing-power-parity doctrine. I have called this obvious. But however obvious it may have been to Hume, Ricardo, Cassel, and Yntema, the doctrine has been bitterly criticized by most writers. And they were right to criticize many of the feeble arguments given for it by Cassel, who rendered his mathematical models poorly into prose. Moreover, this geographical version of the neutral-money model was early confused by Keynes with a trivial doctrine of equality of price for identical goods in zero-transport-cost markets, with which it has no intrinsic connection.[3]

[3] To see this, imagine that substantial transport costs rupture all approximate price equality relations for the same goods in different markets. Thus, let half of all goods melt in the export process. Then we must replace the horizontal lines connection $A_i B_i$ and $a_i b_i$ with the following kinked lines, ⌐ for American exports and ¬ for British exports, the size of the bend representing logarithmically the halving of delivered goods and its effect on arbitraged prices; likewise each country's import arrows will no longer match the length of the other country's export arrows, but instead have to be only half as long. Now let us double money in one country: it is easy to demonstrate in this case as in the no-trade-impediment case that the result must still be a halving of the exchange rate of the depreciating country. Of course, the same argument applies also to tariff impediments. If it is said that changes in tariffs will destroy the *p–p–p* argument, the answer is: "It certainly will. The only thing about purchasing power parity that is valid is its application to situations that closely approximate *pure* money changes with no concomitant real changes. Except in connection with certain dramatic inflations, the *application* of the doctrine is properly subject to criticism." This is to say that in all but the most singular applications neither the absolute nor comparative version of the *p–p–p* doctrine can be expected to be valid. Except in the trivial sense of being applicable to freely-transportable competitive goods, the absolute version is never valid (and even where it is valid it is *trivially* valid as a theory of exchange rate equilibrium). In the singular case of balanced monetary changes, the comparative version is valid since *every* price and wage ultimately shows relative movements over time equal to the relative movements in the exchange rate: this means our index number comparison can involve (i) any single good, (ii) any fixed batch of goods (domestic or international, export or import), (iii) any input rather than output prices, and indeed the *p–p–p* identity will be realized if you compare (iv) an index number of British beer with an index number of American sawdust — for when all things move together one can select incommensurate items by lot and get the same result! For similar points, see Samuelson [6]. In reviewing typical mishandling of purchasing power parity, I have come across a new interpretation in L. B. Yaeger's valuable International Monetary Relations (Harper and Row, New York, 1966) p. 170 ff., where it is gratuitously argued that the essence of the doctrine is denial of the realism of elasticity pessimisms, a notion that would have surprised Cassel, Keynes, Ricardo, and Hume, to say nothing of the dozens of modern writers I have recently reviewed.

3. Mathematical summary

We can summarize the present model by the following behavior equations:

$$P_i = Rp_i \quad (i = 1, 2, \ldots, n) \quad \text{[competitive arbitrage]}$$

$$[D_i(P_i/W) - S_i(P_i/W)] + [d_i(p_i/w) - s_i(p_i/w)] = 0$$

$$\text{[industry market clearing]}$$

$$\sum_1^n (p_j/W)[D_j(P_j/W) - S_j(P_j/W)] = 0$$

$$\text{[balance-of-trade equilibrium]}$$

$$W/M = A, \quad w/m = a \quad \text{[quantity theory]}$$

$$\text{Either } M + m = \bar{G} \text{ and } R = \bar{R},$$

$$\text{or } M = \bar{M} \text{ and } m = \bar{m} \quad \text{[exogenous money supply].} \tag{1}$$

Here upper-case letters denote American variables, P_i being prices and W the dollar wage rate, D_i and S_i demand and supply functions with the usual 'stable' intersections $D_i' - S_i' < 0$, R the dollar price of the pound, and M the American money supply (or gold).

Similar interpretations apply to Britain's lower-case variables, but $r = 1/R$ and Britain's balance-of-trade equality are skipped as redundant.

The first set of equations is shown on the graph in the chosen alignment of the vertical axes.[4] The second set of relations is shown by the equality and opposition of the matching trade arrows at the indicated equivalent latitude levels. The third set of relations is not shown because of the logarithmic scales, but would be depicted on the related back-to-back diagrams of conventional trade theory by the equivalence of the rectangular areas of either country's exports with those of its imports.

The fourth set of relations constitutes each country's adherence to a homogeneity property underlying all long-run Quantity Theory reasoning.[5] It is to be stressed that the expressions A and a are not constants

[4] This will perhaps be seen more clearly if we rewrite the arbitrage relations as $(P_i/W) = (Rw/W)(p_i/w)$, where $A = Rw/W$ is the 'real' exchange rate — the ratio between the British wage expressed in dollars to the American wage (as e.g. $0.5 \times \$ 2.40/\$ 4.00 = 1.2/4 = 0.3$).

[5] Avoiding the self-contradictory assumptions of timelessness, perfect certainty, and frictionless transactions, I have spelled out elsewhere the form of such a neo-classical monetary system [7]. In this model both the money supply and the public debt must double together if the change is to be neutral to interest rates and all real magnitudes and price ratios. So, with Hume, I ignore modern public debts in what follows.

as in various versions of the $MV = PQ$ identity, which gratuitously postulate constancy of V independently of interest rates and everything else and which take full employment for granted. Here A will typically depend upon all the price *ratios* P_i/W, upon interest rates, and the other endogenous *real* variables, and will be a different function depending upon the size of the country and its various institutions and behavior patterns. All that needs emphasizing is that in longest-run equilibrium the A function is homogeneous of first degree in all values, so that balanced changes in all prices and wages do not affect it.

In the final relations, Hume would have taken exchange rates as frozen and total world gold, $M+m$, as exogenously given. But in modern times, one often takes each M and m as exogenously given.

A count of our equations, plus the usual assumptions about elasticities, will show that they suffice to establish one (or sometimes more) equilibrium solution for all the variables, including the exchange rate.[6] It was Hume's triumph to demonstrate that one-way gold drains that go on forever are impossible.[7]

The present model permits, in the two-country case, ranking of commodities to determine which each country will export at high and low exchange rates, just as in the familiar constant-cost case analyzed by Mangoldt, Edgeworth, and Taussig.[8] It will be recalled that if, in that case, $(A_1, \ldots, A_n)$ and $(a_1, \ldots, a_n)$ represent the unit labor requirements

---

[6] A useful procedure for solving the equations might be the following: substitute the first relations into the second, thereby eliminating the P's and enabling the second set to be solved for $p_i/w = f_i[\Lambda]$ and $S_i - D_i = E_i[\Lambda]$ with $f_i' < 0$ and $E_i' > 0$, where $\Lambda = Rw/W$, the 'real' exchange rate. Substituting these functions into the trade balance gives

$$-\Lambda \, \Sigma f_j[\Lambda] \, E_j[\Lambda] = B[\Lambda] = 0,$$

a single equation that must have at least one root Λ^* for the equilibrium real exchange rate. If $B'[\Lambda^*] < 0$, the normal case for Marshall – Lerner elasticities, the equilibrium will be locally stable. Corresponding to Λ^*, all the P_i/W, p_i/w, and other real magnitudes that enter into A and a will be determinate, giving us the absolute wage and price levels and R^* from $W = A^*\bar{M}$, $w = a^*\bar{m}$, $R^* = (\Lambda^* a^*/A^*)\bar{M}/\bar{m}$ — the p–p–p doctrine! If total world gold, $M+m$, is prescribed at G, we solve for $\bar{M}/G = [1+(\Lambda^* a^*/A^*)]^{-1}$, ending up with R^* and all real magnitudes or price ratios independent of G, but with all absolute prices and wages proportional to world gold supply — Hume's global quantity theory.

[7] Ironically, Hume himself proved all that any rational mercantilist could want: namely, that if all countries but one play the rules of the free-trade gold-standard game, that one country by increasing indefinitely its gold reserve ratio (to more than 100%) can hope to accumulate an arbitrarily large fraction of the world's gold, for use in future war emergencies or royal adventures!

[8] Samuelson [6] analyzes n-good comparative advantage.

for the different commodities in America and Britain respectively, we may suppose the numbering to have been done in order of American comparative costs, so that

$$A_1/a_1 \leqq A_2/a_2 \leqq \ldots \leqq A_n/a_n. \tag{2}$$

Then if America produces and exports any goods at all, good 1 will certainly be among them. I.e., as the real exchange rate Rw/W gets ever lower, more and more of the American goods will be priced out of the market and good 1 will be the last good to be competitively viable. Similarly, good n will certainly be in any set of British goods that are internationally competitive. It will depend upon the exchange rate relative to money wage levels, i.e., on $\Lambda = Rw/W$, just where the line will be drawn between our exports and imports; and as Graham used to emphasize, there is some probability of a limbo situation for some intermediate good, $1 < j < n$, for which a trivial purchasing-power-parity relation holds exactly, $(A_j/W)(a_j/w) = Rw/W$.

In this constant-cost case, $S_i(P_i/W)$ and $s_i(p_i/w)$ are not strictly speaking well-defined single-valued functions: the second equations of my (1) above should then be replaced by

$$P_i = \min (WA_i, Rwa_i) \qquad (i = 1, \ldots, n)$$
$$Q_i + q_i = Y_i + y_i,$$
$$Y_i = 0 \quad \text{if} \quad P_i < WA_i \text{ and } y_i = 0 \quad \text{if} \quad p_i < wa_i, \tag{3}$$

where Y_i and y_i represent the amounts produced in the respective countries and Q_i and q_i the amounts consumed.

Now what can be said about the order of exporting and importing in the non-constant-cost case? Surprisingly, we can still give a prior ordering that depends only on wage and exchange rates independently of the compositions of demands and forms of the cost functions. Instead of computing simple A_i/a_i ratios, we must now make a prior computation of all autarky price ratios. I.e., we find the roots of $D_i(p_i/W) = S_i(P_i/W)$ and $d_i(p_i/w) = s_i(p_i/w)$ to define $(P_i/W)_{au}$ and $(p_i/w)_{au}$. Then we imagine the goods numbered to make

$$(P_1/W)_{au}/(p_1/w)_{au} \leqq \ldots \leqq (P_n/W)_{au}/(p_n/w_{au}.) \tag{4}$$

Then much as before we can state that as the dollar appreciates and so to speak becomes progressively overvalued, the higher-numbered goods will become non-competitive and good 1 will become the last American good to be internationally competitive. Likewise Britain's last viable good will be good n. These statements about the qualitative nature of trade should not blind us to the fact that, depending upon the elasticities and shapes of the schedules, it would be possible for the depreciation of an exchange rate to induce greater quantitative changes in goods that are either high or low in order among those eligible for export.

Needless to say the trick of Marshallian bales, which just happens to work in the constant-cost case, is of no avail here. There is no substitute for the full conditions of equilibrium as embodied in all my equations and not just in the second set of them. And no special significance attaches to the trivial purchasing-power-parity equivalence that may now hold in a marginal-cost sense for all goods produced in both countries. This point was already made in my cited 1962 comment on certain Houthakker notions about purchasing-power parity.

When more than two countries are involved, no simple orderings are possible. The determining equations for N countries become

$$P_i^\alpha = R^\alpha P_i^1, \qquad (\alpha = 2, \ldots, N; \quad i = 1, \ldots, n)$$

$$\sum_{\alpha=1}^{N} D_i^\alpha(P_i^\alpha/W^\alpha) = \sum_{\alpha=1}^{N} S_i^\alpha(P_i^\alpha/W^\alpha), \qquad (i = 1, \ldots, n)$$

$$\sum_{j=1}^{n} (P_j^\alpha/W^\alpha)[D_j^\alpha(P_j^\alpha/W^\alpha) - S_j^\alpha(P_j^\alpha/W^\alpha)] = 0, \qquad (\alpha = 2, \ldots, N)$$

$$W^\alpha/M^\alpha = A^\alpha \qquad (\alpha = 1, \ldots, N).$$

Either all M^α prescribed, or

$$\sum_{\alpha=1}^{N} M^\alpha \quad \text{and} \ (R^2, \ldots, R^N) \ \text{prescribed}. \tag{5}$$

Here $W^\alpha = (W^1, W^2, \ldots, W^\alpha, \ldots, W^N)$ are the respective countries' wage rates; $[P_i^\alpha]$ their prices; $R^\alpha = [1, R^2, \ldots, R^N]$ their exchange rates relative to the numeraire country 1; A^α the quantity-theory functions homogeneous of 0th degree in each country's prices and wage; M^α the respective money supplies; and D_i^α and S_i^α being functions whose superscripts denote respective countries. These equations, except for their rigorous justification and expression in terms of P/W variables, are essentially the same as those of Yntema, and his elegant theorems show how prescribed transfer payments from country α to β (or other disturbances) can be analyzed for comparative statics.[9]

The comparative statics of the system are much as in the two-country case. The first three sets of equations can be solved for all $(P_i^\alpha/W^\alpha, Q_i^\alpha, Y_i^\alpha, R^\alpha W^1/W^\alpha)$ independently of the M's. With these solutions substituted into the $W^\alpha/M^\alpha = A^\alpha$ relations, all $(P_i^\alpha/M^\alpha, W^\alpha/M^\alpha)$ are determined in

[9] See Yntema [11]. For $N > 2$, only the two-good case can be handled graphically.

quantity-theory fashion. Combining these solutions with the first set of arbitrage relations completes the purchasing-power-parity relations, according to which all ratios of the form $[M^\alpha/R^\alpha M^1, (M^\alpha/R^\alpha)/M^\beta/R^\beta]$ are determinate independently of the values of $(M^1, \ldots, M^\alpha, \ldots, M^N)$.

No mention has been made of domestic goods, but there can be as many of them as we wish without affecting this model. We merely adjoin to the second set of eqs. (5), autarky equations for every domestic good, of the form

$$S_{n+k}{}^\alpha(P_{n+k}{}^\alpha/W^\alpha) = D_{n+k}{}^\alpha(P_{n+k}{}^\alpha/W^\alpha) \quad (\alpha = 1, \ldots, N; \quad k = 1, 2, \ldots). \quad (6)$$

4. The transfer problem

The traditional transfer problem, in which America permanently pays a reparation payment to Britain, can be handled in this model merely by adding to the balance-of-trade equation a permanent unilateral payment. The incidence of this transfer will be to depreciate the exchange rate of the paying country, with all that is thereby implied, as I showed in [8]. In the Ricardian constant-cost case of horizontal supply curves, there will necessarily be a secondary burden on the payer in the form of worsened terms of trade (save in the limiting case where both countries produce something of a borderline good and no change in exchange rate is needed). But in general one cannot be sure that there is a secondary burden in the form of deterioration of the payer's net terms of trade (as measured by a necessary fall in $P_1/P_2 = p_1/p_2$).[10]

5. Rigorous foundations of partial equilibrium

Partial equilibrium is not general equilibrium: when you must deal with each industry in turn by holding other things constant, you cannot come to grips with mutual interdependence and simultaneous determination. But, as Marshallians and their critics have occasionally realized, there is one singular case in which the mutual interdependences are strictly absent

[10] There is though, generally, an induced secondary burden on the payer in the following sense: if America must pay Britain a given reparation expressed initially in a market basket of American export goods, she will generally be worse off than she would be in the singular situation where Britain — by reason of vast size or peculiarities of tastes and technology — would face America with almost infinitely elastic schedules. Thus, in the present model, the Ohlin criticisms of the orthodox view on the transfer problem are not vindicated.

and in which partial-equilibrium schedules provide an exact general-equilibrium model.

The singular case needed if the separate Cournot–Marshall demand functions are to have an independent, invariant existence must assume (a) all goods have independent, additive utilities $\sum U_j[Q_j]$; (b) one good or service − labor and its counterpart, leisure − has strictly constant marginal (dis)utility. Thus, if we pick units of utility so that one unit of labor has always one unit of disutility, any consumer maximizes an expression of the form $\sum U_j[Q_j] - L$.

To give the rising (or horizontal) supply functions an independent, invariant existence, we must make the Ricardo–Viner assumption that each good is produced by transferable labor working on lands that are, respectively, completely-specific to the industry in question. The labor needed to produce output Y_i of the ith industry can then be written as the convex (from below) function $L_i[Y_i]$, whose slope or marginal-cost function $L_i'[Y_i]$ is a rising function with $L_i'' \geqq 0$ because of the wellknown law of diminishing returns. The $L_i'[Y_i]$ of *marginal cost* (expressed in labor units) is the reciprocal of labor's *marginal productivity* and hence will, in competitive equilibrium, be equal to P_i/W. The rent return to the specific land will be 'price-determined' rather than 'price-determining' and will be competitively set as a function of output Y_i − and hence ultimately as a function of P_i/W − namely by

$$\{P_i Y_i - W_i L_i[Y_i]\}/W = H_i[Y_i] = H_i(P_i/W), \qquad H_i' \geqq 0.$$

In the last expression, the supply relation connecting Y_i and P_i/W, namely $Y_i = S_i(P_i/W)$, has been used to eliminate Y_i. Finally, note that aggregation over all the separate, and possible heterogeneous acres within an industry, can be assumed without loss of precision to have already been done in the background through the familiar process of horizontal summation of curves.[11]

---

[11] One can admit capital goods in this model in the von Neumann–Leontief fashion provided all intermediate goods used in any industry are producible from labor and the specific lands of those industries. (Of course, one must also specify the interest rate in each country or the equations determining it.) Then, in what is a simple generalization of the non-substitution theorem, as discussed in Collected Scientific Papers, Vols. I and II, Chs. 36 (1949), 37 (1961), 70 (1965), the requisite marginal-costs will be monotone functions of the form:

$$Q_j^\alpha = S_j^\alpha(P_j^\alpha/W^\alpha) \leftrightarrow P_j^\alpha/W^\alpha = C_j^\alpha[Q_j^\alpha],$$

where the latter is the 'generalized' derivative of a convex 'net' input-requirement function. The capital goods are there, but they can be kept in the background!

Just as the supply function has been related to the marginal cost function, we can relate the demand function to the marginal utility function. Again, this can be done for a single person, for a large number of 're-presentative', *identical* persons, or by prior horizontal summation of 'diverse persons' marginal utility curves to form a rigorously-valid nation demand curve. The demand response is given by the solution of the following maximum problem:

$$\max_{Q_i,\,L} \left[\sum_1^n U_j(Q_j) - L \right]$$

subject to the budget equation

$$\sum P_j Q_j = \text{income}$$

$$= WL + \text{rents} = WL + W \sum_1^n H_j(P_j/W). \tag{7}$$

Provided both labor and leisure end up positive, the following Gossen conditions for a maximum are assumed to hold

$$U_i'(Q_i) = P_i/W, \qquad U_i'' < 0. \tag{8}$$

In short, our original demand and supply functions are rigorously identified as marginal utility and marginal cost functions invariant for each industry taken by itself. Thus

$$\begin{aligned} U_i'(Q_i) = P_i/W &\leftrightarrow Q_i = D_i(P_i/W), \\ L_i'(Y_i) = P_i/W &\leftrightarrow Y_i = S_i(P_i/W), \end{aligned} \tag{9}$$

where the D_i and S_i functions are those met already in (1).

Everything written down here for America in upper-case letters has its exact counterpart in Britain's lower-case letters: the reader may supply such equations. Fig. 2 summarizes the American relations. Now the scales are not logarithmic, so that the ratio of the shaded rent areas $S_i C_i N_i$ (so-called 'producer's surplus', but here rigorously defined) to the wage areas $0M_i C_i S_i$ will depict factor shares by industry, and, when aggregated, for the economy as a whole.

If autarky prevails, equilibrium is defined at the intersections C_1 and C_2, where

$$U_i'[Q_i] = P_i/W = L_i'[Q_i] \qquad Q_i = Y_i \quad (i = 1, \ldots, n)$$

$$L = \sum_1^n (P_j/W)Q_j - \sum_1^n H_j[Q_j]$$

$$= \sum_1^n L_j[Q_j]. \tag{10}$$

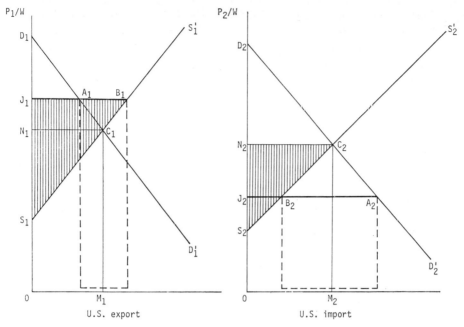

Fig. 2.

The last equivalence holds by virtue of the residual definition of rents, and states that the final total demand for labor by all employing industries equals the amount of labor supplied by maximizing consumers. The equality between value of total product and total incomes earned is also asserted.[12]

Fig. 2 also can show a post-trade situation, in which America is exporting good 1 to Britain, and importing good 2 from Britain. A careful measurement of the value rectangles under $A_1 B_1$ and $A_2 B_2$ will show them to be equivalent in areas, assuring balance-of-trade equilibrium. This also assures that American total labor supplied equals total labor our industries demand.

Note: suppose we ran a balance-of-trade deficit, as for example if our $B_2 A_2$ imports on the right were accompanied by our staying at C_1 on the left. That would destroy the equivalence between the value of what we produce and what we consume; and it would destroy the equivalence

[12] A lump-sum tax would have all its effects on extra labor supplied, there being zero income effects on all goods. If the government uses the tax receipts to buy goods $(G_1, \ldots, G_n)$, the extra labor will be exactly what is needed to produce those goods and realize the conditions: $U_i'(Q_i) = P_i/W = L'_i(Q_i+G_i)$.

between the value of what we consume and what our wage and rent incomes amount to. If we insisted on supplying labor so as to keep our consumptions equal in value to our incomes, our labor supplied as consumers, L, would exceed $\sum L_j[Q_j+E_j]$, the amount of labor demanded by American producers.[13] Thus, we seem near the situation feared by mercantilists and neo-mercantilists, in which an 'overvalued' currency produces involuntary unemployment.

But we have not said how the trade deficit is financed. Suppose it is financed by our sending gold abroad, each of us without the intermediary of governments. Then presumably our excess of consumption is to be financed by voluntary dissaving, rather than by our wanting to work more. So full-employment equilibrium can be envisaged as being preserved through the transition by a trade deficit financed by dissaving.[14]

There remains the final task of going behind the $W/M = A$ relationship of Hume. Without spelling out the cited 1968 version of neoclassical monetary theory, let me give a minimal justification for Hume's quantity theory. Suppose systematic subjective time preference of, say five per cent, sets equilibrium interest rates at $i = 0.05$ in the long run. Suppose to utility of goods $\sum U_j[Q_j]$ we prefix independent utility of cash balance, $U_0[M, P_i, \ldots, P_n, W]$, where U_0 is homogeneous of degree one in reflec-

---

[13] Arithmetically, the deficit $(P_1/W)0-(P_2/W)|E_2|$ would exactly equal in absolute amount the shortfall of employment, $L-\Sigma L_j[Q_j+E_j]$.

[14] I shall not spell out here a Ramsey optimal-control model in which it is shown how maximizing an integral of possibly-discounted utility over infinite time, and in which the utility includes the 'utility of gold holding', will determine the rate at which we gladly give up gold when tempted by a pattern of relatively-lower prices from abroad. The extra leisure induced in this classical process should not be confused with involuntary unemployment. (Outside puritanical mercantilists might object though to this induced reduction in working.)

It should be pointed out that a permanent transfer of reparations payments from Britain to America would finance a permanent trade deficit here and trade surplus there. A lump-sum tax on Britons causes them to work more; the proceeds are sent to our goverment either in kind or in terms of either currency; our government gives these receipts to American citizens who are thereby motivated to work less by exactly the amount needed to match our deficit, our shortfall of production over consumption. It is worth mentioning that the transfer process here described is Pareto-optimal, in the sense that American $U = \Sigma U_j[Q_j]-L$ is at a maximum for each attained level of British $u = \Sigma u_j[q_j]-l$, as can be noted from the equivalences

$$U_1'/u'_1 = U'_2/u'_2 = \ldots = U'_n/u'_n = Rw/W = \Lambda.$$

Aside from welfare implications, this truth enables us to use a Meade trade-indifference diagram to show the transfer, tracing along its contract curve any induced change in the terms of trade.

tion of the fact that money has no intrinsic utility but is only wanted for the sake of the goods it can buy. The form of U_0 might well depend on, among many other things, the amounts and values of the earning assets, lands. The opportunity cost of increasing your M balance permanently is the interest forgone on the extra land that you might put your wealth in. Thus we generalize (7) to solve

$$\max_{M, Q_i, L} U_0[M, P_1, \ldots, P_n, W] + \sum_1^n U_j[Q_j] - L, \tag{11}$$

subject to

$$\sum_1^n P_j Q_j = WL + 0.05 \text{ (capitalized value of lands)} \tag{12}$$

or

$$0.05M + \sum_1^n P_j Q_j = WL + 0.05 \text{ (total wealth)}$$
$$= WL + 0.05 \text{ landvalue} + 0.05\overline{M}.$$

Note M on the left is money demanded and $\overline{M}$ on the right the fixed supply of money that is owned and must end up voluntarily held.

The generalized Gossen maximizing conditions are

$$\frac{1}{W} = \frac{\partial U_0 / \partial M}{0.05} = \frac{U_i'}{P_i} \qquad (i = 1, \ldots, n). \tag{13}$$

Solving these, we get the reduced-form demand relations

$$Q_i = D_i(P_i/W) \qquad (i = 1, \ldots, n)$$

$$M = D_0[W; P_1, \ldots, P_n; \overline{M}]$$
$$= \overline{M} D_0[W/\overline{M}; (P_1/W)(W/\overline{M}), \ldots, (P_n/W)(W/\overline{M}; 1] \tag{14}$$

$$L = \sum_1^n (P_j/W) D_j(P_j/W) - 0.05 \text{ landvalue} - 0.05(M - \overline{M}).$$

If, in equilibrium, we can set $\overline{M} = M = D_0$, the last term on the right will vanish. And we can set

$$D_0[W/\overline{M}; (P_1/W)(W/\overline{M}), \ldots, (P_n/W)(W/\overline{M}); 1] = 1. \tag{15}$$

Since this function is monotone increasing in $W/\overline{M}$, we can solve for

$$W/\overline{M} = A(P_1/W, \ldots, P_n/W). \tag{16}$$

A similar derivation for Britain of $w/\overline{m} = a(p_1/w, \ldots)$ completes the justification of the final Hume quantity-theory relations at the end of eqs. (1) above.

6. Conclusion

A rigorous model has been presented here. No attempt has been made to lighten the strong assumptions needed (as for example in the usual Marshallian rigmarole of postulating some 'approximate' constancy of marginal utility). Although all the strong assumptions made here are needed if the partial-equilibrium diagrams are to be valid, many of the properties of the classical models — e.g. the Hume price-level adjustments — will be valid in much more general models that dispense with simple graphs and are definable by simultaneous equations.

This mathematical appendix is reproduced from P. A. Samuelson, Ohlin Was Right, The Swedish Journal of Economics (1971), 365–384, particularly 377–384 and is reprinted here with the permission of the author and editor. In that article the same production conditions have been assumed; but instead of partial-equilibrium demand conditions of the type that can rigorously be treated by two-dimensional graphs, now the demand conditions are those generated by any 'homothetic' uniform system of tastes that make it immaterial how incomes are distributed. Since this model involves, in addition to labor, at least one resource specialized to the production of each good, we have more factors than goods and complete factor-price equalization in the Heckscher–Ohlin–Lerner–Samuelson fashion can no longer be expected. Nonetheless, it is shown that the original Ohlin position was right in its contention that there would be a tendency for free trade in goods to serve as a *partial* substitute for factor mobility and to thereby serve to reduce but not wipe out differences in factor prices.

Mathematical Appendix

(1) Let the $(i = 1, 2, \ldots, n)$ outputs of the $(j = 1, 2, \ldots, J)$ countries be denoted by $[Q_i^j]$. Each is produced by the inputs (L_i^j, V_i^j), according to the concave homogeneous-first-degree production functions

$$Q_i^j = F_i(L_i^j, V_i^j) = V_i^j Q_i(L_i^j / V_i^j)$$

The total factor endowments of the jth country are given by

$$(L^j, V_1^j, \ldots, V_n^j) = (\sum_i L_i^j, V_1^j, \ldots, V_n^j).$$

(2) Tastes and demand are summarized by a uniform homothetic set of indifference contours in terms of the n goods consumed, either in a region or in the world,

$$u = u[C_1, \ldots, C_n]$$

where u is a homogeneous-first-degree concave function.

For simplicity, regularity conditions are placed on the u and Γ_i functions so that they are smooth, with positive partial derivatives for positive arguments, and satisfying so-called Inada conditions[1] whereby the partial derivative with respect to any variable goes from $+\infty$ to 0 as that variable goes from 0 to $+\infty$ for any positive levels of the other variables.[2]

(3) Autarky equilibrium for any region with $(L, V_1, \ldots, V_n)$ endowment is defined by

$$P_i/W = Q_i'(L_i/V_i)^{-1} = S_i(Q_i) \qquad (i = 1, \ldots, n)$$

$$L_1 + \ldots + L_n = L$$

$$\frac{P_i/W}{P_1/W} = \frac{\partial u[Q_1, \ldots, Q_n]/\partial Q_i}{\partial u[Q_1, \ldots, Q_n]/\partial Q_1} \qquad (i = 2, \ldots, n). \tag{1}$$

Here W is the wage rate, $[P_i]$ the prices, $[W/P_i]$ the real wages in terms of the respective goods, and $S_i(Q_i)$ the rising marginal cost functions easily derivable from the production functions $Q_i(L_i/V_i)$ with $S_i(0) = 0$ and $S_i(\infty) = \infty$. The $3n$ variables, $[Q_i, L_i, P_i/W]$ are uniquely defined by the $2n+1+(n-1)$ equations of (1).

The comparative statics of the equilibrium, as we change any or all of $(L, V_1, \ldots, V_n)$, can be largely summarized in terms of the derivable function of social product

$$U = q(L, V_1, \ldots, V_n) = \underset{L_i}{\text{Max}} \, u[V_1 Q_1(L_1/V_1), \ldots, V_n Q_n(L_n/V_n)]$$

subject to

$$\sum_{i=1}^{n} L_i = L \equiv V_0; \tag{2}$$

namely, by

---

[1] When labour works with more than one specialized land, we need the Inada conditions to rule out the shutting down of production of some goods in some regions. Such specializations are actually realistic.

[2] Inada conditions are more popular in the textbook than in the real world. If marginal productivities and marginal costs begin at positive intercepts, the equations below must be qualified by inequalities. When specialization causes some goods not to be produced at all in a particular region, that enhances Ohlin's case for partial rather than complete equalisation, just as in the Lerner–Samuelson model.

$$w = r_0 = q_0(L, V_1, \ldots, V_n) = \partial q/\partial L = \partial q/\partial V_0$$
$$r_i = q_i(L, V_1, \ldots, V_n) = \partial q/\partial V_i$$
$$\partial r_i/\partial V_j = \partial^2 q/\partial V_i \partial V_j = q_{ij} = q_{ji} \qquad (i, j = 0, 1, \ldots, n). \qquad (3)$$

Here w is the real wage in terms of social product, r_i the similar real rents, and, by convention, L and V_0 are used interchangeably. By concavity and homogeneity (q_{ij}) is negative semi-definite.

Continuing to use real social product, q, as numeraire, with $P_q \equiv 1$, the real prices $P_i/P_q = p_i$ are equal to

$$p_i = \partial u[Q_1, \ldots, Q_n]/\partial Q_i = q_0(L, V_1, \ldots, V_n)/Q_i'(L_i/V_i) \qquad (i = 1, \ldots, n). \qquad (4)$$

Also

$$w = W/P_q = r_0$$
$$r_i = R_i/P_q = (R_i/P_i)p_i = [Q_i(L_i/V_i) - (W/P_i)(L_i/V_i)]p_i$$

For $n = 2$, it is not hard to show that

$$\partial(W/P_i)/\partial L < 0$$
$$\partial(W/P_i)/\partial V_i > 0. \qquad (i = 1, 2).$$

For the limiting cases where the indifference contours are respectively of ∞ and 0 elasticities of substitution, the matrix

$$[\partial r_i/\partial V_j] = \begin{bmatrix} q_{00} & q_{01} & q_{02} \\ q_{10} & q_{11} & q_{12} \\ q_{20} & q_{21} & q_{22} \end{bmatrix}$$

has sign patterns $\begin{bmatrix} - & + & + \\ + & - & - \\ + & - & - \end{bmatrix}$ and $\begin{bmatrix} - & + & + \\ + & - & + \\ + & + & - \end{bmatrix}$,

but I do not see that, for intermediate cases, it is forbidden to have the pattern

$$\begin{bmatrix} - & - & + \\ - & - & + \\ + & + & - \end{bmatrix}$$

(4) Free trade in goods leads to equilibrium defined by

$$P_i/W^j = Q_i'(L_i^j/V_i^j)^{-1} = S_i(Q_i^j), \qquad (i = 1, \ldots, n; j = 1, \ldots, J) \qquad (5a)$$
$$L_1^j + \ldots + L_n^j = L^j \qquad (5b)$$
$$P_1(C_1^j - Q_1^j) + \ldots + P_n(C_n^j - Q_n^j) = 0 \qquad (5c)$$

$$P_i/P_1 = u_i[\sum_j Q_1^j, \ldots, \sum_j Q_n^j]/u_1[\sum_j Q_1^j, \ldots, \sum_j Q_n^j], \quad (i = 2, \ldots, n) \quad (5d)$$

$$(P_i/W^j)/(P_1/W^j) = u_i[C_1^j, \ldots, C_n^j]/u_1[C_1^j, \ldots, C_n^j]. \quad (5e)$$

Here $[C_i^j]$ is the amount consumed of the ith good in the jth country and $u_i[\ ]$ stands for $\partial u[\ ]/\partial C_i$. The P's denote prices in *any* common international unit.

It is of interest to note that, if one is interested only in the equilibrium of international prices and real wages, and not in the pattern of trade and of regional consumption breakdown, all the relations of (5) involving C's, namely (5c) and (5e) can be ignored in this homothetic case: the equations (5a), (5b), (5d), which are $2nJ+J+(n-1)$ in number, suffice to determine uniquely the $nJ[Q_i^j]$, the $nJ[L_i^j]$, the $J[P_1/W^j]$ and the $(n-1)[P_i/P_1]$.

If we then add the J balance-of-payments equations of (5c) and the $J(n-1)$ domestic consumption-demand equations of (5e), we further determine uniquely the remaining Jn consumption unknowns $[C_i]$.

Heuristically, and for that matter rigorously, we can determine all the post-trade real wages and rents from the following maximum problem:

$$U^*(L^1, V_1^1, \ldots, V_n^1; \ldots; L^J, V_1^J, \ldots, V_n^J)$$

$$= \operatorname*{Max}_{L_i^j} u[\sum_{j=1}^J V_1^j Q_1(L_1^j, V_1^j), \ldots \sum_{j=1}^J V_n^j Q_n(L_n^j, V_n^j)]$$

subject to

$$\sum_{i=1}^n L_i^j = L^j \quad (j = 1, \ldots, J). \quad (6)$$

If all prices, wages, and rent are expressed in a single currency unit, one can prove

$$W^j/W^1 = (\partial U^*/\partial L^j)/(\partial U^*/\partial L^1) \quad (j = 2, \ldots, J)$$

$$R_i^j/W^j = (\partial U^*/\partial V_i^j)/(\partial U^*/\partial L^j) \quad (j = 1, \ldots, J; i = 1, \ldots, n). \quad (7)$$

Here R_i denotes the rent of the ith land in the jth country.

(5) Equilibrium with factor mobility, which the text has shown need involve only labour mobility in the Ricardo–Viner model, is defined by the same equations as (5), but with the allocation of total L among regions now to be determined by the additional equations involving geographically-equalised real wages. In a free-trade world, if the real wage in terms of any good, say the first, is equalised regionally, *all* real wages are equalised. Hence, we can adjoin to (5)

$$P_1/W^1 = P_1/W^2 = \ldots = P_1/W^J. \quad (5f)$$

These are the $J-1$ new equations needed to determine the new $J-1$ interregional allocations $[L^j]$ of the given world labor supply to achieve complete equalisation and efficiency.

(6) Again, heuristically, we can determine the equilibrium real wages and real rents when both factors and goods are mobile, without using (5a)–(5f), but merely from (1) applied to world totals

$$w = q_0(\sum_j L^j, \sum_j V_1^j, \ldots, \sum_j V_n^j)$$

$$r_i = q_i(\sum_j L^j, \sum_j V_1^j, \ldots, \sum_j V_n^j) \qquad (i = 1, \ldots, n). \tag{8}$$

(7) A valuable heuristic way of analysing the differences between full and partial factor-price equalisation has been provided by Uzawa in the cited 1959 Econometrica paper. Full equalisation achieves a higher-order of welfare realisation than partial; partial achieves a higher-order than autarky; autarky under perfect competition achieves a higher order than other feasible autarky allocations. All these welfare concepts can be unambiguously handled by the device of production-possibility frontiers; or even better, in our case of uniform homothetic demands, by reckonings of achieved real GNP's.

The following equations characterise the three stages: complete factor-price equalisation, partial, and autarky.

$$q(\sum_j L^j, \sum_j V_1^j, \ldots, \sum_j V_r^j)$$

$$= \underset{L^j}{\text{Max}}\ U^*(L^1, V_1^1, \ldots, V_n^1 : \ldots; L^J, V_1^J, \ldots, V_n^J) \tag{9a}$$

labour mobility and free trade

$$\geqq U^*(L^1, V_1^1, \ldots, V_n^1 : \ldots; L^J, V_1^J, \ldots, V_n^J)$$

$$= \underset{L_i^j}{\text{Max}}\ u[\sum_j F_1(L_1^j, V_1^j), \ldots, \sum_j F_n(L_n^j, V_n^j)] \tag{9b}$$

free trade

$$\geqq \sum_j q(L^j, V_1^j, \ldots, V_r^j)$$

$$= \sum_j \underset{L_i^j}{\text{Max}}\ u[F_1(L_1^j, V_1^j), \ldots, F_n(L_n^j, V_n^j)]. \tag{9c}$$

autarky

Fig. 3 shows, symbolically, these relations. The outer frontier shows the

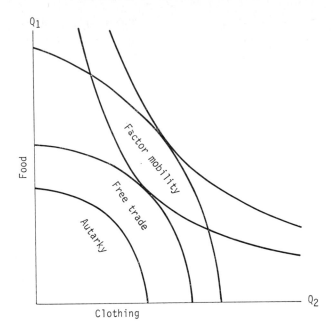

Q_1

Food

Factor mobility

Free trade

Autarky

Clothing

Q_2

Fig. 3. The outer frontier shows world production possibilities when factors can move optimally — or, in the Ricardo–Viner case, when labour can move to equalise the post-trade real wage rate. The intermediate frontier shows world totals produced when goods can move freely in trade but factors are immobile. The inner curve shows what world production totals would be, as tastes changed uniformly in each country toward one good or the other, and when neither goods nor factors can move between regions. If resource endowments were the same in all regions, all three curves would coincide. In singular cases, the present Ricardo–Viner model could have the intermediate curve tangential to the outer frontier. This is in contrast to the Lerner–Samuelson model in which the two outer curves coincide for all regions that are near enough alike.

situation when all factors are mobile, migrating to equalise all factor returns and give the world maximal production possibilities. The middle frontier shows the results of free trade in goods. As each nation is improved by trade, total world GNP (reckoned at the homothetic tastes) is higher than it is at autarky; however, if labour cannot move to wipe out any post-trade geographical differences in the real wage, the aggregate GNP under goods trade falls short of that under factor mobility.

These two frontiers are the productions that would be observed as the homothetic tastes changed their food-clothing intensities, running the gamut from one extreme to the other. What then is the inner frontier? It represents the world sums of all autarky productions that would be engendered by the same change in tastes.[3] The fact that this inner locus lies inside the middle one, represents the production inefficiency attributable to autarky. But, in a sense, there is a further consumption inefficiency as well: thus, suppose all countries under autarky have the same well-being. That 'average level' will be less than the average level that would be read off the homothetic indifference contour going through the relevant point on the inner curve, even after proper allowance is made for the number of people: people are, so to speak, forced under autarky to consume 'unbalanced' diets.

It is possible, as we have seen, for the singular case to occur in which free trade in goods is a full substitute for factor mobility. In such a case the middle frontier must touch the outer frontier in at least one place. However, save in the uninteresting case of identical geographical endowments – when all these curves are identical and no mobility will ever be used – the inner curve can never touch the intermediate frontier.

The mathematical condition for the singular case to occur can be written down briefly for the case of two regions, A and B. Suppose with balanced endowments, equilibrium would take place with uniform world prices proportional to $(W, P_1, \ldots, P_n, R_1, \ldots, R_n)$ and with industry i everywhere using, per unit of output, a_{oi} of labour and a_{ii} of V_i. Let the migration of the ith factor from A to B be written as ΔV_i. Then, full factor-price equalisation will be preserved by free trade provided

$$\Delta V_0 = \sum_{i=1}^{n} (a_{0i}/a_{ii})\Delta V_i, \tag{10}$$

even though factor endowments have now become relatively different. After such migration, the same equilibrium prices will prevail under free trade, and the same total world productions and consumptions. However, were all tastes now to change, it would be virtually impossible for free trade in goods to continue to keep real wages geographically the same. Thus, if A now has relatively much food production and tastes turn toward food rather than clothing, how can that help but give B lower real wages? So the intermediate locus is touched only at the one singular point.

Examination of (9c) shows that (1) expresses the necessary condition for its maximum condition. Similarly, for (9b), the conditions (5a, b, d) are necessary. To achieve (9a), (5f) must be satisfied as well.

---

[3] E.g., write a Cobb–Douglas $u = Q_1^k Q_1^{1-k}$ and let k go from zero to one. Or write a fixed-proportions $u = \text{Min}\ [Q_1/k, Q_2/(1-k)]$ with $0 < k < 1$. These two alternatives will generate the same two outer frontiers, for the reason that those frontiers each represent solutions to maximal production problems under specified constraints. But the precise shape of the inner locus need not be the same.

(8) If labour works with more than one specialized resource in any industry, V_i must be interpreted as a vector, being short for $(V_{i1}, V_{i2}, \ldots, V_{ik_i})$, where k_i is the number of non-labour factors in the ith industry. Then (5a) must be replaced by

$$P_i/W^j = \partial F(L_i^j, V_i^j)/\partial L_i^j = S_i(Q_i^j), \qquad (i = 1, \ldots, n) \qquad (11)$$
$$P_i/R_{ik}^j = \partial F(L_i^j, V_i^j)/\partial V_{ik}^j, \qquad (k = 1, \ldots, k_i),$$

and a similar rewriting of (1) is needed.

But now, migration of labour alone will not suffice to achieve complete factor price equalisation. The single condition of (5f) must be augmented, so that the numerous following all hold:

$$\frac{P_i}{R_{ik}^1} = \frac{P_i}{R_{ik}^2} = \ldots = \frac{P_i}{R_{ik}^J}, \qquad (i = 1, \ldots, n; k = 1, \ldots, k_i) \qquad (12)$$

Only if all (or all but one) of the $r = 1 + k_1 + \ldots + k_n$ factors can migrate freely, singular cases aside, will these conditions be guaranteed.

(9) What if goods involve transport costs? The simplest case is the following: as any good goes from region A to B, or vice versa, only the fraction f_i arrives there. Clearly, as every $f_i \to 1$, the Ohlin rule of partial factor-price equalisation will prevail. But now two regions that differ only by a trifle in factor endowments will not be able to trade; and their factor returns will necessarily differ by a trifle permanently. Free labour migration will almost, but not quite, equalise factor returns. It will equalise the real wage reckoned in terms of the homothetic tastes; but in regions of food-land abundance, the real wage in food will be compensatingly high and in clothing will be compensating low, with the rents unequal in the opposite directions. In real life, tastes are not uniform, and sun lovers migrate toward the sun.

References

[1] Bickerdike, C. F., 1920, The instability of foreign exchange, Economic Journal 30, 118–122.

[2] Cournot, A. A., 1838, Mathematical principles of the theory of wealth, transl. by Nathaniel T. Bacon, 1927, New York: Macmillan, Ch. X.

[3] Haberler, G., 1949, The market for foreign exchange and the stability of the balance of payments: A theoretical analysis, Kyklos 3, 193–218. Reprinted in: R. N. Cooper, ed., 1969, International finance, Harmondsworth: Penguin Books, Ltd., 107–134.

[4] Haberler, G., 1952, Currency depreciation and the terms of trade, in: E. Lagler and J. Messner, eds., Wirtschaftliche Entwicklung und Soziale Ordnung, Vienna: Verlag Herold, 149–158.

[5] Robinson, J., 1937, Essays in the theory of employment, London and New York: Macmillan, 183–228.

[6] Samuelson, P. A., 1964, Theoretical notes on trade problems, Review of Economics and Statistics 46, 145–154, reproduced in: my Collected Scientific Papers, Vol. 2, Cambridge: MIT Press, 1966, Ch. 56, pp. 821–830.

[7] Samuelson, P. A., 1968, What neoclassical monetary theory really was, Canadian Journal of Economics 1, 1–15.

[8] Samuelson, P. A., 1972, in: Trade, Balance of Payments and Growth, Papers in International Economics in Honor of Charles P. Kindleberger, Amsterdam: North-Holland Publishing Company.

[9] Viner, J., 1937, Studies in the theory of international trade, New York: Harper and Brothers, 319.

[10] Yaeger, L. B., 1966, International monetary relations, New York: Harper and Row, 170 ff.

[11] Yntema, O., 1932, A mathematical reformulation of the general theory of international trade, Chicago, Illinois: The University of Chicago Press.

PART IV

PUBLIC AND PRIVATE PLANNING MODELS

CHAPTER 32

National and interregional models of water demand for land use and agricultural policies

EARL O. HEADY and HOWARD C. MADSEN

Iowa State University

1. Introduction

Over the past decade we have developed a family of programming or systems models encompassing the whole of U.S. agriculture and land use relating thereto. The most interesting application and set of outputs from these models results from a recent study we completed for the National Water Commission. The latter study incorporates all major agricultural commodities into a supply-demand and resource use interaction reflecting restraints in land resources for 223 agricultural producing regions, water resources for 51 water supply regions in the 17 Western States and 27 consumer markets. Incorporating a transportation submodel for the various commodities and water and product transfer activities, the models applied allow selection of optimal resource use patterns for the nation in future time periods. The models allow reflection of comparative advantage in the allocation of land and water to competing alternatives as reflected in relative yields, technologies, production costs, location and transport costs. They allow substitution of land at one location for water at another location a thousand miles away (or vice versa). Finally, they allow evaluation of various policy alternatives in use of land and water resources, in interaction with commercial agricultural policies, in meeting the nation's future requirements or demands for food, fiber and water. However, before we detail the nature of the models applied, we will summarize the evolution in the development and application of this set of models over the last decade. Because of the data base generated for these models, we have been able to extend their dimensions over broader problems such as the study recently completed for the National Water Commission. While this study dealt only with the quantity of water, our next large-scale study will include water quality and a general analysis of environmental alternatives through the flow of inputs and outputs through agriculture.

Actually, our initial national model for agriculture which was reported in Egbert and Heady [2], was initiated in 1955. It included only feed grains and wheat and demand for these commodities specified at the national level. Transportation activities were not included and the objective function was one of profit maximization (or cost minimization in attaining a 'national bill of goods' for meeting projected domestic and export demand for the commodities included). As well as national commodity demands, restraints included land restraints for each feed grains and wheat in each of 100 producing regions. The major forage and pasture areas of the nation were not included in the model because of constraints in data availability, funds and time. While this linear programming model included only 225 equations and 411 real variables, it taxed computing facilities and funds for computations at that time. The models were used to generate solutions allowing evaluation of optimal land use patterns and various supply control policies for agriculture. A large initial effort went into developing a detailed technical matrix for the crops of each region and in delineating producing or land use regions on an agro-climatic basis.

With time and additional funds, the models were expanded. In the next round of models, cotton and soybeans were added, a transportation sub-model was incorporated, consuming regions with appropriate commodity demands (reflected as a 'fixed bill of goods' in each) were included and solutions provided a pattern of land use which would minimize the total costs of producing and transporting the 'bill of goods' representing domestic and export demands for the commodities included [3, 4]. The 140 regions still excluded major pasture and hay producing regions and livestock products. (Livestock was assumed to follow historic patterns in allocation among producing regions.) The dozen models applied were used for numerous research objectives such as appraising the potential of food supplies, prospective national patterns and structures of agriculture, the treasury costs of different farm policies and the farm and commodity income impact of these alternative futures. As an average, these models included 450 equations and 2000 real variables. In the next stage of development, livestock commodities and all hay and forage producing regions were incorporated [1]. A great deal of background empirical work, as in previous models, went into developing technical coefficients expressing labor, capital, land and transportation costs or requirements for each crop and livestock commodity. As an average, this set of models included 190 producing regions, 31 consuming and market regions, 1900 total equations and 5500 real variables including transportation activities. In a recent extension of these models, restraints for three classes of farms (industrial, family commercial and small) were incorporated for each producing region. Three soil types were added for each of the 200 producing regions [5]. Including the demand equations for the 31 market regions, the total dimension of this model is 5500 equations and 60 000 real variables. More recent models have incorporated food demand functions so that the objective functions are non-linear [6]. However, considerable effort is required in refining estimates of demand functions before these models are to be operable in assessment of policy alternatives.

2. Current water models

2.1.

The current water models are modifications and extensions (in certain respects) of the above models. Availability of data from the bank generated in the evolution of these models made it possible for us to make the study for the National Water Commission in the time allowed. Because of restraints in time and funds, and also because certain detail (e.g. the impact of different alternatives on income of various farm classes in each region), some of the detail of the above models was dropped.

2.2. Objectives of water models

The programming models formulated for the water study were designed to conform with the charge before the National Water Commission. In our case, the overall objective was to determine whether (or under what conditions) the nation has enough water to produce its future food and fiber requirements, given projections of urban, industrial and other non-farm demand for water as reflected in various levels and distributions of population and national economic activity in the year 2000. An alternative statement of the overall objective is: through a more efficient allocation of land and water resources in agriculture and a modification of agricultural policies, how much water could be released from agriculture for other uses? The amount of water used in agriculture is partly a function of the prices or costs of water for irrigation purposes. Hence, an auxiliary objective of the study was the formulation of the models so that they would reflect (normatively) the demand for water under different pricing policies. But water demand in agriculture also is a function of other policies in agriculture. Because of the large supply capacity and low income of agriculture in previous times, the nation implemented a supply control program based on land retirement. Through payments to farmers for keeping their land idle, cropland retired under federal programs averaged 56 million acres over the decade 1961–70. These land retirement and associated price support programs now have an annual public cost of around $ 5 billion. But the land retired, plus the higher price from these supply control and associated programs, increased the demand for irrigation water in the Western States. At the same time that farmers over the rest of the nation have been given direct payments to idle their land and reduce production, the public has also invested in irrigation projects in the 17 Western States, which increases production. Hence, the nation tends to pay double for certain programs which cancel each other out; once to increase production in development of irrigated land and once to retire land and reduce production elsewhere in the nation. Accordingly, the models were formulated to evaluate different policy alternatives such as (a) free markets and a long-run equilibrium wherein land can be used in conformance with comparative advantage and substituted for water in other locations (or vice versa) in optimizing the objective function of the models, (b) greater investment, as a substitute for either land or water elsewhere, in technology to increase yields in the Southeast where farm progress has lagged other regions, (c) farm supply policies which constrain land use and distribute supply control over the nation in a manner paralleling that of the past, and (d) alternatives in international trade policies.

3. Nature of models

3.1.

To illustrate the general nature of the models involved, we use a model projecting to the year 2000 for a population of 300 million, free market conditions and trend levels of agricultural technology in each of the 223 agricultural producing regions and the 51 water supply regions. The objective is to minimize the cost of producing and transporting the various crop and livestock commodities among producing regions of origin, regions of processing and regions (or parts) of consumption. The costs of water consumption and transfer are included in Z. The costs cover factor costs (except land rents which are reflected in shadow prices) and thus allow simulation of a long-run market equilibrium for each commodity with a national allocation reflecting the comparative advantage of each of the 223 producing regions and the 51 water supply regions. The objective function is

$$Z = \sum_{j=1}^{25} \sum_{e=1}^{223} c_{ij} X_{ij} + \sum_{m=1}^{51} \left(p_m^B W_m^B + \sum_{m'=1}^{51} p_{m'm}^T W_{m'm}^T \right)$$
$$+ \sum_{k=1}^{27} \sum_{k'=1}^{27} \sum_{q=1}^{8} z_{qk'k} T_{qk'k} \quad (1)$$

where

Z = total costs of crop and livestock production, total costs of transportation and certain water costs to meet domestic and export demands;

c_{ij} = the cost per acre or livestock unit of the jth crop or livestock activity in the ith producing region; livestock costs do not include certain feed costs determined internally to the programming model;

X_{ij} = is the level of the jth product activity in the ith producing region;

p_m^B = the cost of water per foot consumed in the mth water supply region;

W_m^B = the acre feet of water bought for consumptive uses in the mth water supply region;

$p_{m'm}$ = the difference between the cost of water per acre foot consumed in the m'th and mth water supply regions (the cost defined only for adjoining supply regions connected by natural flows);

$W_{m'm}^T$ = the acre feet of water transferred by natural flows from the m'th water supply region to the mth water supply region;

$z_{qk'k}$ = the cost of transporting a unit of the qth type of commodity from the kth consuming region to the kth consuming region where k and k' regions are contiguous except for certain long haul routes; and

$T_{qk'k}$ = the amount transported of the qth type of commodity from the kth consuming region to the kth consuming region where $k+k'$ must be contiguous except for certain long hauls.

3.2. Restraints and variables

Both dryland and irrigated crop variables are included for producing regions in the 17 Western States which can produce irrigated crops. A range of livestock rations (livestock variables) are allowed in all producing regions since the least-cost feed mix can be drawn from crop grown in the region or imported from others. The objective function is subject to each of the following land restraints in all 223 producing regions.

cropland

total land

$$\sum_{j=1}^{14} a_{ij} X_{ij} \leq L_{Ci} \qquad (2)$$

$$\sum_{j=1}^{16} a_{ij} X_{ij} \leq L_{Ti} \qquad (3)$$

irrigated cropland

irrigated total land

$$\sum_{j=8}^{14} a_{ij} X_{ij} \leq L_{Ci}^{I} \qquad (4)$$

$$\sum_{j=8}^{15} a_{ij} X_{ij} \leq L_{Ti}^{I} \qquad (5)$$

dryland wild hayland

irrigated wild hayland

$$a_{i20} X_{i20} \leq L_{Wi}^{D} \qquad (6)$$

$$a_{i20} X_{i21} \leq L_{Wi}^{I} \qquad (7)$$

dryland cropland and improved
pasture land

irrigated cropland and improved
pasture land

$$a_{i17} X_{i17} \leq L_{CPi}^{D} \qquad (8)$$

$$a_{i18} X_{i18} \leq L_{CPi}^{I} \qquad (9)$$

dryland unimproved pasture,
woodland pasture and public grazing
lands

agronomic restraint for soybeans

$$a_{i19} X_{i19} \leq L_{Oi} \qquad (10)$$

$$X_{i3} \leq 0.5L_{Ci} \qquad X_{i10} \leq 0.5L_{Ci} \quad (11)$$

population restraint

$$N_i \geq \bar{N}_i. \qquad (12)$$

For the policy model simulating an annual land retirement program, the following additional restraints prevail:

cropland

acreage quota restraint for wheat and
feed grains

$$\sum a_{ij} X_{ij} + R_i = L_{Ci} \qquad (2')$$

$$\sum_{\substack{j=1 \\ j \neq 3,6,7,10}}^{12} r_{ij} X_{ij} \leq Q_i \qquad (13)$$

acreage restraint for cotton

acreage restraint for sugar beets

$$X_{i6} + X_{i13} \leq C_i \qquad (14)$$

$$X_{i7} + X_{i14} \leq S_i \qquad (15)$$

land retirement minimum and maximum

$$R_i \geq R_{Li} \qquad R_i \leq 0.5L_{Ti} \qquad (16)$$

The objective function is subject to the following restraint in water supply region m:

water restraint[1]

$$W_m^B + \sum_{j'=1}^{51} [W_{m'm}^T - W_{mm'}^T + W_{m'm}^I - W_{mm'}^I] - W_m^X - W_m^O - W_m^F$$

$$- \sum_{i \in m} [\sum_{\substack{j=8 \\ j \neq 16,17,19,20}}^{25} w_{ij} X_{ij} + w_{iN} N_i] - \sum_{p=1}^{4} w_{mp} G_p \geq 0 \qquad (17)$$

The objective function is subject to the following types of restraints in consuming region k:

for the qth crop commodity[2]

$$\sum_{i \in k} [\sum_{j=1}^{21} Y_{ij} X_{ij} - b_{iq} N_i] - \sum_{j=22}^{25} F_{kjq} - e_{kq} E_q - \sum_{p=1}^{5} f_{kpq} G_p$$

$$+ \sum_{k'=1}^{27} [T_{qk'k} - T_{qkk'}] \geq 0 \qquad q = 1, \ldots, 6 \quad (18)$$

for the qth livestock commodity[2]

$$\sum_{i \in k} [\sum_{j=22}^{25} Y_{ij} X_{ij} - b_{iq} N_i] + N_{kq} I_q + \sum_{k'=1}^{27} [T_{qk'k} - T_{qkk'}] \geq 0 \qquad (19)$$

TDN requirement for the jth type of livestock

$$\sum_{q=1}^{6} t_{kjq}^{TDN} F_{kjq} - \sum_{i \in k} f_{ij}^{TDN} X_{ij} \geq 0 \qquad (20)$$

protein requirement for the jth type of livestock

$$\sum_{q=1}^{6} t_{kjq}^{P} F_{kjq} - \sum_{i \in k} f_{ij}^{P} X_{ij} \geq 0 \qquad (21)$$

roughage requirement for beef cows

$$\sum_{q=5}^{6} t_{k24q}^{R} F_{k24q} - \sum_{i \in k} f_{i24}^{R} X_{i24} \geq 0 \qquad (22)$$

roughage requirement for dairy cows and beef feeding

$$\sum_{q=5}^{6} t_{kjq}^{R} F_{kjq} - \sum_{i \in k} f_{ij}^{R} X_{ij} \leq 0 \qquad (23)$$

[1] For water transfer activities $(W_{m'm}^T, W_{mm'}^T, W_{m'm}^I, W_{mm'}^I)$ the first subscript represents the origin and the second subscript the destination of the water.

[2] For commodity transportation activities $(T_{qk'k}, T_{qkk'})$ the first subscript represents the origin and the second subscript the destination of the commodity.

Finally, the objective function is subject to the following national restraints:

national restraint for cotton

$$\sum_{i=1}^{150} [Y_{i6} X_{i6} + Y_{i13} - b_{i11} N_i] \geq 0 \tag{24}$$

national restraint for sugar beets

$$\sum_{i=1}^{150} [Y_{i7} X_{i7} + Y_{i14} - b_{i12} N_i] \geq 0 \tag{25}$$

for the pth exogenous type of livestock

$$G_p \geq \bar{G}_p \tag{26}$$

for exports of the qth type of commodity

$$E_q \geq \bar{E}_q \tag{27}$$

for imports of the qth type of commodity

$$I_q \leq \bar{I}_q \tag{28}$$

The following non-negativity constraints also must hold:

$$F_{kjq}, X_{ij}, T_{qk'k}, W_m^B, W_{m'm}^I \geq 0 \tag{29}$$

The subscripts and variables are defined as follows:

i = subscript denoting the producing areas, $i = 1, 2, \ldots 223$;

j = subscript denoting the type of endogenous crop or livestock activity, $j = 1, 2, \ldots 25$;

k = subscript denoting the consuming region, $k = 1, 2, \ldots 27$;

m = subscript denoting the water supply region, $m = 1, 2, \ldots 51$;

p = subscript denoting the type of exogenous livestock activity, $p = 1, 2, \ldots 5$;

q = subscript denoting the type of commodity, $q = 1, 2, \ldots 12$;

a_{ij} = amount of land used by the jth crop activity in the ith producing area;

b_{iq} = per capita consumption of the qth type of commodity in the ith producing region, $q = 1, 2, \ldots 12$;

e_{kq} = the proportion of U.S. exports of the qth type of commodity exported historically from the kth consuming region;

f_{ij}^{TDN} = the amount of total digestible nutrients (TDN) consumed per unit of the jth type of livestock in the ith producing region;

f_{ij}^{P} = the amount of protein consumed per unit of the jth type of livestock in the ith producing area;

f_{ij}^{R} = the amount of roughage (in hay equivalent) consumed per unit of the jth type of livestock activity in the ith producing area;

f_{kpq} = the amount of the qth type of crop commodity consumed by the pth type of exogenous livestock in the kth consuming region;

n_{kq} = the proportion of the qth type of livestock commodity imported into the kth consuming region based on the relative distribution of U.S. population in the year 2000;

p_{m}^{B} = the cost of water per acre foot consumed in the mth water supply region;

r_{ij} = the amount of the acreage quota, Q_i, used by the jth type of crop activity (wheat and feed grains only) in the ith producing area;

t_{kjq}^{TDN} = the amount of total digestible nutrients (TDN) per unit of the qth type of commodity transformed into feed to be used by the jth type of livestock activity in the kth consuming region;

t_{kjq}^{P} = the amount of protein per unit of the qth type of commodity transformed into feed to be used by the jth type of livestock activity in the kth consuming region;

t_{kjq}^{R} = the amount of roughage (in hay equivalents) per unit of the qth type of commodity transformed into feed to be used by the jth type of livestock activity in the kth consuming region;

w_{ij} = the amount of water consumed per unit of the jth type of crop or livestock activity in the ith producing area;

w_{mp} = the amount of water consumed by the pth type of exogenous livestock activity in the mth water supply region;

w_{iN} = the per capita consumption of water for municipal, industrial, recreation and thermal electric power uses in the ith producing area;

y_{ij} = the yield per acre or per unit of activity of the jth type of crop or livestock activity in the ith producing area;

E_{q} = the national export activity for the qth type of commodity;

$\bar{E}_{q}$ = the national level of exports (lower bound) of the qth type of commodity;

F_{kjq} = the amount of the qth type of commodity transformed into feed (TDN, protein and roughage) for use by the jth type of livestock activity in the kth consuming region;

G_{p} = the national activity for the pth type of exogenous livestock;

$\bar{G}_{p}$ = the national level (lower bound) of the pth type of exogenous livestock (includes exports and imports)

I_q = the national import activity for the qth type of commodity;

$\bar{I}_q$ = the national level of imports (upper bound) of the qth type of commodity;

N_i = the population-industry activity in the ith producing area;

$\bar{N}_i$ = the lower bound or level of population in the ith producing area;

$W^T_{m'm}$ = the acre feet of water transferred by natural flows from the m'th water supply region to the mth water supply region;

W^O_m = the acre feet of water consumed by other uses for water including fish and wildlife, wetlands, swamps and in some special cases mining in the mth water supply region;

W^X_m = the acre feet of water exported to regions outside the 17 Western States from the mth water supply region;

L_{Ci} = the acres of cropland available for annual crops production in the ith producing area;

L_{Ti} = the acres of total land (crop and hayland) available for annual crops and tame hay production in the ith producing area;

L^I_{Ci} = the acres of irrigated cropland available for irrigated annual crops production in the ith producing area;

L^I_{Ti} = the acres of irrigated total land available for irrigated annual crops and irrigated tame hay production in the ith producing area;

L^D_{CPi} = the acres of land available for dryland cropland–improved pasture production in the ith producing area;

L^I_{CPi} = the acres of land available for irrigated cropland–improved pasture production in the ith producing area;

L_{Oi} = the acres of land available for dryland unimproved pasture, woodland pasture and public grazing lands pasture production in the ith producing area;

L^D_{Wi} = the acres of land available for dryland wild hay production in the ith producing area;

W^F_m = the acre feet of water consumed by fruits, nuts, rice and vegetables in the mth water supply region;

L^I_{Wi} = the acres of land available for irrigated wild hay production in the ith producing area;

Q_i = the acres of acreage quota available, in the annual land retirement policy model, for annual crops production (wheat and feed grains only) in the ith producing area;

C_i = the harvested acreage of cotton in 1964 in the ith producing area (220);

S_i = the harvested acreage of sugar beets in 1964 in the ith producing area (220) multiplied by two;

R_i = the acres retired, in the annual land retirement policy model, in the ith producing area;

R_{Li} = the minimum (lower limit) acreage retired, in the annual land retirement policy model, in the ith producing area.

Commodities included in the analysis are corn, sorghum, wheat, barley, oats, soybeans, cotton, sugar beets, tame hay, wild hay, improved pasture, unimproved and woodland pasture, cropland pasture, public grazing lands, fruits, nuts, rice, vegetables, all dairy products, pork, beef, broilers, turkeys, eggs, mutton and other livestock. All projections are for the year 2000. The model includes 5426 real variables (excluding transportation) and 3220 equations, including 1650 bounds.

4. Regions and their delineation

4.1.

This model of interregional competition determines the location of crop and livestock production given resource availability and commodity demands in the year 2000. To reflect the interregional nature of the analysis the U.S. was partitioned into sets of regions appropriate for various restraints and demands.

4.2. Producing regions

Producing regions are delineated such that (a) a single activity can be legitimately defined to represent production of a crop in that area, and (b) the set of producing areas can be used as the elements of sets of market and water supply regions. Each of the 223 production regions, which are identified in fig. 1, is an aggregation of contiguous counties. The producting regions also are composed of subsets of the counties with the water resources subregions defined by the Water Resources Council [10].

4.3. Water supply regions

The water supply regions are defined as the smallest watersheds for which surface runoff data are readily available. The 51 water supply regions for the 17 Western States are, given in figure 2, defined such that each water supply region is an aggregate of contiguous producing areas and each is a

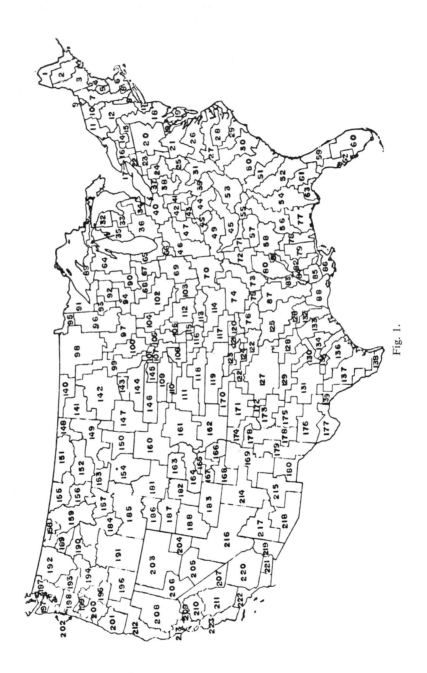

Fig. 1.

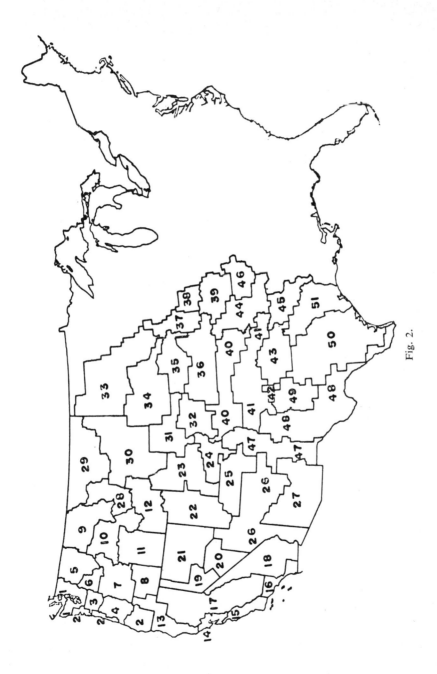

Fig. 2.

subset of a river basin. The water supply regions closely approximate those defined by the Water Resources Council [11].

4.4. Consuming regions

The 27 consuming regions are based on 'central place theory' and each consuming region is an aggregate of contiguous producing areas.

Results of the models can be analyzed by individual producing, water or consumption regions, or they can be aggregated to 18 river basins.

5. Water supplies and detail

5.1.

The water supply in each water supply region is a function of the total reservoir storage and the mean annual runoff in the region.[3] First, the total storage capacities of reservoirs in each of the water supply regions were determined by adding the active conservation and joint use capacities[4] for storage dams in the region as obtained from the Bureau of Reclamation[5] the Army Corps of Engineers[6], and a survey of reservoirs in the U.S. [9]. Second, the mean annual runoffs reported were determined from *The Nation's Water Resources* [11]. Then using the relationships between storage and mean annual flow developed by Lof and Hardison [8] the net water supply as a proportion of the mean annual runoff was determined.

It was assumed that all water supply regions in a given river basin have the same relationship between the gross water supply and total reservoir storage. The gross surface runoff in each water supply region was determined as reported in [7]. Water supplies were first calculated for all water supply regions and then the gross water supplies were adjusted for reservoir evaporation, giving a net water supply in each water supply region [7]. Mining of underground water supplies is not allowed in any of the water

---

[3] See Heady *et al.* [7, table 3.3] for the annual supplies in the 51 water regions.

[4] Active conservation capacity is water storage available for irrigation, municipal and industrial uses, power, fish and wildlife or other direct uses. The joint use capacity includes that storage area of the dam allocated for flood control during part of the year and to active conservation for the remainder of the year.

[5] Unpublished data obtained through private communications with D. W. Davies, U.S. Department of the Interior, Bureau of Reclamation, Denver, Colorado, March, 1971.

[6] See refs. [68–88] in Heady *et al.* [7], ibid.

supply regions. We assume that most closed underground water supplies will be depleted by the year 2000 and the amount of water available on a continuous basis from the others is not known with any degree of accuracy.

5.2. Water use coefficients

Water use coefficients for each crop activity in the model reflect the net diversion requirement to provide the crop with the amount of water needed for growth in addition to that provided by precipitation. Withdrawal coefficients are also calculated to indicate the diversion requirements needed to supply the water consumed. Gross delivery requirements in area i for crop j are

$$GDR_{ij} = \frac{CU_{ij} EP_i}{(IE_j)(CE_i)} \tag{30}$$

where: CU_{ij} is the amount of water required by crop j in producing area i as determined from regional publications on consumptive use of water by crops [7]; EP_i is the effective precipitation in producing area i representing water available after evaporation and deep percolation are subtracted from the rainfall; and IE_j is the irrigation efficiency or the efficiency of the crops in using the water applied (as affected by the surface of the land exposed between plants and the ability of the plants to hold the water in the ground for use); and CE_i the canal efficiency or efficiency of the delivery system between the diversion point and the farm delivery gate (calculated for each region from data on Bureau of Reclamation projects).

The net diversion requirements, NDR_{ij}, or the consumptive water coefficients for each of the activities are calculated as

$$NDR_{ij} = CU_{ij} - EP_i + (1 - RF)[GDR_{ij} - (CU_{ij} - EP_i)]$$
$$= CIR_j + (1 - RF)[GDR_{ij} - CIR_{ij}] \tag{31}$$

where GDR_{ij}, CU_{ij} and EP_i are defined above, CIR_{ij} is the crop irrigation requirement of the jth crop in the ith producing area; RF is percent of the water not used by the plant which is returned for re-use in the region. This return flow is assumed to be 55 % for all river basins except the Columbia–North Pacific where 60 % is used; and $GDR_{ij} - (CU_{ij} - EP_i)$ is the water diverted but not directly used by the crops.

5.3. Current water prices

The price presently paid by farmers for water in water supply region j,

p_j, was determined by using a weighted average of present water costs in Bureau of Reclamation irrigation projects or

$$P_j = \sum_{i \in j} (CA_i/AF_i)(WD_i) / \sum_{i \in j} WD_i, \qquad (32)$$

where CA_i is the cost per acre to farmers in project i; AF_i is the acre feet of water applied per acre in project i; and WD_i is the total acre feet of water delivered to the farms in project i. For regions in which Bureau of Reclamation data are not available the water price in the most immediate upstream region is used. These water prices were then increased to account for farm waste and deep percolation and are measured as cost per acre of water consumed. No correction is required for canal losses since the deliveries, WD_i, are measured at the farm.

5.4. Water transfers

Water transfer activities are defined to allow water in upstream regions to flow along the natural slopes to downstream water supply regions. Each of these activities is bound at a maximum level equal to 70.0 % of the upstream water supply. Since losses occur from evaporation, removal by natural vegetation and some deep percolation, this restraint prevents downstream movement of water with 100.0 % efficiency. The costs associated with these natural flow transfers are set at a level such that the upstream water price plus the transfer cost is greater than the price of water in the receiving region. For some of these activities, the cost would be zero if water in the upstream region is priced higher than water in the downstream region.

Existing interbasin transfers are simulated by transfer activities. Due to the fixed nature of the facilities and since present water prices reflect their variable cost, no cost is associated directly with these transfers. An upper bound on each activity is set at the projected capacity of the project to transfer water in the year 2000.

One water export activity is defined to transfer water (1.5 million acre feet) in accord with the Mexican Treaty of 1944, [7]. The lower bound on this activity is set at 1.5 million acre feet and the water is transferred from water supply region 26 (the Lower Colorado basin). Another activity allows for the transfer of 1.1 million acre feet from water supply region 33 (the Dakotas) to the Souris-Red-Rainy river basin as is projected with the completion of the Garrison diversion project [7]. A depletion activity is defined for water supply region 29 (northern Montana) to account for the expected increased depletion of the Milk River by Canada in the year 2000, [7].

Unbounded desaltation activities are defined for all sea cost water supply regions to allow for augmentation of the water supply. The price of $ 100.00 per acre foot placed on these activities approximates the best estimates available of the cost of large scale desalting schemes under present technologies [7]. A water augmenting activity is placed in water supply region 26 (the Lower Colorado basin) with a high cost in the event of a water shortage to satisfy the exogenous water requirements projected for that region in 2000.

6. Models used and results

6.1.

Solutions were made for seven models representing different futures in population, farm policies, export levels, water pricing and farm technology. They are summarized in table 1. Models A, A-1, A-2 and A-3 all assume a 2000 population of 300 million, 1967–69 levels of exports for all farm commodities and technology (yields and feed transformation) projected by time-series trends to 2000. They differ only in the price of water charged farmers in the 17 Western States. Model B uses a 280 million population. Model C assumes an annual land retirement policy to restrain supply with land forced into the program over the entire country as at the present. All other models assume a free market for farm commodities. Model D uses a

Table 1

Summary of models and parameter levels for 2000

Model	Population (mil)	Farm policy	Water price	Export level	Farm technology
A	300	market	present	67–69	trend
A-1	300	market	$ 15.00	67–69	trend
A-2	300	market	$ 22.50	67–69	trend
A-3	300	market	$ 30.00	67–69	trend
B	280	market	present	67–69	trend
C	280	land	present	67–69	trend
D	325	market	present	double	advanced

population of 325 million in 2000, exports averaging 100 % greater than in
the period 1967–69 and a level of technology in the Southeast equal to that
of other regions of the country.

Each of these models provides a vast amount of output by commodities in
each individual producing, water supply and consuming region; in use of
water and its shadow prices by supply regions; interregion commodity flows
and water transfers, costs; and other information. Because of time and space
restraints, we present a few details only for Model A.

6.2. Summary results for Model A

Under the assumptions of Model A, total acreage of dryland crops in
2000 is 12.3 million higher than in 1964. Acreages of corn for grain and
cotton acres are significantly lower while wheat, grain sorghum and soybeans acres are significantly higher. Based on total dryland acres, the rank
of river basins generally is the same as in 1964, except the Texas–Gulf basin
increases feed grain acreage by 6.9 million acres as grain sorghum expands
in the basin. Added feed grain is needed in the Texas–Gulf basin to satisfy
the beef demand for an increased population in the Houston–Dallas area.
Also, the dryland production of grain sorghum substitutes for some currently irrigated grain production. This substitution is especially important
in water supply region 49 Northern California where ground-water is
projected to be depleted by 2000. Dryland acres of cotton decrease in 2000
due to the continued decline in domestic use of cotton and an increase in
average cotton yield. Cotton production also moves into the Lower Mississippi basin (Southeastern U.S.) in response to the increased competition for
water from nonagricultural water requirements and increased forage production in the West. Compared with 1964 the total acres harvested (dryland
and irrigated) of major field crops is 7.2 million higher due to the higher
food and fiber demand in 2000 and the substitution of dryland acres for
some currently irrigated land. Since dryland yields are less than irrigated
yields, especially in the West, more land is used for food and fiber production.

Total dryland acres of tame hay and silages are projected to increase
41.9 million acres over 1964. This large increase in dryland forage production is necessary for: (a) the increased cattle fed in 2000, (b) the increased beef cow herd to provide feeder cattle for the increased fed beef
production, and (c) because dryland production is substituted for irrigated
production. Pasture and hay are large users of water. Considerable adjustment would be made in these uses of water. Some regions would reduce

greatly the use of water for hay and pasture, but because of the large demand for beef, some would increase use.

For the 9 western river basins, the largest increases (a total of 3.8 million acres) in irrigated acreage of tame hay and silage are in the Missouri, California–South Pacific and Columbia–North Pacific basins. Compared with 1969, both the Missouri and California–South Pacific basins have significant decreases in irrigated acreage of annual crops. In 2000, most of the land so released is shifted to irrigated tame hay and silages production. Irrigated acreage of tame hay and silages decreases slightly due to the shortage of water in the Texas–Gulf basin in 2000. Irrigated acreage of fruits, nuts, rice and vegetables for 2000 in the West are projected to increase 15.0 % over 1964. Over 90 % of the increase is in the California–South Pacific basin.

In terms of the objective function of the model, irrigated acreage of annual crops in 2000 declines by 5.1 million acres from the 1964 level. The supply of both land and water is large enough to a low this shift while attaining a greater total output. It should be remembered that this model allows land now held out of production under government supply programs to be returned to cropping. The use of less irrigated land and the return to production of land now idled by supply control programs would allow the nation's overall agriculture to be optimized by this pattern and shift. Agriculture could either (a) produce the nation's food needs at a lower total factor cost, or (b) produce a given amount at a greater national farm profit by this pattern. However, the shift to a smaller dependence on irrigated acreage would have important effects on the interregional distribution of income.

The Texas–Gulf, Missouri and California–South Pacific basins show the largest decrease (4.6 million acres) of irrigated land. This decrease of irrigated annual crops in 2000, compared with 1969, can be explained by a number of factors. First, in conformity with the objective function of the model, it is economic for dryland production in either the East or West to be substituted for water and irrigated production in the West. Dryland acres of annual crops increase 12.3 million acres and dryland acreage of tame hay and silages increases by 41.9 million acres over 1969. In this comparison, it should be remembered that Model A does not include a land retirement or supply control program of the 1969 type for the year 2000. The model allows non-irrigated land to be brought back into production and substituted for water or irrigated land where (a) municipal and industrial water requirements indicate the need, and (b) where the national economic objectives of the model are furthered by the substitution. In other words, land idled under current supply control programs is released for substitution for water and irrigated land for meeting these objectives. Water in some specific areas is not available for irrigation after exogenous water requirements (municipal, industrial, fruits and vegetables, etc.) are satisfied. This outcome explains some of the decrease in irrigated annual crops in the Southwest and the Texas–Gulf basin. Since use of ground water above recharge rates is not allowed in the model, certain areas presently using water for irrigation have reduced supplies in 2000. Some of the decrease in irrigated annual crop production in the Texas–Gulf basin the Southwest and the Missouri basin may result similarly by 2000. Finally, some water and irrigable land are needed for forage production for greater beef production. Under model solutions, irrigated tame hay and silages increase by 4.0 million acres over the 1964 level. The increase in forage production, as already outlined, is used for the increased fed beef and beef cow production in 2000.

Even with the higher food and fiber requirements in 2000, 16.4 million acres of land could remain unused. The term *unused* refers to the amount of land not needed to meet the domestic and export food demands at the numerical levels specified in the restraint equations of the programming model. Of course, in a completely free market, we would expect the acreage denoted as *unused* to be absorbed into agricultural or urban uses. Also it poses a supply of land to be used for public purposes such as parks and recreation. The greatest proportion of land designated as not needed for agricultural production (in terms of the specific demand restraints of the programming model) is in the Appalachian, Smokey and other mountainous areas of the East. Also a large proportion of the unused land is along the heavily populated area of the Eastern Seabord, where the demand for recreational lands will be large over the next three decades. Most of the remaining unused land occurs in the 17 Western States as either land is reduced from irrigation or as supply controls are relaxed and more productive soil in the Corn Belt or elsewhere are substituted.

Consumptive use and supplies of water by river basin. Projected withdrawals and consumptive use of water were also generated by the model. Total consumptive use of water in the 17 Western States is projected to increase 21.0 million acre feet or 128 % per year over the 1965 level. Only the Arkansas-White-Red and Rio Grande basins have a projected 2000 consumption which is less than the 1965 level. Food and fiber production in the Arkansas-White-Red basin is predominantly from dryland acreage in 2000. In the Rio Grande basin, only a small amount of available water is surplus. In certain areas of both the Arkansas-White-Red and Rio Grande basins, current use of ground water predominates. Since ground water use above recharge rates is not allowed in Model A, water for consumptive use in 2000 is less than presently available supplies. Irrigated acreage of annual crops in both of these basins declines in 2000 from 1969 levels.

Of the total increased water for consumptive use in 2000, 110.0 million acre feet (45.5 %) is in the California–South Pacific basin. The Missouri, Texas–Gulf and Columbia–North Pacific basins also increase water consumption to much higher levels. The increase in the California–South Pacific basin is due to population growth and increased fruit, nut, rice and vegetable production by 2000. In the Texas–Gulf basin, municipal and industrial water requirements give rise to the major increase. Crops are the primary water user in both the Missouri and Columbia–North Pacific basins. The increases in water consumed in the Lower Colorado and Great Basin basins are relatively small and irrigated acreage less in 2000 under Model A than 1964 levels. Currently, ground water is an important supply source in both these areas. About 40 % of the estimated total water supply is consumed in 2000. Only the Texas–Gulf basin has a water deficit. The Rio Grande, Great Basin and Lower Colorado basins have a relative scarcity, however. All remaining basins, including the Upper Colorado, have adequate water and need no further surface reservoir construction after 1980. The Upper Colorado basin has a surplus of 0.9 million acre feet per year. In addition, by the model solution, it should release 5.3 million acre feet for consumptive use in the Lower Colorado basin. The Columbia–North Pacific basin has the largest surplus, 98.9 million acre feet per year. The results of Model A do not indicate a national water shortage by 2000. Neither is an overall water shortage indicated for the 17 Western States. While one specific area has an indicated deficit, the problem ahead is one of the distribution or allocation of water rather than of a shortage per se. When land now idle under government supply control programs is allowed to return to production, it is substituted for water on irrigated land and prevents an overall shortage, either for the U.S. or the 17 Western States, and poses the problem as one of water allocation rather than an absolute physical or economic scarcity.

6.3. Supply potential and policy alternatives

The projections to 2000 under Model A indicate neither a land nor an overall water shortage for agriculture. The prospect is for continued large supply capacity relative to projected domestic and export demand for U.S. farm products. Farm commodity prices are not likely to rise to high real levels under the supply-demand relationships expected to prevail at that time. While the nation averaged 56 million acres retired from production under federal supply control programs over the period 1961–70, the model indicated that some cropland still will not be needed for crops in meeting the projected demands for 2000. However, the amount of land not needed for crops is projected to decline from the 58.0 million acres out of production in 1969 to 16.4 million in 2000. At the same time, the amount of water used for irrigation and the amount of land irrigated can decline by 2000 if resources are allocated optimally in terms of Model A to meet national food and water needs. Under Model A, the amount of irrigated acreage declines from the estimated 38.5 million acres in 1969 to 27.3 million acres in the 17 Western States in 2000. Hence, the nation can readily meet its food needs under the assumptions of Model A and some water can be released for other uses accordingly. Even if urban, municipal and manufacturing demand for water proves larger than that projected for the year 2000, under Model A, more water can be diverted from agriculture where locational aspects of water supply and demand mesh. The locational linkage is necessary only for water and not for agricultural production. With even more water withdrawn from agriculture to meet non-farm demand at particular locations, land elsewhere in the nation can be used for crops on land shifted from irrigated practices.

6.4. Summary for models and outlook

The various futures or policy alternatives represented by the models summarized in Table 2 can all be attained without a national water shortage.

Table 2

Summary of land and water use under seven models

	Actual 1964	Model						
		A	A-1	A-2	A-3	B	C	D
Dryland [a]	1555	1227	1232	1238	1242	1192	1197	1238
Irrigated [a]	31.3	27.2	22.6	17.2	12.4	26.0	29.2	28.6
Unused [a]	55.5	16.4	15.1	12.9	12.5	51.0	44.9	4.5
Water withdrawal [b]	151.7	115.9	139.3	120.3	105.0	147.1	154.6	163.3
Consumptive use [b]	76.0	97.3	85.9	71.8	61.1	92.0	96.6	100.9
Water surplus [b]	n.a.	142.1	153.5	167.6	178.3	147.4	142.8	138.5

[a] Million acres of land for U.S.
[b] Million acre feet for U.S.

Additionally, agriculture can supply food abundantly and at very favorable real prices (in terms of the 'equilibrium prices' for commodities generated for each model) for consumers. A summary of land and water use for agriculture at the national level under the seven models is indicated in table 2. Dryland acreage increases and irrigation use of water declines as water price is increased. Other obvious shifts are implied in land and water use for parameter variations in population levels, farm programs, technology and exports in the year 2000. However, in no case is a shortage of land or water for agricultural production indicated. In all cases, water could be shifted from farm uses to urban and manufacturing uses. The supply of food needed to meet 2000 demands can be sufficiently large that the prospects for farmers are more those of burdened markets and low prices rather than the opposite. These are important findings for national planning since many people propose that future magnitudes of population will place a very great pressure on our food-producing capacity.

6.5. Water demand under pricing policies

Time prevents us from summarizing many other results from the various models. One set of data of special interest are the shadow prices on land and water. These provide indication of compensation levels which might be used as a foundation in payments to farmers for their water rights should re-allocation of water from farm to urban and industrial uses occur.

Models A, A-1, A-2 and A-3 provide some basis for indicating the aggregate demand relations (for the nation or by water supply regions). Accordingly, we present fig. 3 which relates consumptive use of water in agriculture to the four water price levels represented in the four models. The 'free hand' curve is 'drawn in' for illustrative purposes, but many additional points on relevant water and land demand functions could be derived from the general model format.

As the water price is increased (i.e., Model A-1, Model A-2 and Model A-3), land and its production in the East is substituted for water and its production in the West. Also, the same type of land–water substitution in the West occurs. Movement from right to left along the demand curve in fig. 1 conforms with substitution of land in the East and West for water in the West.

In summary, when the price of water increases to $ 30.00 per acre foot, total irrigated land in the West decreases 14.9 million acres; irrigated annual crops and tame hay and silages decrease by 10.7 million acres. At the same time, dryland production of annual crops and tame hay increases by 4.0

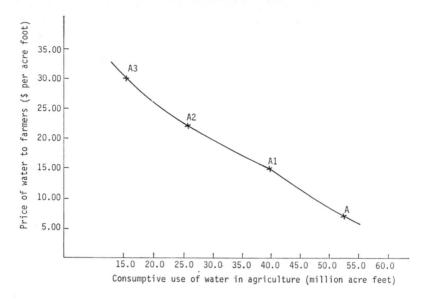

Fig. 3. Agricultural demand for water in the 17 Western States.

million acres in the East and by 10.5 million acres in the West. When one acre is removed from irrigated production in the West, on the average, one acre of dryland production replaces it. The replacement acre is composed of about one-third of an acre in the East and two-thirds of an acre in the West. This one-to-one substitution is possible because (a) the mix of annual crop changes (e.g., wheat decreases relative to corn for grain), and (b) the relative mix of hays to grain changes.

7. Future models

The models summarized above relate only to water quality. Under planning are models which will encompass the nation's agriculture and its many commodity and resource supply areas in relation to water quality and the environment. These models will incorporate variables representing the inflow of potential pollutants (insecticides, nitrogen, phosphates, etc.) and the outflow of by-product outputs (water runoff, animal wastes, chemicals, insecticides, etc.) On the crop side, there will be subsets for each producing region of variables for crops produced with various levels of chemicals and insecticides, or under various rotational mixes of crops to generate fertility and plant protection through organic means. Further, sets of equations, containing these variables representing environmental or pollutant effects and their appropriate coefficients, will place upper bounds on levels of nitrates, phosphates, animal wastes either imported by streams or exported from relevant farm producing regions or watersheds. In addition to these environmental models, we also are extending more conventional models to include the employment and income generation effects of various farm programs and structures, as well as national policies directed towards the dispersion of population and economic activity.

References

[1] Broken, R. F. and E. O. Heady, 1968, Interregional Adjustments in Crop and Livestock Production; a Linear Programming Analysis, U.S.D.A. Technical Bul. 1396, Washington, D.C., Government Printing Office.

[2] Egbert, A. and E. O. Heady, 1961, Regional Adjustments in Grain Production – A Linear Programming Analysis, USDA Tech. Bul. 1241, Washington, D.C., Government Printing Office, 1–66.

[3] Heady, E. O. and N. Whittlesley, 1965, Projections of United States Agriculture Capacity and Interregional Adjustments in Production and Land Use with Spatial Programming Models, Iowa Agr. and Home Econ. Exp. Sta. Res. Bul. 539, Ames.

[4] Heady, E. O. and M. Skold, 1965, Programming analysis of interregional competition and surplus capacity of American agriculture, Iowa Agr. and Home Econ. Exp. Sta. Res. Bul. 528, Ames.

[5] Heady, E. O. and R. Eyvidson, A Programming Model Incorporating Producing Regions, Consumer Markets and Individual Farms for Optimizing National Agricultural Patterns and Comparative Advantage, to be published.

[6] Heady, E. O. and H. Hall, 1969, Applications of Linear and Nonlinear Programming Models in Specifying Land Use, Spatial Equilibrium and Prices for Agriculture, in: Economic Models, Estimation and Risk Programming; Essays in Honor of Gerhard Tintner, Berlin, Springer-Verlag, 190–222.

[7] Heady, E. O., H. C. Madsen, K. J. Nicol and S. H. Hargrove, Future Water and Land Use: Effects of Selected Public Agricultural and Irrigation Policies on Water Demand and Land Use. National Water Commission, National Technical Service PB206493.

[8] Lof, G. O. G. and C. H. Hardison, 1966, Storage requirements for water in the United States, Water Resources Research, 2, 323–354.

[9] Maritin, R. O. R. and R. L. Hansen, 1966, Reservoirs in the United States, Water Supply Paper 1838, Washington, D.C., Geological Survey, U.S. Department of the Interior.

[10] U.S. Water Resources Council, 1970, Water Resources Regions and Subregions for the National Assessment of Water and Related Land Resources, Washington, D.C., Government Printing Office.

[11] U.S. Water Resources Council, 1968, The Nation's Water Resources, Washington, D.C., Government Printing Office.

CHAPTER 33

Evaluation of the effect of alternative agricultural systems on water quality: a linear programming approach*

EARL R. SWANSON and A. V. S. NARAYANAN

University of Illinois

1. Introduction

1.1. General considerations

Environmental quality is a topic of continuing concern not only to the public, but also to the various disciplines. Because the solutions suggested for most environmental quality problems involve rearrangement of production and consumption processes, both in space and time, it is not surprising that economists are now extending traditional mathematical programming analysis to include aspects of environmental quality, e.g. see [9] and [12].

1.2. The agricultural–environmental complex

Environmental quality problems are, in a sense, natural resource use problems. Consequently, recognition of the interactions between agriculture and the environment is important in public policy and planning related to the environment. Agricultural activity not only produces commodities which enter market channels, but it also generates certain by-products which may have an undesirable effect on environmental media (air, water and land). In particular, agricultural activity may impair the quality of nearby surface water in terms of the intended use or uses of the water. Such impairment from agricultural sources may occur in the form

* The research reported in this chapter was conducted under a project, Economic Evaluation of the Effects of Selected Crop Practices on Non-Agricultural Uses of Water, supported in part by funds provided by the U.S. Department of Interior under the Water Resources Research Act of 1964, P.L. 88-379, Agreement No. 14-31-0001-3272.

of sedimentation, excessive plant nutrient run-off, animal waste, and pesticides. The traditional basis for economic analysis of such problems has been the concept of 'externality' [10]. More recently, Kneese and his associates [6, 7, 12] have utilized the framework of management of common property resources for problems of this nature. It is this latter formulation which underlies the linear programming analysis presented in this chapter. Viewing the agricultural-environmental complex as a problem in common property resource management, it is important that public bodies charged with decision making have estimates of the impact on the private sector of increasing the level of quality in the publicly-held environmental media (air, water and land). The analysis which follows provides an example of a procedure for generating this kind of information. The specific example deals with estimating the consequences for private farm income of improving water quality in a reservoir by shifting to agricultural practices which reduce erosion.

1.3. The scope and importance of the erosion–sedimentation problem

Although the economic and social importance of the impact of agriculture on the environment cannot accurately be ascertained by examining physical magnitudes, nevertheless, such examination does provide a perspective. In the case of soil erosion and sedimentation, it has been estimated that nearly 3 million tons of soil are washed annually from cultivated, barren or overgrazed land in the United States [5]. This loss usually leads to decreased agricultural productivity.

In addition, when the sediment is deposited in water it causes damage in the form of reduced reservoir capacity and undesirable effects on water quality. Deterioration of water quality affects aquatic organisms and also the uses of water for drinking and recreation. Closely related to the effect of the sediment itself on water quality is the role of sediment in transport of certain plant nutrients which, in high concentrations, may also have a detrimental effect on water quality.

Sedimentation damage for the Upper Mississippi Basin alone has been estimated to be $ 25 million per year (1960 dollars) [14]. Much of this damage can be attributed to agricultural practices adopted to increase individual farm income. Thus, an important public policy question involves the income consequences of reducing sedimentation.

2. Empirical setting for analysis

2.1. Description of watershed

A 1200-acre watershed, Forest Glen, in eastern Illinois was selected as the
site for our study (fig. 1). A watershed has a distinct advantage over a
political unit for erosion–sedimentation analysis. The source of water-
borne sediment entering the reservoir or lake must come from land in the
watershed. Consequently, a more complete accounting can be made of the
sources of sediment than would be the case if the unit of analysis contained
parts of several watersheds. However, this advantage is often offset by the
need for an additional governmental administrative unit, organized to deal
with problems on a watershed basis, to plan and control the economic
activities of the watershed.

The soils in the watershed are of six different types (fig. 1). Because
these types range from level and highly-productive soils to rather steep and
unproductive soils it is important that the watershed be subdivided into
soil and slope classes to estimate agricultural income. From the standpoint
of the effect on sedimentation in the reservoir, it is also important to sub-
divide the watershed; the susceptibility of the soil to erosion depends on
soil type and slope. The fraction of soil which actually erodes from a
particular field and which, in turns, enters the reservoir depends largely on
the distance of the field from the reservoir. Consequently, the watershed
was further subdivided into four classes based on the elevation of the land
above the reservoir. Thus, the watershed area was divided into 51 separate
land areas (table 1).

There are presently 12 farms within the watershed boundary. Corn and
soybeans are the main crops presently grown on these farms. Since these
are cultivated row crops, the amount of soil erosion is presently higher
than it would be if, for example, the watershed had more of the area in
meadow.

2.2. Description of planned reservoir use

The reservoir of approximately 55 acres will be used primarily for recreation. Fishing, boating, and various water sports are planned for the reservoir. It is also possible that, at some time in the future, the need for such
other uses as water for human consumption or irrigation may emerge.
However, the immediate purpose is recreational.

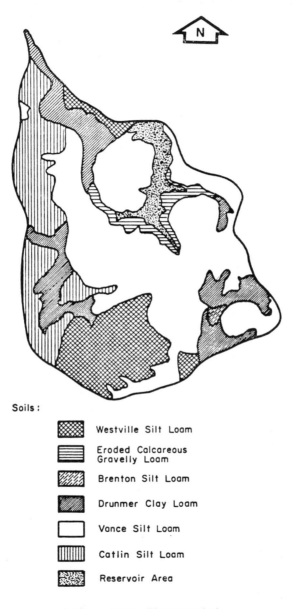

Soils:

Westville Silt Loam

Eroded Calcareous
Gravelly Loam

Brenton Silt Loam

Drunmer Clay Loam

Vance Silt Loam

Catlin Silt Loam

Reservoir Area

Fig. 1. Forest Glen watershed.

Table 1

Land area by soil type, elevation, and slope. Forest Glen watershed

Soil type, elevation, and slope [a]	Area in acres	Soil type, elevation, and slope	Area in acres	Soil type, elevation, and slope	Area in acres
1 WAE	52.57	18 HDF	0.92	35 VAT	57.16
2 WAS	84.70	19 BCF	5.05	36 VBD	4.13
3 WAF	6.43	20 BDT	2.30	37 VBE	22.50
4 WAT	3.21	21 DAS	0.23	38 VBF	39.30
5 WBE	1.15	22 DAF	1.38	39 VBT	99.60
6 WBS	11.48	23 DAT	91.15	40 VCD	12.63
7 WBF	1.84	24 DBD	0.46	41 VCE	30.77
8 WBT	6.66	25 DBS	0.61	42 VCT	152.90
9 NCD	2.29	26 DBF	0.92	43 VDD	98.00
10 WCS	1.38	27 DBT	20.43	44 VDE	6.66
11 WCF	6.98	28 DCD	0.69	45 VDF	3.40
12 WDD	2.98	29 DCF	5.28	46 VDT	36.50
13 HCE	0.92	30 DCT	53.00	47 CAF	16.99
14 HCF	2.53	31 DDD	0.23	48 CAT	170.10
15 HCT	0.69	32 DDF	0.46	49 CBF	0.92
16 HDD	25.94	33 DDT	9.64	50 CBT	25.74
17 HDE	1.61	34 VAF	15.15	51 CCT	1.38

[a] The first letter gives the soil type, the next letters gives the contour divisions and the last letter gives the slope. The key is as follows:

W – Westville soil   A – 50 feet or more elevation above reservoir
H – Hennepin soil   B – 40 to 50 feet   ,,   ,,   ,,
B – Brenton soil   C – 30 to 40 feet   ,,   ,,   ,,
D – Drummer soil   D – less than 30 feet   ,,   ,,   ,,
V – Vance soil   D – 12% slope
C – Catlin soil   E –   8% slope
    S –   6% slope
    F –   4% slope
    T –   3% and less than 4% slope

3. The linear programming model

3.1. Constraints

The land areas in each of the soil type-elevation-slope classes in table 1 form a set of 51 constraints on maximization of farm income in the watershed. The final constraint is the permitted level of annual sedimentation in the reservoir. As shown later, this constraint is parameterized and the consequences on net farm income are estimated.

3.2. Activities

For each of the land areas, except the very unproductive Hennepin soil, nine crop sequences are considered as alternatives (table 2). These crop sequences span a wide range in farm income per acre. The crop sequences also vary greatly in their susceptibility to soil erosion and hence the rate of sedimentation into the reservoir. The gross soil erosion for each activity was estimated by the Universal Soil Loss Equation [15]. Estimates of sediment deposited in the reservoir for each activity were based on a method proposed by Roehl [11].

Table 2

Net returns for various crop sequences

Soil type slope (%)	Westville		Hennepin			Brenton	Drummer		Vance		Catlin
	0–4	4–12	0–4	4–8	8–12	0–4	0–4	4–12	0–4	4–12	0–4
Crop Sequence [a]					(dollars per acre) [b]						
Continuous corn	32.70	30.80	–	–	–	68.85	67.15	56.50	46.60	36.69	62.65
CSbCOx	25.20	21.23	–	–	–	51.39	50.98	46.00	33.81	26.43	46.95
CSbOx	23.00	18.69	–	–	–	46.38	46.41	38.80	29.76	23.32	41.86
COx	21.20	17.88	–	–	–	43.40	41.24	34.30	28.63	21.67	39.83
CSbCOM	28.60	23.27	–	–	–	49.88	49.01	43.90	34.47	26.82	45.93
CCOM	29.11	24.38	–	–	–	49.44	47.56	41.23	35.25	26.99	46.10
CSbWM	26.80	21.63	–	–	–	45.92	45.64	38.91	31.30	24.83	42.11
COMM	28.66	23.52	–	–	–	42.15	39.76	34.23	31.73	24.00	39.65
OMMM	27.42	22.34	16.50	18.31	11.87	34.09	31.49	26.21	27.72	20.52	32.72

[a] C = corn; Sb = soybeans; O = oats; Ox = oats with legume catch crop; M = meadow.
[b] Net returns above direct costs, labor costs and fertilizer costs.

3.3. Objective function

Each crop sequence contributes an expected net income per acre to the objective function which is total net income for the watershed (table 2). These incomes differ according to the soil type and slope.

3.4. Summary of model

To summarize, we maximize

$$\sum_i \sum_j \sum_k \sum_s C_{ijks} X_{ijks}$$

subject to

$$\sum_s X_{ijks} \leqq B_{ijk} \qquad \text{for all } i, j, k$$

and

$$\sum_i \sum_j \sum_k \sum_s Q_{ijks} X_{ijks} \leqq Q$$

where X_{ijks} is the acreage of the sth crop sequence on the ith soil type, jth slope group, and kth elevation class; C_{ijks} is the net return above direct costs for the indicated crop sequence on the indicated area of land; B_{ijk} is the area of land in the ith soil type, jth slope group, and kth elevation class; Q is the maximum annual quantity of sediment permitted to be deposited in the reservoir; Q_{ijks} is the amount of sediment deposited from the indicated area of land and crop sequence.

4. Results

4.1. Choice of sediment restriction level

Because there is no explicit, easily calculated market price for the sedimentation damage in the reservoir, the consequences of a range of values were estimated (fig. 2). Given the present agricultural practices in the watershed, it is estimated at approximately 3400 tons per year. From the standpoint of capacity alone, this would mean a reservoir life of about 670 years. However, the quality of the water in terms of turbidity and its suitability for recreation is estimated to be adequate at one-half (1700 tons) of that expected under present agricultural practices. It should be noted that achieving this level of sedimentation reduces farm income from $ 55,000 to $ 50,570 (fig. 2).

There is also a productivity loss to the soil as a result of erosion. The Soil Conservation Service has made estimates for each soil of the loss that could be tolerated and still maintain soil productivity at an adequate level. Although these tolerances are somewhat arbitrary, they do provide a set of guidelines. Using these soil loss tolerances as a standard, the sediment would be restricted to 1500 tons per year, a more demanding restriction than that assumed necessary to meet water quality standards.

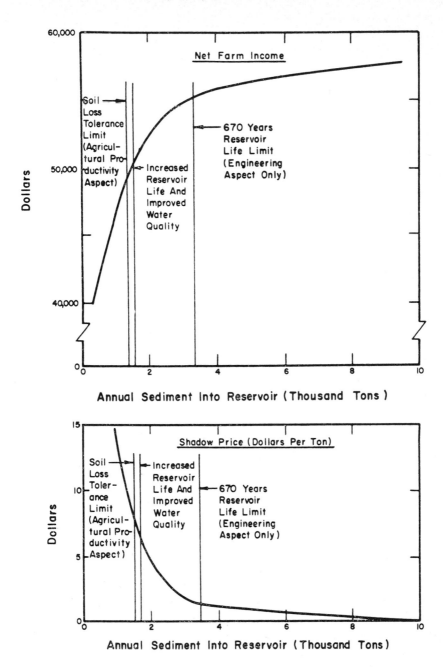

Fig. 2. Relationship between net farm income, shadow price and sediment level.

4.2. Shadow prices

Each level of sedimentation has an associated shadow price (fig. 2). These indicate the agricultural income foregone by decreasing the sediment entering the reservoir by one ton. These may be used as guides by decision-making agencies in their deliberations concerning the 'correct' standard for sedimentation and they may also be useful in certain incentive systems (see below). Further, they may also be useful in comparing the cost of keeping the soil in place by conservation practices with removal of sediment from the reservoir by dredging. Of course, dredging would alleviate the storage capacity problem but would not deal directly with the turbidity aspect.

5. Policy implications

5.1. Effluent charges

The results indicate the minimum-cost method of achieving various levels of sedimentation control, or viewed in another way, the highest-return set of agricultural activities for each of various levels of sedimentation. This trade-off itself provides useful information but does not imply any particular form of incentive system, i.e. subsidies, effluent charges, or regulation. Baumol and Oates [1] have suggested that arbitrary standards be established and that a set of charges be imposed that will approximately meet these standards. In the case of soil erosion, the watershed shadow cost (fig. 2) would need to be adjusted to reflect differences in soils, crops, and distance from the reservoir.

5.2. Subsidies

Subsidization is also an alternative method of implementation of a policy to achieve a given level of sediment control. The level of subsidy for each field could too be based on the loss of income (shadow cost) incurred by shifting to agricultural practices which reduce erosion. Again, the nature of such a shift would be specified in the watershed solution and it could vary from field to field. A subsidization scheme, as well as regulation with enforcement by fines and penalties, would require sufficient administrative surveillance to insure that the subsidized practices were indeed being followed. If the effluent charge has a satisfactory technical base and is periodically adjusted according to results, the charge provides an implementation method with a smaller enforcement burden than either subsidization or direct regulation.

6. Concluding remarks

6.1. Modification of watershed model

The preceding analysis of the trade-off between farm income and sedimentation in a 1200-acre watershed represents only an illustration of the logic and method which is needed in a wide variety of environmental problem areas. Given the watershed as a unit of analysis, there are a number of straightforward extensions of the model which can, in principle, be easily made. For example, in addition to sediment, agricultural activity generates other possible pollutants, such as excess plant nutrients and pesticides. The levels of these pollutants in the receiving waters can be treated as additional constraints. This would permit a more comprehensive analysis of the implications of water quality improvement. However, in contrast to the description of the movement of sediment from various locations to the reservoir, very little is known about the dynamic changes in form and location of the other potential pollutants.

In addition to extending the list of potential pollutants, the production processes might also be extended to include other means of reducing soil erosion. Further, the possibility of removing sediment from the reservoir might be added as an alternative with a specified cost.

While the above extensions would require no conceptual modification of the model, there are others, more difficult, which demand attention. Clearly, the problem of pricing the quality of the water is a critical one. The analysis presented above gives only the opportunity cost of achieving various levels of water quality (with respect to only one quality characteristic – sedimentation). Nothing is said about the gains from such quality improvement. Even if standards are established, pricing of the benefits is implicit. Among others, Castle *et al.* [2] and Lave [8] have discussed the difficulties in valuing environmental quality and the need for improved estimates of such values. At the core of the valuation problem is the manner by which institutions provide for aggregation of individual preferences regarding environmental quality and the translation of such collective preferences into decisions. The operational value of the type of analysis presented above would be enhanced if these essentially political processes were more adequately recognized [3].

6.2. Units of analysis larger than watersheds

Many of the extensions to the watershed model suggested above could also be made to a model covering a larger geographic area such as a river basin. The larger model would be appropriate if, for example, substantial sedimentation or pollution damage occurred beyond the limits of the watershed.

Further, as we extend to a larger geographic area, the prices of products and costs of inputs no longer can be assumed to be independent of quantities sold or purchased and some type of non-linear programming might be employed [13, pp. 18–20]. The close connection between the rates of use of the natural resources over periods of time and the environmental quality problem implies that an intertemporal extension may be important in some applications [13, Part VI]. The spatial aspects of the watershed analysis presented above consisted primarily of the area-to-area flow of sediment within the four areas of the watershed. A larger river-basin model might consider separation of the basin into production and consumption regions with provision for transport costs for interregional transfers of commodities [4, Part III, and 13].

The above represent the modifications of the basic programming model for which we have precedents and experience. More difficult, and also more important for operational realism, are those modifications which incorporate the institutional alternatives for reflecting individual preferences in the management of the publicly-held environmental media. The pay-offs to successful research in this area will be substantial. Some work on this difficult topic has been started by, among others, Haefle [3], but much remains to be done.

References

[1] Baumol, W. J. and W. E. Oates, 1971, The use of standards and prices for protection of the environment, Swedish Journal of Economics, 73(1), 42–54.
[2] Castle, E. N. et al., 1972, Multi-Disciplinary Study of Water Quality Relationships: A Case Study of Yaquina Bay, Oregon, Special Report 348, Agricultural Experiment Station, Oregon State University, Corvallis, Oregon.
[3] Haefle, E. T., 1972, Environmental Quality as a Problem of Social Choice, in: A. V. Kneese and B. T. Bower, eds., Environmental Quality Analysis: Theory and Methods in Social Sciences, Baltimore and London: The Johns Hopkins Press, ch. 8.
[4] Heady, E. O., ed., 1971, Economic Models and Quantitative Methods for Decisions and Planning in Agriculture, Ames, Iowa: The Iowa State University Press.
[5] Klein, C. L., 1969, Sediment Pollution and Water Quality. Proceedings of the National Conference on Sediment Control, U.S. Department of Housing and Urban Development, September 14–16, 1969.

[6] Kneese, A. V., 1971, Environmental pollution: economics and policy, American Economic Review, 61(2), 153–166.

[7] Kneese, A. V. and B. T. Bower, eds., 1972, Environmental Quality Analysis: Theory and Method in the Social Sciences, Baltimore and London: The Johns Hopkins Press.

[8] Lave, L. B., 1972, Air Pollution Damage: Some Difficulties in Estimating Value of Abatement, in: A. V. Kneese and B. T. Bower, eds., Environmental Quality Analysis: Theory and Methods in Social Sciences, Baltimore and London: The Johns Hopkins Press, ch. 6.

[9] Mayer, L. V. and S. H. Hargrove, 1971, Food Costs, Farm Incomes, and Crop Yields With Restrictions on Fertilizer Use, CAED Report No. 38. Center for Agricultural and Economic Development, Ames, Iowa: Iowa State University.

[10] Mishan, E. J., 1971, The post war literature on externalities: an interpretive essay, Journal of Economic Literature, 9(1), 1–28.

[11] Roehl, J. W., 1962, Sediment source areas, delivery ratios and influencing morphological factors, International Association Hydrologists Pub. No. 59.

[12] Russell, C. S. and W. O. Spofford, Jr., 1972, A Quantitative Model for Residuals Management Decisions, in: A. V. Kneese and B. T. Bower, eds., Environmental Quality Analysis: Theory and Methods in Social Sciences, Baltimore and London: The Johns Hopkins Press, ch. 4.

[13] Takayama, T. and G. G. Judge, 1971, Spatial and Temporal Price and Allocation Models, Amsterdam: North-Holland Publishing Company.

[14] U.S. Department of the army, Corps of Engineers, 1970, Fluvial Sediment, Upper Mississippi River Comprehensive Basin Study Report, Vol. III, Appendix G.

[15] Wischmeier, W. H. and D. D. Smith, 1965, Predicting Rainfall-Erosion Losses from Cropland East of the Rocky Mountains, Guide for Selection of Practices for Soil and Water Conservation. Soil and Water Conservation Research Division, Agricultural Research Service, U.S. Department of Agriculture in cooperation with Purdue Agricultural Experiment Station, Agriculture Handbook No. 282, Washington, D.C.

CHAPTER 34

Capital budgeting and financial management in linear programming models

C. B. BAKER

University of Illinois

1. Introduction

Capital budgeting is a method for evaluating investment expectations. Following Bierman and Smidt [3] we define an investment as a commitment of resources to produce returns expected over a "reasonably long period" of time. Any production activity might be considered an investment. 'Investments' are production activities that involve several accounting periods. For most investments of empirical significance, relevant evaluations often are complicated. Outcomes of a given investment may effect and be affected by outcomes of the current firm and outcomes of other investments being considered either in or without association with the given investment. Expectations may also be uncertain. And means to counter uncertainty may be costly.

Capital budgeting is applicable over a wide range of problems common to firms in the private sector. Examples are technical and organizational innovations; replacement decisions; comparisons of leasing, buying or custom-hiring; retirement and estate planning; credit and debt management; and many related problems. Indeed, as will be shown below, many of these problems are interrelated. Hence appropriately specified linear programming models can vastly facilitate comparisons among alternatives in terms relevant to the decision maker and subject to constraints he must take into account.

Capital budgeting is also applicable over a wide range of problems met by decision makers in the public sector. Indeed it is the method basic to cost-benefit analyses, designed to yield estimates on which public investments will be judged feasible or otherwise. Despite formal similarity, however, public sector applications are complicated by the necessity to identify socially-relevant objective functions; to incorporate the externalities that are ignored in private sector models, but which may be the essence of the public sector model; to specify the socially relevant constraints, and to decide upon rates of discount that reflect appropriate opportunity costs of resources proposed for the public investment. While many suggestions below may apply to models appropriate to public sector models, they are, in fact, developed in the specific context of private sector decision making.

2. Objectives in capital budgeting

The managerial objectives of the capital budgeter are straightforward: to arrive at a basis for comparing investment alternatives in terms appropriate to managerial objectives with respect to the firm as a whole. To identify the firm-wise objective as utility maximization is not especially helpful, without further specification. It seems plausible to assume that an expectation of higher income or equity in assets is preferred to an expectation of lower income or equity, though there may well be important short-run trade-offs between income and equity. In either case the mean expectation may well be subject to trade-off with respect to variation of the mean expectation, and/or, to financial capacity to bear the consequences of adverse outcomes. Given perfect expectations with respect to relevant markets, claims on income expectations do not differ from expected equity in assets. Hence the choice of income and/or equity is intimately related to the management of uncertain expectations. The management alternatives relevant to uncertainty are, broadly: to avoid it; to shift its costs; or to develop the means to bear the consequences of uncertainty.

3. Financial constraints in investment decisions

For many economists, investment analysis is a topic in production economics. As already noted, it is but a special case of a production activity analysis. For others, however, investment is a topic in financial management, inasmuch as it deals with resource acquisition and/or portfolio adjustment. Models for investment analysis often have been weakened by a failure to integrate both production and finance in the model specification. We propose to do this without ignoring important subtleties that reveal the interactions between financial and production relationships. Many are linked closely with the concept of liquidity, a valuable attribute in the presence of uncertain expectations.

It is difficult to conceive of a rational decision maker who makes an investment that is not *expected* to increase the value of the firm. However, the first effect of an investment is to transform the asset structure of the firm, ordinarily reducing its liquidity. The investment transaction leaves the decision maker's accounting equity in the firm unchanged. The outright purchase of a new machine, a unit of land, or a materials-handling system simply substitutes the value of the new asset(s) for the cash used in the purchase. A debt-financed purchase leaves a part of the new purchase represented among liabilities — claims held by others on the firm's assets — and a substitution of cash for new asset value, in the amount of the down payment. In either case, liquidity of the firm is lessened by the investment transaction.

We define liquidity as the ability to generate cash on demand. Liquidity is, of course, relatively high in a firm whose main assets are money and close substitutes for money. Liquidity is lessened as cash diminishes relative to the value of other assets. The diminution is slight when the other assets are highly marketable and can be detached from the firm for conversion to cash with little or no effect on the total value of the firm. An asset may be said to be completely liquid if its sale would result in cash receipts equal to its pre-sale contribution to total firm value. It may be said to be completely illiquid if it could not be sold without dissolution of the firm. Virtually all assets in real firms lie on a continuum between complete liquidity and complete illiquidity. Even cash, as normally held in the firm, can hardly be said to be completely liquid. And there are few resources that could not be sold without complete destruction of the capacity to preserve some value of the firm.

However, we introduce the concept of credit to identify an important added source of liquidity. We define cr as the ability to borrow, representing cr of type L as given by:

$$cr_L = a + b_1 x_1 + b_2 x_2 + \ldots b_n x_n,$$ \hfill (1)

where a is the borrowing capacity associated with 'personal characteristics' of the applicant: individual, corporate or group; b_1 and b_2 are coefficients that describe the reaction of lender L to his perceptions of the borrower's income expectations and equity position(s), respectively; and $b_3 \ldots b_n$ describe other rules of action in the lender's behavior. Total credit of the borrower is the total of cr, summed over all available lenders. It is worthwhile to note in this concept that credit is not an asset of the lender that is provided to the borrower. We shall call *those* quantities 'loan funds'. Rather, credit is an asset of the borrower, exchanged for loan funds in the borrowing transaction. We make this obvious note in recognition of the confused state of the literature with respect to nomenclature in loan transactions.

In our concept, credit provides a useful source of liquidity in the firm. Insofar as it remains unused, it provides the decision maker with a source of cash that can be generated on demand. Credit liquidity is especially valuable, relative to sales liquidity, in that cash provided by a loan transaction does not require detaching an asset from the production organization of the firm, though it does modify the financial organization through the claim it provides to the lender. However, owing to rules of thumb used by lenders, borrowing reduces credit by an amount that is equal to or in excess of loan proceeds. This result derives from the usual requirement of most lenders for safety margins in the loan transaction.

This digression is to establish the plausibility of conceiving credit as a primary financial constraint in capital budgeting. The other financial constraints are cash, debt obligations and other financial requirements to be observed in comparing investment alternatives. The final point to be made here is that these constraints are most usefully employed in relation to production alternatives and constraints, not separately and independent of the production relationships [1]. We shall find that this procedure provides for the use of appealing alternatives in the specification of linear programming models that include investment choices where uncertain expectations cannot be ignored.

4. Modifying linear programming specifications to account for uncertain expectations

4.1.

Let x_j^t be a unit of investment in the jth alternative in period t; and r_j^t, the contribution made by the unit to the investor's economic objective. We can form a model in which x_j^t can be compared with alternatives within t and in other periods relevant within the investor's planning horizon: To maximize

$$Z = \sum_{j=1}^{n} \sum_{t=1}^{T} r_j^t x_j^t, \tag{2}$$

subject to

$$\sum_{i=1}^{m} \sum_{j=1}^{n} a_{ij}^t x_j^t \lesseqgtr b_i^t \quad (t = 1 \dots T); \tag{2a}$$

and

$$x_j^t \gtreqqless 0; \qquad\qquad\qquad (2b)$$

where a_{ij}^t is the amount of constraint (or requirement), b_j^t, used (or contributed) by a unit of x_j^t. Each of the resulting column vectors represents a 'capital budget' in the sense that the coefficient, r_j^t, is the contribution to Z of a unit of (investment) activity, x_j^t, produced with specified inputs, a_{ij}, in each of the time periods relevant to the capital investment. The quantities, r_j^t and b_i^t, can, of course, include cash. But they also can include such other resources and requirements as may be relevant in the choice environment.

Thus Model 2 is highly flexible in representing investment alternatives in a useful decision and planning context. Z can be specified as a cash flow, with suitable adjustments in r_j^t and x_j^t. Cash requirements can be represented in the definitions of r_j^t and/or a_{ij}^t. Otherwise, Z can be specified as an income residual, with appropriate imputations reflected in the definitions of r_j^t and/or a_{ij}^t. Z can be specified as a present value, V_0, a sum of $r_j^t x_j^t$, each suitably discounted prior to summations indicated in Model 2. Finally, Z can be specified as a value at the planning horizon, V_T, of accumulated equity [4]. Moreover, combinations are possible among the first two alternatives and either of the last two. This is an important feature of multi-period models. In multi-period models, the planning period is finite. Hence assets unused at the planning horizon remain to be valued. So also do unpaid debts. In summary, the objective in Model 2 can be stated in terms of income, summed over time, a net value, present or future, or combinations of both.

The parameters in Model 2 are specified as single-valued expectations. This representation clearly violates the empirical conditions of most important investment choices. Prices at which products are sold and inputs bought are subject to uncertainty. So also are resource capacities, productivities, and other constraints and requirements. Were the effects among certain expectations evenly distributed among alternatives to be compared, perhaps Model 2 could be used as at least a guide to choices in levels and combinations in which to activate investment alternatives. But there is no a priori basis for assuming homogeneity in outcome variations and many empirical bases for supposing the variations to differ among important alternatives. Hence there is a need to improve upon the way uncertainty is accounted for in modelling investment alternatives. An important method for doing this is found in quadratic programming models.

4.2. Quadratic programming models

Let Z, in alternative terms already discussed, be given by:

$$Z = \sum_{j=1}^{n} \sum_{t=1}^{T} \bar{r}_j^t x_j^t - \sum_{t=1}^{T} \alpha_t \sum_{j=1}^{n} \sum_{k=1}^{n} \sigma_{jk}^t x_j^t x_k^t = \text{a maximum,} \qquad (3)$$

subject to

$$\sum_{i=1}^{m} \sum_{j=1}^{n} a_{ij}^t x_j^t \lessgtr b_i^t \qquad (t = 1 \ldots T); \qquad (3a)$$

and

$$x_j^t \geqq 0. \qquad (3b)$$

The parameters, $\bar{r}_j^t$, a_{ij}^t and b_i^t, already have been identified, except that in (3), $\bar{r}$ is the mean of a probability distribution of values for r. The parameter, α_t reflects the contribution of the interaction terms, $\sigma_{jk}^t x_j^t x_k^t$ to the value of Z. Thus the objective function in Model 3 provides a basis for introducing explicitly the variances and covariances expected in the outcomes from the various investment alternatives. Conceptually, this represents a considerable improvement over the specifications made possible in Model 2. However, Model 3 is subject to important limitations.

The first is the limited number of alternatives and constraints that can be considered in one model. Algorithms currently available limit the operational size of Model 3, relative to that of Model 2. Moreover, given the operational limit in model size, the number of real alternatives that can be compared is reduced in Model 3 by the need to incorporate the variance–covariance matrix into the tableau.

A second limitation is perhaps more serious. The intellectual appeal of introducing variance–covariance properties of expectations is quite clear. And the size limitations may well be temporary, given reasonably expected progress in computer hardware and computer programs. But the plain truth is that there exists little empirical evidence to support the hypothesis that decision makers in fact make decisions on the basis of outcomes that include the variance (or other measures of dispersions) with respect to mean expectations. And even if there were, the estimation of α_t is a heroic empirical problem.[1] Therefore, it may be useful to investigate alternative model specifications that may reflect decision behavior with a reasonable amount of intellectual appeal and perhaps greater empirical plausibility.

---

[1] The alternative remains, of course, of generating solutions over a range of values for α_t, leaving to the decision maker the task of selecting the solution consistent with his utility function [5]. Even this procedure presupposes, however, that the mean and variance of outcome distributions are relevant in the decision maker's utility function.

Before turning to alternatives, however, we digress to suggest a simple modification of linear programming modelling to introduce variance–covariance properties. In Model 2, let the row constraints include cash rows suitable to represent a cash flow. Such a specification is provided in table 1. The column vectors specify cash transfers between S seasons in each of T periods, and from the last season of one period to the first season of the following period. The last column transfers any cash surplus to the objective function, Z, which is to be maximized.

Table 1

Cash flow component of a multi-period linear programming tableau

Cash rows	Cash transfers: within and between periods									Constraint	
	In Period 1: From			In period 2: From			In Period T: From				
	Season		to next	Season		to next	Season				
	1–2	2...	Period	1–2	2...	Period	1–2	2...	to Z	Relation	Level
Period 1:											
Cash 1	1									$\leqslant$	b
Cash 2	-1	1								$=$	0
...		...								...	
Cash S			1							$=$	0
Period 2:											
Cash 1			-1	1						$=$	0
Cash 2				-1	1					$=$	0
...					...					...	
Cash S						1				$=$	0
...										...	
Period T:											
Cash 1						-1	1			$=$	0
Cash 2							-1	1		$=$	0
...								...		...	
Cash S									1	$=$	0
...										...	
Z							...		1	$=$ maximum	

If the model is specified to reflect all inflows and outflows *in the cash components* of the model, there need be no entries in the objective function other than for the single entry in the last column. This simple property provides the means for introducing variance–covariance expectations in a manner particularly relevant to the study of investment alternatives of the firm. Two variances are computationally relevant: the variance of outcomes of the firm as a whole, currently organized; and the variance associated with outcomes of the activity proposed for addition to the firm. The other term to be considered is the covariance of the two. But the variance of outcome of the firm as currently organized is represented simply by the variance of the cash flow, the activity unit in the last column vector in table 1. Hence the variance–covariance matrix relevant in the computation is the simple 2×2 matrix of table 2. The remainder of the variance–covariance matrix would consist of zeros.

Table 2

Variance–covariance matrix for a firm modelled with two entries in the objective function: current organization and added activity

Source of variation in Z	Measure of variation associated with	
	Current firm organization	Added activity
Current firm organization	σ_{CC}	σ_{CA}
Added activity		σ_{AA}

A footnote might be added for those critical of representing all final outcomes in a cash flow. Two alternatives are possible: (1) include in the cash row(s) the value of assets and debts accumulated at the horizon of the planning period; or (2) add a row in which to collect these values, providing for a separate value transfer to the objective function. The second alternative would add to the size of the variance–covariance matrix. But the addition to the total matrix size still would fall far short of additions typical of the usual specification of quadratic programming models.[2]

4.3. Liquidity management specifications

In conventional specifications of linear programming models, liquidity values are largely ignored. If a cash row is specified as an inequality, a

---

[2] The total savings in size of matrix is greater than might be obvious by reference to table 1, in the case of a multi-period model. The suggested modification would leave only one (or two) variance(s) to be represented regardless of the number of periods in the model. Otherwise, the number of variances to be represented would be multiplied by the number of periods.

C. B. Baker

slack vector is provided with a c_j value of zero. For example, see the first row in table 1. If credit constraints are specified, comparable slack vectors are provided for, all with zero values in the objective function. Insurance is not likely to appear at all.

An appealing alternative provided by Model 2 lies in specifying column vectors for reserving cash, assigning objective function values for each dollar of cash in season S that is reserved for that reason. This value would represent an opportunity cost of the specified cash in a non-reserved use: a value that must be exceeded by the return in any use to which the cash would otherwise be allocated. Relevant specifications are suggested for S seasons in table 3. As a practical matter, a minimum might well be the savings in transactions costs charged against a demand deposit. 'Transaction motives' generate a demand for cash in general, and furnish a basis for estimating the size of the relevant c_j. Clearly the alternative is plausible. Equally clearly, the proper assignment of c_j is an empirical problem. In general, the value may be expected to vary among seasons (and periods), for a given decision maker, and among decision makers as well.

Table 3

Specifying reservation prices for cash in linear programming models

Cash rows	Transfer cash		Reserve cash		Constraint	
	1 2	S Z	$S1$	SS	Relation	Level
C1	1		1 $\ldots$	1	$=$	b
C2	-1				$=$	0
$\ldots$	$\ldots$				$\ldots$	$\ldots$
CS		1			$=$	0
Z		1	C_1 $\ldots$	C_S	$=$	M

It also is plausible to assume the value of reserved cash to be related to organizational features of the firm. For the firm organized to yield a small variance in Z, it is plausible to assume a relatively low reservation price for cash. The reverse might hold for the firm organized for a higher mean expectation of Z despite a large variation in Z. On the other hand, in a positivistic sense, a manager might be observed to reflect his aversion to risk in both ways: high reservation prices on liquidity and organizational choices that reduce variance in Z.

Insurance alternatives may also affect the reservation price of cash: level of indemnity and/or scope of events against which insurance is purchased. Let the cost of an indemnifiable event (for example, fire) be insurable at an annual cost, P. The decision maker's alternative is to set aside a reserve, R, to meet the cost of the event, should it materialize. The cost of the reserve is the rate, e, that could be earned with the fund, allocated to its best use(s) within the firm. To offset a part of this cost, perhaps the reserve could be invested at rate, i, in financial instruments that could be readily liquidated. The alternatives are thus (1) insure, at a cost, P; or (2) reserve, at a cost, $R(e-i)$. In this comparison, the decision maker is led to insure if

$$\frac{P}{e-i} \leqq R. \tag{4}$$

Credit, too, furnishes a source of liquidity, insofar as it is reserved — that is, left unused, in contrast with use in borrowing. Credit constraints can be treated in a manner similar to that suggested for cash constraints. For each source and type of loan available to the decision maker, a slack vector can be replaced by a 'reserving' vector, in which a reservation price can be specified. The reservation price will represent an opportunity cost of credit exchanged for a loan. Hence to activate a borrowing vector would require the value of the loan proceeds to exceed the interest cost of the loan (and, of course, the transaction costs of borrowing) by enough to offset the reservation price. The empirical problem of proper specifications is met by determining responses of decision makers to the use of credit in borrowing. The reservation price of those averse to debt financing will be high relative to the reservation price of those willing to use credit more widely and freely. The empirical problems are not easily resolved. Yet they are not insoluble either [2]. With resources comparable to those used in finding other parameter estimates, considerable empirical as well as logical relevance can be added to investment models by introducing credit management vectors.

In table 4 we display the vectors required in a linear programming specification to allow for a comparison of cash, credit and insurance as alternatives in providing liquidity. The reserving vectors include objective function values for the increments reserved. The values decline over the range, $c_{1...j}(j = C, I, CC$ for cash, insurance and credit, respectively), reflecting a diminishing value associated with greater quantities reserved. In the row constraints, we include maximum limits in each of the classes, $1...i$ ($i = C, I, CC$, for cash, insurance and credit, respectively), for each of the values of reserved liquidity. Thus the activation of $V_1(CR)$ is subject to

Table 4

Liquidity management vectors: cash, insurance, credit

Row description		Transfer cash S 1 2 ... Z	Acquire reserves C to CR (Insure) 1 ... 1	Acquire reserves CC to CCR	Cash V(CR) 1 2 ... C	Insurance V(Ins.) 1 2 ...	Credit V(CCR) 1 2 ... CC	Relation	Level
Cash	C1	1	1 1 ... 1					$=$	$b(C)$
	C2	-1						$=$	0
	...								
	CS	1						$=$	0
Credit	CC			1				$=$	$b(CC)$
Reserves	CR		-1		1 1 ... 1			$=$	0
	IR		$-\frac{I}{P}$ ... $-\frac{I}{P}$			1 1 ... 1		$=$	0
	CCR			-1			1 1 ... 1	$=$	0
Cash reserve limits	CR1				1			$\leqq$	$b(CR1)$
	CR2				1			$\leqq$	$b(CR2)$
	...								
	CRC				1			$\leqq$	$b(CRC)$
Insurance limits	IR1					1		$\leqq$	$b(IR1)$
	IR2					1		$\leqq$	$b(IR2)$
	...								
	IRI					1		$\leqq$	$b(IR1)$
Credit reserve limits	CCR1						1	$\leqq$	$b(CCR1)$
	CCR2						1	$\leqq$	$b(CCR2)$
	...								
	CCRCC						1	$\leqq$	$b(CCRCC)$
	Z	1			$C_1^c C_2^c ... C_C^c C_C^c$	$C_1^I C_2^I ... C_I^I$	$C_1^{cc} C_2^{cc} ... C_{cc}^{cc}$	$=$	Maximum

the limit, $b(CR\ 1)$, each unit valued at c_1^C. We have specified cash to be reserved only in the first season, but clearly this specification could, as relevant, be used in any or all seasons.

Similarly, insurance is specified only in terms of a total insurance purchase. However, a set of vectors could be specified, one for each of the insurance alternatives available to the firm. The row constraints, $b(IRI\ \ldots\ IRI)$, are defined as the quantities, R, in (4). The values, $c_1^I \ldots c_I^I$, are defined as the values, $e-i$, in (4). The model is specified to yield optimal quantities of P, as identified in (4).

Credit too, is reflected in table 4 as a single aggregate. In most real world situations, loans are available in a variety of sources and subject to a wide range of terms. Sources and terms of loan could, in turn, be represented in an expanded version of the credit vectors shown in table 4. The result would be a specification, in the constraint set, of a 'credit profile': a structure of credit that characterizes the loan limits, by source and terms, that constrain the decision maker's choices.

The assumptions on which linear programming is based preclude the specification of values for objective function coefficients as being related to levels of activities. The specification of reservation prices that diminish with respect to quantities of liquidity reserved tend to overcome some of the limitations inherent in this limited characteristic of linear programming models. Any further explorations would require use of the linear programming model in a set of simulation runs, designed around a grid of liquidity value specifications.

5. A hypothetical example

In fig. 1 we represent in a simple diagram a plausible assumption on the general relation that might be expected between the value of an increment of cash in reserve and the percent of all cash allocated to use (or reserved). The convex (from below) slopes suggest diminishing utility of such increments. The positions of the relations suggest that the value of given reserved cash might be expected to increase with respect to time. Two factors can be suggested: age, in the case of an unincorporated decision maker; and increasing uncertainty of expectations, regardless of the business form of the decision maker. Numerical approximations are provided in table 5.

In table 6 we indicate a specification of cash reservation that is more efficient (uses less model space) than that of table 4. The efficiency is gained

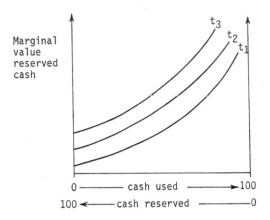

Fig. 1. Hypothetical relation of values of reserved cash to percent of cash used (reserved).

Table 5

Liquidity value of cash reserves (hypothetical)

Percent of cash		Marginal value of reserved cash		
Used	Reserved	Period 1	Period 2	Period 3
90–100	0– 10	0.30	0.32	0.34
61– 90	10– 39	0.15	0.17	0.19
31– 60	40– 69	0.05	0.07	0.09
0– 30	70–100	0.02	0.04	0.06

by elimination of the reserve limit rows required by the more straightforward representation of table 4. The coefficients in table 6 are drawn from the hypothetical values shown in table 5 for period 1. The example values are the same between the two seasons illustrated. They need not be, should reserves have values that differ seasonally. Values in Z may be higher, for example, in a season especially subject to costly uncertain events. Non-reserving uses of cash will be reflected by coefficients in $CR1 \dots CRS$ rows, in the cash-using vectors (e.g. production requirements, debt payments, etc.). Cash-producing vectors (e.g. sales, borrowing, etc.) will be specified with coefficients in the $C1 \dots CS$ rows.

The activity value in the first column vector reflects a high value of a dollar-increment reserved when the reservation level is zero. Thus any cash use (e.g., a_1), draws upon $CA1$ at an opportunity cost of 0.30. Hence cash will first be reserved in this column vector. The opportunity cost, subject

Table 6

Cash liquidity submatrix

| Row description | Reserved C1 at (percent): | | | | | ... | Reserved CS at (percent): | | | | | Cash use | | | Constraint | |
	0	10	40	70	100		0	10	40	70	100	S1	...	SS	Relation	Level
	C11	C12	C13	C14	C15		CS1	CS2	CS3	CS4	CS5					
C1	1	1	1	1	1										$=$	3
...													...		...	
CS							1	1	1	1	1				$=$	0
CA1	-1	-0.9	-0.6	-0.3								a_1			$=$	0
...													...		...	
CAS							-1	-0.9	-0.6	-0.3				a_s	$=$	0
...															...	
Z	0.30	0.15	0.05	0.02		...	0.30	0.15	0.05	0.02			...		$=$	maximum

to which cash is used, is 30 cents until 10 % of all cash in season 1 has been reserved. The value of cash reserved beyond 70 % is zero, the value typically specified for all cash in the usual linear programming model. The values in Z reflect an increasing opportunity cost, as cash reserves are drawn to successively lower levels. The functional relation of fig. 1 can be approximated more closely, the more column vectors that are specified to divide the range of cash reservation between 0 and 100 % of cash available.

Credit may in general be expected to have a lower value in reserve than does cash. Access to credit is less certain than access to cash. However, the difference may be slight, likely something less than the rate of interest. Otherwise, it would be rational for the decision maker to borrow for purposes of providing a cash reserve! Over small ranges of cash levels, this action may indeed be observed, and could well be provided for in a combination of cash-reserving vectors, such as are shown in table 6 and credit-reserving vectors, such as are shown in table 7. The specifications in table 8[3] are drawn from the hypothetical values given in table 7.

Table 7

Liquidity value of B, D credit reserves (hypothetical)

Percent of credit		Marginal value of reserved credit	
Used	Reserved	Source B	Source D
90–100	0– 10	0.25	0.20
61– 90	10– 39	0.20	0.15
31– 60	40– 69	0.02	0.01
0– 30	70–100	0.01	0.005

In table 7 we identify two sources of loan funds, banks (B) and dealers (D), available to the decision maker. The rates of interest might be, respectively, 9 and 15 % per annum. The greater versatility of bank credit makes it more useful as a reserve than is dealer credit. This is reflected in the relative schedules of values, given in table 7.

The first two sets of column vectors in table 8 describe activities comparable to the cash-reserving vectors of table 6, and will not be discussed in detail. Borrowing to provide cash can be done at the bank (BB) or dealer (BD), drawing primarily upon bank and dealer credit at rates A_B and A_D respectively. 'Interaction coefficients' A_D^B and A_B^D reflect a diminution in dealer (bank) credit when borrowing occurs at the bank (dealer). They reflect the plausible assumption that each creditor is responsive, in terms of

---

[3] Table 8 is a modification of a table first published by Vandeputte and Baker [6].

Table 8

Credit liquidity submatrix

Row description	Reserved bank credit at (%)					Reserved dealer credit at (%)					Borrow		Repay		Constraint	
	0 $B11$	10 $B12$	40 $B13$	70 $B14$	100 $B15$	0 $D11$	10 $D12$	40 $D13$	70 $D14$	100 $D15$	B^* BB	D^{**} BD	B^* RB	D^{**} RD	Relation	Level
Cash, by season — $C1$											-1	-1			$=$	C
⋮															⋮	
CS													$1+I$	$1+I$	$=$	0
Credit Capacity, by source — CCB		1	1	1	1										$\leqq$	BC
⋮															⋮	
CCD							1	1	1	1					$\leqq$	BD
Credit Accounting, by source — $CCBA$	-1	-0.9	-0.6	-0.3							A_B	A_B^D			$=$	0
⋮															⋮	
$CCDA$						-1	-0.9	-0.6	-0.3		A_D^B	A_D			$=$	0
Debt Balance, Bank, by season — $DB1$											-1				$=$	0
⋮															⋮	
DBS													$1+I$		$=$	0
Dealer, by season — $DD1$												-1			$=$	0
⋮															⋮	
DDS														$1+I$	$=$	0
Z	0.25	0.20	0.02	0.01		0.20	0.15	0.01	0.005						$=$	maximum

* B is bank.

** D is dealer.

loan limits, to debt outstanding to another creditor. Debt transfers among
seasons have been omitted. In fact, a rather elaborate specification is required
if terms of loan provide for much flexibility in debt management. Repayment
vectors in table 8 show cash used in season S to repay principle plus accumulated interest.

The coefficients in Z show, on the one hand, the value of credit reserved
at selected levels, and as differentiated by source. On the other hand, they
represent opportunity costs of credit used for borrowing. A model specified
with liquidity preference functions, in both cash and credit, would be considerably enriched, from an empirical viewpoint. One minor note: the interpretation of Z, as generated in such a model, must take account of these added sources of value. Although they may be real in the preference patterns
of the decision maker, they are not a part of the accounting orthodoxy.
But the 'liquidity values' can easily be subtracted from the solution value of
Z.

6. Critique

Specification of capital budgets in linear programming models that include
liquidity management components requires considerable information with
respect to behavior of the decision maker. The slopes of functions such as
those shown in fig. 1 are critical, in that they represent an array of opportunity costs for cash, to which all cash-using activities are subjected. The
same is true for comparable slopes of credit-reservation functions (see [6]).
The behavior reflected in these parameter estimates must be closely associated with the behavior that generates values of α_t in Model 3. The
empirical requirements in providing relevant estimates will doubtless be
similar also.

Two advantages seem apparent in the use of liquidity-management
components. The first is the fact that they can be accommodated in *linear*
programming specifications, yet reflecting (cheaply) certain aspects of
diminishing returns. This advantage may be temporary, given the considerable talent and effort currently allocated to the improvement of quadratic
programming algorithms.

The second advantage may be more lasting. The provision for means to
counter the effects of adverse outcomes may well be a more accurate description of actual decision behavior, in many empirical situations. The wide-
spread purchase of insurance contracts, where available, attests to this
conclusion. Where insurance is unavailable, the next best alternative is to

provide for liquidity in the financial structure of the firm. Cash and credit are obvious candidates as liquidity sources. Perhaps other assets could be used, but their liquidity values are most likely reflected most usefully in sales and credit liquidity.

Liquidity preference relations can, of course, be used in addition to the risk aversion coefficient associated with interaction terms in the objective function of Model 3, and the related variance–covariance matrix. Indeed, a model so specified could be used in a simulation design to generate variations in prescriptions that can be associated with variations in parameters of liquidity preference functions, on the one hand, and in the risk aversion coefficient, on the other. That is, if *both* have empirical relevance, liquidity preference specifications can complement those of quadratic programming.

We introduced this chapter with a brief note on applications of capital budgeting in the public sector. The issues in liquidity management specific to the private sector firm may differ in detail from those reflected in models of the public sector policy maker or administrator. Yet if they are relevant to the private sector, they are essential components among assumptions made in the public sector when estimates are required on reactions in the private sector to alternate public programs. Also, many public programs have a direct bearing on constraint levels that influence private decisions, especially those determining credit of the private firm. Thus the whole system is seen as a set of interacting decision units, related principally through markets, but related also through other social media that influence decision behavior in private firms and political response among decision makers in the public sector.

References

[1] Baker, C. B., 1968, Credit in the production organization of the firm, American Journal of Agricultural Economics, 50, 3, 507–520.
[2] Barry, P. J. and C. B. Baker, 1971, Reservation prices on credit use, American Journal of Agricultural Economics, 53, 2, 222–227.
[3] Bierman, H. and S. Smidt, 1971, The Capital Budgeting Decision, Macmillan, 3rd ed., 482.
[4] Boussard, J.-M., 1971, Time horizon, objective function, and uncertainty in a multi-period model of firm growth, American Journal of Agricultural Economics, 53, 3, 467–477.
[5] Scott, Jr., J. T. and C. B. Baker, 1972, A practical way to select an optimum farm plan under risk, American Journal of Agricultural Economics, 54, 4.
[6] Vandeputte, J. M. and C. B. Baker, 1971, Specification of credit and liquidity preference schedules in linear programming models, Tijdschrift voor Economie, 4, 483–492.

CHAPTER 35

An econometric model of supply, demand and wages of educated workers

HECTOR CORREA*

University of Pittsburgh

1. Introduction

The assumption that education contributes to the productivity of labor has a long history in economics [39]. In recent years this assumption has served as the basis for the manpower approach to educational planning, as seen, for example, in refs. [7, 8, 9, 33], and numerous studies based on this approach. It also provides the basis for computing returns on investments in education, as in [2] and [36], and for evaluating the contribution of education to economic development, as in [8, 10, 12, 13].

In the initial attempts to test this hypothesis, income was related to education, and a high correlation coefficient was interpreted as a sign of causal relationship. This approach was widely criticized [28, 35, 39]. Vaisey [39], in particular, suggests that these correlation coefficients might be due to parental wealth, income, social class and innate abilities, which would explain easy access to educational opportunity, motivation in education, access to the better jobs, and success in later life. More recent studies, such as those in refs. [1, 6, 25, 29, 30, 38, 41] attempt to avoid such deficiencies. For this purpose, the endogenous variable income is related to exogenous variables that describe several personal characteristics of the recipients of that income, such as age, sex, race, and personal ability, together with quality, quantity, and content of education. The usual result of these studies is that quantity, quality, and content of education have a positive effect on income. However, even these results offer at best extremely weak evidence of the contribution of workers' education to production. This is because

* The author is grateful for the suggestions of Professor Arnold Katz of the Department of Economics of the University of Pittsburgh.

only under the assumption of perfect competition can income differentials reflect different contributions to production.

A second approach to testing the hypothesis includes papers such as those in references [3, 16–21, 37, 41], in which the endogenous variable is some index of production, and attention is centered on the production process. In this case the exogenous variables, in addition to indices of the education of the labor force, include indices of other factors of production such as number of workers and volume of capital. The results obtained with this approach will be commented upon briefly. Welch [41] reports inconsistencies between two different estimates of the contribution of education to agricultural production. The educational index introduced by Hildebrand and Liu [21] did not perform as desired in their study of the manufacturing industries, and they do not discuss it in detail. Griliches [17, p. 298] says, "All the coefficients of the labor-quality variables have the expected signs and are in general significant at the conventional levels, but the contribution of these variables becomes small if all the between-industry and between-regions variance is eliminated using the dummy variables procedure". Finally, the educational index used by Bensen [3] was significant at a 5 % confidence level in only six of the 18 industries studied, and in seven is not significant even at a 10 % confidence level. Scully [37], studying interstate wage differentials by industry, reports that education appears as a significant factor at a 5 % confidence level in only ten out of 18 manufacturing industries that he studied, while in five industries, education of the labor force is not significant even at a 10 % confidence level. A more detailed study of these results will be presented later. As a conclusion, the evidence provided on the contribution of education to production, based on the analysis of production functions, can be considered inconclusive. This is not only because of the differences in the results of different studies, but also because the single equation models of the production process are likely to be under-identified [32].

The study of production functions that include educational indices leads to the question of complementarity between human and physical capital. In refs. [15] and [16], demand equations for labor are used to test the hypothesis that such complementarity exists. The results obtained − like those in ref. [8] − support the hypothesis. However, additional explorations on this topic would be useful, because of the limitations of the data used in the tests, and also because single equation models of demand for factors of production are likely to be under-identified.

The methods proposed to avoid under-identification can be classified in two groups. The first is based on hypotheses about the characteristics of the

error term. It has been applied mainly to the analysis of production functions as in refs. [22, 31, 42]. Since the assumptions on which these methods
are based are somewhat restrictive, their applicability is limited. The second
group includes those approaches based on the construction of multiple
equation models. A first possibility is that described in ref. [32] where
production and demand for inputs functions are identified, using a model
in which it is assumed that the income of the factors of production is equal
to their marginal productivities, i.e., to their contribution to production.
As a consequence, any attempt to apply any of these methods to the
hypothesis studied in this paper is unacceptable, because all of them take
for granted the hypothesis of the contribution to production of the education
of the workers. To avoid this problem, the model has to be expanded to
include the assumption that the workers' income is determined in the
market by supply and demand conditions. Such a model would also include production as an endogenous variable. A step in the direction of
such a model is taken in this paper, where the relationship between supply,
demand, and wages of educated workers will be studied. However, the
production process will be considered to be exogenously determined. The
impact of this assumption on the identification of the equations will be
studied later.

It should be observed that only with a system of assumptions including
perfect competition as one of its main elements is it possible to show that
a unique relationship exists between supply, demand and wages [34]. This
might suggest that a statistical analysis of this relationship has the same
limitations as those of income and education, or of production and education, already discussed. However, this is not the case, because the analysis
of the interaction between supply, demand, and wages is an explicit test
of the assumption of perfect competition. The consistency of the statistical
data with the relationship can be interpreted as meaning that (a) there is
some degree of competition, and (b) since in the data explicit attention is
paid to the education of the workers, this education — or any other variable
correlated with education, such as innate ability — influences production.

2. *The econometric models*

As mentioned before, the theory of production provides a starting point for
the development of a model to test the interaction between supply and
demand and the wages of qualified labor. On the basis of this theory, assume a production function of the form

$$V = f(K, N_1, N_2, N_3),\tag{1}$$

where V = production, K = capital, and N_j = number of workers with educational level j. $j = 1, 2, 3$. $j = 1$, up to 8 years of schooling; $j = 2$, 8+ to 12 years of schooling; $j = 3$, 12+ years of schooling.

In the production function (1), the stocks of capital and qualified labor are used as indices of the services they provide over the production period. The use of number of workers by level of education is limited by the fact that it does not take into consideration the quality of the education received. The importance of this aspect as a determinant of income differentials has frequently been studied, as in refs. [1, 27, 30]. However, the approach used, i.e., considering an index of educational quality as an explanatory variable of the income differentials will not be applied in the present case. What is needed is a means of expressing the fact that every worker embodies a certain quality and quantity of education. The method used in refs. [8, 10, 12, 13], i.e., the multiplication of the index of educational quality by that of quantity, will be used in this case. Expenditures per student in each state will be used as an index of quality. This index has been successfully employed by Morgan and Sirageldin [30]. Labor by level of education, corrected for quality, will be denoted by QN_j. This notation will be used in the presentation of the results. In the derivation of the basic model, only N_j will be used. In every case, similar results can be obtained with QN_j.

The profits of the production unit take the form

$$\Pi = V - rK - W_1 N_1 - W_2 N_2 - W_3 N_3,\tag{2}$$

where Π = profits, r = cost of capital per unit of time, and W_j wages per worker with educational level j, $j = 1, \ldots, 3$. Prices are defined so that the price of the product is equal to one. Eqs. (1) and (2), together with the assumption that profits are maximized, can be used to derive the following equations for the demand of factors of production:

$$W_j = g_j(K, N_1, N_2, N_3) \text{ for } j = 1, \ldots, 3.\tag{3}$$

where

$$\delta f / \delta N_j = g_j \qquad j = 1, \ldots, 3.\tag{4}$$

and a similar equation can be written for capital.

For the econometric analysis, it will be assumed here that eqs. (3) include V among the explanatory variables. This will make it possible to consider explicitly the influence of volume of production on demand for labor and on wages. It will also be assumed that eqs. (3) are linear. Two alternative specifications of this linear form are considered below:

$$N_j = \alpha_{j1} + \alpha_{j2} V + \alpha_{j3} K + \alpha_{j4} W_j + \alpha_{j5} N_i + \alpha_{j6} N_h \qquad (5)$$

where $j = 1, \ldots, 3$ and $j \neq h, j \neq i, h \neq i$ and

$$N_j = \beta_{j1} + \beta_{j2} V + \beta_{j3} K + \beta_{j4} W_j \qquad \text{for } j = 1, \ldots, 3. \qquad (6)$$

When quality of education is also considered, the variables N_j are replaced by QN_j in eqs. (5) and (6). The choice between using the demand equation in (5) or (6) with or without quality will be made on the basis of statistical results. The convenience of this approach is discussed in ref. [11].

To complete the construction of an econometric model of the supply, demand, and wages of qualified workers, the equations in (5) or (6) should be extended in two directions. First, the mechanisms of supply and demand determining production, and second, the supply of the qualified labor and its influence on wages, should be considered.

Since the question to be studied in this paper is not directly related to the determination of total output, no attempt will be made here to expand the model in the first direction mentioned above. As a consequence, V and K will be considered exogenous variables. Arbitrary limitations such as this — as Liu [26] observes — cannot be avoided in the construction of any scientific model. Without them, the basic model would have to be extended without limits. However, the specification and statistical analysis of an all-compromising model is clearly impossible. Working from this basis, Liu proceeds to state that all equations in econometric models are mis-specified and under-identified, and that the use of estimation techniques for multiple equation models does not improve the estimates. Valavanis [40], and in particular, Fisher [14], refute Liu, and Fisher shows that the estimation of the parameters can be improved by the use of approximate specification and identification, meaning that an equation is correctly specified and identified when all the variables with significant parameters are included. These results bring theoretical comfort, because to discover in practice all the variables that should be included in an equation is an im-possible task. However, Valavanis and Fisher show that the use of progres-sively more complex models is helpful. In this sense, the model to be studied here is a step in the right direction, despite the fact that it is not — and never will be — as comprehensive as would be desirable.

The supply of labor with educational level j is equal to the services pro-vided per unit of time by persons having that level of education. As men-tioned before, the number of workers by level of education will be used as indices of these services.

The first determinant of the services provided is the number of persons having a certain level of education. This number will be denoted by P_{jt}, where j refers to level of education, and t to date. Using the simplest form of the theory of labor supply derived from the assumption of maximization of utility, the rate of participation in the labor force is a function of the current wage rate. From this observation, it follows that a reasonable specification of the supply function to be studied is

$$N_{jt} = \xi(W_{jt})P_{jt} \qquad \text{for } j = 1, \ldots, 3 \qquad (7)$$

where $\xi(W_{jt})$ denotes the participation rate as a function of the wage rate.

To complete the analysis of the determinants of N_{jt}, the factors influencing P_{jt} must be studied. This can be written

$$P_{jt} = \sum_{h=-\infty}^{t} (i_{jh} - e_{jh} - d_{jh} + b_{jh}) \qquad (8)$$

where i = number of immigrants, e = number of emigrants, d = number of deaths, b = number of persons leaving the educational system, and j (subscript) = educational level of the number subscripted, j 1, 2, 3, h (subscript) = number subscripted in the period between $h-1$ and h.

The next step is to specify each of the components of the right hand side of eq. (8). In this specification, attention should be paid to the availability of data, and to the fact that, even if all the data needed were available, their analysis would have serious problems.

As a starting point it should be observed that according to (8) $P_{jh} = 0$ for $-\infty < h < t'$ for some $t' < t$. The reason for this is that the number of deaths cancel out the net effect of migration plus output of the educational system. Here it will be assumed that $t' = t-60$, i.e., it is assumed that persons with elementary education live about 70 years and those with college education live about 80 years.

In the specification of the function determining i_{jh} and e_{jh} it will be assumed that only migratory movements in the period between $t-1$ and t have to be considered, because only they reflect the adaptation of the population to changes in the demand for labor. In this sense the migrations in year t cancel out those of previous years. This means that in the accounting identity in (8) only i_{jt} and e_{jt} have some behavioral meaning. The net result of migrations plus deaths of migrants for years $t-1, t-2 \ldots$ determines a constant not influenced by any of the variables considered in the analysis. It will be assumed that

$$i_{jt} = \mu(W_{jt}) \quad \text{and} \quad e_{jt} = \phi(W_{jt}) \qquad \text{for } j = 1, \ldots, 3 \qquad (9)$$

where ϕ and μ denote unspecified functions. Unfortunately, at the present, the estimation of these functions does not seem feasible, because — according to information provided by the Bureau of the Census — no data are available on interstate migration by educational level.

To complete the analysis of eq. (8) it remains to explain the influence on P_{jt} of the persons leaving the educational system who do not migrate and of the deaths of these persons in order to obtain the net effect in year t. To do so it will be assumed that the b_{jh} are a fixed proportion of enrollment say k years before h, and that enrollment grows at a constant rate.

These assumptions permit the expression of all the b_{jh} as a fraction of enrollment in one year in the educational system. In the following enrollment in year t-20 will be used and denoted with $T_{jt\text{-}20}$. To obtain any T_{jh} the value of $T_{jt\text{-}20}$ is modified by the value of the rate of growth of enrollment raised to the appropriate power. Once the value of T_{jh} is expressed in terms of $T_{jt\text{-}20}$, that of b_{jh} can be obtained using the assumed fixed proportions. The observations above show that the total of b_{jh} for t-60 $\leq h \leq t$ can be expressed as equal to a constant multiplied by $T_{jt\text{-}20}$.

The assumption that the death rate is constant permits us to express the number of deaths among the school leavers who did not migrate as a fraction of the b_{jh} and, as a consequence of $T_{jt\text{-}20}$.

In summary it is possible to write

$$\sum_{h=t-60}^{t} (d'_{jh} + b_{jh}) = \beta'_j T_{jt\text{-}20} \tag{10}$$

where d'_{jh} denotes deaths among the persons counted in b_{jh}, and β'_j is a parameter.

If the results of the previous observations are incorporated in eq. (7), the following result is obtained

$$N_{jt} = \xi(W_{jt})(C_{jt} + \mu(W_{jt}) - \phi(W_{jt}) + \beta'_j T_{jt\text{-}20})$$

where C_{jt} is a constant.

For the statistical analysis this equation will be written

$$N_{jt} = \beta_{j1} + \beta_{j2} W_j + \beta_{j3} T_j. \tag{11}$$

The simplifications introduced in eq. (11) do not require any explanation. It should be observed that to simplify printing, $T_{jt\text{-}20}$ is written T_j. All the coefficients in eq. (11) should be positive.

Again in eq. (11), N_i is replaced with QN_i when the quality of educated labor is also considered.

In summary, four models have been specified. The first one is formed by eqs. (5) and (11), and the second by eqs. (6) and (11). These two models have as endogenous variables N_j and W_j for $j = 1, \ldots, 3$. The other two models are obtained from the first two when N_j is replaced by QN_j $j = 1, \ldots 3$. It should be observed that the second and fourth models can be divided into three sets of independent equations, each set dealing with supply and demand of labor for one level of education. As a consequence, these models eliminate any possibility of studying complementarity or substitutability among workers having different levels of education. Such a study would be a useful consequence of the analysis made here. However, it is not the main object of this paper.

The four models specified are determined so that each has the same number of equations as of endogenous variables. The remaining variables, i.e., production, capital, and number of students, are assumed to be predetermined.

In checking for identification, it can be observed that the demand equations are exactly identified, while the supply equations are over-identified.

The parameters of eqs. (5), (6), and (11) were evaluated using cross-section data for the states of the United States. When the N_j are among endogenous variables, 48 observations are used (Alaska and Hawaii excluded). When the QN_i are among the endogenous variables, 47 observations are used (Delaware is also excluded). Judging from the studies published so far, these are the only data available. The sources of the data are presented in the appendix. The figures for capital and production were expressed in 10^6 1960 dollars, those of annual wages in 10^3 1960 dollars, and those of workers for 1960 in 10^3 units.

Despite efforts to avoid it, multi-collinearity remained an important problem. Since it is known that limited information, maximum likelihood, and full information-maximum likelihood estimators are more sensitive to multi-collinearity than the two stages-least squares estimators [24], this last method of estimation was used.

3. The empirical results

Before proceeding to analyze the results obtained, the final form of the model must be determined, i.e., one model must be selected from among those in eqs. (5) and (11) or (6) and (11). Since these two models differ only in the form of the demand equations, these equations will be considered first. They are presented in tables 1 and 2. The results in table 1 are not ac-

Table 1

TSLS estimators of the demand equations, when the model in eqs. (5) and (11) is used

$$N_1 = 836.89 + 153.00V + 47.74K - 0.80N_2 - 1.44^*N_3 - 311.50^*W_1$$
$$(3.72) \quad (2.49) \quad (0.40) \quad (9.34) \quad (1.80)$$
$$R = 0.99 \qquad F_{(5.43)} = 332.1$$

$$N_2 = 1352.46 + 125.82V + 59.26K - 0.77N_1 - 0.60N_3 - 356.04W_2$$
$$(3.63) \quad (2.47) \quad (1.00) \quad (0.50) \quad (1.04)$$
$$R = 0.99 \qquad F_{(5.43)} = 829.74$$

$$N_3 = 3089.09 - 118.14^*V + 15.70K - 1.30N_1 + 3.29^*N_2 - 628.62^*W_3$$
$$(11.02) \quad (0.45) \quad (12.12) \quad (23.91) \quad (10.14)$$
$$R = 0.99 \qquad F_{(5.43)} = 497.49$$

* Significant at least at 0.95 confidence level.

The figures in parentheses under the coefficients are the F values for the coefficient.

Table 2

TSLS estimators of the parameters in the demand equations when the model in eqs. (6) and (11) is used

$$N_1 = 728.86 + 45.62^*V + 54.94^*K - 286.89^*W_1$$
$$(169.87) \quad (30.38) \quad (50.88)$$
$$R = 0.98 \qquad F_{(3.45)} = 430.54$$

$$N_2 = 66.86 + 67.51^*V + 19.75^*K - 10.18W_2$$
$$(780.25) \quad (7.97) \quad (0.06)$$
$$R = 0.99 \qquad F_{(3.45)} = 1404.39$$

$$N_3 = -305.01 + 37.87^*V - 24.55^*K + 66.92^*W_3$$
$$(470.28) \quad (21.96) \quad (4.16)$$
$$R = 0.99 \qquad F_{(3.45)} = 551.63$$

$$QN_1 = -268.34 + 2.32V + 188.88^*K + 152.53W_1$$
$$(0.44) \quad (56.54) \quad (0.77)$$
$$R = 0.91 \qquad F_{(3.44)} = 49.36$$

$$QN_2 = 1476.50 + 109.51^*V + 3.02K - 458.78^*W_2$$
$$(46.59) \quad (0.01) \quad (46.10)$$
$$R = 0.94 \qquad F_{(3.44)} = 89.45$$

$$QN_3 = 131.31 + 62.76^*V - 49.63^*K - 37.80^*W_3$$
$$(57.74) \quad (5.06) \quad (56.63)$$
$$R = 0.93 \qquad F_{(3.44)} = 69.13$$

* Significant at least at a 0.95 confidence level.

The figures in parentheses under the coefficients are the F values for the coefficient.

ceptable because (a) production V and capital K are not significant except in the case of the demand for N_3, in which case, the coefficient of V is negative and, as a consequence, without meaning; (b) the coefficient of N_3 in the equation for N_1, and of N_1 in the equation for N_3 suggest that they are substitutes, and this result does not seem reasonable; finally, the coefficients of N_3 in the equation for N_2 and of N_2 in the equation for N_3 are not consistent. On the other hand, it will be seen below that the results in table 2 are meaningful in terms of economic theory. Using stepwise regression, it can be found that the change from the results in table 1 to those in table 2 is due to the high multicollinearity among the variables in eq. (5). As a consequence of the previous observations, only the model in eqs. (6) and (11) will be analyzed below using both N_j and QN_j as indices of the services of educated labor. The results of the statistical analysis of these models appear in tables 2 and 3.

Table 3

TSLS estimators of the parameters in the supply equations

$$N_1 = -863.77 + 348.42 + W_1 + 1.74 + T_1$$
$$(57.43) \qquad (764.64)$$
$$R = 0.97^* \qquad F_{(2.46)} = 401.79$$

$$N_2 = -1622.81 + 465.83^* W_2 + 4.28^* T_2$$
$$(17.39) \quad (236.73)$$
$$R = 0.95^* \qquad F_{(2.46)} = 245.15$$

$$N_3 = -1132.19 + 243.32^* W_3 + 6.67^* T_3$$
$$(24.27) \quad (138.21)$$
$$R = 0.95^* \qquad F_{(2.46)} = 196.47$$

$$QN_1 = -1668.13 + 654.50^* W_1 + 2.17^* T_1$$
$$(41.62) \qquad (197.00)$$
$$R = 0.95^* \qquad F_{(2.45)} = 140.56$$

$$QN_2 = -258.80 + 15.71 W_2 + 6.71^* T_2$$
$$(1.21) \quad (164.24)$$
$$R = 0.93^* \qquad F_{(2.45)} = 88.23$$

$$QN_3 = -61.00 - 2.05^* W_3 + 12.23^* T_3$$
$$(4.92) \quad (137.41)$$
$$R = 0.93^* \qquad F_{(2.45)} = 88.85$$

* Significant at least at 0.95 confidence level.

The figures in parentheses under the coefficients are the F values for the coefficient.

The results for the demand equations appear in table 2. With some exceptions, which will be explained below, the coefficients are significant and have the proper signs. The first exception appears for the coefficients of W_j, $j = 2, 3$, in the equations explaining N_j. For $j = 2$ the coefficient is not significant and $j = 3$ the coefficient is positive. It should be observed that Welch [41] also found that the relationship between wages and labor having a college education did not show the characteristics that could be expected from the point of view of economic theory. He attributed this result to misspecification. The same reasoning is valid in the present case. When the specification of the equations is corrected with the use of QN_j, $j = 2, 3$, W_j appears as significant and with the proper sign. However, the significance of W_1 disappears when explaining QN_1. These results make perfectly good sense. In the demand for labor with up to 8 years of education, quantity is the important element, while quality can be disregarded. This demand is mainly determined by volume of production, measured by V and K, and in this case wages are influential. In the demand for labor with high-school and college education, quality becomes a significant element.

A point which has not yet been discussed is the negative sign of the significant coefficients for capital in the equations for N_3 and QN_3. These results in table 2 suggest that there is some substitutability between N_3, QN_3 and K, particularly when quality is excluded. This is surprising, because such results would apparently contradict those in [8, 15, 16].

The substitutability observed can be explained by the shift from production of physical goods, requiring high volumes of capital and labor which is not highly qualified, to the production of services requiring less capital and more highly qualified workers. This modification of the type of production does not seem to affect the requirements for workers with elementary and intermediate levels of education. This point has theoretical and empirical support. Kenen [23] shows that additions to capital invested in humans are more likely to raise the efficiency in the least capital-intensive industries. As a consequence, these industries are more likely to demand more qualified labor. The empirical results of Bensen [3] and Scully [37] can also be used to substantiate the point. As mentioned in the introduction, these two authors, one studying the production function of different industries and the other studying wage differentials by industry, found that the index of education of the labor force they used was significant in some, but not all the industries they studied. In table 4 it can be observed that Bensen's and Scully's results are quite similar. They agree in classifying industries where the educational variable is either significant or non-significant in 13 out of 17 cases. In table 5, the average value of capital per worker in the industries

Table 4

Comparison of the results obtained by Bensen and Scully

Bensen [a] ⟍ Scully	Significant up to 10%		Non-significant	
Industries where educational variables present coefficients significant up to 10% level	22	Textile	33	Primary metals
	23	Apparel		
	24	Lumber		
	25	Furniture		
	27	Printing		
	32	Stone and clay		
	34	Fab. metals		
	35	Non-elect. mach.		
	36	Elect. mach.		
Industries where educational variables present non-significant coefficients	20	Food	28	Chemicals
	26	Paper	29	Petroleum
	31	Leather	30	Rubber
			37	Transport

[a] *Industry 38 instruments* is excluded from the table because it is considered only in Bensen's study. The educational variable for this industry is significant at a 10% confidence level.

Table 5

Average of capital per worker in industries classified by the levels of significance obtained by Bensen and Scully

	Average values	
	Bensen	Scully
Up to 5%	4736	⎫ 5756
More than 5% up to 10%	7175	⎭
Not significant	11 855	15 056
F value in A.V.	33.15 (2446) [a]	127.93 (1431) [a]

[a] Number of degrees of freedom.

classified by level of significance is presented. The values per state and industry were used as observations. These results show that capital per worker tends to increase with the reduction of the level of significance of the educational variables, reaching their highest values when education is not significant. The one-way classification analysis of variance of the differences among the means gives highly significant *F* values.

The contradiction between our results and those in [8, 15, 16] is more apparent than real, because in these references composite indices of the quality of the labor force as determined by education are used. In these indices, the weight of the labor force with $8+$ to 12 years of education is substantially higher than that of the labor force with $12+$ years of education. As a consequence, the complementarity observed with respect to N_2, QN_2 and K in table 2 is likely to overshadow the substitutability that seems to exist in certain industries between labor with $12+$ years of education and capital.

In table 3 both the number of students and wages appear as the determinants of the supply of workers in the three levels of education, regardless of whether educational quality is considered. The impact of number of students seems to be more important than that of wages, since their F coefficients are substantially larger. This is reasonable. Most employed persons do not have the choice of not working, whatever the level of salaries. Their choice is limited to where or in what they can work. On the other hand, a person can choose whether he wishes to continue to attend school.

In each of the three equations explaining N_j, the levels of significance of W_j and T_j are higher than in those explaining QN_j. This also seems reasonable. The quantity of education to be received can be determined on a more rational basis than the quality of education to be received. A rational choice of the quality of education is difficult, due to lack of information. Also the choice of quality of education is but one of the elements considered in deciding on the domicile of a family.

As a consequence of the previous analysis, it can be concluded that the results in tables 2 and 3 strongly support the hypothesis that supply and demand for qualified labor are influenced by economic factors. From this it follows that the differences in income of workers having different levels of education are actually due to differences in their productivity, attributable to differences both in education and in innate ability. They also show that capital and college-educated labor are, in certain cases, substitutable.

It should be clear that the conclusions reached are valid only for the United States, the country of origin of the data used, and might not hold for other countries. This is particularly true for the developing countries, in which market imperfections exert stronger influences.

4. Implications of the results

Most, if not all, the methods for integrating economic and educational planning, and the actual plans prepared, are based on the model in refs. [7] and

[33]. The object of this model is to determine: first, the educational structure of the labor force needed to achieve a target GNP, and second, the flows of students in the educational system needed to bring about the required educational structure of the labor force. In the model, the numbers of workers by level of education are estimated, using some simple relationships between number of workers and production. In the simplest case, it is assumed that the number of workers maintains a constant proportion with value of production. Logarithmic functions have also been used. Next, assuming constant labor participation ratios, the required educational structure of the population is computed. Finally, the output of the educational system is made equal to the gross (including deaths) increment of population by level of education.

In the model described, no attention is paid to the influence of wages on supply or demand of qualified workers. However, the results of the analysis in sects. 2 and 3 of the present paper show that this might lead to substantial errors.

Two obstacles seem to exist to the inclusion of wages in the model in refs. [7] and [33]. The first is the lack of statistical data. Despite that this obstacle has taken most of the blame, the fact is that even in cases where some data exist, they have not been used for the estimation of manpower requirements. This suggests that the main obstacle is the second one, namely, the lack of a theoretical model.

This second obstacle is somewhat more serious. Little attention has been paid in planning models of all the economic sectors to the actual — as opposed to the shadow — prices of goods and services. This means that the problem affects not only the manpower approach to educational planning, but also most of economic planning in general. It also means that there is not much similarity on which to begin constructing a model for the educational approach to manpower planning that includes wages.

The problem raised by the inclusion of wages in manpower planning is that the direct links between targets of production and educational structure of the labor force, between labor force and population, and between population and the educational system are broken. More specifically, and adopting an extreme position, it can be said that an infinite set of educational structures of the labor force could, with positive wages, produce the target fixed for GNP. In other terms, and assuming complete flexibility of positive wage rates, there is a feasible wage rate that would create demand for any stock of qualified labor. If this is the case, no reason exists for educational planning. Any educational structure of the labor force that is produced by the educational system would be demanded.

The previous observations, in addition to the extreme assumption on wage flexibility that they include, ignore the investment and current costs of education. As a consequence of the expenditures needed for education, each of the educational structures of the labor force that could be produced has a cost. If this is the case, it makes sense to state the problem of the manpower approach to educational planning as that of minimizing the educational costs of reaching a GNP target. In this minimization the fact that changes in wages are needed to bring about equality between supply and demand of qualified labor should be considered.

A detailed analysis of the idea presented above, of the modifications needed in it to include the substitutability between capital and qualified labor and between different types of qualified labor, and of its relations with the usual optimization models in economics that have as a by-product shadow prices, will not be presented here.

Appendix

Data

Workers by level of education 1960
1960 Census of Population, Volume 1, "Characteristics of the Population. Results by State." Table: Income in 1959 of persons 25 years and over by years of school completed, color, sex, for the state, urban and rural 1960 (Persons with income). Figures in 10^0.

Wages 1960
See Source for data on workers by level of education. Medium income. Figures in 10^0 1960 dollars per year.

Number of workers by level of education 1960, with correction for educational quality
Morgan and Sirageldin [30] use average expenditure per pupil by state as an index of the quality of education. Their data (table 1) are used here as a starting point. The index Q_i of educational quantity in state i is equal to

$$Q_i = E_i/\bar{E}$$

where E_i is the expenditures per pupil in state i, and $\bar{E}$ is the average of expenditures per pupil over all the states.

The number of workers corrected for quality is computed with

$$QN_i = Q_i{}^*N_i.$$

It should be observed that the product quality times number of workers is used in refs. [8, 10, 12 and 13] to evaluate the contribution of the quality of the labor force to economic growth.

Students by level of education 1939–1940
U.S. Office of Education, Biennial Survey of Education in the U.S. Table: Enrollment by grade in public day schools, by state and institution of higher education — Faculty, Enrollment and Recipients of Degrees, by states, territories and Outlying Possessions. 10^0.

Capital by state 1960
Computed using as a starting point the data on expenditures on new capital from the Department of Commerce, Bureau of the Census, Annual Survey of Manufactures. The available figures for 1939 up to 1960 appropriately weighted to represent several years when necessary, were added without depreciation. The total is used as index of capital equipment by states. 10^3.

Production 1960
Total personal income by state, Department of Commerce, Office of Business Economics, Survey of Current Business, August 1961. 10^6 dollars, 1960.

Capital by manufacturing industry and region
From U.S. Bureau of the Census, Annual Survey of Manufactures, 1957, Washington, Government Printing Office, 1959, and from U.S. Bureau of the Census, Census of Manufactures, 1958, Washington: Government Printing Offices 1968.

References

[1] Ashenfelter, O. and D. J. Mooley, 1968, Graduate education, ability and earnings, The Review of Economics and Statistics, XLX, no. 1, 78–86.
[2] Becker, G. S., 1964, Human Capital, New York: Columbia University Press.
[3] Bensen, S. M., 1968, Education and productivity in U.S. manufacturing: some cross section evidence, Journal of Political Economy, 76, no. 3, 494–497.
[4] Blaug, M., 1966, An economic interpretation of the private demand for education, Economica, 33.
[5] Campell, R. and B. N. Siegel, 1967, The demand for higher education in the U.S., The American Economic Review, LVII, no. 3, 482–494.

[6] Carnoy, M., 1967, Earning and schooling in Mexico, Economic Development and Cultural Change, 15, no. 4.

[7] Correa, H. and J. Tinbergen, 1962, The quantitative adaptation of education to economic growth, Kyklos, XV.

[8] Correa, H., 1963, The Economics of Human Resources, Amsterdam: North-Holland Publishing Company.

[9] Correa, H., 1969, Quantitative Methods of Educational Planning, Scranton: International Textbook, 242

[10] Correa, H., 1970, Sources of economic growth in Latin America, Southern Economic Journal, XXXVII, no. 1.

[11] Christ, C. E., 1966, Econometric Models and Methods, New York: John Wiley and Sons.

[12] Denison, E., 1962, The Sources of Economic Growth in the U.S.A., New York: Committee for Economic Development.

[13] Denison, E., 1967, Why Growth Rates Differ, Washington: The Brooking Institute.

[14] Fisher, F. M., 1961, On the cost of approximate specification in simultaneous equation estimation, Econometrica, 29, 139–170.

[15] Griliches, Z., 1969, Capital skill complementarity, The Review of Economics and Statistics, LI, no. 4, 465–468.

[16] Griliches, Z., 1970, Notes on the role of education in production functions and growth accounting, in: W. L. Hansen, ed., Education, Income and Human Capital. Papers presented at the Conference on Education and Income held at the University of Wisconsin in November 1968, New York: Columbia University Press.

[17] Griliches, Z., 1967, Production functions in manufacturing: some preliminary results, in: M. Brown, ed., The Theory and Empirical Analysis of Production, New York: National Bureau of Economic Research.

[18] Griliches, Z., 1964, Research expenditures, education and the aggregate agricultural production function, American Economic Review, LIV, 961–974.

[19] Griliches, Z., 1963, The sources of measured productivity growth: United States agriculture, 1940–60, Journal of Political Economy, LXXI, 331–346.

[20] Griliches, Z., 1963, Estimates of the aggregate agricultural production function from cross-sectional data, Journal of Farm Economics, XLV, 419–428.

[21] Hildebrand, G. H. and T. Liu, 1965, Manufacturing Production Function in the U.S., 1957: An Interindustry and Interstate Comparison of Productivity Ithaca: Cornell University Press, xi, 224.

[22] Hoch, I., 1958, Simultaneous equation bias in the context of the Cobb–Douglas production function, Econometrica, 26, no. 4, 566–578.

[23] Kenen, P. E., 1966, Efficiency differences and factor intensities in the CES production function, Journal of Political Economy, LXXIV, no. 6, 635–636.

[24] Klein, L. R. and M. Nakamura, 1962, Singularity in the equations systems of econometrics: some aspects of the problems of multicollinearity, International Economic Review, 3.

[25] Lassiter, R. L., 1965, The association of income and education for males by region, race and age, The Southern Economic Journal, XXXII, no. 1, Part 1, 15–22.

[26] Liu, T. C., 1955, A simple forecasting model of the U.S. economy, International Monetary Fund Staff Papers, 434–466.

[27] McClelland, D. C., 1966, Does education accelerate economic growth?, Economic Development and Cultural Change, 14, no. 3.

[28] Merrett, S., 1966, The rate of return to education: a critique, Oxford Economic Papers, 289–303.

[29] Morgan, J. N. and M. H. David, 1963, Education and income, Quarterly Journal of Economics, 423–437.

[30] Morgan, J. and I. Sirageldin, 1968, A note on the quality dimension in education, Journal of Political Economy, no. 5, 1069–1077.

[31] Mundlak, Y. and I. Hoch, 1965, Consequences of alternative specifications in estimation of Cobb–Douglas production functions, Econometrica, 33, no. 4, 814–828.

[32] Nerlove, M., 1965, Estimation and Identification of Cobb-Douglas Production Functions, Chicago: Rand McNally, 193.

[33] Parnes, H. S., 1962, Forecasting Educational Needs for Economic and Social Development, Paris: OECD.

[34] Quirk, J. and R. Saposnik, 1968, Introduction to General Equilibrium Theory and Welfare Economics, New York: McGraw-Hill, 218.

[35] Renshaw, E. F., 1960, Estimating the returns to education, Review of Economics and Statistics, 42, 318–324.

[36] Schultz, T. W., 1960, Capital formation by education, The Journal of Political Economy, December.

[37] Scully, G. W., 1969, Interstate wage differentials: a cross-section analysis, American Economic Review, LIX, no. 5, 757–773.

[38] Thias, H. H. and M. Carnoy, 1969, Cost-Benefit Analysis in Education: A case Study on Kenya International Bank for Reconstruction and Development, Report No. EC-173 (mimeograph).

[39] Vaisey, J., 1962, The Economics of Education, New York: The Free Press of Glencoe.

[40] Valavanis, S., 1959, Econometrics, New York: McGraw-Hill, 223.

[41] Welch, F., 1970, Education in production, Journal of Political Economy, 78, no. 1, 35–59.

[42] Zellner, A., J. Kmenta and J. Dreze, 1966, Specification and estimation of Cobb-Douglas production function models, Econometrica, 34, no. 4, 784–795.

Subject Index